Until Death do us Part

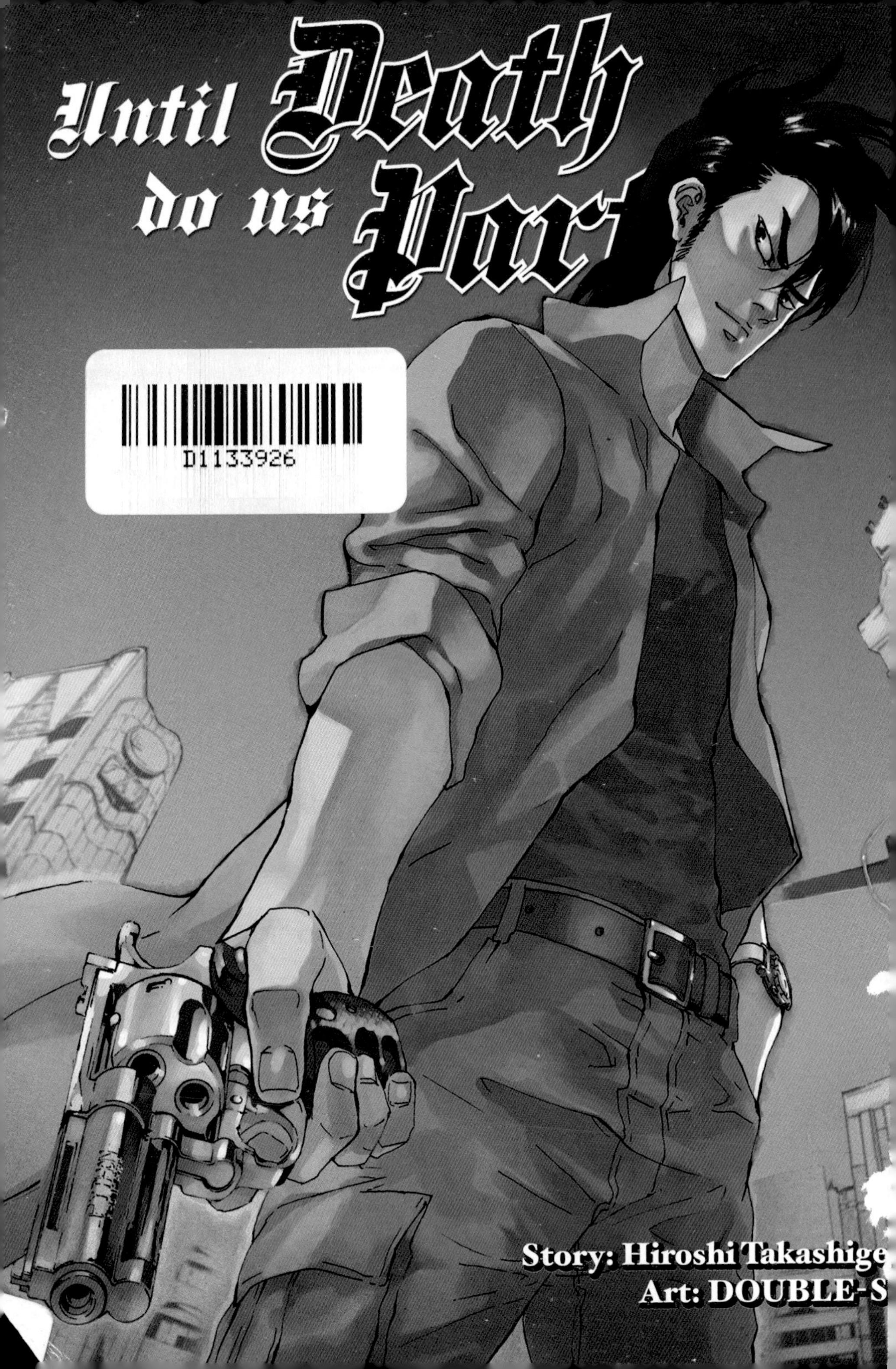

Story: Hiroshi Takashige

Art: DOUBLE-S

Until Death do us Part

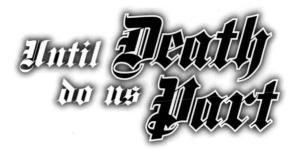

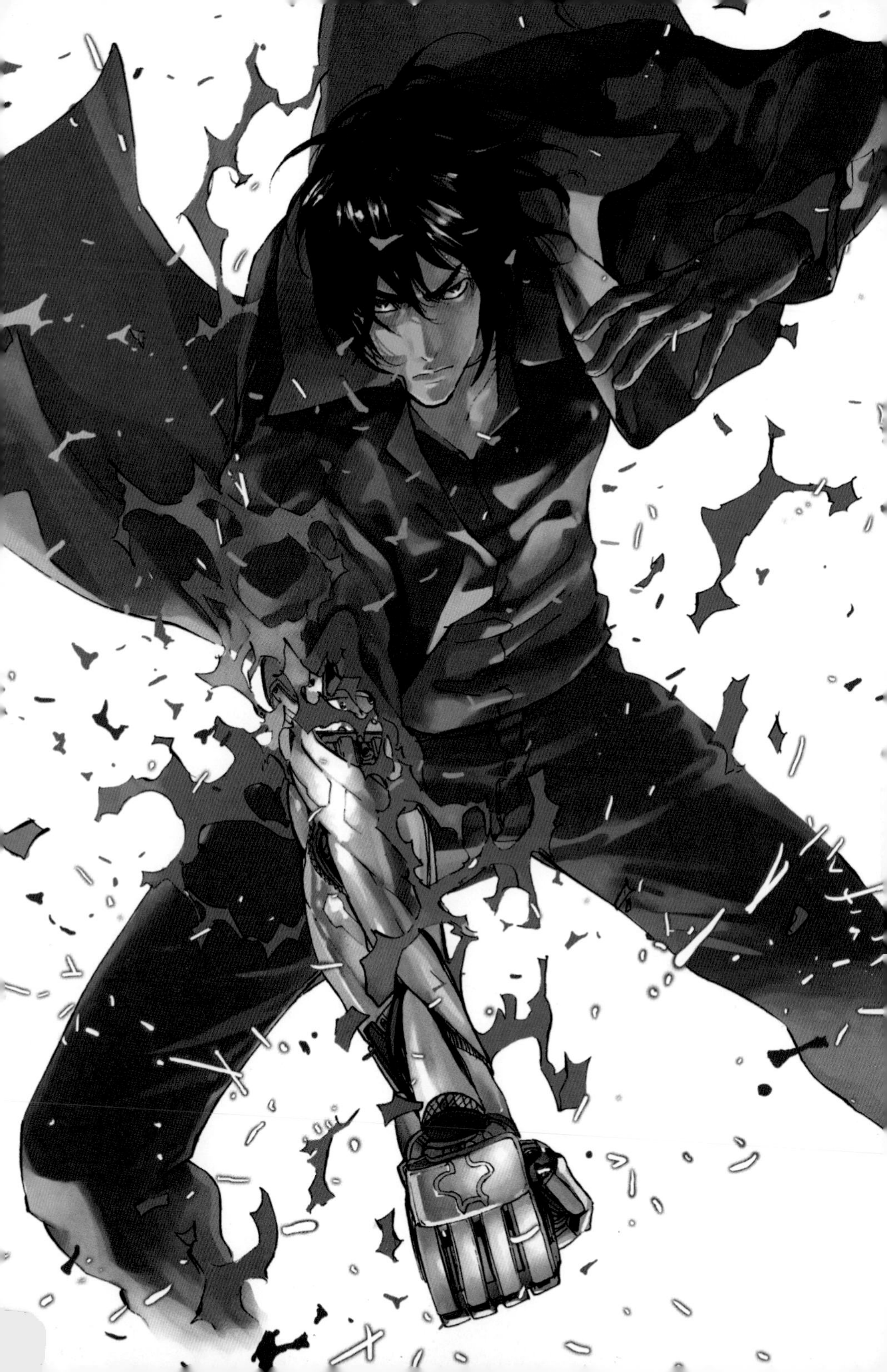

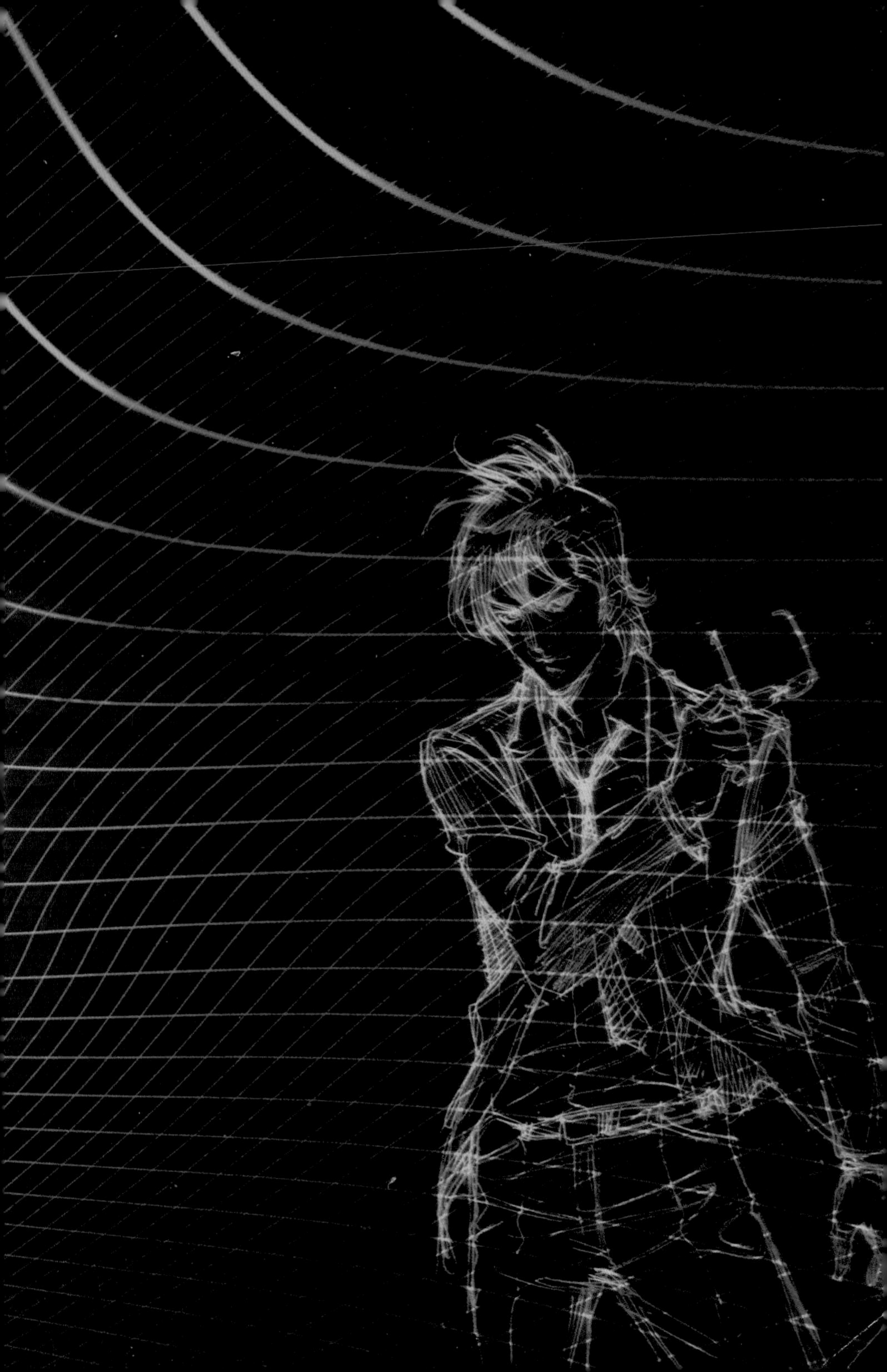

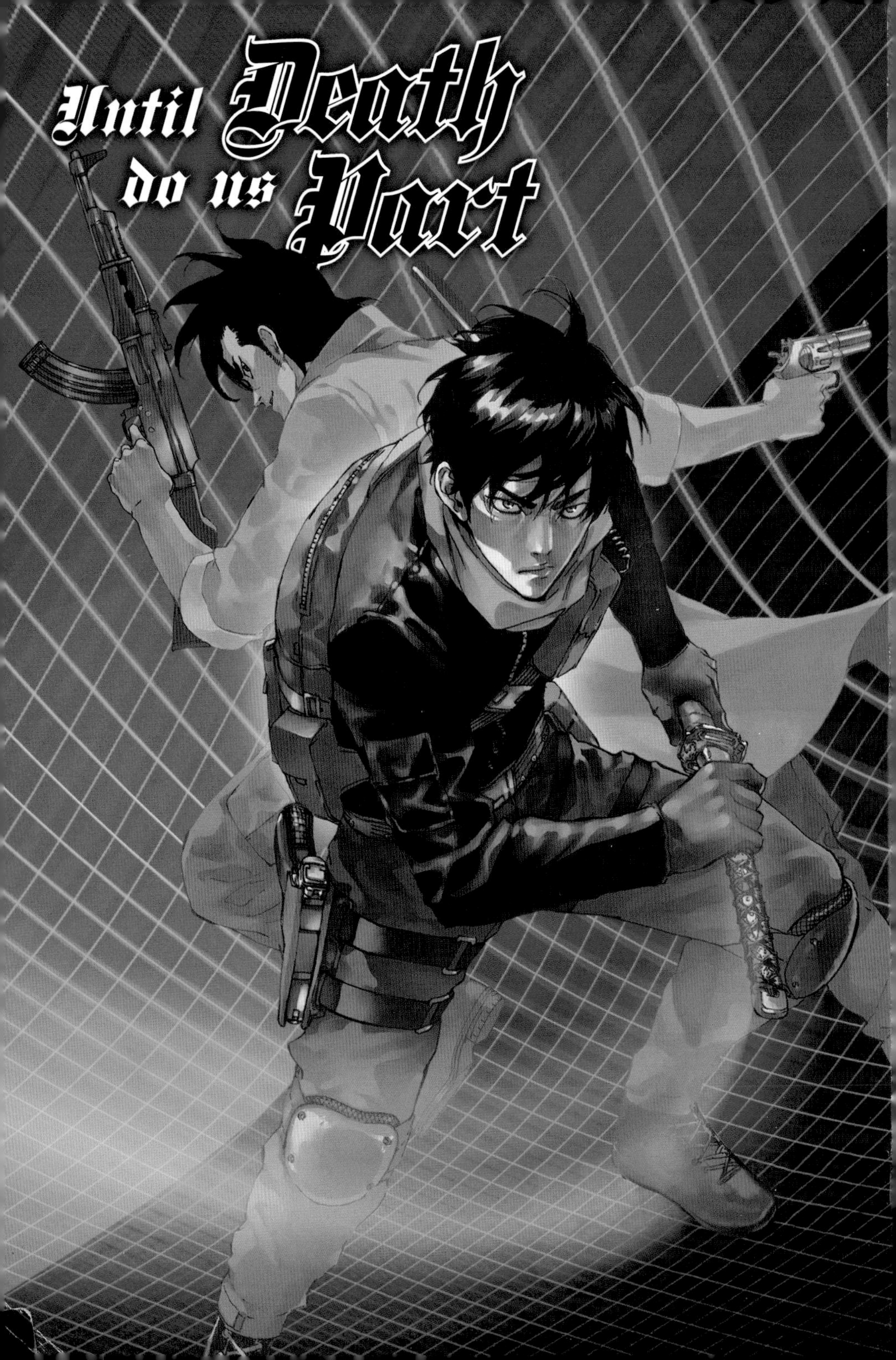
Until Death do us Part

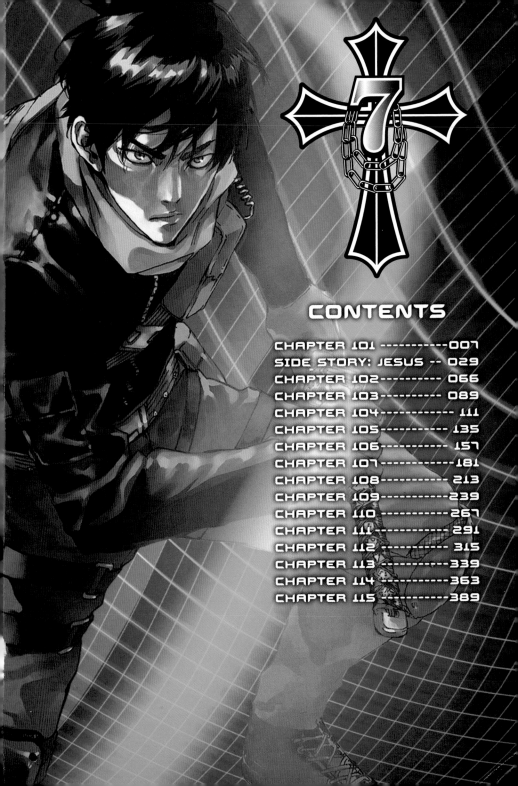

CONTENTS

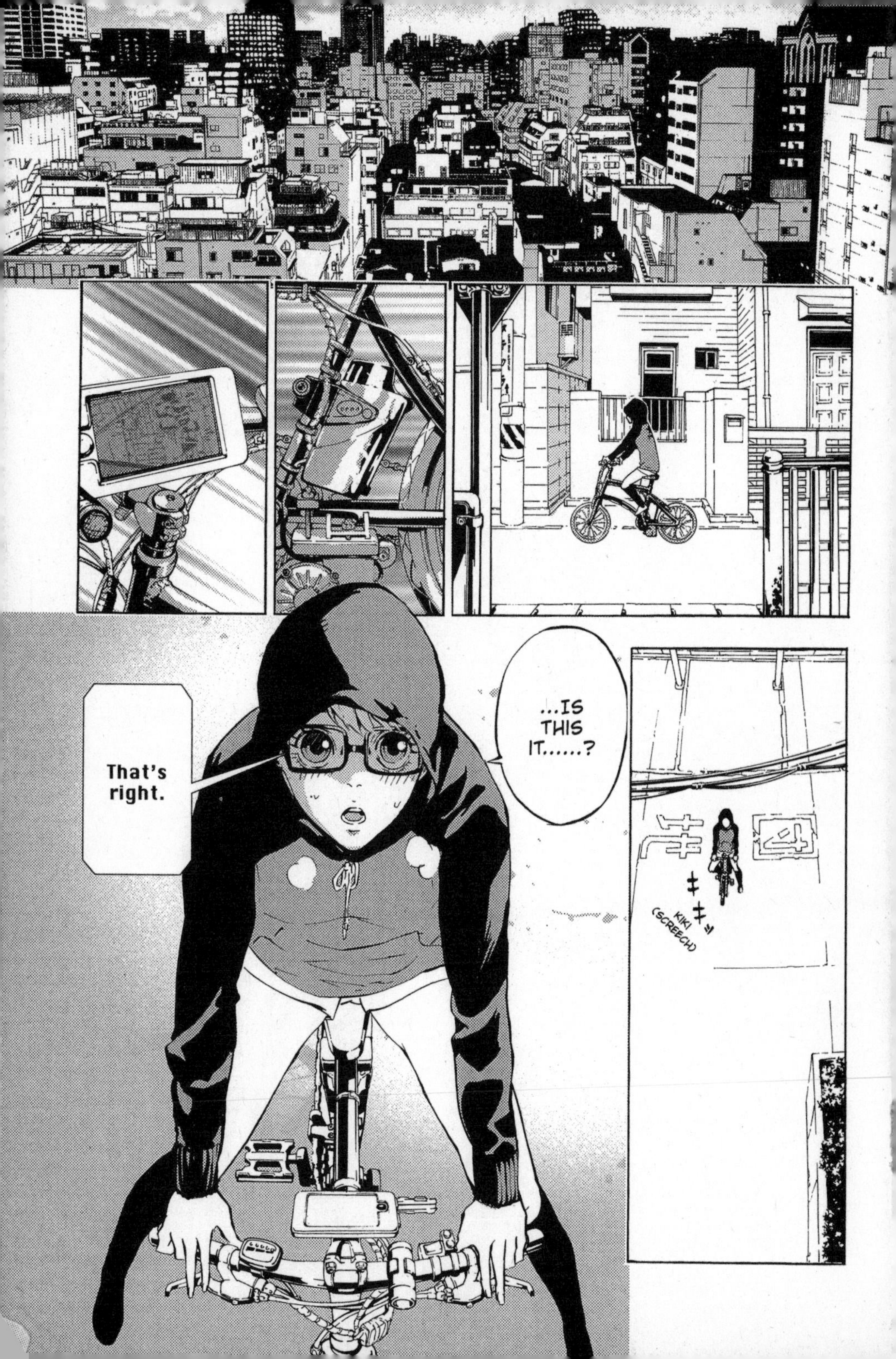
キキッ
KIKI (SCREECH)
...IS THIS IT......?
That's right.

chapter 101

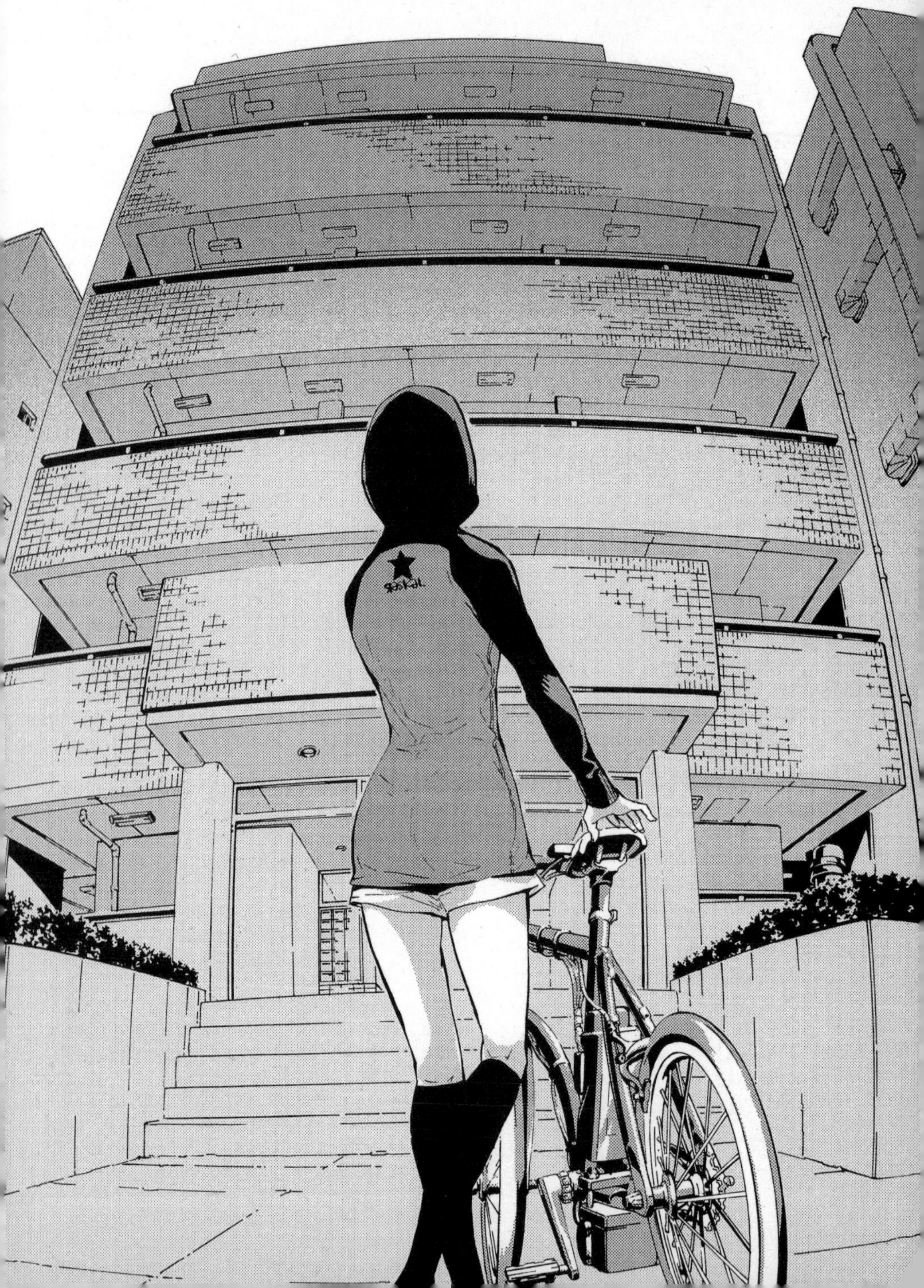

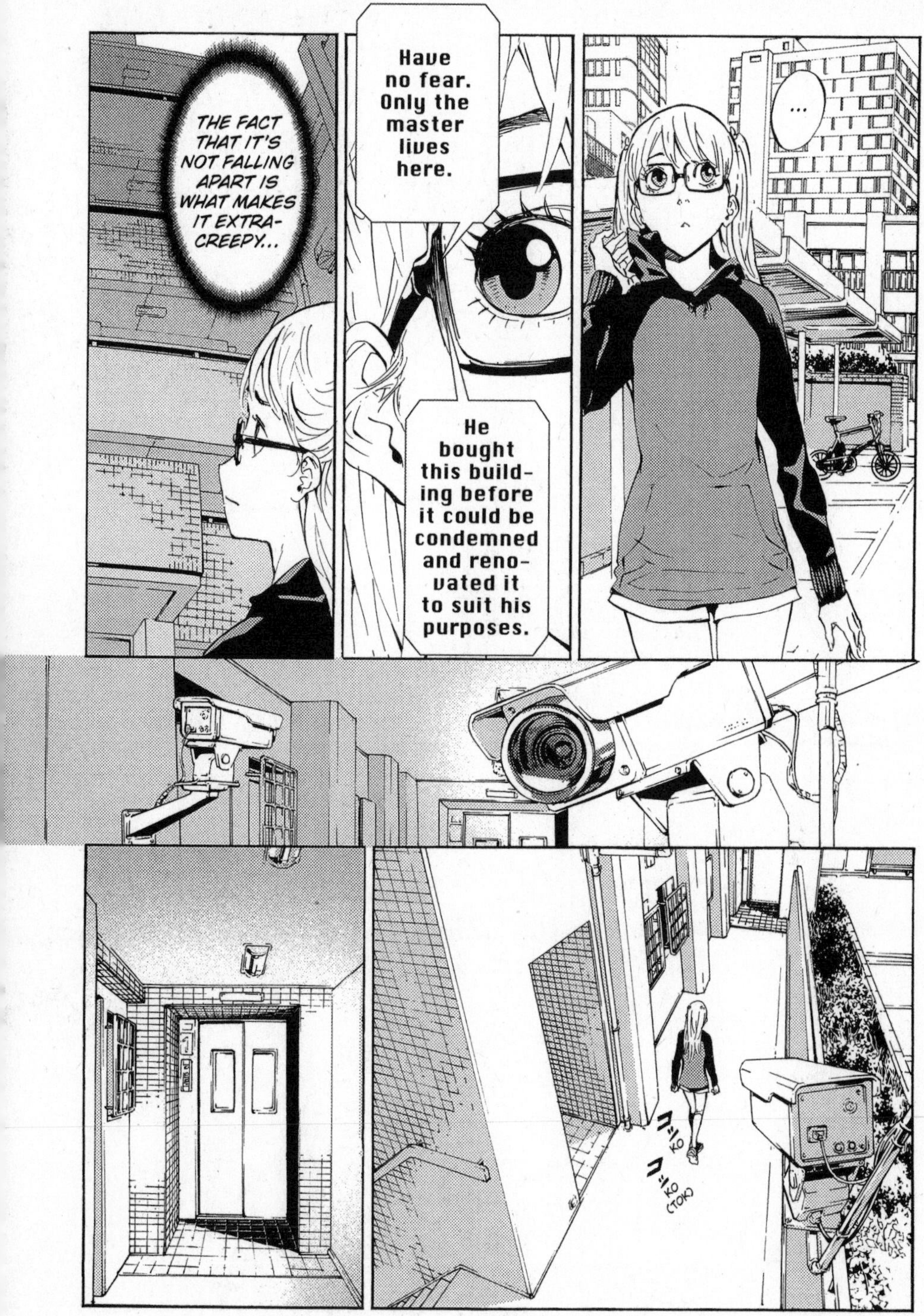
...
Have no fear. Only the master lives here.
He bought this building before it could be condemned and renovated it to suit his purposes.
THE FACT THAT IT'S NOT FALLING APART IS WHAT MAKES IT EXTRA-CREEPY...
コッ KO
コッ KO (TOK)

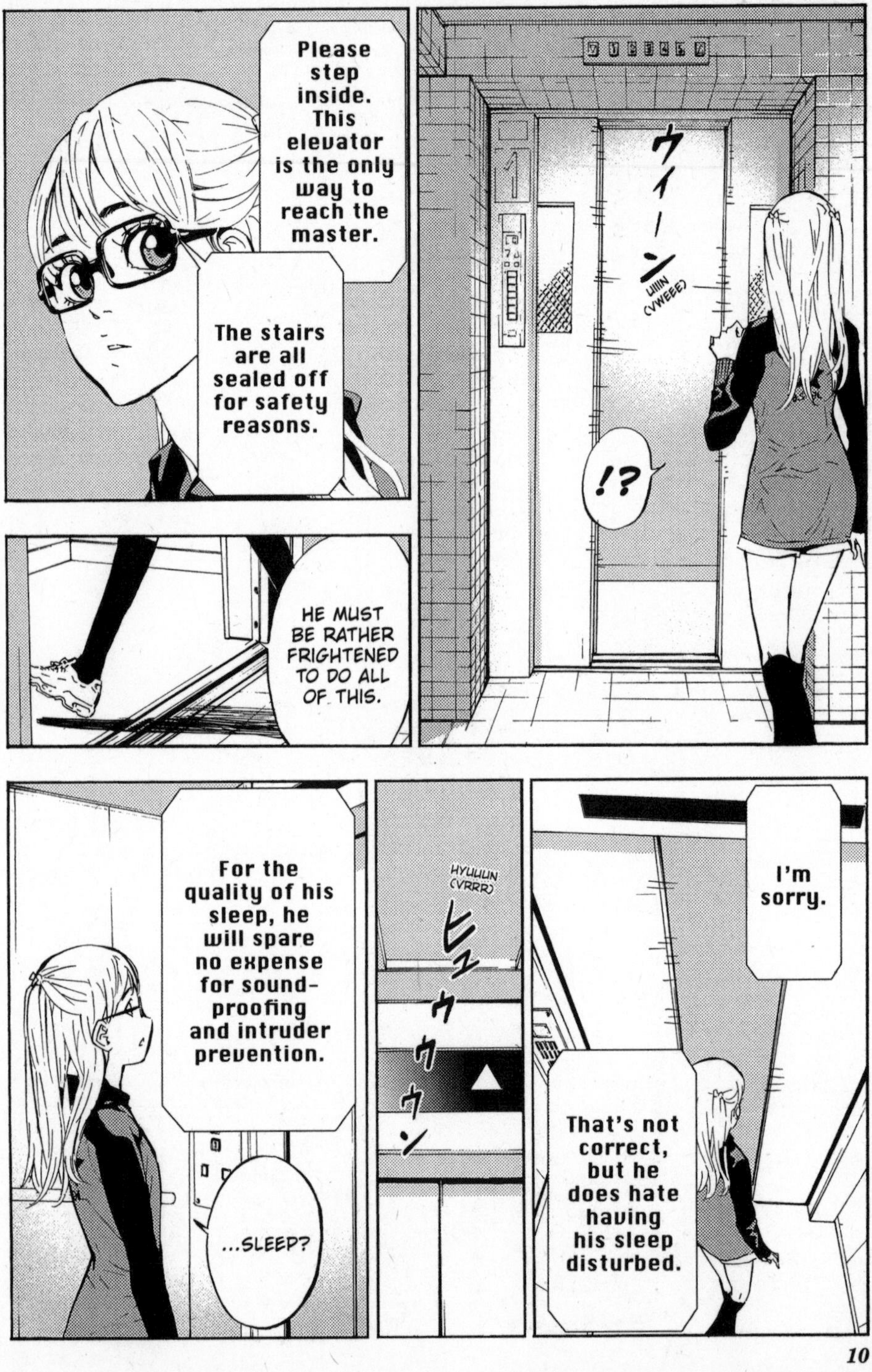
Please step inside. This elevator is the only way to reach the master.
The stairs are all sealed off for safety reasons.
HE MUST BE RATHER FRIGHTENED TO DO ALL OF THIS.
ウイーン
UIIIN (VWEEE)
!?
For the quality of his sleep, he will spare no expense for sound-proofing and intruder prevention.
...SLEEP?
HYUUUN (VRRR)
ヒュウウウン
I'm sorry.
That's not correct, but he does hate having his sleep disturbed.

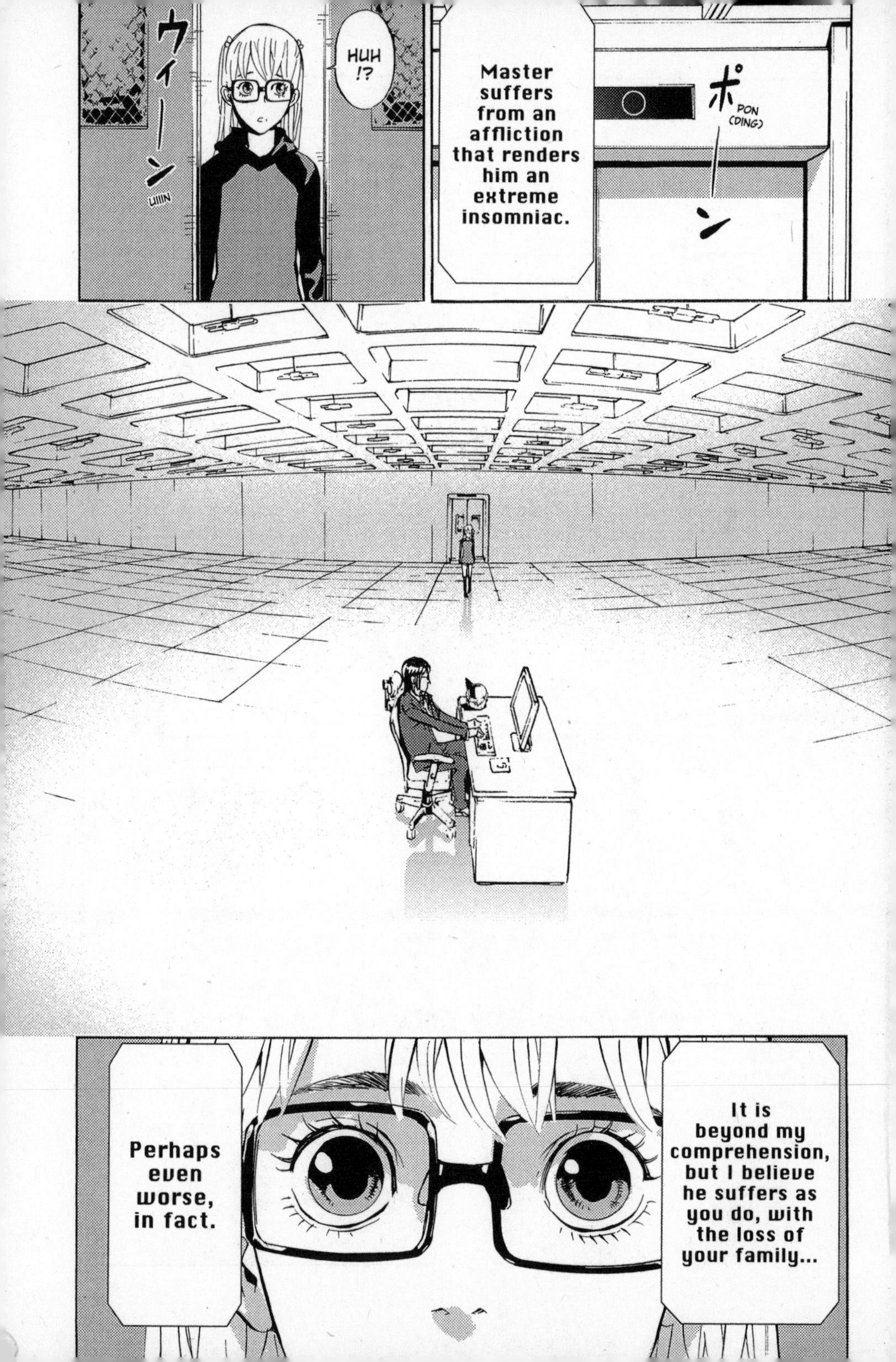

Master suffers from an affliction that renders him an extreme insomniac.
ポン
PON (DING)
ウィーン
UIIIN
HUH !?
It is beyond my comprehension, but I believe he suffers as you do, with the loss of your family...
Perhaps even worse, in fact.

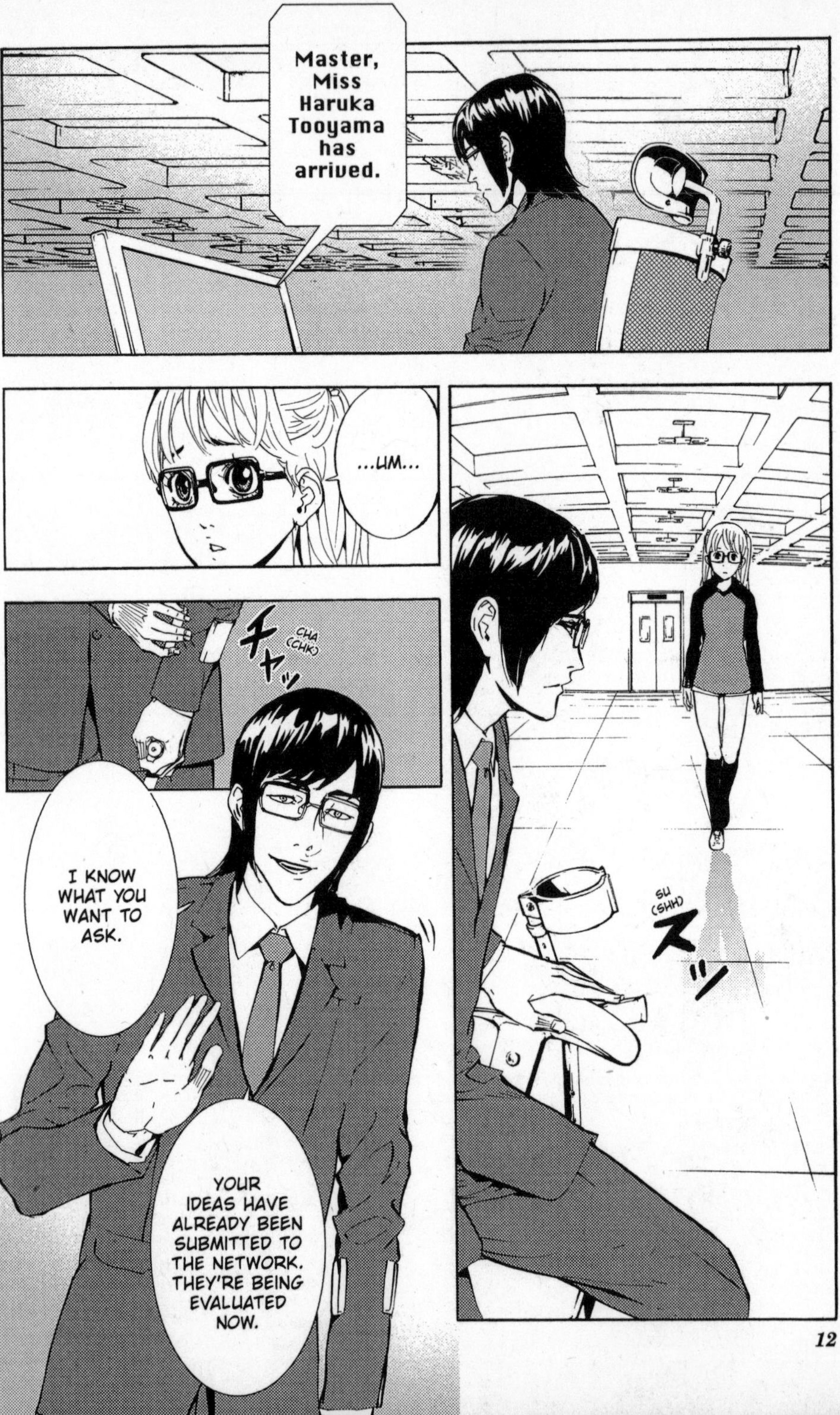
Master, Miss Haruka Tooyama has arrived.
スッ
SU (SHH)
...UM...
チャッ
CHA (CHK)
I KNOW WHAT YOU WANT TO ASK.
YOUR IDEAS HAVE ALREADY BEEN SUBMITTED TO THE NETWORK. THEY'RE BEING EVALUATED NOW.

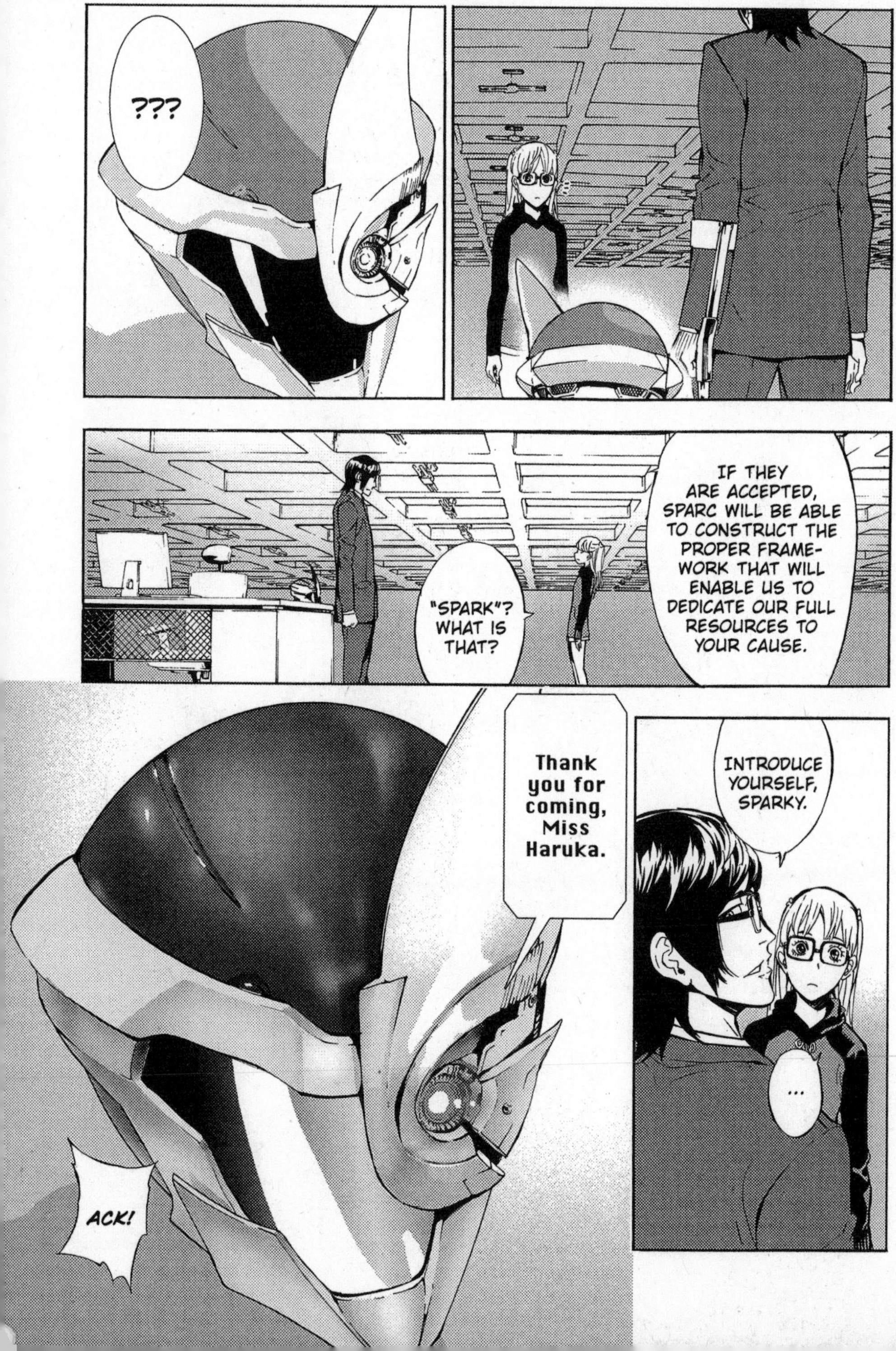
???
IF THEY ARE ACCEPTED, SPARC WILL BE ABLE TO CONSTRUCT THE PROPER FRAME-WORK THAT WILL ENABLE US TO DEDICATE OUR FULL RESOURCES TO YOUR CAUSE.
"SPARK"? WHAT IS THAT?
INTRODUCE YOURSELF, SPARKY.
...
Thank you for coming, Miss Haruka.
ACK!

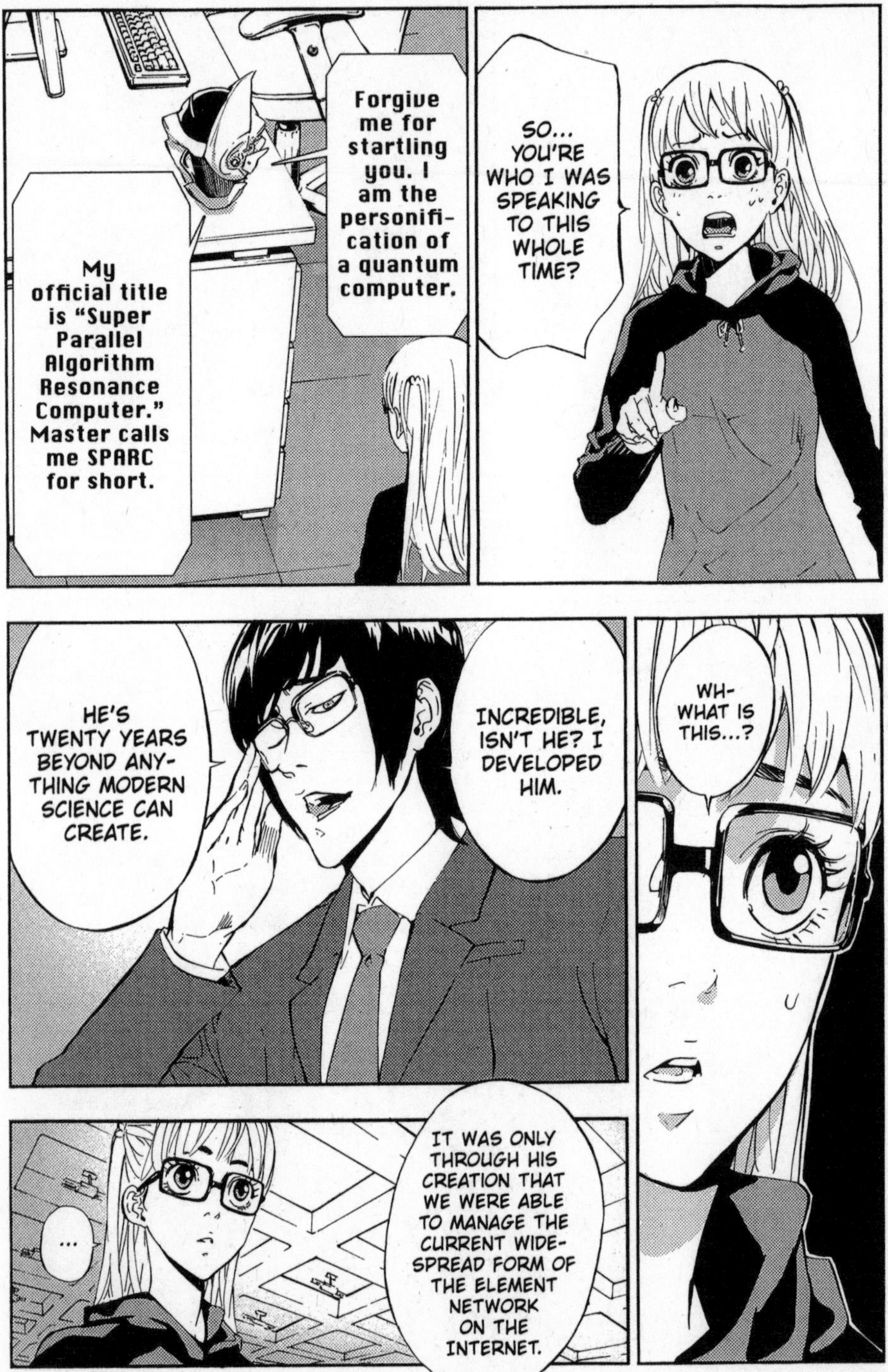
SO... YOU'RE WHO I WAS SPEAKING TO THIS WHOLE TIME?
Forgive me for startling you. I am the personifi-cation of a quantum computer.
My official title is "Super Parallel Algorithm Resonance Computer." Master calls me SPARC for short.
WH-WHAT IS THIS...?
INCREDIBLE, ISN'T HE? I DEVELOPED HIM.
HE'S TWENTY YEARS BEYOND ANY-THING MODERN SCIENCE CAN CREATE.
IT WAS ONLY THROUGH HIS CREATION THAT WE WERE ABLE TO MANAGE THE CURRENT WIDE-SPREAD FORM OF THE ELEMENT NETWORK ON THE INTERNET.
...

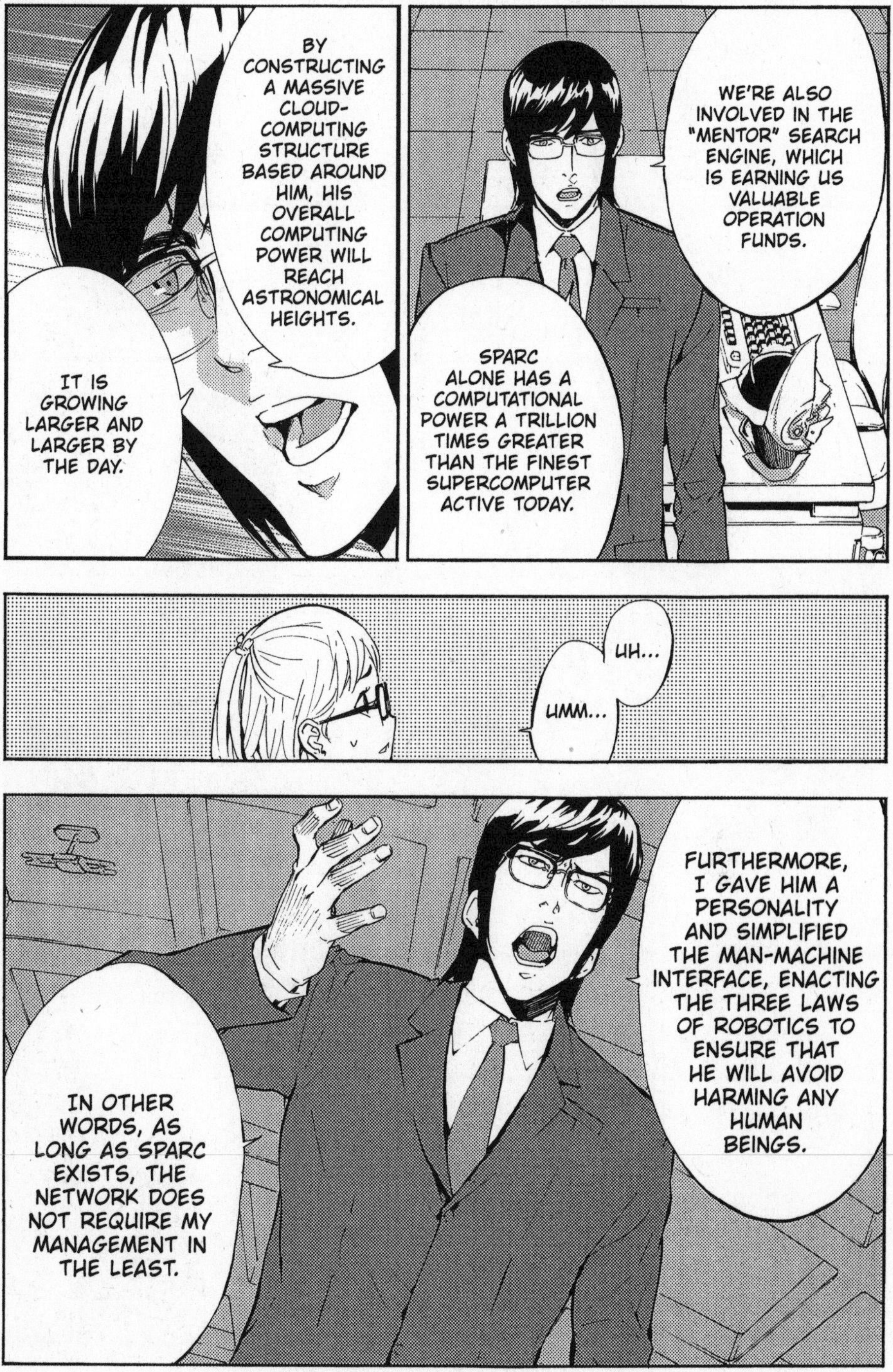
WE'RE ALSO INVOLVED IN THE "MENTOR" SEARCH ENGINE, WHICH IS EARNING US VALUABLE OPERATION FUNDS.
SPARC ALONE HAS A COMPUTATIONAL POWER A TRILLION TIMES GREATER THAN THE FINEST SUPERCOMPUTER ACTIVE TODAY.
BY CONSTRUCTING A MASSIVE CLOUD-COMPUTING STRUCTURE BASED AROUND HIM, HIS OVERALL COMPUTING POWER WILL REACH ASTRONOMICAL HEIGHTS.
IT IS GROWING LARGER AND LARGER BY THE DAY.
UH...
UMM...
FURTHERMORE, I GAVE HIM A PERSONALITY AND SIMPLIFIED THE MAN-MACHINE INTERFACE, ENACTING THE THREE LAWS OF ROBOTICS TO ENSURE THAT HE WILL AVOID HARMING ANY HUMAN BEINGS.
IN OTHER WORDS, AS LONG AS SPARC EXISTS, THE NETWORK DOES NOT REQUIRE MY MANAGEMENT IN THE LEAST.

...

HUH!?

OH, GREAT. I DID IT *AGAIN*. I'M SORRY.

THAT'S... AMAZING...

TO HELP OTHERS?

THE POINT IS, I NEEDED HIM IN ORDER TO HELP OTHERS.

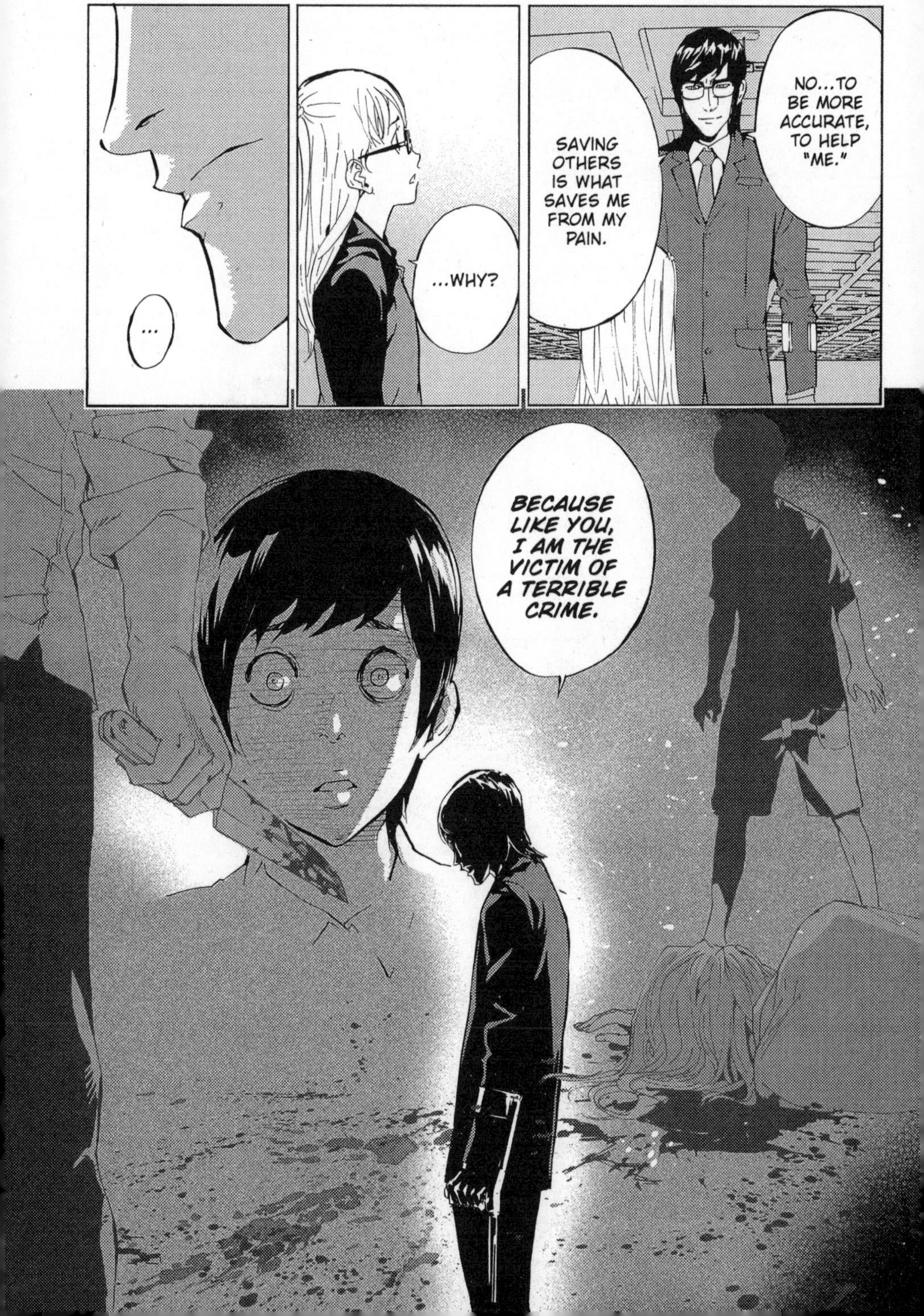
NO...TO BE MORE ACCURATE, TO HELP "ME."
SAVING OTHERS IS WHAT SAVES ME FROM MY PAIN.
...WHY?
...
BECAUSE LIKE YOU, I AM THE VICTIM OF A TERRIBLE CRIME.

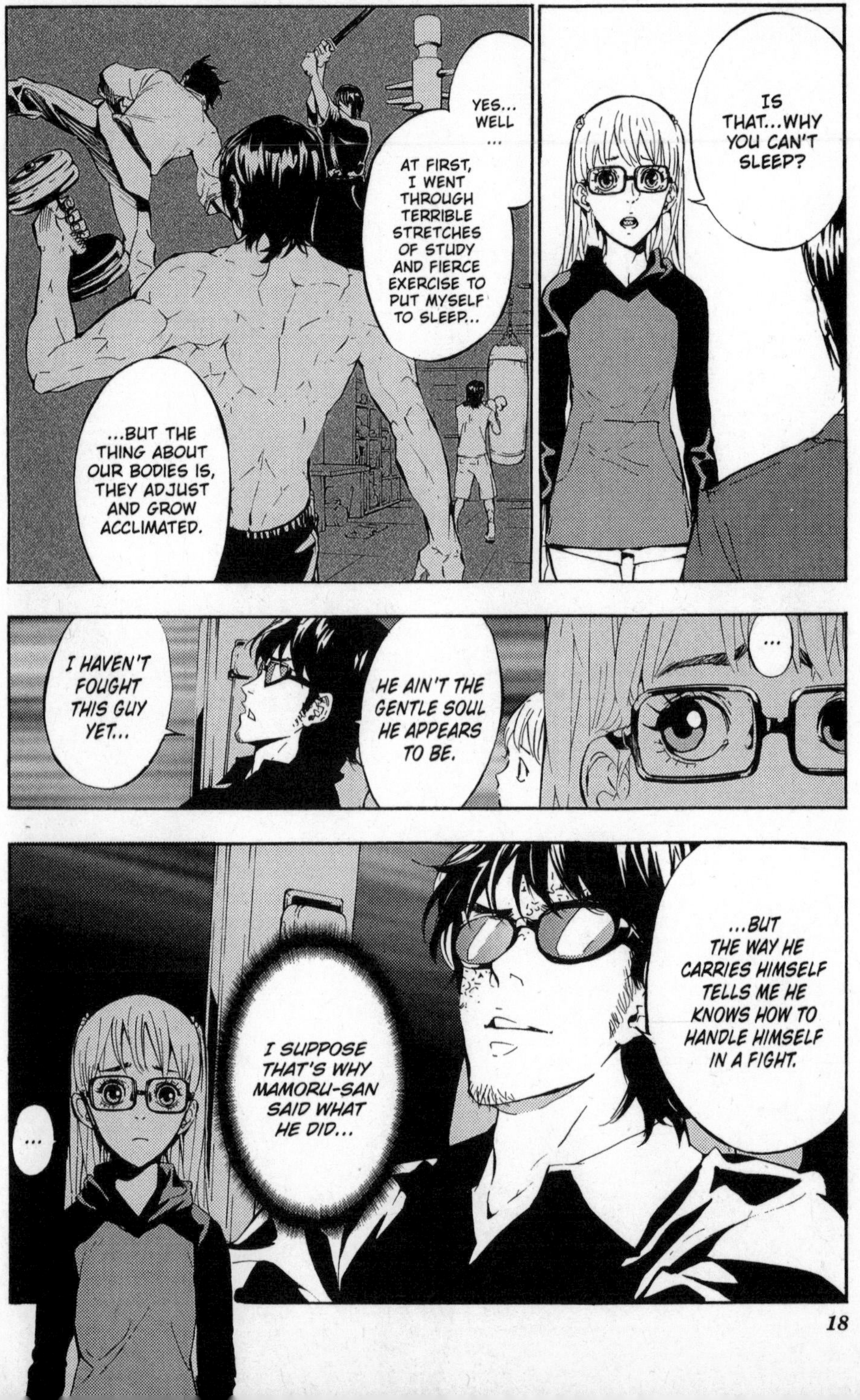
IS THAT...WHY YOU CAN'T SLEEP?
YES... WELL ...
AT FIRST, I WENT THROUGH TERRIBLE STRETCHES OF STUDY AND FIERCE EXERCISE TO PUT MYSELF TO SLEEP...
...BUT THE THING ABOUT OUR BODIES IS, THEY ADJUST AND GROW ACCLIMATED.
...
HE AIN'T THE GENTLE SOUL HE APPEARS TO BE.
I HAVEN'T FOUGHT THIS GUY YET...
...BUT THE WAY HE CARRIES HIMSELF TELLS ME HE KNOWS HOW TO HANDLE HIMSELF IN A FIGHT.
I SUPPOSE THAT'S WHY MAMORU-SAN SAID WHAT HE DID...
...

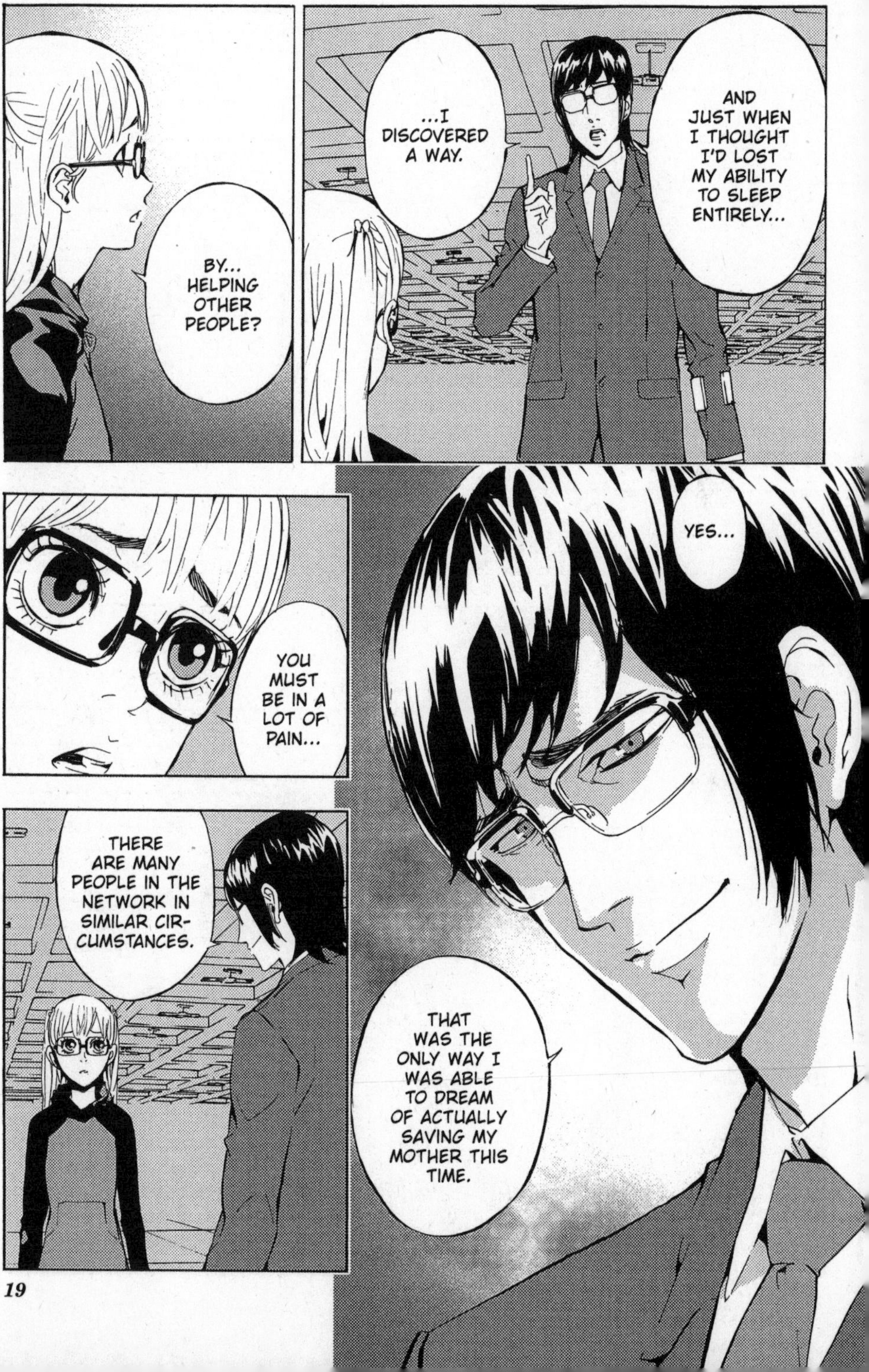
AND JUST WHEN I THOUGHT I'D LOST MY ABILITY TO SLEEP ENTIRELY...
...I DISCOVERED A WAY.
BY... HELPING OTHER PEOPLE?
YES...
THAT WAS THE ONLY WAY I WAS ABLE TO DREAM OF ACTUALLY SAVING MY MOTHER THIS TIME.
YOU MUST BE IN A LOT OF PAIN...
THERE ARE MANY PEOPLE IN THE NETWORK IN SIMILAR CIR-CUMSTANCES.

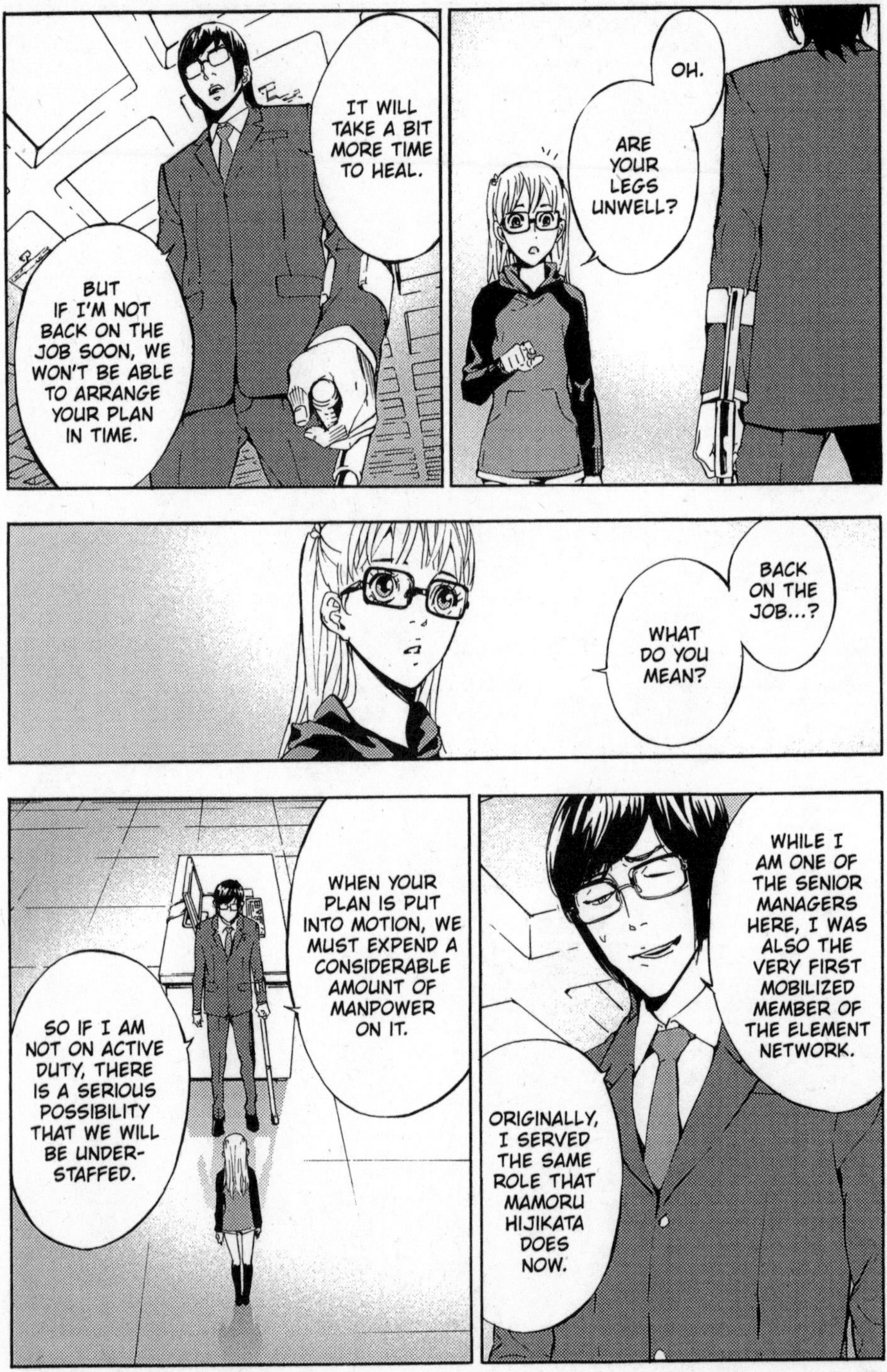
OH.
ARE YOUR LEGS UNWELL?
IT WILL TAKE A BIT MORE TIME TO HEAL.
BUT IF I'M NOT BACK ON THE JOB SOON, WE WON'T BE ABLE TO ARRANGE YOUR PLAN IN TIME.
BACK ON THE JOB...?
WHAT DO YOU MEAN?
WHILE I AM ONE OF THE SENIOR MANAGERS HERE, I WAS ALSO THE VERY FIRST MOBILIZED MEMBER OF THE ELEMENT NETWORK.
ORIGINALLY, I SERVED THE SAME ROLE THAT MAMORU HIJIKATA DOES NOW.
WHEN YOUR PLAN IS PUT INTO MOTION, WE MUST EXPEND A CONSIDERABLE AMOUNT OF MANPOWER ON IT.
SO IF I AM NOT ON ACTIVE DUTY, THERE IS A SERIOUS POSSIBILITY THAT WE WILL BE UNDER-STAFFED.

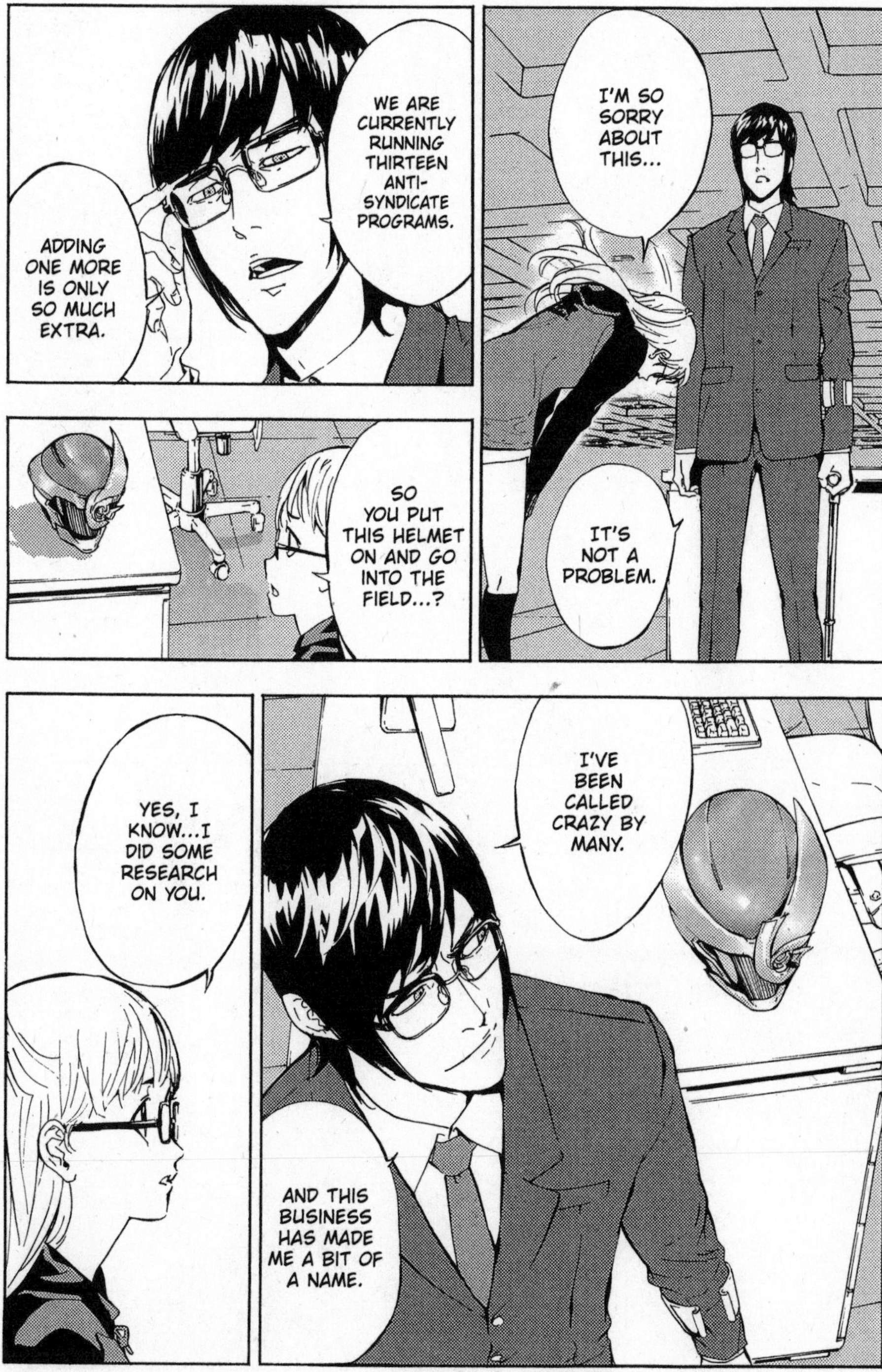
I'M SO SORRY ABOUT THIS...
IT'S NOT A PROBLEM.
WE ARE CURRENTLY RUNNING THIRTEEN ANTI-SYNDICATE PROGRAMS.
ADDING ONE MORE IS ONLY SO MUCH EXTRA.
SO YOU PUT THIS HELMET ON AND GO INTO THE FIELD...?
I'VE BEEN CALLED CRAZY BY MANY.
AND THIS BUSINESS HAS MADE ME A BIT OF A NAME.
YES, I KNOW...I DID SOME RESEARCH ON YOU.

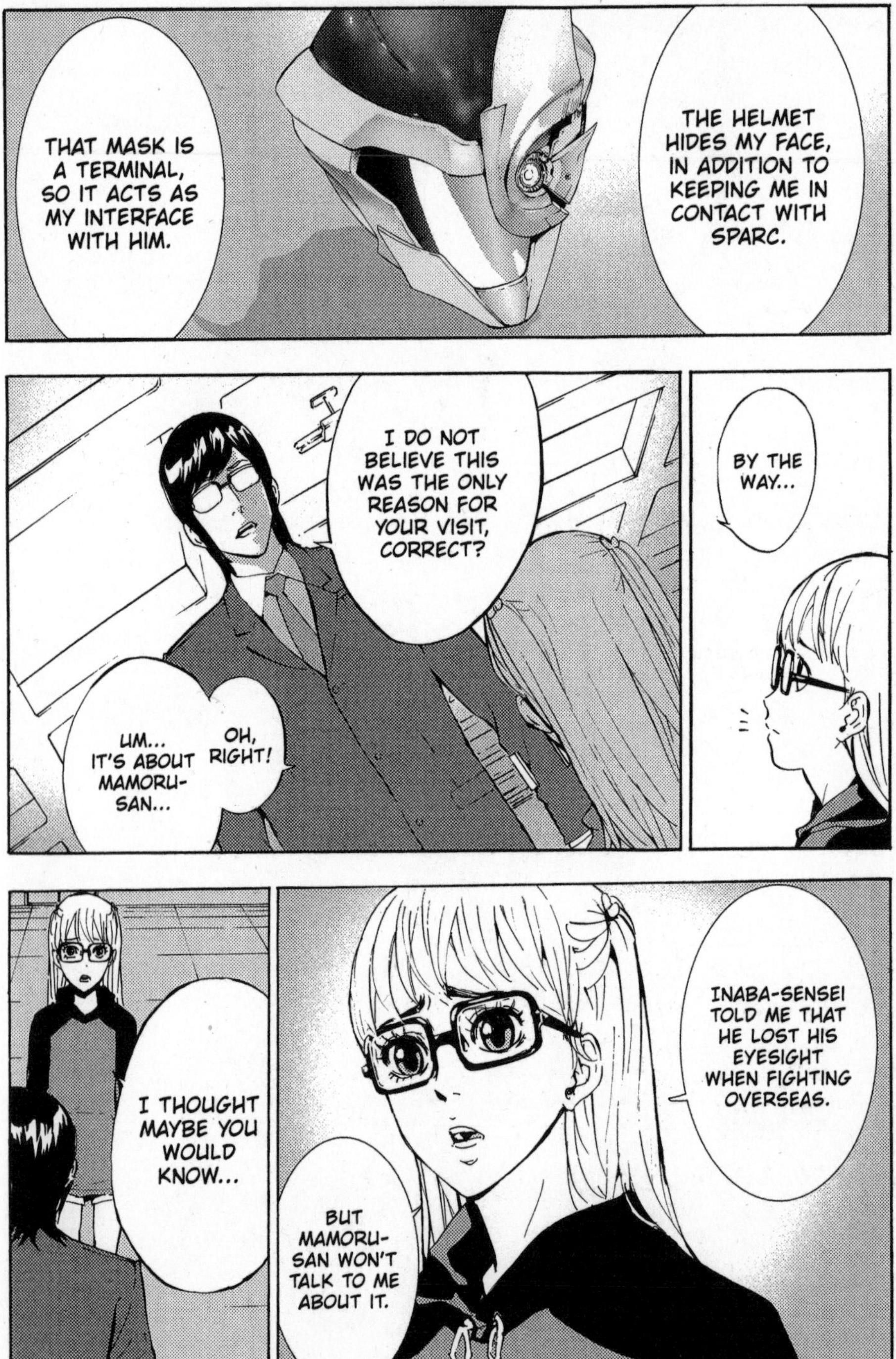
THE HELMET HIDES MY FACE, IN ADDITION TO KEEPING ME IN CONTACT WITH SPARC.
THAT MASK IS A TERMINAL, SO IT ACTS AS MY INTERFACE WITH HIM.
BY THE WAY...
I DO NOT BELIEVE THIS WAS THE ONLY REASON FOR YOUR VISIT, CORRECT?
OH, RIGHT!
UM... IT'S ABOUT MAMORU-SAN...
INABA-SENSEI TOLD ME THAT HE LOST HIS EYESIGHT WHEN FIGHTING OVERSEAS.
BUT MAMORU-SAN WON'T TALK TO ME ABOUT IT.
I THOUGHT MAYBE YOU WOULD KNOW...

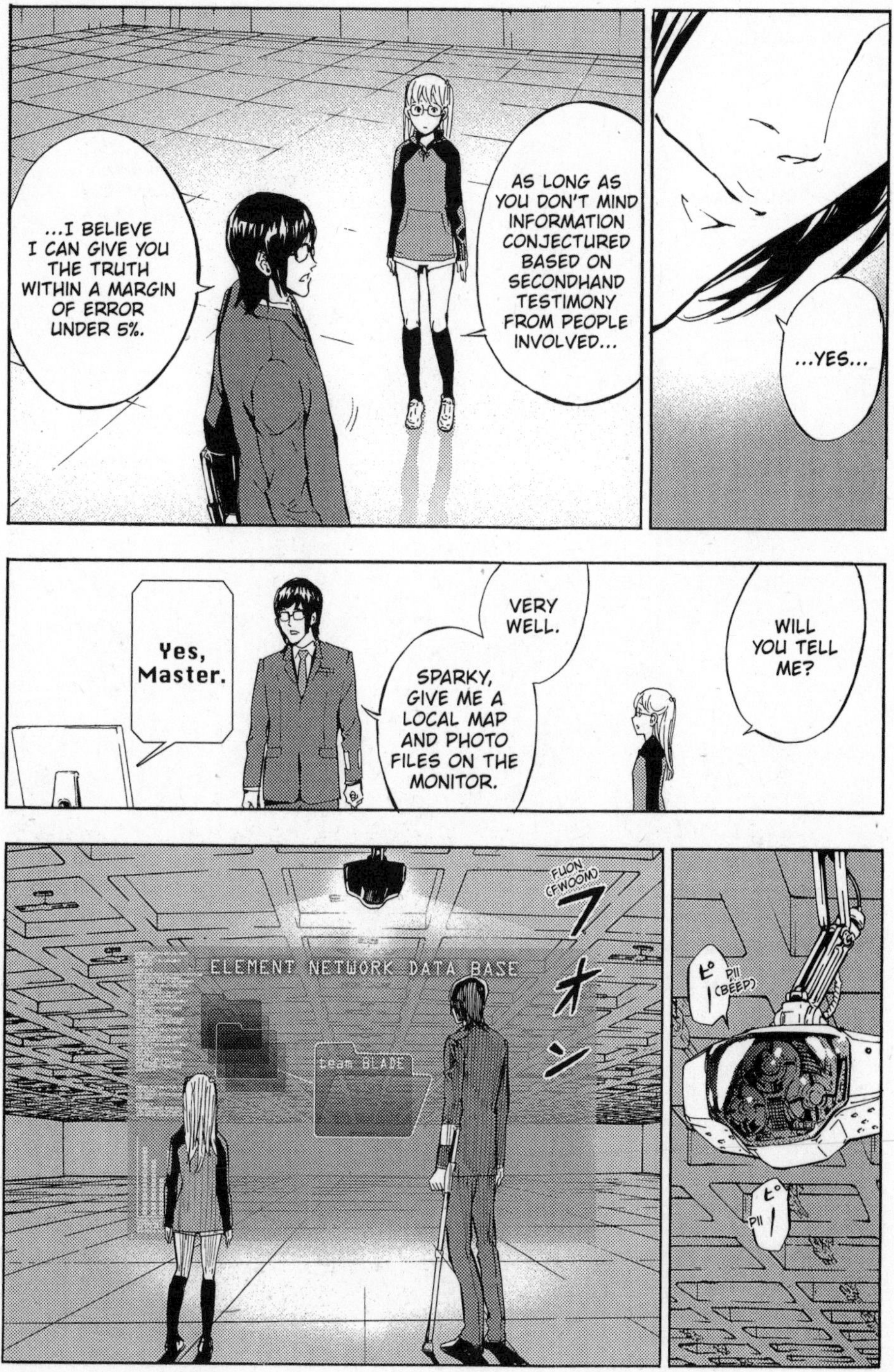
...YES...
AS LONG AS YOU DON'T MIND INFORMATION CONJECTURED BASED ON SECONDHAND TESTIMONY FROM PEOPLE INVOLVED...
...I BELIEVE I CAN GIVE YOU THE TRUTH WITHIN A MARGIN OF ERROR UNDER 5%.
WILL YOU TELL ME?
VERY WELL.
SPARKY, GIVE ME A LOCAL MAP AND PHOTO FILES ON THE MONITOR.
Yes, Master.
ピー
PII (BEEP)
ピー
PII
フォン
FUON (FWOOM)
ELEMENT NETWORK DATA BASE
team BLADE

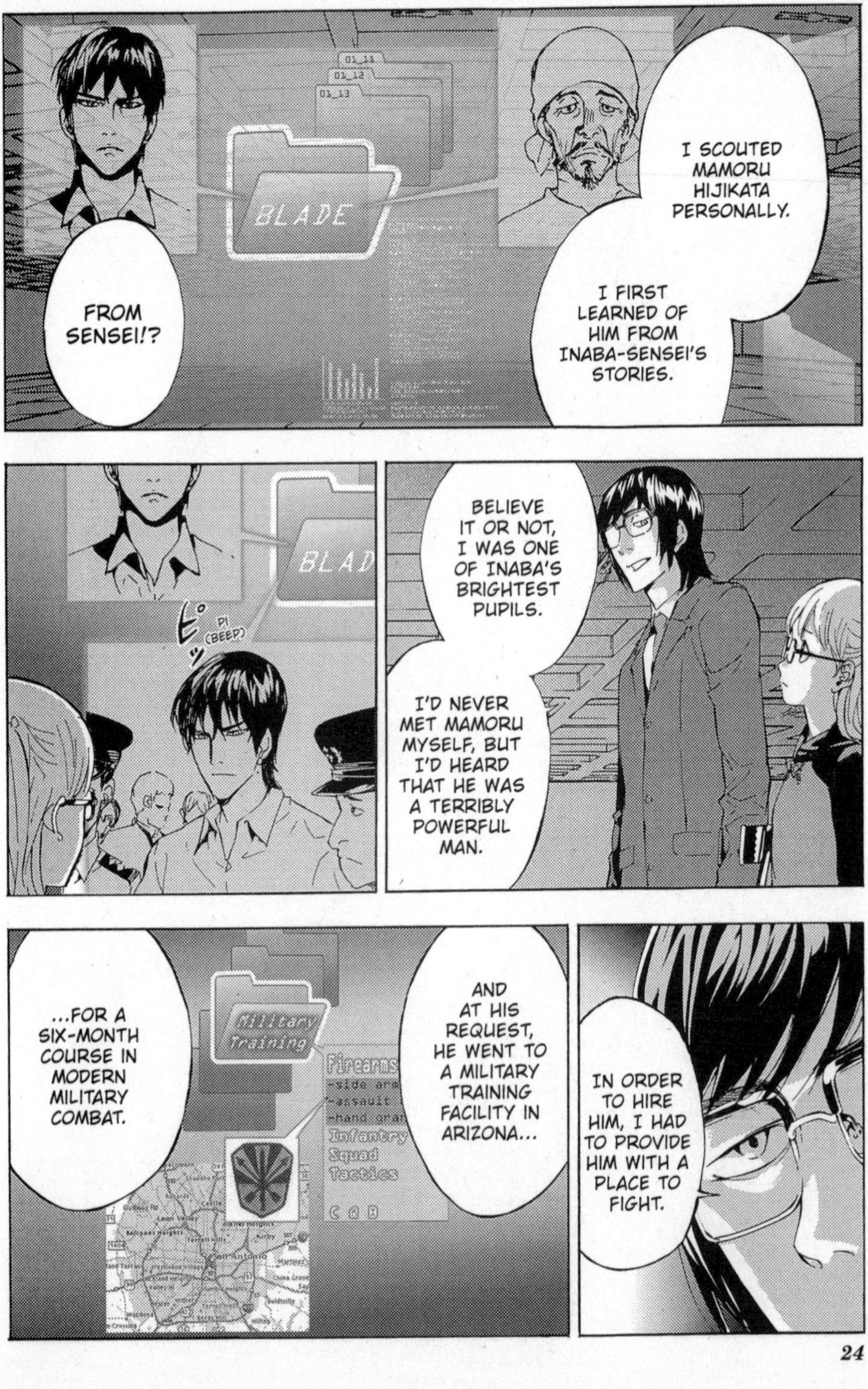
I SCOUTED MAMORU HIJIKATA PERSONALLY.
I FIRST LEARNED OF HIM FROM INABA-SENSEI'S STORIES.
01_11
01_12
01_13
BLADE
FROM SENSEI!?
BELIEVE IT OR NOT, I WAS ONE OF INABA'S BRIGHTEST PUPILS.
I'D NEVER MET MAMORU MYSELF, BUT I'D HEARD THAT HE WAS A TERRIBLY POWERFUL MAN.
BLAD
PI (BEEP)
IN ORDER TO HIRE HIM, I HAD TO PROVIDE HIM WITH A PLACE TO FIGHT.
AND AT HIS REQUEST, HE WENT TO A MILITARY TRAINING FACILITY IN ARIZONA...
Military Training
Firearms
-side arm
-assault
-hand gran
Infantry
Squad
Tactics
...FOR A SIX-MONTH COURSE IN MODERN MILITARY COMBAT.

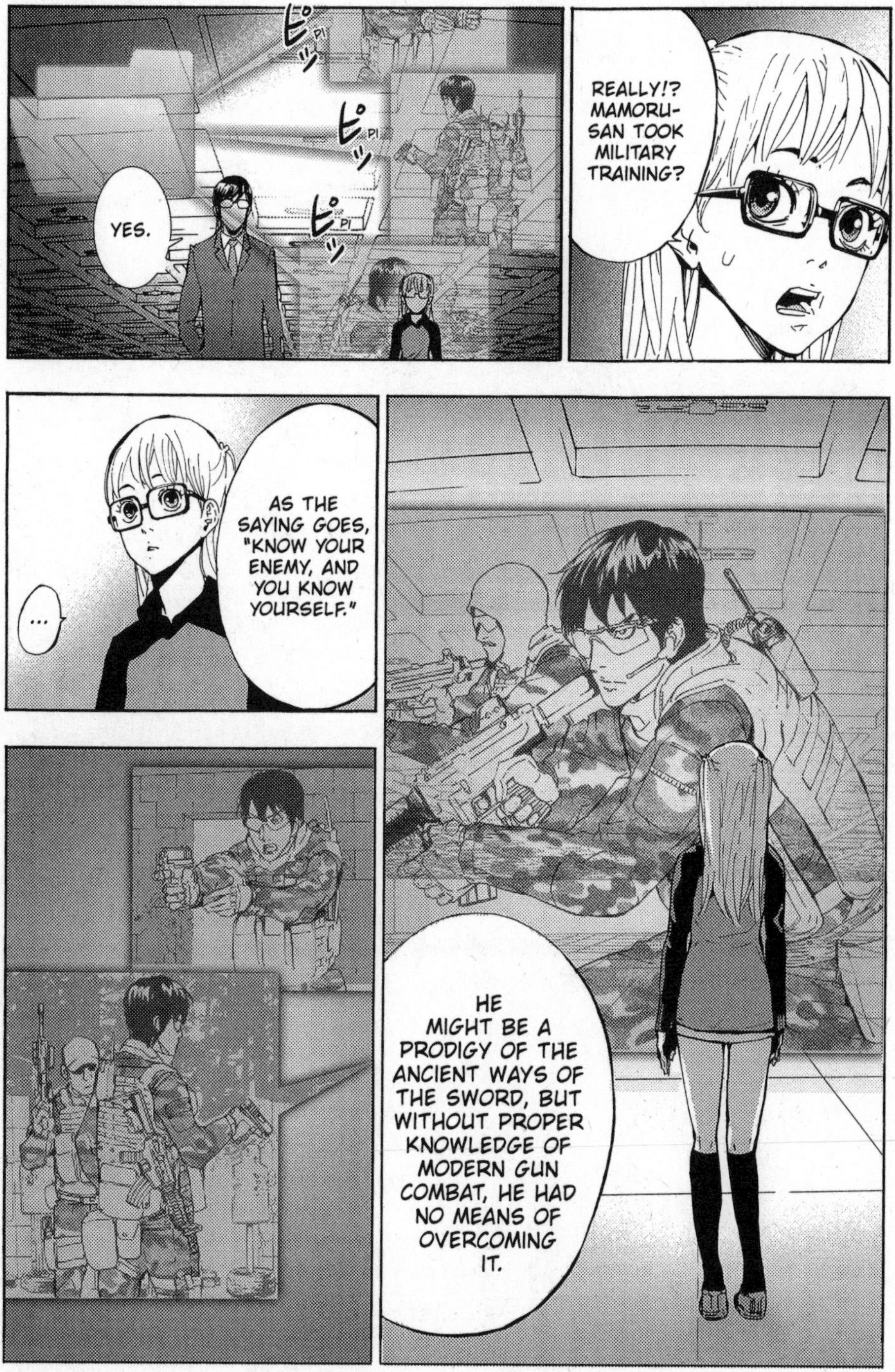
REALLY!? MAMORU-SAN TOOK MILITARY TRAINING?
ピッ PI
ピッ PI
ピッ PI
YES.
HE MIGHT BE A PRODIGY OF THE ANCIENT WAYS OF THE SWORD, BUT WITHOUT PROPER KNOWLEDGE OF MODERN GUN COMBAT, HE HAD NO MEANS OF OVERCOMING IT.
AS THE SAYING GOES, "KNOW YOUR ENEMY, AND YOU KNOW YOURSELF."
...

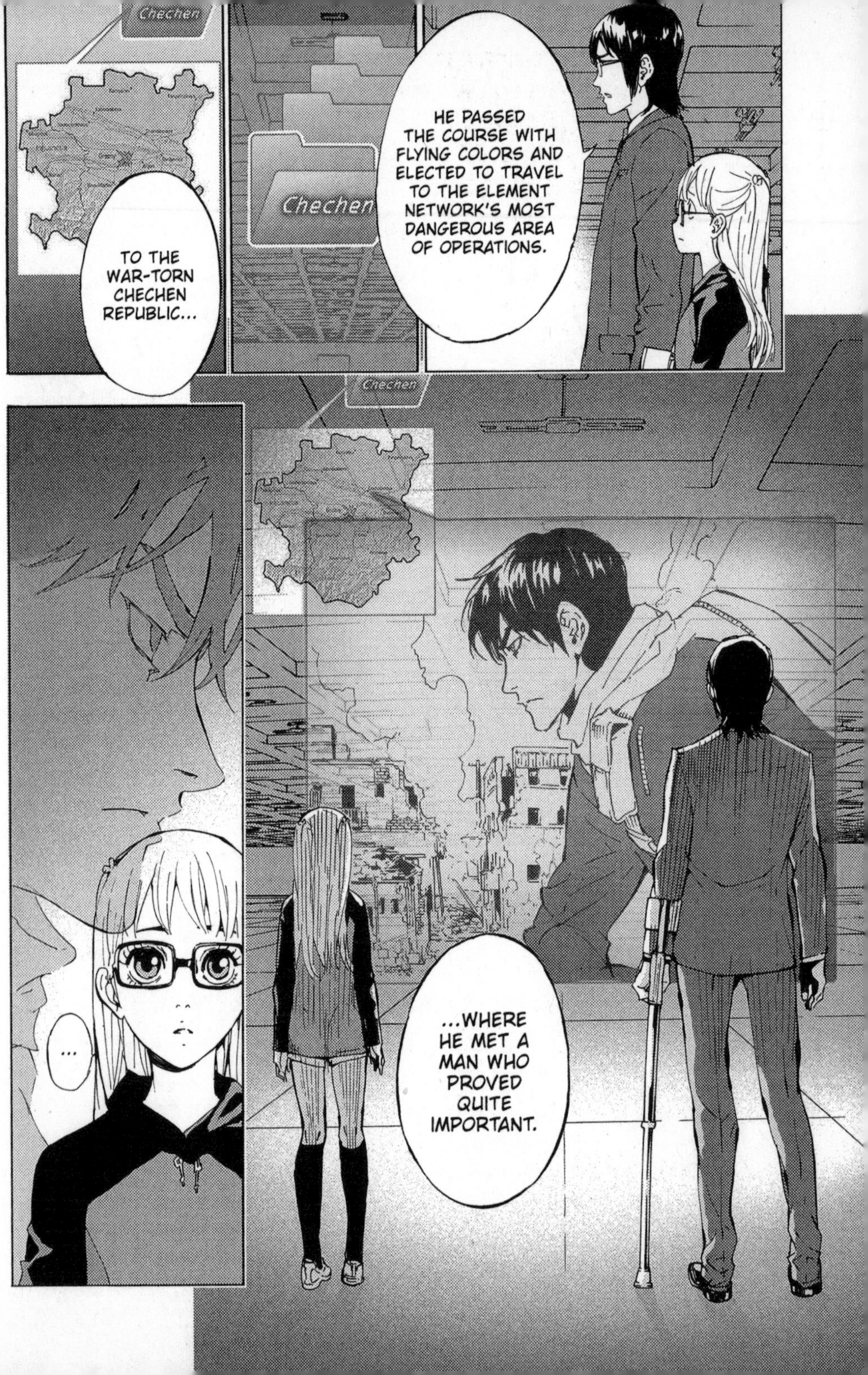
HE PASSED THE COURSE WITH FLYING COLORS AND ELECTED TO TRAVEL TO THE ELEMENT NETWORK'S MOST DANGEROUS AREA OF OPERATIONS.
Chechen
Chechen
TO THE WAR-TORN CHECHEN REPUBLIC...
Chechen
...WHERE HE MET A MAN WHO PROVED QUITE IMPORTANT.
...

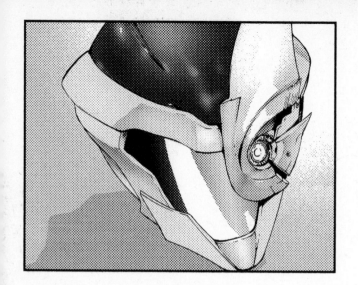

Until Death do us Part

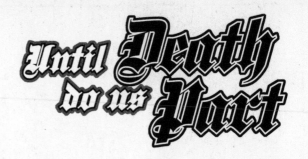

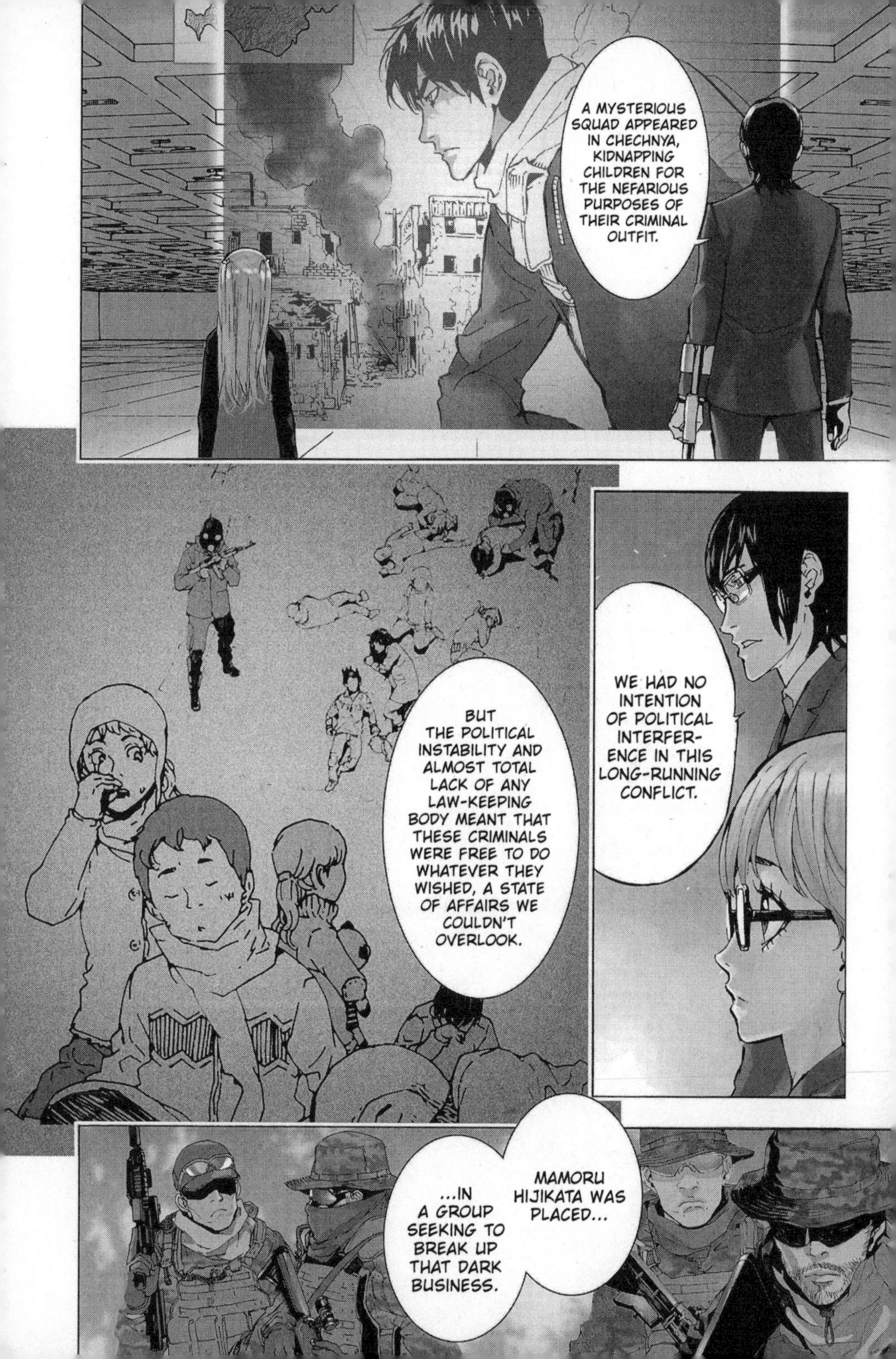
A MYSTERIOUS SQUAD APPEARED IN CHECHNYA, KIDNAPPING CHILDREN FOR THE NEFARIOUS PURPOSES OF THEIR CRIMINAL OUTFIT.
WE HAD NO INTENTION OF POLITICAL INTERFER-ENCE IN THIS LONG-RUNNING CONFLICT.
BUT THE POLITICAL INSTABILITY AND ALMOST TOTAL LACK OF ANY LAW-KEEPING BODY MEANT THAT THESE CRIMINALS WERE FREE TO DO WHATEVER THEY WISHED, A STATE OF AFFAIRS WE COULDN'T OVERLOOK.
MAMORU HIJIKATA WAS PLACED...
...IN A GROUP SEEKING TO BREAK UP THAT DARK BUSINESS.

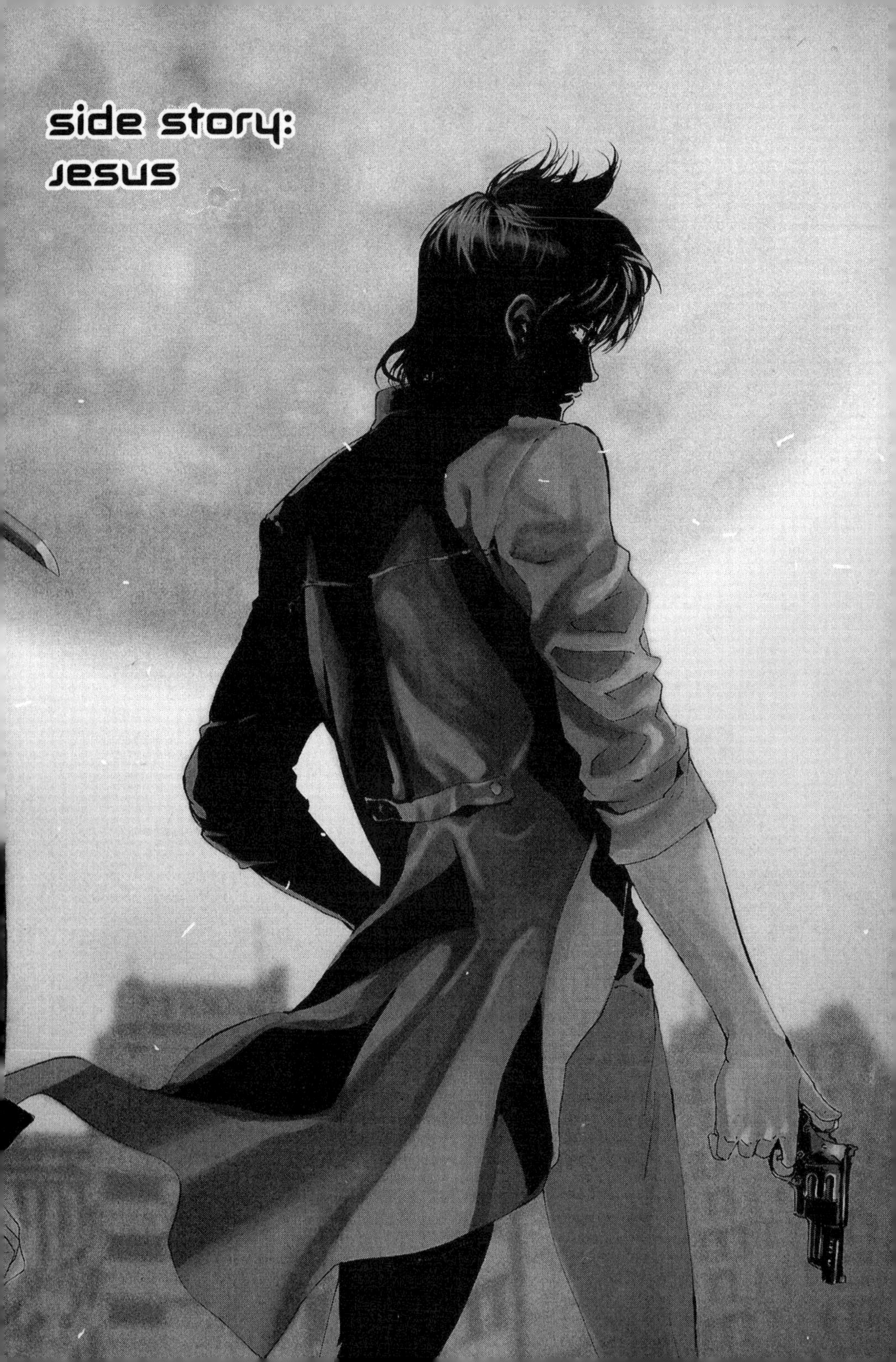
side story:
jesus

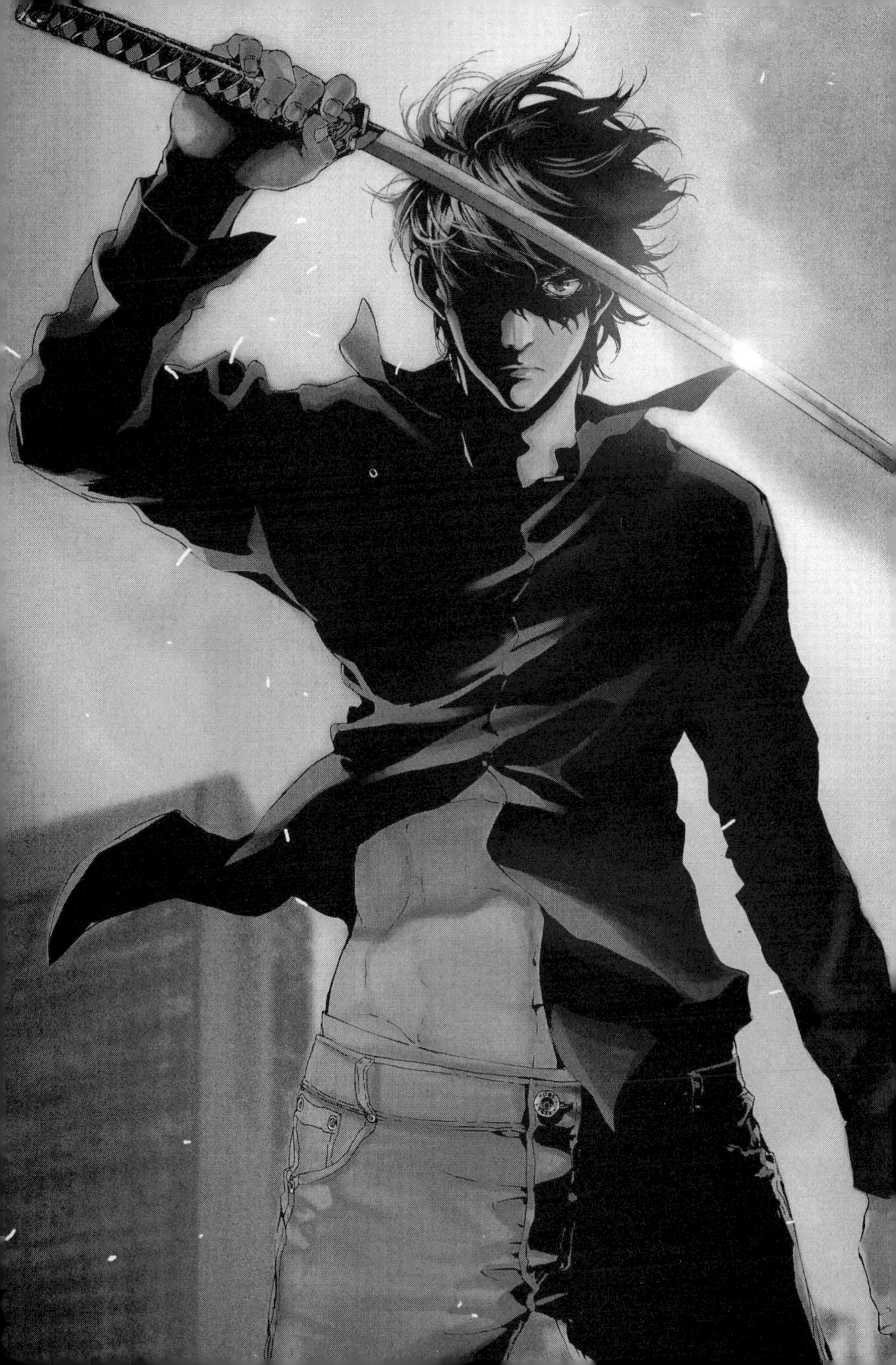

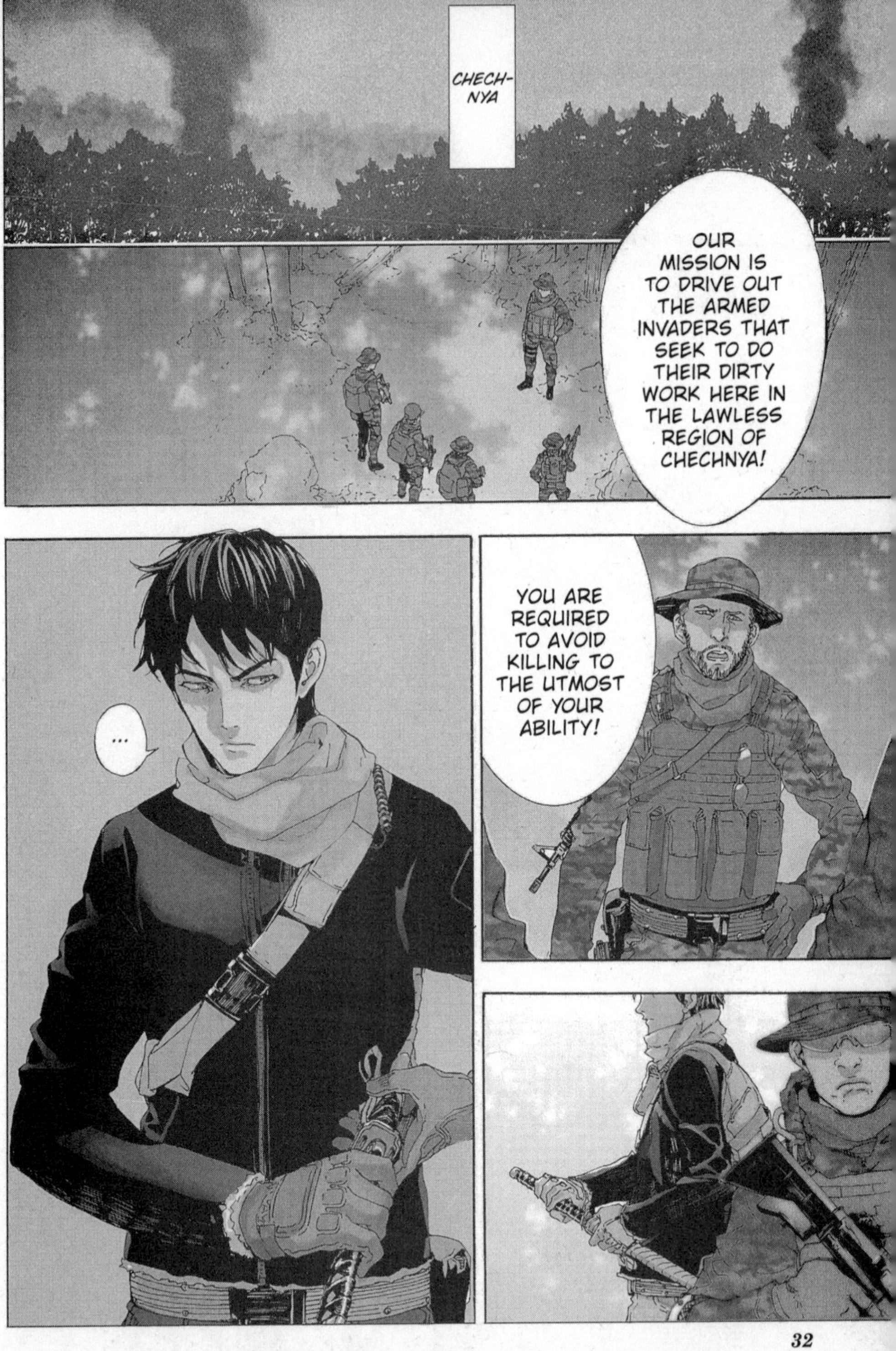
CHECH-NYA
OUR MISSION IS TO DRIVE OUT THE ARMED INVADERS THAT SEEK TO DO THEIR DIRTY WORK HERE IN THE LAWLESS REGION OF CHECHNYA!
YOU ARE REQUIRED TO AVOID KILLING TO THE UTMOST OF YOUR ABILITY!
...

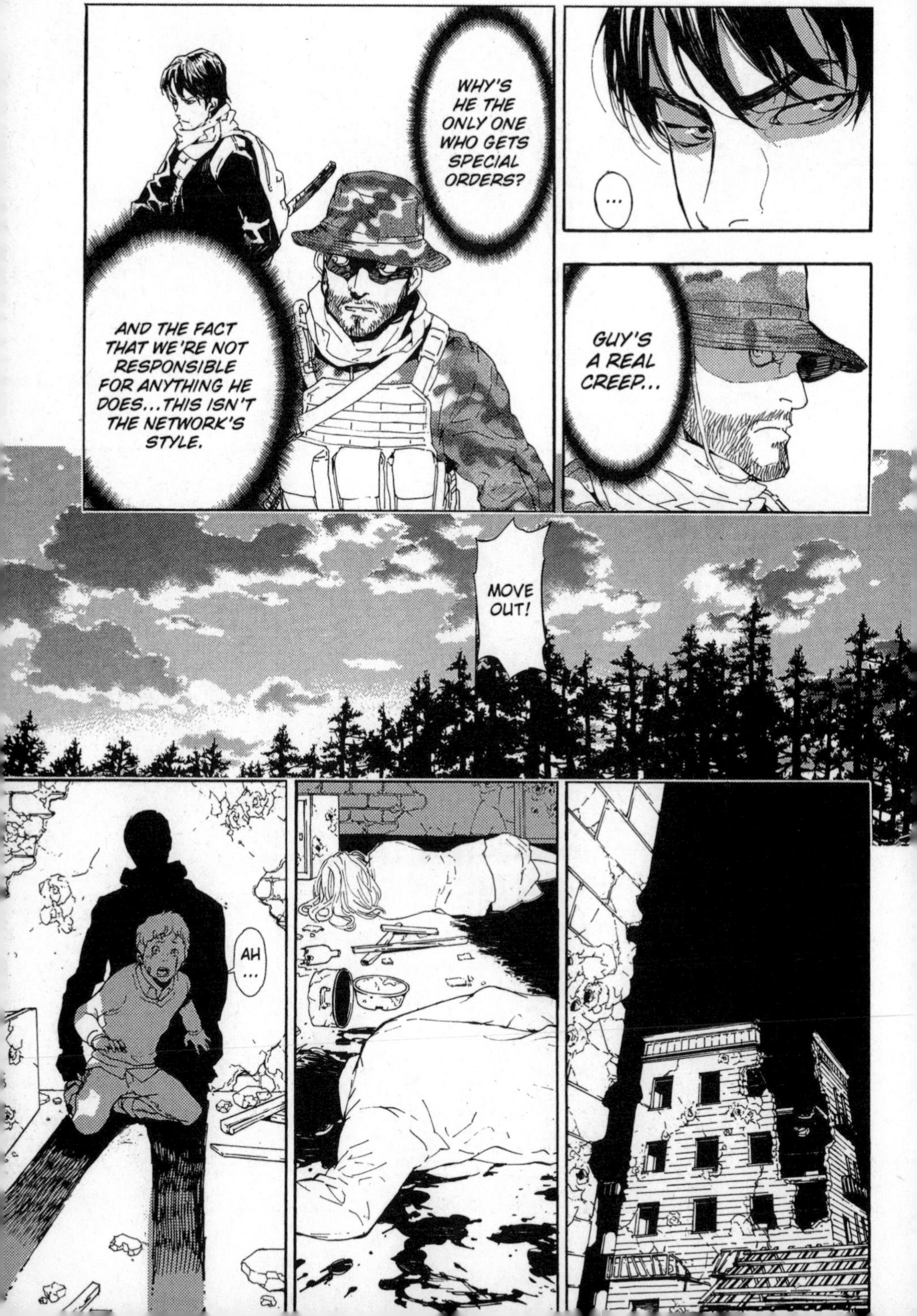
...
GUY'S A REAL CREEP...
WHY'S HE THE ONLY ONE WHO GETS SPECIAL ORDERS?
AND THE FACT THAT WE'RE NOT RESPONSIBLE FOR ANYTHING HE DOES...THIS ISN'T THE NETWORK'S STYLE.
MOVE OUT!
AH ...

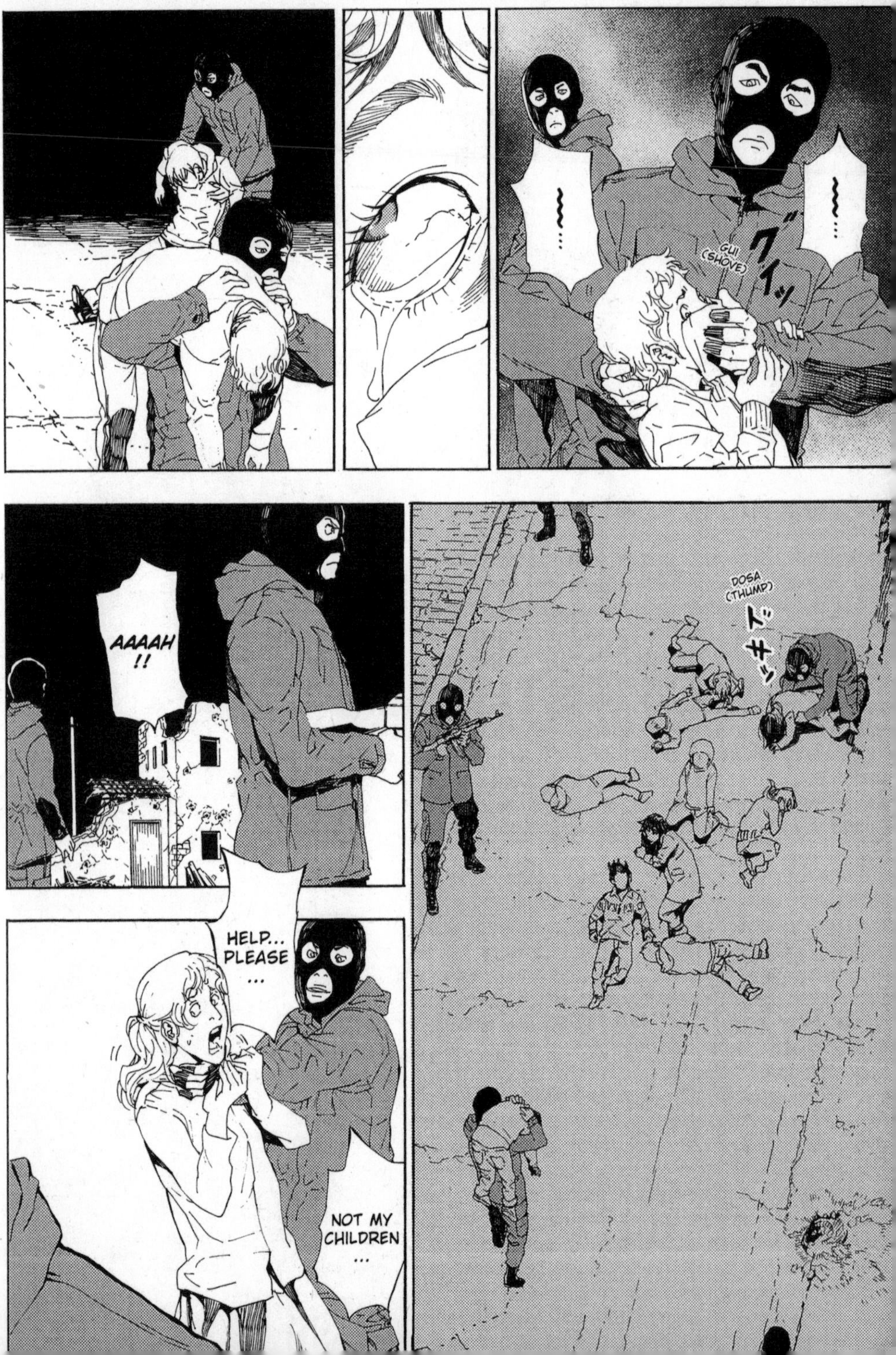

...
...
GUI (SHOVE)
グイッ
DOSA (THUMP)
ドサッ
AAAAH !!
HELP... PLEASE ...
NOT MY CHILDREN ...

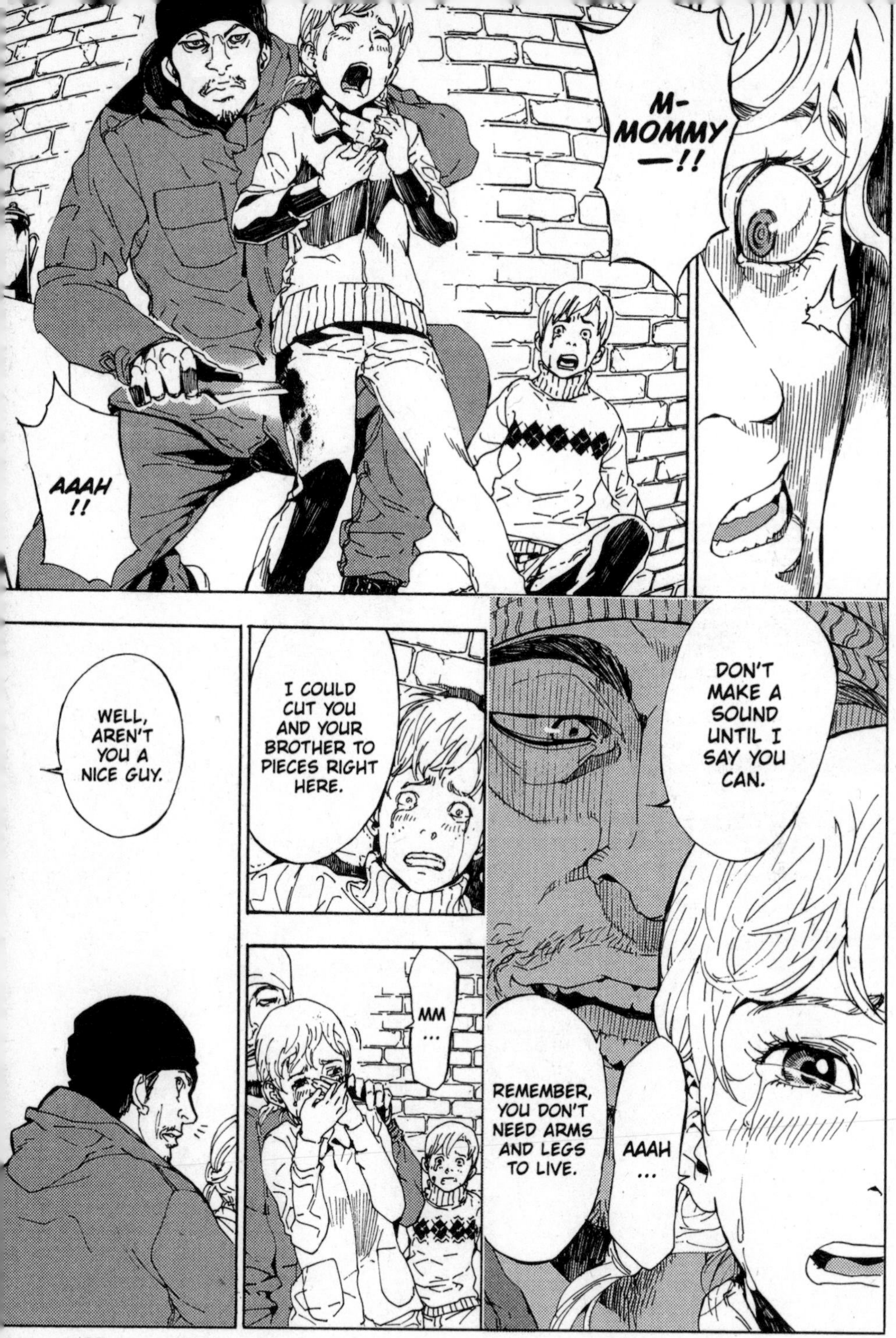
M-MOMMY—!!
AAAH !!
DON'T MAKE A SOUND UNTIL I SAY YOU CAN.
AAAH ...
REMEMBER, YOU DON'T NEED ARMS AND LEGS TO LIVE.
I COULD CUT YOU AND YOUR BROTHER TO PIECES RIGHT HERE.
MM ...
WELL, AREN'T YOU A NICE GUY.

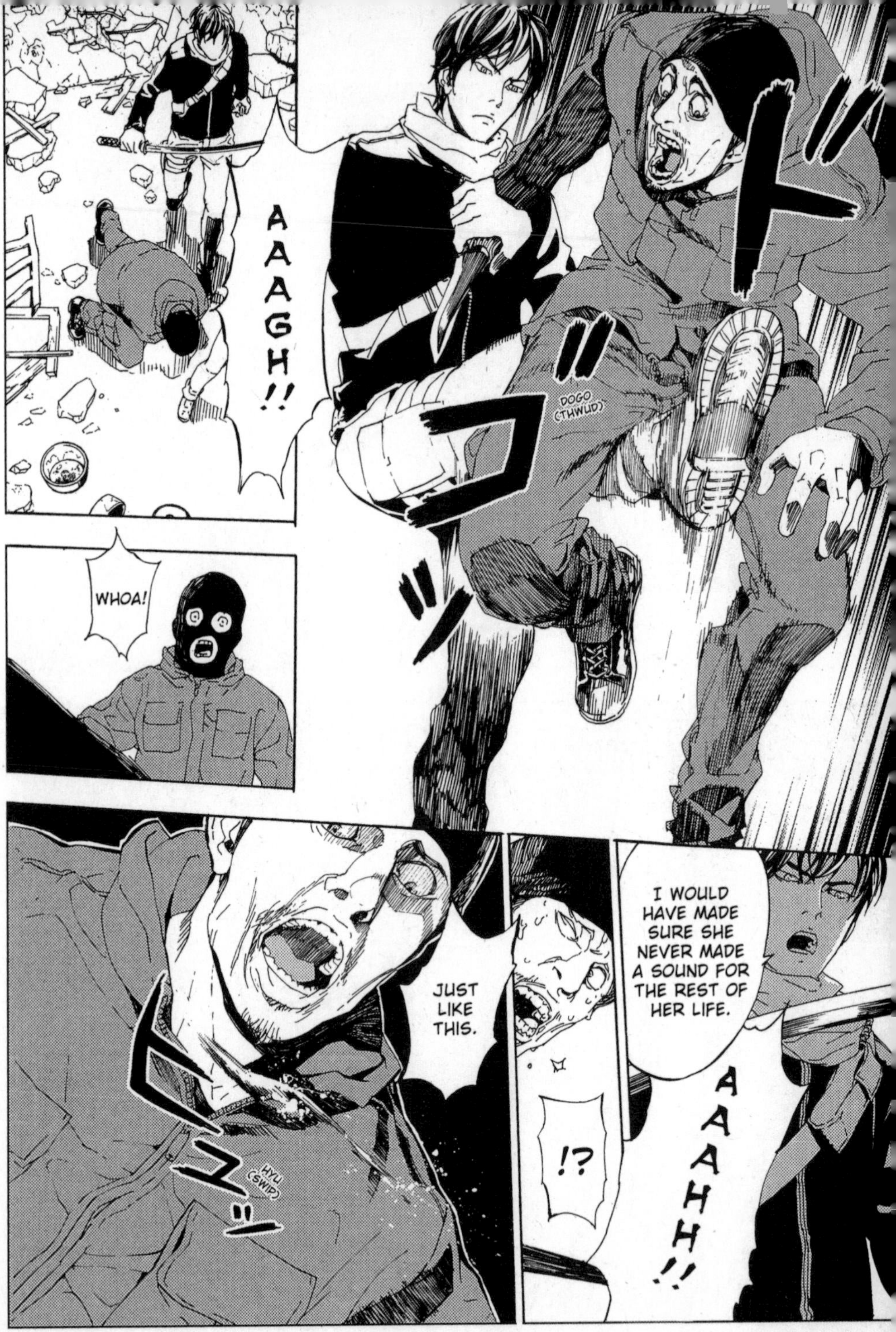
DOGO (THWUD)
AAAAGH!!
WHOA!
I WOULD HAVE MADE SURE SHE NEVER MADE A SOUND FOR THE REST OF HER LIFE.
AAAAHH!!
!?
JUST LIKE THIS.
HYU (SWIP)

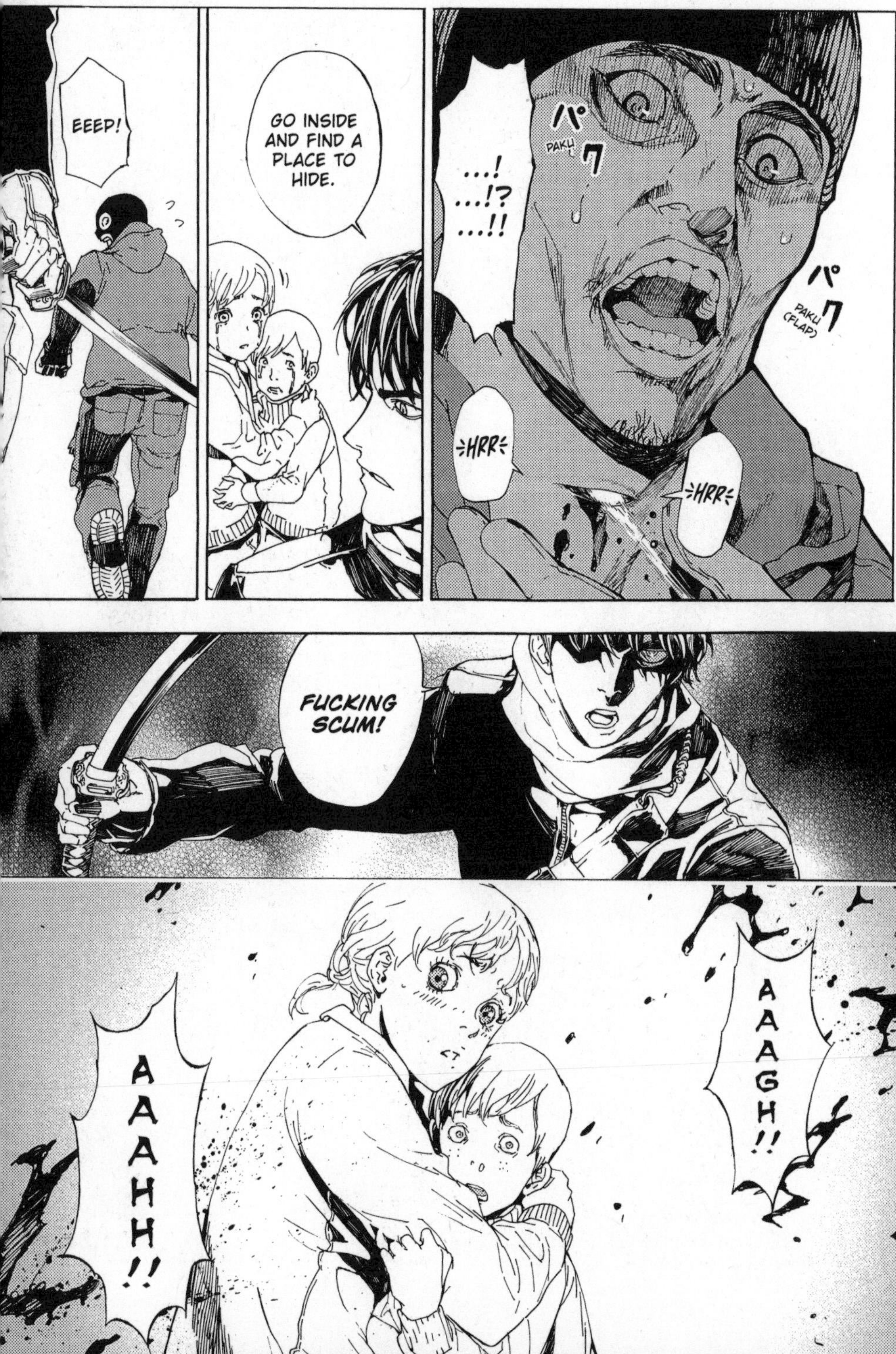
パク
PAKU
...!
...!?
...!!
パク
PAKU (FLAP)
HRR
HRR
GO INSIDE AND FIND A PLACE TO HIDE.
EEEP!
FUCKING SCUM!
AAAGH!!
AAAHH!!

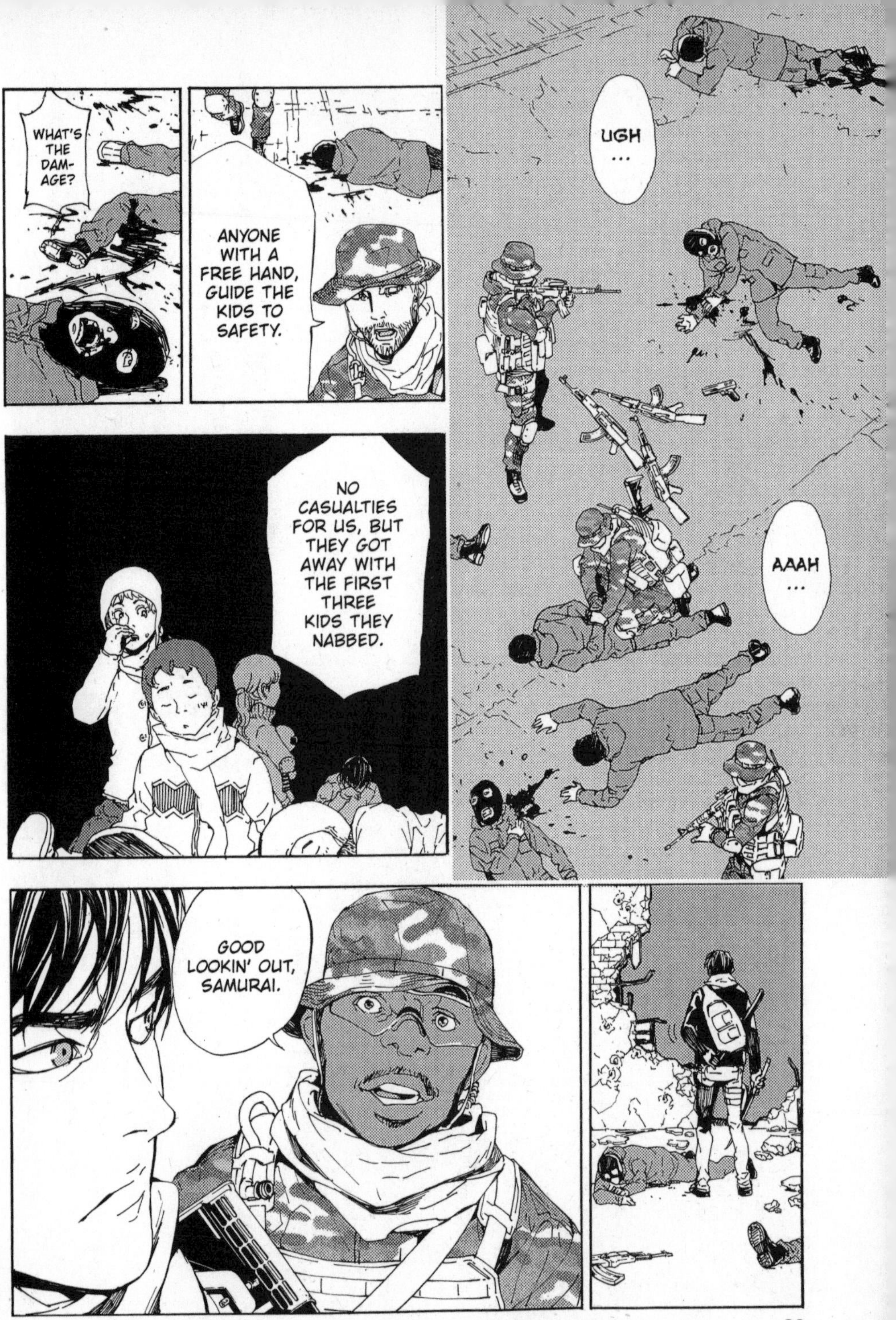
UGH ...
AAAH ...
ANYONE WITH A FREE HAND, GUIDE THE KIDS TO SAFETY.
WHAT'S THE DAM-AGE?
NO CASUALTIES FOR US, BUT THEY GOT AWAY WITH THE FIRST THREE KIDS THEY NABBED.
GOOD LOOKIN' OUT, SAMURAI.

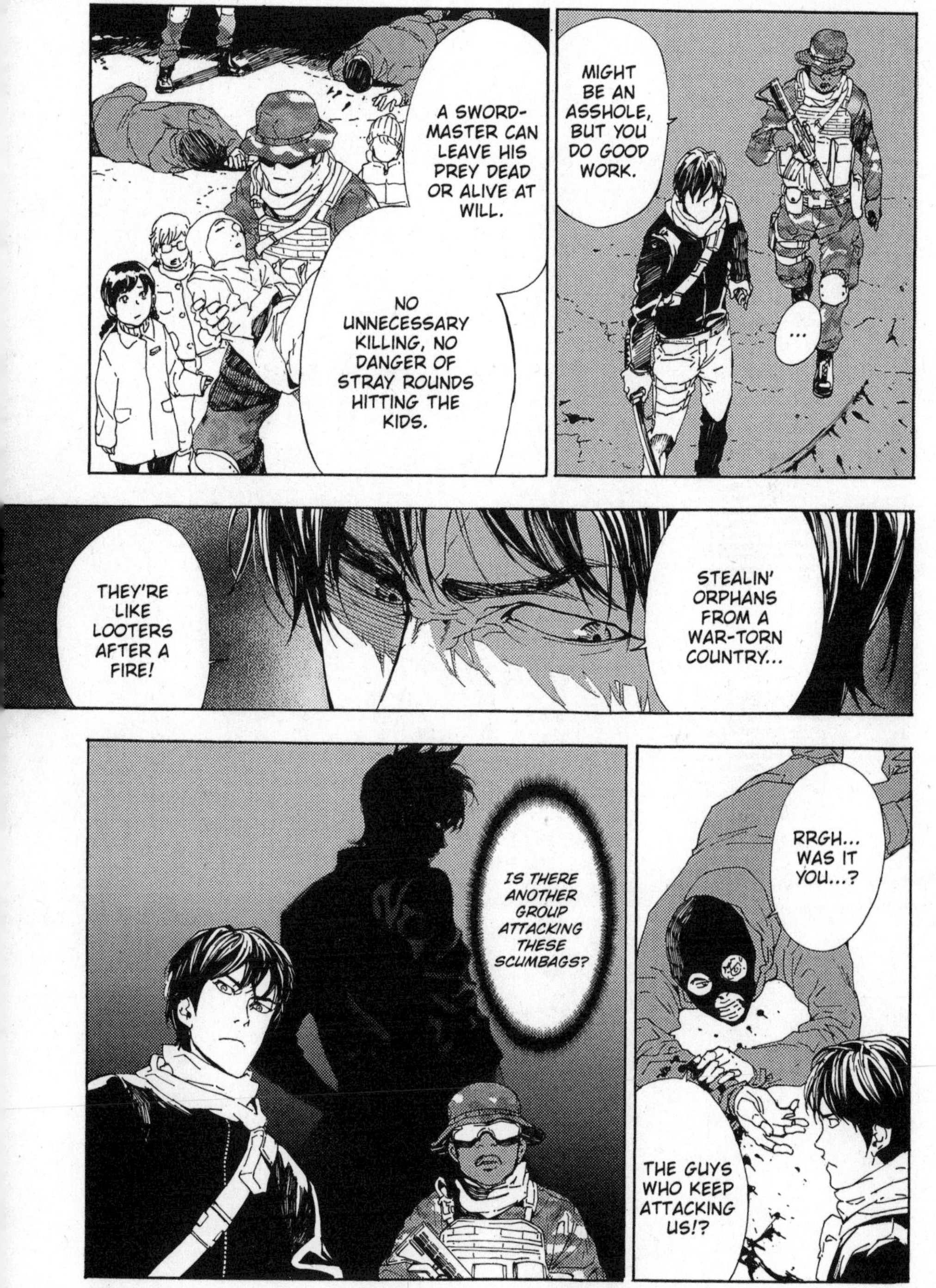
MIGHT BE AN ASSHOLE, BUT YOU DO GOOD WORK.
...
A SWORD-MASTER CAN LEAVE HIS PREY DEAD OR ALIVE AT WILL.
NO UNNECESSARY KILLING, NO DANGER OF STRAY ROUNDS HITTING THE KIDS.
STEALIN' ORPHANS FROM A WAR-TORN COUNTRY...
THEY'RE LIKE LOOTERS AFTER A FIRE!
RRGH... WAS IT YOU...?
THE GUYS WHO KEEP ATTACKING US!?
IS THERE ANOTHER GROUP ATTACKING THESE SCUMBAGS?

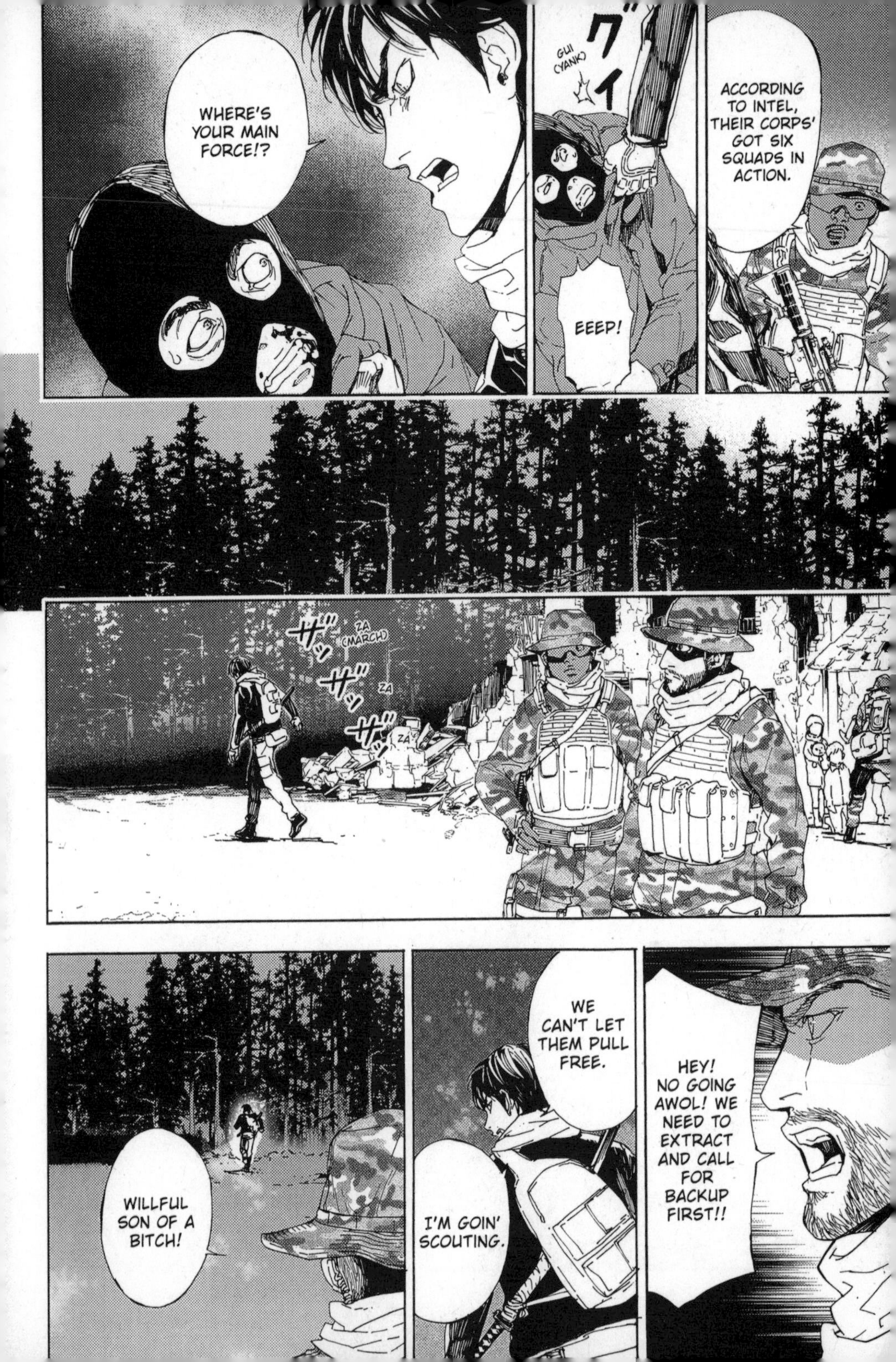
ACCORDING TO INTEL, THEIR CORPS' GOT SIX SQUADS IN ACTION.
グイ
GUI (YANK)
EEEP!
WHERE'S YOUR MAIN FORCE!?
ザッ
ZA (MARCH)
ザッ
ZA
ザッ
ZA
HEY! NO GOING AWOL! WE NEED TO EXTRACT AND CALL FOR BACKUP FIRST!!
WE CAN'T LET THEM PULL FREE.
I'M GOIN' SCOUTING.
WILLFUL SON OF A BITCH!

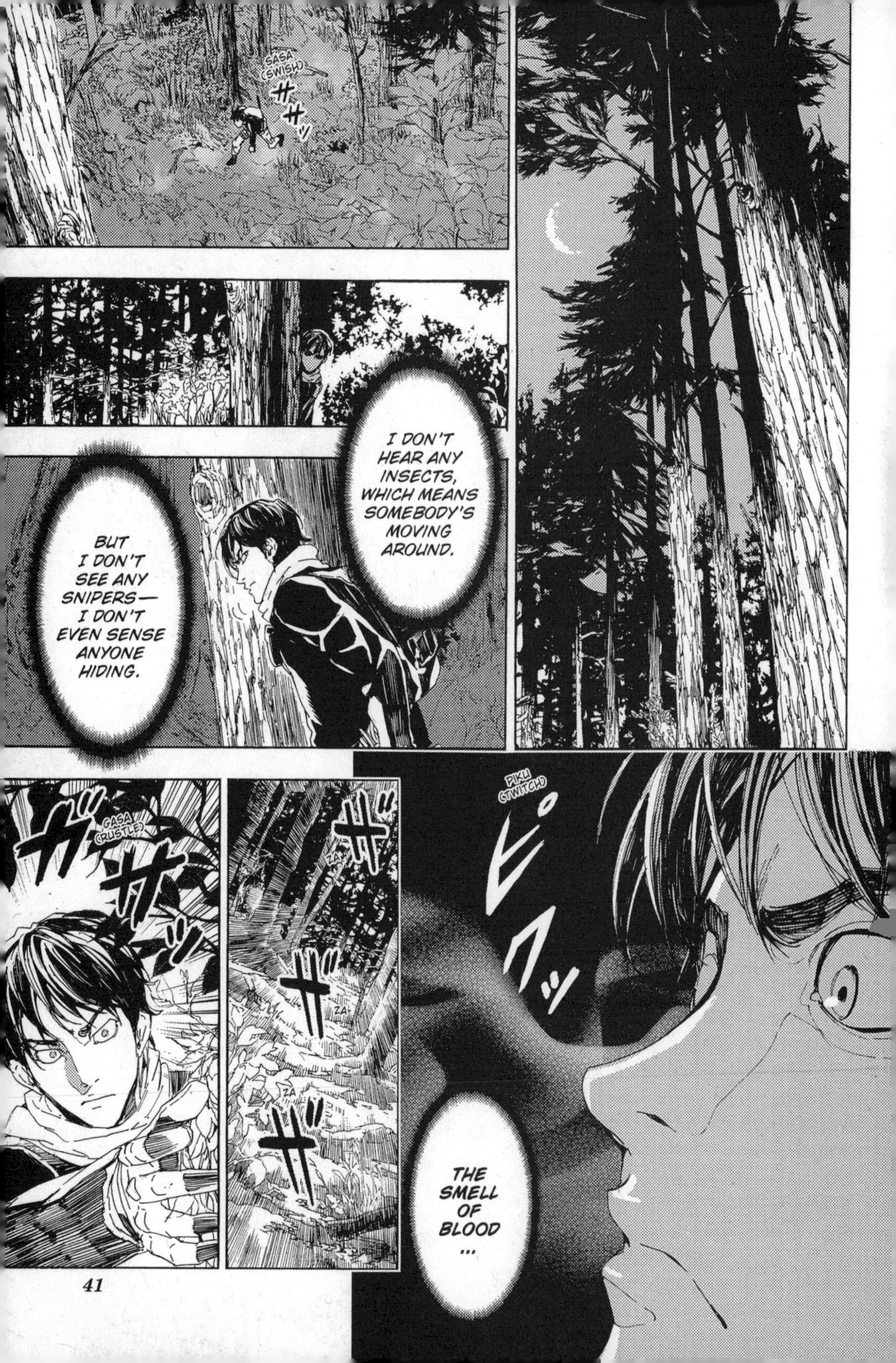
SASA (SWISH)
I DON'T HEAR ANY INSECTS, WHICH MEANS SOMEBODY'S MOVING AROUND.
BUT I DON'T SEE ANY SNIPERS— I DON'T EVEN SENSE ANYONE HIDING.
PIKU (TWITCH)
THE SMELL OF BLOOD ...
ZA
ZA
ZA
GASA (RUSTLE)

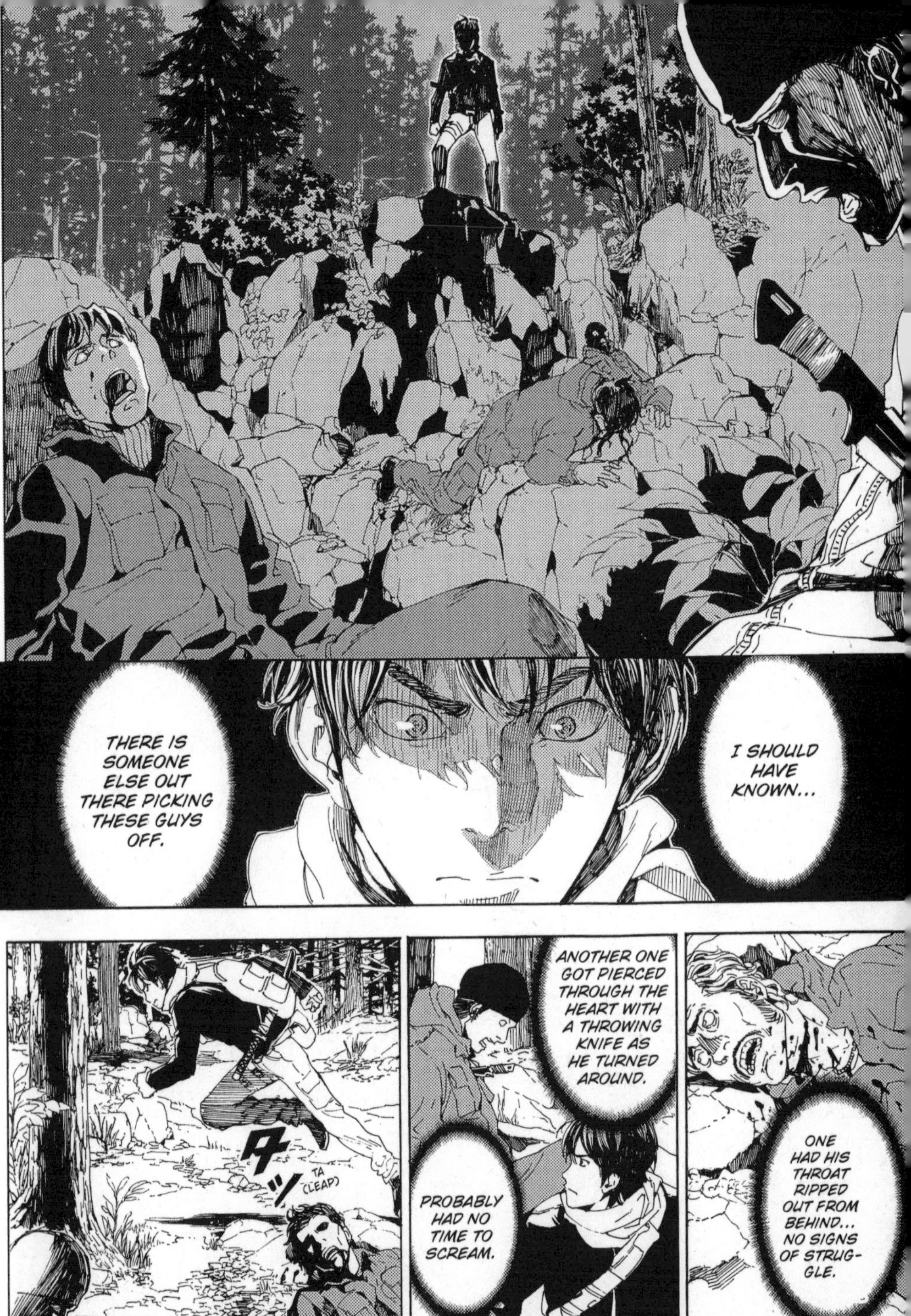
I SHOULD HAVE KNOWN...
THERE IS SOMEONE ELSE OUT THERE PICKING THESE GUYS OFF.
ONE HAD HIS THROAT RIPPED OUT FROM BEHIND... NO SIGNS OF STRUG-GLE.
ANOTHER ONE GOT PIERCED THROUGH THE HEART WITH A THROWING KNIFE AS HE TURNED AROUND.
PROBABLY HAD NO TIME TO SCREAM.
タッ
TA (LEAP)

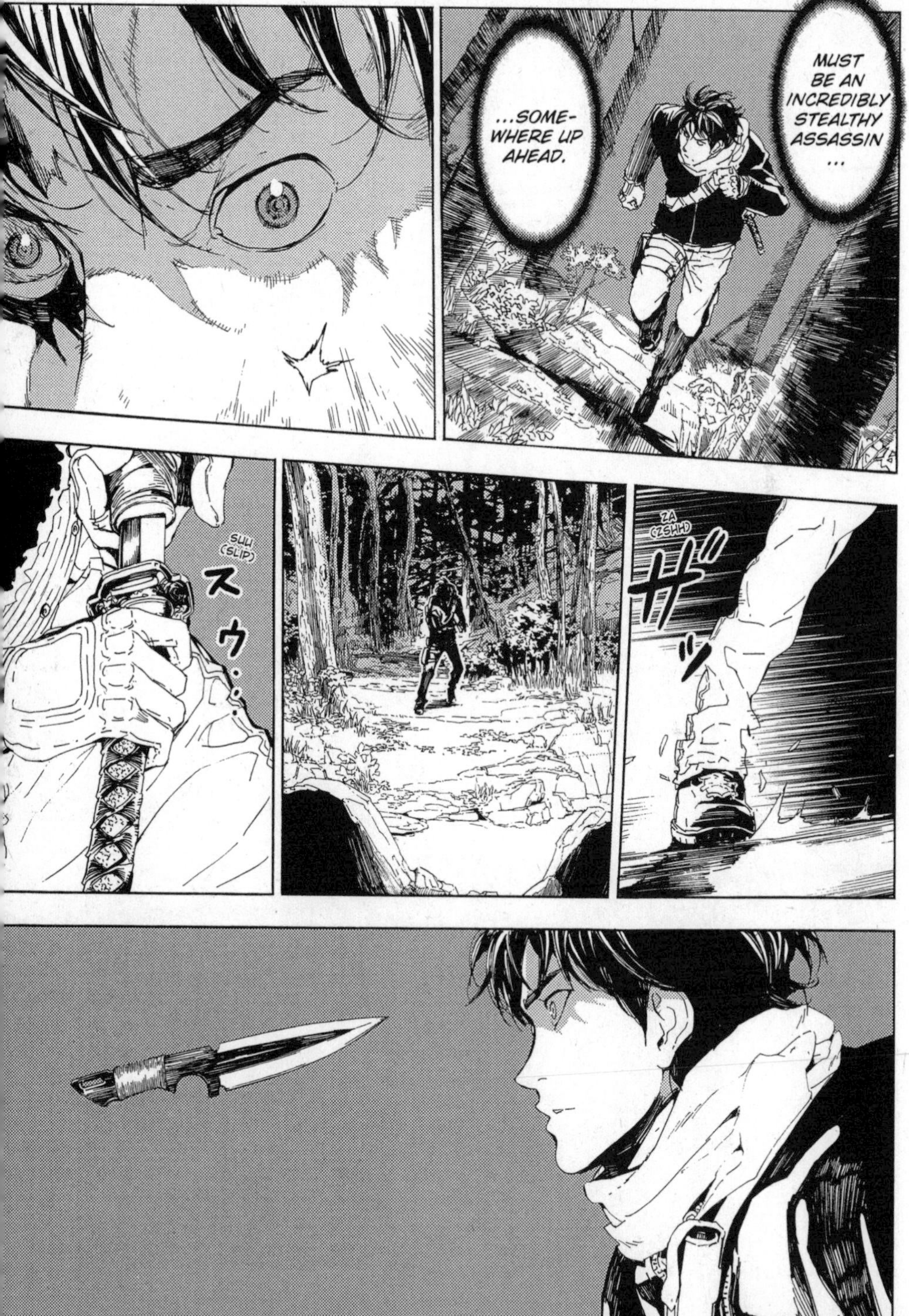
MUST BE AN INCREDIBLY STEALTHY ASSASSIN...
...SOME-WHERE UP AHEAD.
ZA (ZSHH)
ザッ
SUU (SLIP)
スウ...

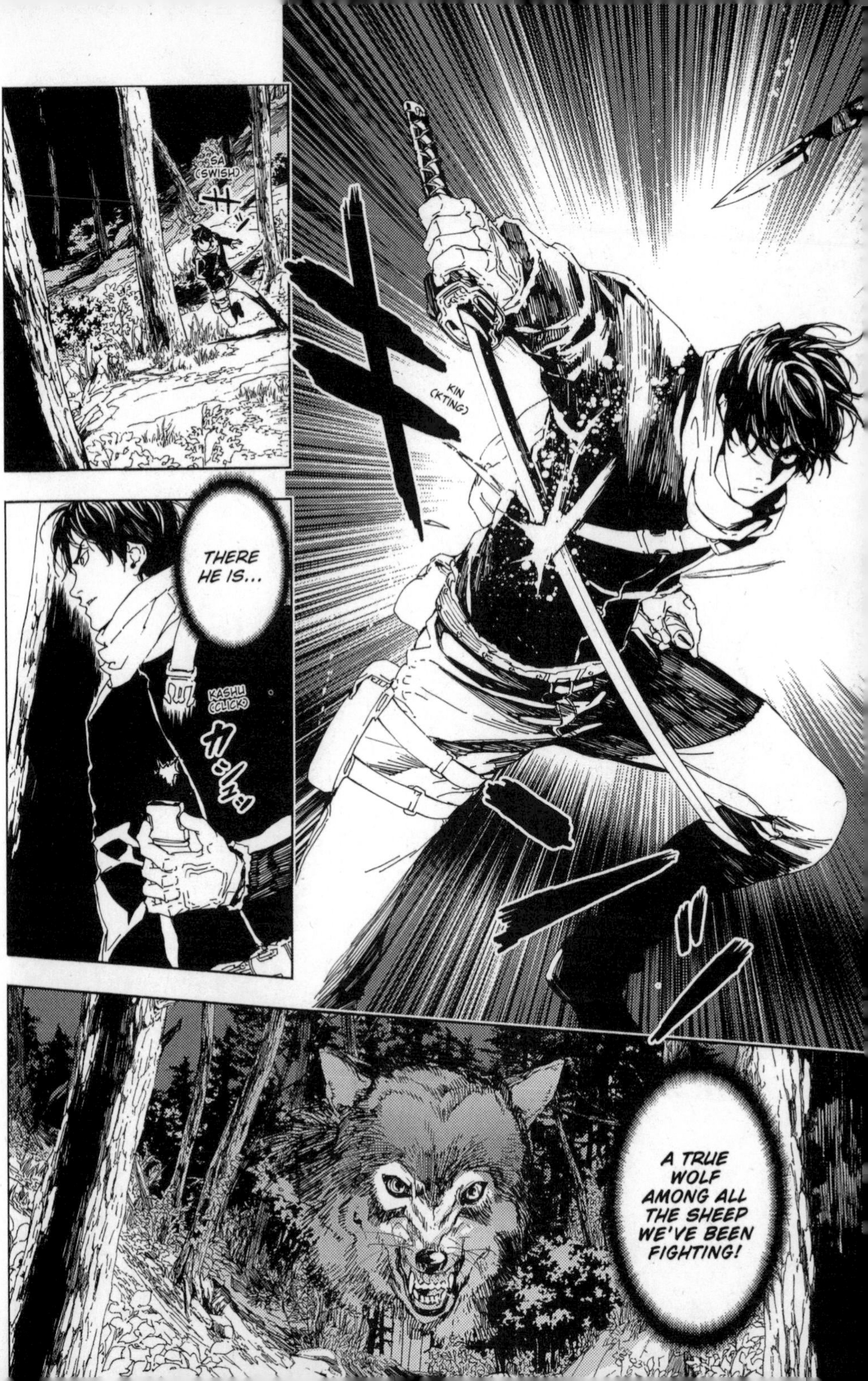
KIN (KTING)
SA (SWISH)
THERE HE IS...
KASHU (CLICK)
A TRUE WOLF AMONG ALL THE SHEEP WE'VE BEEN FIGHTING!

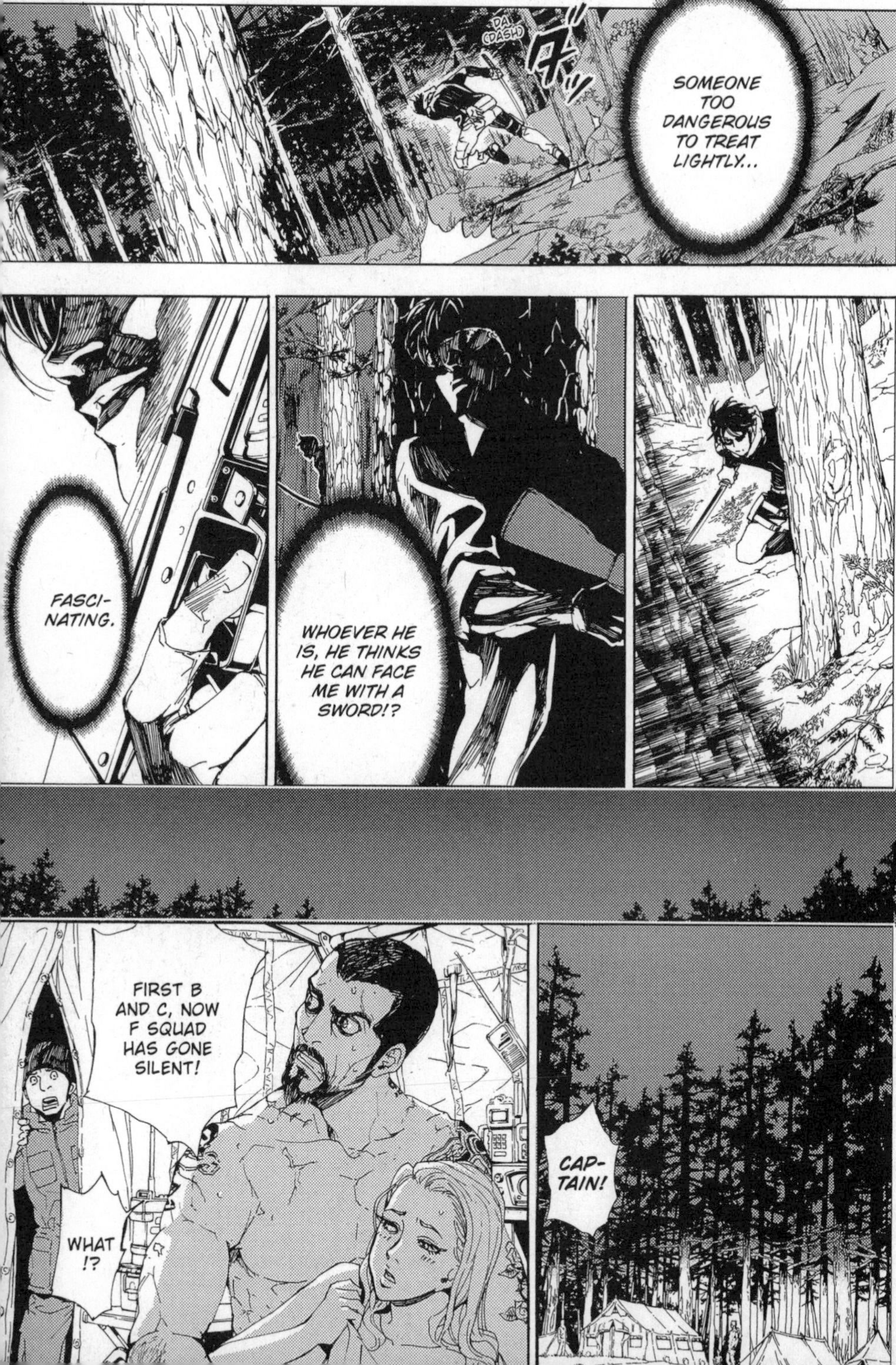
SOMEONE TOO DANGEROUS TO TREAT LIGHTLY...
DA (DASH)
ダッ
WHOEVER HE IS, HE THINKS HE CAN FACE ME WITH A SWORD!?
FASCI-NATING.
CAP-TAIN!
FIRST B AND C, NOW F SQUAD HAS GONE SILENT!
WHAT!?

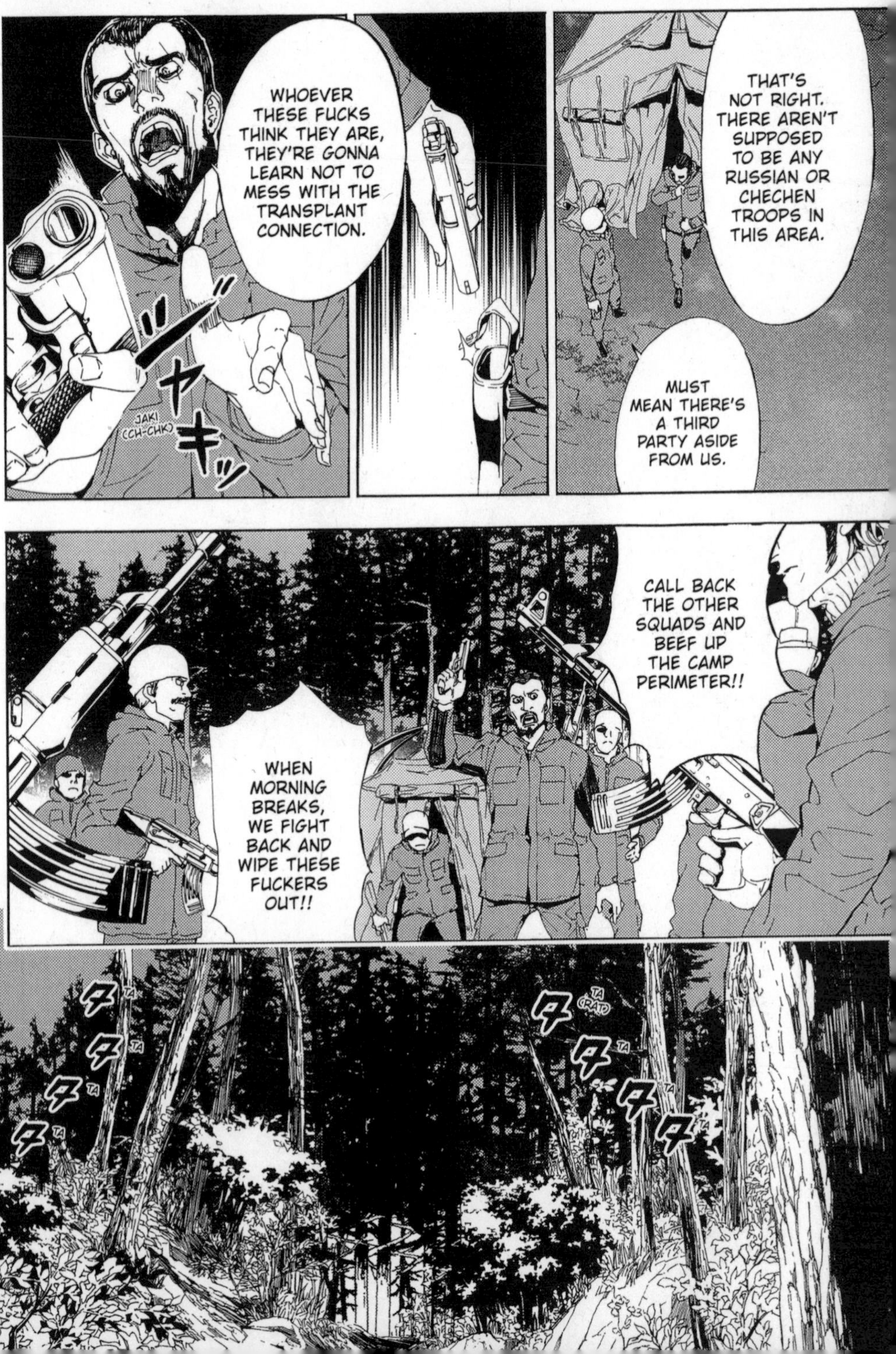
THAT'S NOT RIGHT. THERE AREN'T SUPPOSED TO BE ANY RUSSIAN OR CHECHEN TROOPS IN THIS AREA.
MUST MEAN THERE'S A THIRD PARTY ASIDE FROM US.
WHOEVER THESE FUCKS THINK THEY ARE, THEY'RE GONNA LEARN NOT TO MESS WITH THE TRANSPLANT CONNECTION.
JAKI (CH-CHK)
CALL BACK THE OTHER SQUADS AND BEEF UP THE CAMP PERIMETER!!
WHEN MORNING BREAKS, WE FIGHT BACK AND WIPE THESE FUCKERS OUT!!
TA (RAT)
TA
TA
TA
TA
TA
TA
TA

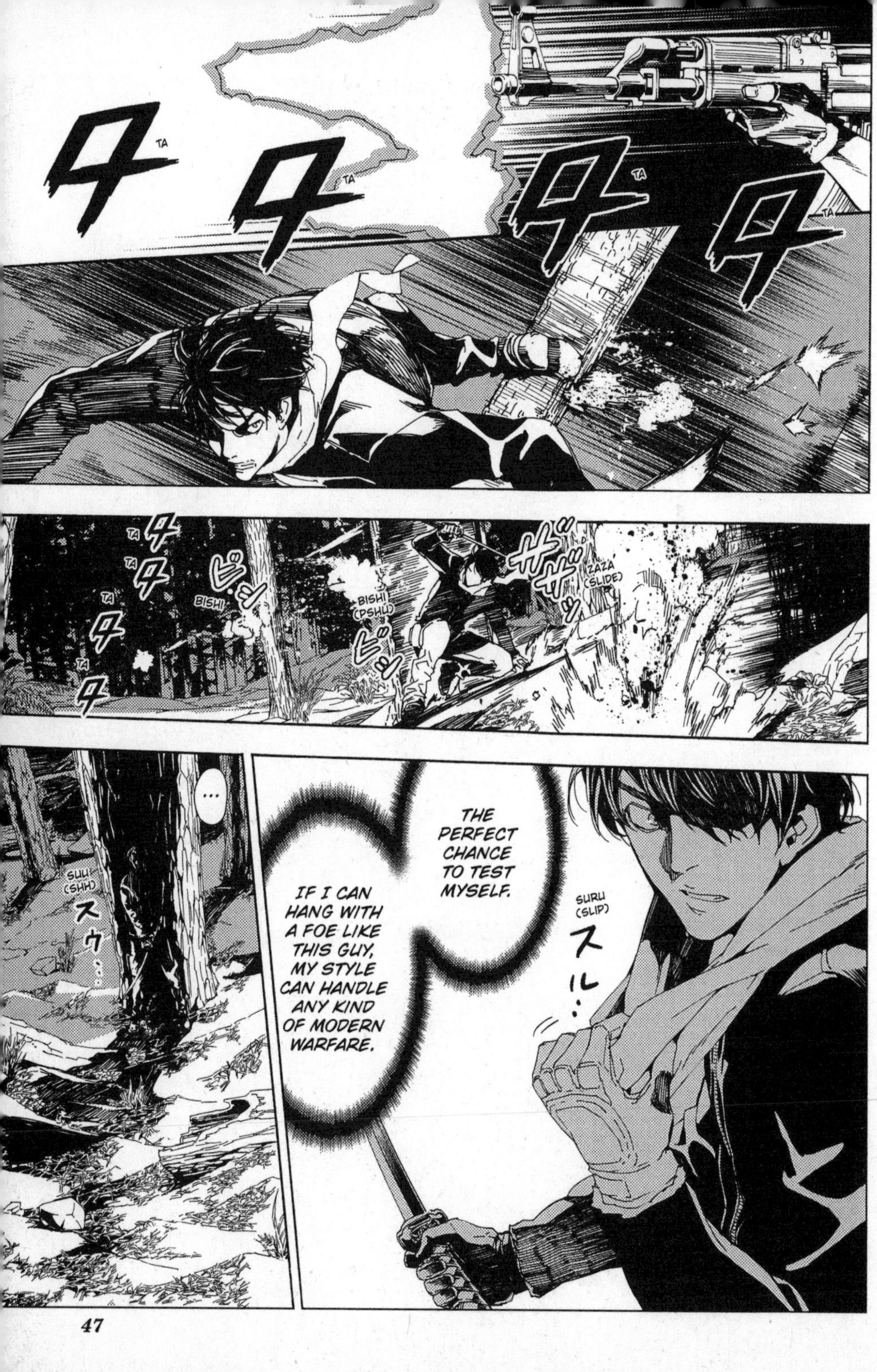
TA TA TA TA
ZAZA (SLIDE)
BISHI (PSHU)
BISHI
TA TA TA TA
THE PERFECT CHANCE TO TEST MYSELF.
IF I CAN HANG WITH A FOE LIKE THIS GUY, MY STYLE CAN HANDLE ANY KIND OF MODERN WARFARE.
SURU (SLIP)
...
SUU (SHH)

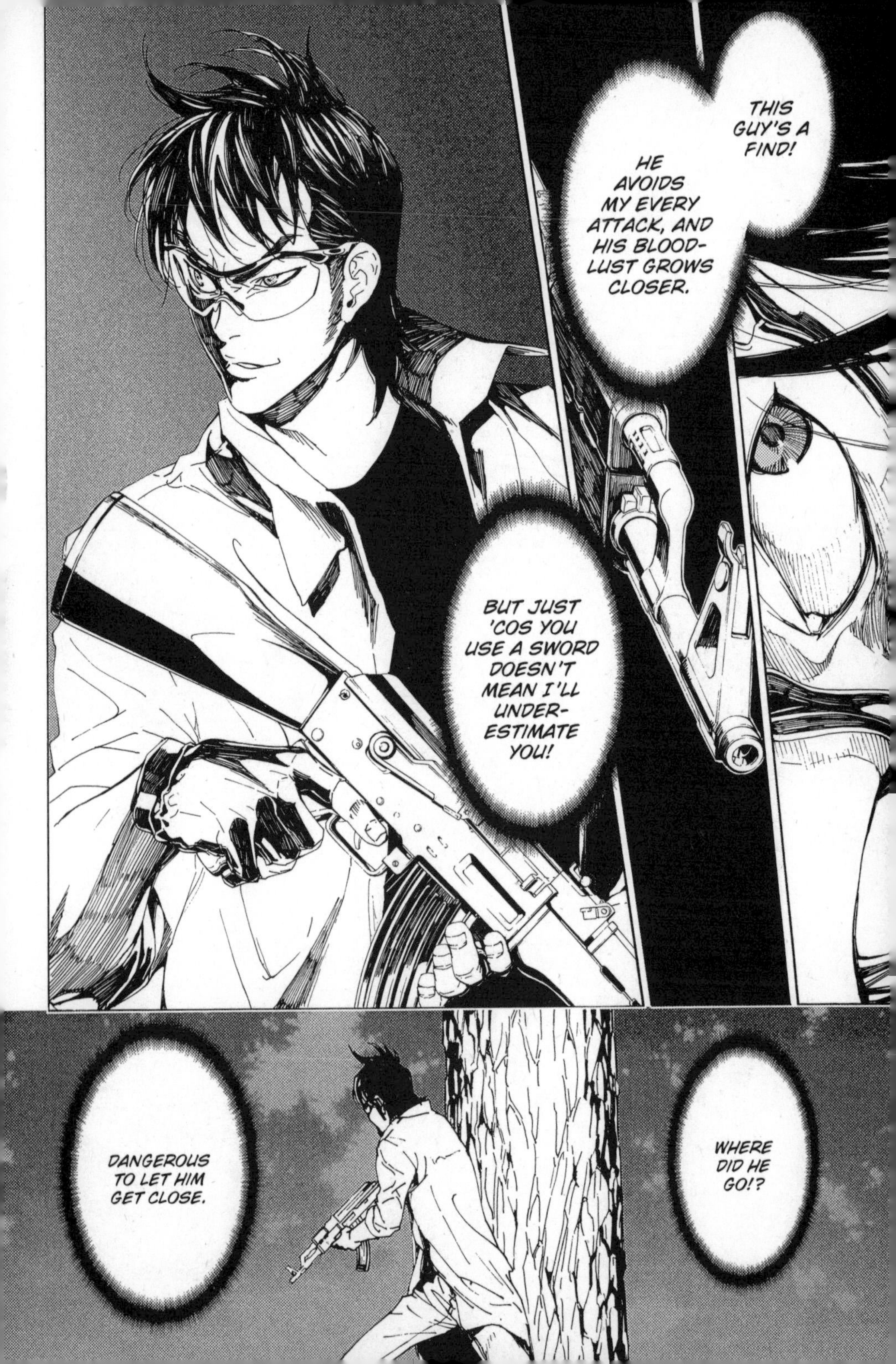
THIS GUY'S A FIND!
HE AVOIDS MY EVERY ATTACK, AND HIS BLOOD-LUST GROWS CLOSER.
BUT JUST 'COS YOU USE A SWORD DOESN'T MEAN I'LL UNDER-ESTIMATE YOU!
WHERE DID HE GO!?
DANGEROUS TO LET HIM GET CLOSE.

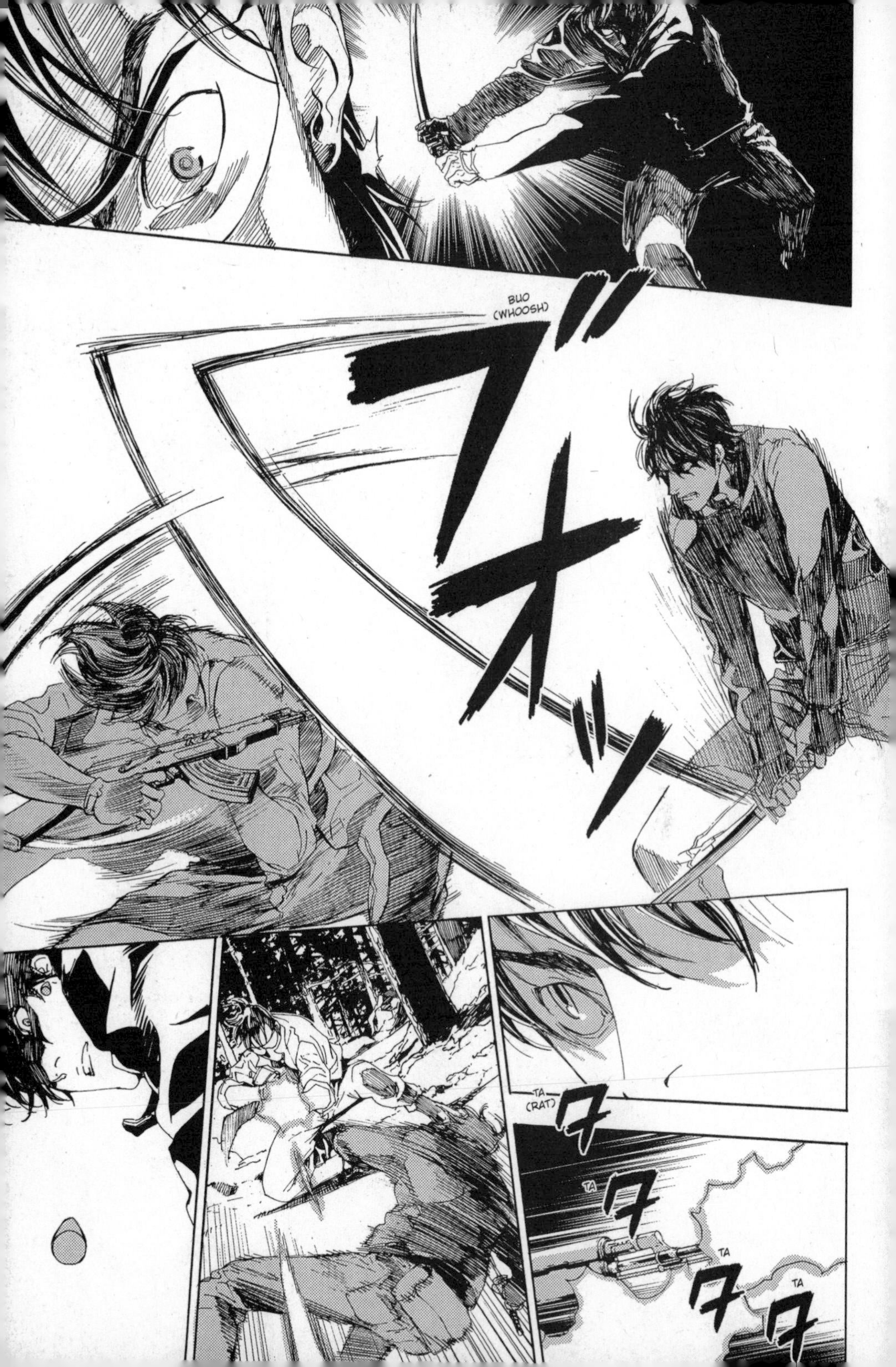

BUO (WHOOSH)
ブオッ
TA (RAT)
タ
TA
タ
TA
タ
TA
タ

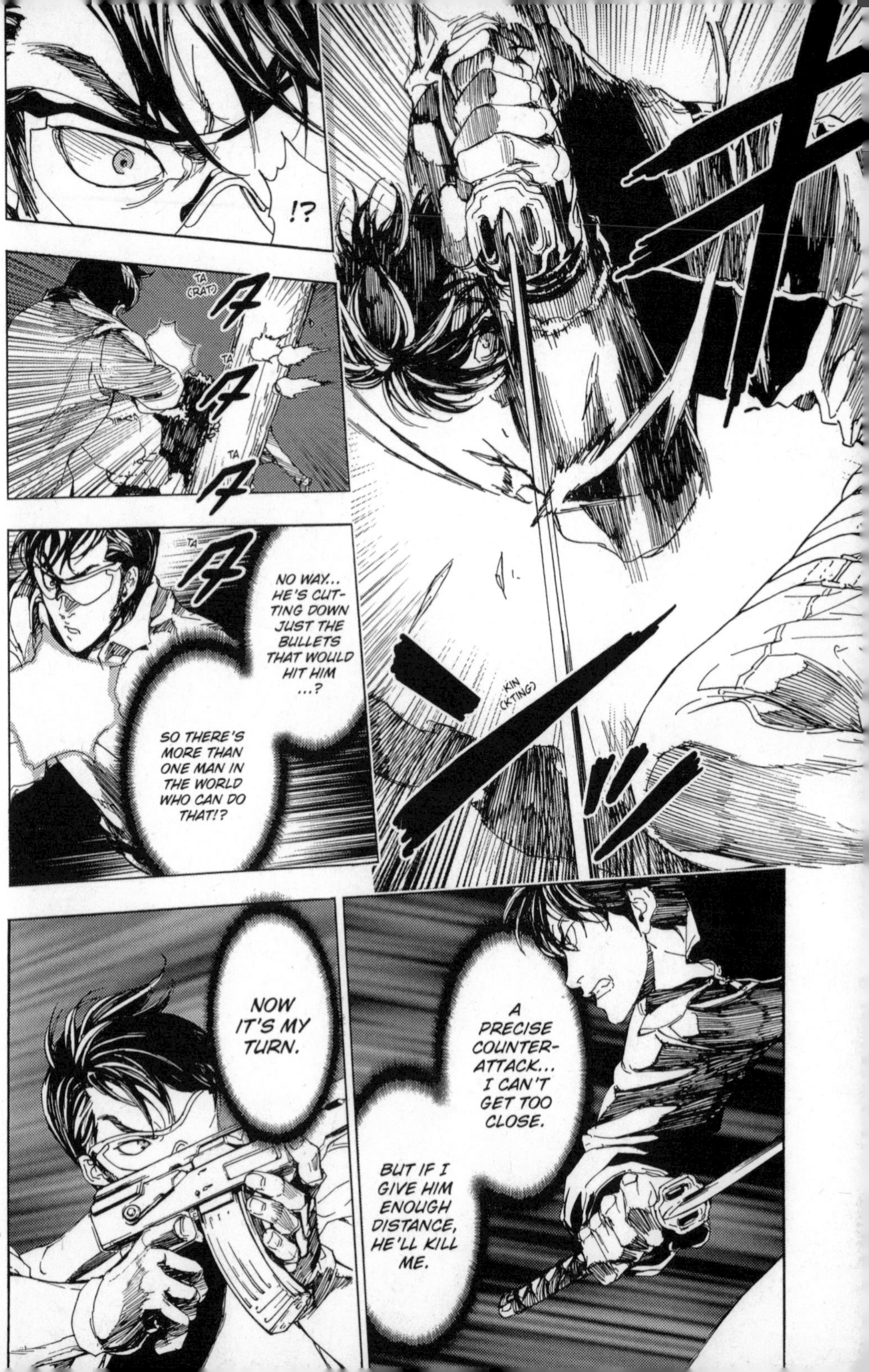
KIN (KTING)
!?
TA (RAT)
TA
TA
TA
NO WAY... HE'S CUTTING DOWN JUST THE BULLETS THAT WOULD HIT HIM ...?
SO THERE'S MORE THAN ONE MAN IN THE WORLD WHO CAN DO THAT!?
A PRECISE COUNTER-ATTACK... I CAN'T GET TOO CLOSE.
BUT IF I GIVE HIM ENOUGH DISTANCE, HE'LL KILL ME.
NOW IT'S MY TURN.

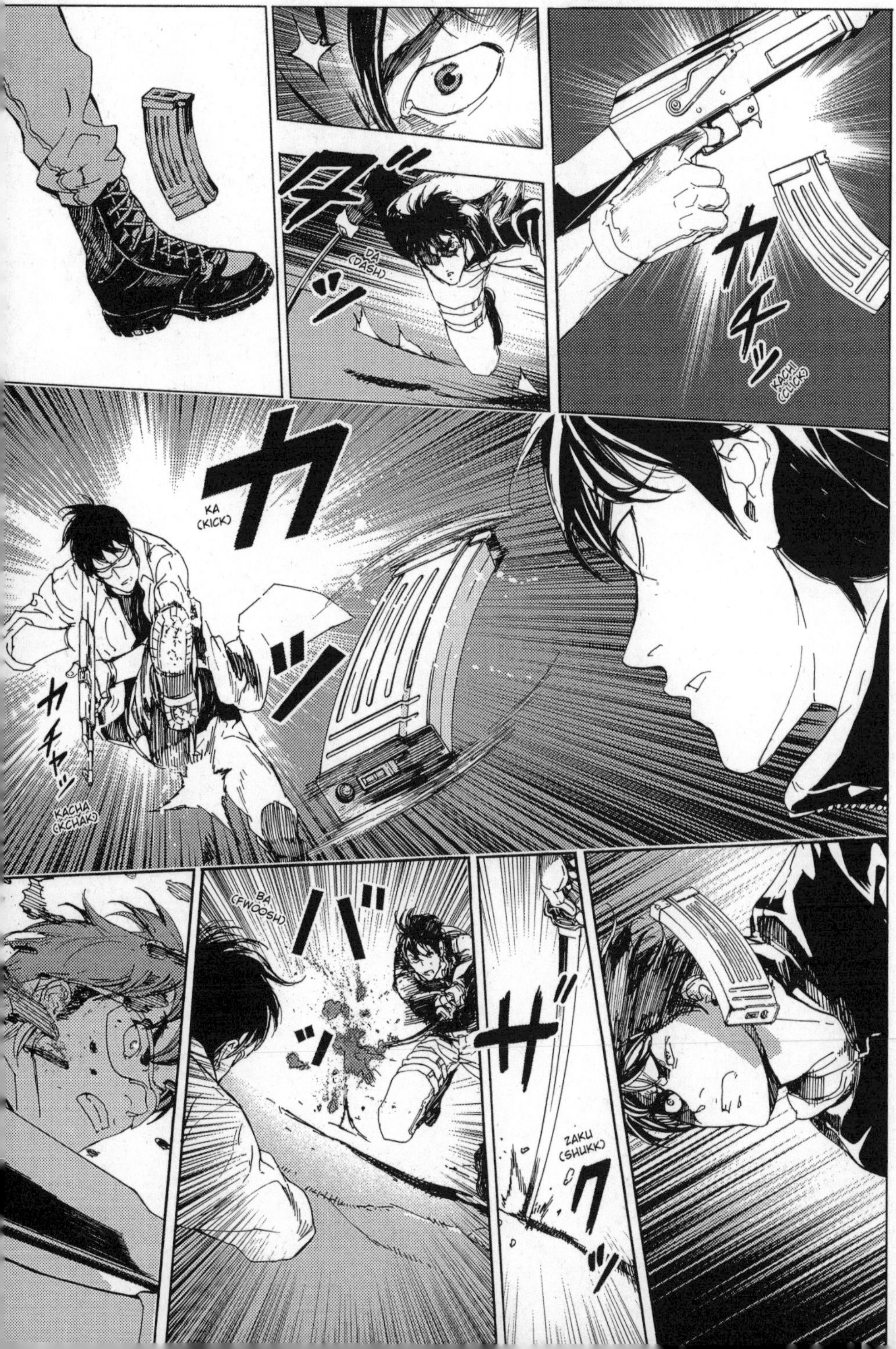
KACHI (CLICK)
DA (DASH)
KA (KICK)
KACHA (KCHAK)
ZAKU (SHUKK)
BA (FWOOSH)

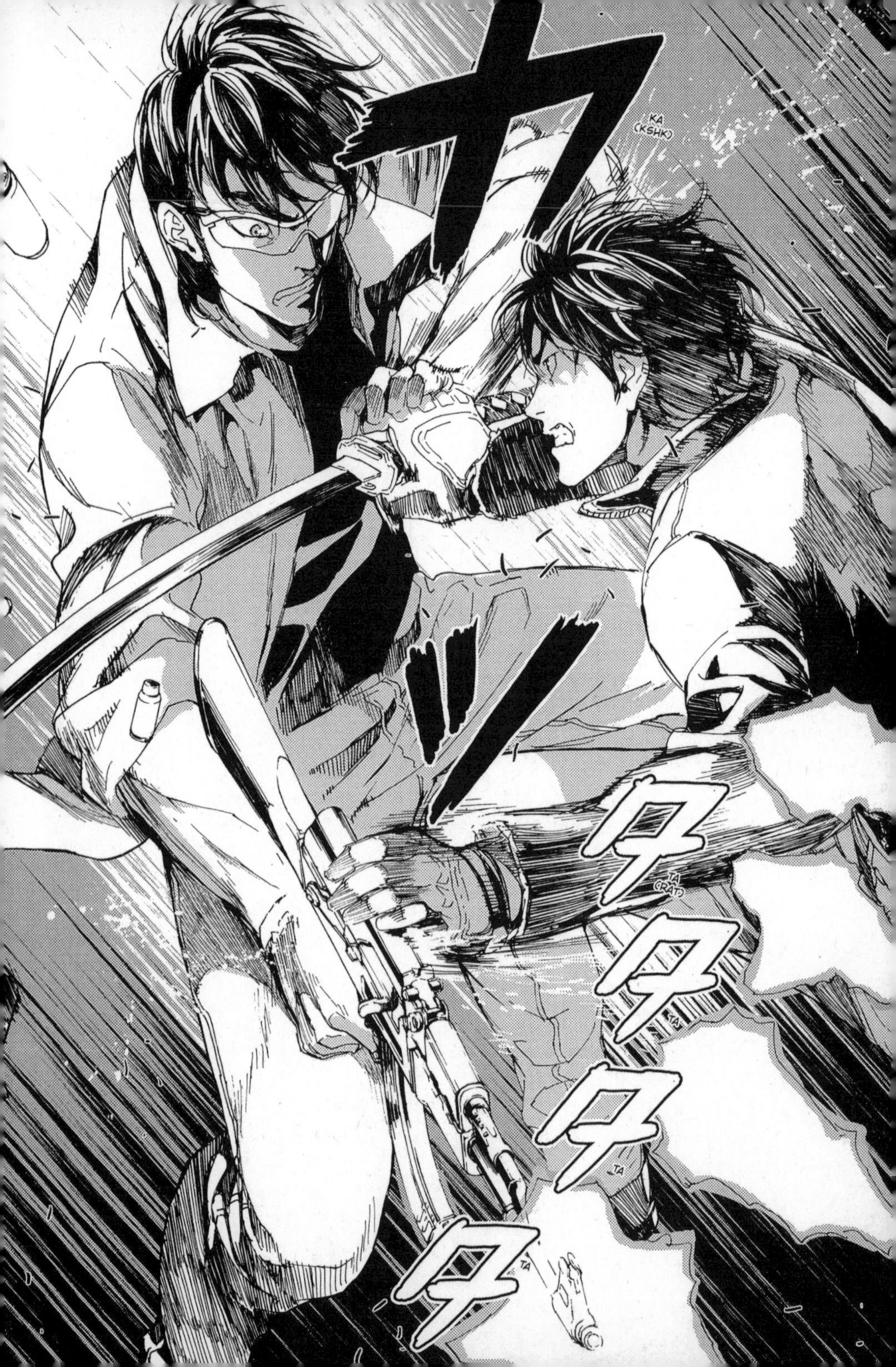
カッ
KA
(KSHK)
タタタタ
TA
(RAT)
TA
TA
TA

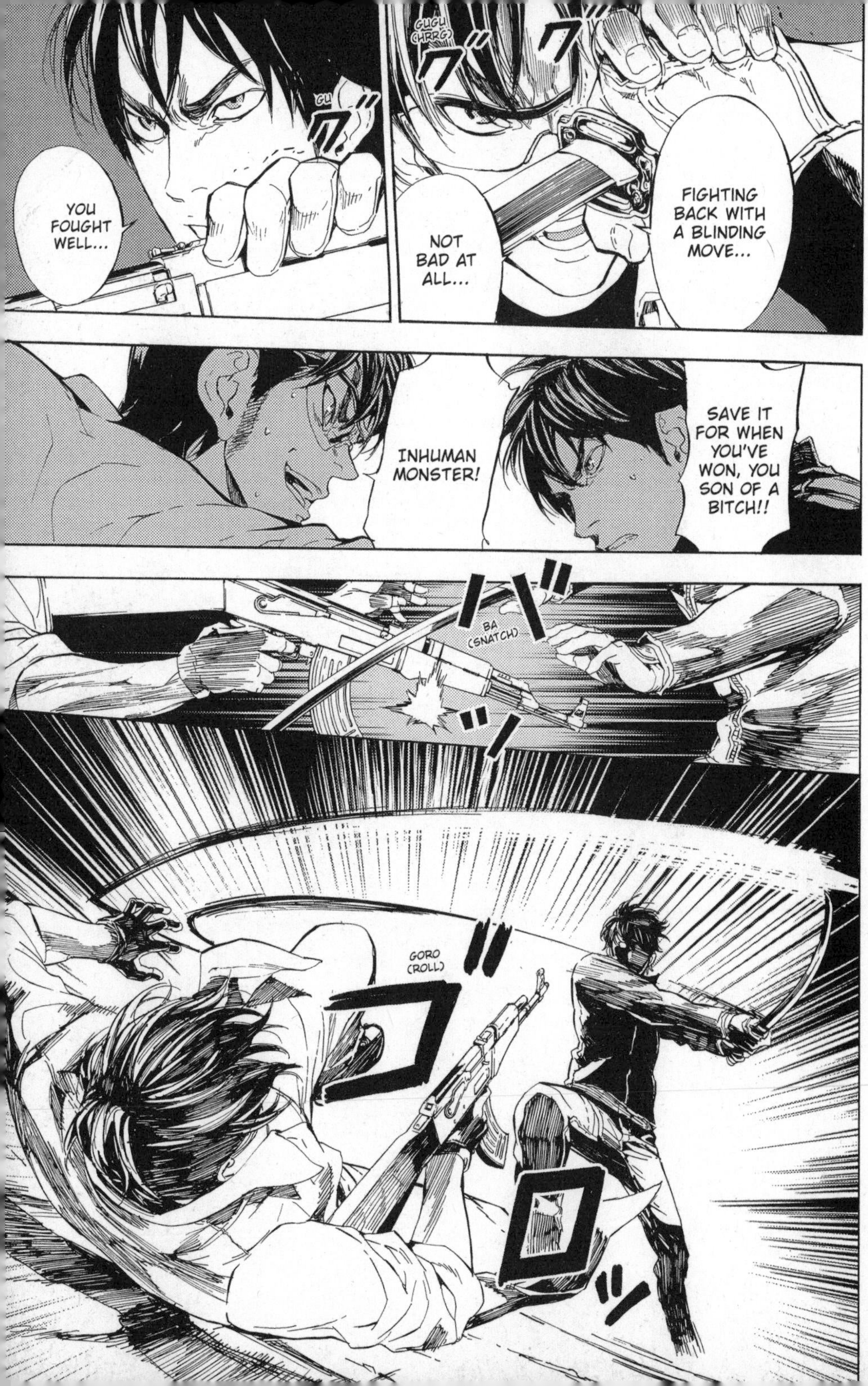
GUGU (HRRG)
FIGHTING BACK WITH A BLINDING MOVE...
NOT BAD AT ALL...
GU
YOU FOUGHT WELL...
SAVE IT FOR WHEN YOU'VE WON, YOU SON OF A BITCH!!
INHUMAN MONSTER!
BA (SNATCH)
GORO (ROLL)

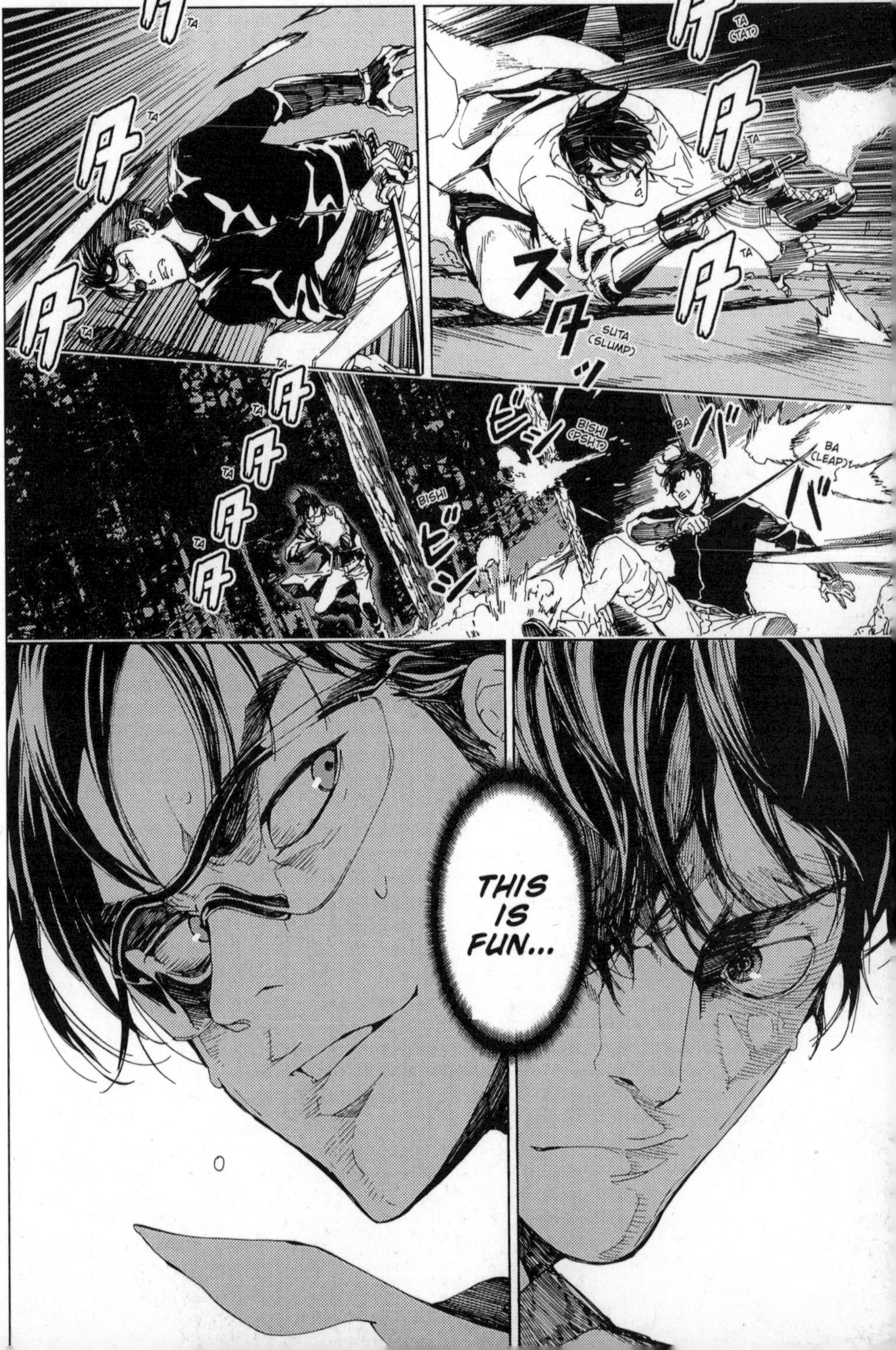

TA (TAT)
TA
TA
SUTA (SLUMP)
TA
TA
TA
BA
BA (LEAP)
BISHI (PSHT)
BISHI
TA-
TA
TA
TA
THIS IS FUN...

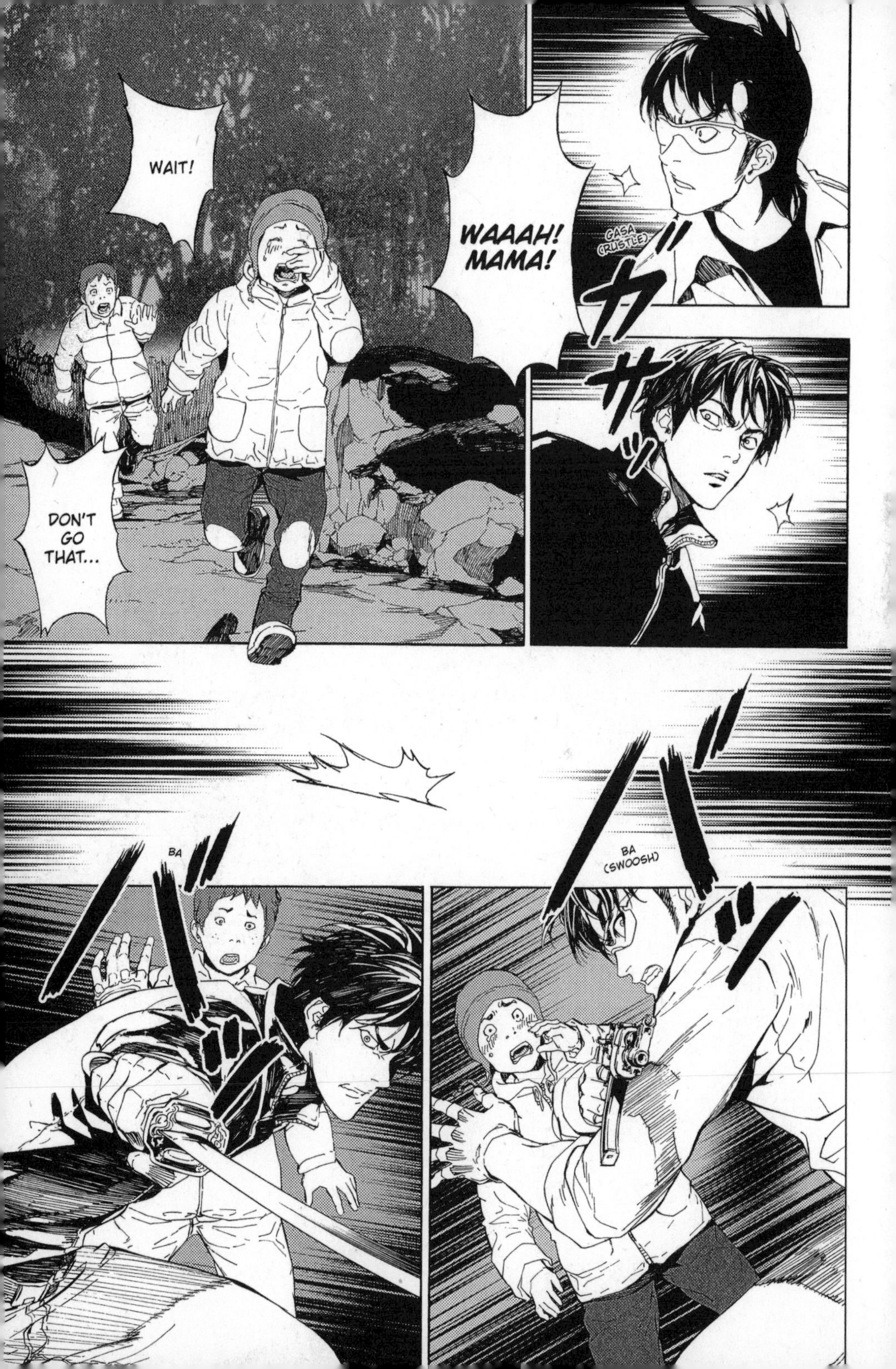
GASA (RUSTLE)
WAAAH! MAMA!
WAIT!
DON'T GO THAT...
BA (SWOOSH)
BA

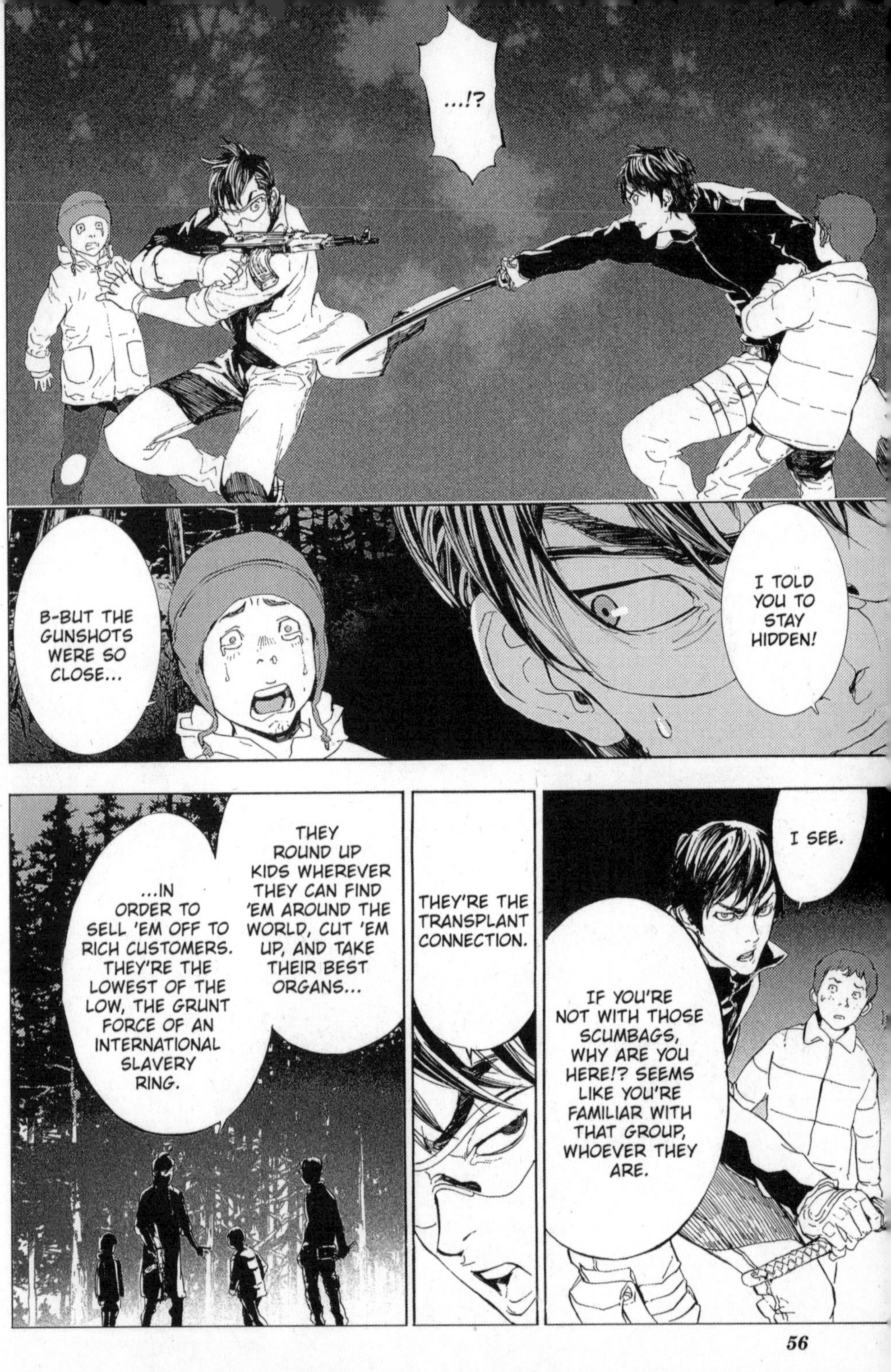
...!?
I TOLD YOU TO STAY HIDDEN!
B-BUT THE GUNSHOTS WERE SO CLOSE...
I SEE.
IF YOU'RE NOT WITH THOSE SCUMBAGS, WHY ARE YOU HERE!? SEEMS LIKE YOU'RE FAMILIAR WITH THAT GROUP, WHOEVER THEY ARE.
THEY'RE THE TRANSPLANT CONNECTION.
THEY ROUND UP KIDS WHEREVER THEY CAN FIND 'EM AROUND THE WORLD, CUT 'EM UP, AND TAKE THEIR BEST ORGANS...
...IN ORDER TO SELL 'EM OFF TO RICH CUSTOMERS. THEY'RE THE LOWEST OF THE LOW, THE GRUNT FORCE OF AN INTERNATIONAL SLAVERY RING.

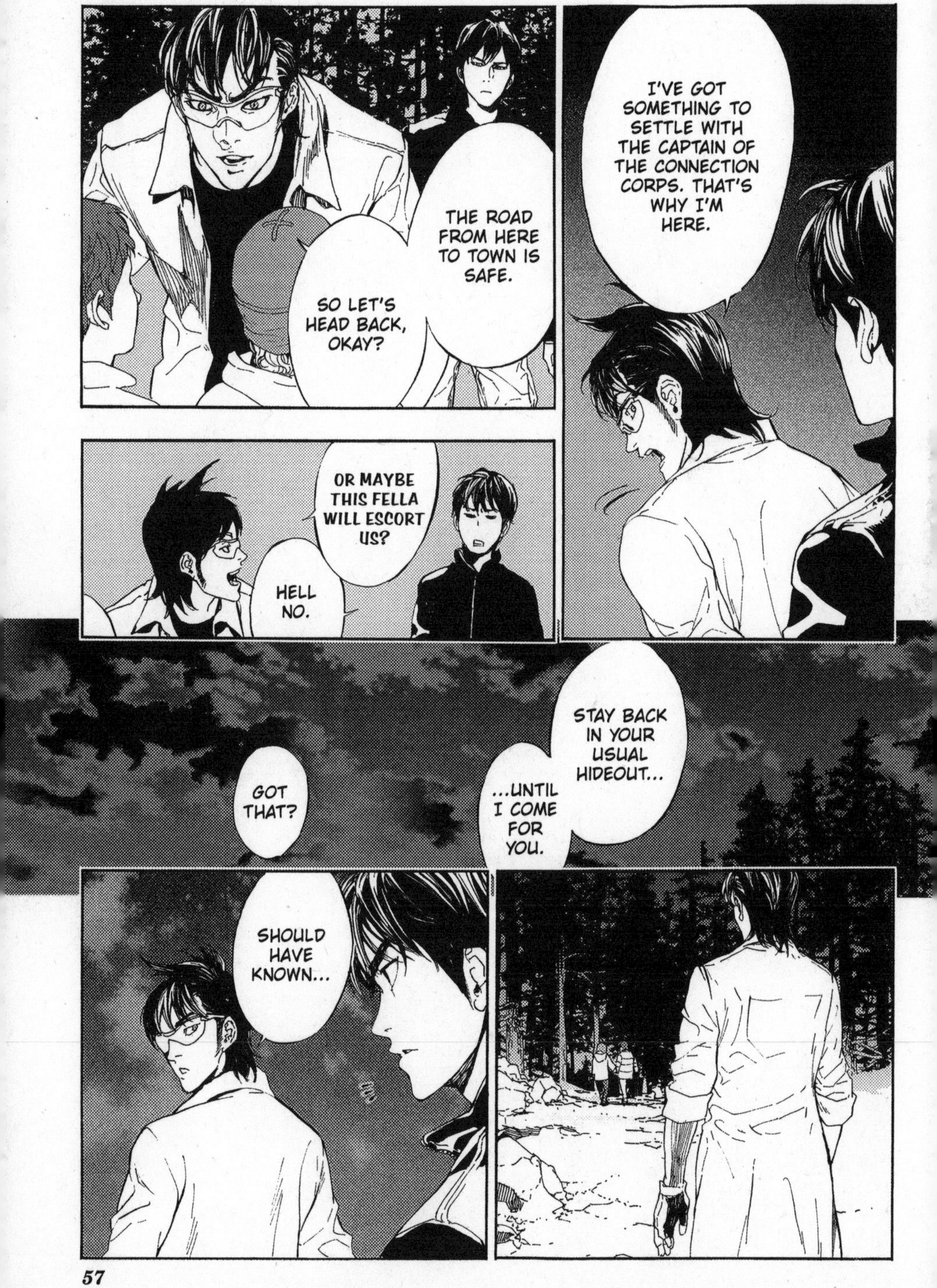
I'VE GOT SOMETHING TO SETTLE WITH THE CAPTAIN OF THE CONNECTION CORPS. THAT'S WHY I'M HERE.
THE ROAD FROM HERE TO TOWN IS SAFE.
SO LET'S HEAD BACK, OKAY?
OR MAYBE THIS FELLA WILL ESCORT US?
HELL NO.
STAY BACK IN YOUR USUAL HIDEOUT...
...UNTIL I COME FOR YOU.
GOT THAT?
SHOULD HAVE KNOWN...

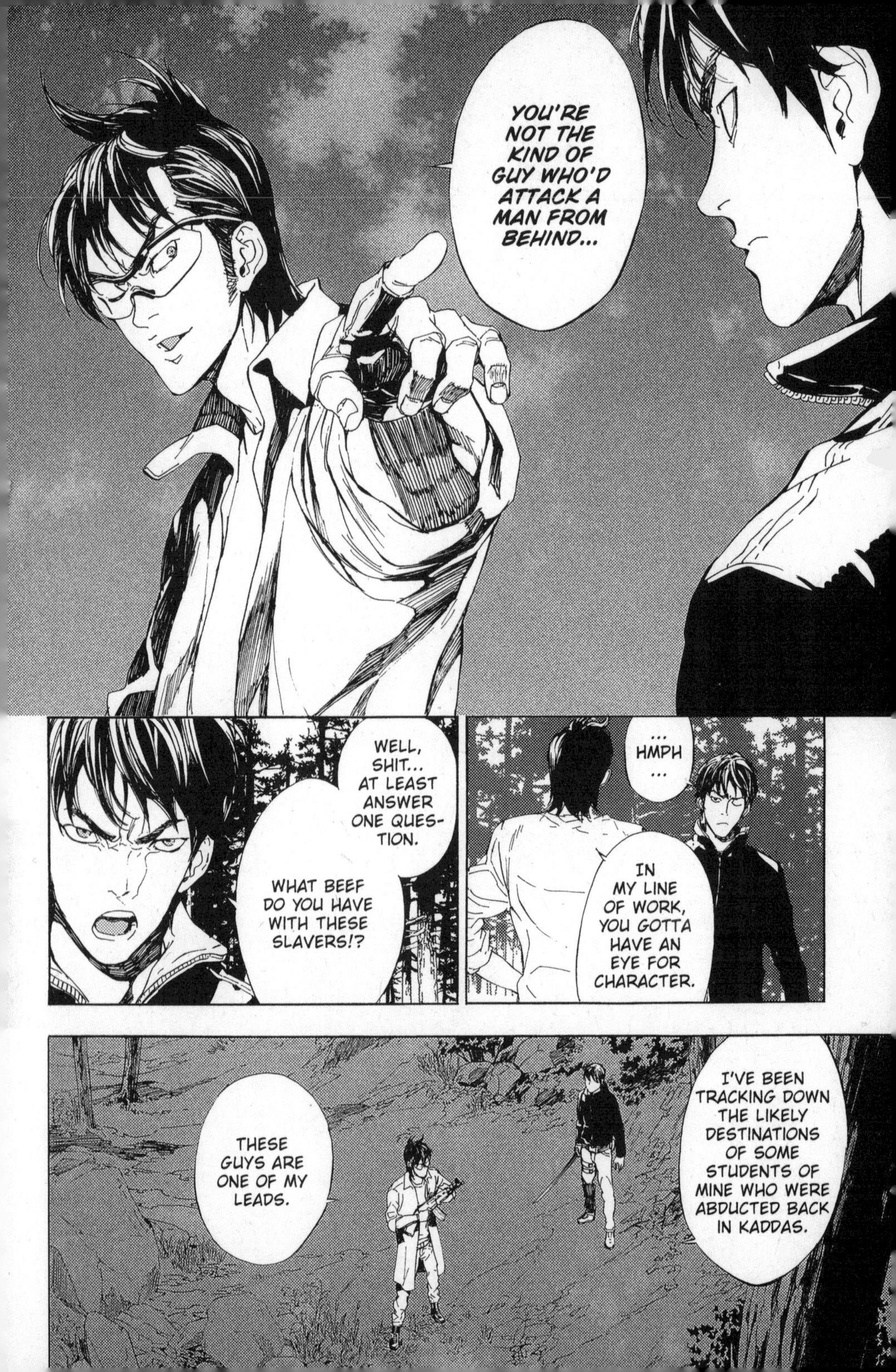
YOU'RE NOT THE KIND OF GUY WHO'D ATTACK A MAN FROM BEHIND...
...HMPH...
IN MY LINE OF WORK, YOU GOTTA HAVE AN EYE FOR CHARACTER.
WELL, SHIT... AT LEAST ANSWER ONE QUESTION.
WHAT BEEF DO YOU HAVE WITH THESE SLAVERS!?
I'VE BEEN TRACKING DOWN THE LIKELY DESTINATIONS OF SOME STUDENTS OF MINE WHO WERE ABDUCTED BACK IN KADDAS.
THESE GUYS ARE ONE OF MY LEADS.

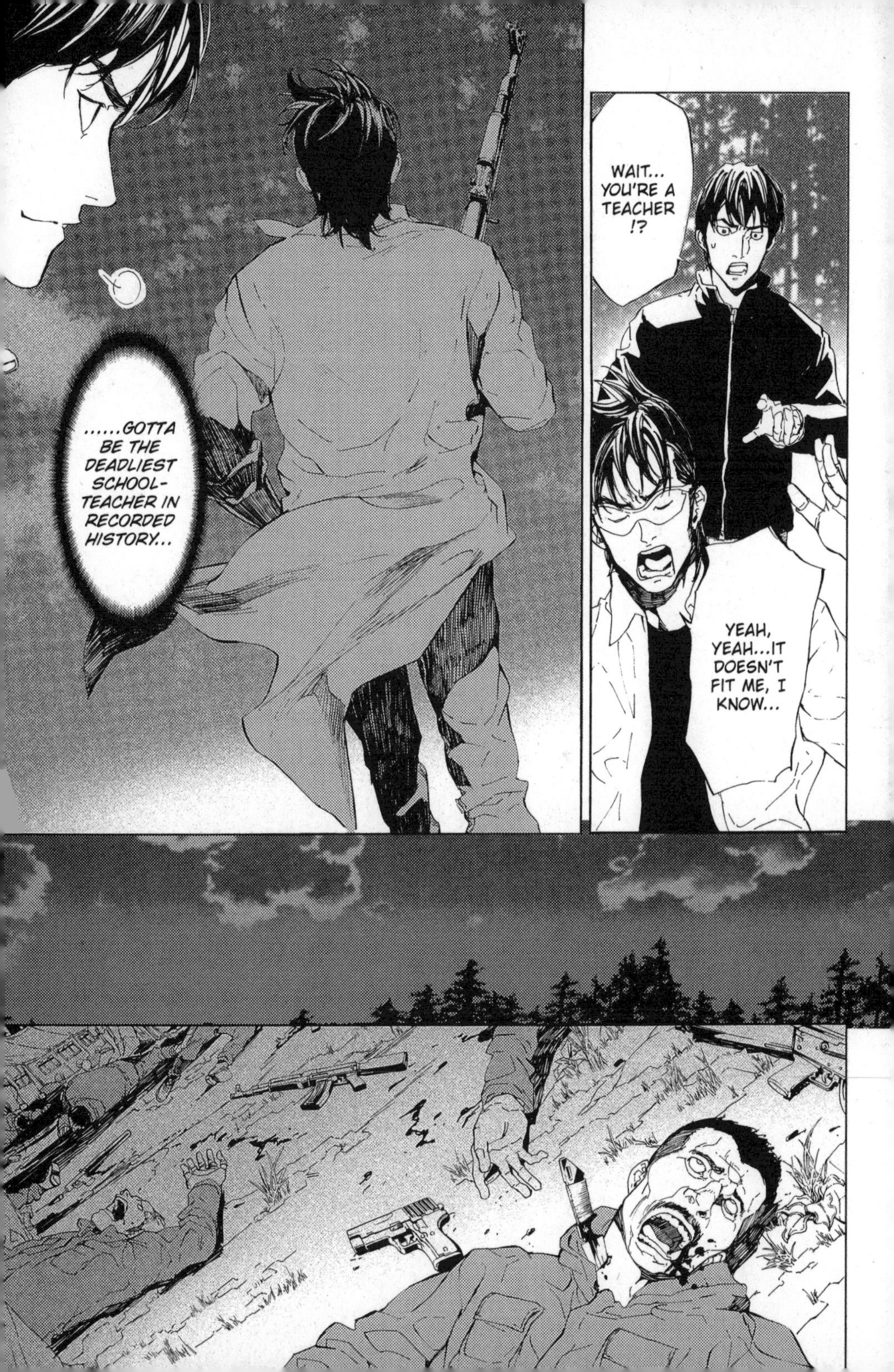
WAIT... YOU'RE A TEACHER !?
YEAH, YEAH...IT DOESN'T FIT ME, I KNOW...
......GOTTA BE THE DEADLIEST SCHOOL-TEACHER IN RECORDED HISTORY...

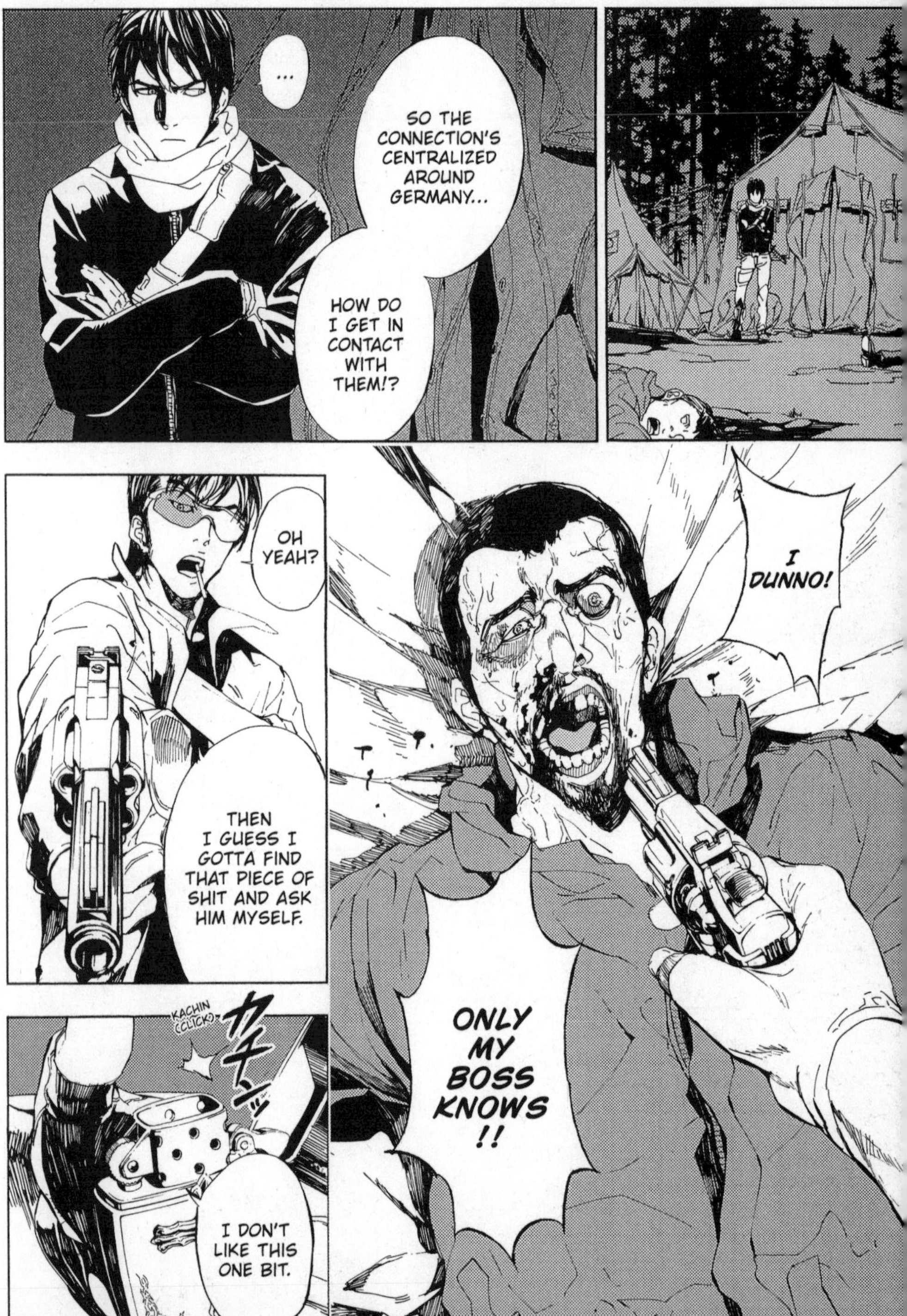
SO THE CONNECTION'S CENTRALIZED AROUND GERMANY...
...
HOW DO I GET IN CONTACT WITH THEM!?
I DUNNO!
ONLY MY BOSS KNOWS!!
OH YEAH?
THEN I GUESS I GOTTA FIND THAT PIECE OF SHIT AND ASK HIM MYSELF.
KACHIN (CLICK)
I DON'T LIKE THIS ONE BIT.

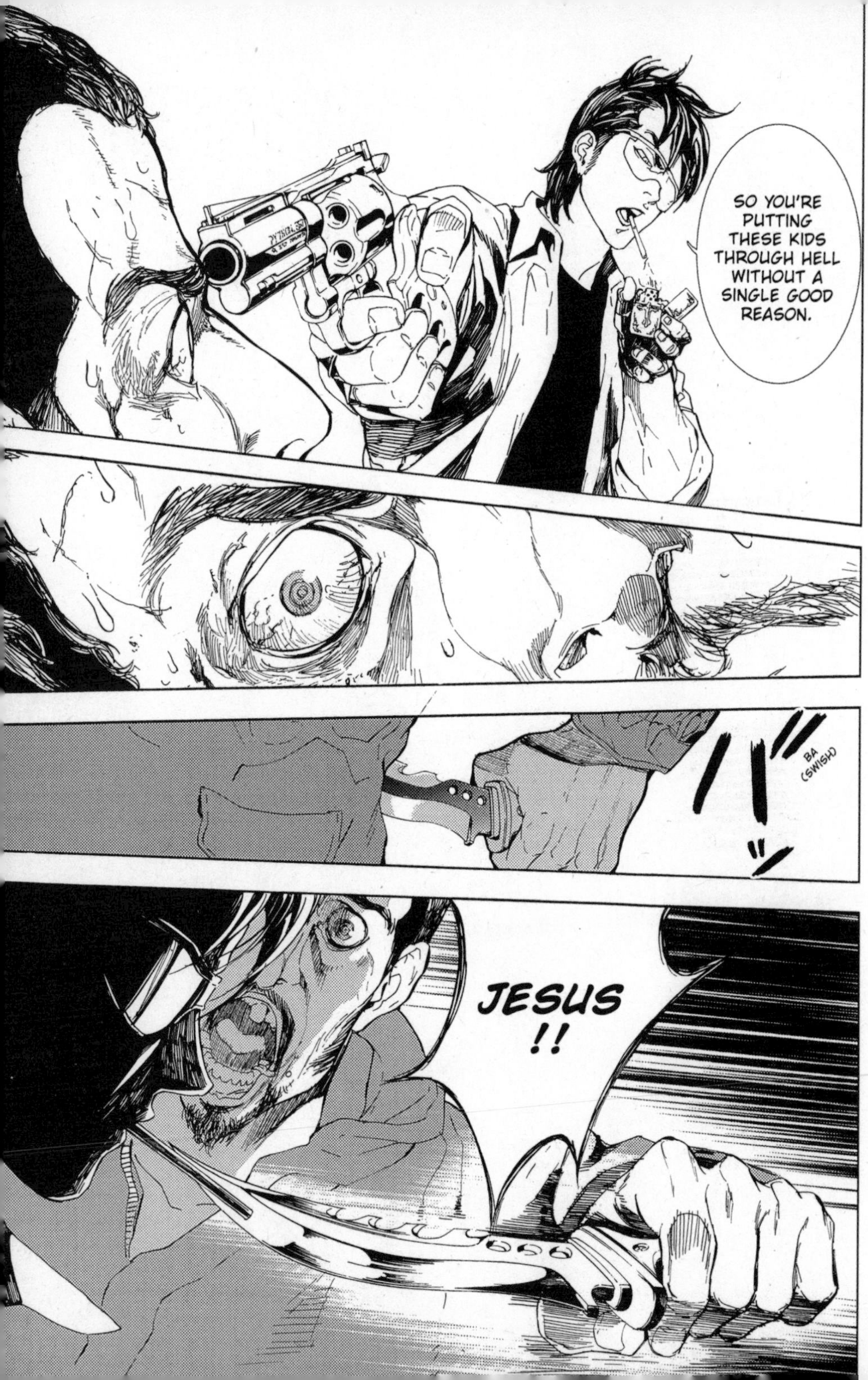
SO YOU'RE PUTTING THESE KIDS THROUGH HELL WITHOUT A SINGLE GOOD REASON.
BA (SWISH)
JESUS !!

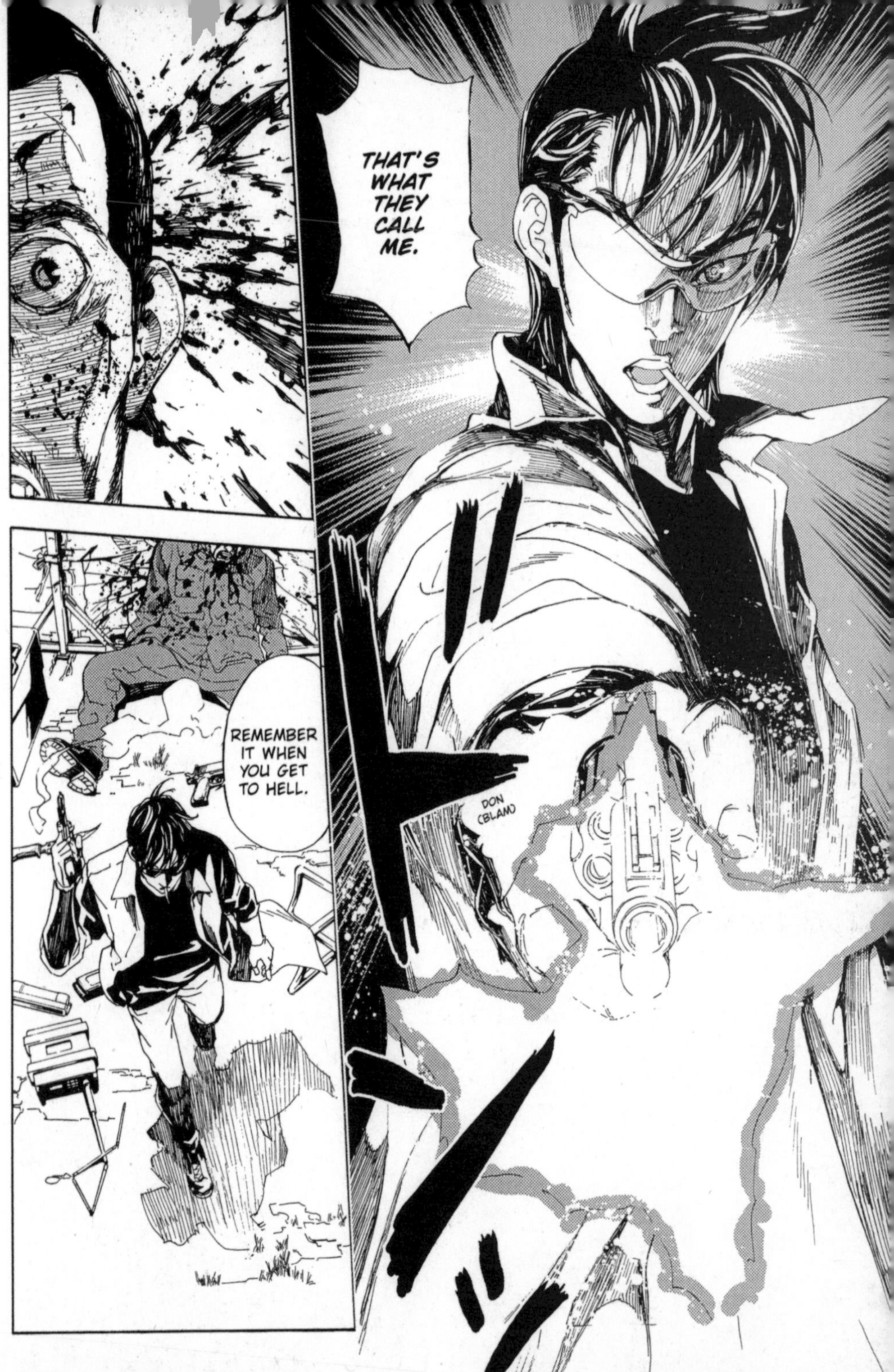
THAT'S WHAT THEY CALL ME.
DON (BLAM)
REMEMBER IT WHEN YOU GET TO HELL.

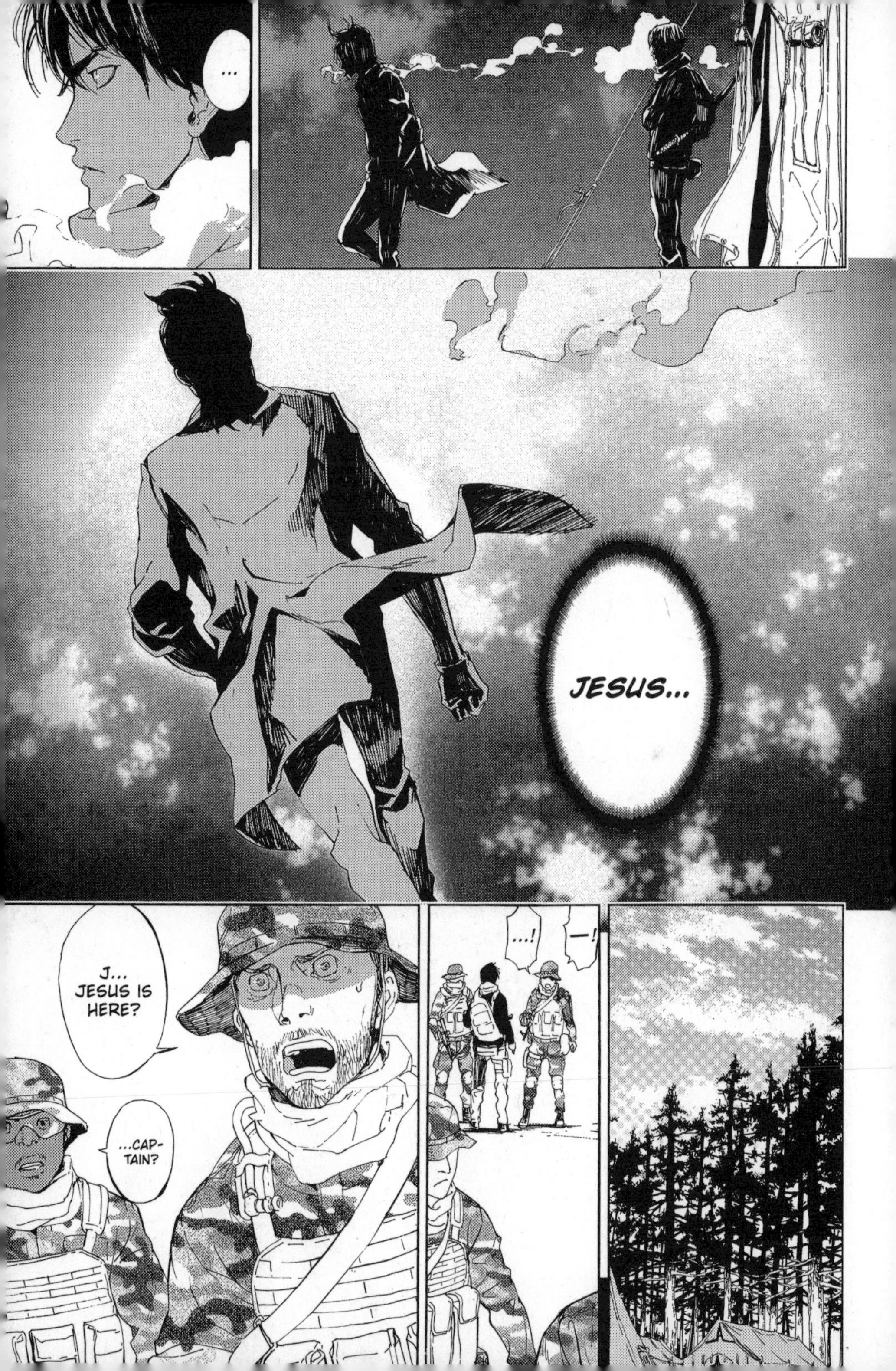
...
JESUS...
—!
...!
J... JESUS IS HERE?
...CAP-TAIN?

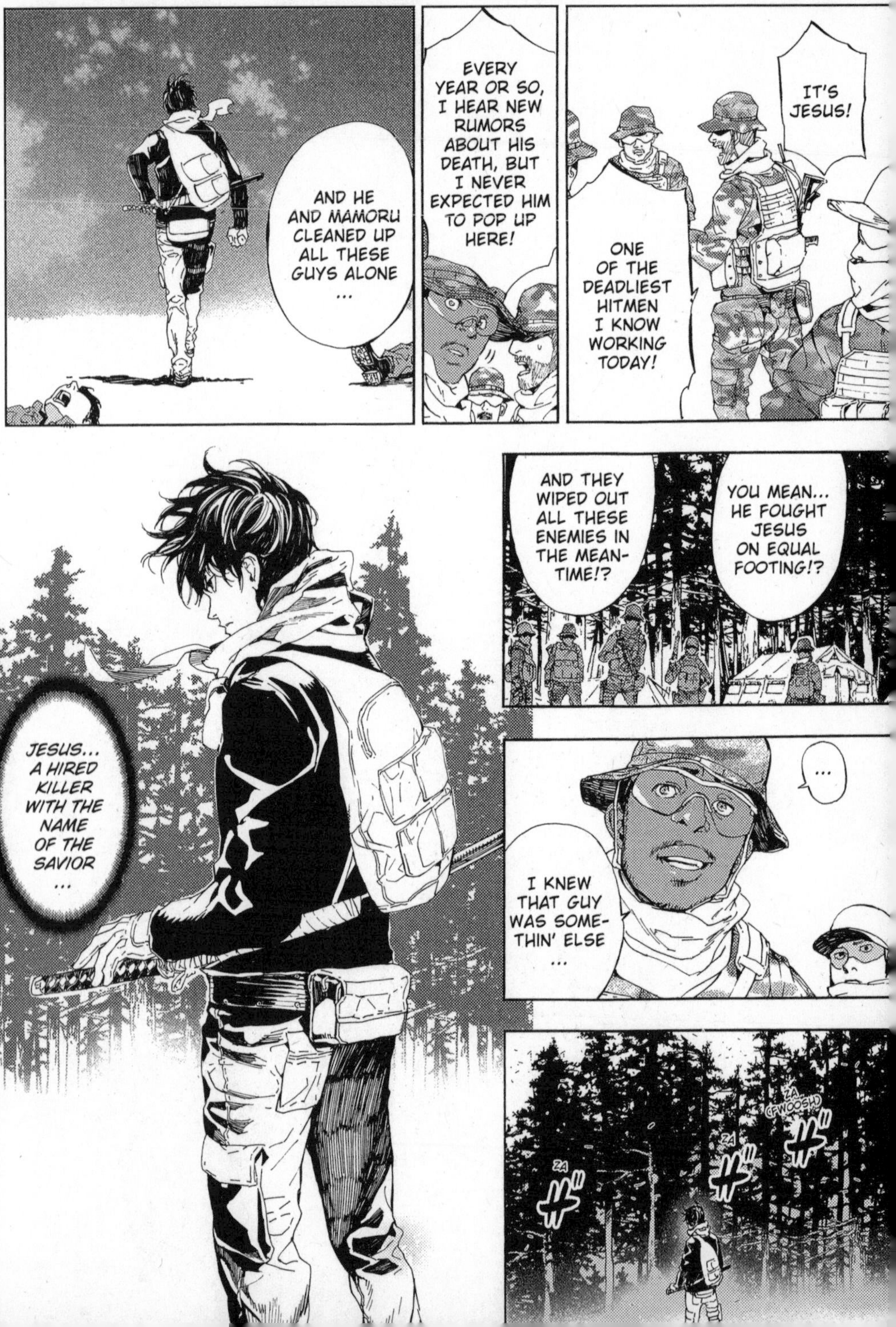
IT'S JESUS!
ONE OF THE DEADLIEST HITMEN I KNOW WORKING TODAY!
EVERY YEAR OR SO, I HEAR NEW RUMORS ABOUT HIS DEATH, BUT I NEVER EXPECTED HIM TO POP UP HERE!
AND HE AND MAMORU CLEANED UP ALL THESE GUYS ALONE ...
YOU MEAN... HE FOUGHT JESUS ON EQUAL FOOTING!?
AND THEY WIPED OUT ALL THESE ENEMIES IN THE MEAN-TIME!?
...
I KNEW THAT GUY WAS SOME-THIN' ELSE ...
ZA (FWOOSH)
ZA
ZA
JESUS... A HIRED KILLER WITH THE NAME OF THE SAVIOR ...

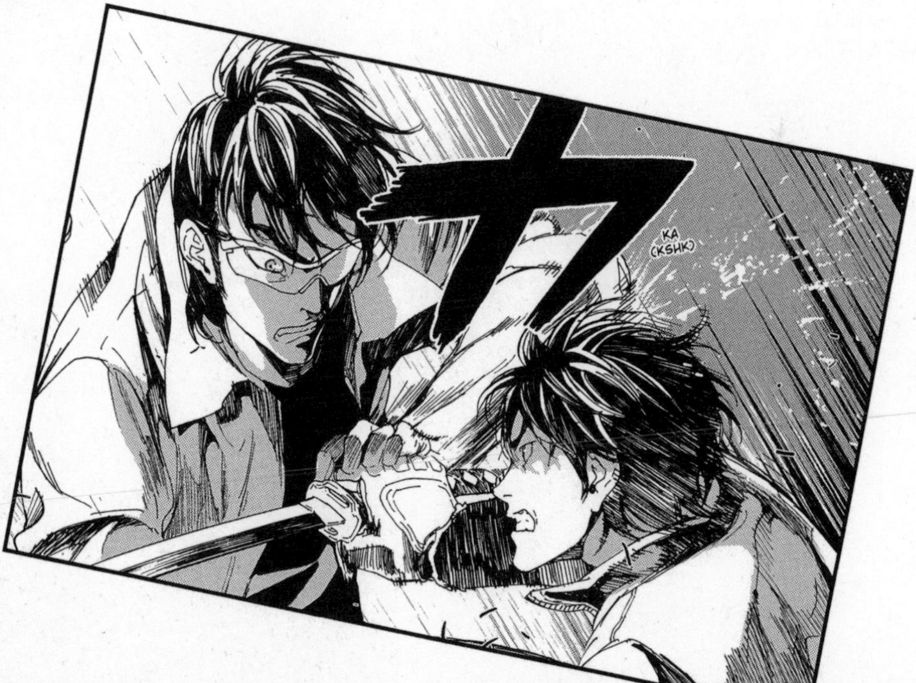
KA
(KSHK)

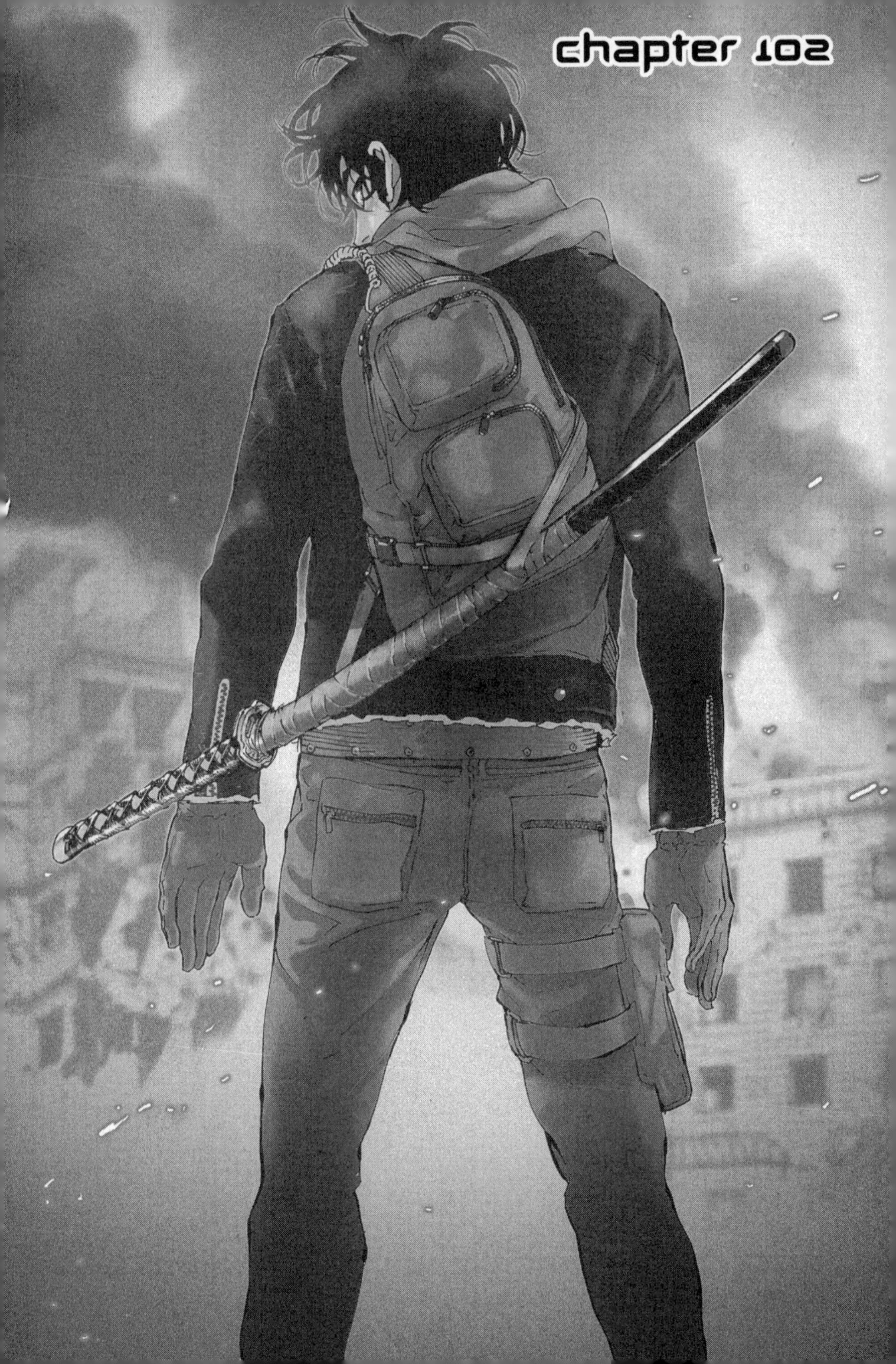
chapter 102

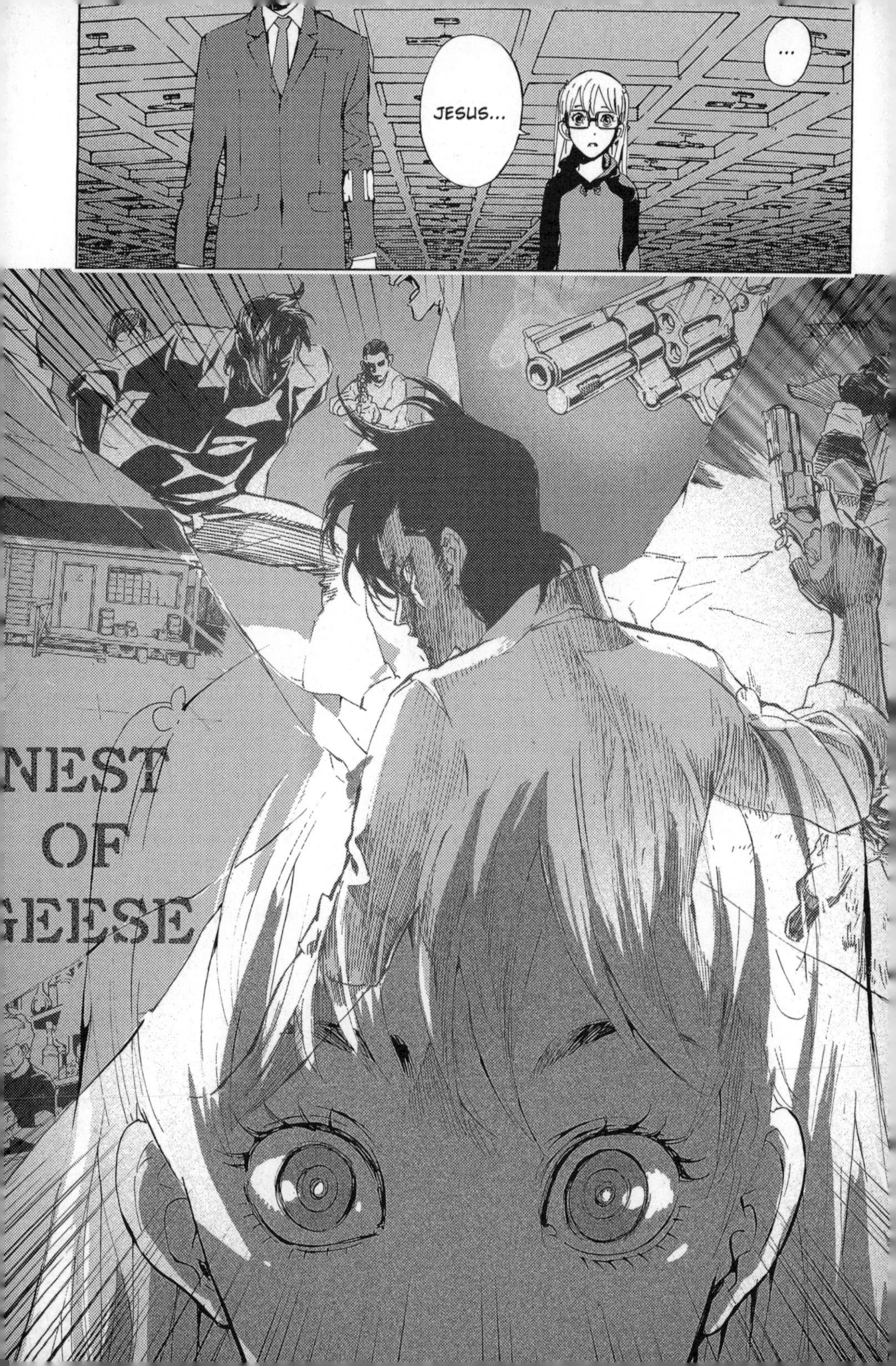
...
JESUS...
NEST OF GEESE

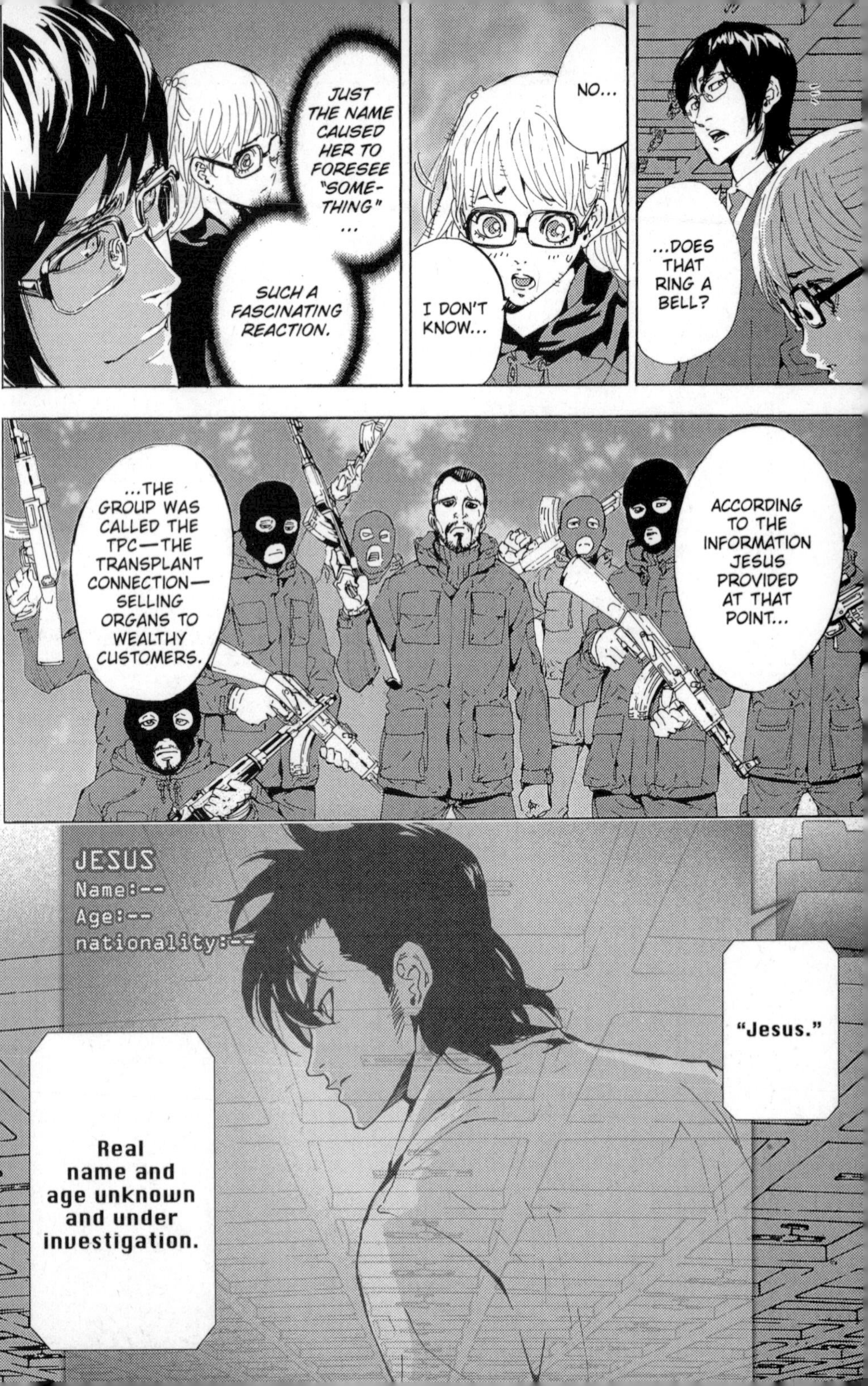
...DOES THAT RING A BELL?
NO...
I DON'T KNOW...
JUST THE NAME CAUSED HER TO FORESEE "SOMETHING" ...
SUCH A FASCINATING REACTION.
ACCORDING TO THE INFORMATION JESUS PROVIDED AT THAT POINT...
...THE GROUP WAS CALLED THE TPC—THE TRANSPLANT CONNECTION—SELLING ORGANS TO WEALTHY CUSTOMERS.
JESUS
Name:--
Age:--
nationality:--
"Jesus."
Real name and age unknown and under investigation.

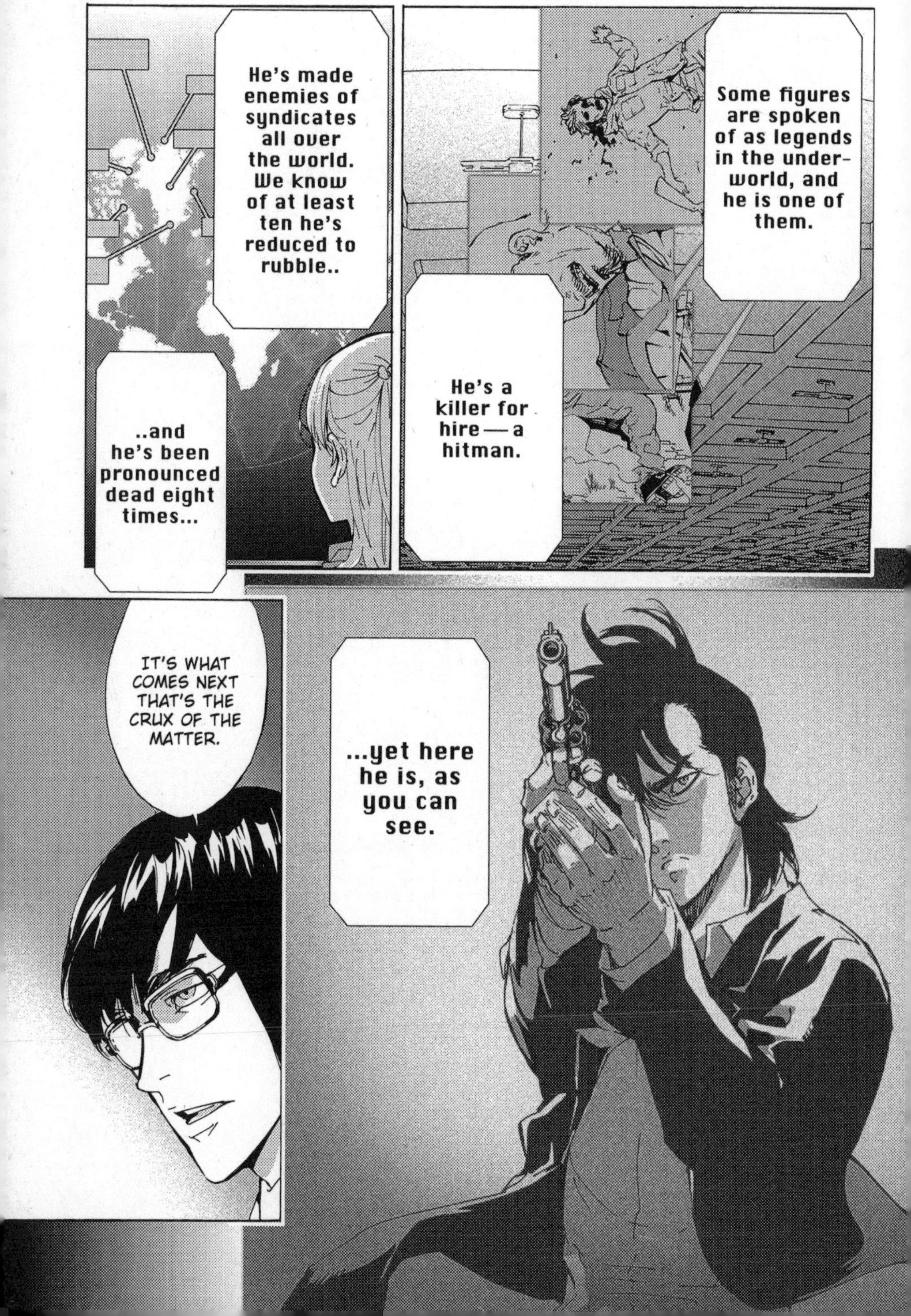
Some figures are spoken of as legends in the under-world, and he is one of them.
He's a killer for hire — a hitman.
He's made enemies of syndicates all over the world. We know of at least ten he's reduced to rubble..
..and he's been pronounced dead eight times...
...yet here he is, as you can see.
IT'S WHAT COMES NEXT THAT'S THE CRUX OF THE MATTER.

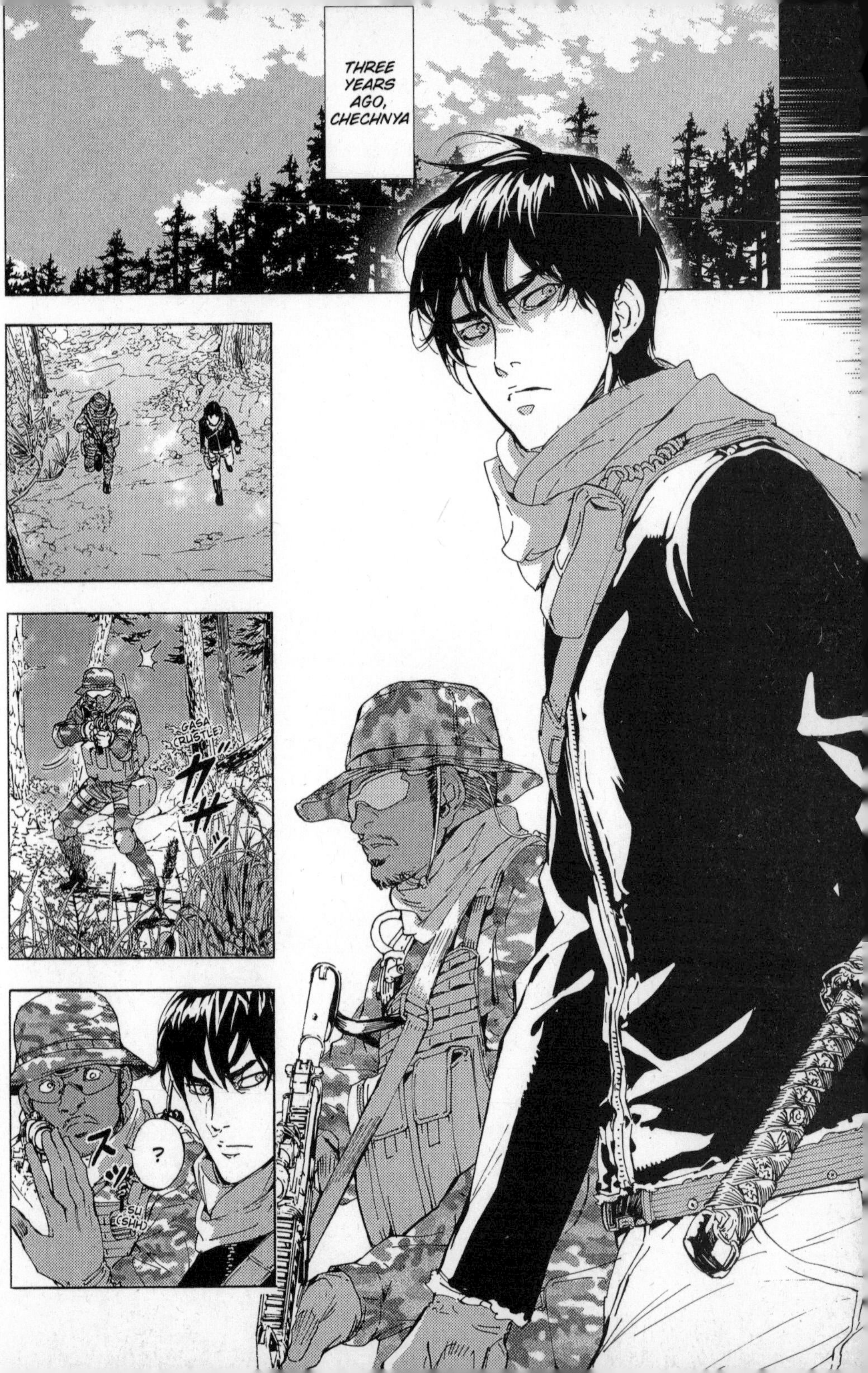
THREE YEARS AGO, CHECHNYA
GASA (RUSTLE)
?
SU (SHH)

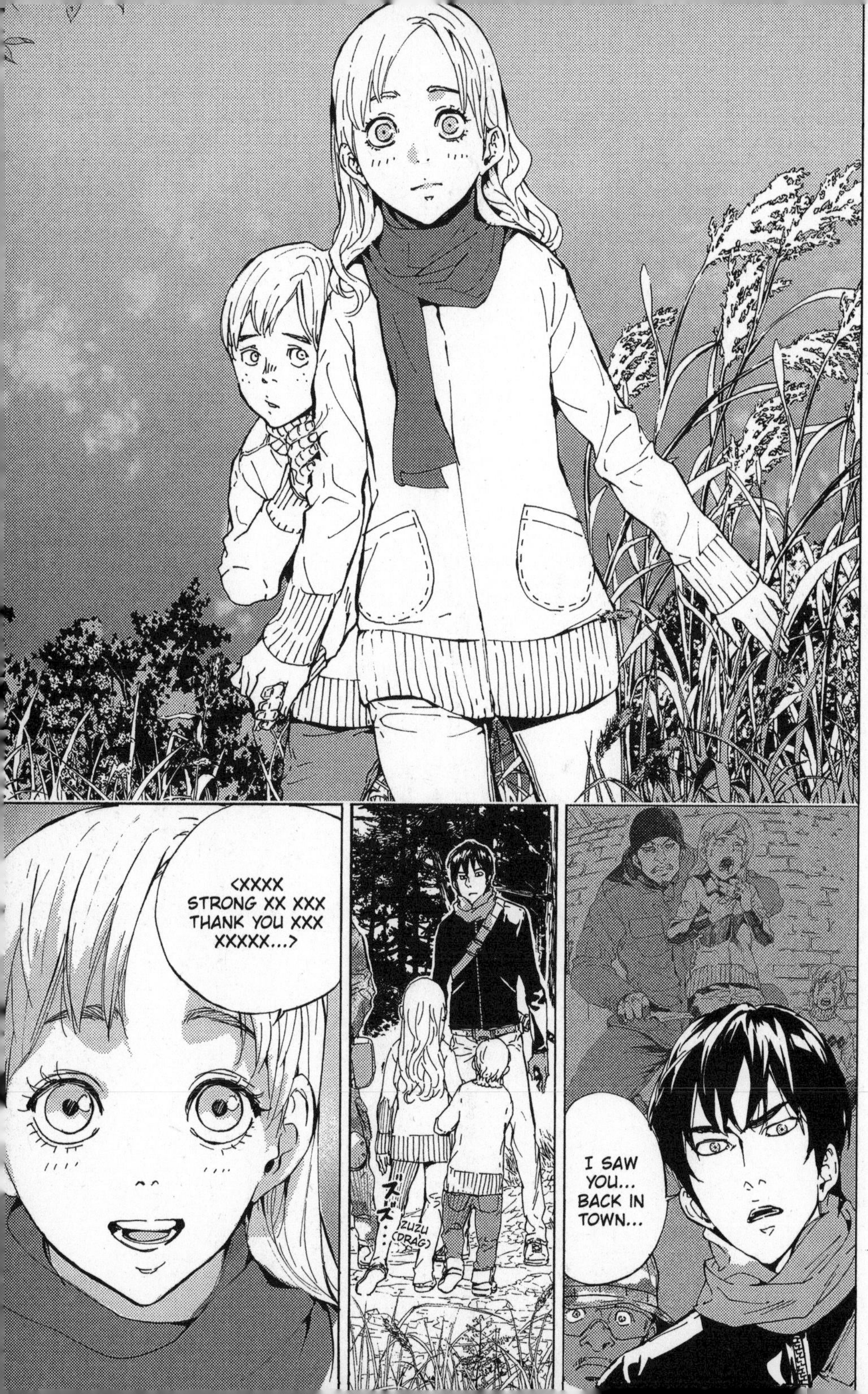
I SAW YOU... BACK IN TOWN...
ズズ…
ZUZU (DRAG)
<XXXX STRONG XX XXX THANK YOU XXX XXXXX...>

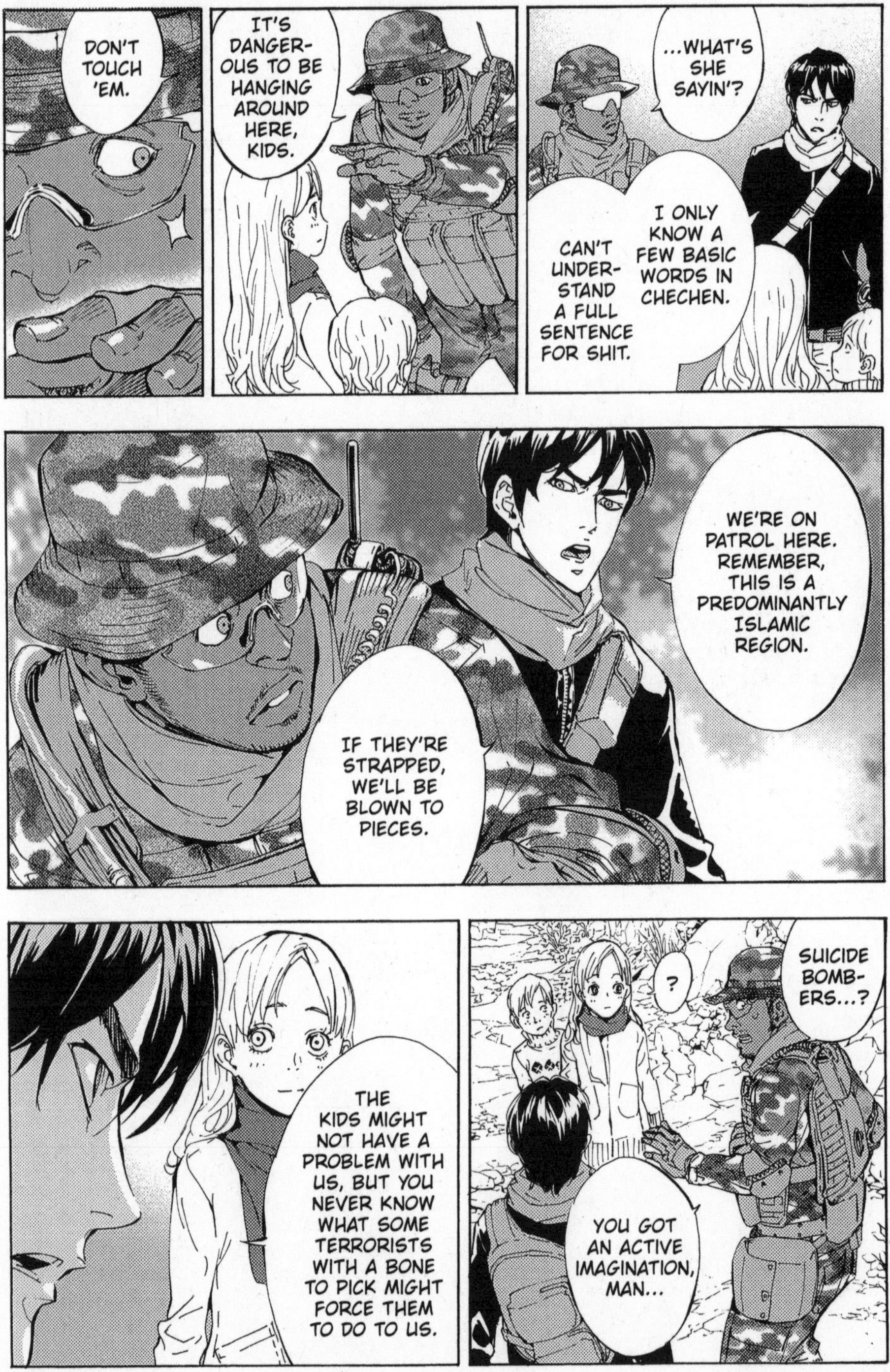
...WHAT'S SHE SAYIN'?
I ONLY KNOW A FEW BASIC WORDS IN CHECHEN.
CAN'T UNDERSTAND A FULL SENTENCE FOR SHIT.
IT'S DANGEROUS TO BE HANGING AROUND HERE, KIDS.
DON'T TOUCH 'EM.
WE'RE ON PATROL HERE. REMEMBER, THIS IS A PREDOMINANTLY ISLAMIC REGION.
IF THEY'RE STRAPPED, WE'LL BE BLOWN TO PIECES.
SUICIDE BOMBERS...?
?
YOU GOT AN ACTIVE IMAGINATION, MAN...
THE KIDS MIGHT NOT HAVE A PROBLEM WITH US, BUT YOU NEVER KNOW WHAT SOME TERRORISTS WITH A BONE TO PICK MIGHT FORCE THEM TO DO TO US.

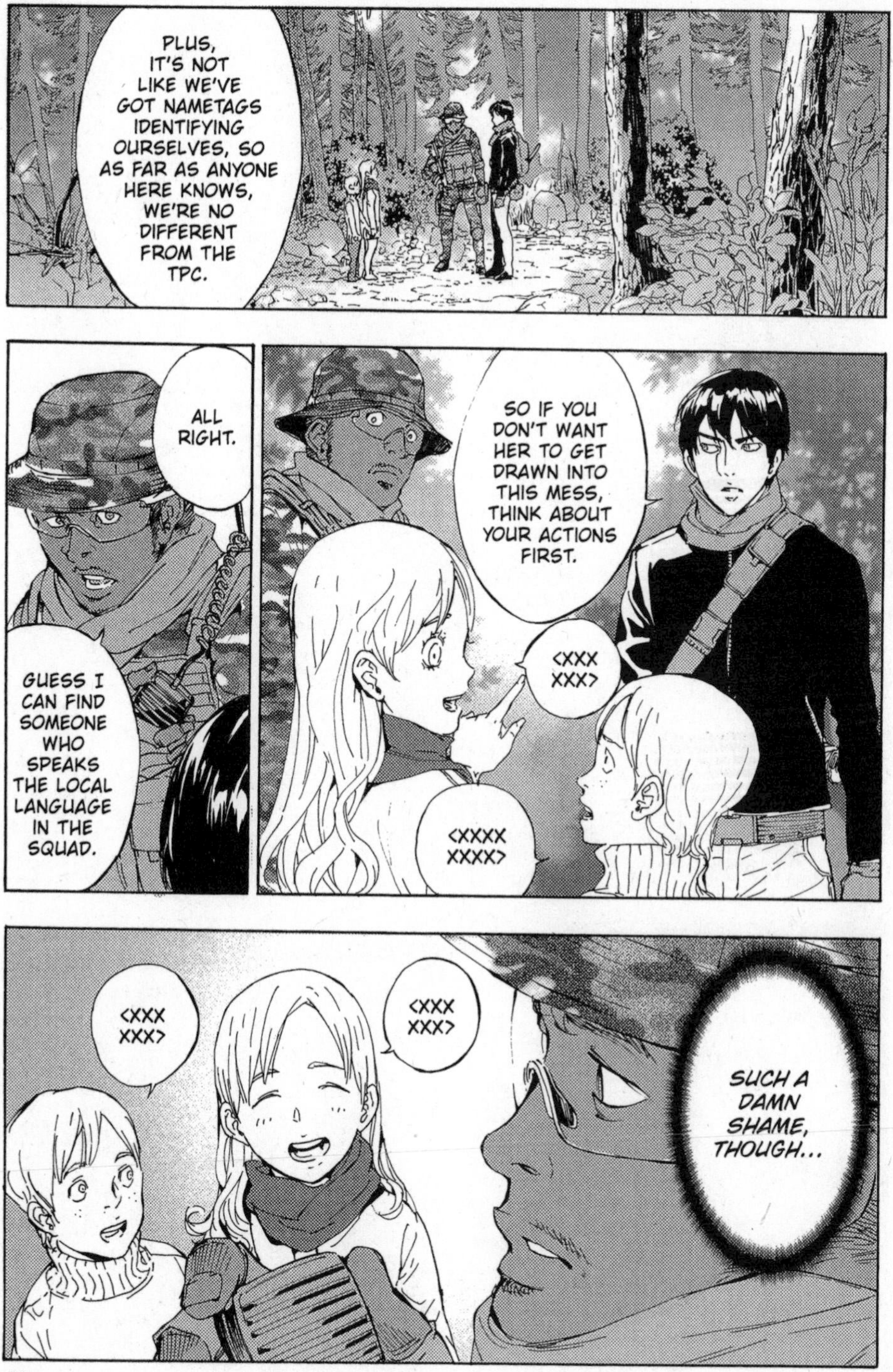
PLUS, IT'S NOT LIKE WE'VE GOT NAMETAGS IDENTIFYING OURSELVES, SO AS FAR AS ANYONE HERE KNOWS, WE'RE NO DIFFERENT FROM THE TPC.
SO IF YOU DON'T WANT HER TO GET DRAWN INTO THIS MESS, THINK ABOUT YOUR ACTIONS FIRST.
<XXX XXX>
<XXXX XXXX>
ALL RIGHT.
GUESS I CAN FIND SOMEONE WHO SPEAKS THE LOCAL LANGUAGE IN THE SQUAD.
SUCH A DAMN SHAME, THOUGH...
<XXX XXX>
<XXX XXX>

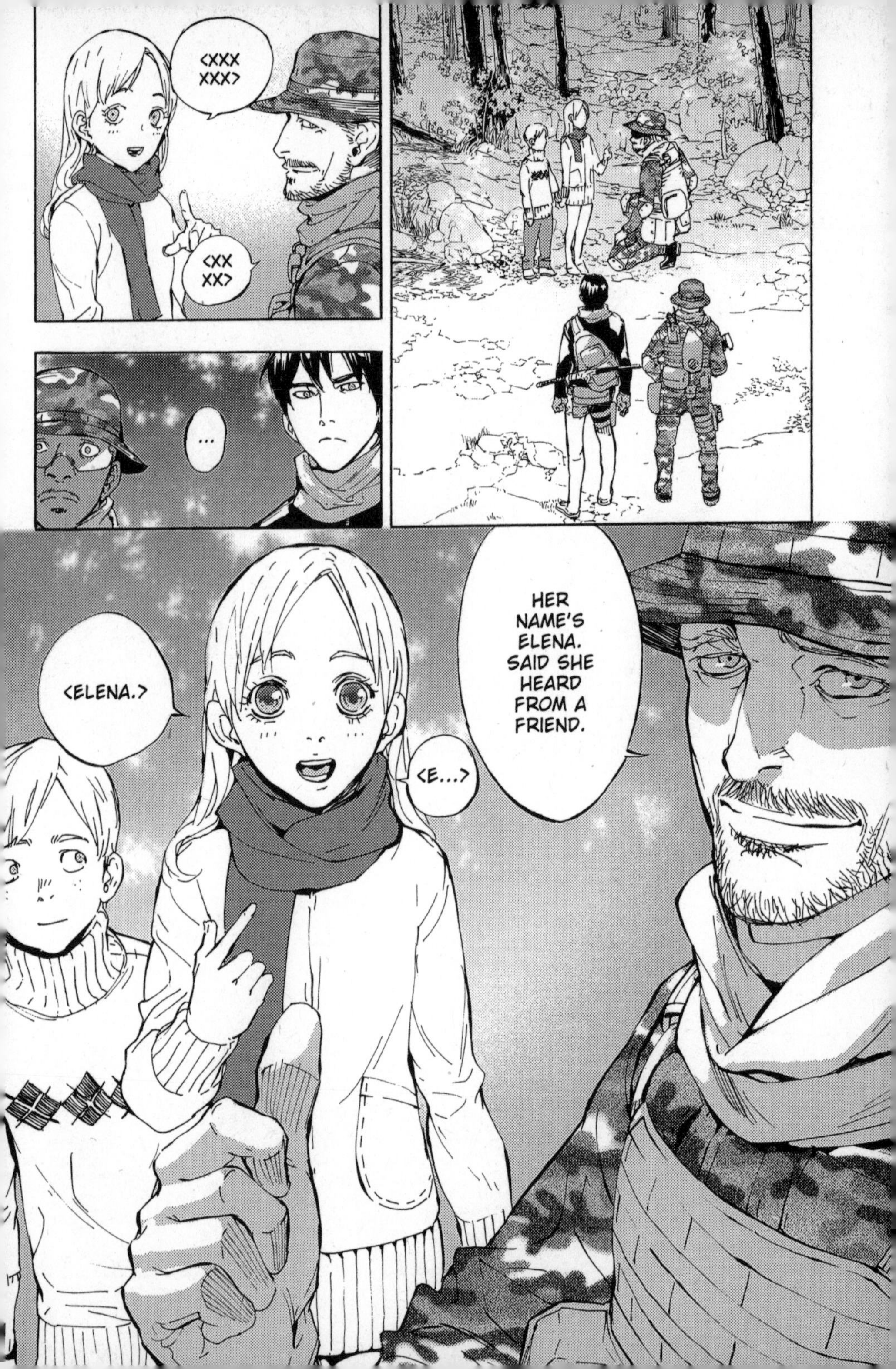
<XXX XXX>
<XX XX>
...
HER NAME'S ELENA. SAID SHE HEARD FROM A FRIEND.
<E...>
<ELENA.>

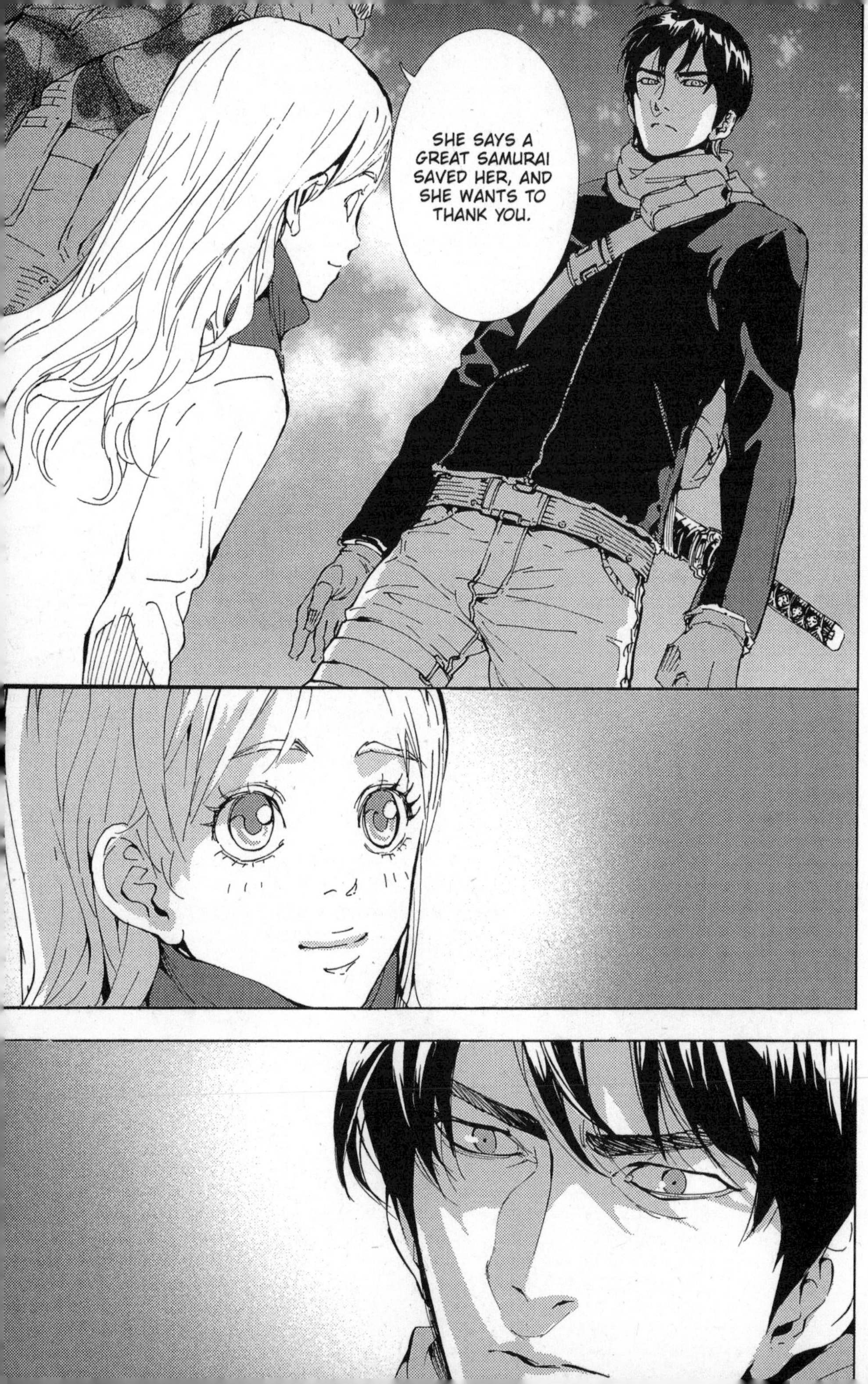
SHE SAYS A GREAT SAMURAI SAVED HER, AND SHE WANTS TO THANK YOU.

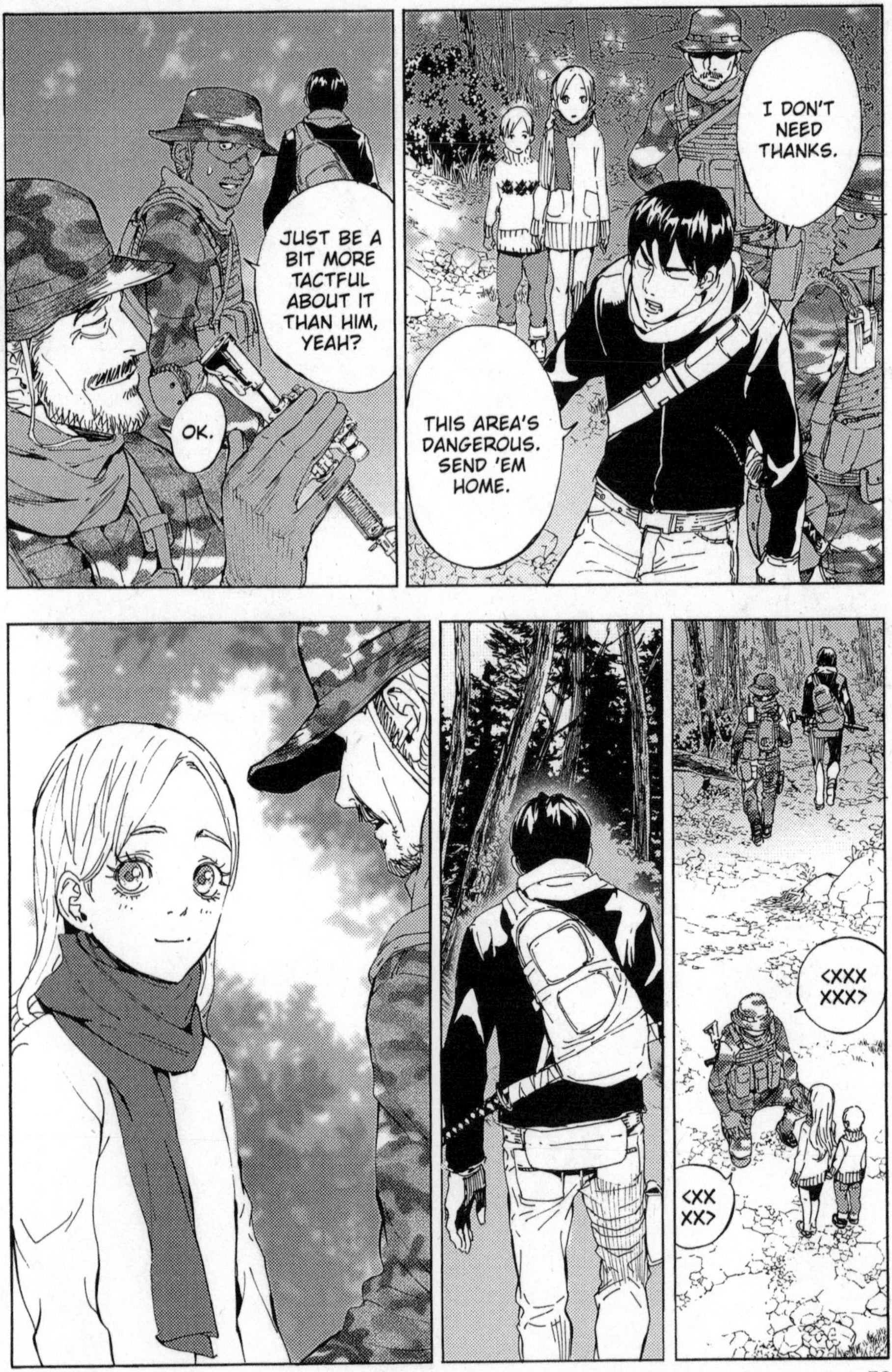
I DON'T NEED THANKS.
THIS AREA'S DANGEROUS. SEND 'EM HOME.
JUST BE A BIT MORE TACTFUL ABOUT IT THAN HIM, YEAH?
OK.
<XXX XXX>
<XX XX>

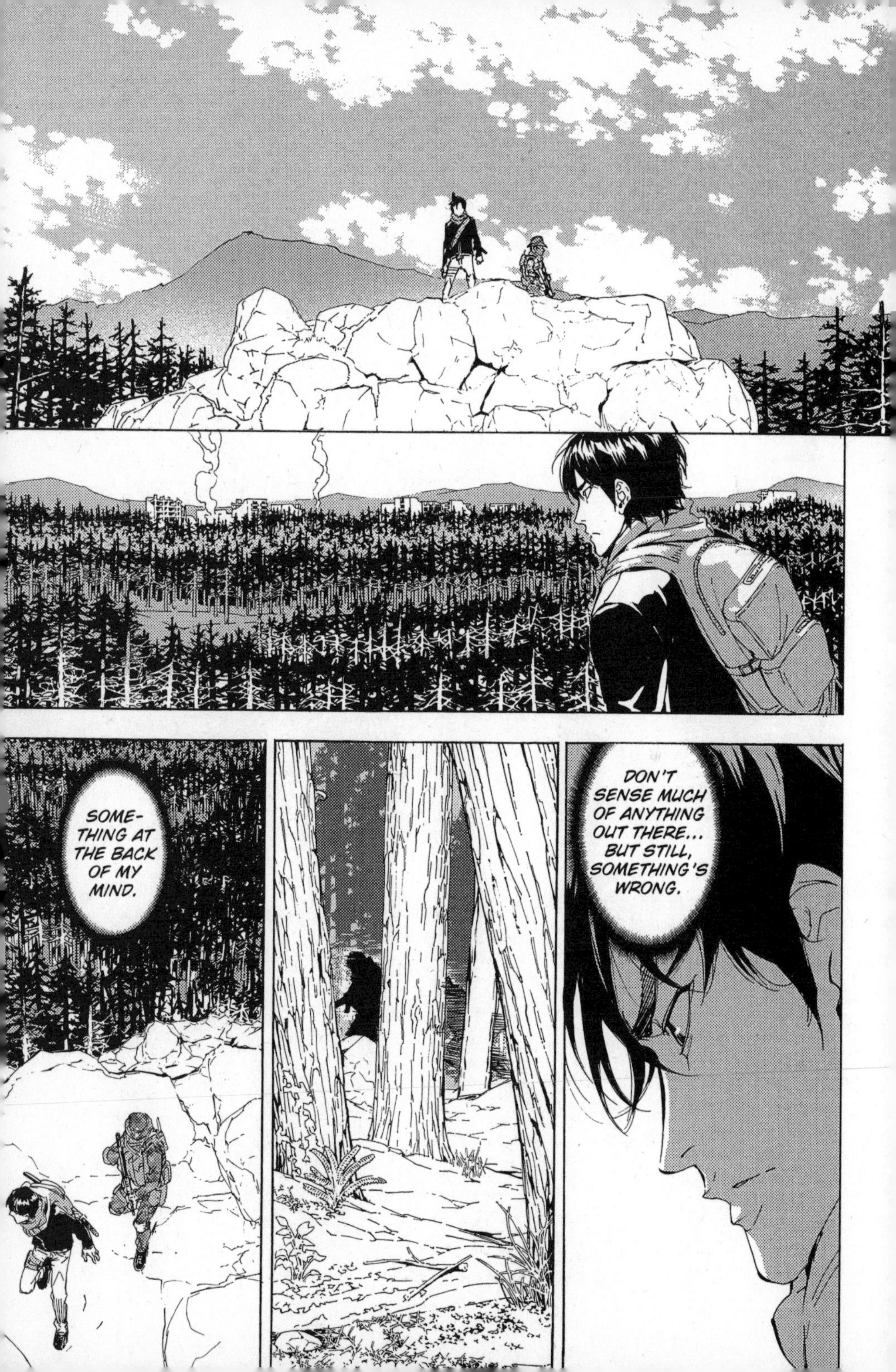
DON'T SENSE MUCH OF ANYTHING OUT THERE... BUT STILL, SOMETHING'S WRONG.
SOME-THING AT THE BACK OF MY MIND.

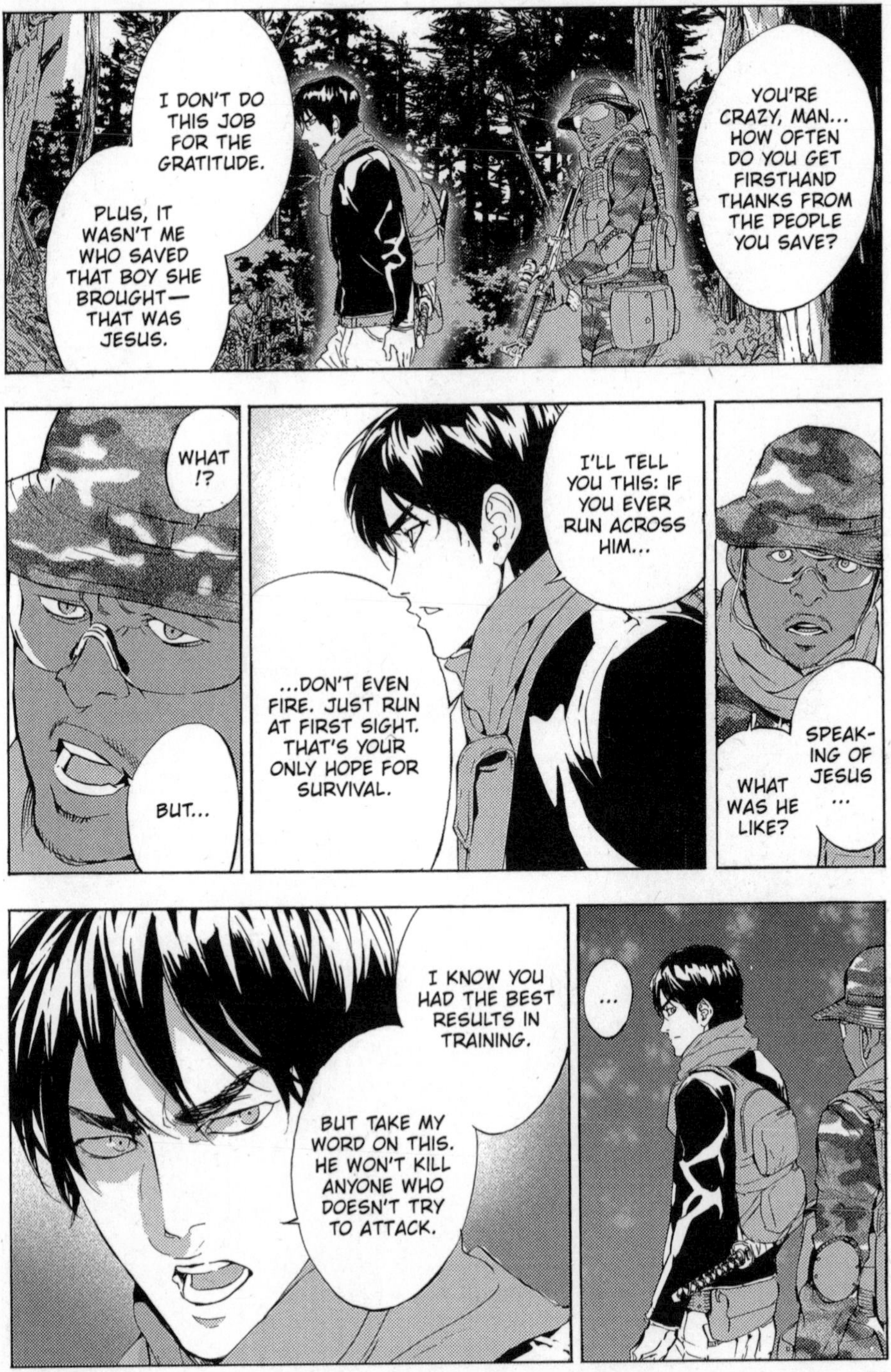

YOU'RE CRAZY, MAN... HOW OFTEN DO YOU GET FIRSTHAND THANKS FROM THE PEOPLE YOU SAVE?
I DON'T DO THIS JOB FOR THE GRATITUDE.
PLUS, IT WASN'T ME WHO SAVED THAT BOY SHE BROUGHT— THAT WAS JESUS.
SPEAK-ING OF JESUS...
WHAT WAS HE LIKE?
I'LL TELL YOU THIS: IF YOU EVER RUN ACROSS HIM...
...DON'T EVEN FIRE. JUST RUN AT FIRST SIGHT. THAT'S YOUR ONLY HOPE FOR SURVIVAL.
WHAT!?
BUT...
...
I KNOW YOU HAD THE BEST RESULTS IN TRAINING.
BUT TAKE MY WORD ON THIS. HE WON'T KILL ANYONE WHO DOESN'T TRY TO ATTACK.

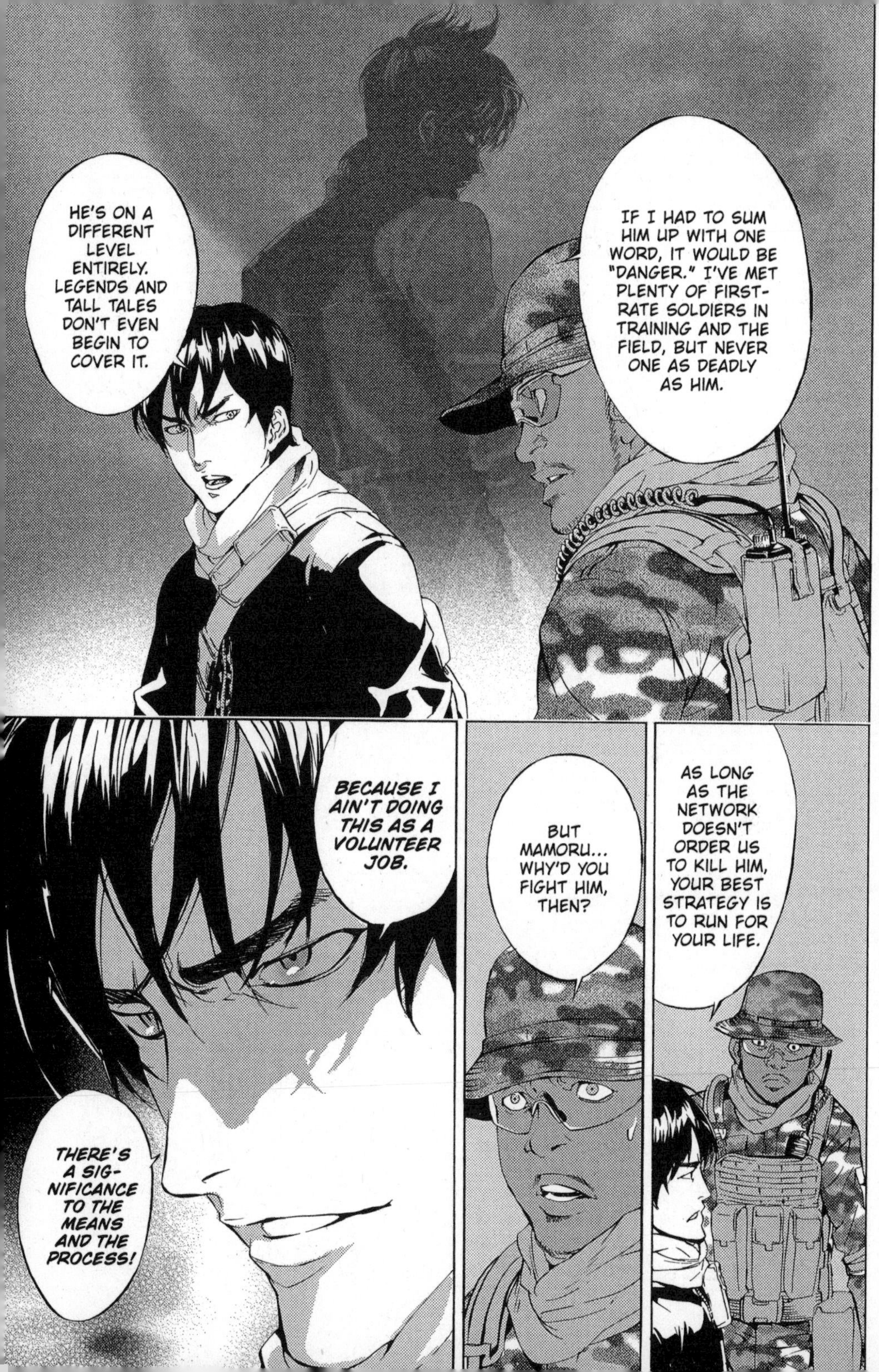
IF I HAD TO SUM HIM UP WITH ONE WORD, IT WOULD BE "DANGER." I'VE MET PLENTY OF FIRST-RATE SOLDIERS IN TRAINING AND THE FIELD, BUT NEVER ONE AS DEADLY AS HIM.
HE'S ON A DIFFERENT LEVEL ENTIRELY. LEGENDS AND TALL TALES DON'T EVEN BEGIN TO COVER IT.
AS LONG AS THE NETWORK DOESN'T ORDER US TO KILL HIM, YOUR BEST STRATEGY IS TO RUN FOR YOUR LIFE.
BUT MAMORU... WHY'D YOU FIGHT HIM, THEN?
BECAUSE I AIN'T DOING THIS AS A VOLUNTEER JOB.
THERE'S A SIG-NIFICANCE TO THE MEANS AND THE PROCESS!

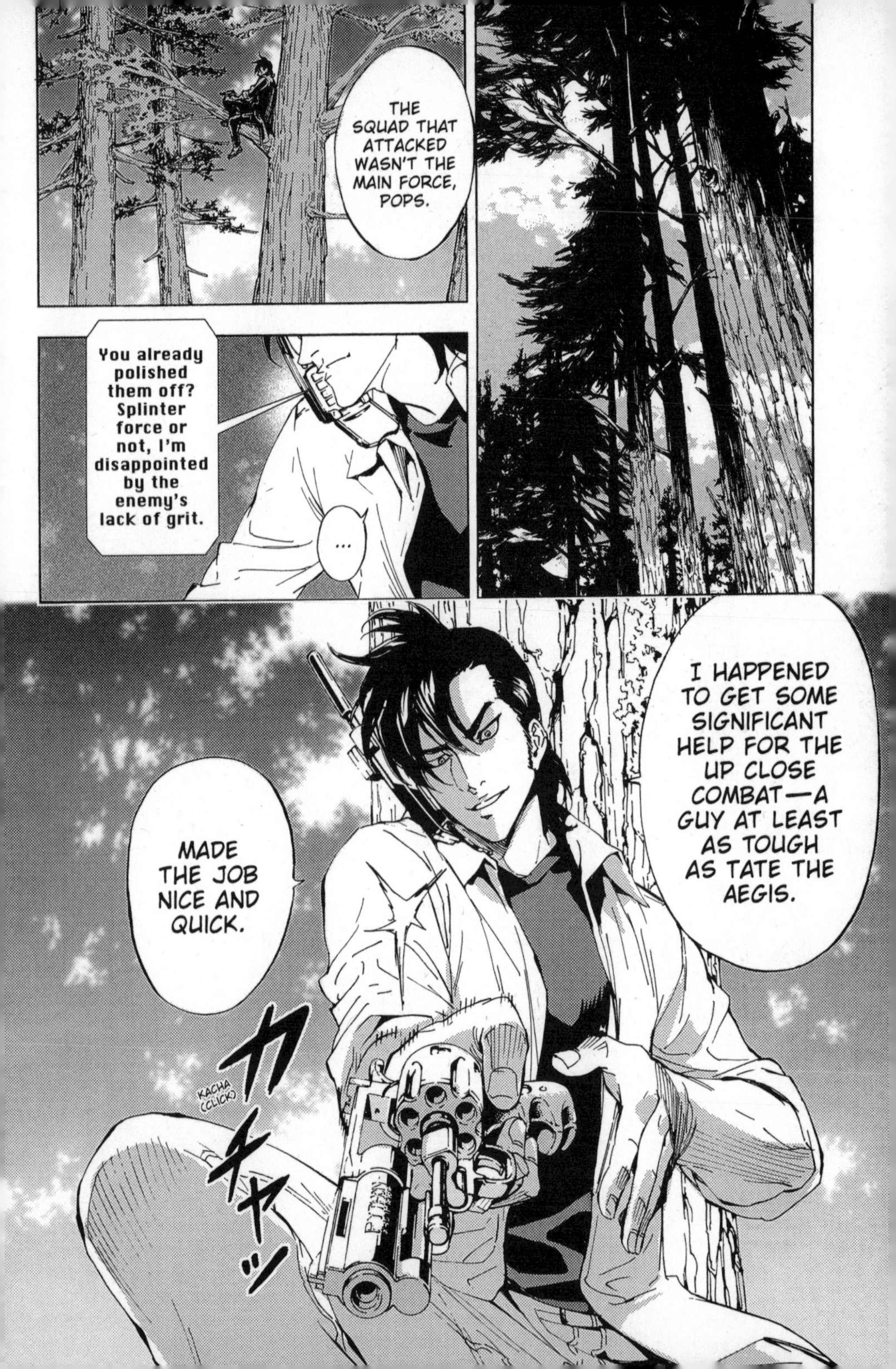
THE SQUAD THAT ATTACKED WASN'T THE MAIN FORCE, POPS.
You already polished them off? Splinter force or not, I'm disappointed by the enemy's lack of grit.
...
I HAPPENED TO GET SOME SIGNIFICANT HELP FOR THE UP CLOSE COMBAT—A GUY AT LEAST AS TOUGH AS TATE THE AEGIS.
MADE THE JOB NICE AND QUICK.
KACHA (CLICK)
カチャッ

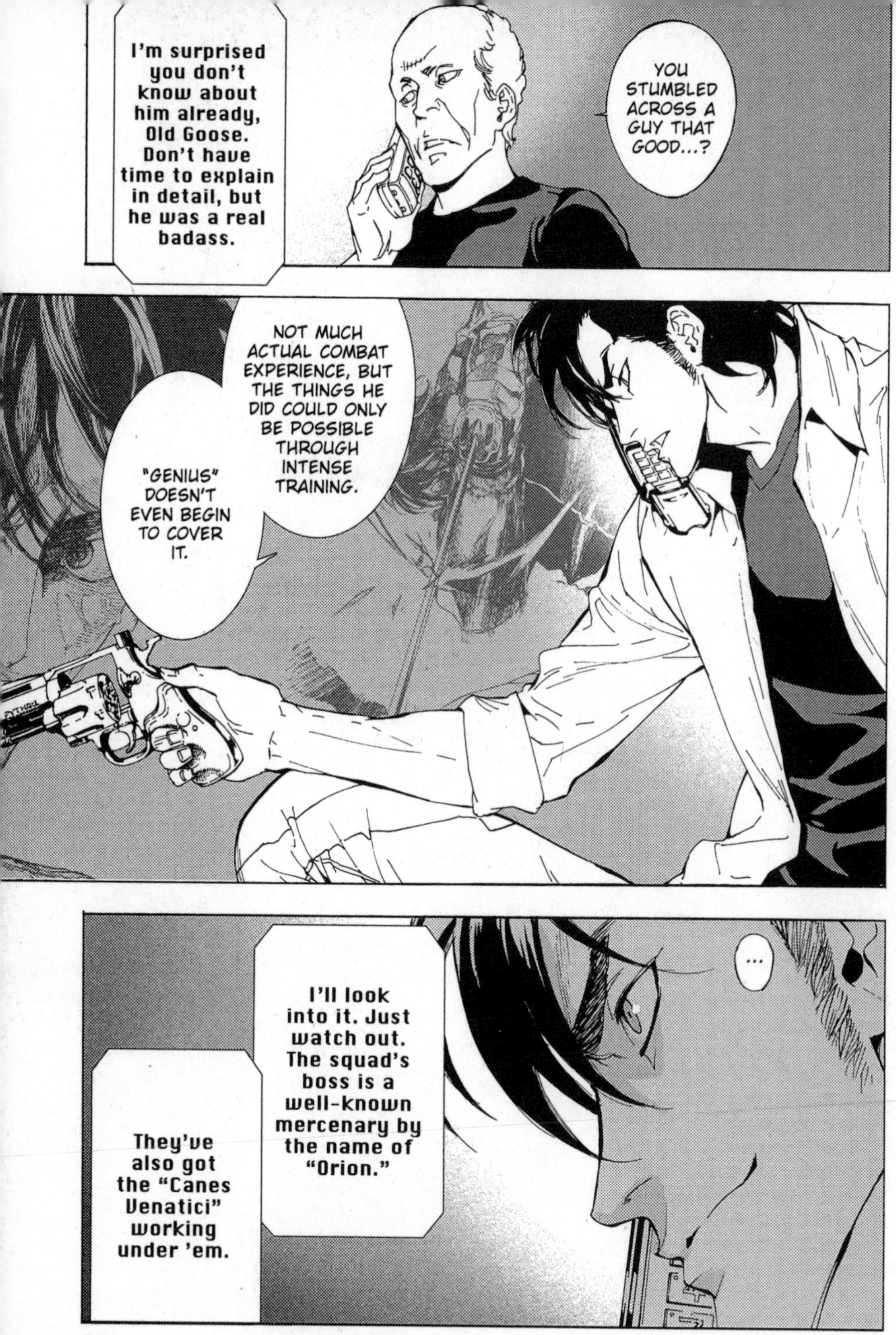
YOU STUMBLED ACROSS A GUY THAT GOOD...?
I'm surprised you don't know about him already, Old Goose. Don't have time to explain in detail, but he was a real badass.
NOT MUCH ACTUAL COMBAT EXPERIENCE, BUT THE THINGS HE DID COULD ONLY BE POSSIBLE THROUGH INTENSE TRAINING.
"GENIUS" DOESN'T EVEN BEGIN TO COVER IT.
...
I'll look into it. Just watch out. The squad's boss is a well-known mercenary by the name of "Orion."
They've also got the "Canes Venatici" working under 'em.

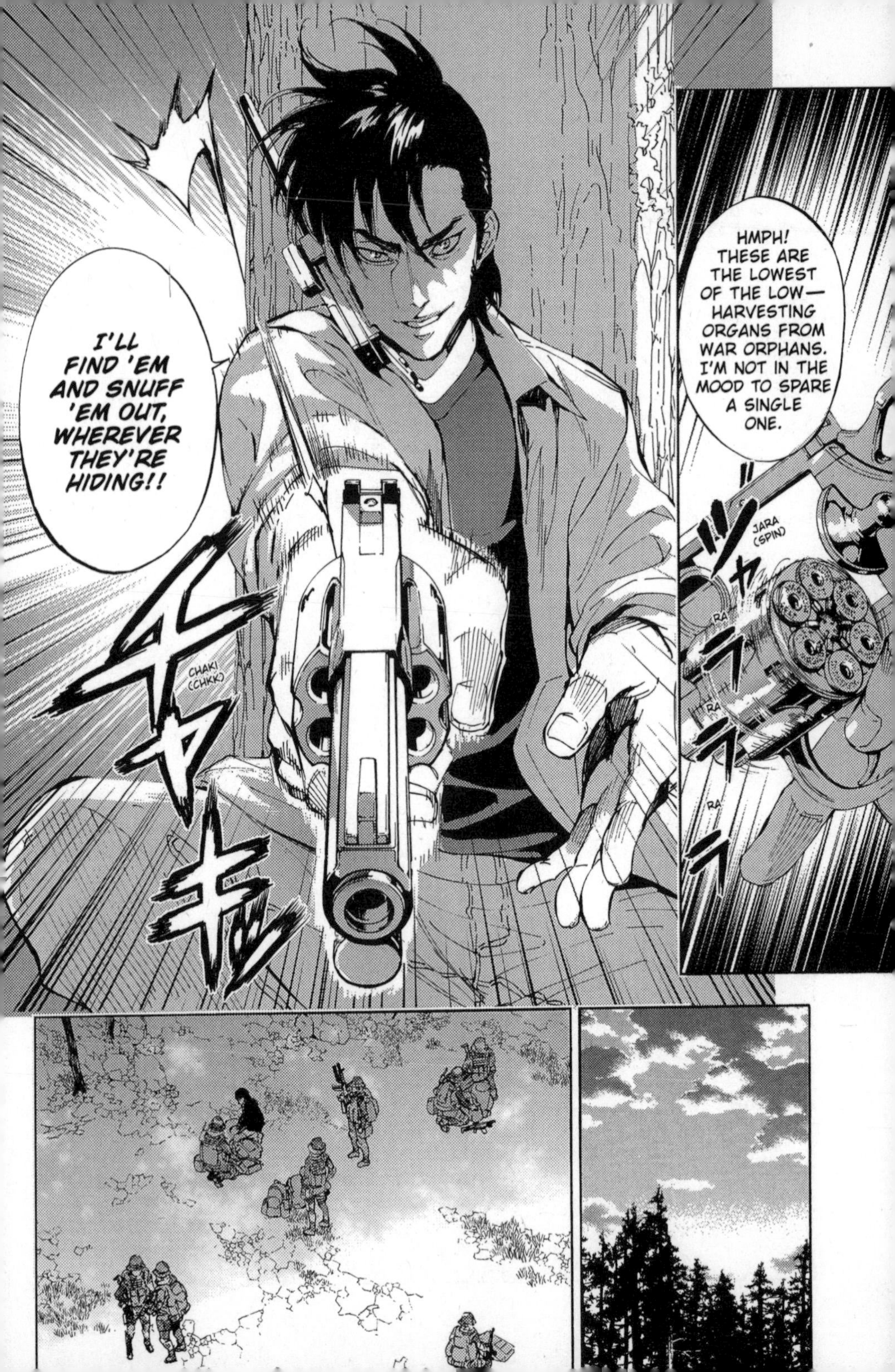
HMPH! THESE ARE THE LOWEST OF THE LOW— HARVESTING ORGANS FROM WAR ORPHANS. I'M NOT IN THE MOOD TO SPARE A SINGLE ONE.
JARA (SPIN)
RA
RA
RA
I'LL FIND 'EM AND SNUFF 'EM OUT, WHEREVER THEY'RE HIDING!!
CHAKI (CHKK)

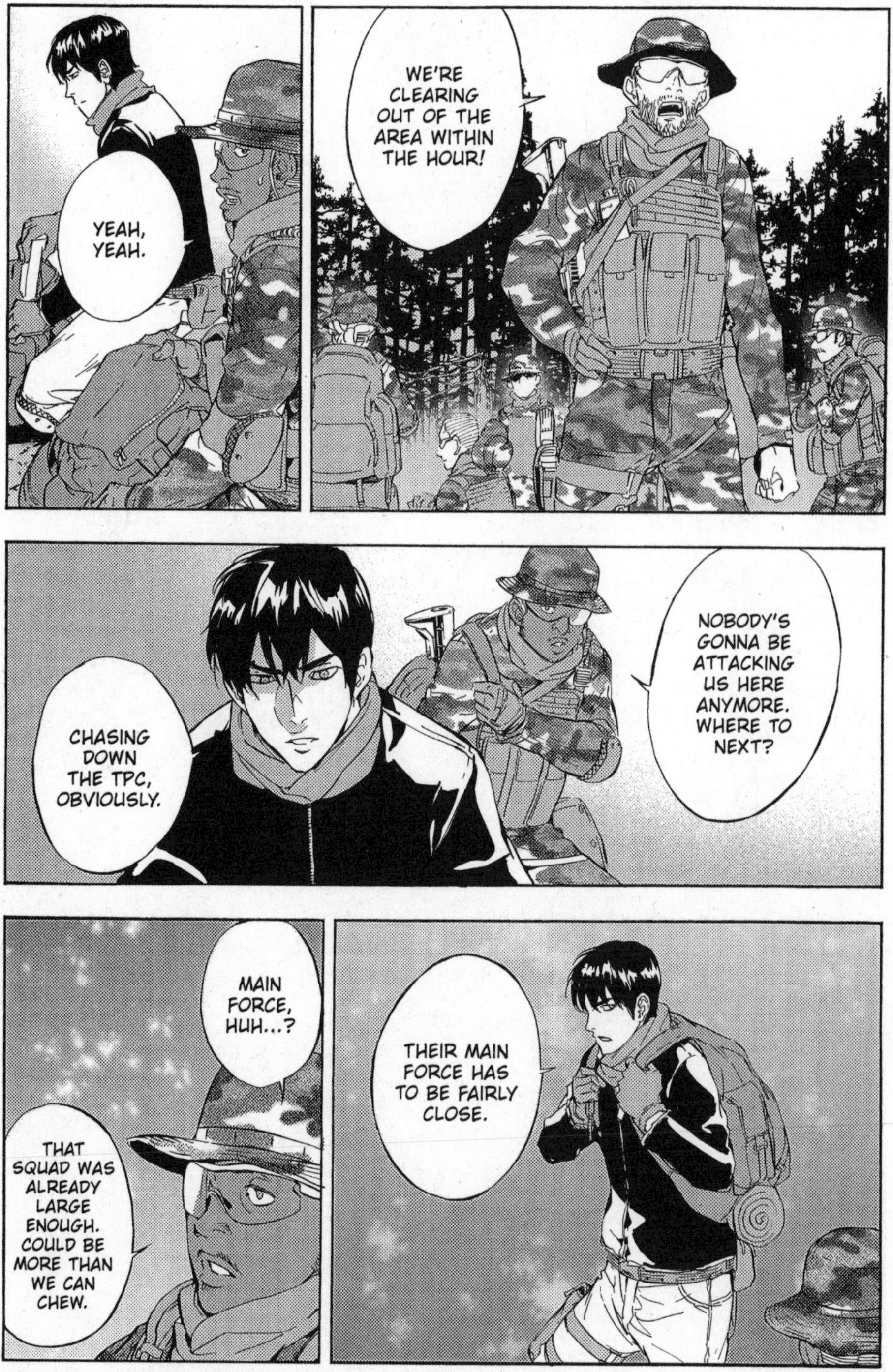
WE'RE CLEARING OUT OF THE AREA WITHIN THE HOUR!
YEAH, YEAH.
NOBODY'S GONNA BE ATTACKING US HERE ANYMORE. WHERE TO NEXT?
CHASING DOWN THE TPC, OBVIOUSLY.
THEIR MAIN FORCE HAS TO BE FAIRLY CLOSE.
MAIN FORCE, HUH...?
THAT SQUAD WAS ALREADY LARGE ENOUGH. COULD BE MORE THAN WE CAN CHEW.

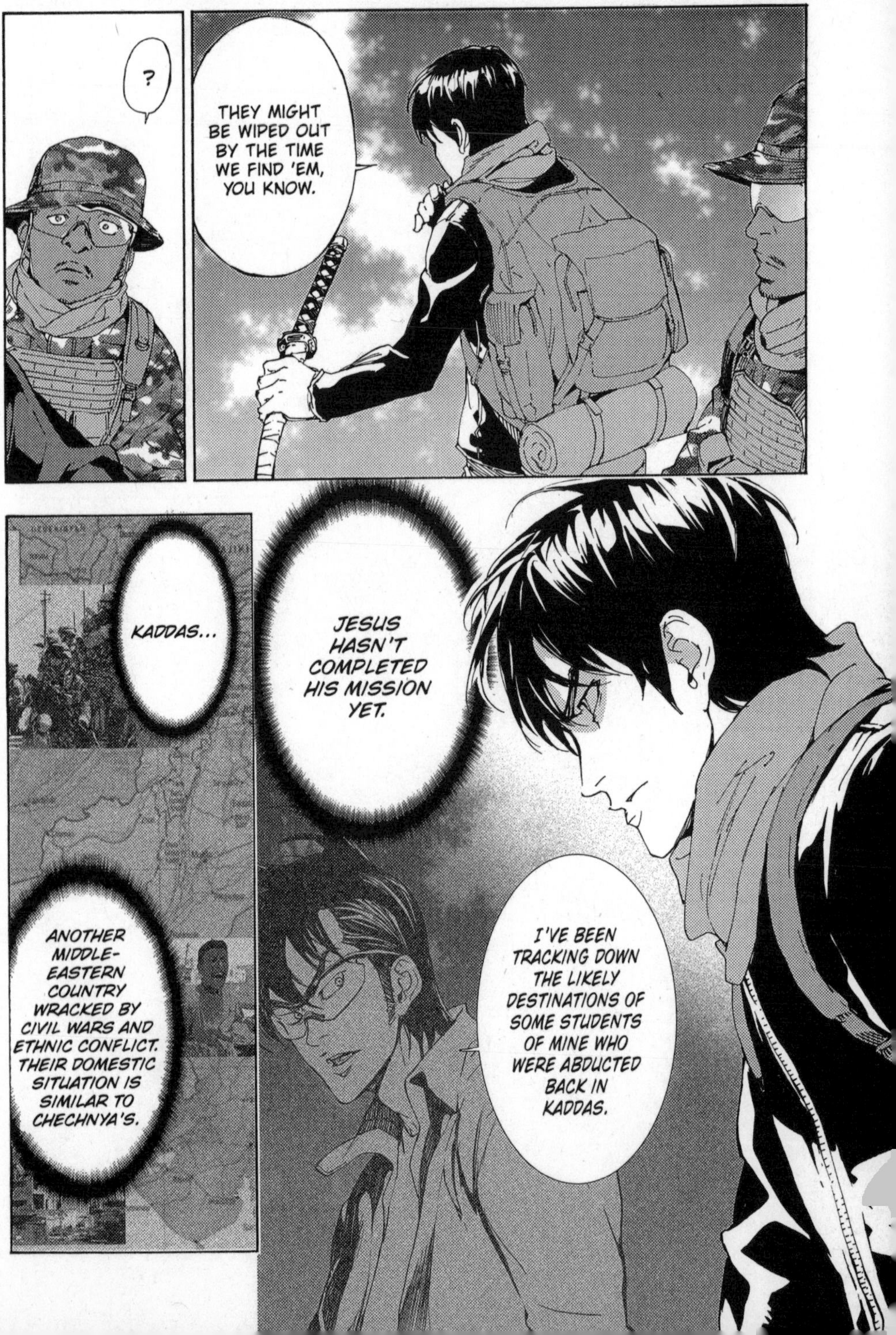
THEY MIGHT BE WIPED OUT BY THE TIME WE FIND 'EM, YOU KNOW.
?
JESUS HASN'T COMPLETED HIS MISSION YET.
I'VE BEEN TRACKING DOWN THE LIKELY DESTINATIONS OF SOME STUDENTS OF MINE WHO WERE ABDUCTED BACK IN KADDAS.
KADDAS...
ANOTHER MIDDLE-EASTERN COUNTRY WRACKED BY CIVIL WARS AND ETHNIC CONFLICT. THEIR DOMESTIC SITUATION IS SIMILAR TO CHECHNYA'S.

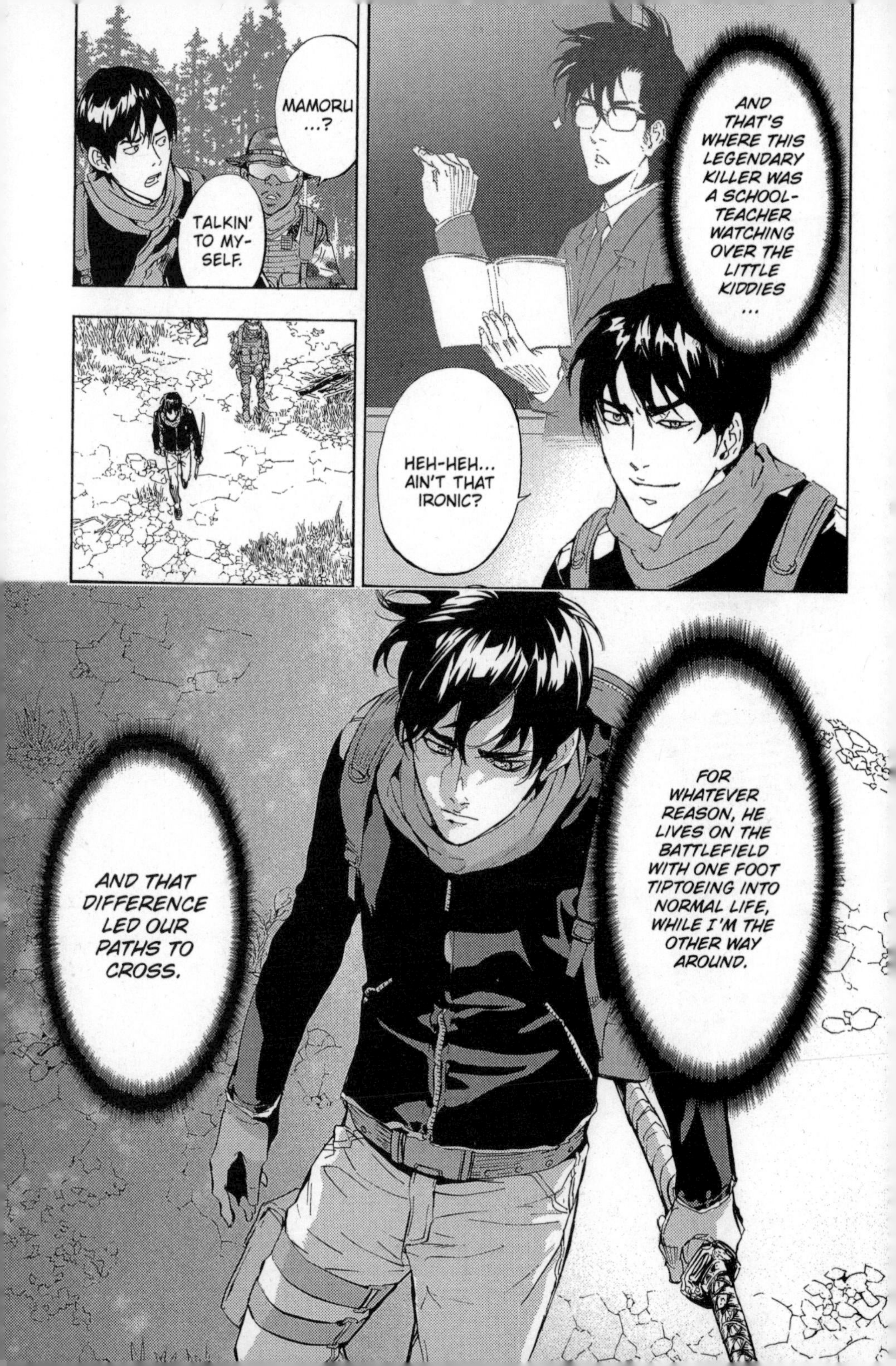
AND THAT'S WHERE THIS LEGENDARY KILLER WAS A SCHOOL-TEACHER WATCHING OVER THE LITTLE KIDDIES ...
HEH-HEH... AIN'T THAT IRONIC?
MAMORU ...?
TALKIN' TO MY-SELF.
FOR WHATEVER REASON, HE LIVES ON THE BATTLEFIELD WITH ONE FOOT TIPTOEING INTO NORMAL LIFE, WHILE I'M THE OTHER WAY AROUND.
AND THAT DIFFERENCE LED OUR PATHS TO CROSS.

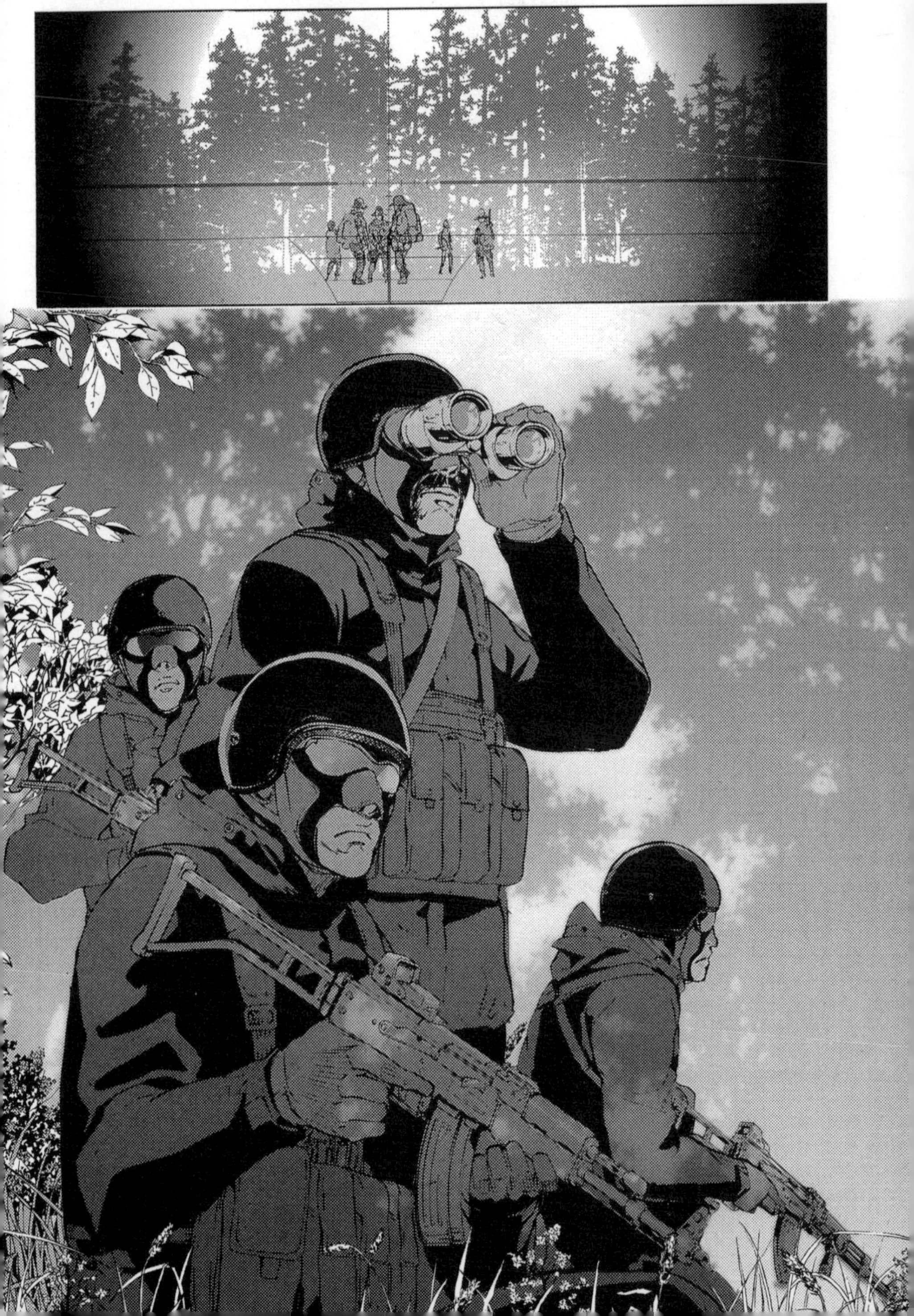

Until Death do us Part

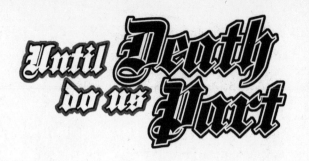

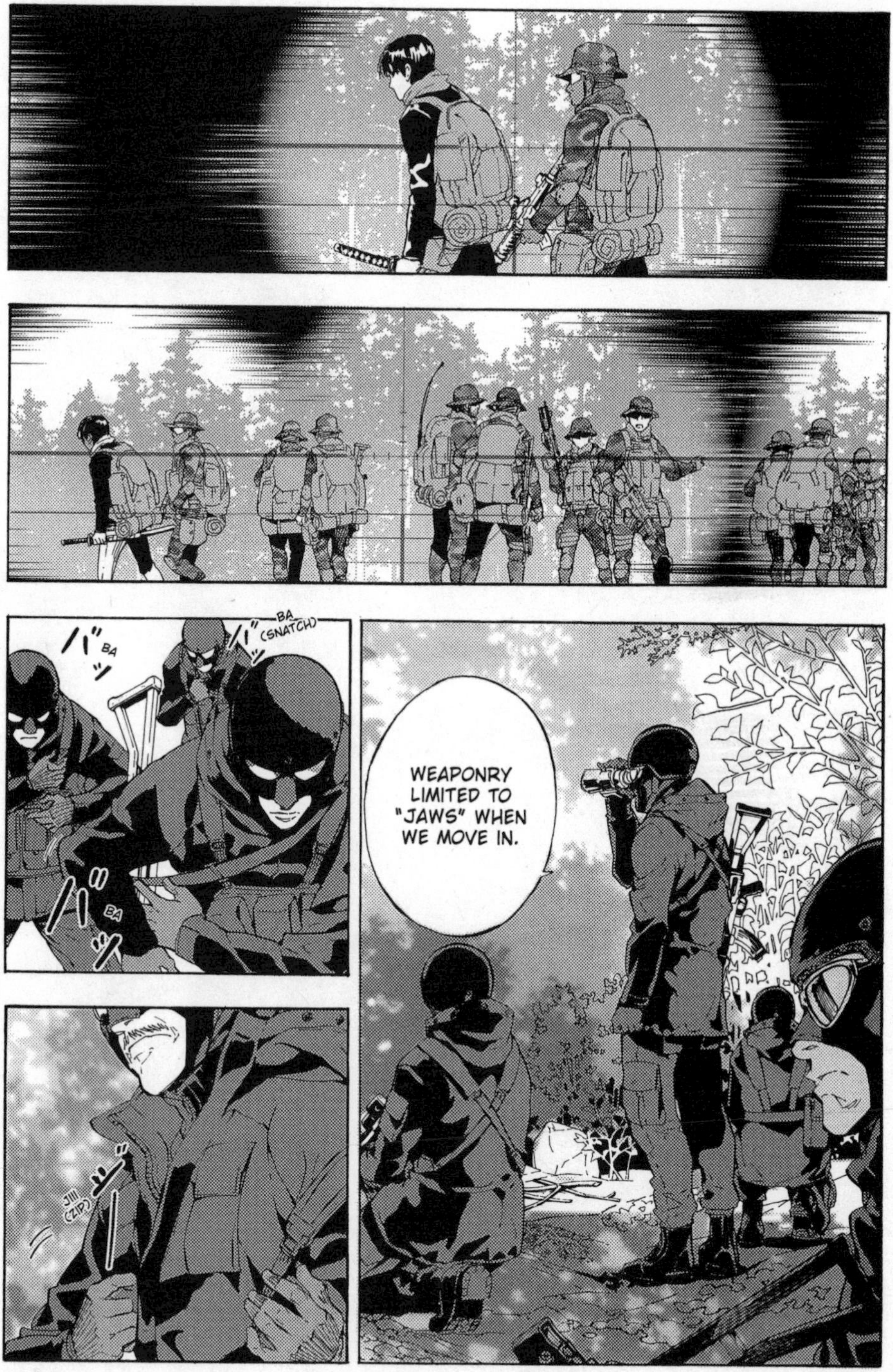
WEAPONRY LIMITED TO "JAWS" WHEN WE MOVE IN.
BA
BA (SNATCH)
BA
JIII (ZIP)

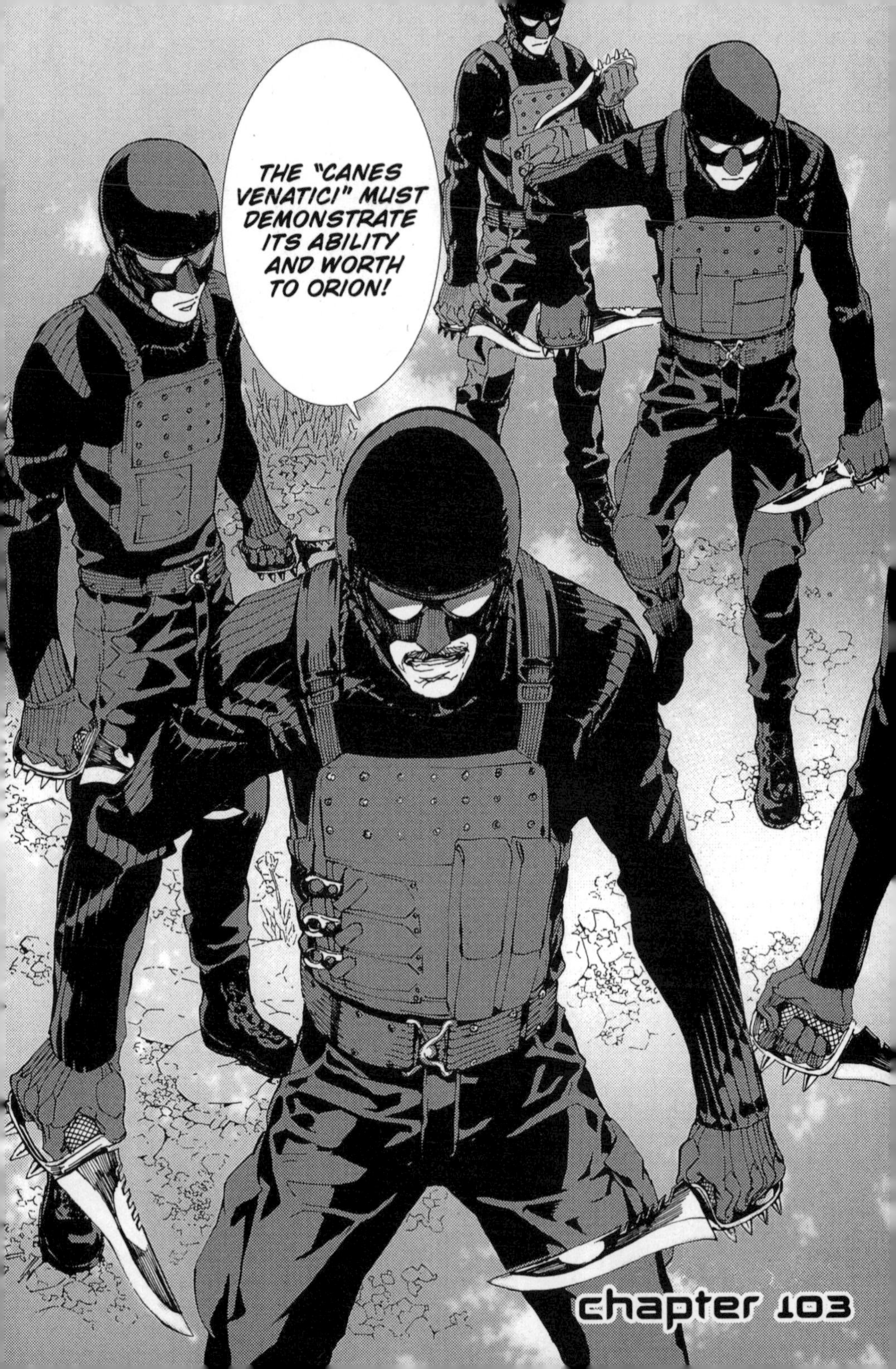
THE "CANES VENATICI" MUST DEMONSTRATE ITS ABILITY AND WORTH TO ORION!
chapter 103

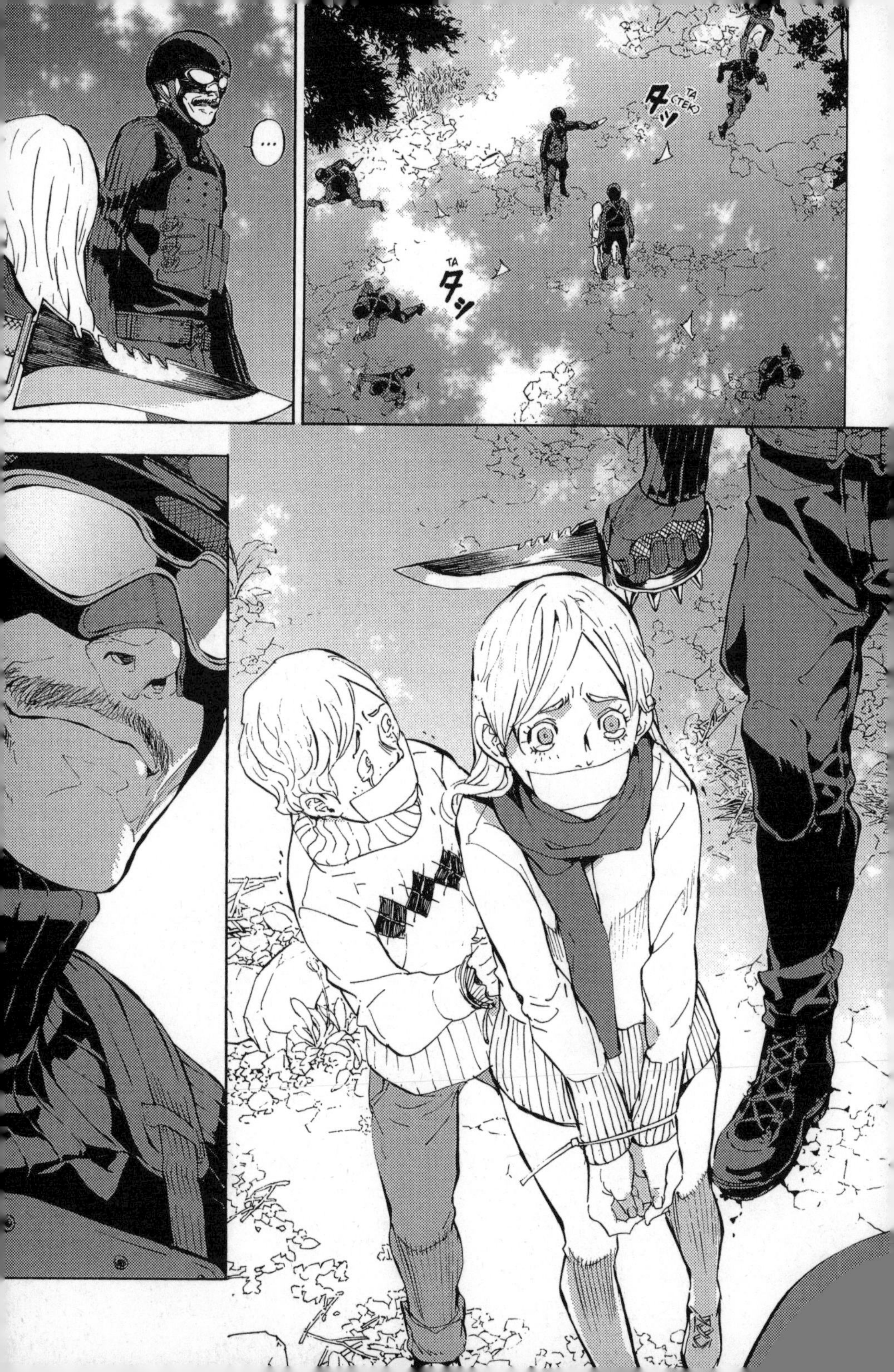
タッ TA (TEK)
TA タッ
...

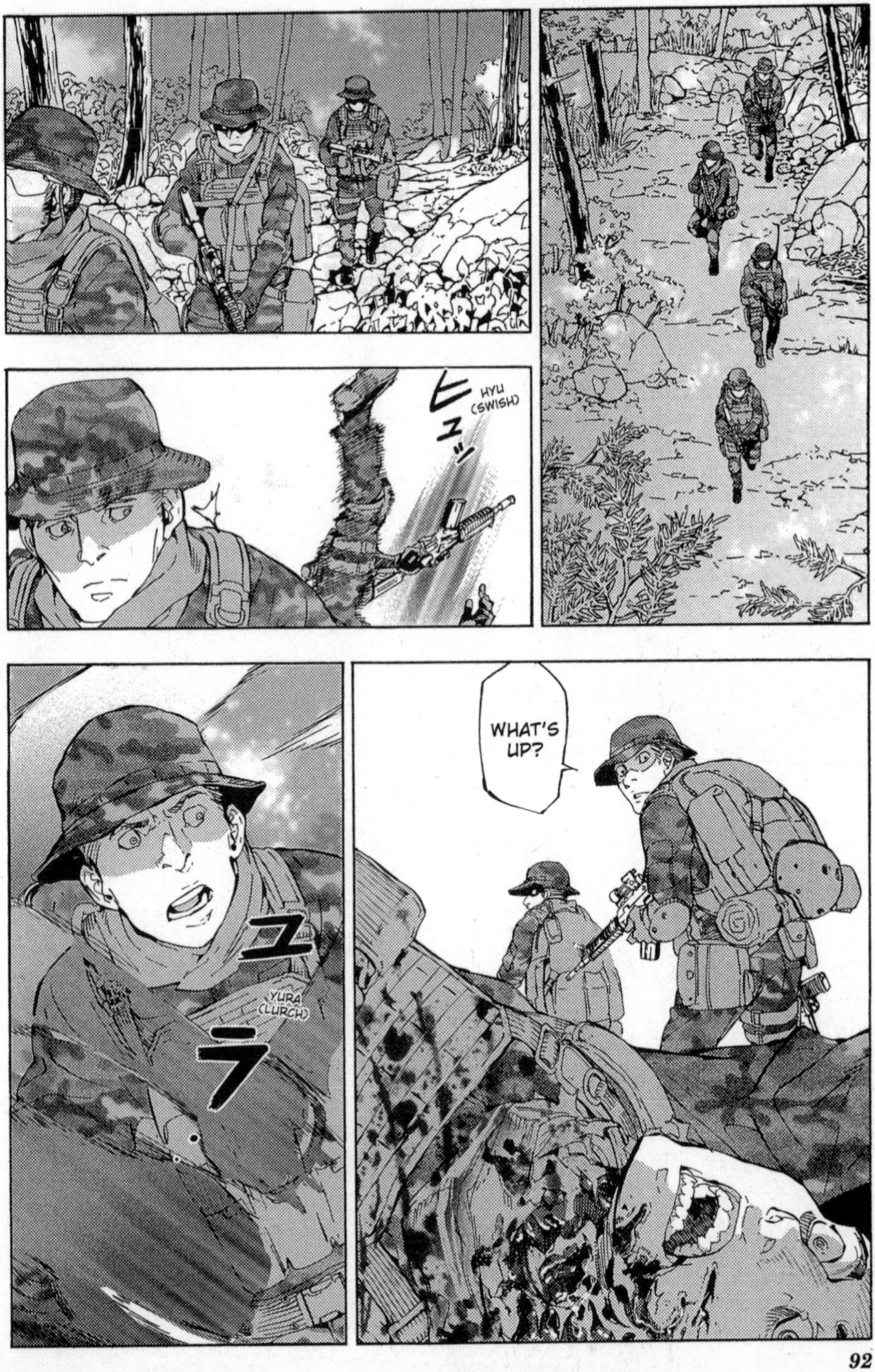
ヒュッ
HYU (SWISH)
WHAT'S UP?
ユラ
YURA (LURCH)

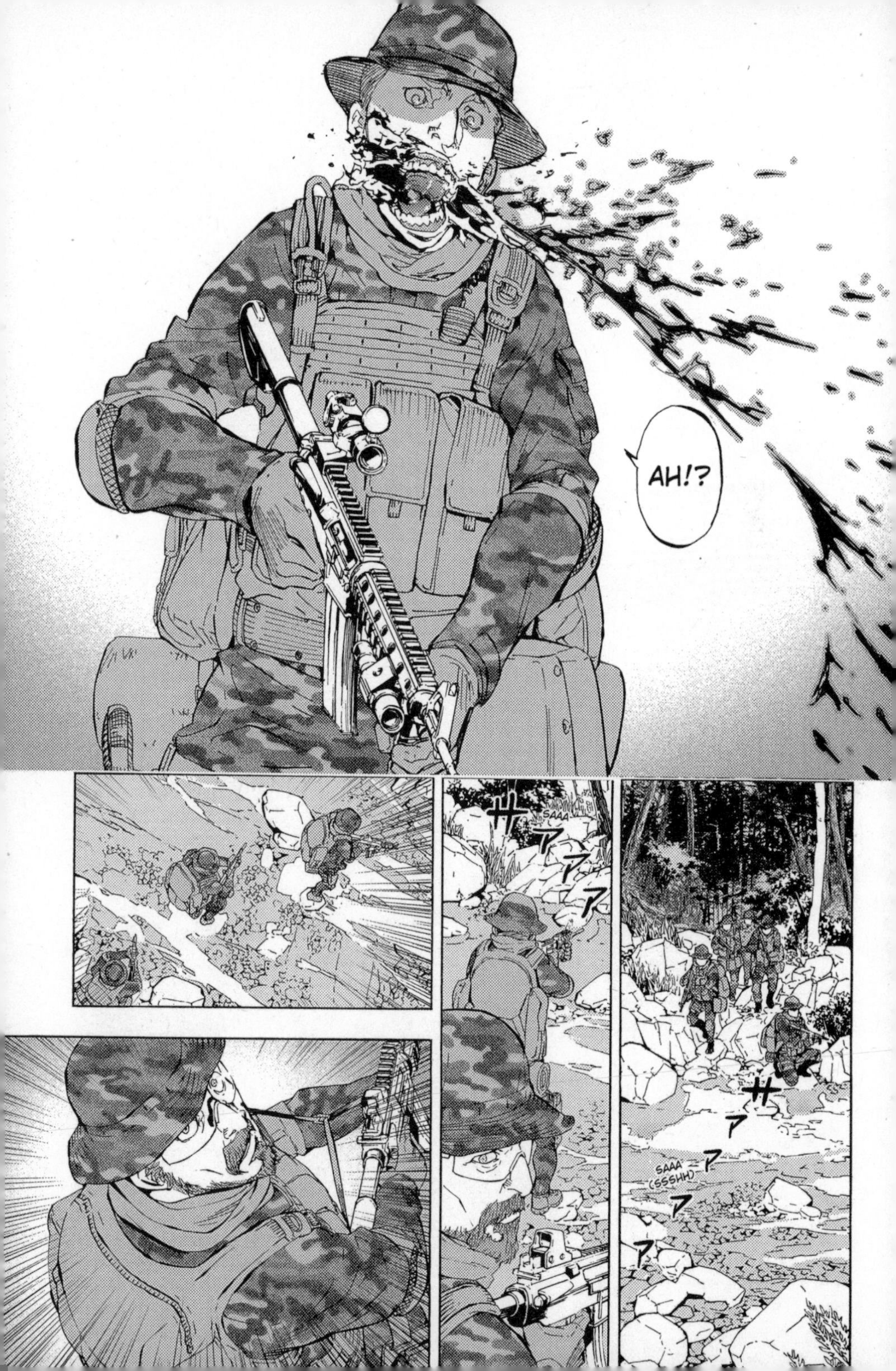
AH!?
サアアアア
SAAA (SSSHH)
サアアア
SAAA

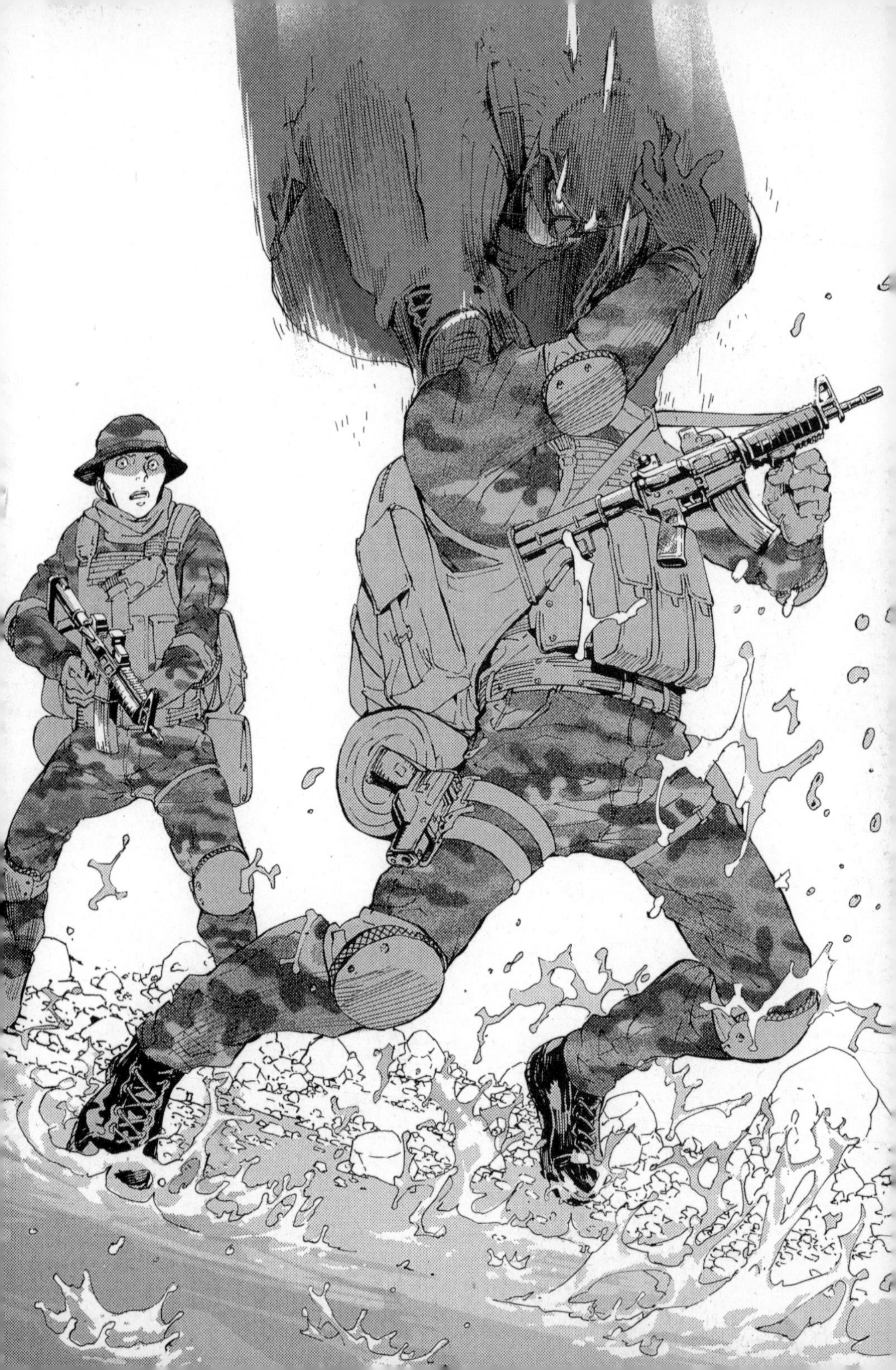

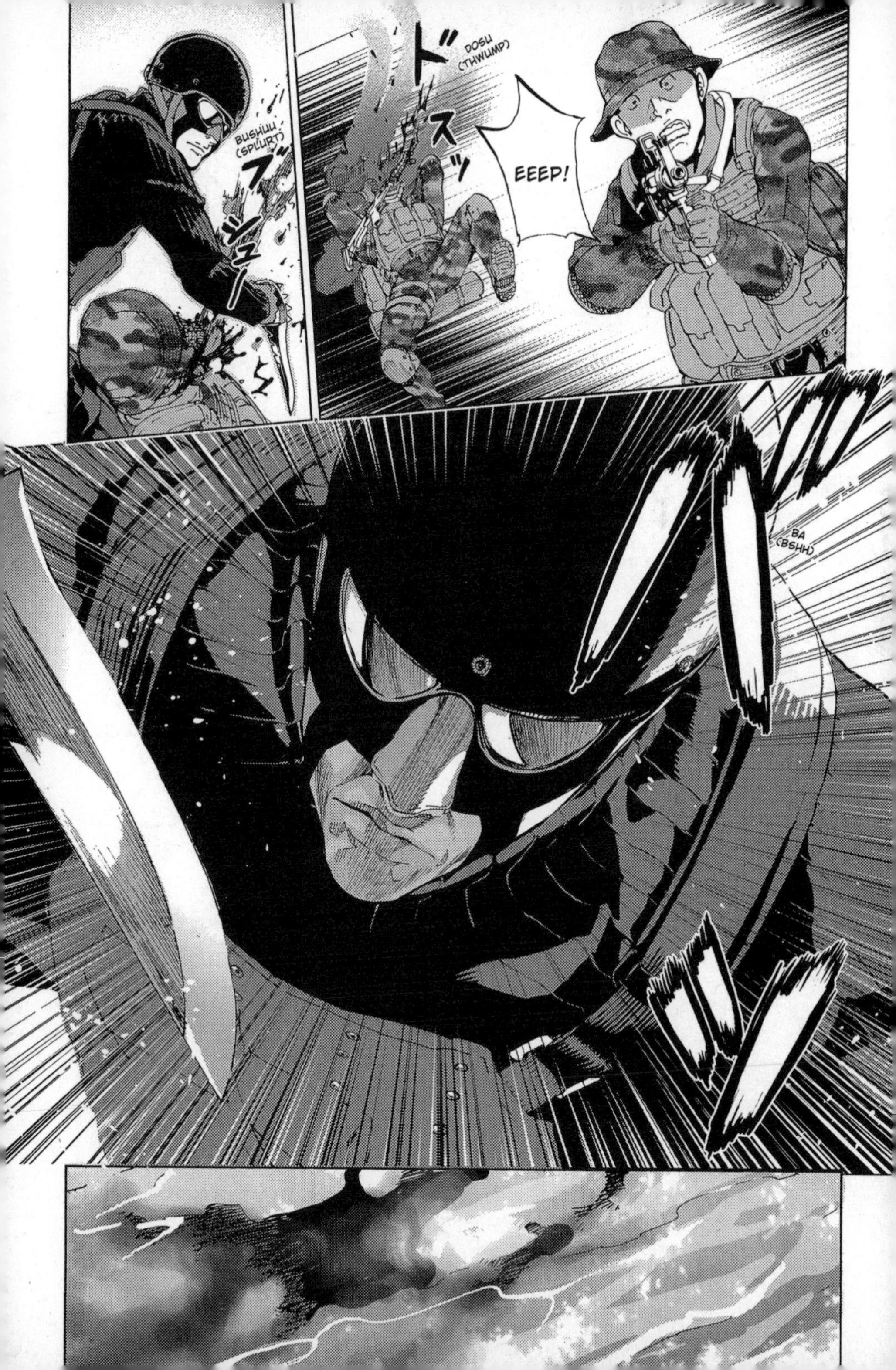
DOSU (THWUMP)
EEEP!
BUSHUU (SPLURT)
BA (BSHH)

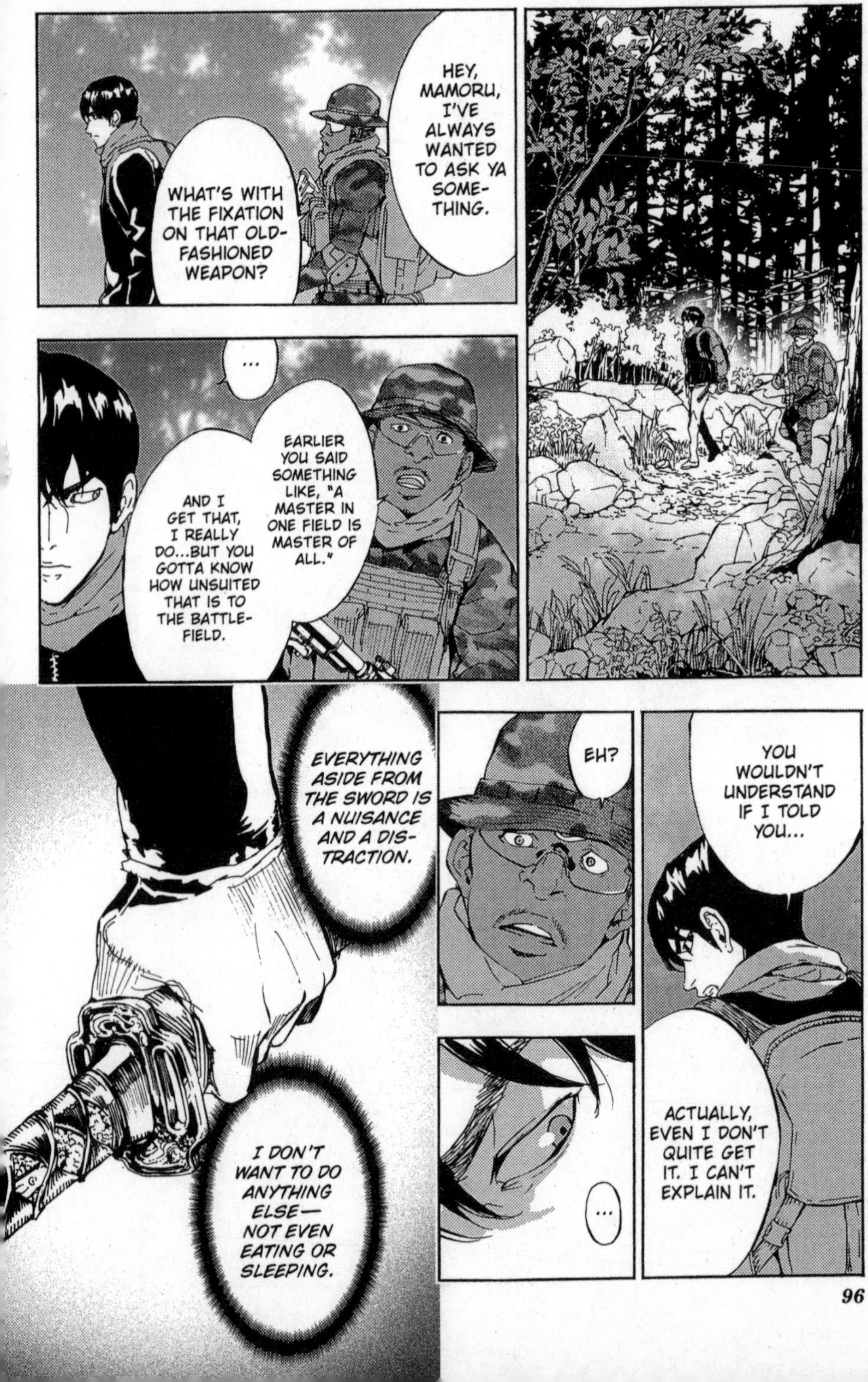
HEY, MAMORU, I'VE ALWAYS WANTED TO ASK YA SOME-THING.
WHAT'S WITH THE FIXATION ON THAT OLD-FASHIONED WEAPON?
...
EARLIER YOU SAID SOMETHING LIKE, "A MASTER IN ONE FIELD IS MASTER OF ALL."
AND I GET THAT, I REALLY DO...BUT YOU GOTTA KNOW HOW UNSUITED THAT IS TO THE BATTLE-FIELD.
YOU WOULDN'T UNDERSTAND IF I TOLD YOU...
ACTUALLY, EVEN I DON'T QUITE GET IT. I CAN'T EXPLAIN IT.
EH?
...
EVERYTHING ASIDE FROM THE SWORD IS A NUISANCE AND A DIS-TRACTION.
I DON'T WANT TO DO ANYTHING ELSE— NOT EVEN EATING OR SLEEPING.

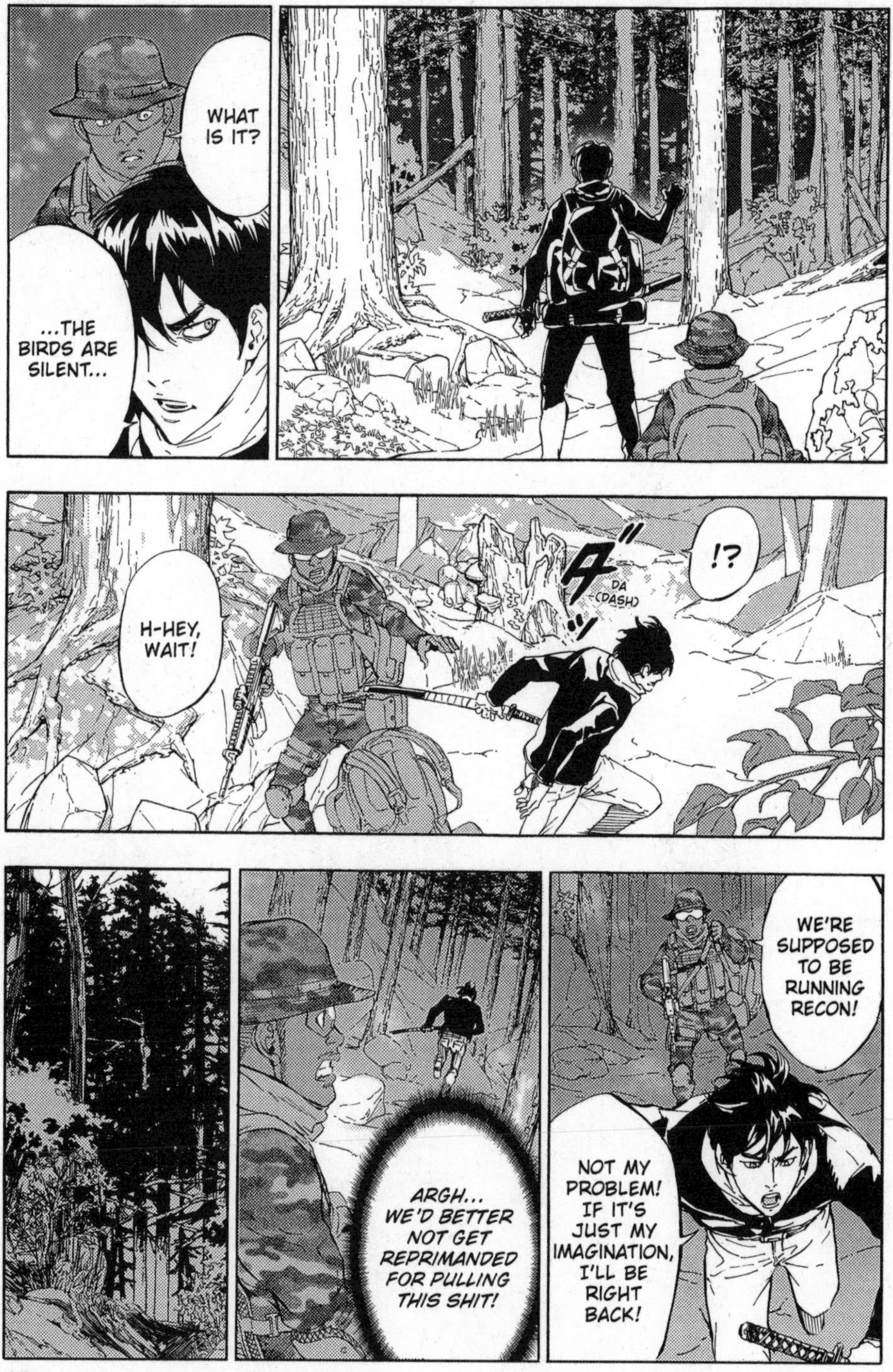
WHAT IS IT?
...THE BIRDS ARE SILENT...
!?
DA (DASH)
H-HEY, WAIT!
WE'RE SUPPOSED TO BE RUNNING RECON!
NOT MY PROBLEM! IF IT'S JUST MY IMAGINATION, I'LL BE RIGHT BACK!
ARGH... WE'D BETTER NOT GET REPRIMANDED FOR PULLING THIS SHIT!

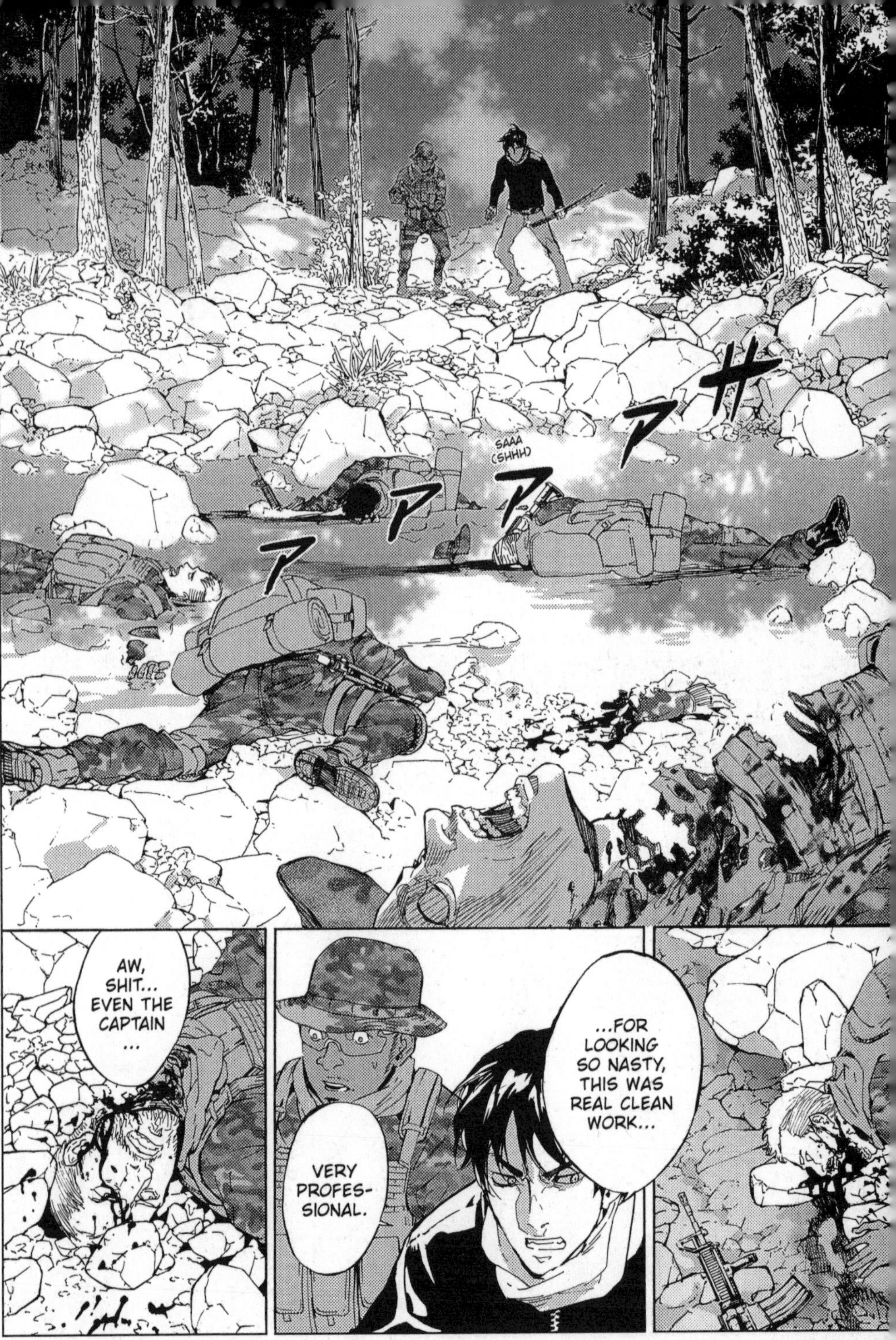
サアアアア
SAAA (SHHH)
...FOR LOOKING SO NASTY, THIS WAS REAL CLEAN WORK...
VERY PROFES-SIONAL.
AW, SHIT... EVEN THE CAPTAIN ...

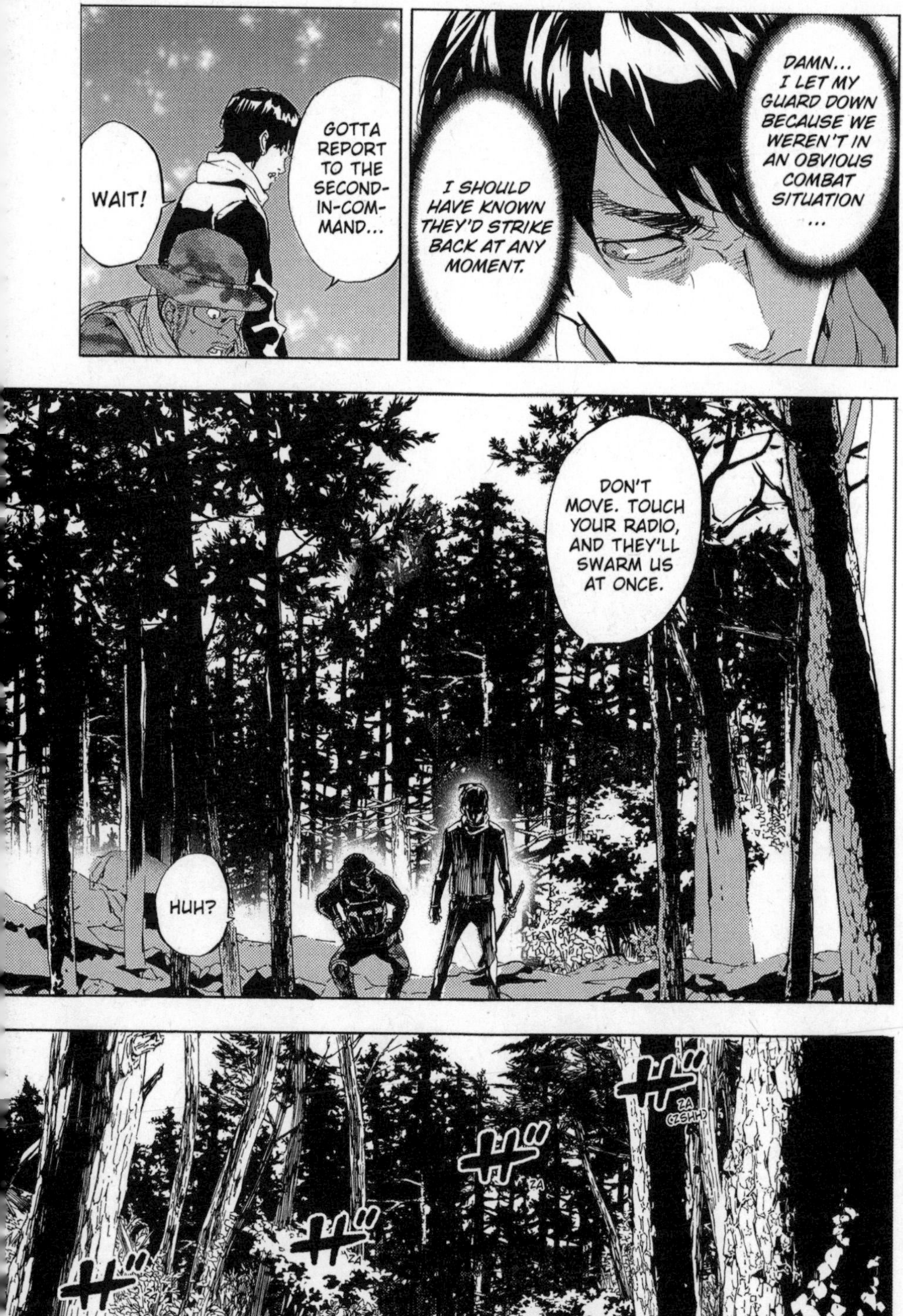
DAMN... I LET MY GUARD DOWN BECAUSE WE WEREN'T IN AN OBVIOUS COMBAT SITUATION...
I SHOULD HAVE KNOWN THEY'D STRIKE BACK AT ANY MOMENT.
GOTTA REPORT TO THE SECOND-IN-COMMAND...
WAIT!
DON'T MOVE. TOUCH YOUR RADIO, AND THEY'LL SWARM US AT ONCE.
HUH?
ZA GZSHHD
ZA
ZA
ZA

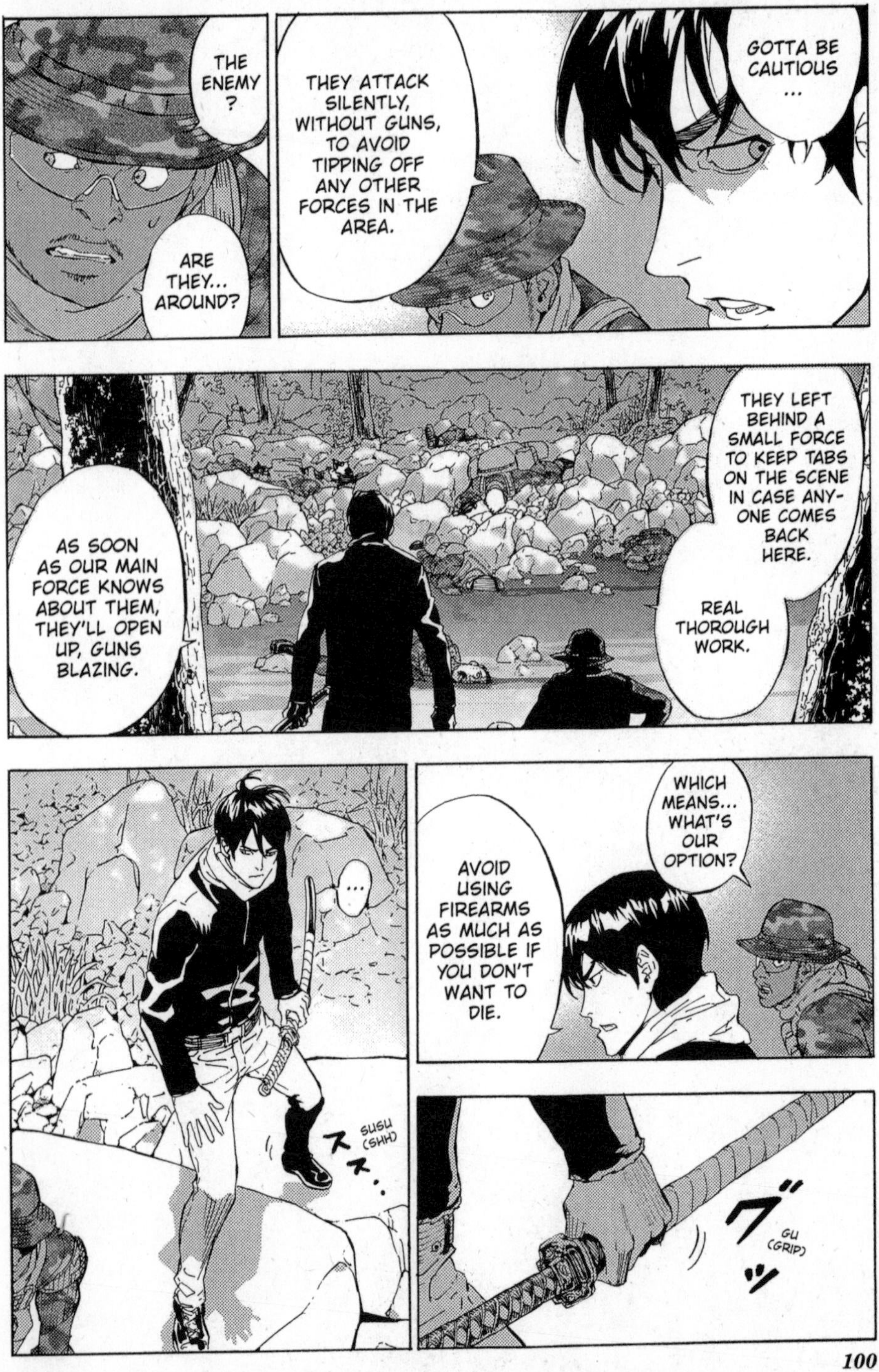
GOTTA BE CAUTIOUS ...
THEY ATTACK SILENTLY, WITHOUT GUNS, TO AVOID TIPPING OFF ANY OTHER FORCES IN THE AREA.
THE ENEMY ?
ARE THEY... AROUND?
THEY LEFT BEHIND A SMALL FORCE TO KEEP TABS ON THE SCENE IN CASE ANY-ONE COMES BACK HERE.
REAL THOROUGH WORK.
AS SOON AS OUR MAIN FORCE KNOWS ABOUT THEM, THEY'LL OPEN UP, GUNS BLAZING.
WHICH MEANS... WHAT'S OUR OPTION?
AVOID USING FIREARMS AS MUCH AS POSSIBLE IF YOU DON'T WANT TO DIE.
GU (GRIP)
...
SUSU (SHH)

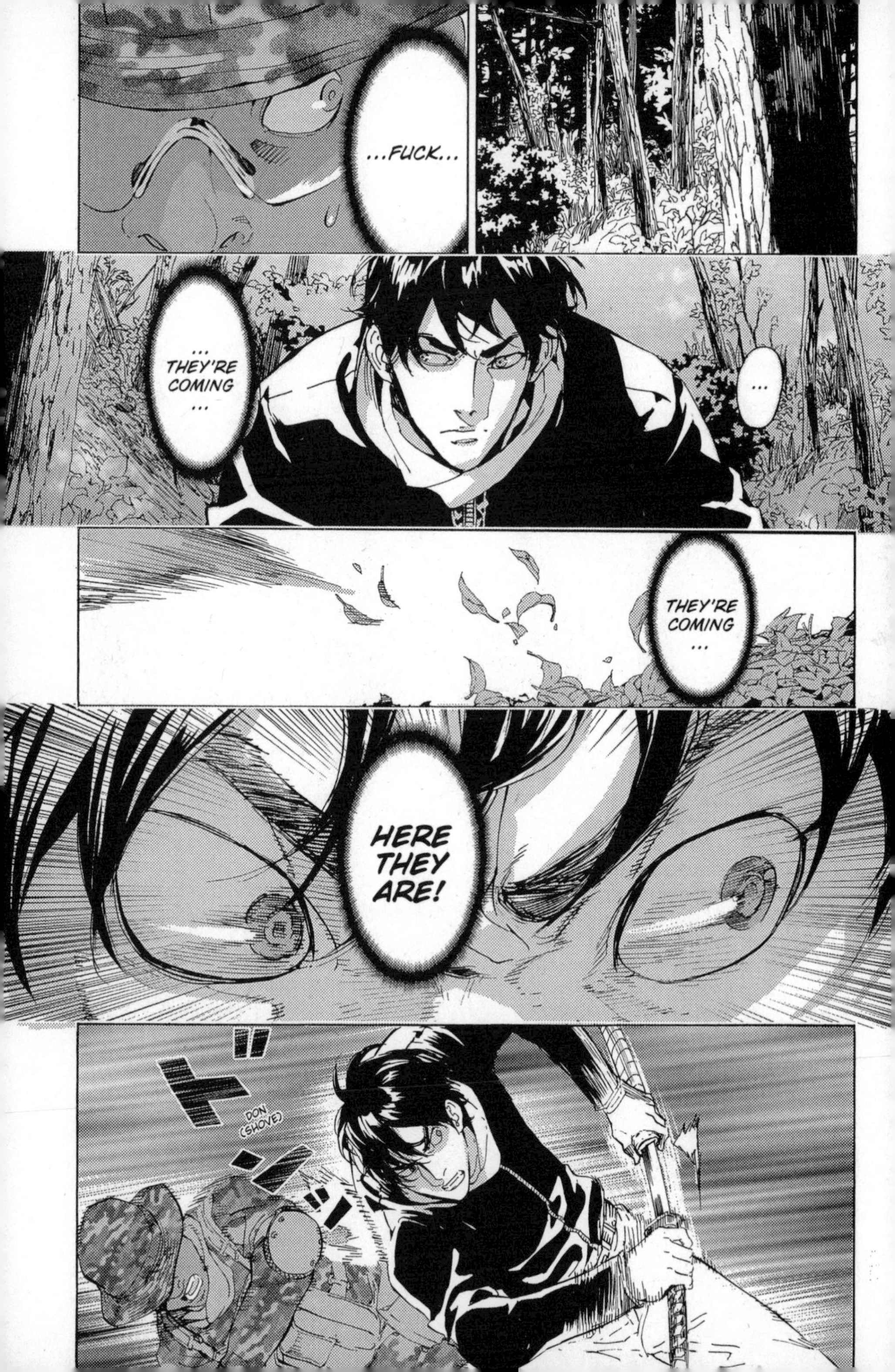
...FUCK...
...
... THEY'RE COMING ...
THEY'RE COMING ...
HERE THEY ARE!
DON (SHOVE)

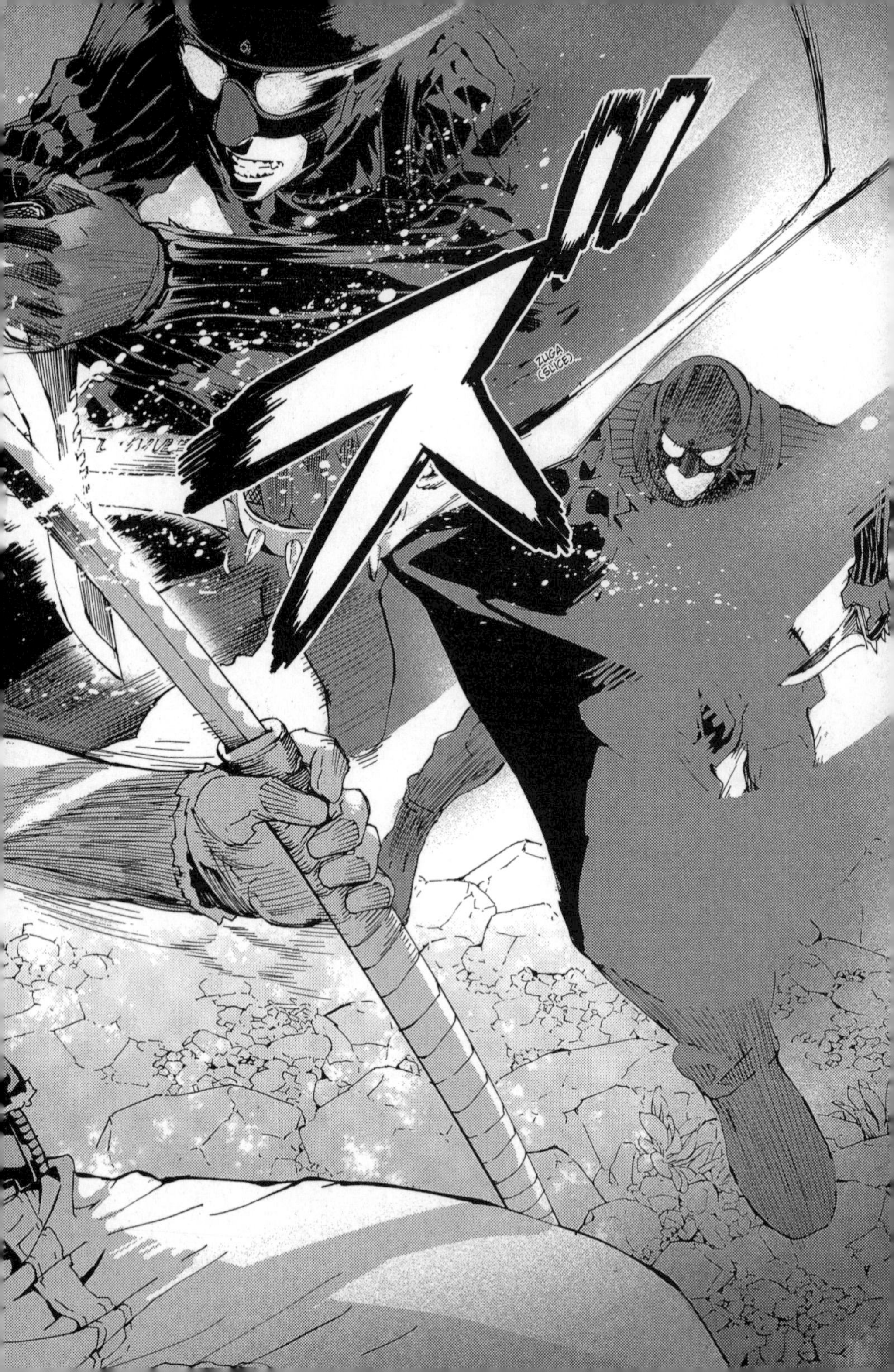
ZUGA
(SLICE)

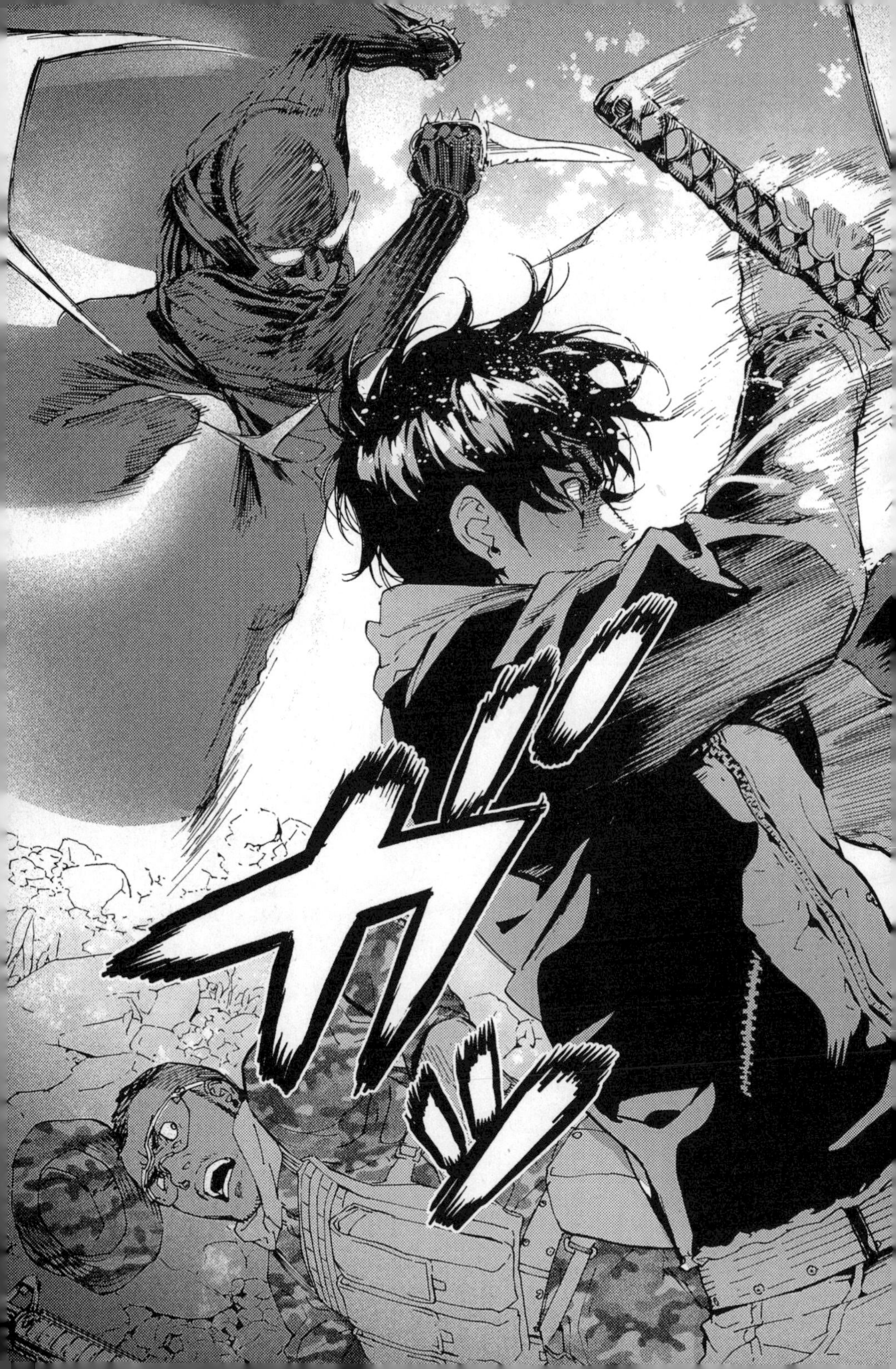

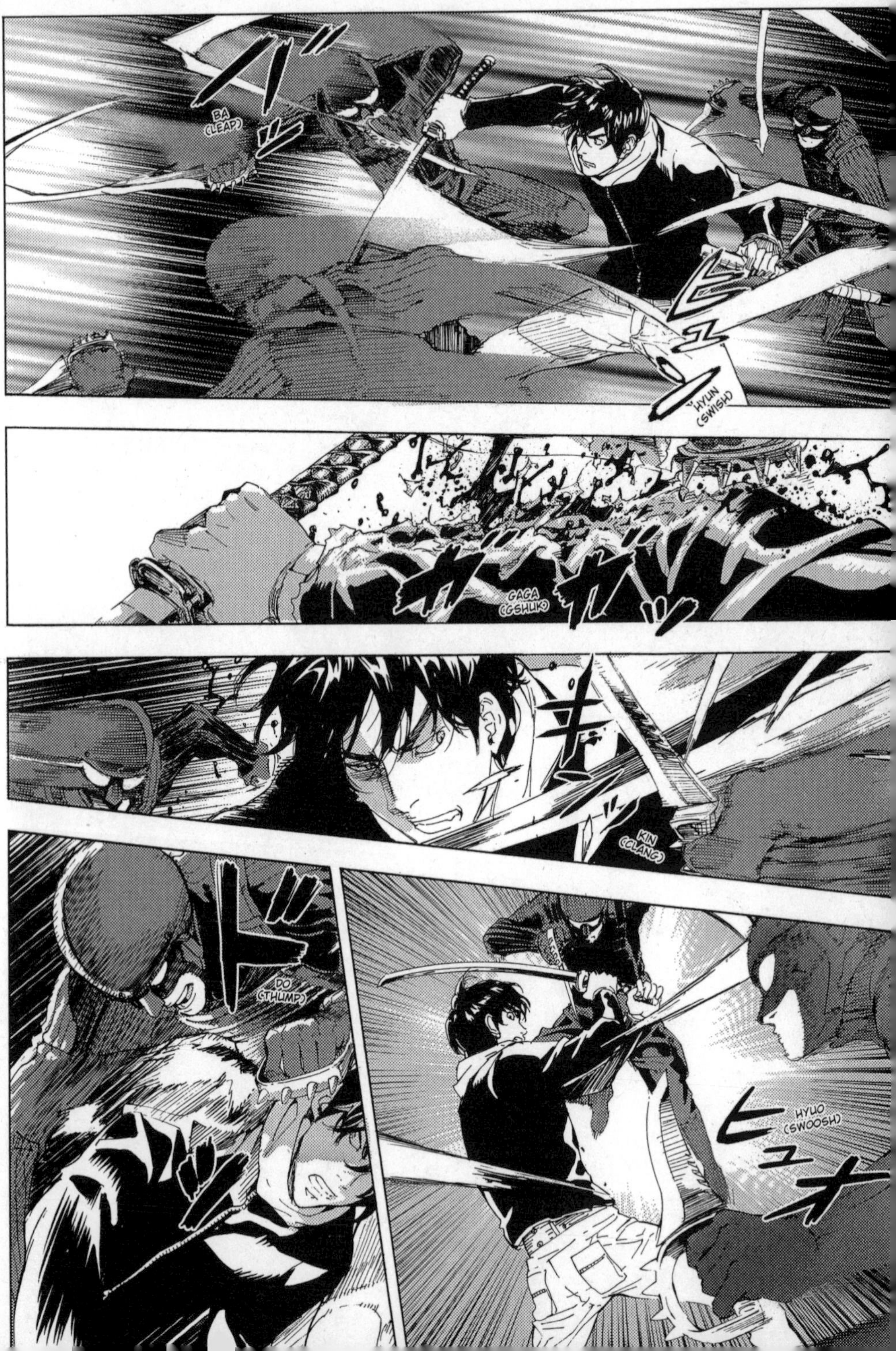
HYUN (SWISH)
BA (LEAP)
GAGA (GSHLK)
KIN (CLANG)
HYUO (SWOOSH)
DO (THUMP)

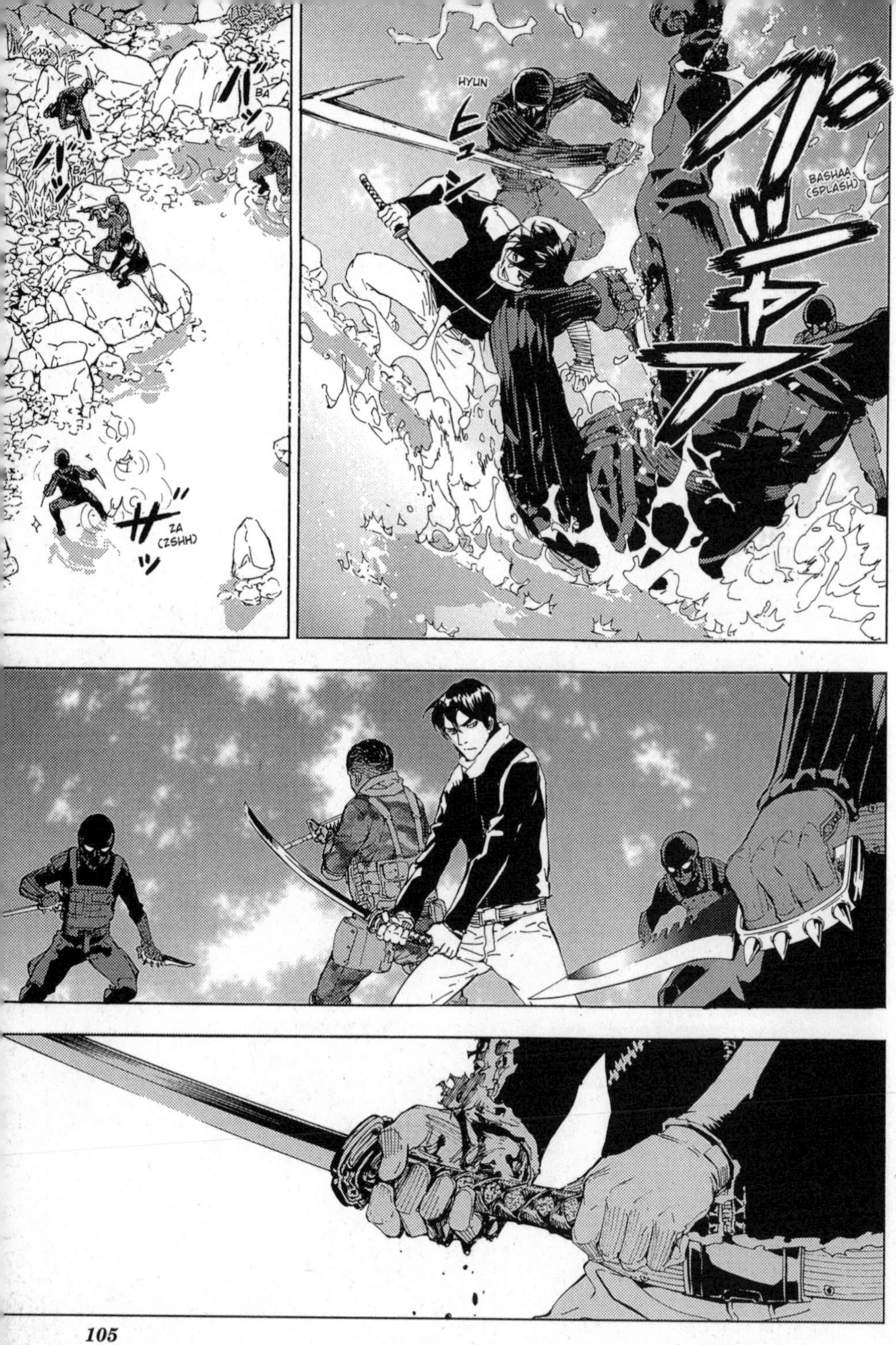
HYUN
BASHAA (SPLASH)
BA
BA
ZA (ZSHH)

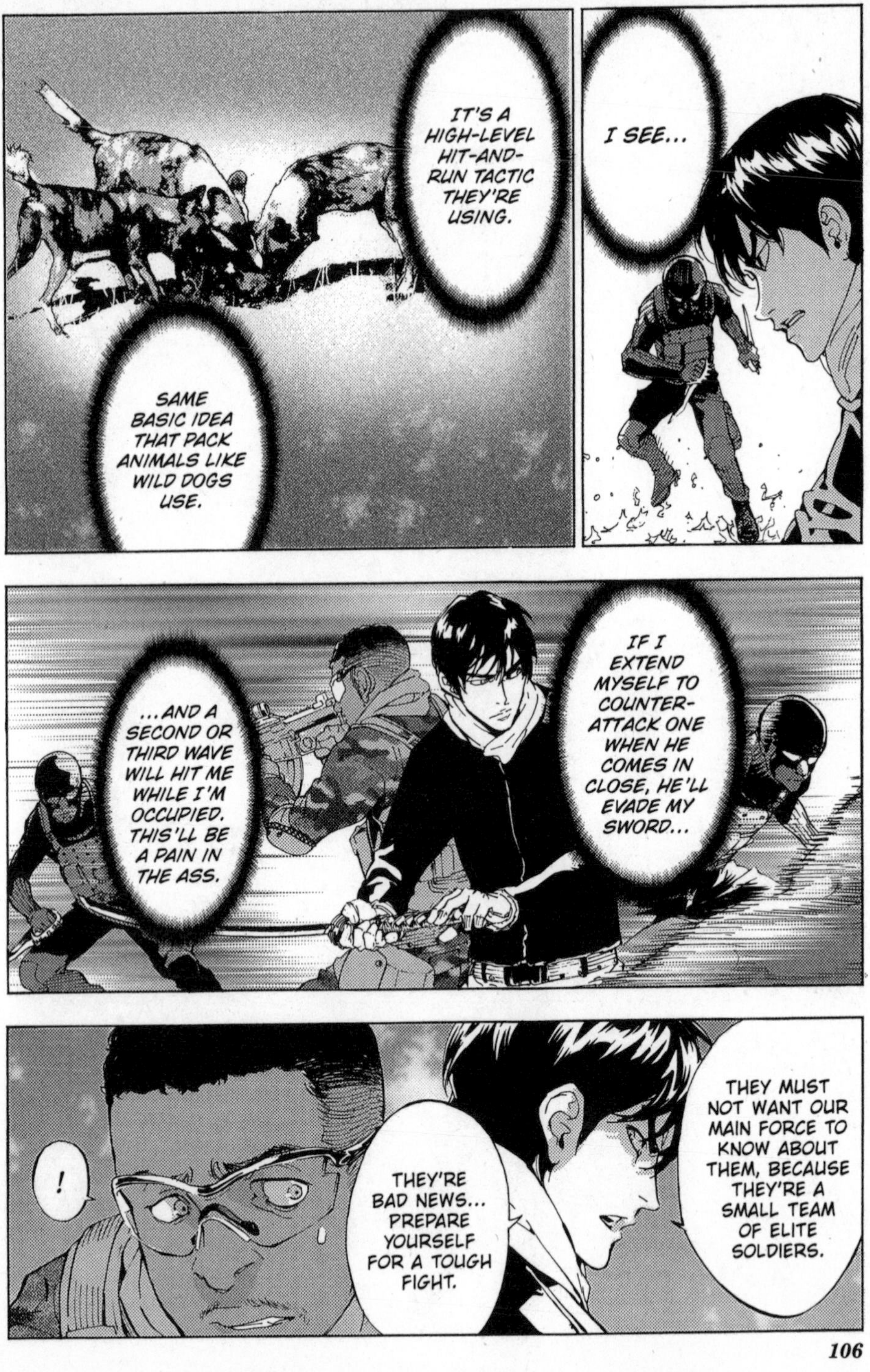
I SEE...
IT'S A HIGH-LEVEL HIT-AND-RUN TACTIC THEY'RE USING.
SAME BASIC IDEA THAT PACK ANIMALS LIKE WILD DOGS USE.
IF I EXTEND MYSELF TO COUNTER-ATTACK ONE WHEN HE COMES IN CLOSE, HE'LL EVADE MY SWORD...
...AND A SECOND OR THIRD WAVE WILL HIT ME WHILE I'M OCCUPIED. THIS'LL BE A PAIN IN THE ASS.
THEY MUST NOT WANT OUR MAIN FORCE TO KNOW ABOUT THEM, BECAUSE THEY'RE A SMALL TEAM OF ELITE SOLDIERS.
THEY'RE BAD NEWS... PREPARE YOURSELF FOR A TOUGH FIGHT.
!

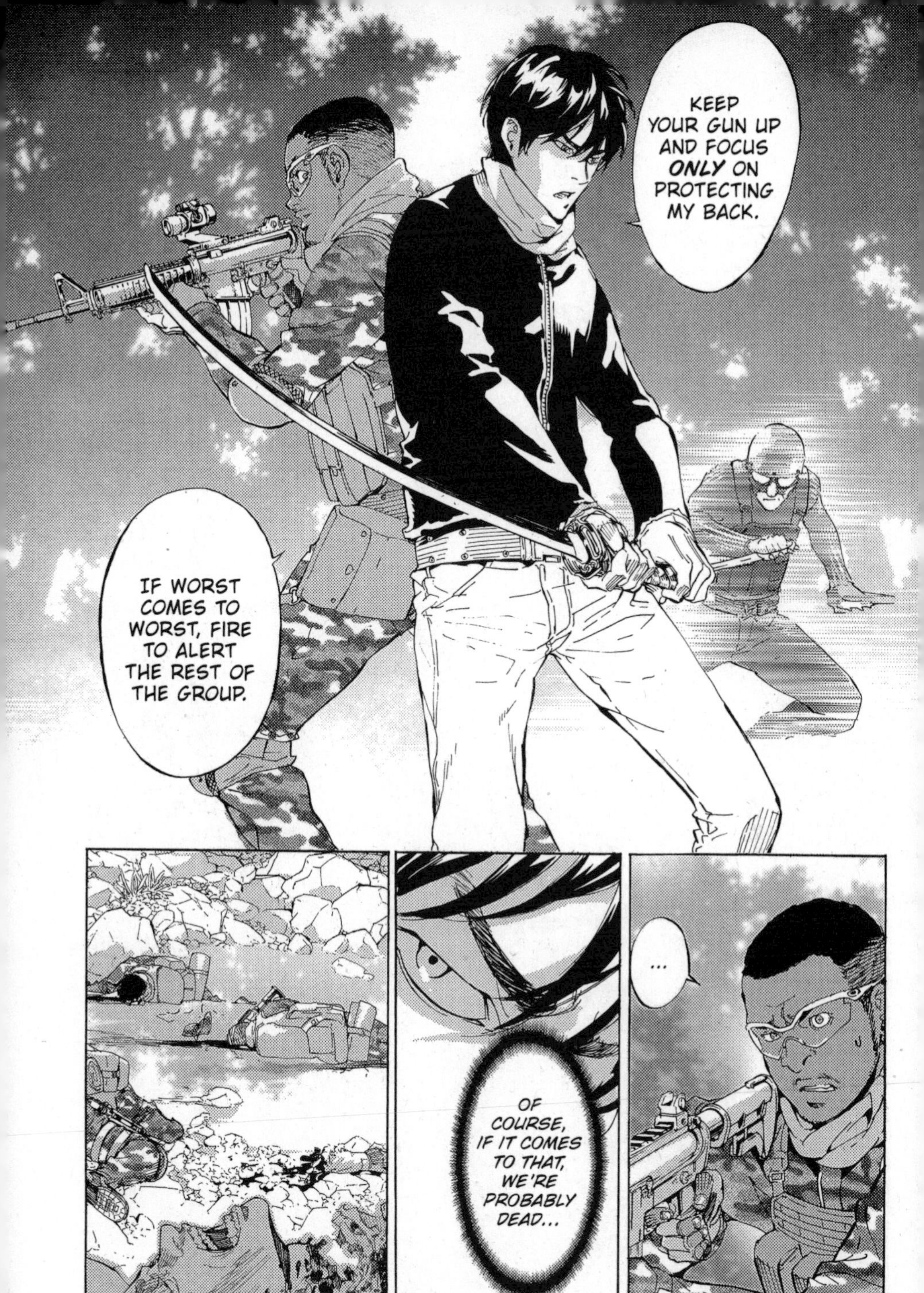
KEEP YOUR GUN UP AND FOCUS ONLY ON PROTECTING MY BACK.
IF WORST COMES TO WORST, FIRE TO ALERT THE REST OF THE GROUP.
...
OF COURSE, IF IT COMES TO THAT, WE'RE PROBABLY DEAD...

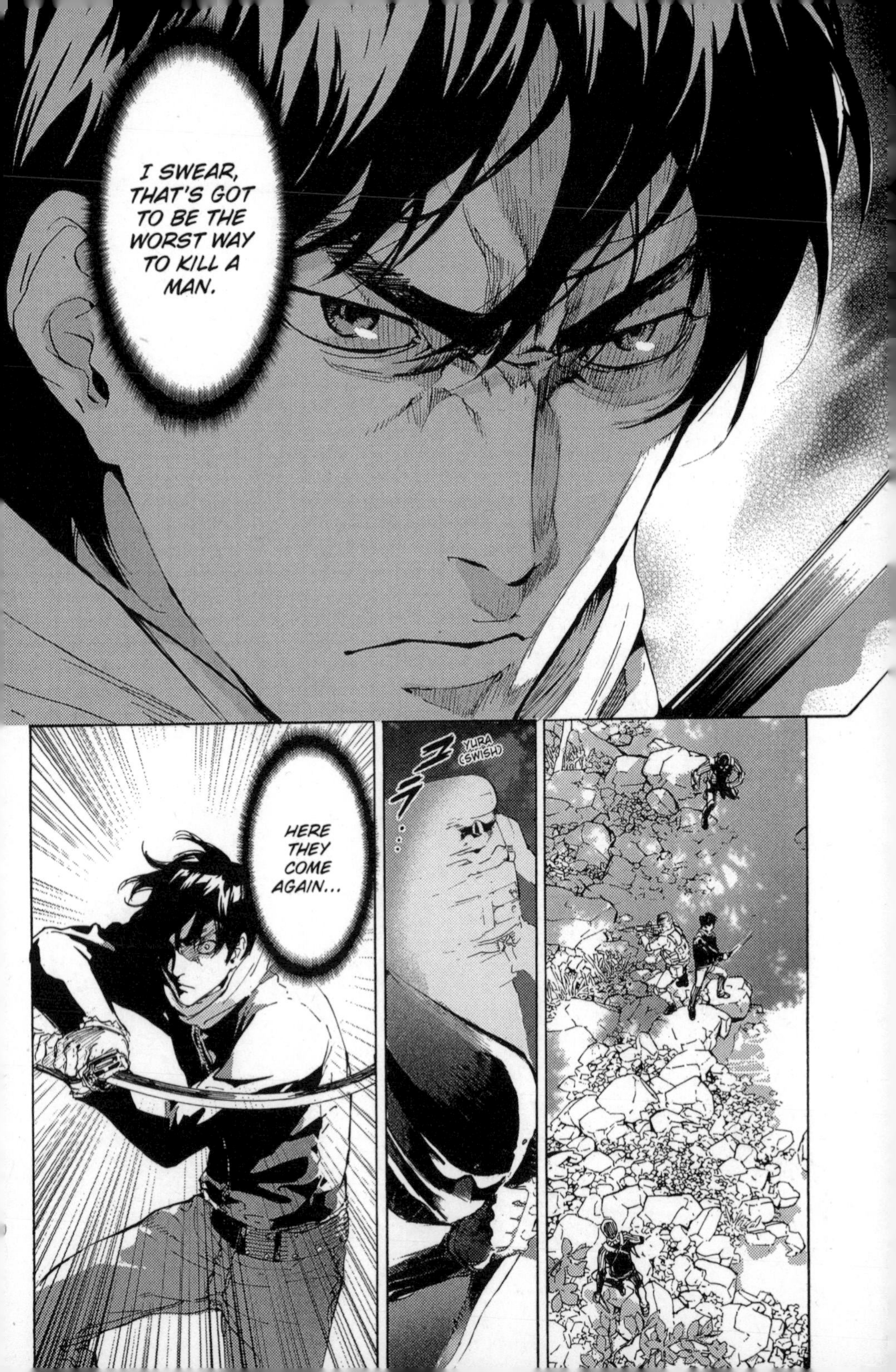
I SWEAR, THAT'S GOT TO BE THE WORST WAY TO KILL A MAN.
YURA (SWISH)
...
HERE THEY COME AGAIN...

Until Death do us Part

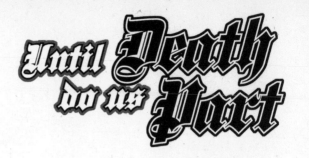

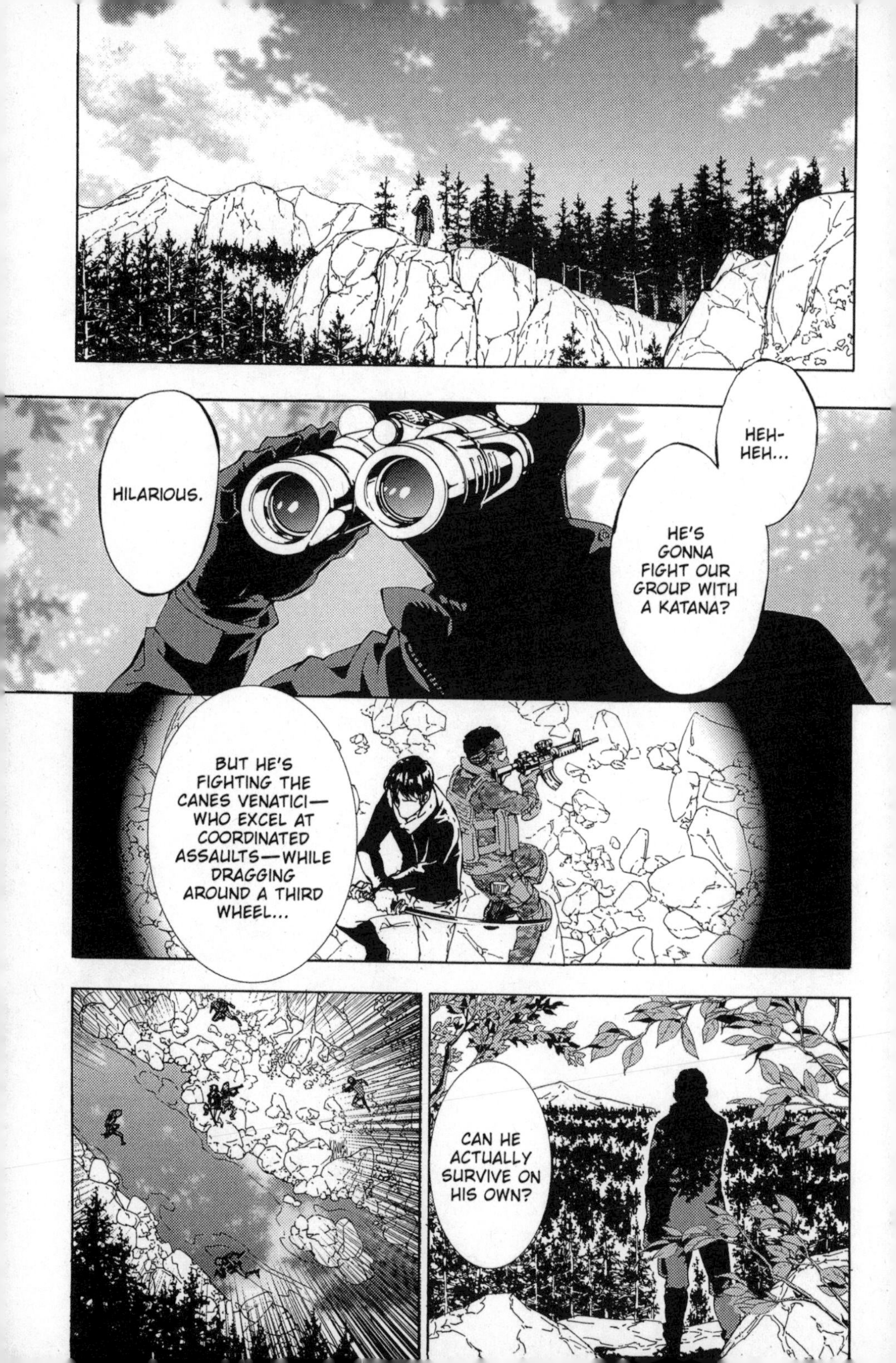
HEH-HEH...
HE'S GONNA FIGHT OUR GROUP WITH A KATANA?
HILARIOUS.
BUT HE'S FIGHTING THE CANES VENATICI—WHO EXCEL AT COORDINATED ASSAULTS—WHILE DRAGGING AROUND A THIRD WHEEL...
CAN HE ACTUALLY SURVIVE ON HIS OWN?

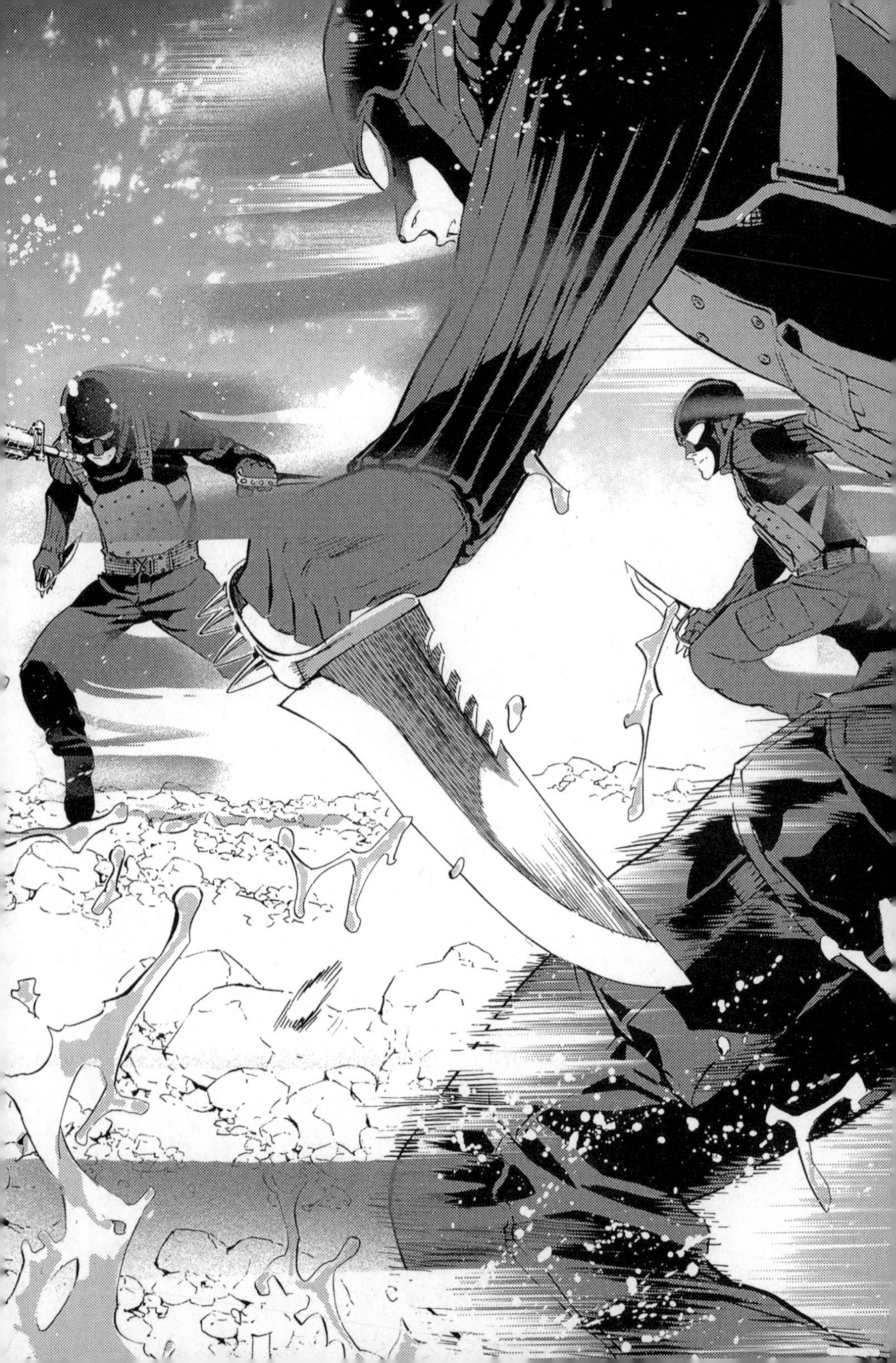

chapter 104

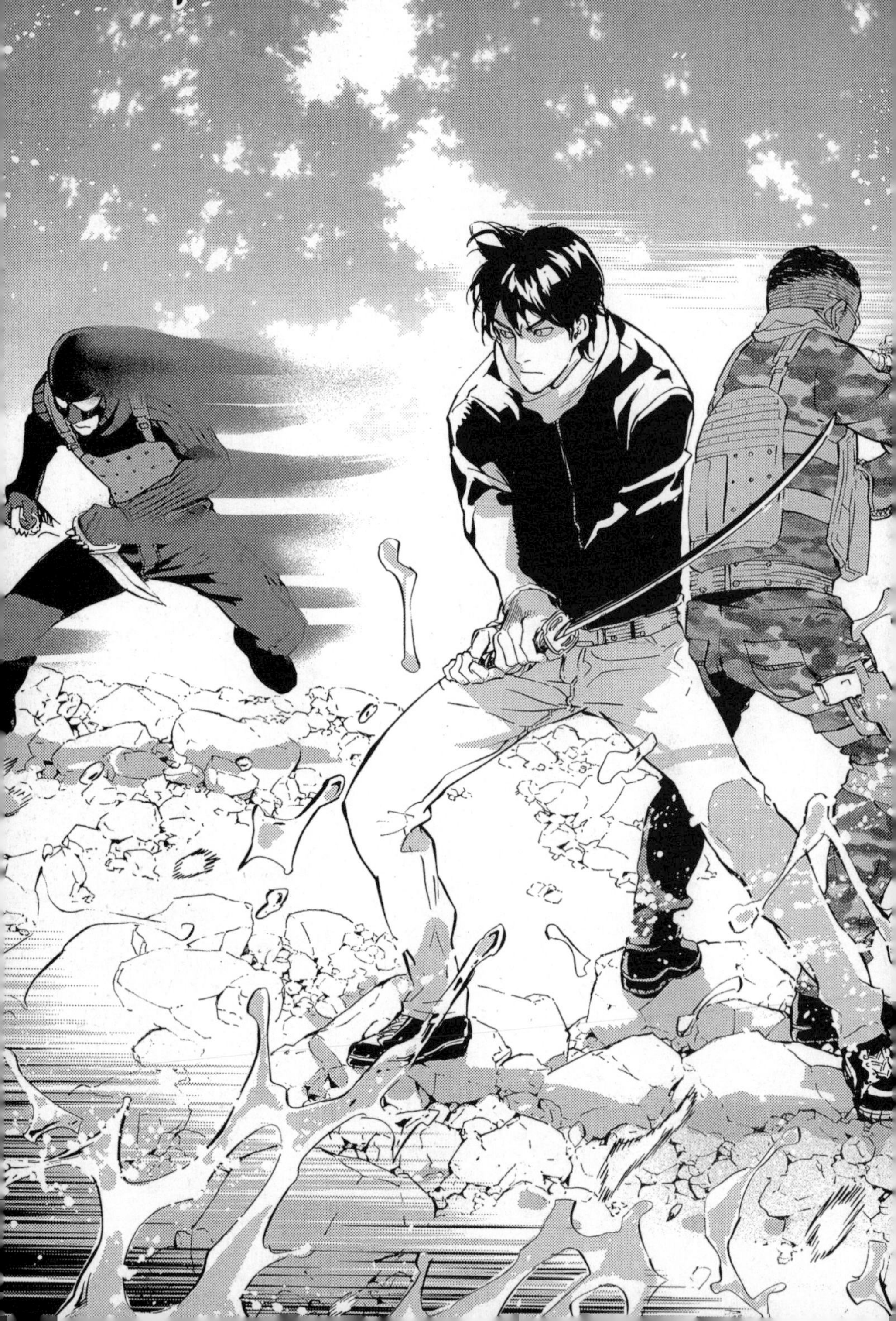

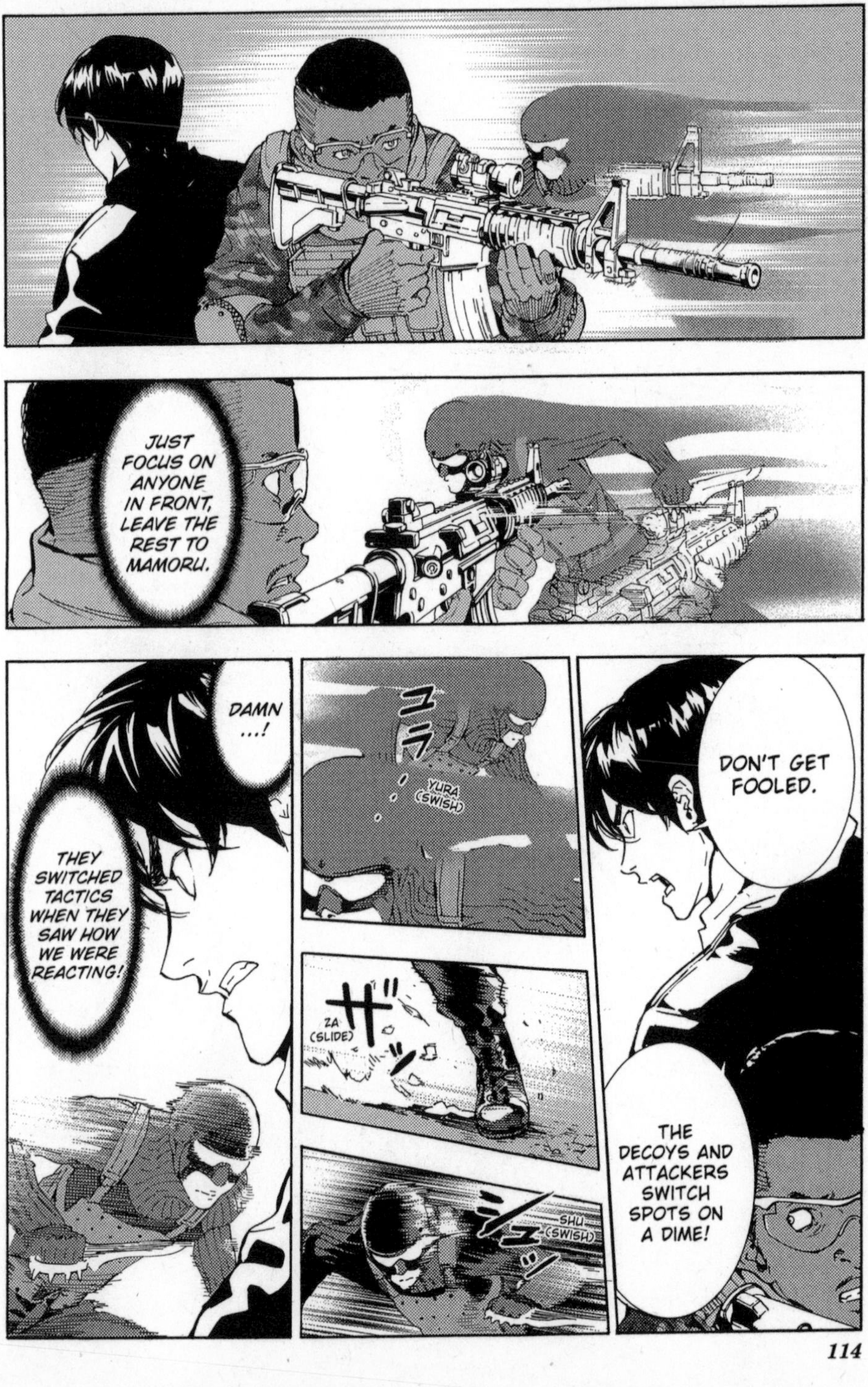
JUST FOCUS ON ANYONE IN FRONT, LEAVE THE REST TO MAMORU.
DON'T GET FOOLED.
THE DECOYS AND ATTACKERS SWITCH SPOTS ON A DIME!
YURA (SWISH)
ZA (SLIDE)
SHU (SWISH)
DAMN ...!
THEY SWITCHED TACTICS WHEN THEY SAW HOW WE WERE REACTING!

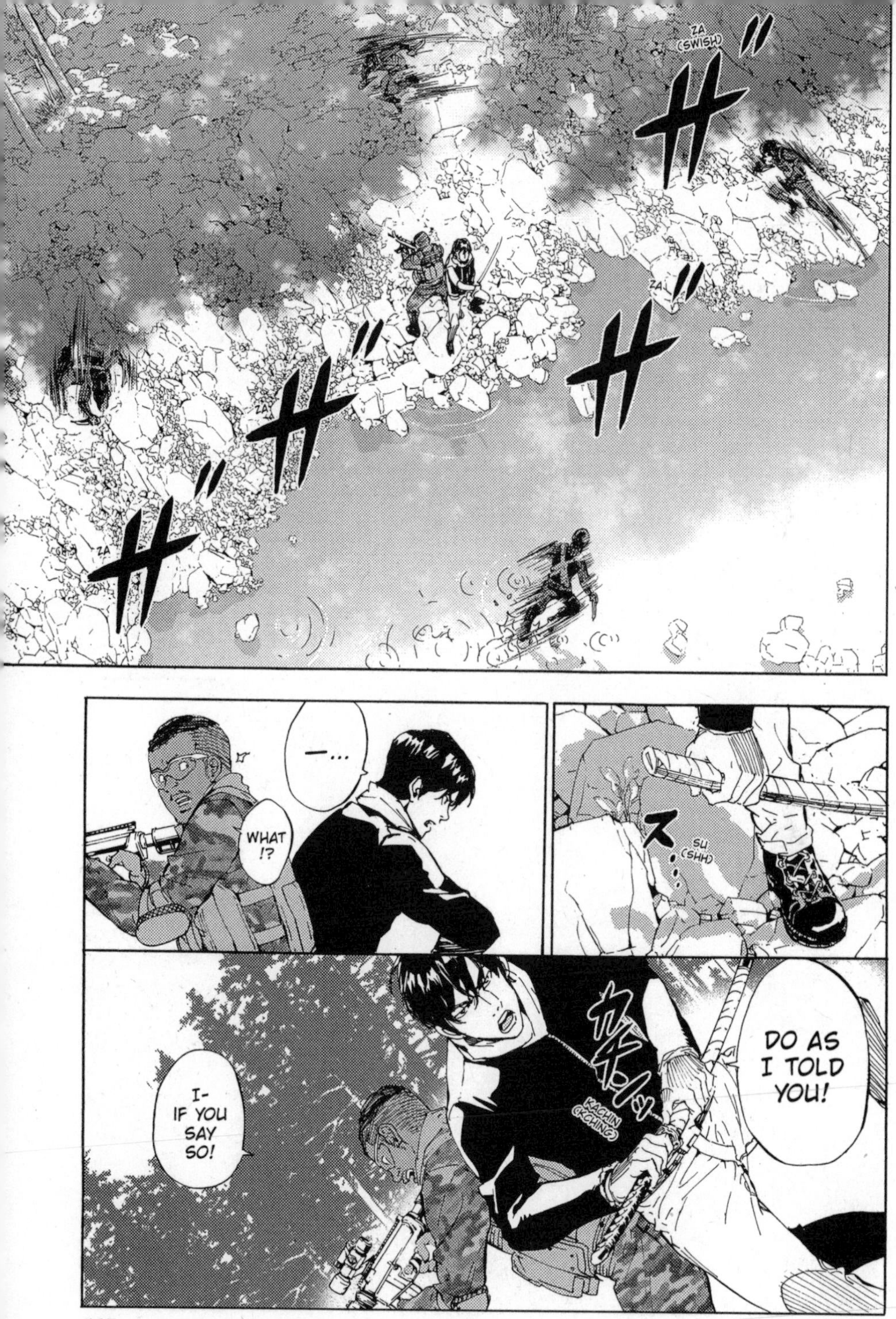
ZA (SWISH)
ZA
ZA
ZA
SU (SHH)
—...
WHAT !?
DO AS I TOLD YOU!
KACHIN (KCHING)
I- IF YOU SAY SO!

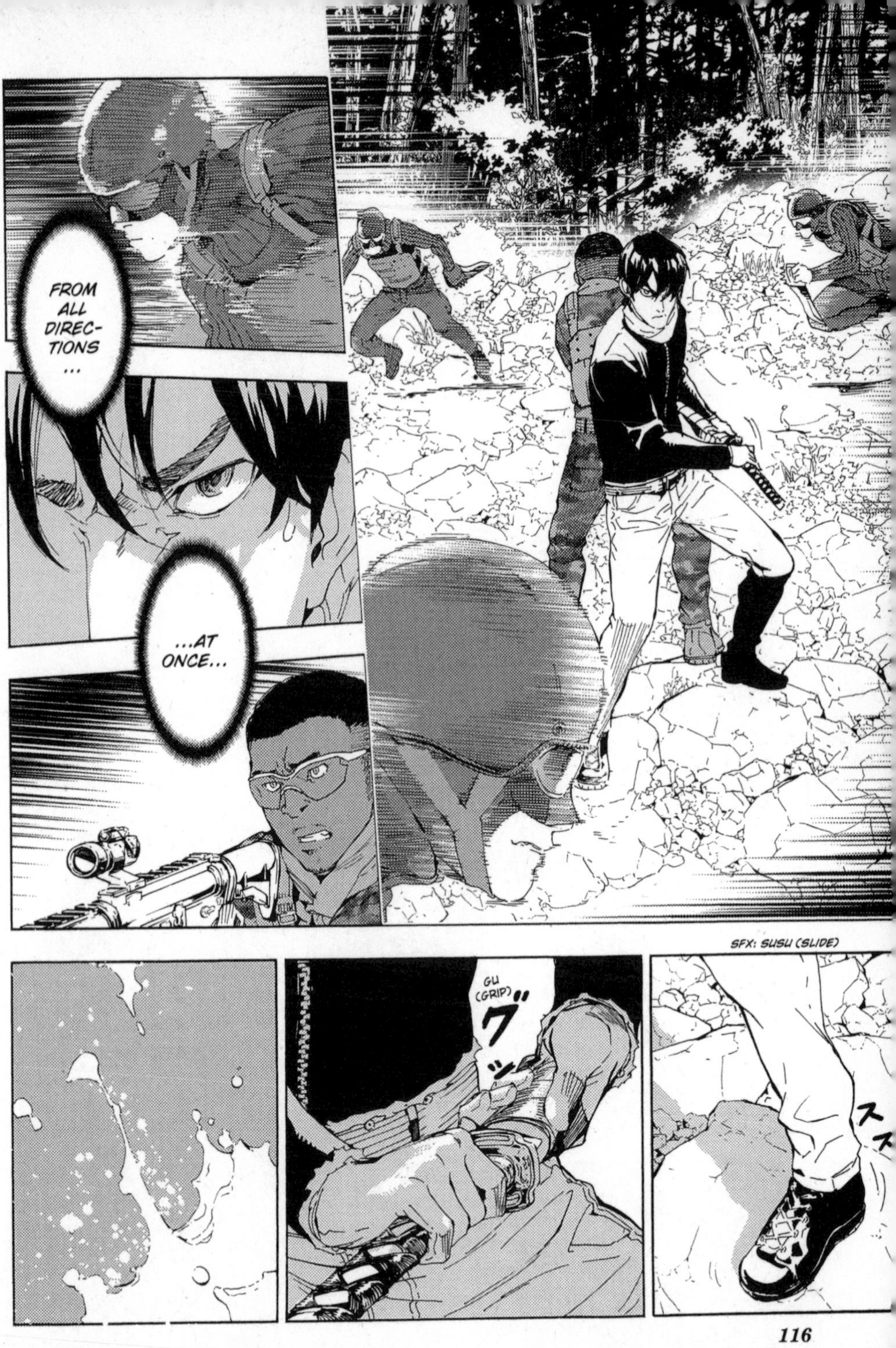
FROM ALL DIRECTIONS...
...AT ONCE...
SFX: SUSU (SLIDE)
スス
GU (GRIP)
グッ

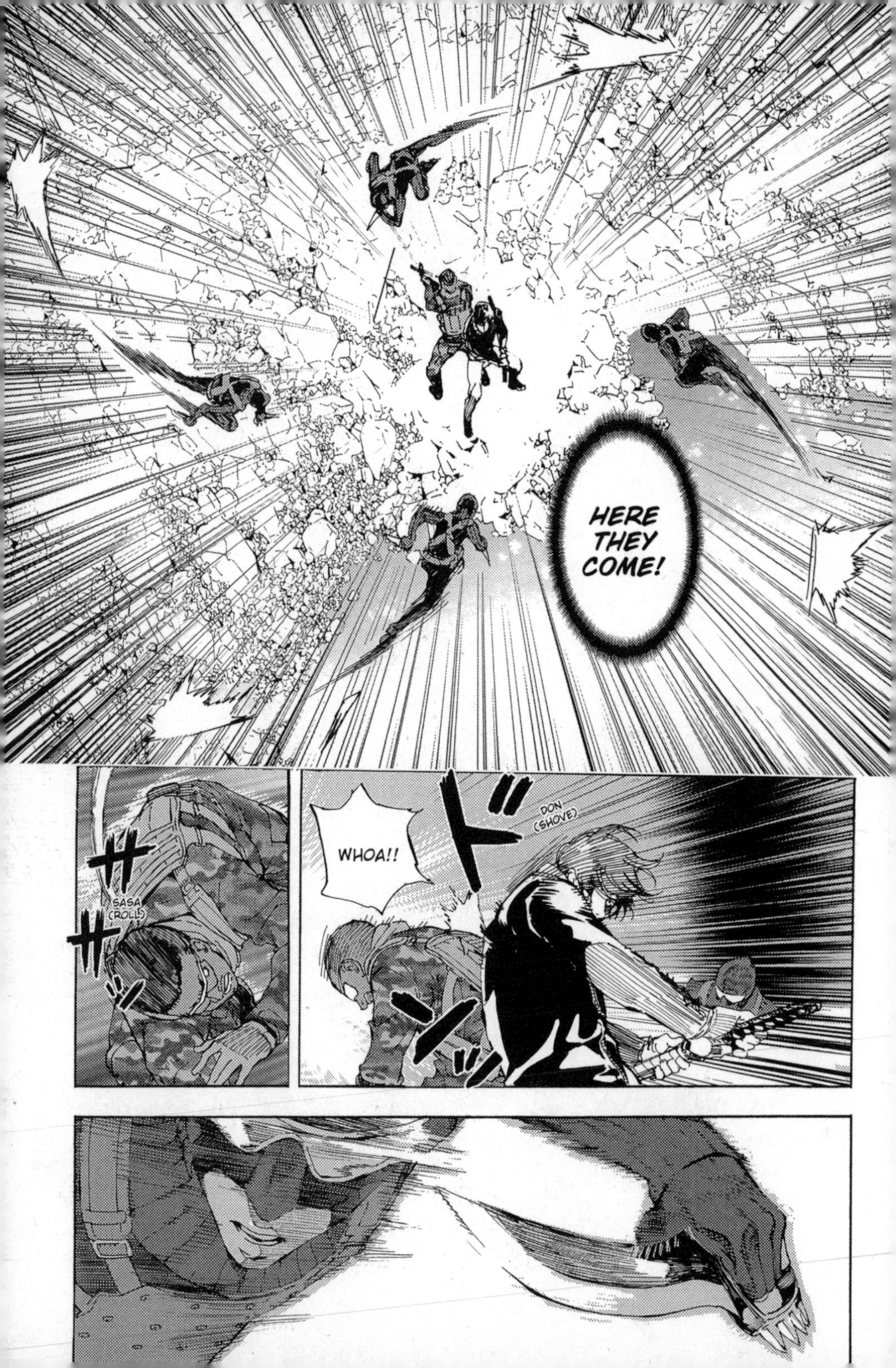
HERE THEY COME!
WHOA!!
DON (SHOVE)
SASA (ROLL)

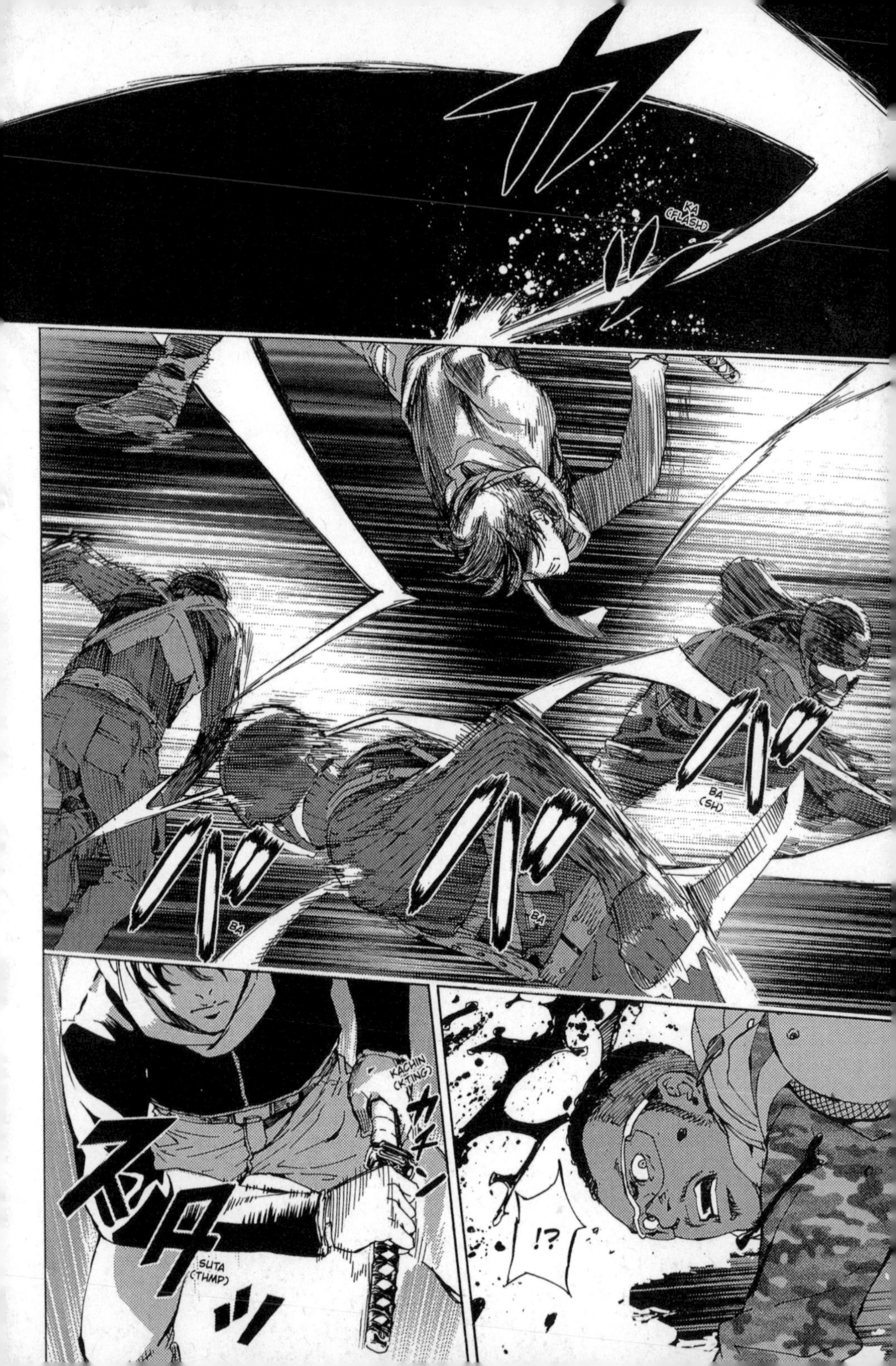
KA (FLASH)
BA (SH)
BA
BA
!?
KACHIN (KTING)
SUTA (THMP)

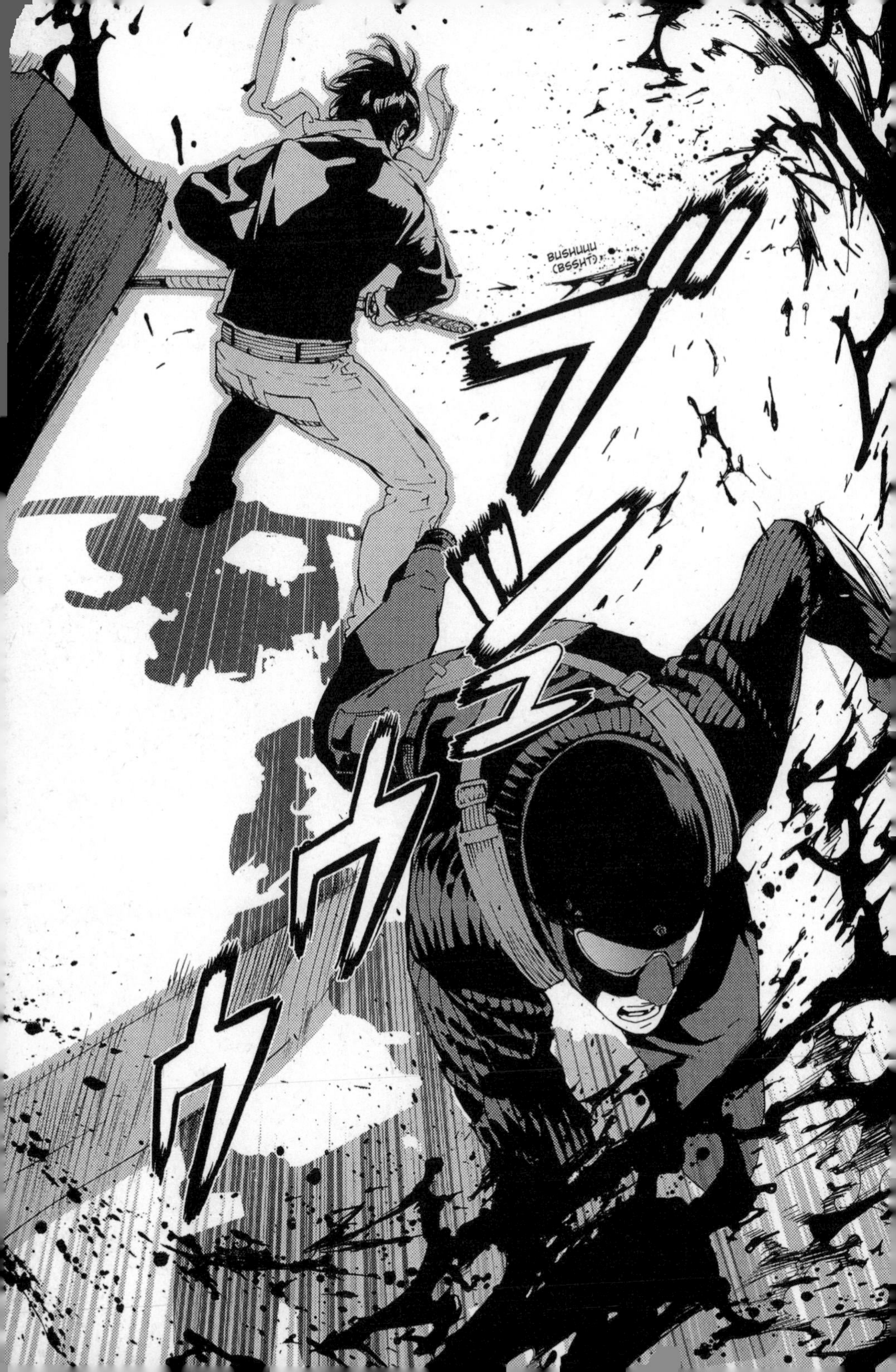
BUSHUUU
(BSSHT)

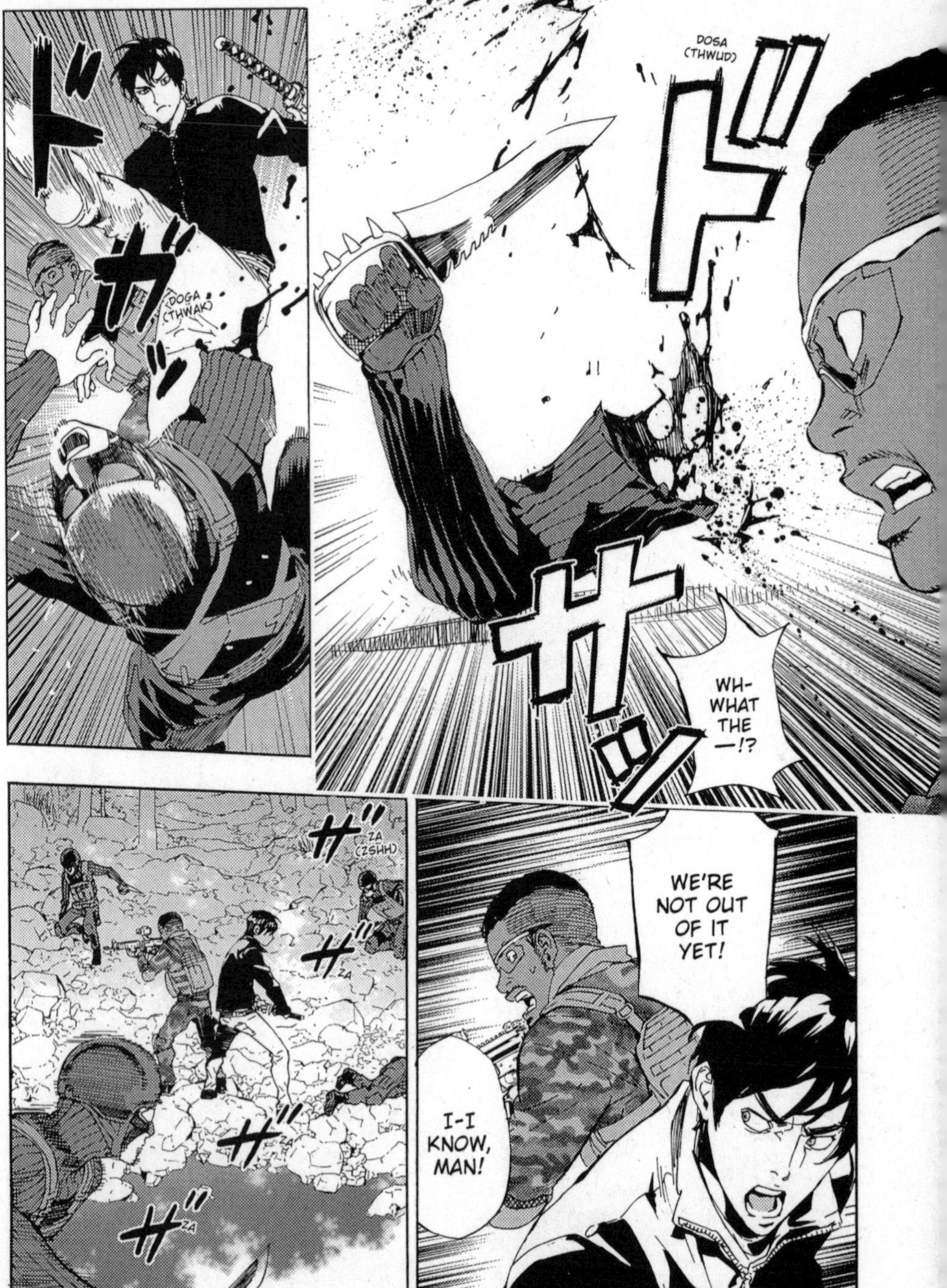
DOSA
(THWUD)
DOGA
(THWAK)
WH-
WHAT
THE
—!?
ZA
(ZSHH)
ZA
ZA
ZA
WE'RE
NOT OUT
OF IT
YET!
I-I
KNOW,
MAN!

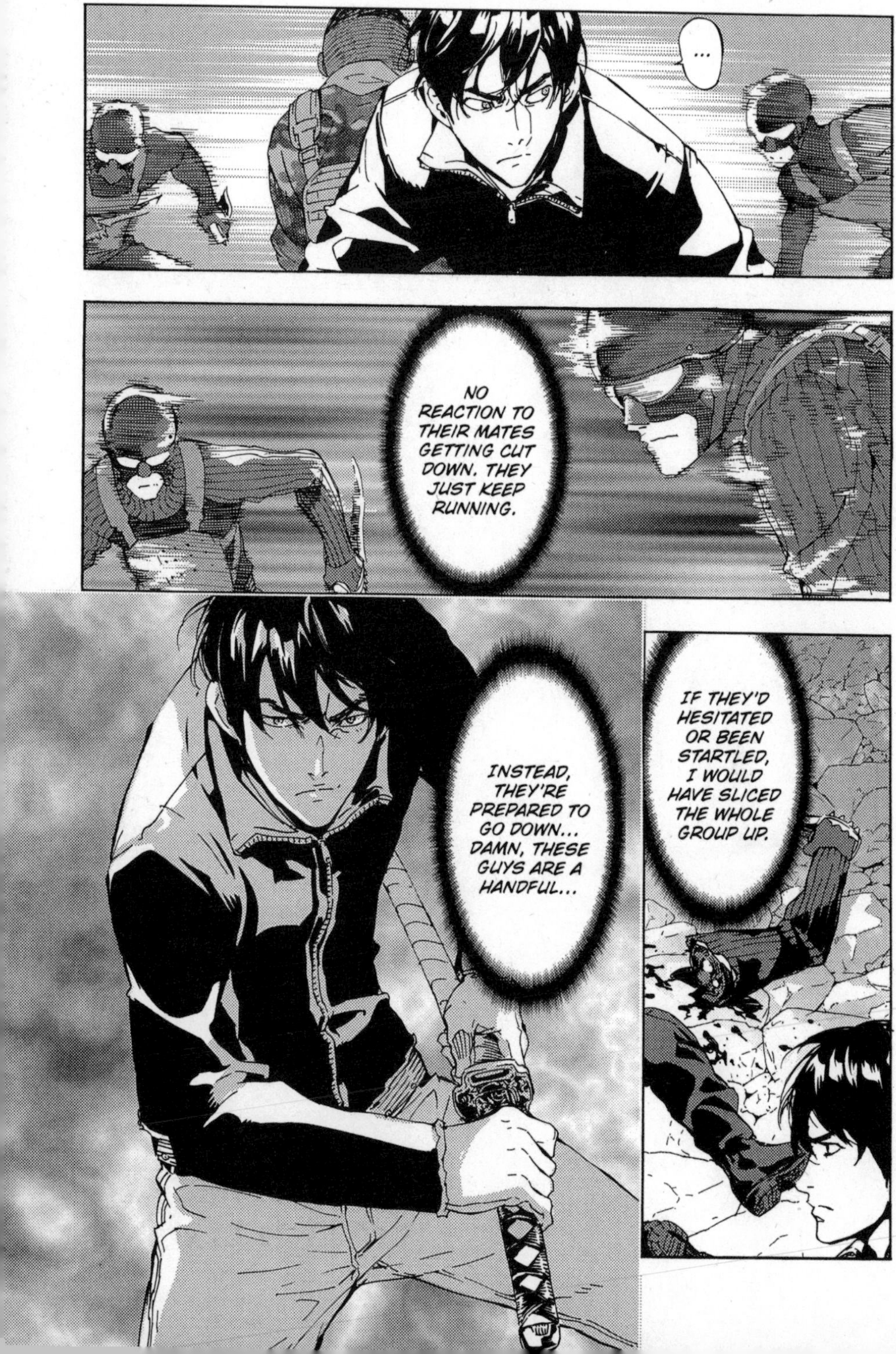
...
NO REACTION TO THEIR MATES GETTING CUT DOWN. THEY JUST KEEP RUNNING.
IF THEY'D HESITATED OR BEEN STARTLED, I WOULD HAVE SLICED THE WHOLE GROUP UP.
INSTEAD, THEY'RE PREPARED TO GO DOWN... DAMN, THESE GUYS ARE A HANDFUL...

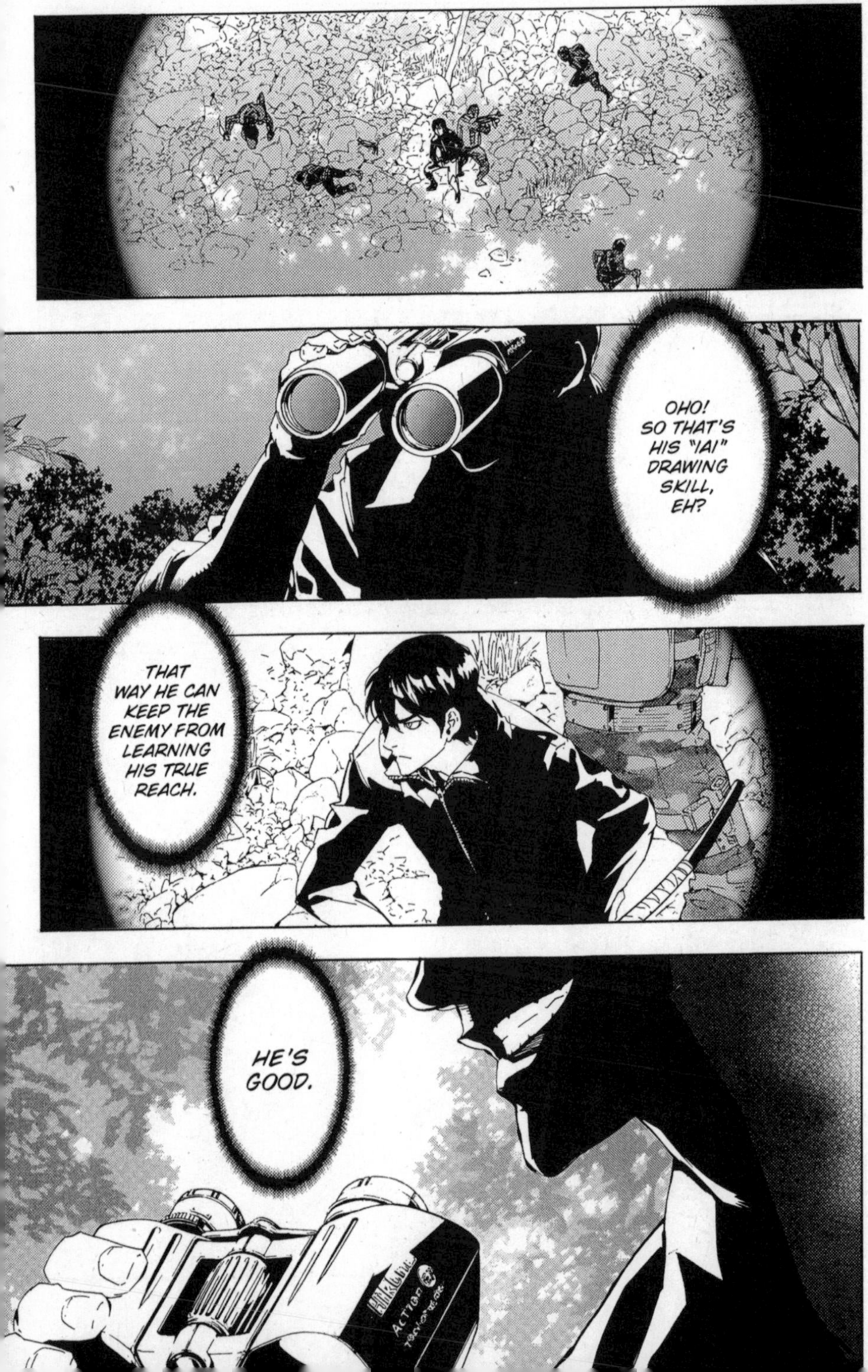
OHO! SO THAT'S HIS "IAI" DRAWING SKILL, EH?
THAT WAY HE CAN KEEP THE ENEMY FROM LEARNING HIS TRUE REACH.
HE'S GOOD.

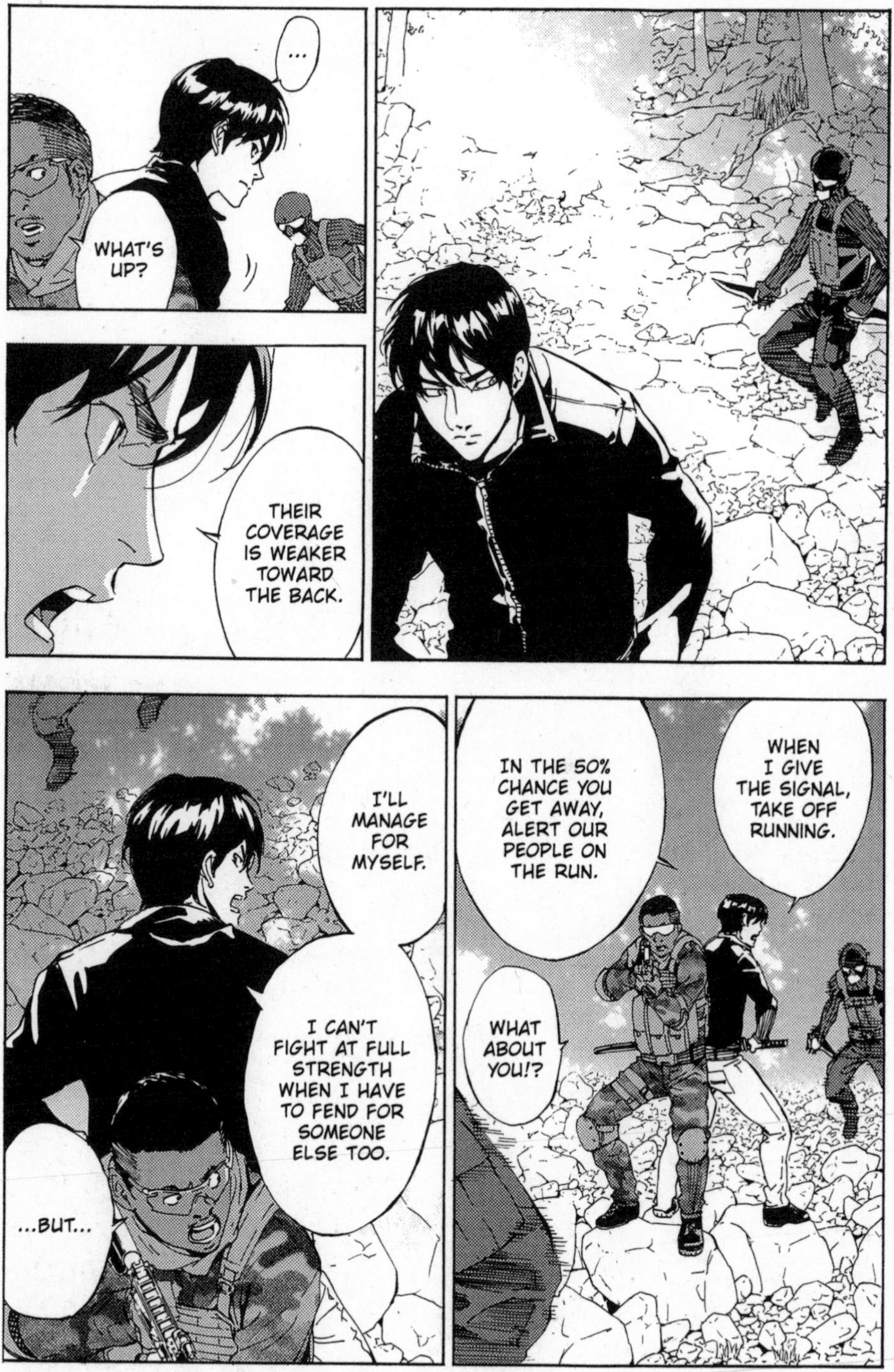
...
WHAT'S UP?
THEIR COVERAGE IS WEAKER TOWARD THE BACK.
WHEN I GIVE THE SIGNAL, TAKE OFF RUNNING.
IN THE 50% CHANCE YOU GET AWAY, ALERT OUR PEOPLE ON THE RUN.
WHAT ABOUT YOU!?
I'LL MANAGE FOR MYSELF.
I CAN'T FIGHT AT FULL STRENGTH WHEN I HAVE TO FEND FOR SOMEONE ELSE TOO.
...BUT...

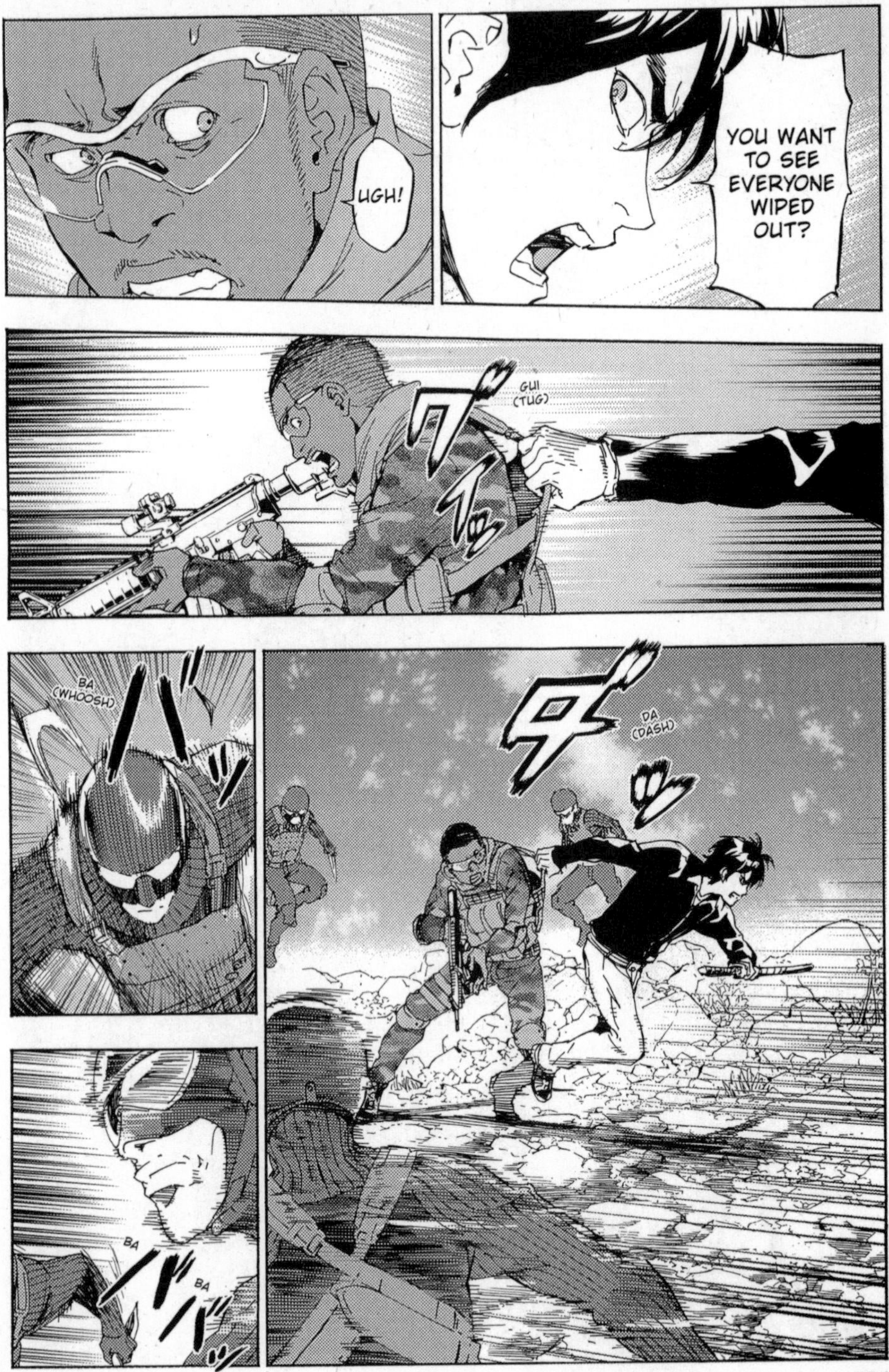
YOU WANT TO SEE EVERYONE WIPED OUT?
UGH!
GUI (TUG)
DA (DASH)
BA (WHOOSH)
BA
BA

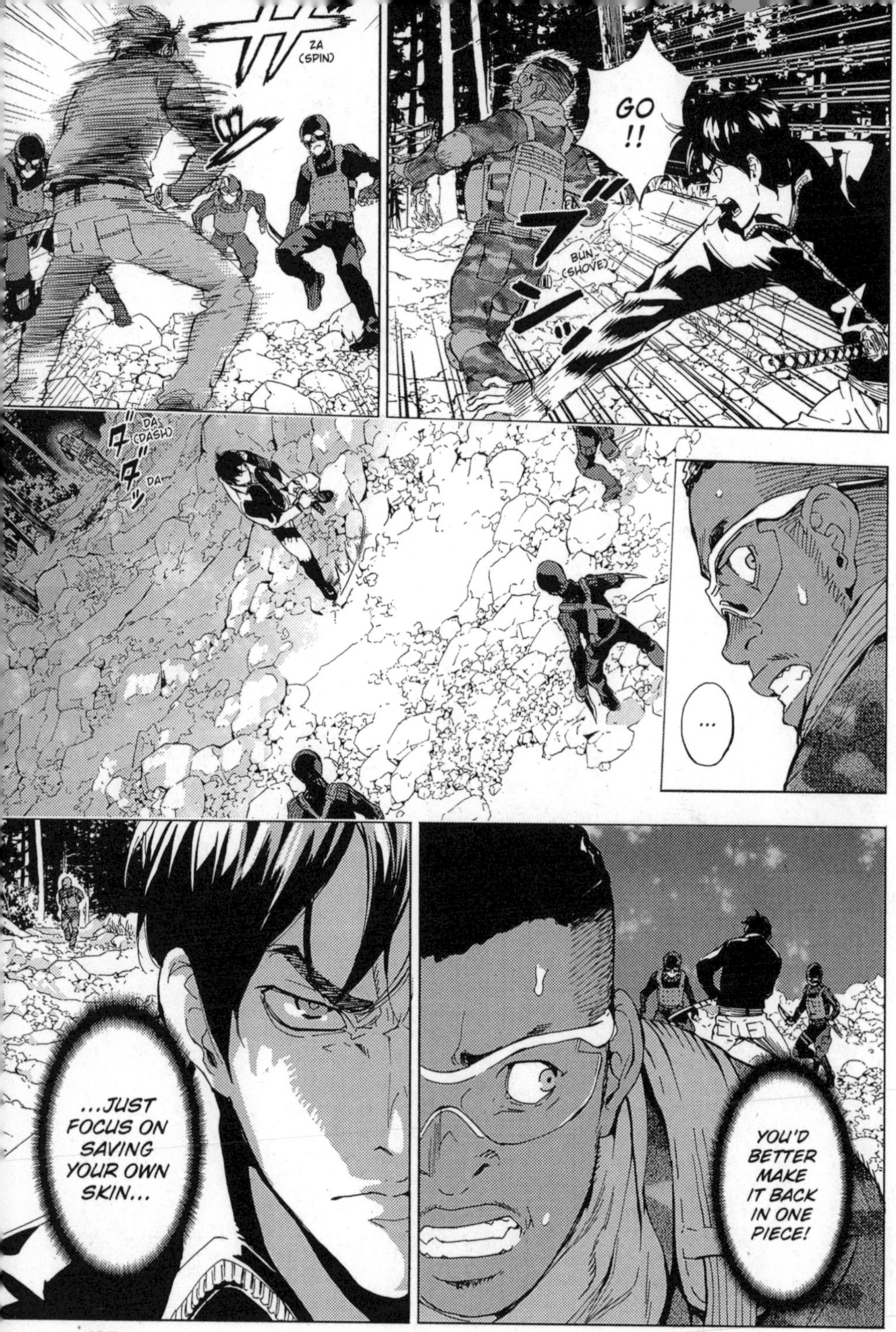
GO !!
BUN (SHOVE)
ZA (SPIN)
...
DA (DASH)
DA
YOU'D BETTER MAKE IT BACK IN ONE PIECE!
...JUST FOCUS ON SAVING YOUR OWN SKIN...

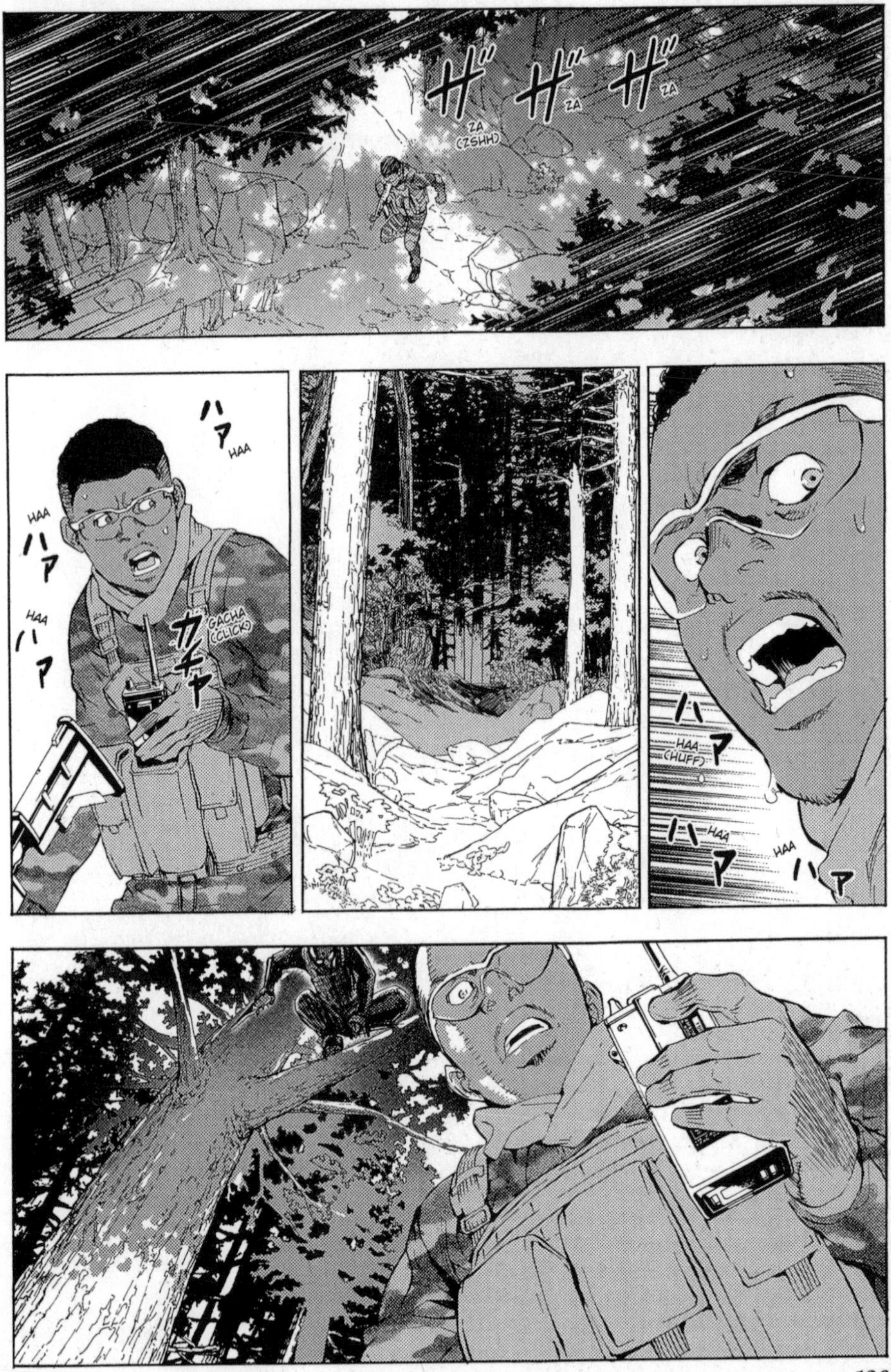
ザ ZA (ZSHH)
ザ ZA
ザ ZA
ハア HAA (HUFF)
ハア HAA
ハア HAA
ハア HAA
ハア HAA
ハア HAA
ガチャ GACHA (CLICK)

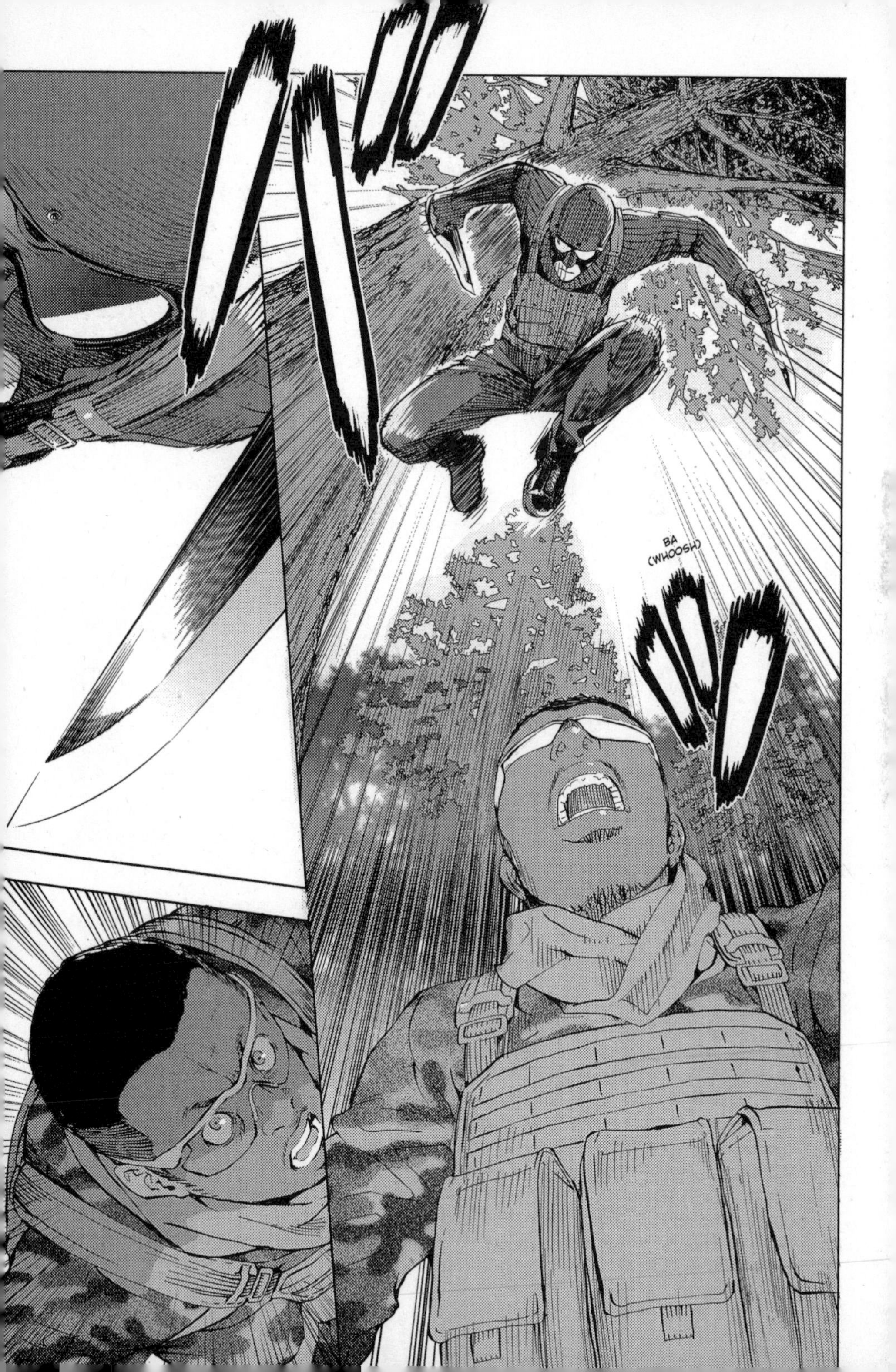
BA
(WHOOSH)

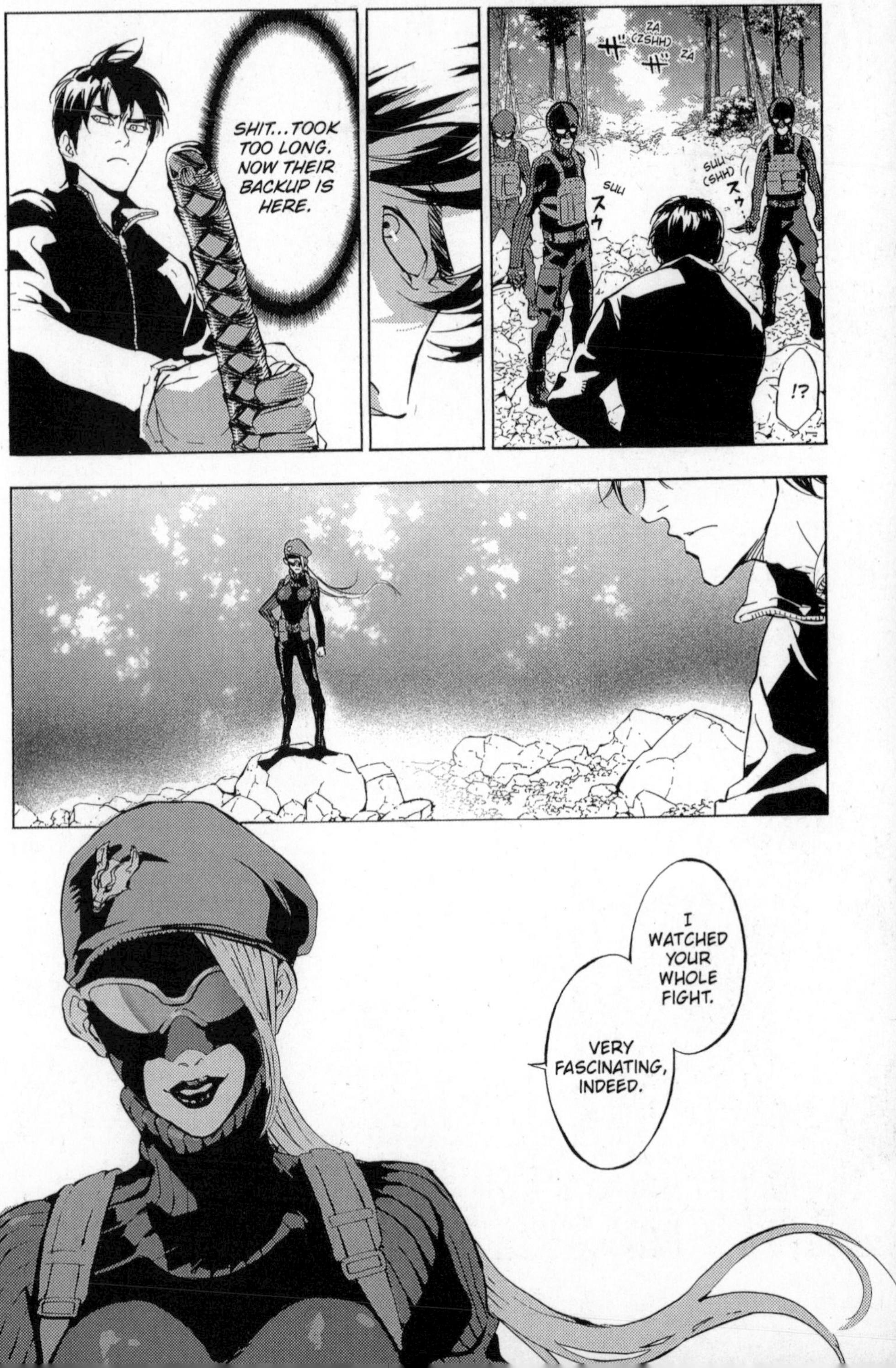

ザ ZA (ZSHH)
ザ ZA
スゥ SUU
スゥ… SUU (SHH)
!?
SHIT...TOOK TOO LONG. NOW THEIR BACKUP IS HERE.
I WATCHED YOUR WHOLE FIGHT.
VERY FASCINATING, INDEED.

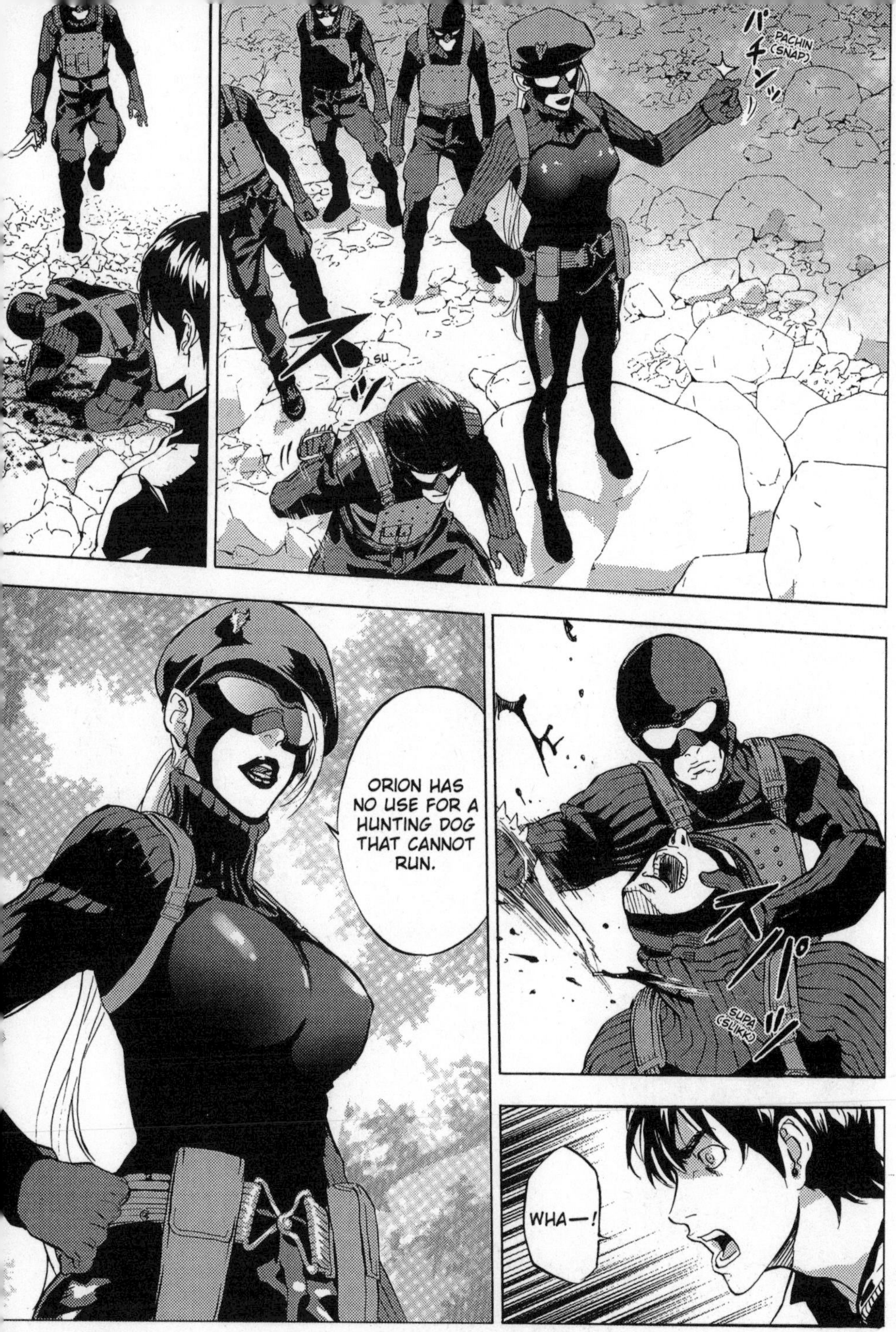
PACHIN (SNAP)
SU
SUPA (SLIKK)
WHA—!
ORION HAS NO USE FOR A HUNTING DOG THAT CANNOT RUN.

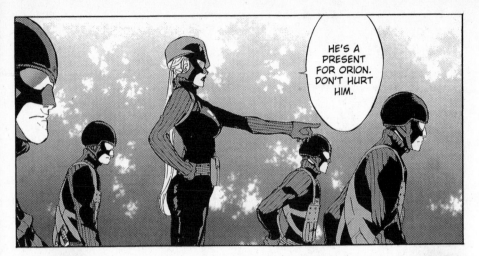

HE'S A PRESENT FOR ORION. DON'T HURT HIM.
HAH! YOU THINK YOU CAN TAKE ME UNHARMED?
YOU REALLY DON'T THINK MUCH OF MY SKILL, DO YOU?
DON'T GET SO UPSET, VOLUNTEER.

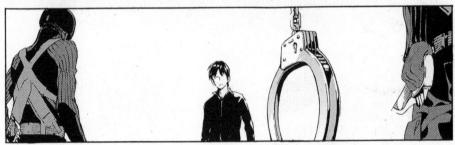

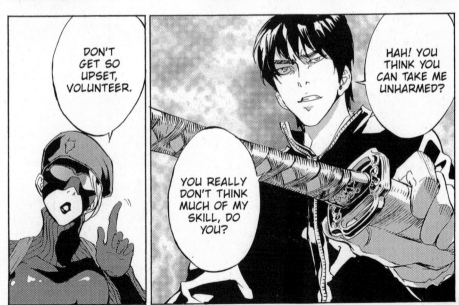

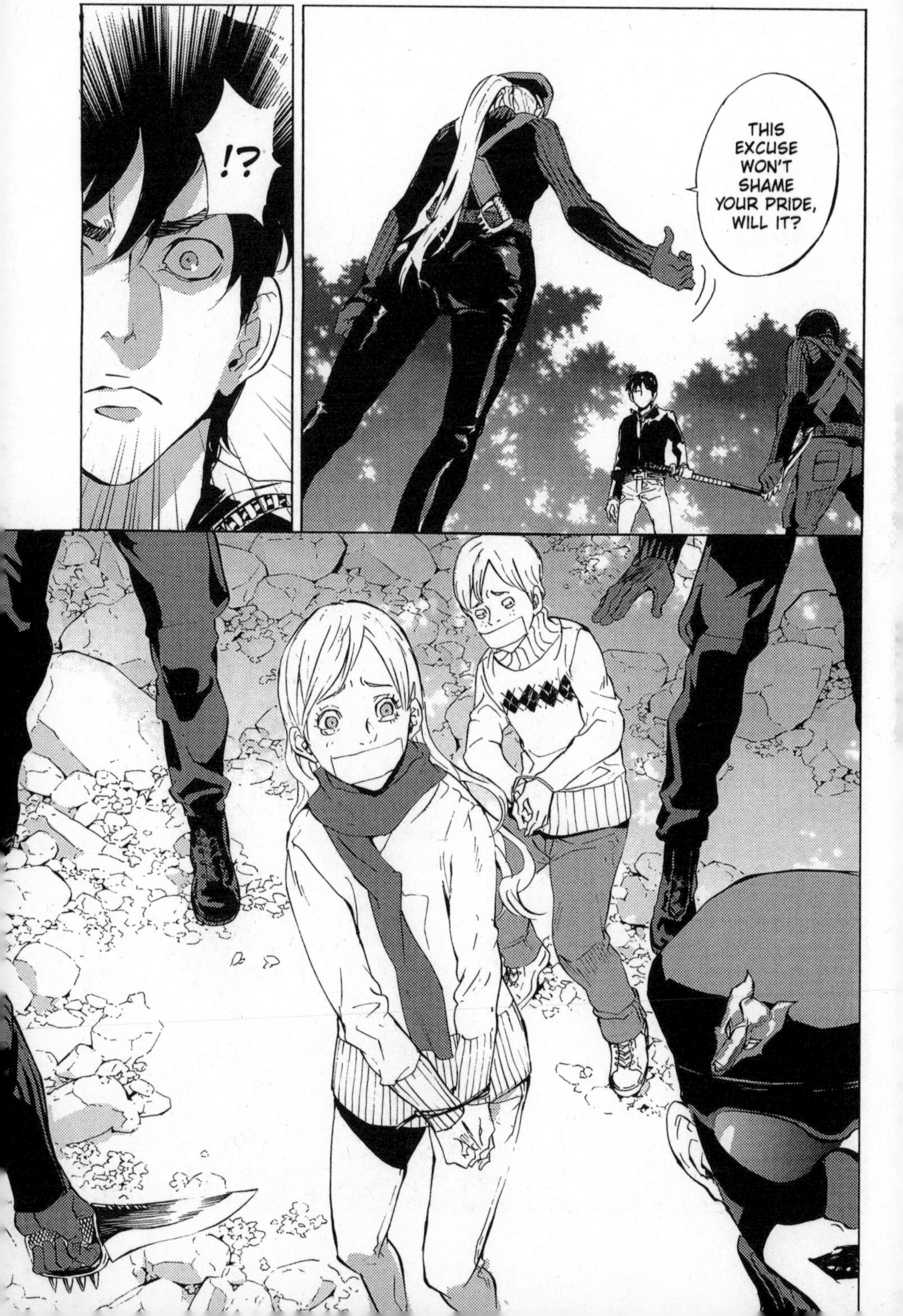
THIS EXCUSE WON'T SHAME YOUR PRIDE, WILL IT?
!?

......YOU THINK THAT'S ENOUGH TO STOP ME!?

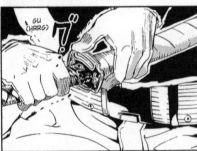

ABSOLUTELY. YOU'RE ONE OF THE GOOD GUYS.

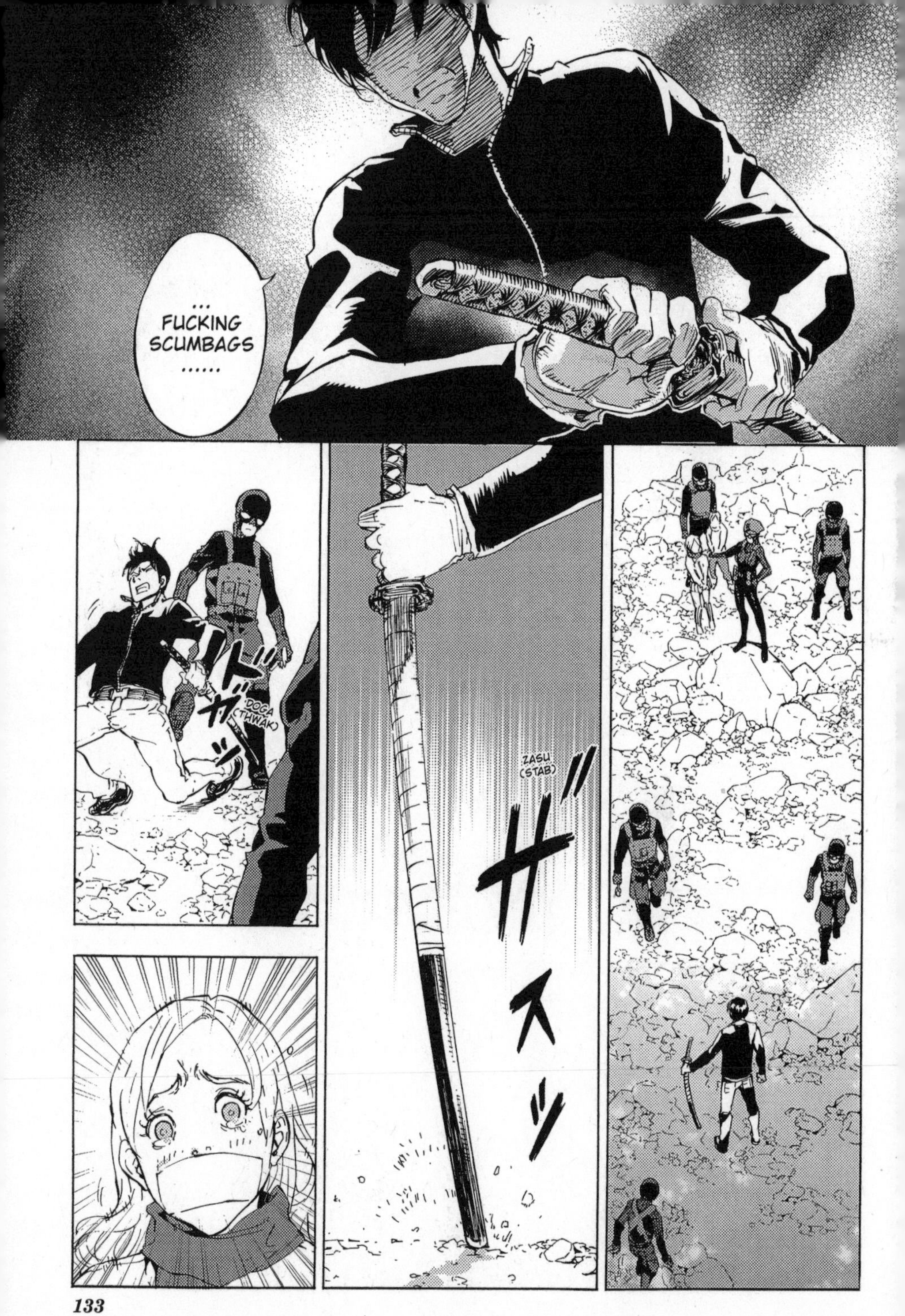

... FUCKING SCUMBAGS ......
ザスッ
ZASU (STAB)
ドガッ
DOGA (THWAK)

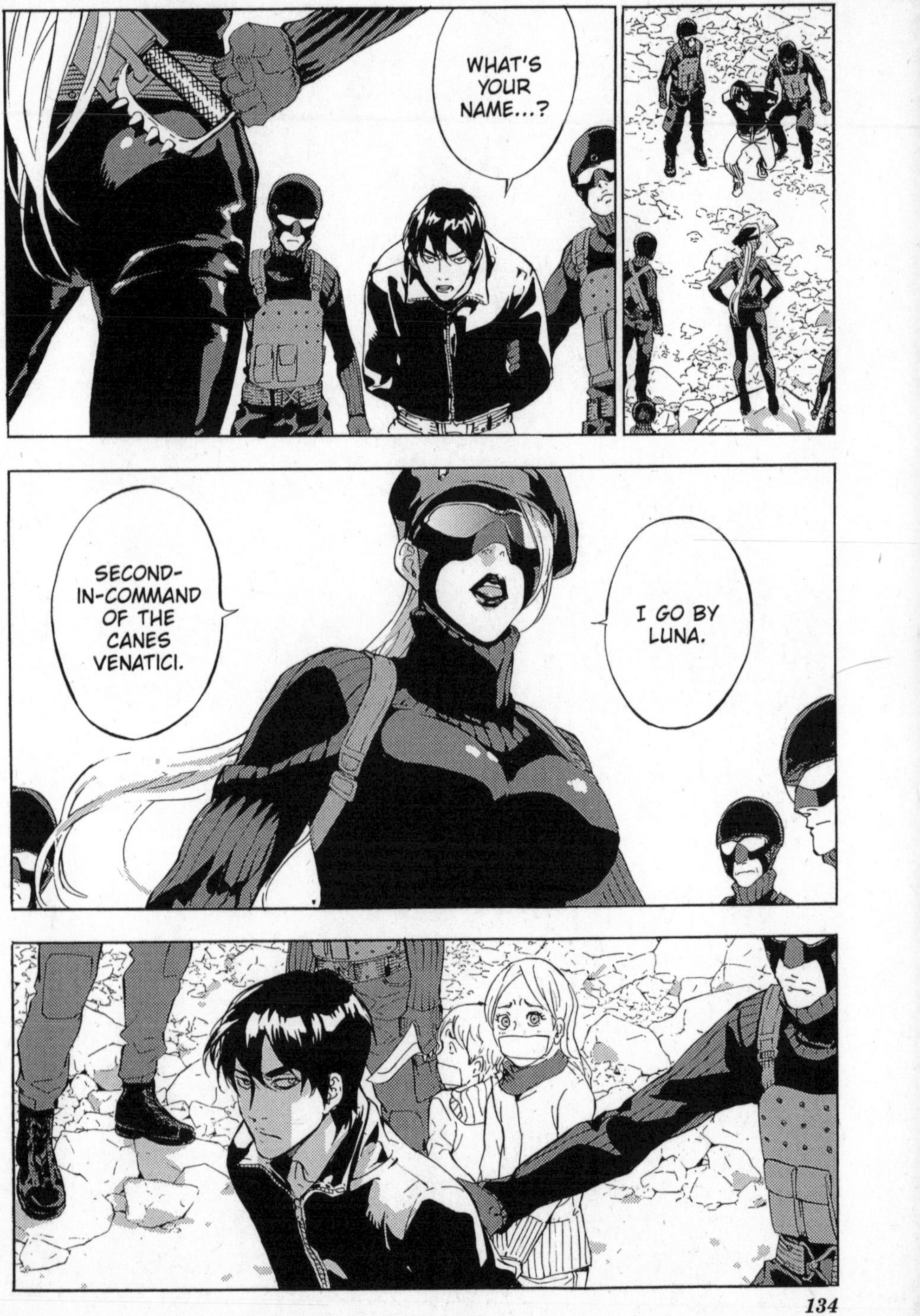
WHAT'S YOUR NAME...?
I GO BY LUNA.
SECOND-IN-COMMAND OF THE CANES VENATICI.

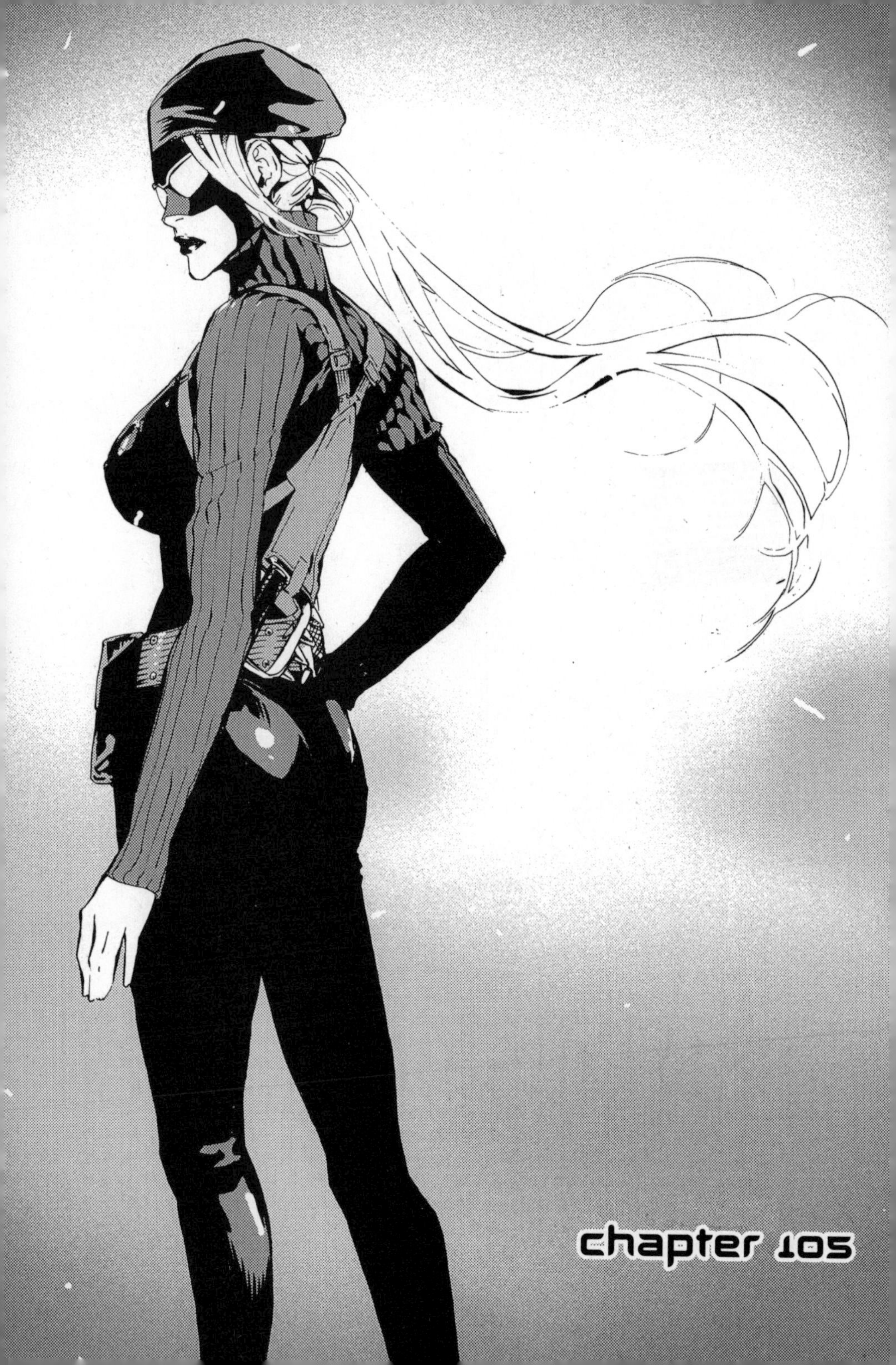
chapter 105

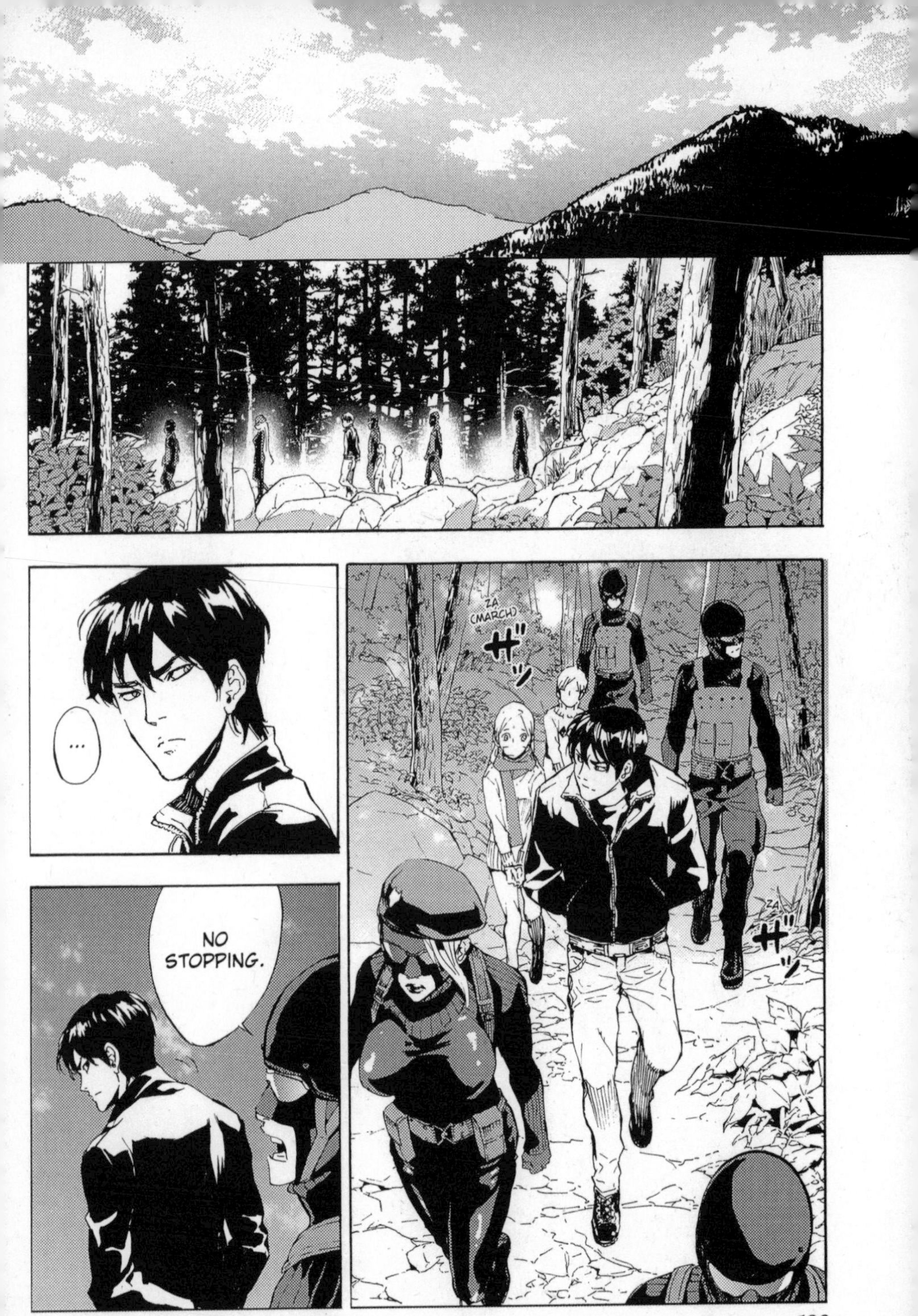
ZA (MARCH)
ザッ
ZA
ザッ
...
NO STOPPING.

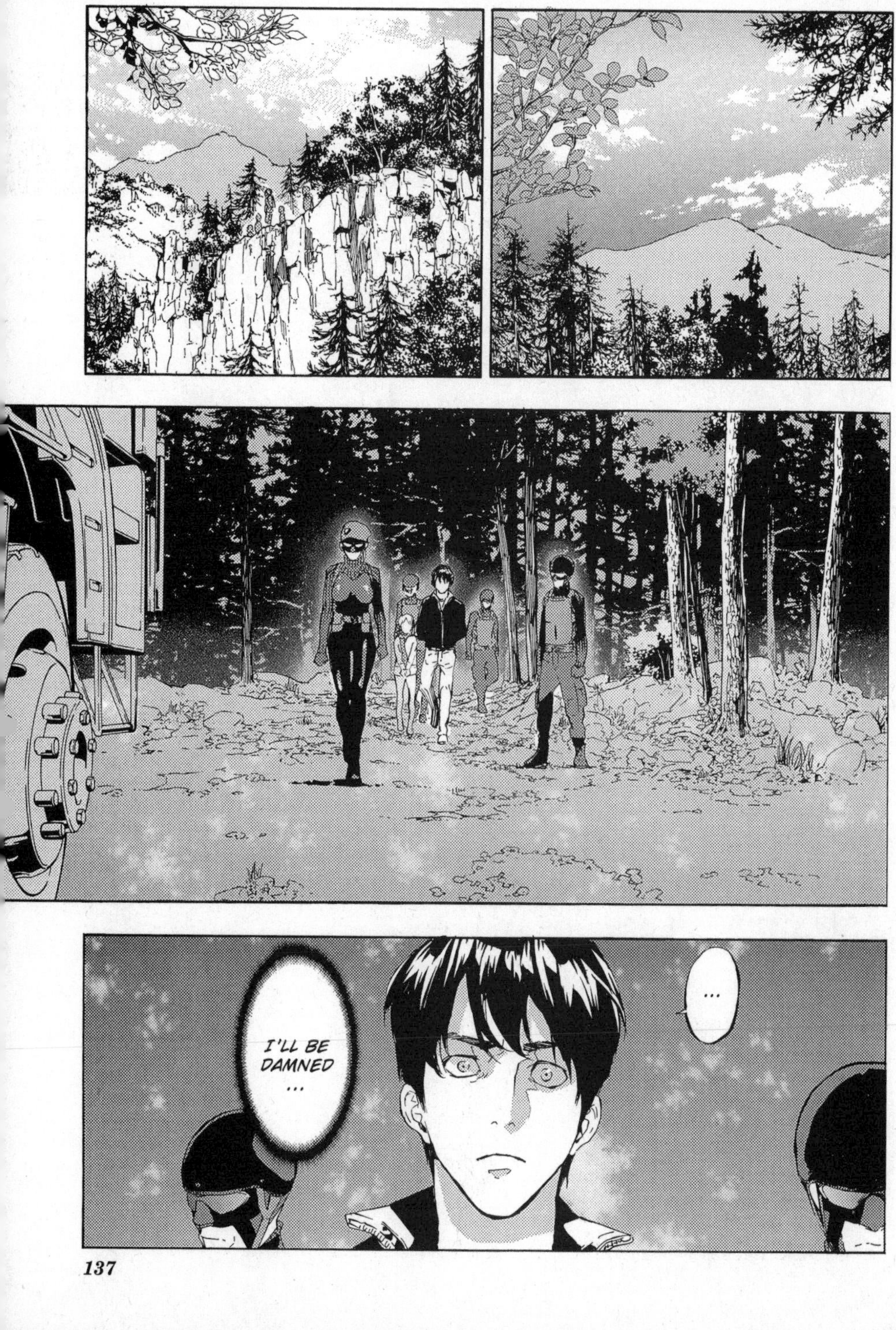
...
I'LL BE DAMNED ...

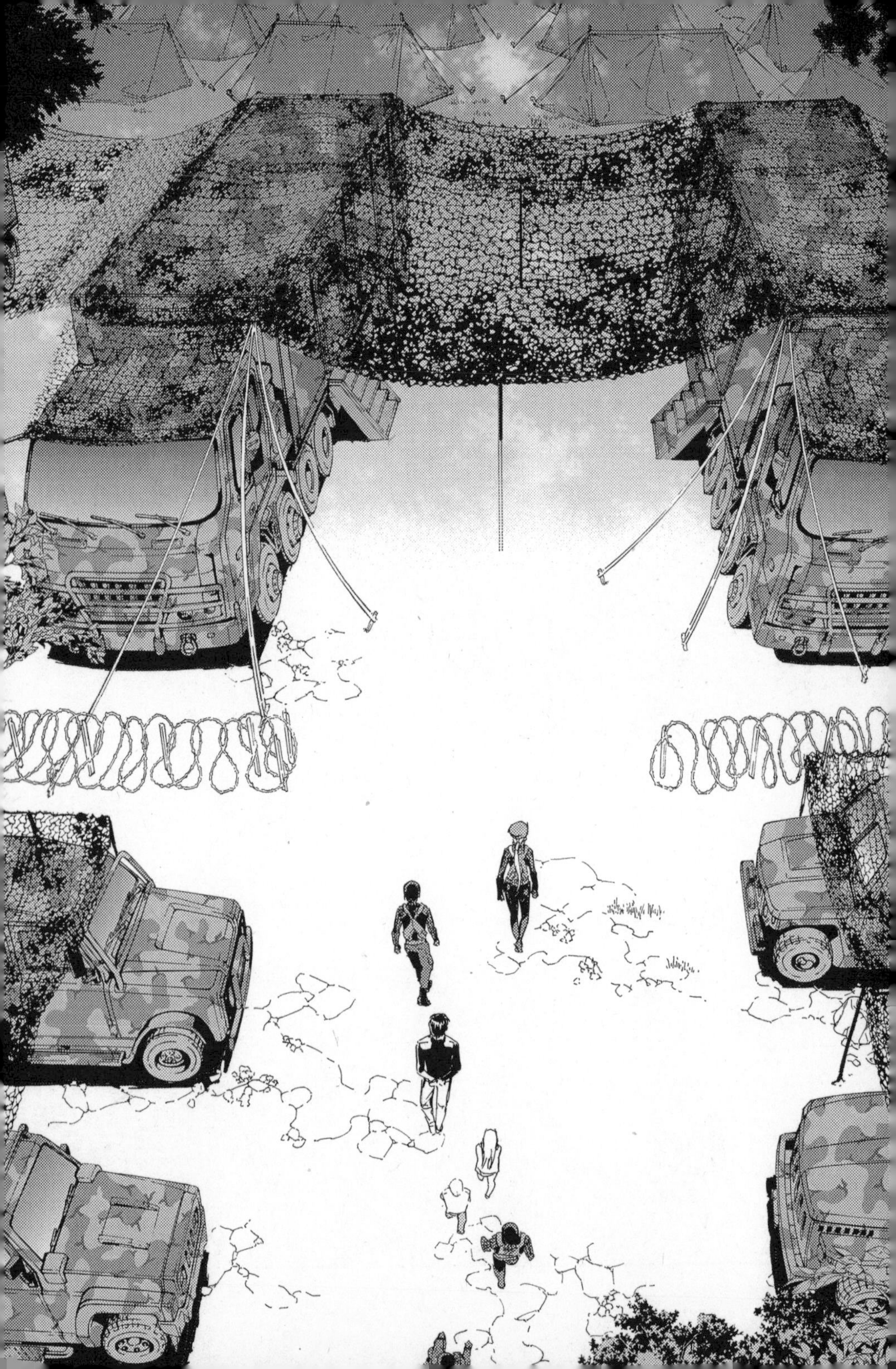

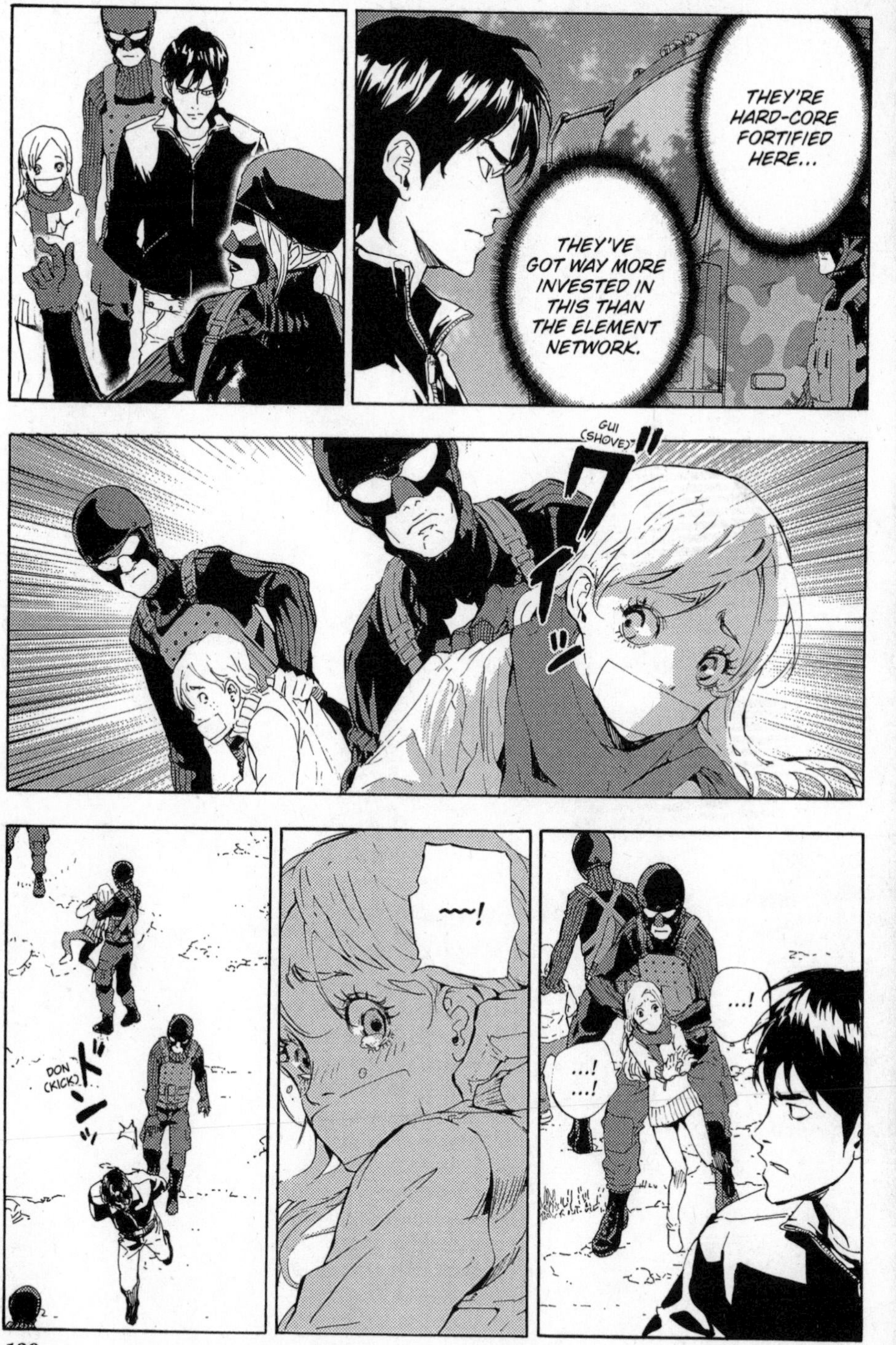
THEY'RE HARD-CORE FORTIFIED HERE...
THEY'VE GOT WAY MORE INVESTED IN THIS THAN THE ELEMENT NETWORK.
GUI (SHOVE)
...!
...! ...!
~~!
DON (KICK)

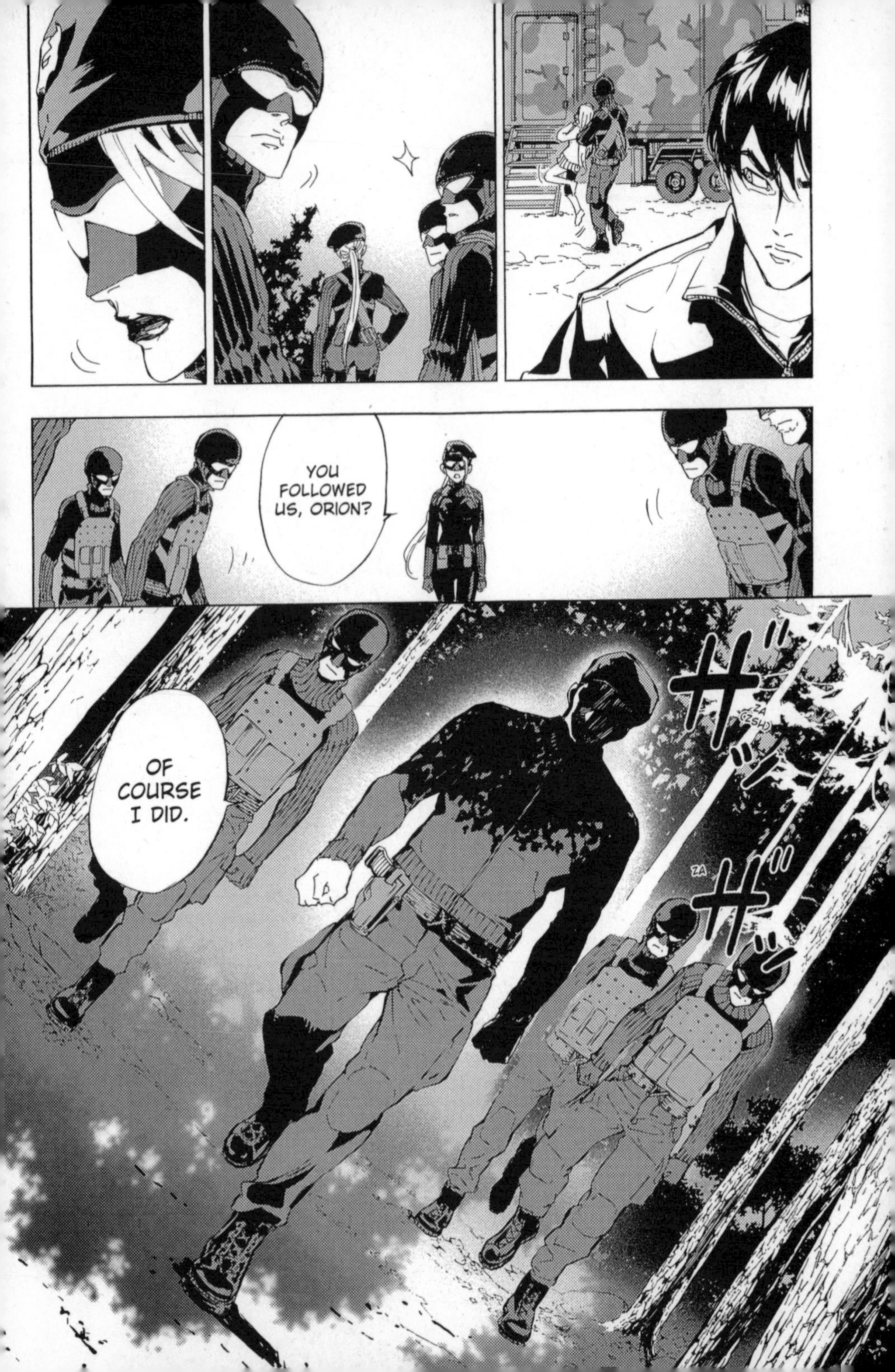
YOU FOLLOWED US, ORION?
ザッ
ZA (ZSH)
ザッ
ZA
OF COURSE I DID.

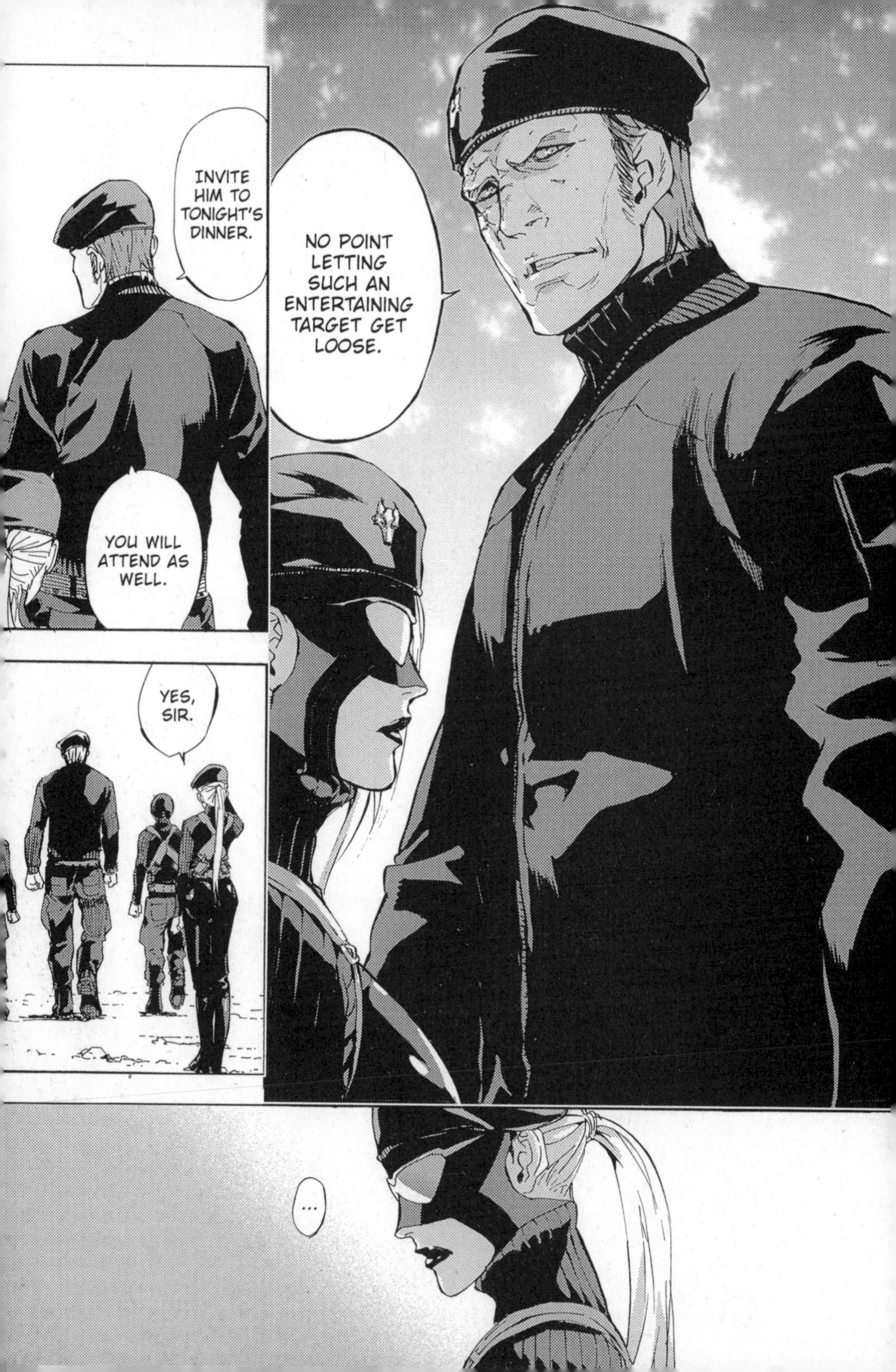
NO POINT LETTING SUCH AN ENTERTAINING TARGET GET LOOSE.
INVITE HIM TO TONIGHT'S DINNER.
YOU WILL ATTEND AS WELL.
YES, SIR.
...

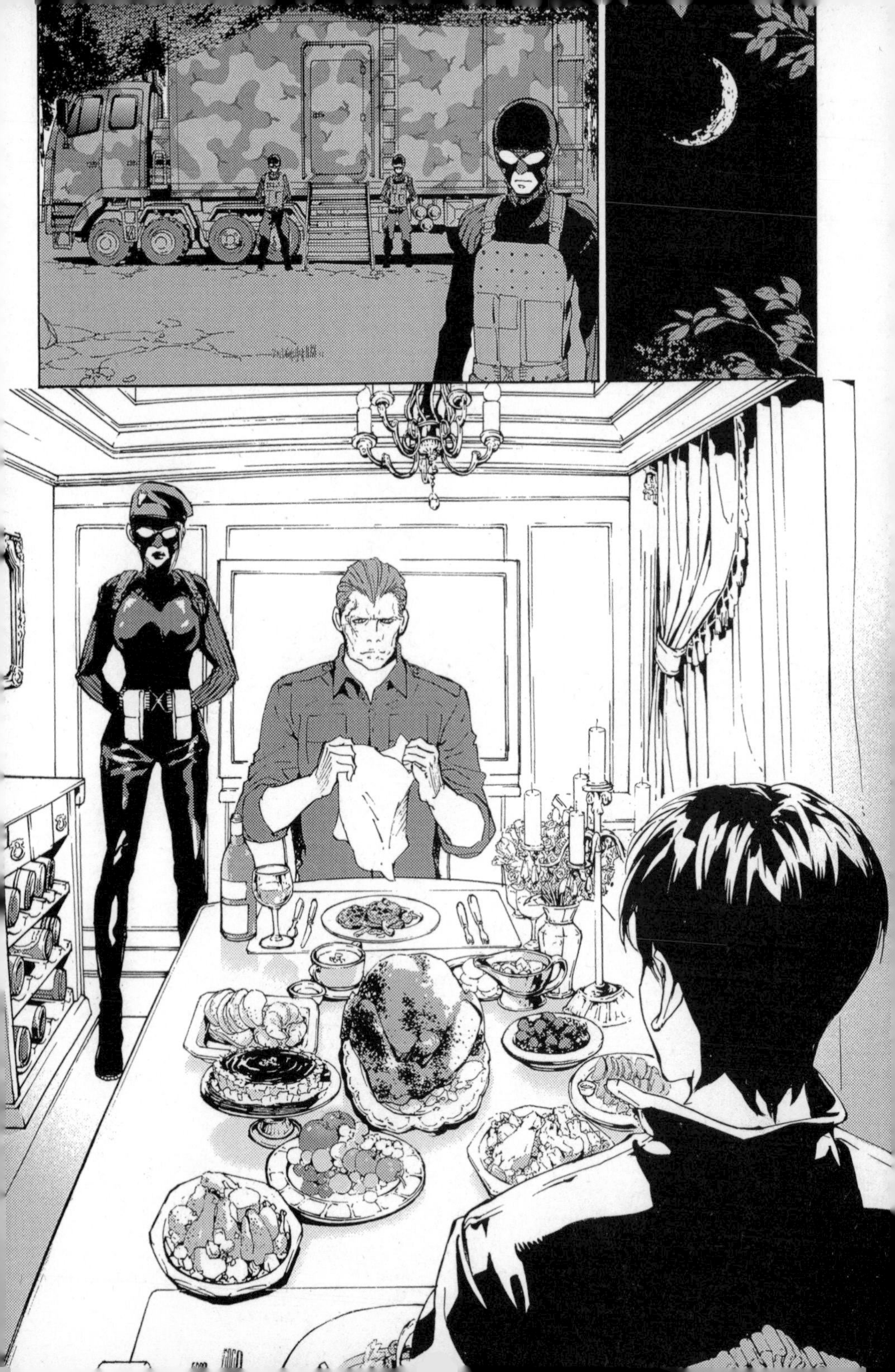

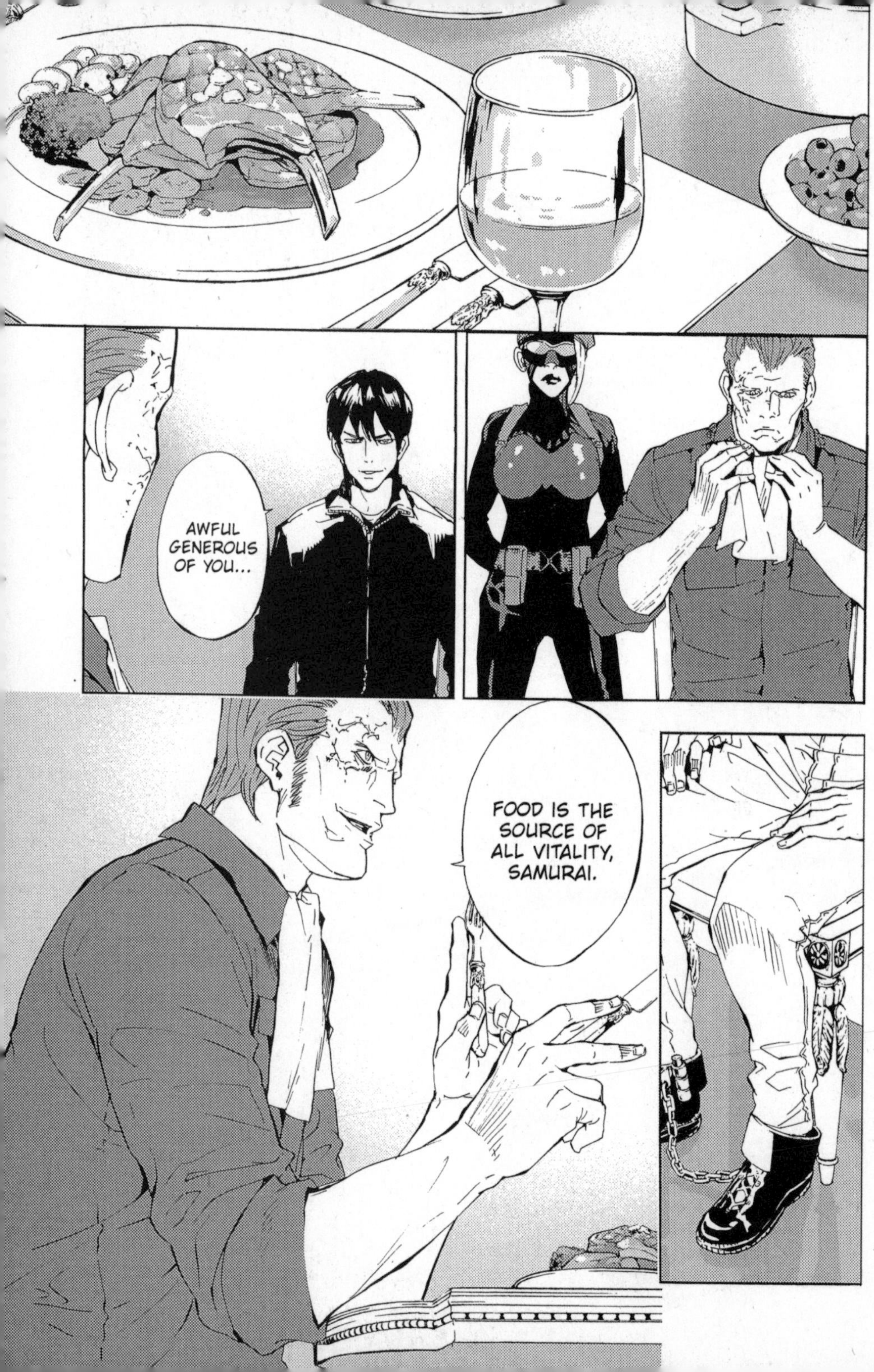
AWFUL GENEROUS OF YOU...
FOOD IS THE SOURCE OF ALL VITALITY, SAMURAI.

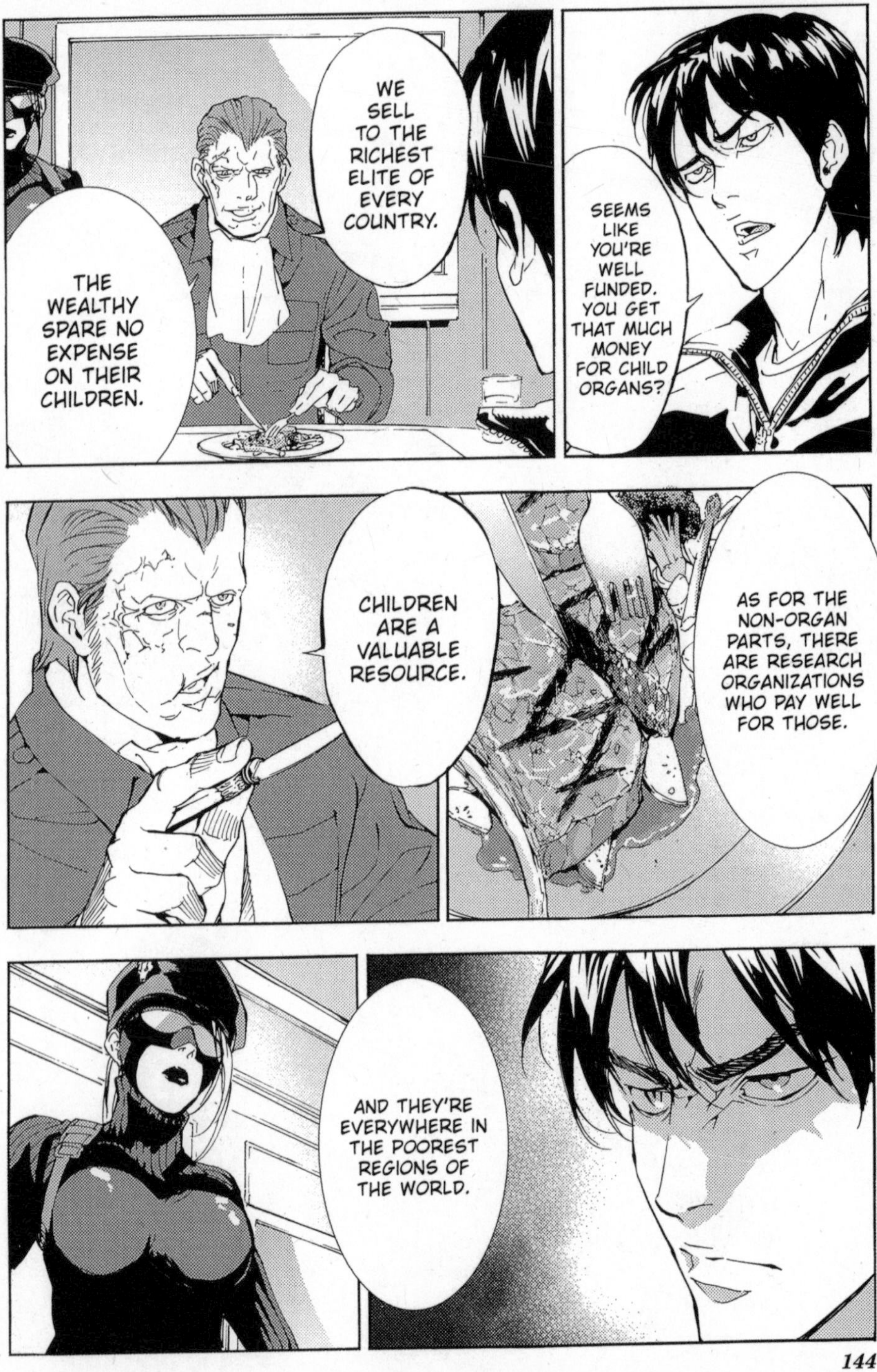
SEEMS LIKE YOU'RE WELL FUNDED. YOU GET THAT MUCH MONEY FOR CHILD ORGANS?
WE SELL TO THE RICHEST ELITE OF EVERY COUNTRY.
THE WEALTHY SPARE NO EXPENSE ON THEIR CHILDREN.
AS FOR THE NON-ORGAN PARTS, THERE ARE RESEARCH ORGANIZATIONS WHO PAY WELL FOR THOSE.
CHILDREN ARE A VALUABLE RESOURCE.
AND THEY'RE EVERYWHERE IN THE POOREST REGIONS OF THE WORLD.

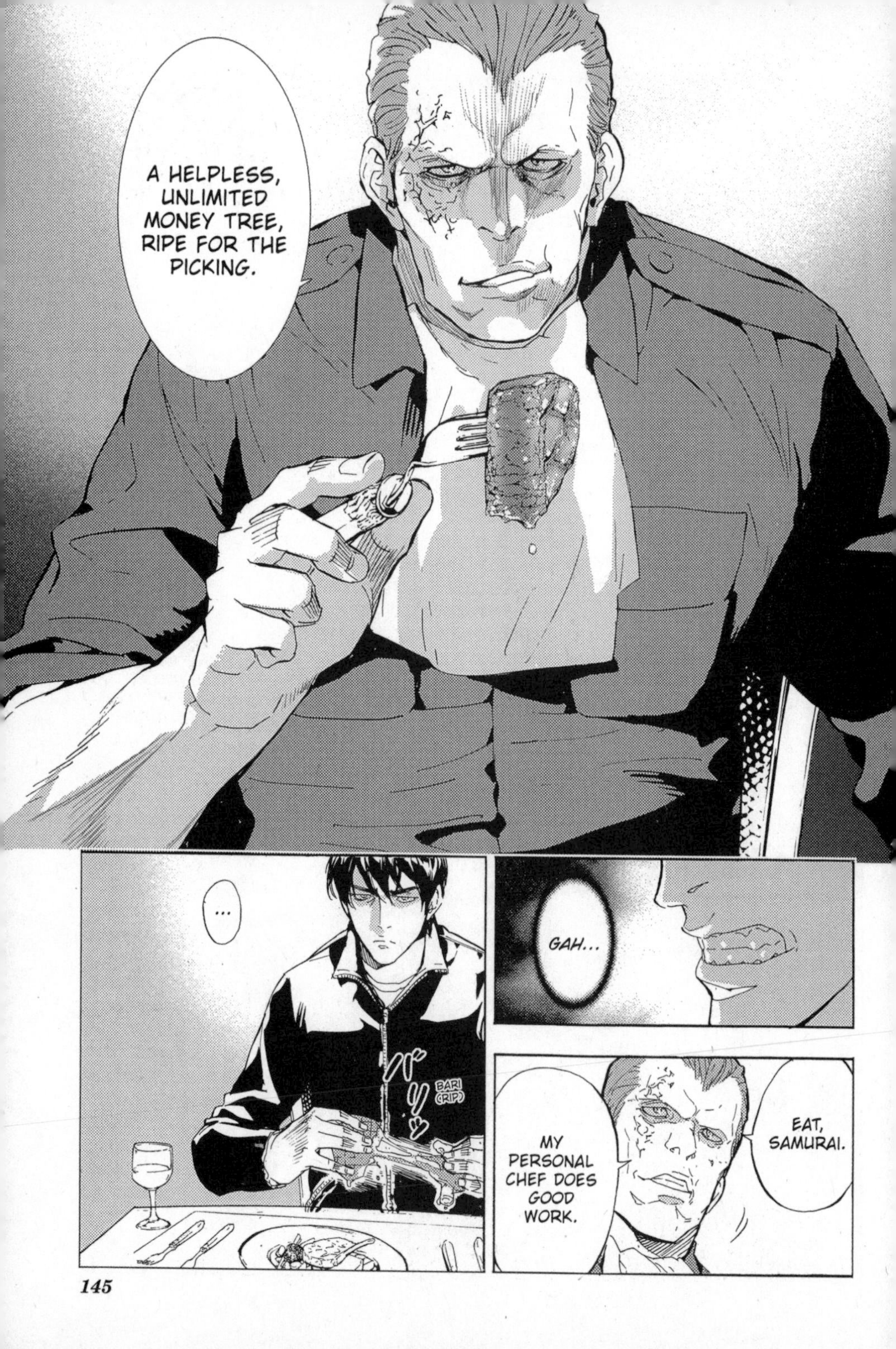
A HELPLESS, UNLIMITED MONEY TREE, RIPE FOR THE PICKING.
GAH...
EAT, SAMURAI.
MY PERSONAL CHEF DOES GOOD WORK.
...
BARI (RIP)

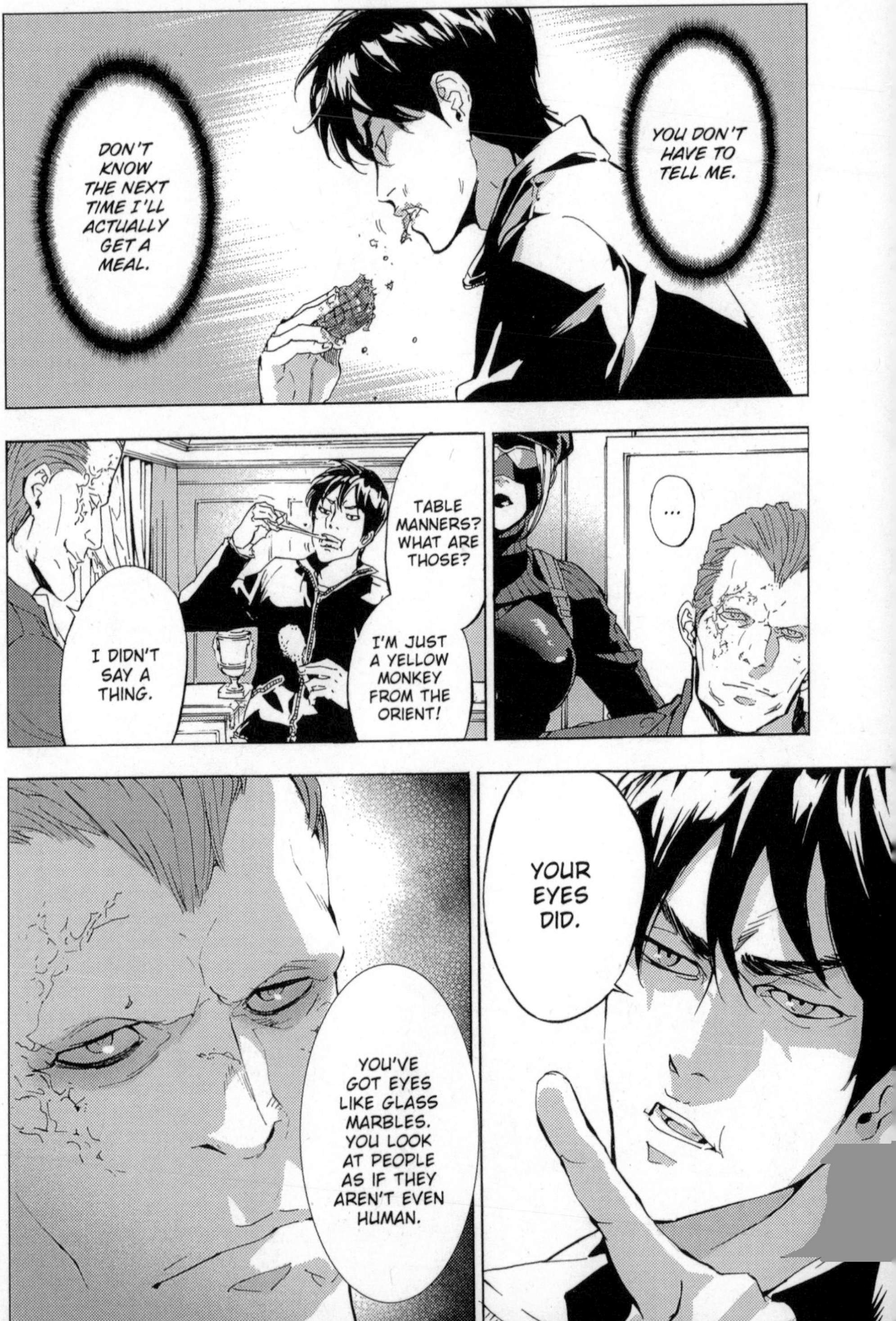
YOU DON'T HAVE TO TELL ME.
DON'T KNOW THE NEXT TIME I'LL ACTUALLY GET A MEAL.
...
TABLE MANNERS? WHAT ARE THOSE?
I'M JUST A YELLOW MONKEY FROM THE ORIENT!
I DIDN'T SAY A THING.
YOUR EYES DID.
YOU'VE GOT EYES LIKE GLASS MARBLES. YOU LOOK AT PEOPLE AS IF THEY AREN'T EVEN HUMAN.

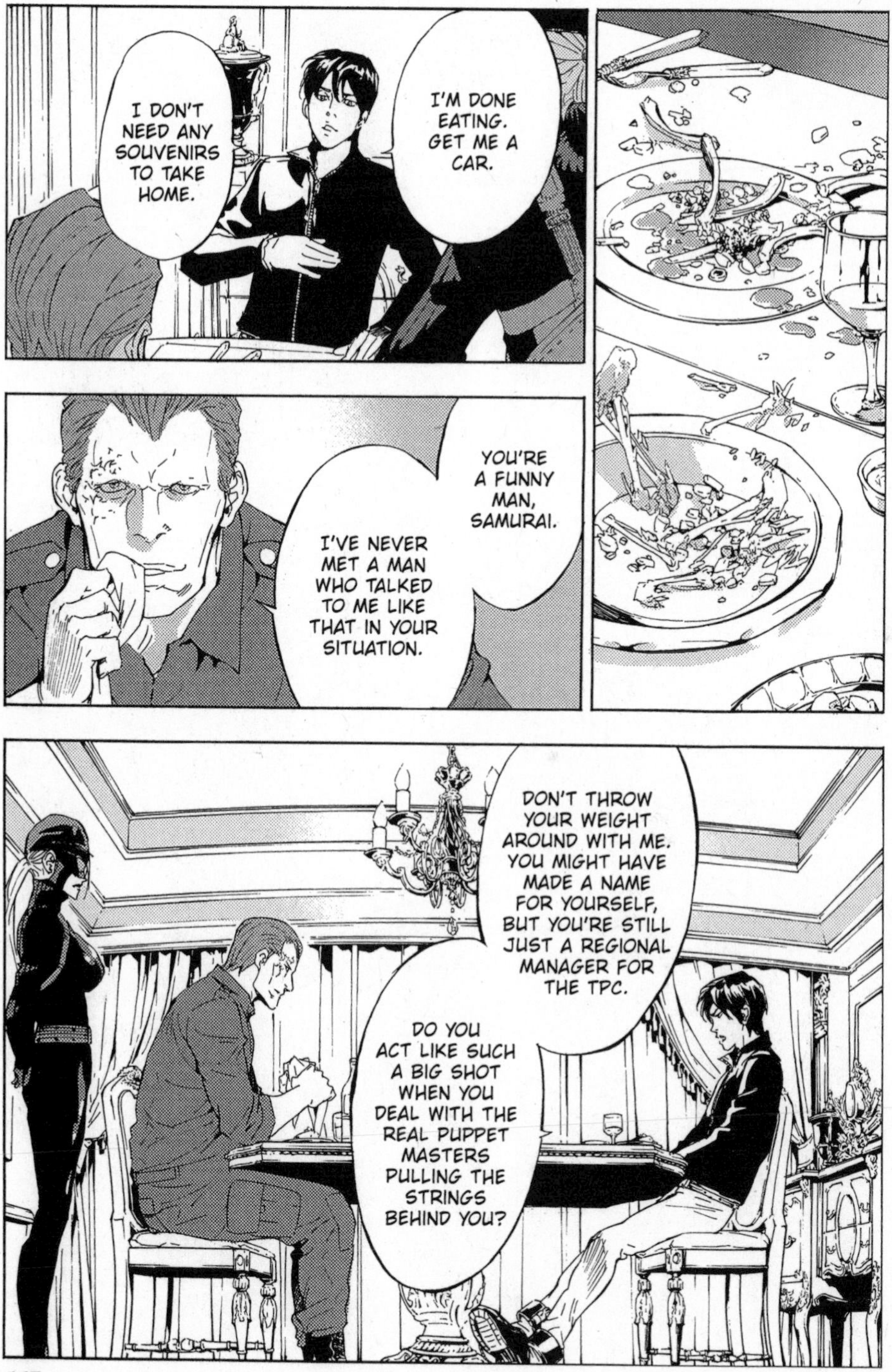
I'M DONE EATING. GET ME A CAR.
I DON'T NEED ANY SOUVENIRS TO TAKE HOME.
YOU'RE A FUNNY MAN, SAMURAI.
I'VE NEVER MET A MAN WHO TALKED TO ME LIKE THAT IN YOUR SITUATION.
DON'T THROW YOUR WEIGHT AROUND WITH ME. YOU MIGHT HAVE MADE A NAME FOR YOURSELF, BUT YOU'RE STILL JUST A REGIONAL MANAGER FOR THE TPC.
DO YOU ACT LIKE SUCH A BIG SHOT WHEN YOU DEAL WITH THE REAL PUPPET MASTERS PULLING THE STRINGS BEHIND YOU?

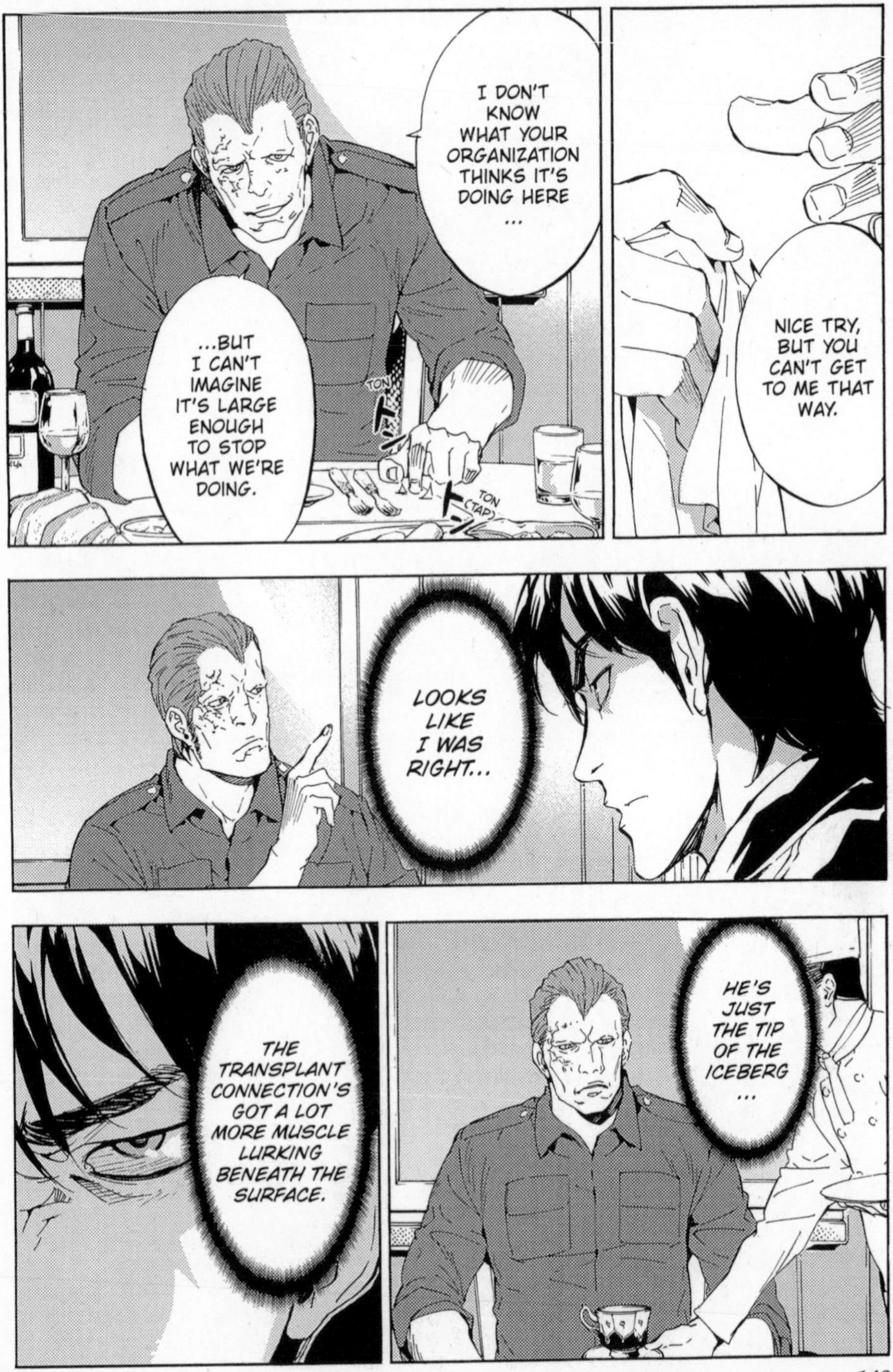
NICE TRY, BUT YOU CAN'T GET TO ME THAT WAY.
I DON'T KNOW WHAT YOUR ORGANIZATION THINKS IT'S DOING HERE ...
...BUT I CAN'T IMAGINE IT'S LARGE ENOUGH TO STOP WHAT WE'RE DOING.
TON
TON (TAP)
LOOKS LIKE I WAS RIGHT...
HE'S JUST THE TIP OF THE ICEBERG ...
THE TRANSPLANT CONNECTION'S GOT A LOT MORE MUSCLE LURKING BENEATH THE SURFACE.

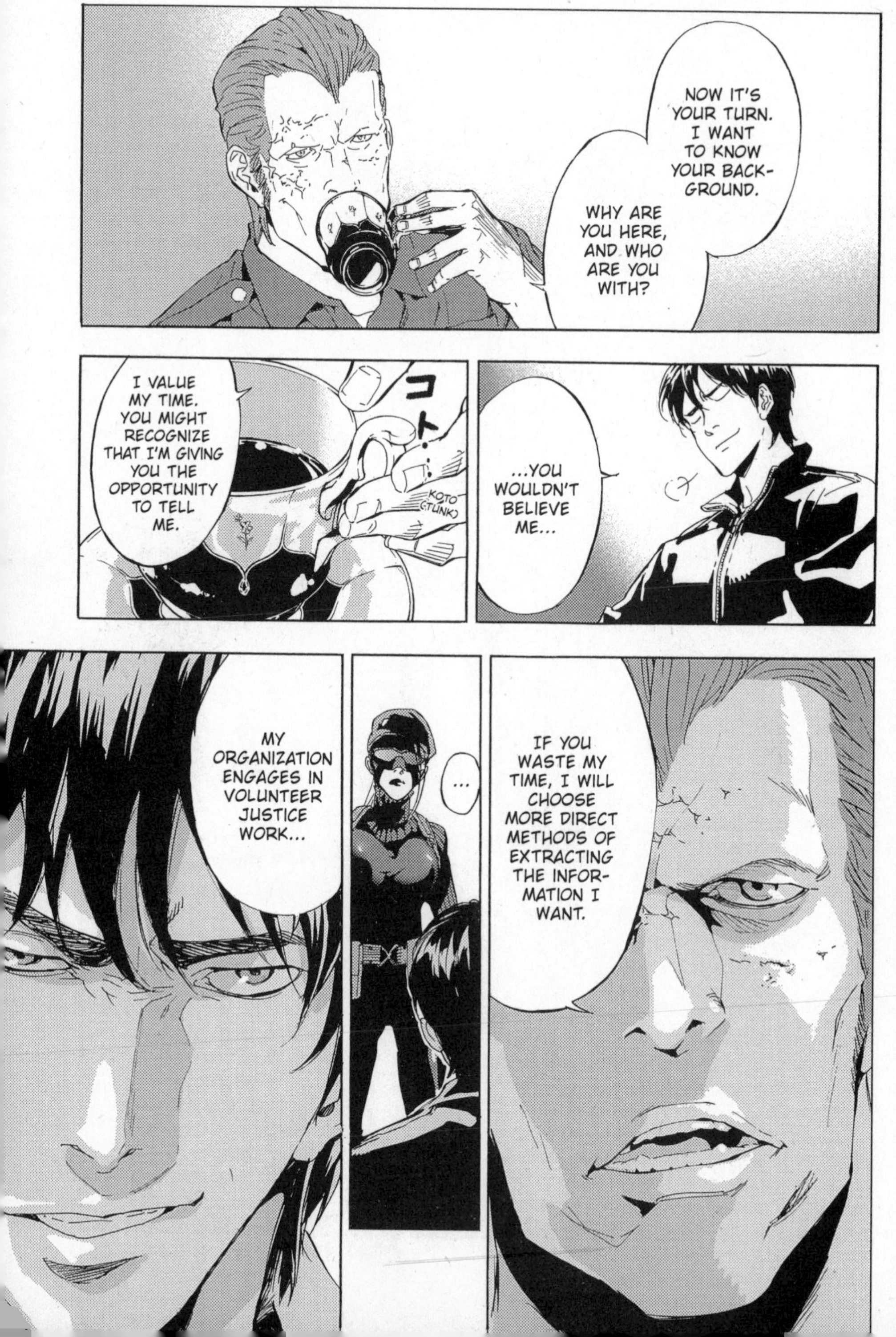
NOW IT'S YOUR TURN. I WANT TO KNOW YOUR BACK-GROUND.
WHY ARE YOU HERE, AND WHO ARE YOU WITH?
...YOU WOULDN'T BELIEVE ME...
コト
KOTO (TUNK)
I VALUE MY TIME. YOU MIGHT RECOGNIZE THAT I'M GIVING YOU THE OPPORTUNITY TO TELL ME.
IF YOU WASTE MY TIME, I WILL CHOOSE MORE DIRECT METHODS OF EXTRACTING THE INFOR-MATION I WANT.
...
MY ORGANIZATION ENGAGES IN VOLUNTEER JUSTICE WORK...

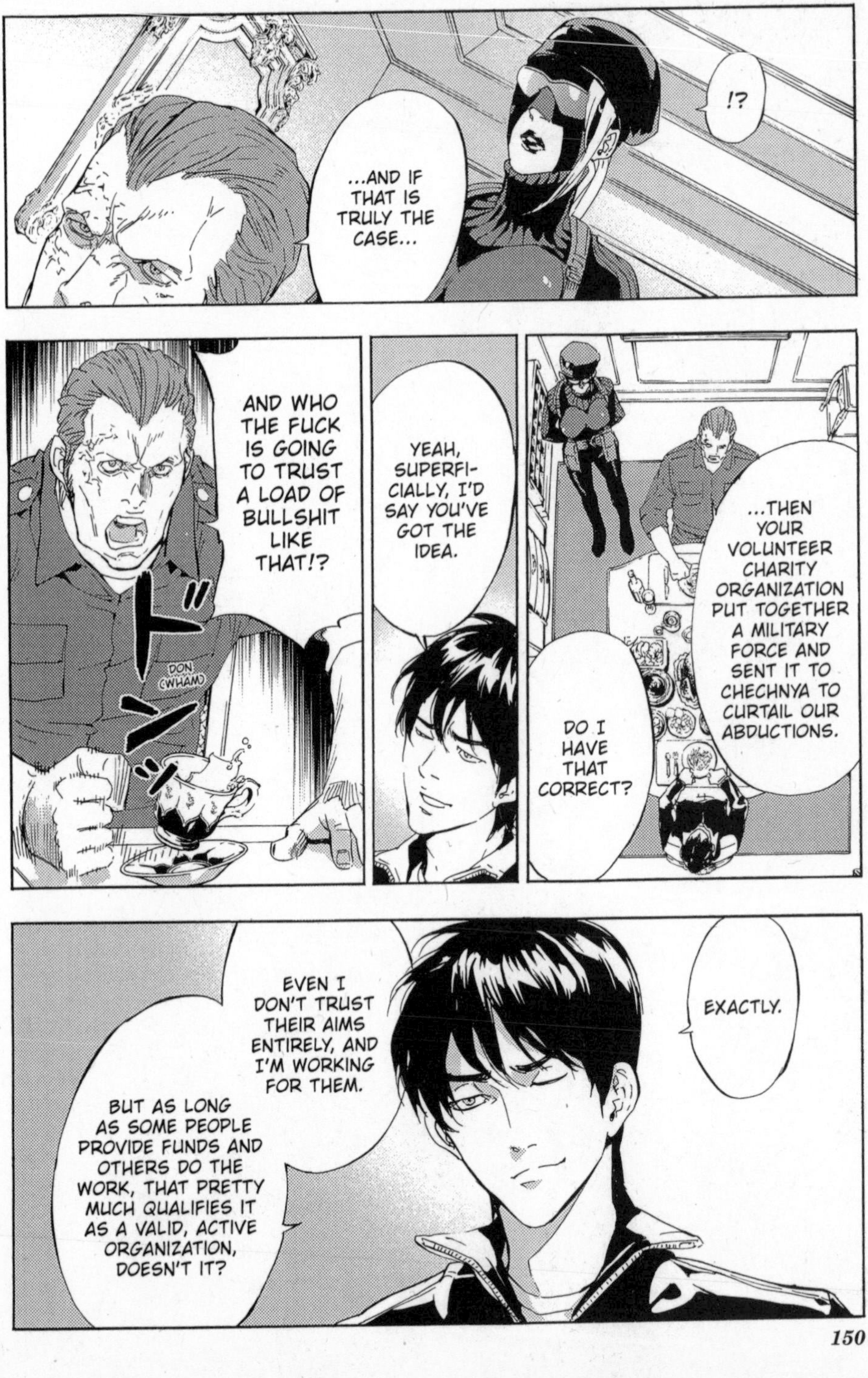
!?
...AND IF THAT IS TRULY THE CASE...
...THEN YOUR VOLUNTEER CHARITY ORGANIZATION PUT TOGETHER A MILITARY FORCE AND SENT IT TO CHECHNYA TO CURTAIL OUR ABDUCTIONS.
DO I HAVE THAT CORRECT?
YEAH, SUPERFICIALLY, I'D SAY YOU'VE GOT THE IDEA.
AND WHO THE FUCK IS GOING TO TRUST A LOAD OF BULLSHIT LIKE THAT!?
DON (WHAM)
EXACTLY.
EVEN I DON'T TRUST THEIR AIMS ENTIRELY, AND I'M WORKING FOR THEM.
BUT AS LONG AS SOME PEOPLE PROVIDE FUNDS AND OTHERS DO THE WORK, THAT PRETTY MUCH QUALIFIES IT AS A VALID, ACTIVE ORGANIZATION, DOESN'T IT?

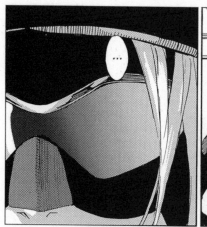

...

AND THE FACT THAT WE DON'T ALLOW ANY FACET OF OUR EXISTENCE TO BE BROUGHT TO LIGHT MAKES US NO DIFFERENT FROM YOU.

...

NONE OF THIS MATTERS TO ME. THEY GAVE ME A "BATTLEFIELD" AND A "REASON TO FIGHT." THAT'S ALL I NEED.

GET HIM OUTTA MY SIGHT...

...!

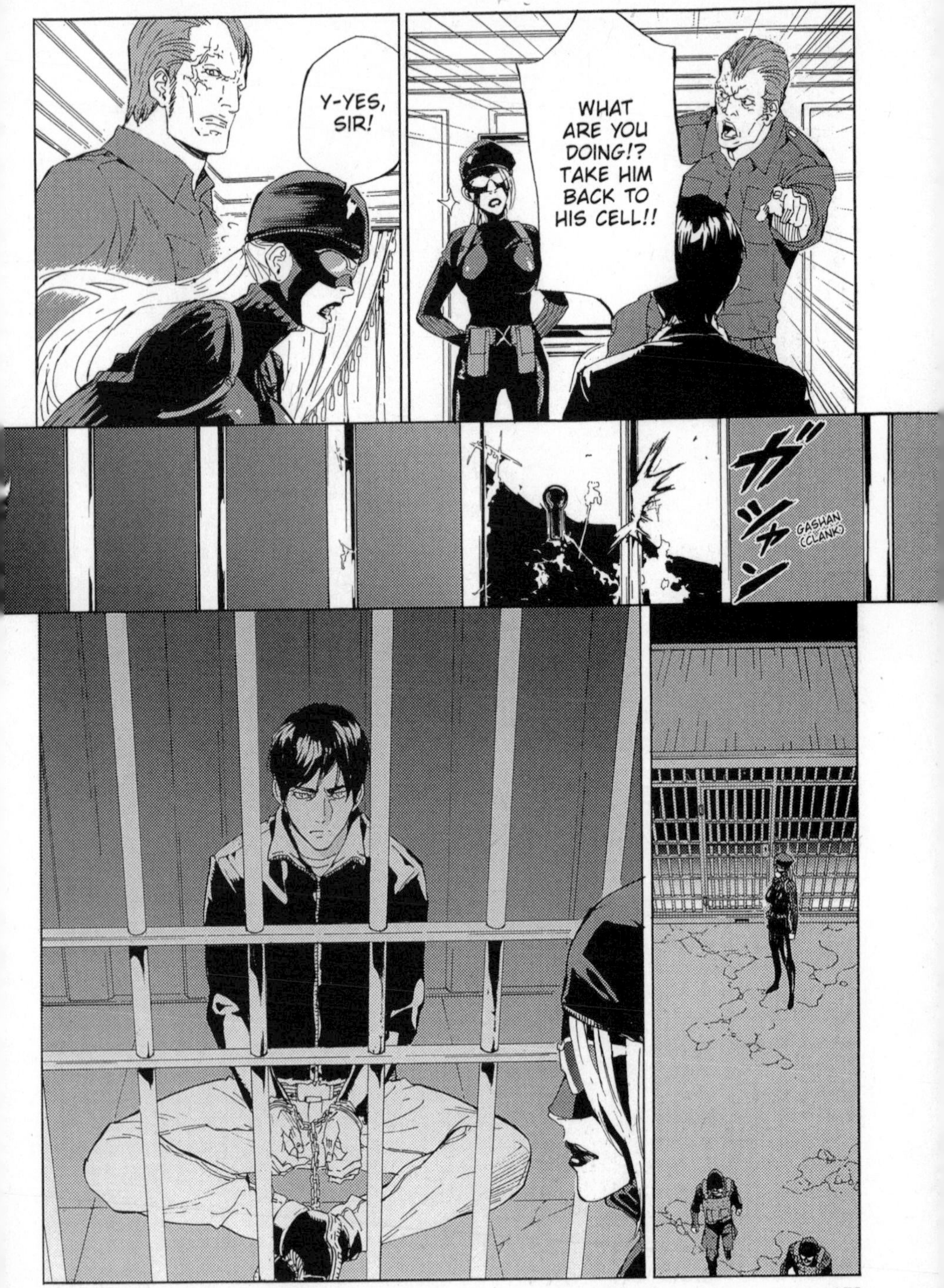
WHAT ARE YOU DOING!? TAKE HIM BACK TO HIS CELL!!
Y-YES, SIR!
ガシャン
GASHAN (CLANK)

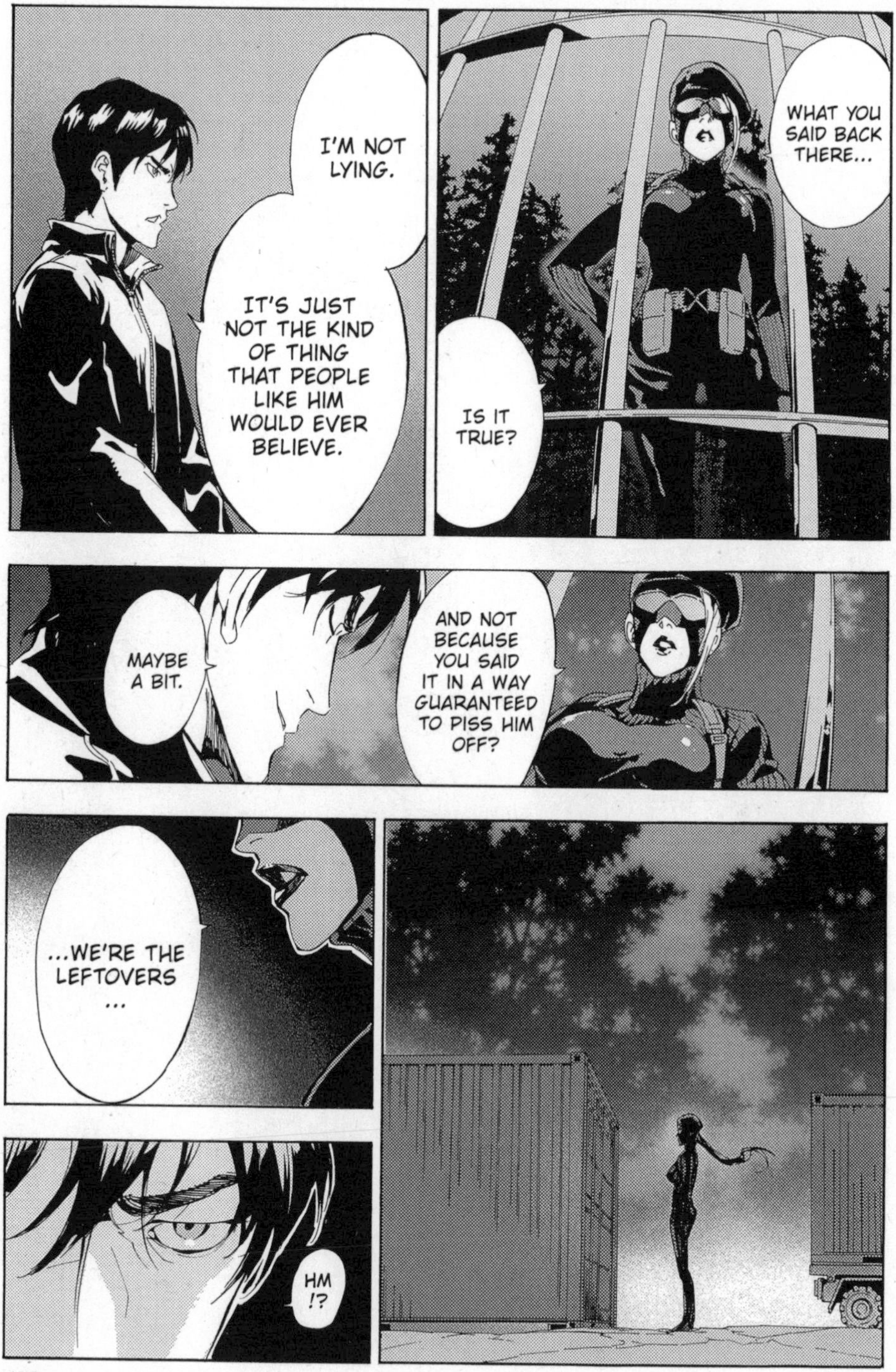
WHAT YOU SAID BACK THERE...
IS IT TRUE?
I'M NOT LYING.
IT'S JUST NOT THE KIND OF THING THAT PEOPLE LIKE HIM WOULD EVER BELIEVE.
AND NOT BECAUSE YOU SAID IT IN A WAY GUARANTEED TO PISS HIM OFF?
MAYBE A BIT.
...WE'RE THE LEFTOVERS ...
HM !?

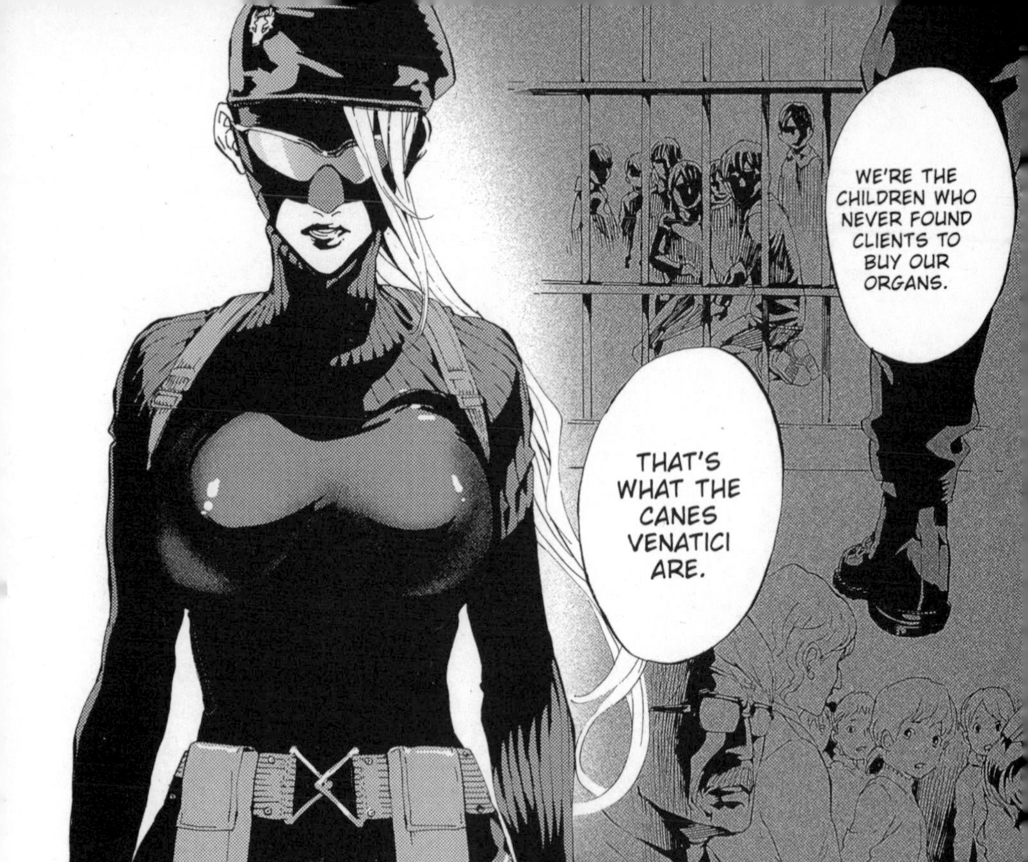
WE'RE THE CHILDREN WHO NEVER FOUND CLIENTS TO BUY OUR ORGANS.
THAT'S WHAT THE CANES VENATICI ARE.
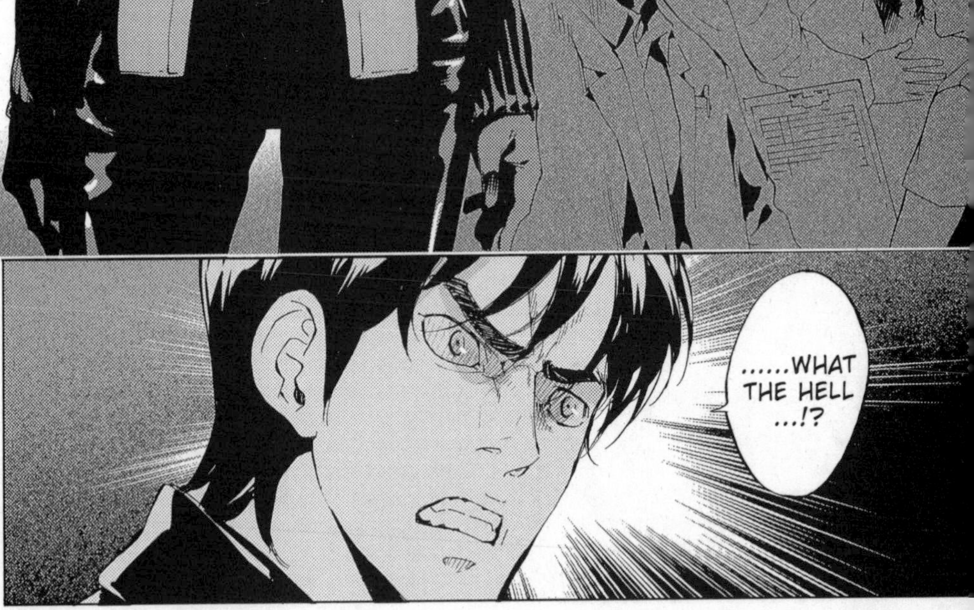
......WHAT THE HELL ...!?

Until Death do us Part

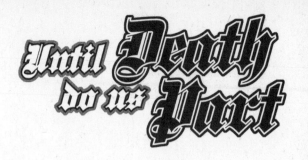

chapter 106

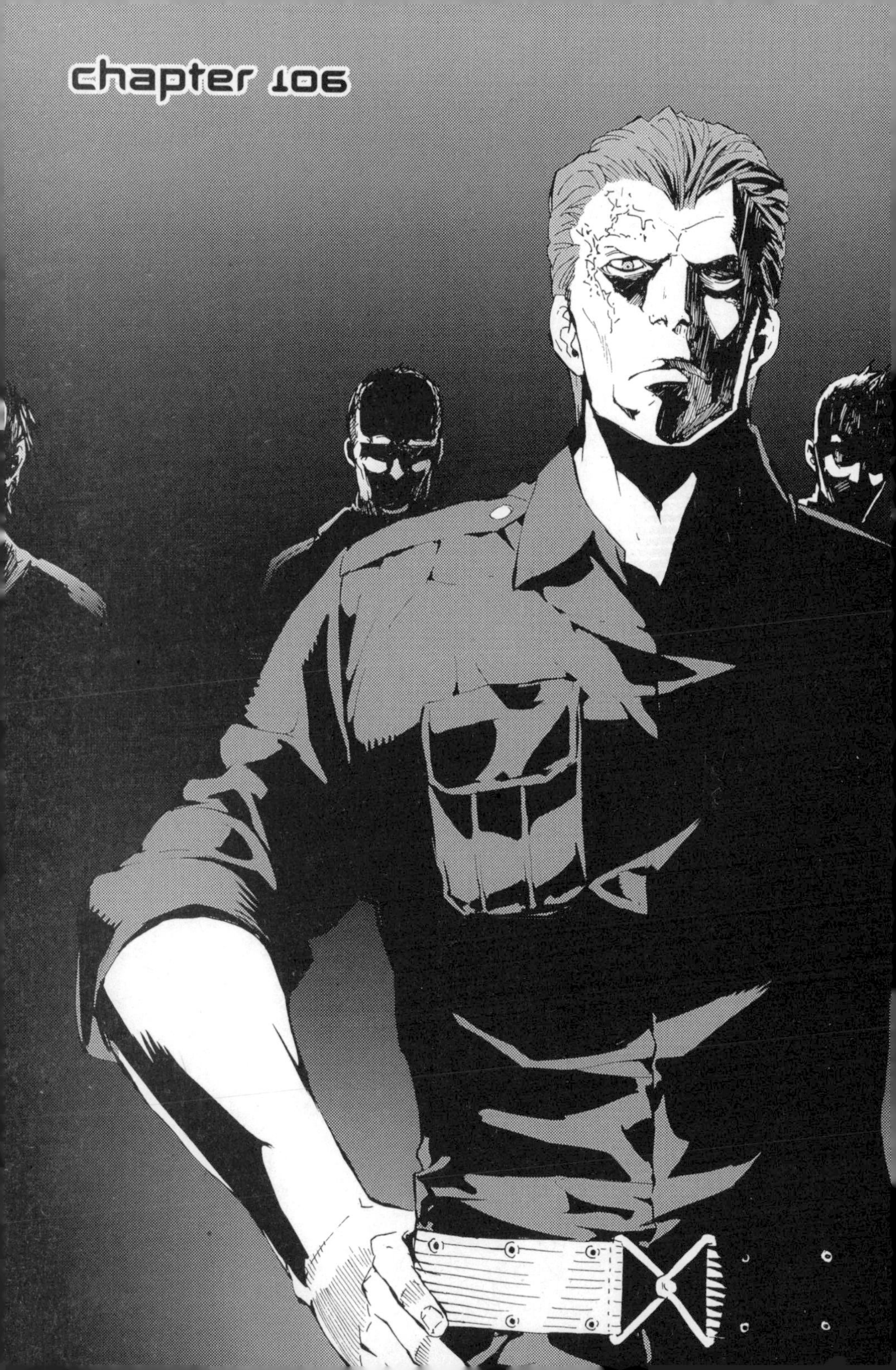

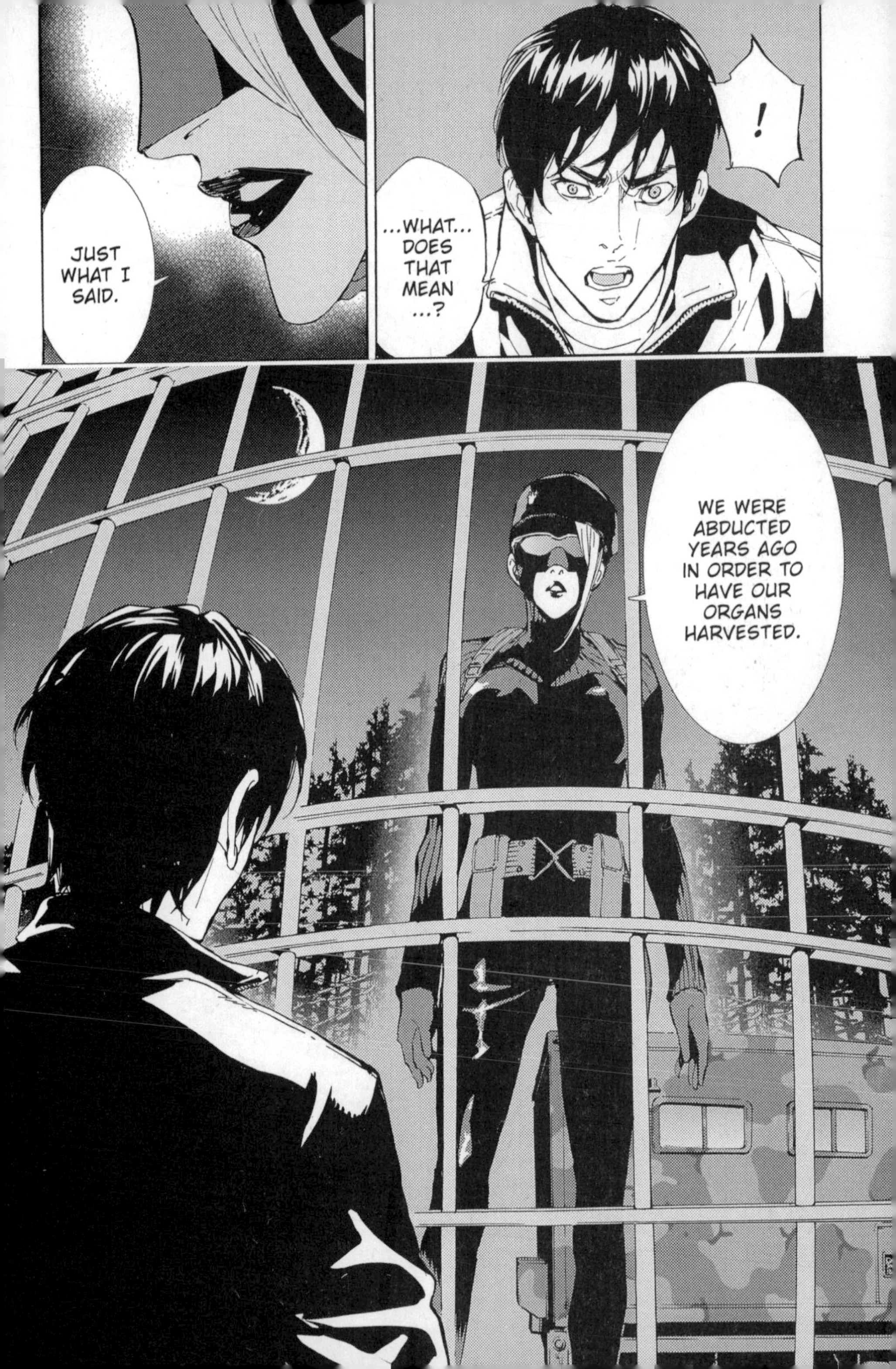
!
...WHAT... DOES THAT MEAN ...?
JUST WHAT I SAID.
WE WERE ABDUCTED YEARS AGO IN ORDER TO HAVE OUR ORGANS HARVESTED.

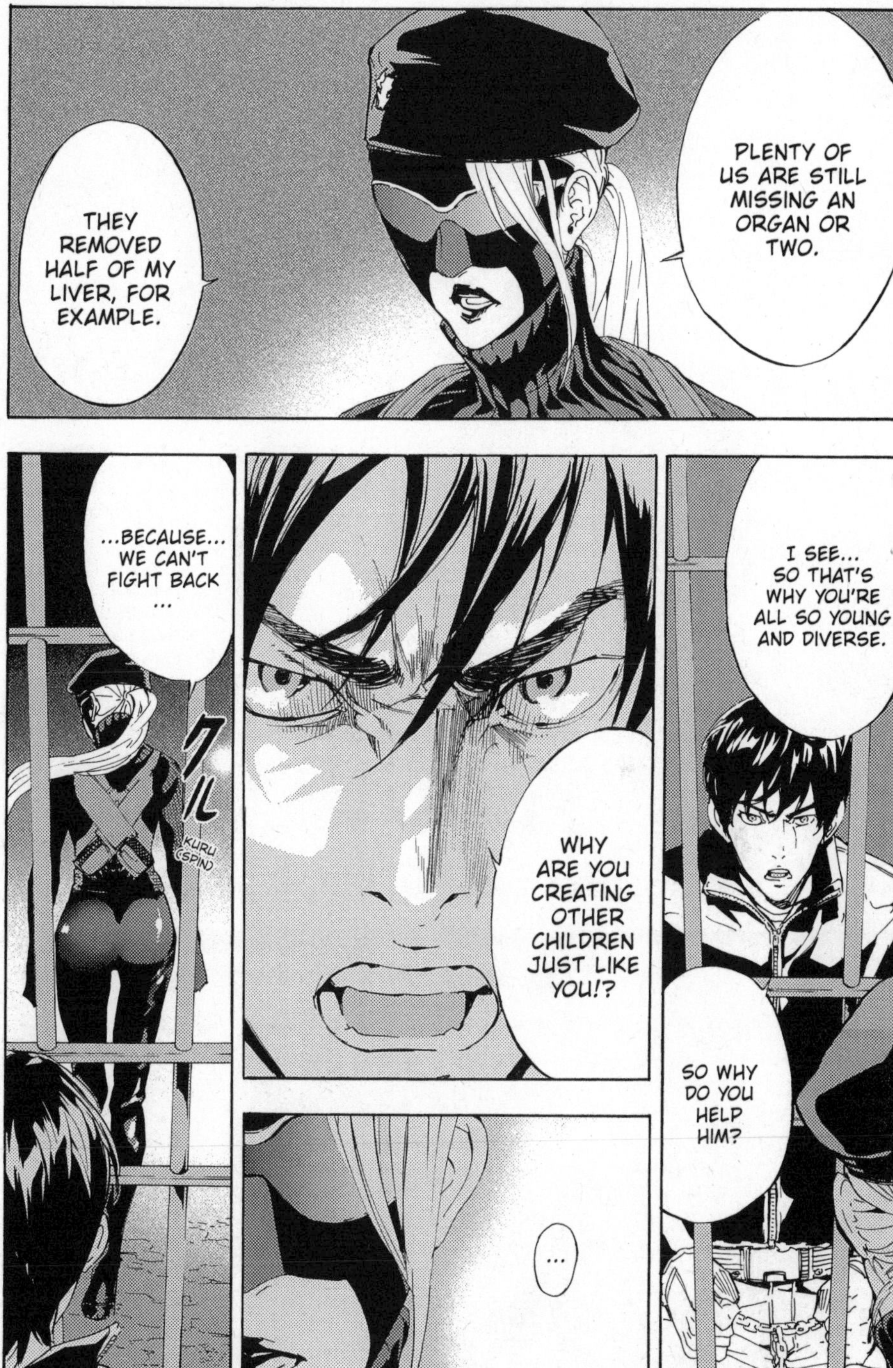
PLENTY OF US ARE STILL MISSING AN ORGAN OR TWO.
THEY REMOVED HALF OF MY LIVER, FOR EXAMPLE.
I SEE... SO THAT'S WHY YOU'RE ALL SO YOUNG AND DIVERSE.
WHY ARE YOU CREATING OTHER CHILDREN JUST LIKE YOU!?
...BECAUSE... WE CAN'T FIGHT BACK ...
クル
KURU (SPIN)
SO WHY DO YOU HELP HIM?
...

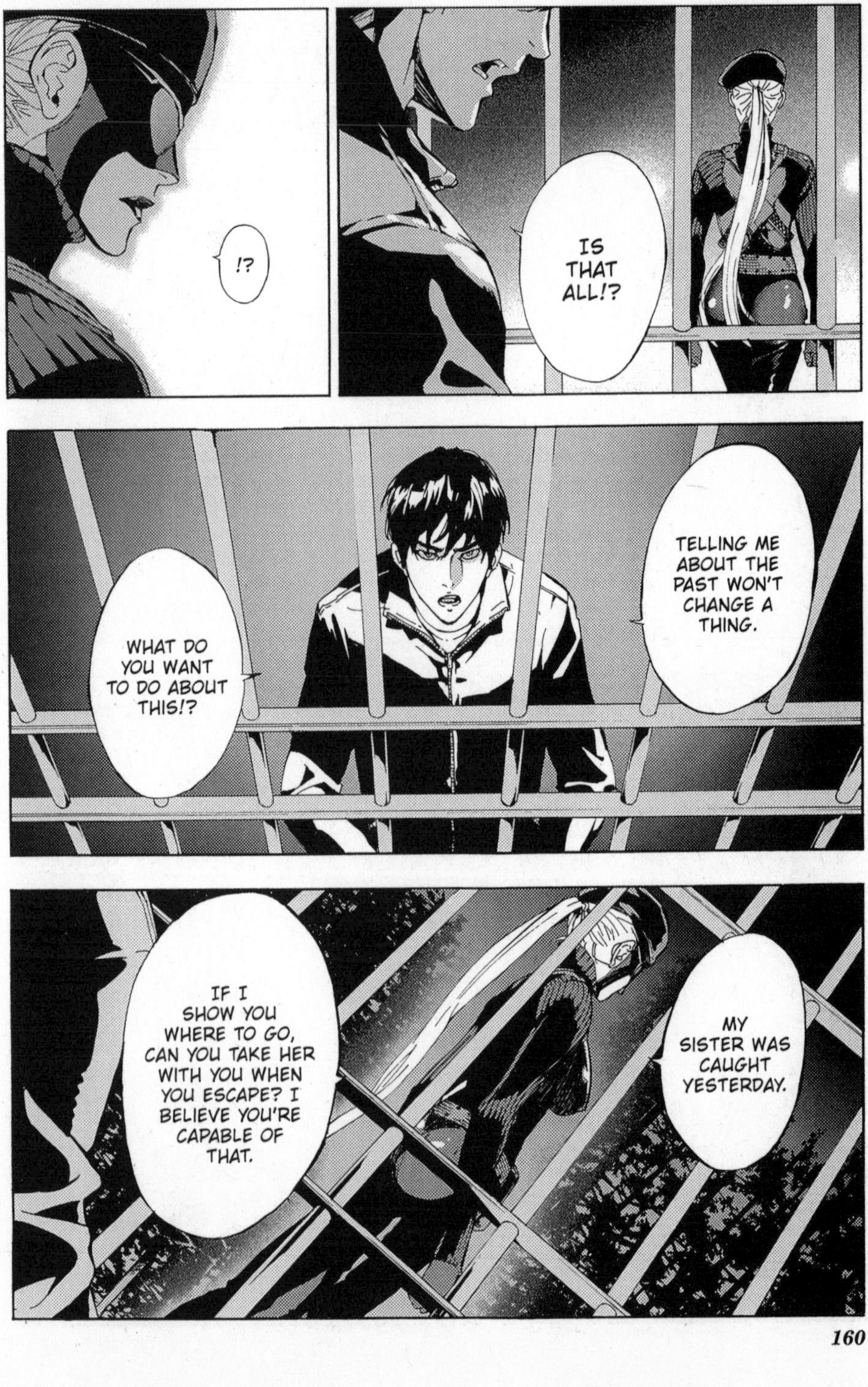
IS THAT ALL!?
!?
TELLING ME ABOUT THE PAST WON'T CHANGE A THING.
WHAT DO YOU WANT TO DO ABOUT THIS!?
MY SISTER WAS CAUGHT YESTERDAY.
IF I SHOW YOU WHERE TO GO, CAN YOU TAKE HER WITH YOU WHEN YOU ESCAPE? I BELIEVE YOU'RE CAPABLE OF THAT.

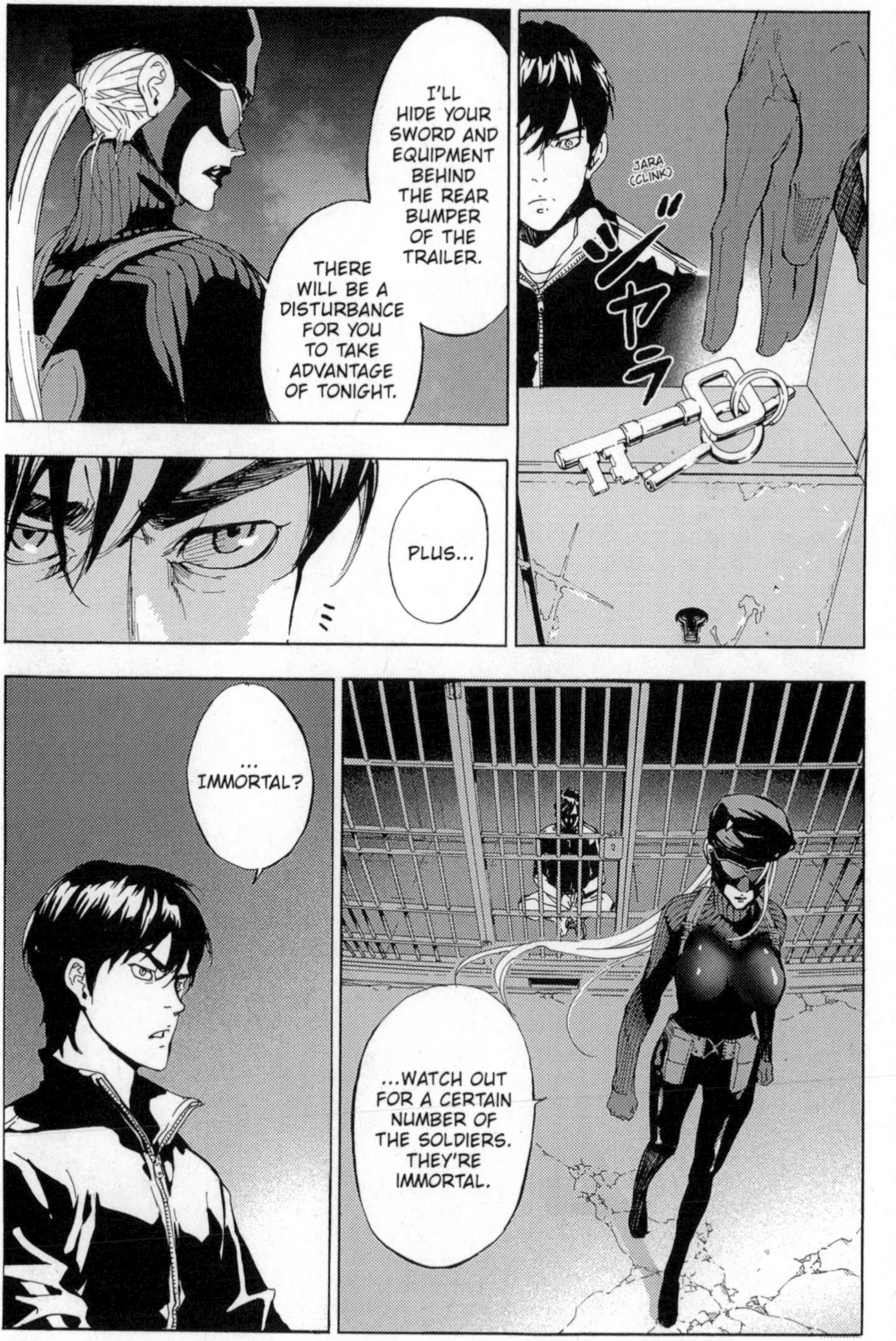
JARA (CLINK)
ジャラ
I'LL HIDE YOUR SWORD AND EQUIPMENT BEHIND THE REAR BUMPER OF THE TRAILER.
THERE WILL BE A DISTURBANCE FOR YOU TO TAKE ADVANTAGE OF TONIGHT.
PLUS...
...WATCH OUT FOR A CERTAIN NUMBER OF THE SOLDIERS. THEY'RE IMMORTAL.
...IMMORTAL?

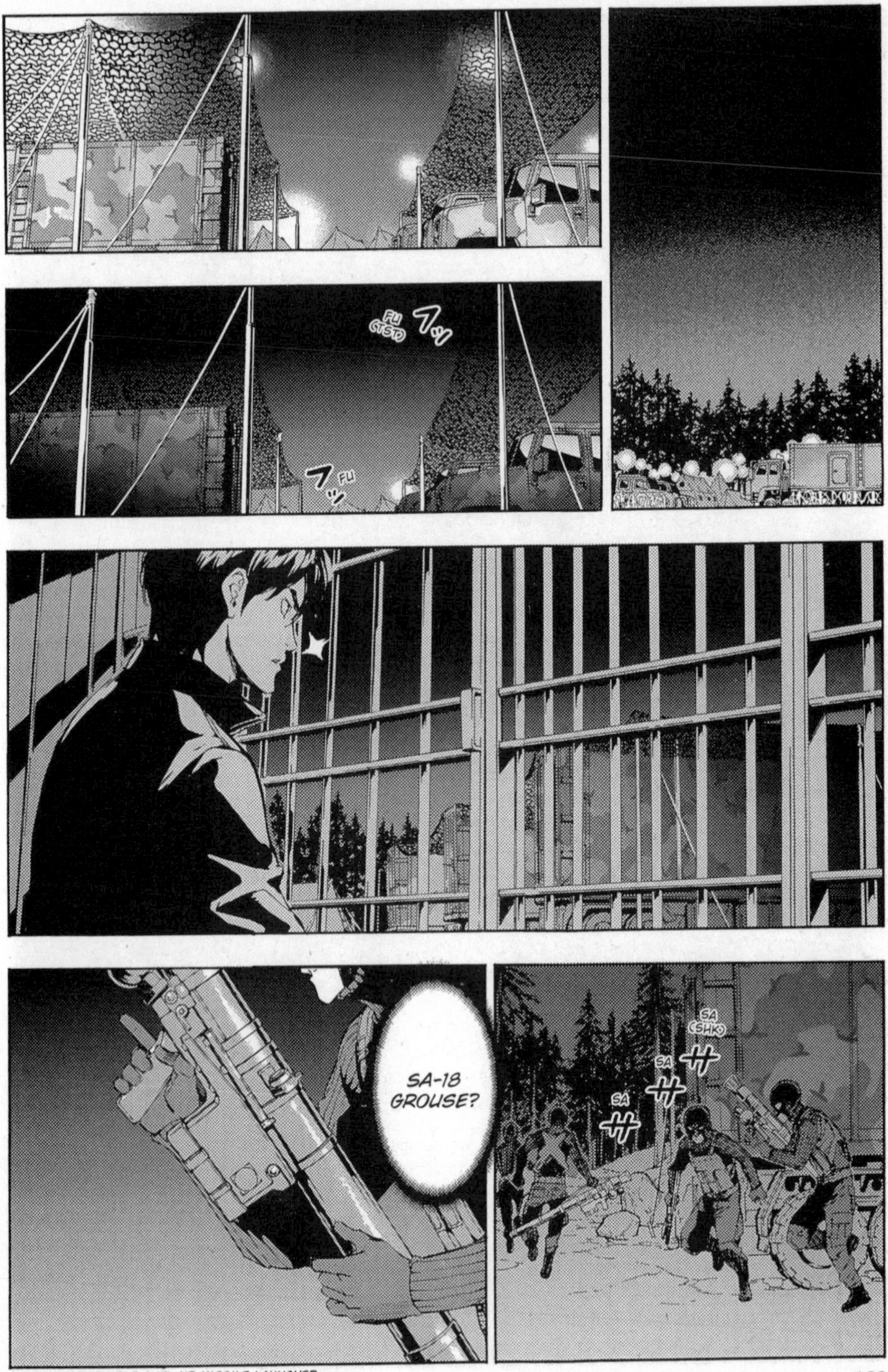
FU (TST)
フッ
フッ
FU
SA (SHK)
サ
SA
サ
SA
サ
SA-18 GROUSE?

SA-18: A PORTABLE ANTI-AIR MISSILE LAUNCHER.

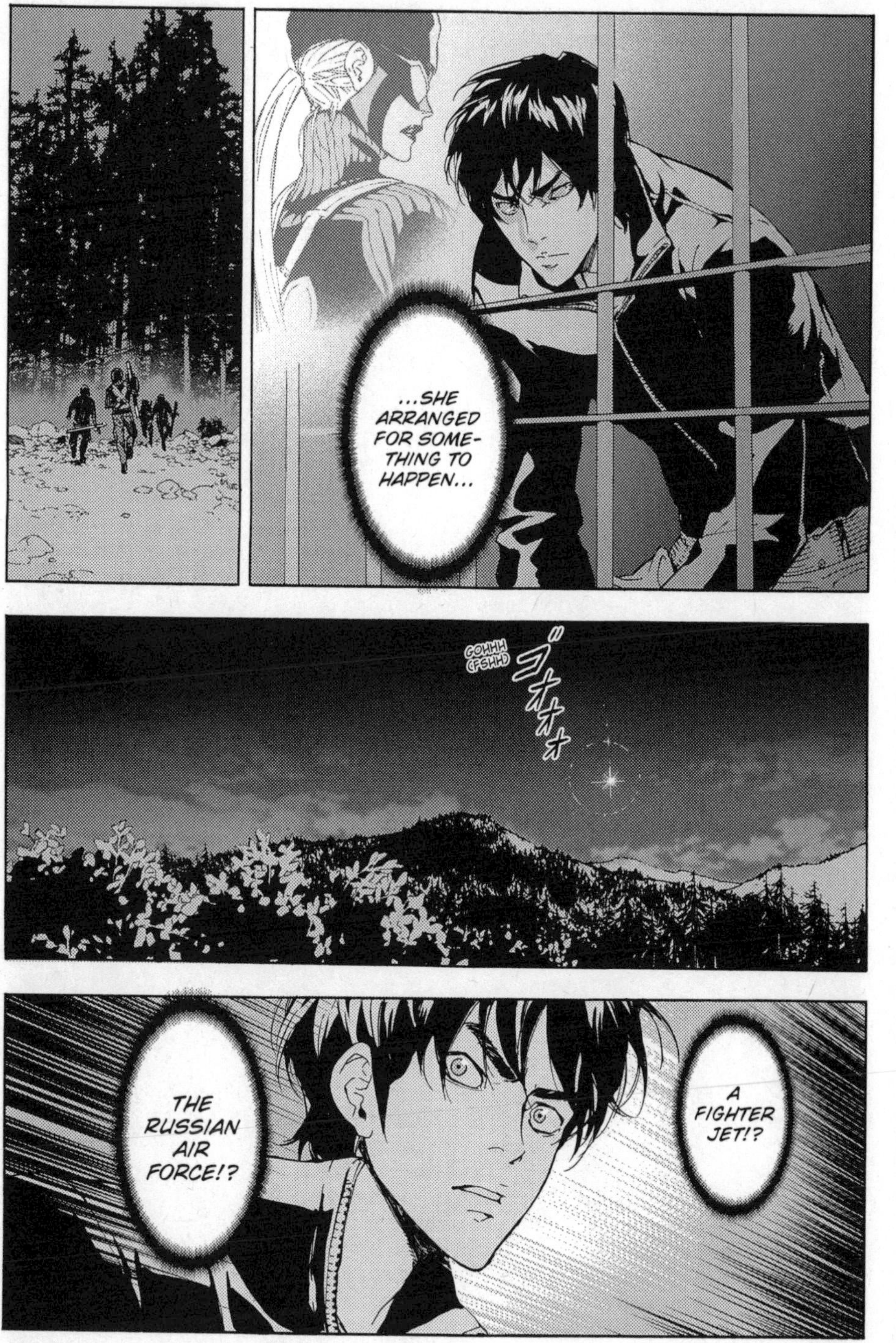
...SHE ARRANGED FOR SOME-THING TO HAPPEN...
GOHHH (FSHH)
A FIGHTER JET!?
THE RUSSIAN AIR FORCE!?

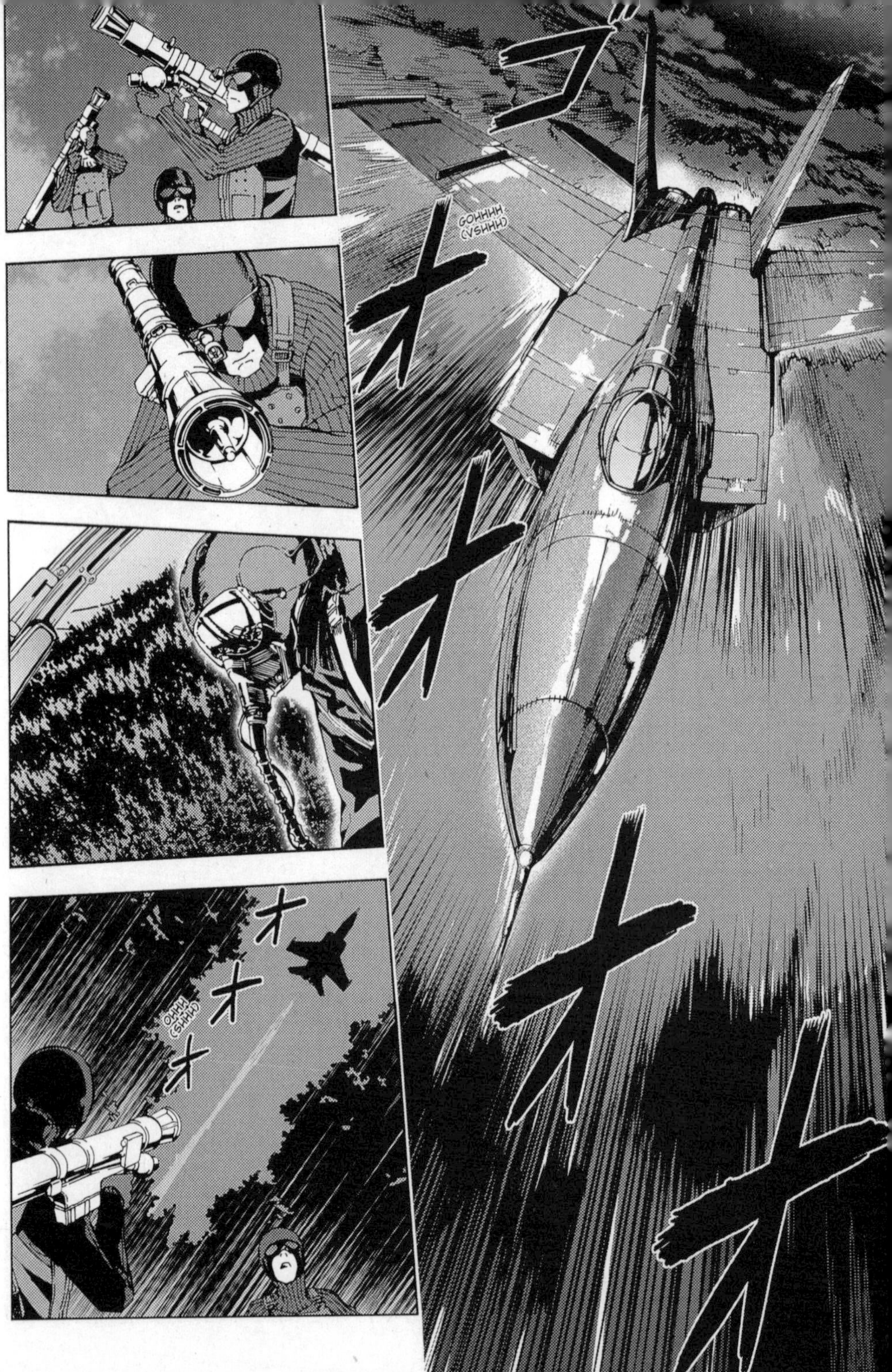
GOHHHH (VSHHH)
OHHH (SHHH)

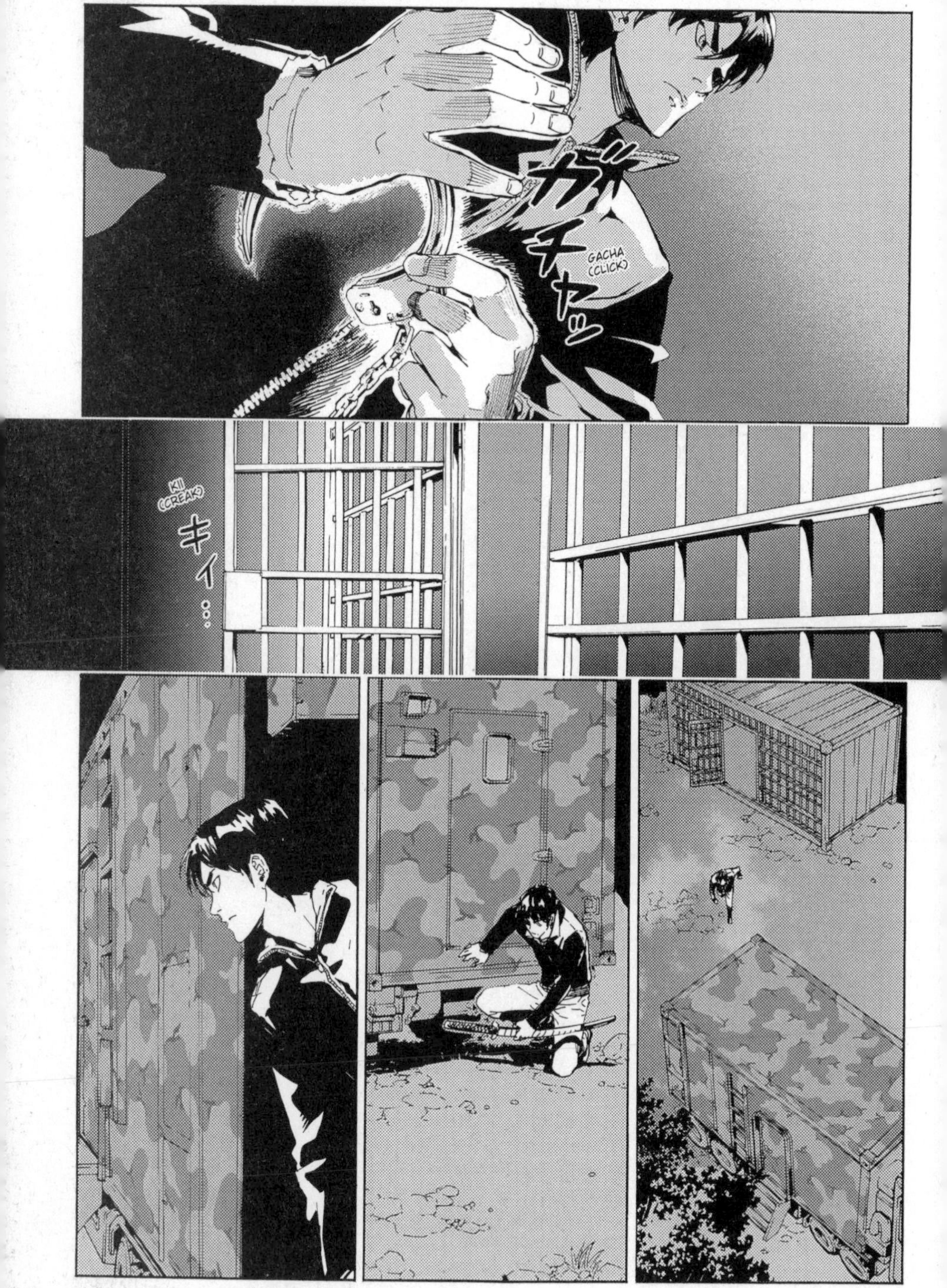
ガチャッ
GACHA (CLICK)
KII (CREAK)
キイ…

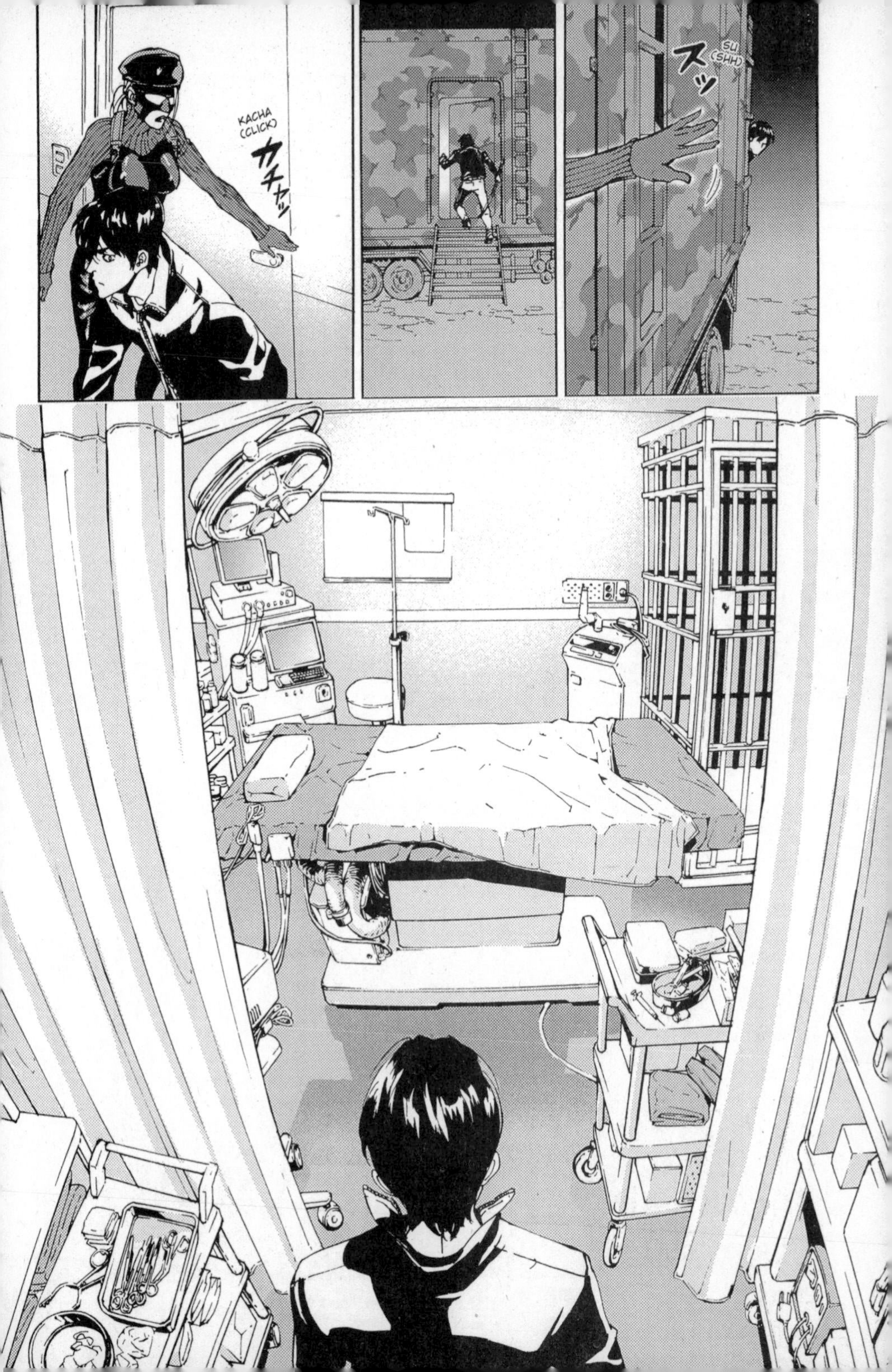
SU (SHH)
スッ
KACHA (CLICK)
カチャッ

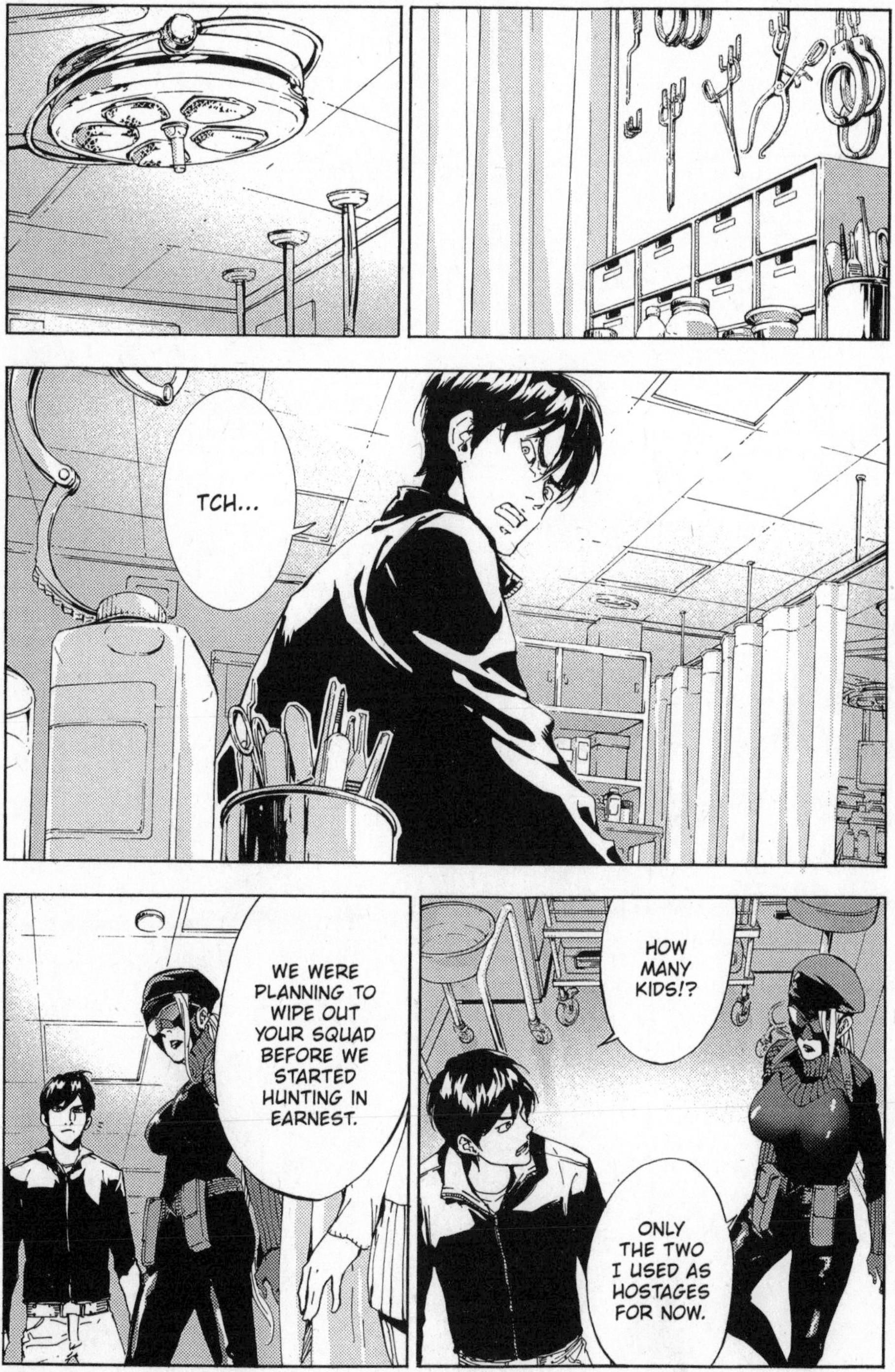
TCH...
HOW MANY KIDS!?
ONLY THE TWO I USED AS HOSTAGES FOR NOW.
WE WERE PLANNING TO WIPE OUT YOUR SQUAD BEFORE WE STARTED HUNTING IN EARNEST.

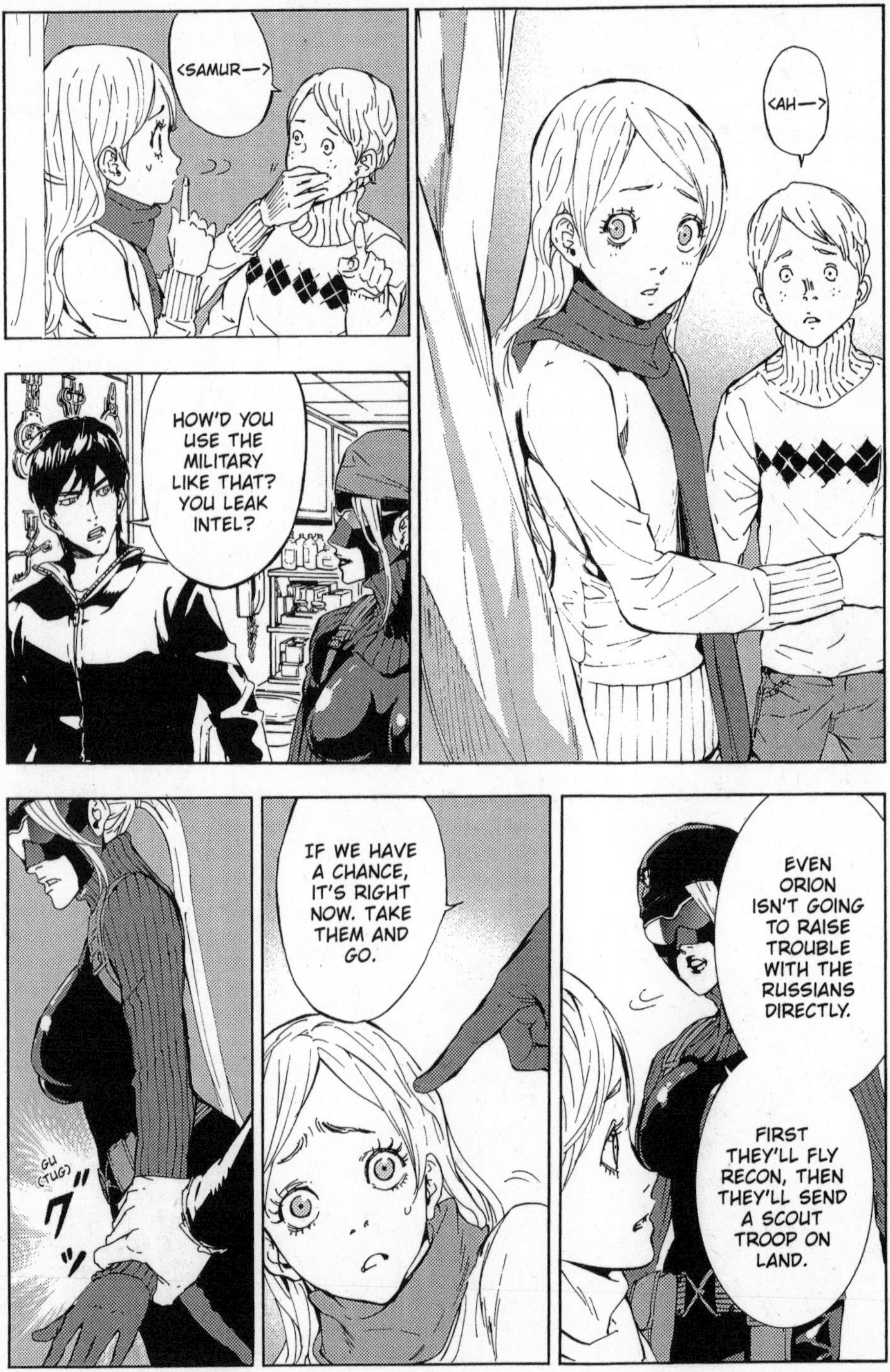
<AH—>
<SAMUR—>
HOW'D YOU USE THE MILITARY LIKE THAT? YOU LEAK INTEL?
EVEN ORION ISN'T GOING TO RAISE TROUBLE WITH THE RUSSIANS DIRECTLY.
FIRST THEY'LL FLY RECON, THEN THEY'LL SEND A SCOUT TROOP ON LAND.
IF WE HAVE A CHANCE, IT'S RIGHT NOW. TAKE THEM AND GO.
GU (TUG)

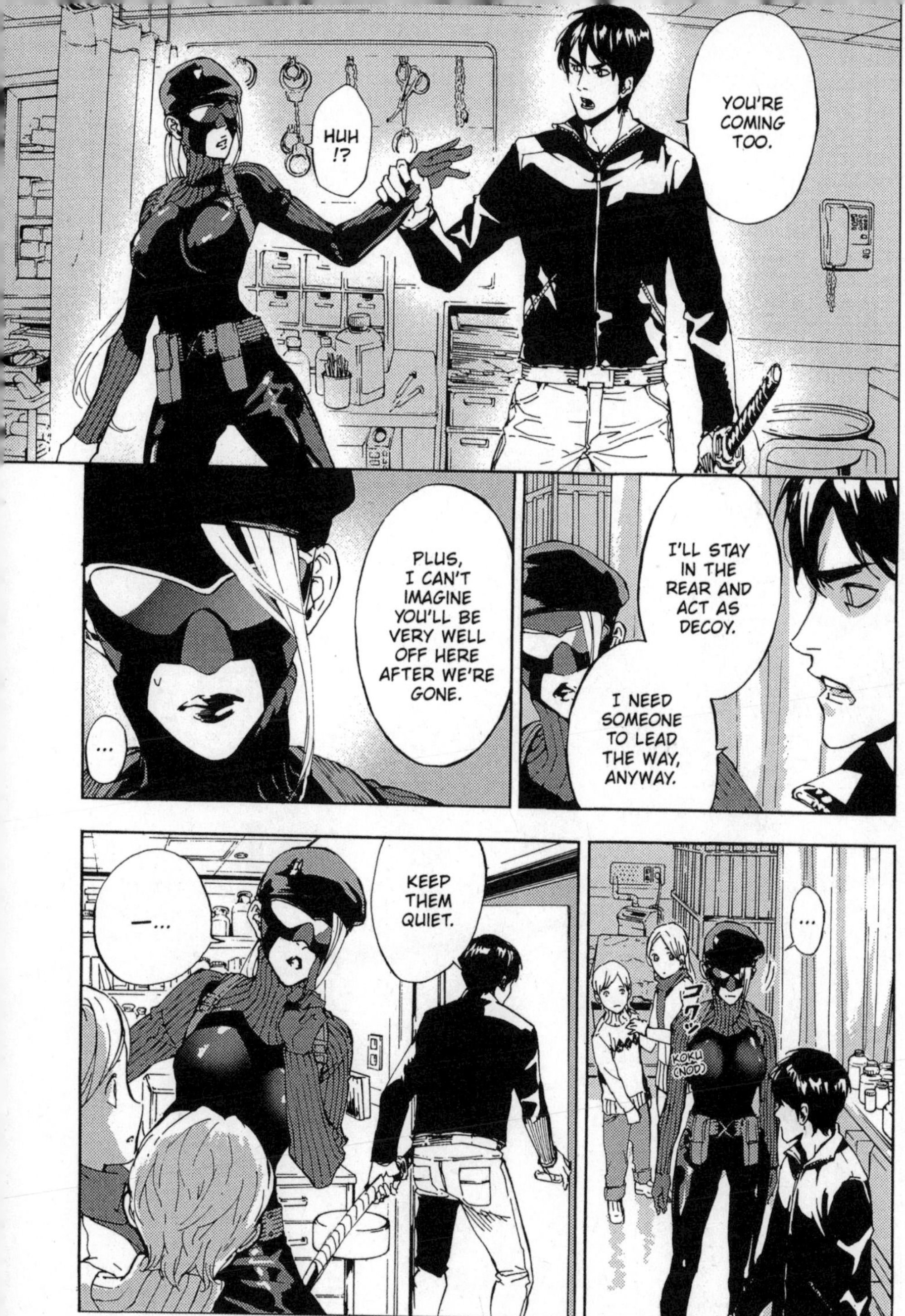
YOU'RE COMING TOO.
HUH !?
I'LL STAY IN THE REAR AND ACT AS DECOY.
I NEED SOMEONE TO LEAD THE WAY, ANYWAY.
PLUS, I CAN'T IMAGINE YOU'LL BE VERY WELL OFF HERE AFTER WE'RE GONE.
...
...
KOKU (NOD)
KEEP THEM QUIET.
—...

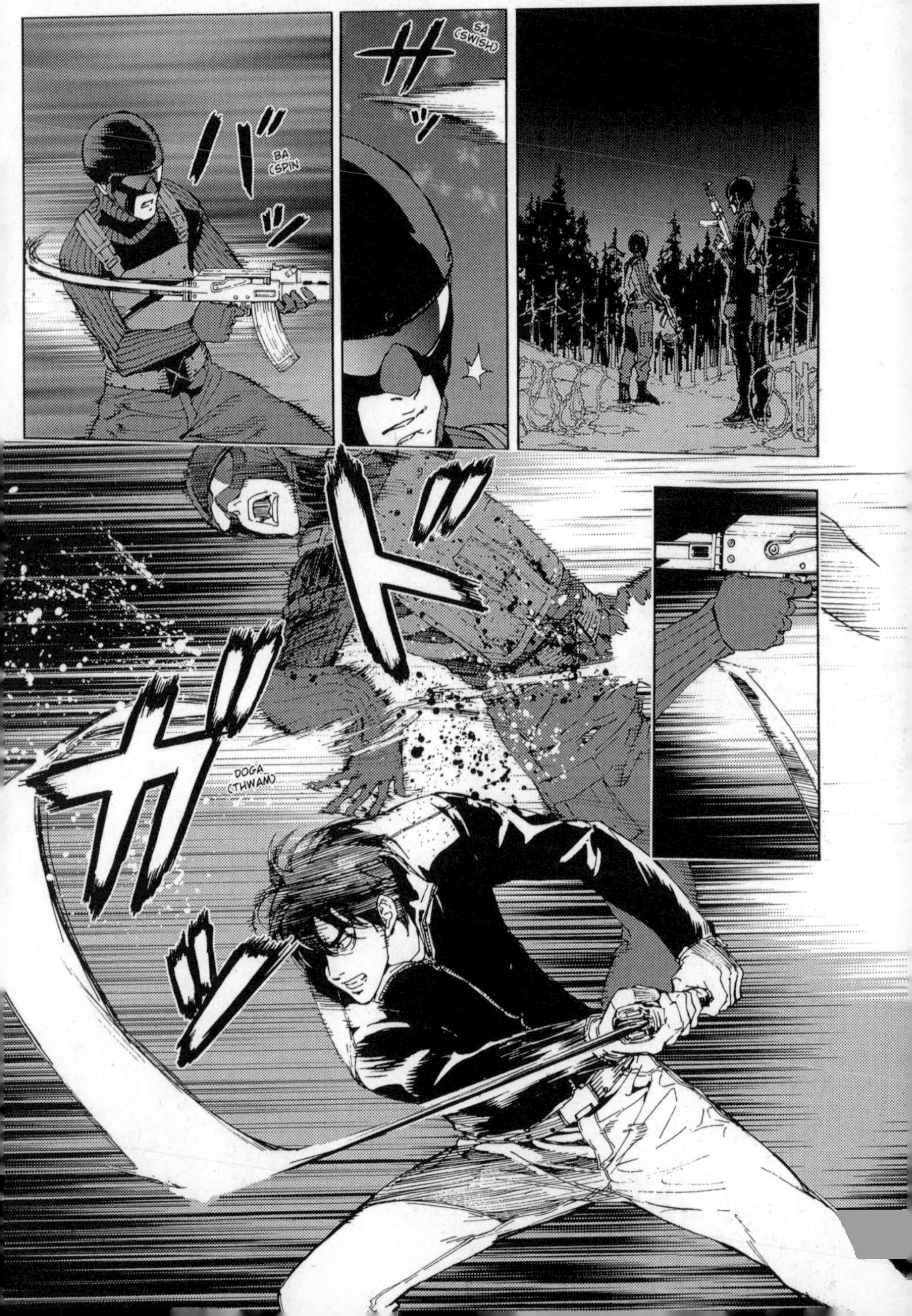
SA (SWISH)
BA (SPIN
DOGA (THWAM)

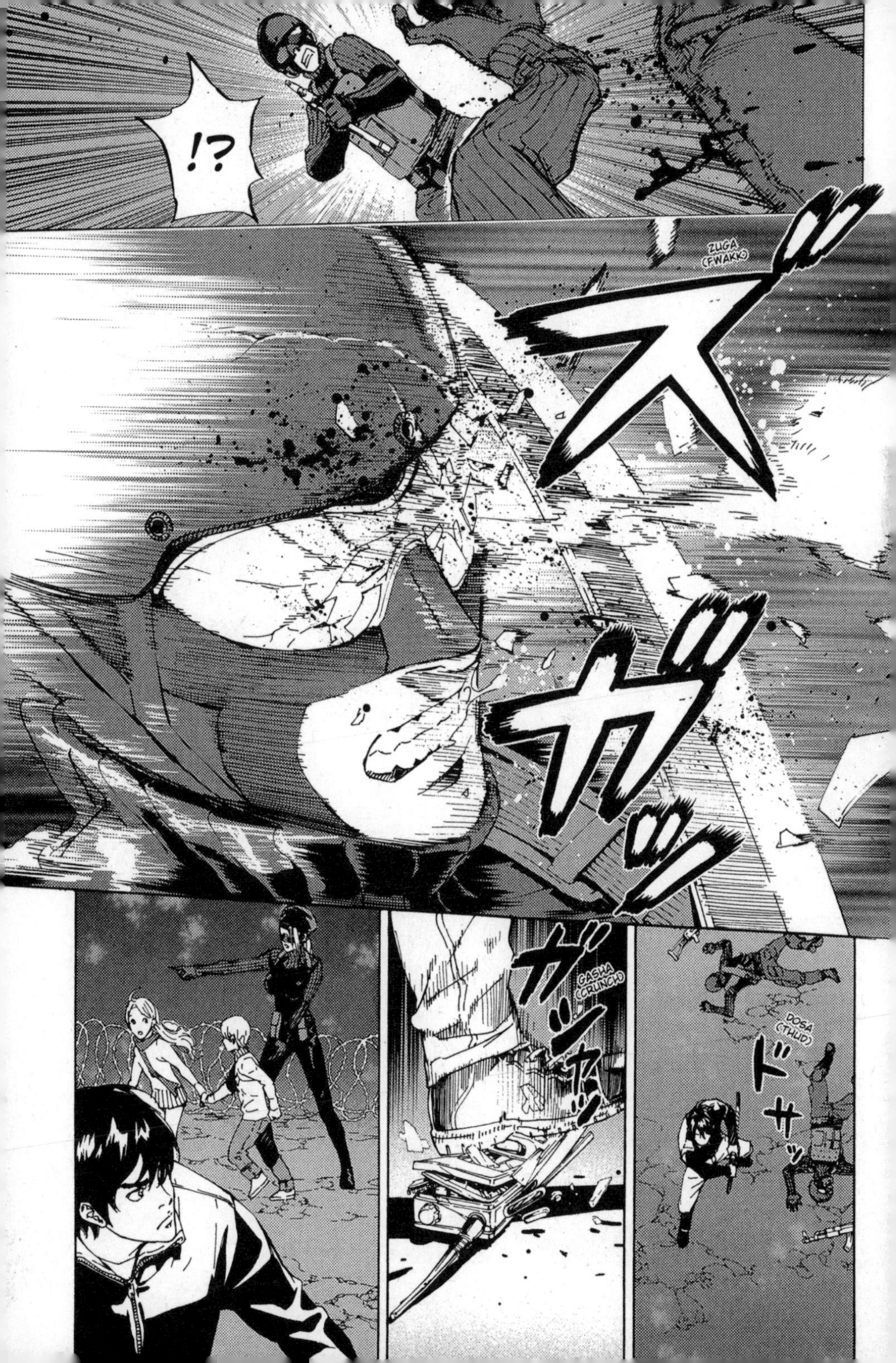
!?
ZUGA (FWAKK)
ズガッ
DOSA (THUD)
ドサッ
GASHA (CRUNCH)
ガシャッ

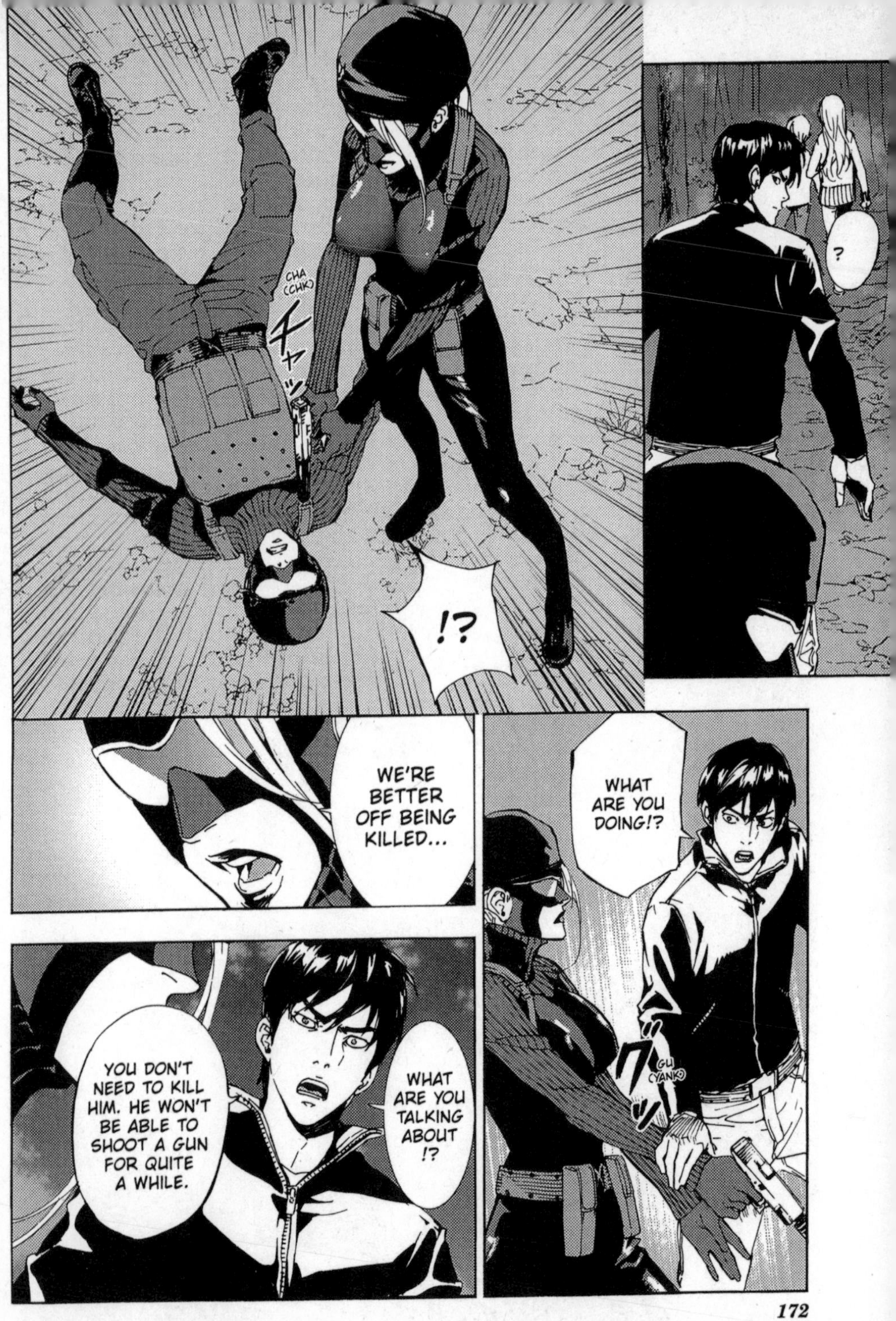
?
CHA (CHK)
!?
WHAT ARE YOU DOING!?
GU (YANK)
WE'RE BETTER OFF BEING KILLED...
WHAT ARE YOU TALKING ABOUT !?
YOU DON'T NEED TO KILL HIM. HE WON'T BE ABLE TO SHOOT A GUN FOR QUITE A WHILE.

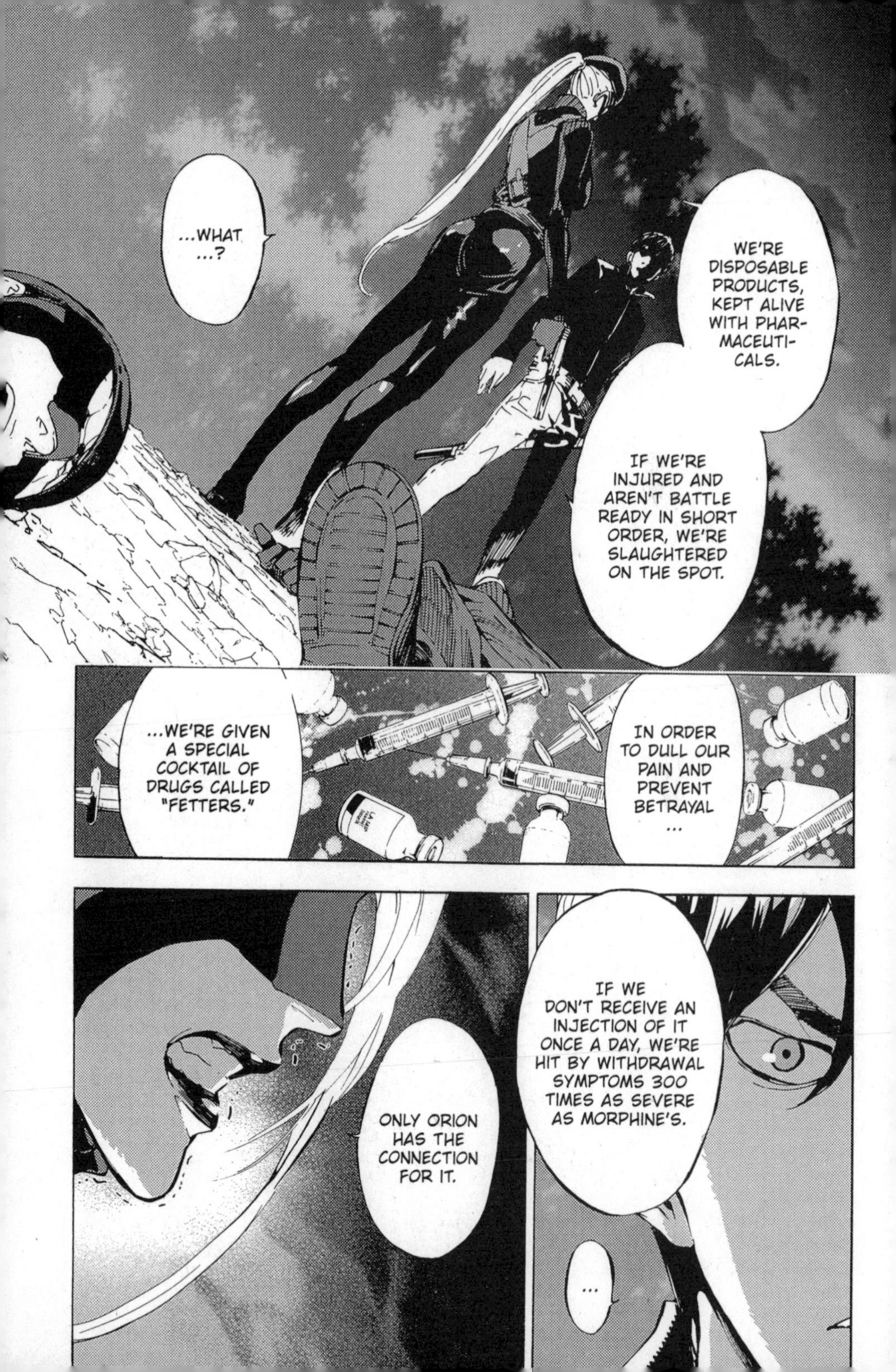

WE'RE DISPOSABLE PRODUCTS, KEPT ALIVE WITH PHARMACEUTICALS.
...WHAT ...?
IF WE'RE INJURED AND AREN'T BATTLE READY IN SHORT ORDER, WE'RE SLAUGHTERED ON THE SPOT.
IN ORDER TO DULL OUR PAIN AND PREVENT BETRAYAL ...
...WE'RE GIVEN A SPECIAL COCKTAIL OF DRUGS CALLED "FETTERS."
IF WE DON'T RECEIVE AN INJECTION OF IT ONCE A DAY, WE'RE HIT BY WITHDRAWAL SYMPTOMS 300 TIMES AS SEVERE AS MORPHINE'S.
...
ONLY ORION HAS THE CONNECTION FOR IT.

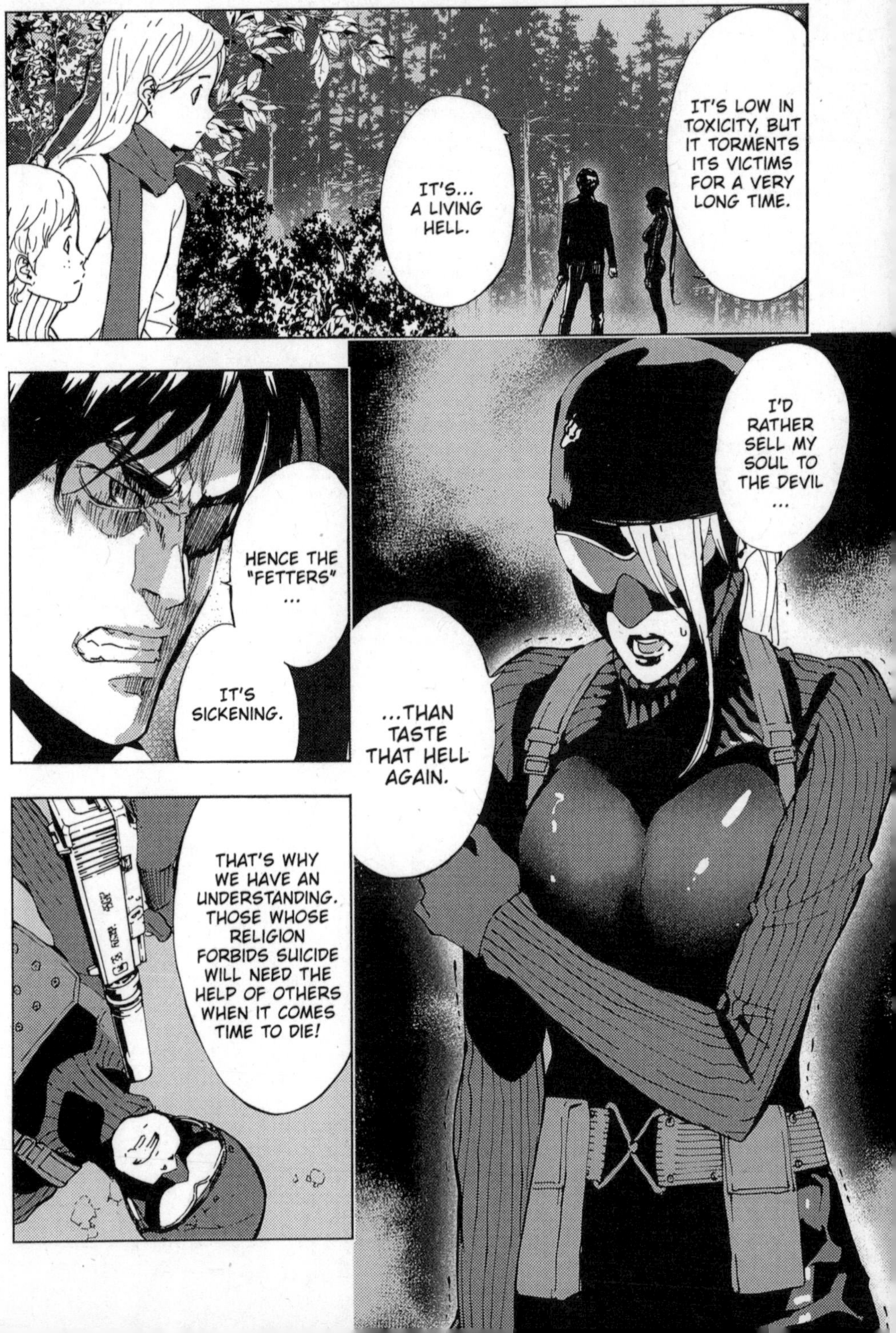
IT'S LOW IN TOXICITY, BUT IT TORMENTS ITS VICTIMS FOR A VERY LONG TIME.
IT'S... A LIVING HELL.
I'D RATHER SELL MY SOUL TO THE DEVIL ...
...THAN TASTE THAT HELL AGAIN.
HENCE THE "FETTERS" ...
IT'S SICKENING.
THAT'S WHY WE HAVE AN UNDERSTANDING. THOSE WHOSE RELIGION FORBIDS SUICIDE WILL NEED THE HELP OF OTHERS WHEN IT COMES TIME TO DIE!

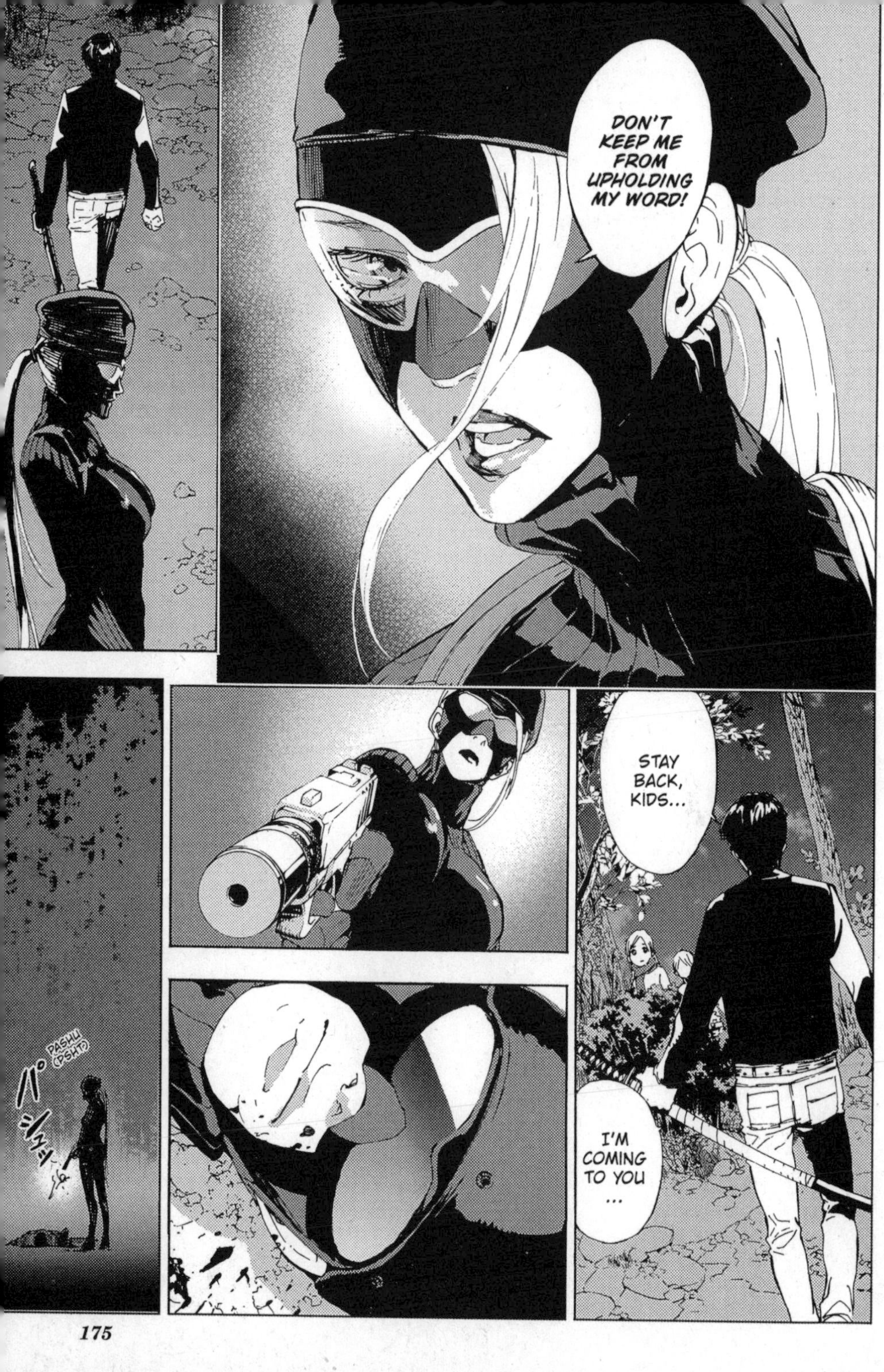
DON'T KEEP ME FROM UPHOLDING MY WORD!
STAY BACK, KIDS...
I'M COMING TO YOU ...
PASHU (PSHT)

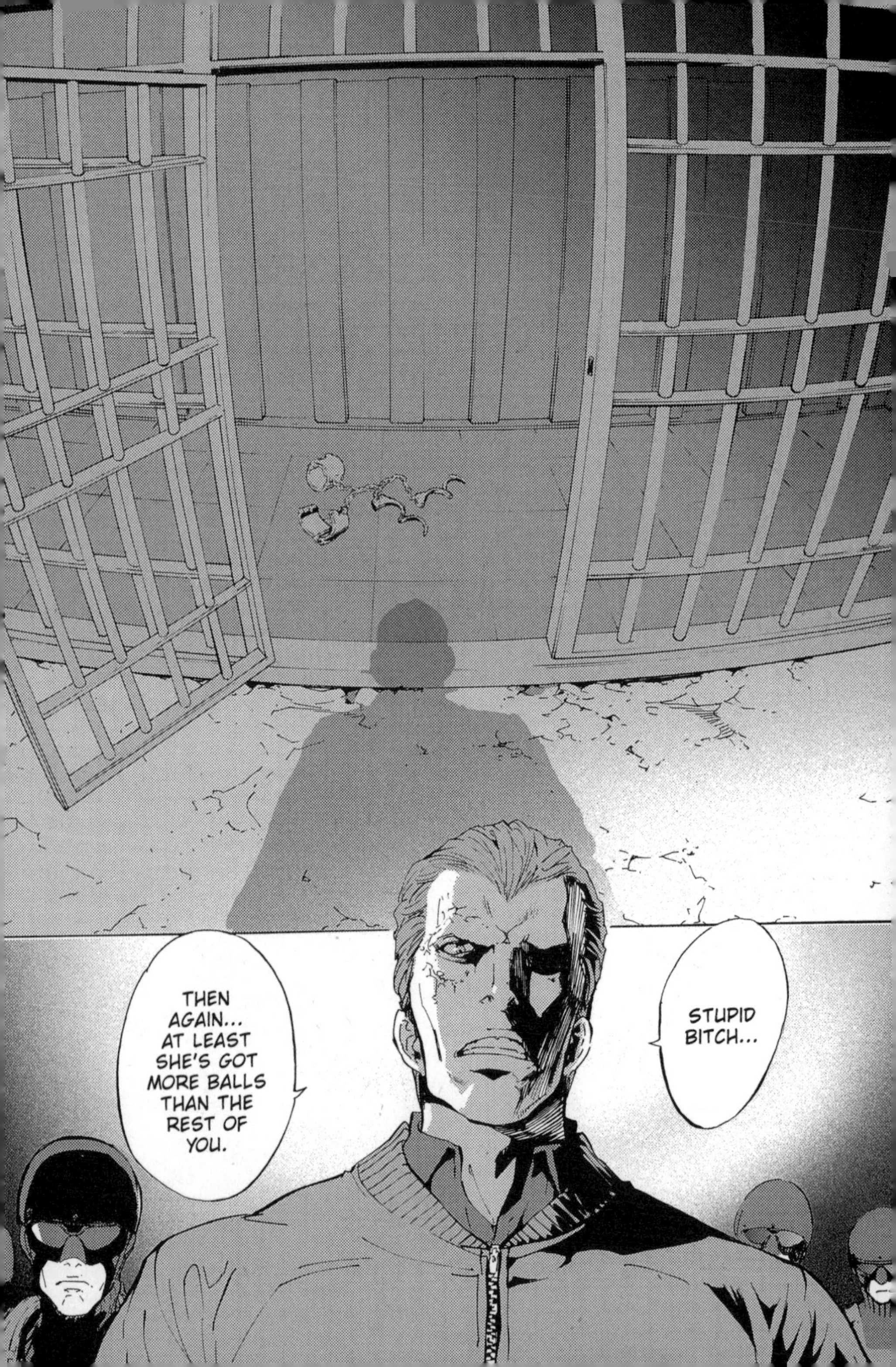
STUPID BITCH...
THEN AGAIN... AT LEAST SHE'S GOT MORE BALLS THAN THE REST OF YOU.

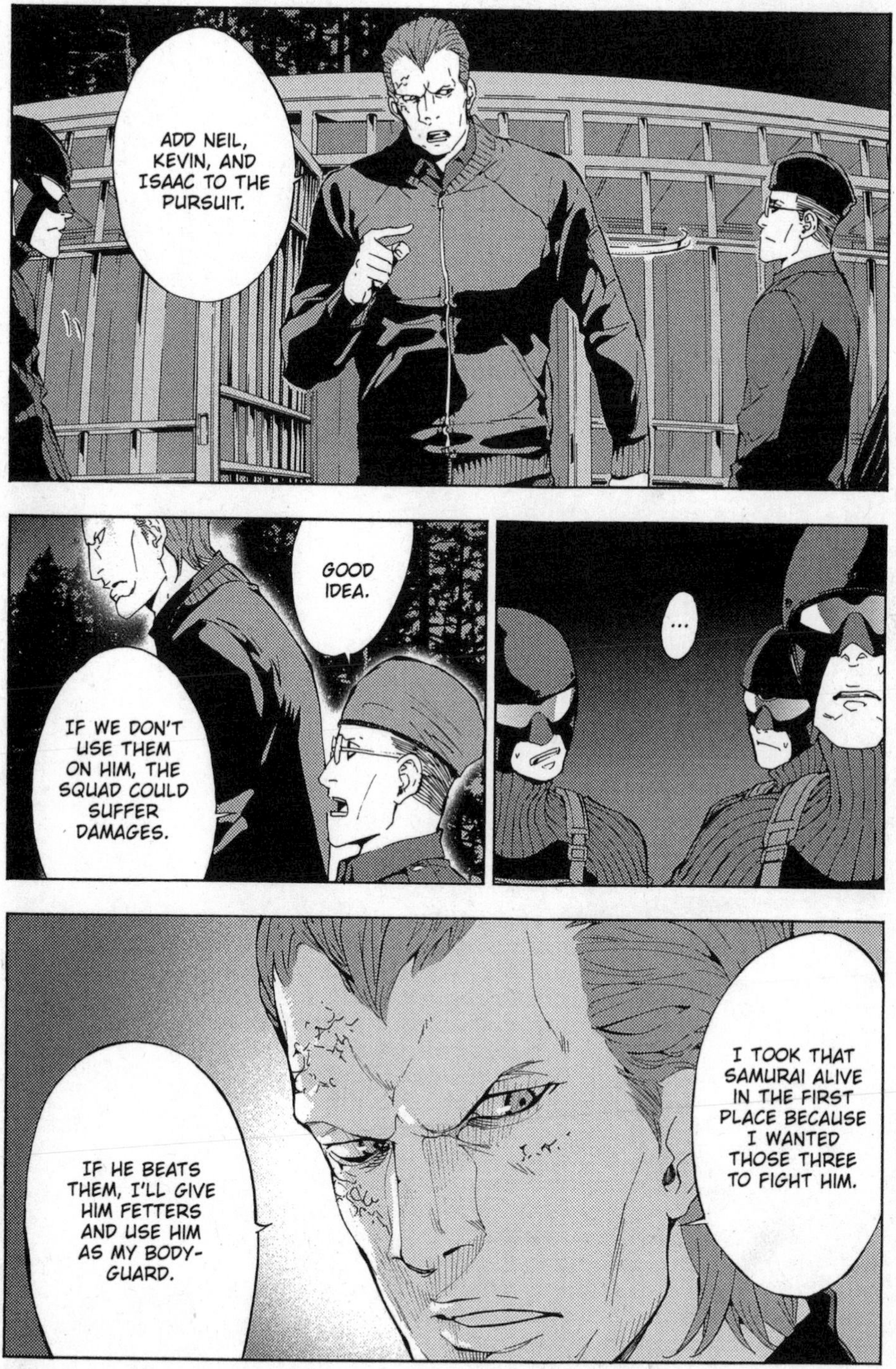
ADD NEIL, KEVIN, AND ISAAC TO THE PURSUIT.
...
GOOD IDEA.
IF WE DON'T USE THEM ON HIM, THE SQUAD COULD SUFFER DAMAGES.
I TOOK THAT SAMURAI ALIVE IN THE FIRST PLACE BECAUSE I WANTED THOSE THREE TO FIGHT HIM.
IF HE BEATS THEM, I'LL GIVE HIM FETTERS AND USE HIM AS MY BODY-GUARD.

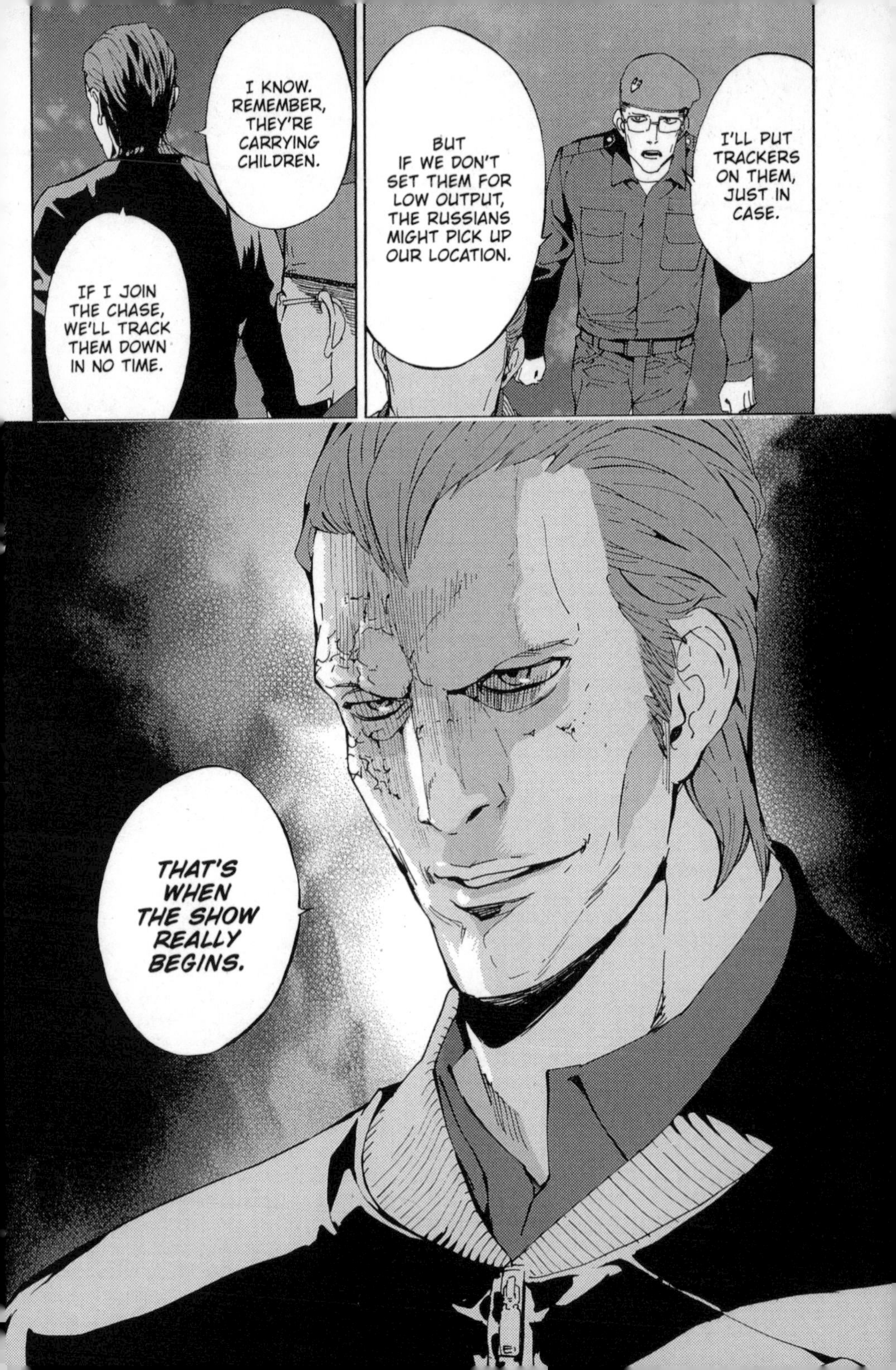
I'LL PUT TRACKERS ON THEM, JUST IN CASE.
BUT IF WE DON'T SET THEM FOR LOW OUTPUT, THE RUSSIANS MIGHT PICK UP OUR LOCATION.
I KNOW. REMEMBER, THEY'RE CARRYING CHILDREN.
IF I JOIN THE CHASE, WE'LL TRACK THEM DOWN IN NO TIME.
THAT'S WHEN THE SHOW REALLY BEGINS.

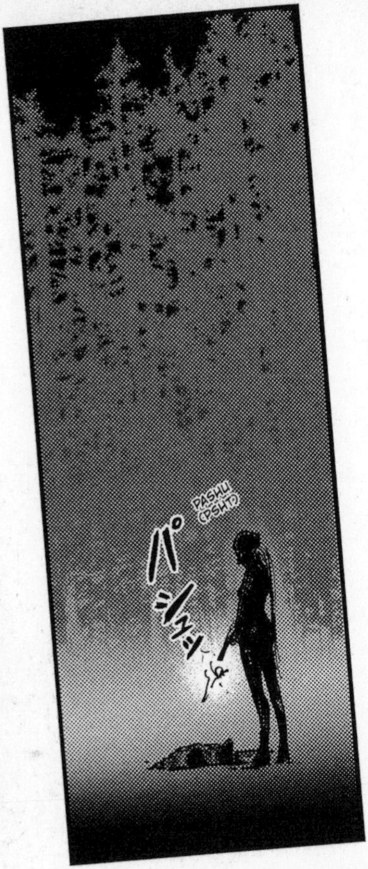

パシュッ
PASHU (PSHT)

Until Death do us Part

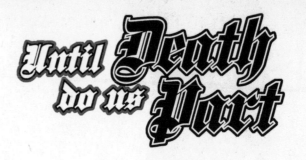

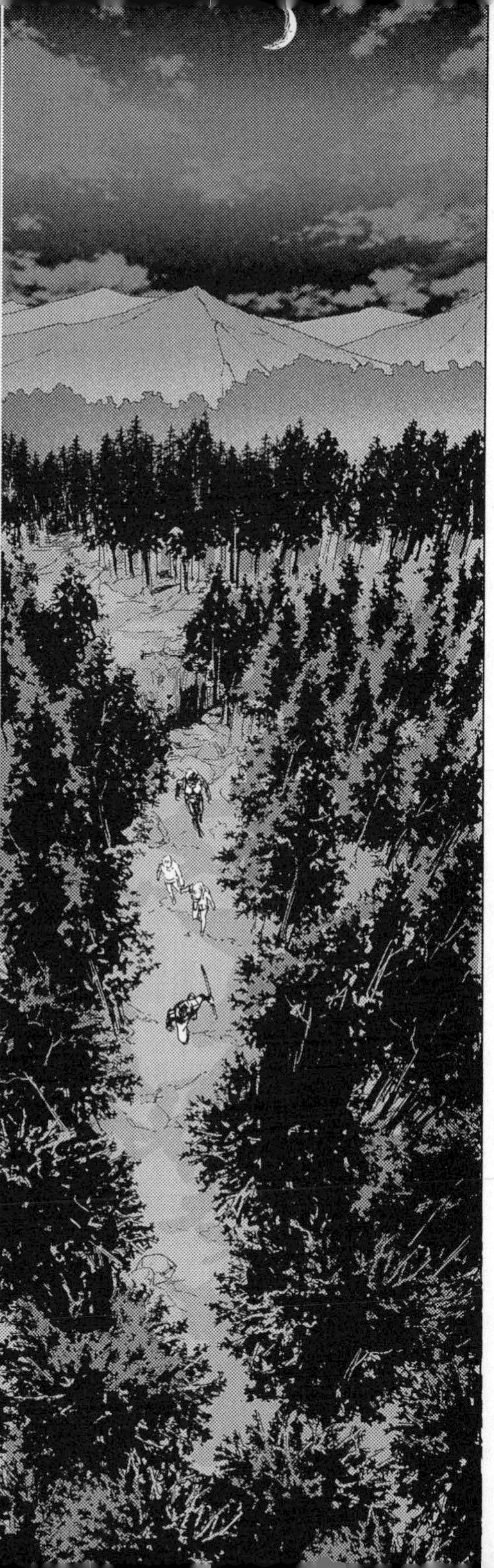

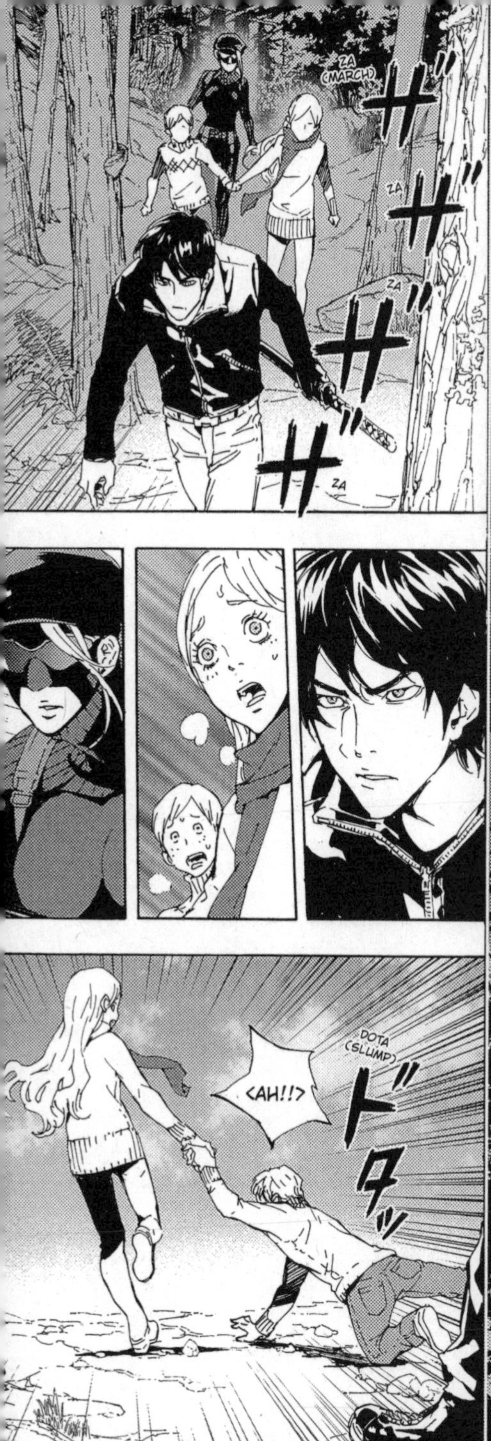
ZA
(MARCH)
ZA
ZA
ZA
DOTA
(SLUMP)
<AH!!?>

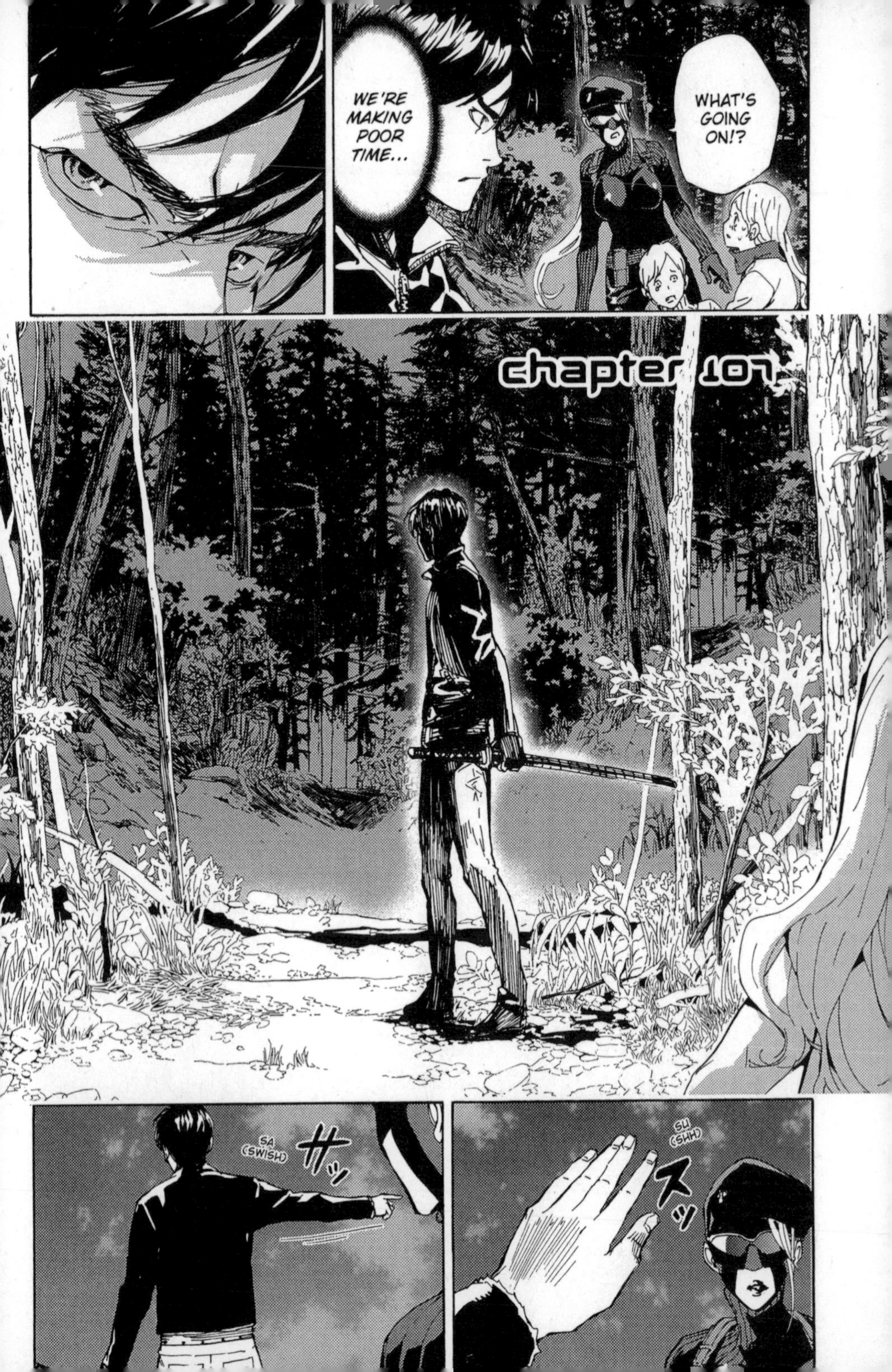
WHAT'S GOING ON!?
WE'RE MAKING POOR TIME...
chapter 107
SU (SHH)
スッ
SA (SWISH)
サッ

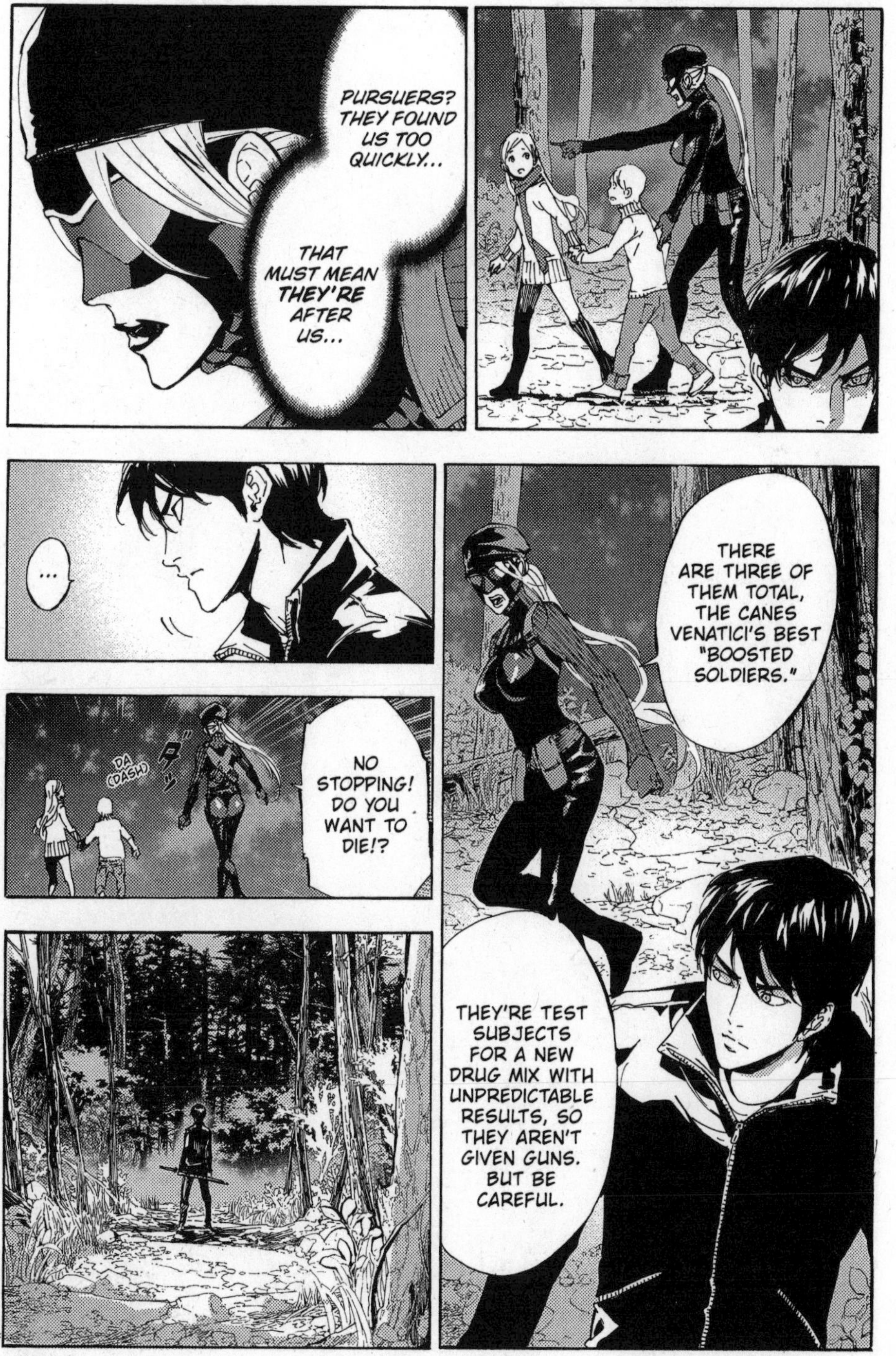
PURSUERS? THEY FOUND US TOO QUICKLY...
THAT MUST MEAN THEY'RE AFTER US...
THERE ARE THREE OF THEM TOTAL, THE CANES VENATICI'S BEST "BOOSTED SOLDIERS."
THEY'RE TEST SUBJECTS FOR A NEW DRUG MIX WITH UNPREDICTABLE RESULTS, SO THEY AREN'T GIVEN GUNS. BUT BE CAREFUL.
...
DA (DASH)
NO STOPPING! DO YOU WANT TO DIE!?

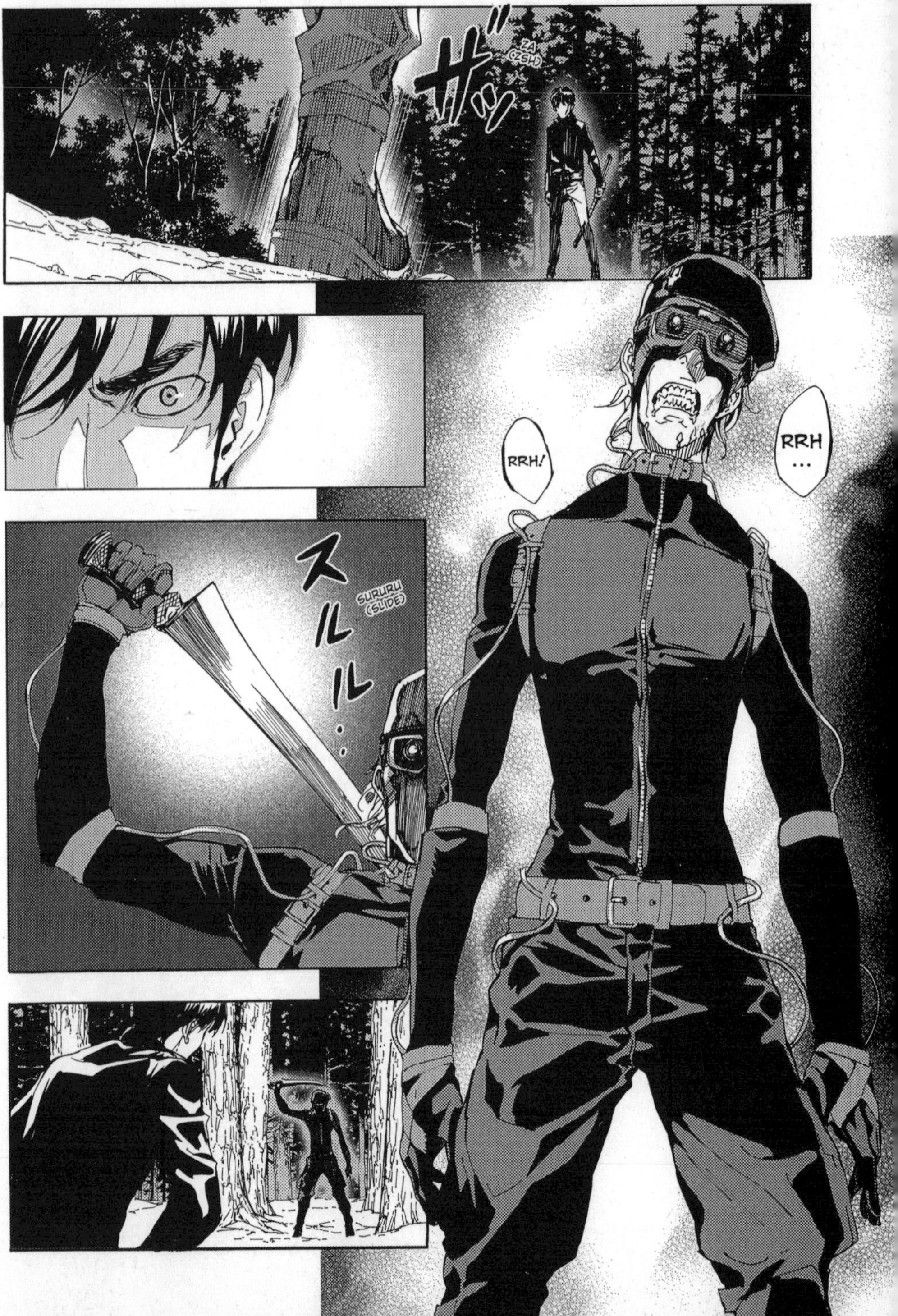
ザッ
ZA (ZSH)
RRH ...
RRH!
スルル・・
SURURU (SLIDE)

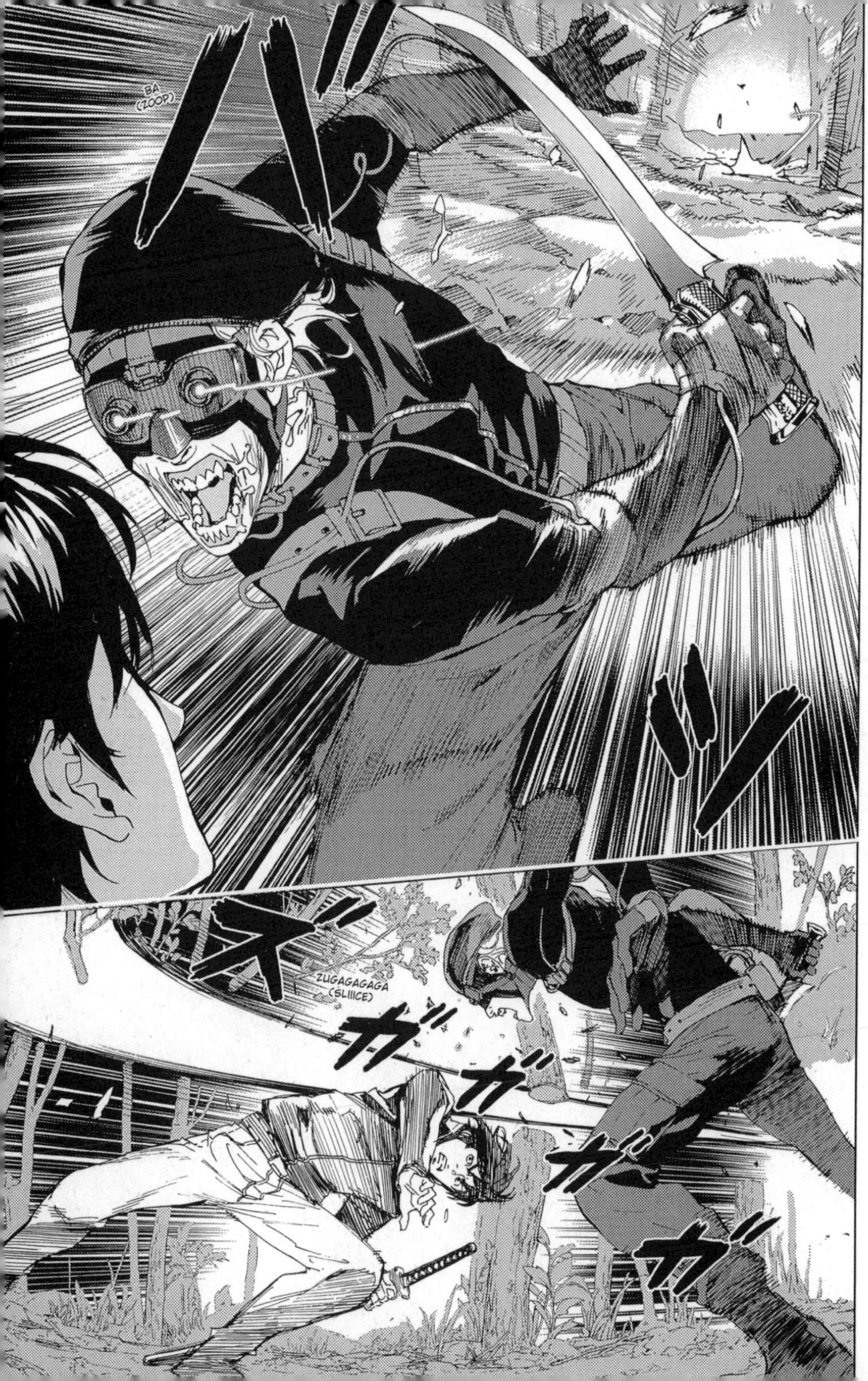
BA
(ZOOP)
ZUGAGAGAGA
(SLIIICE)

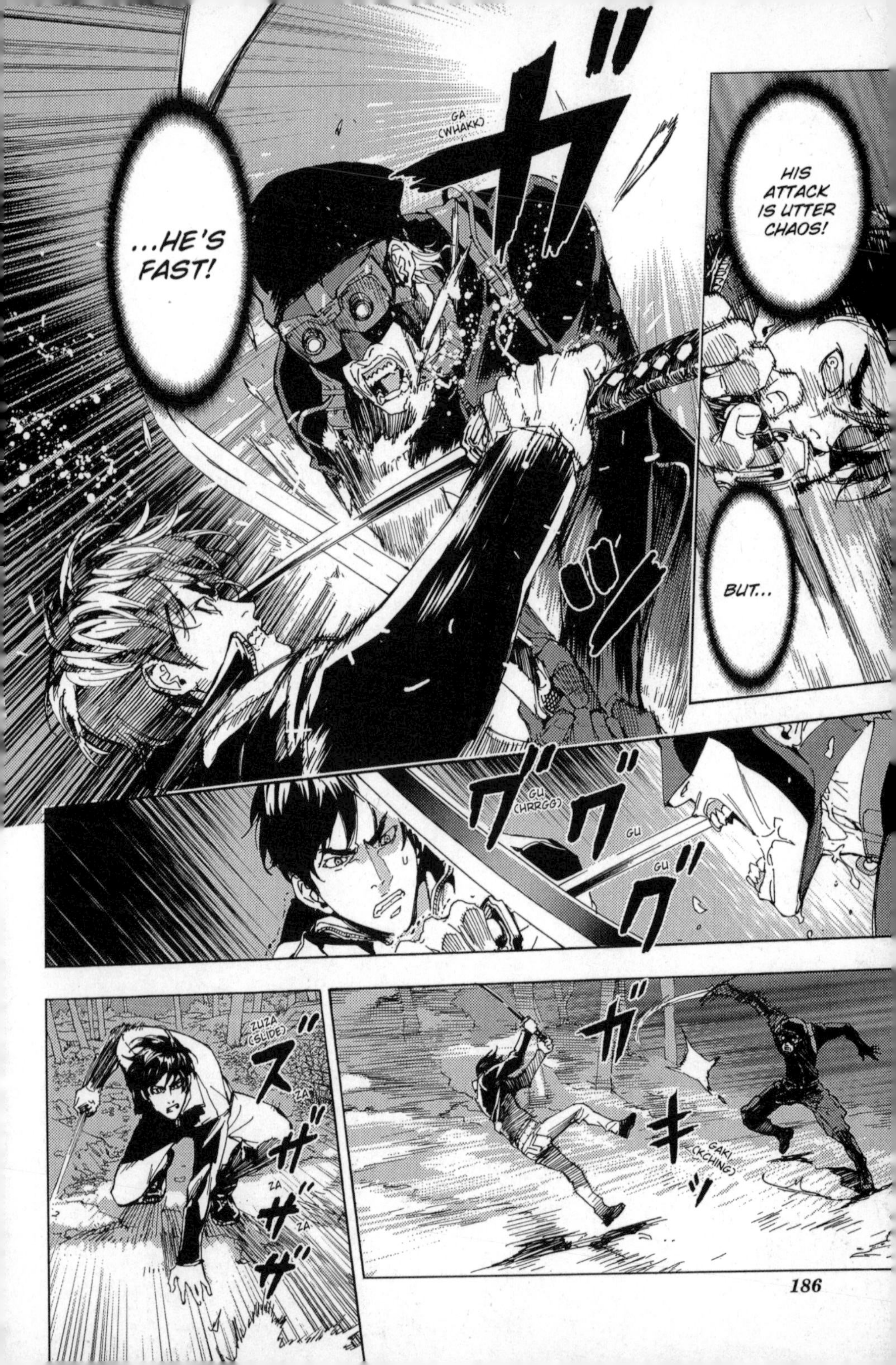
HIS ATTACK IS UTTER CHAOS!
BUT...
GA (WHAKK)
...HE'S FAST!
GU (HRRGG)
GU
GU
GAKI (KCHING)
ZUZA (SLIDE)
ZA
ZA
ZA

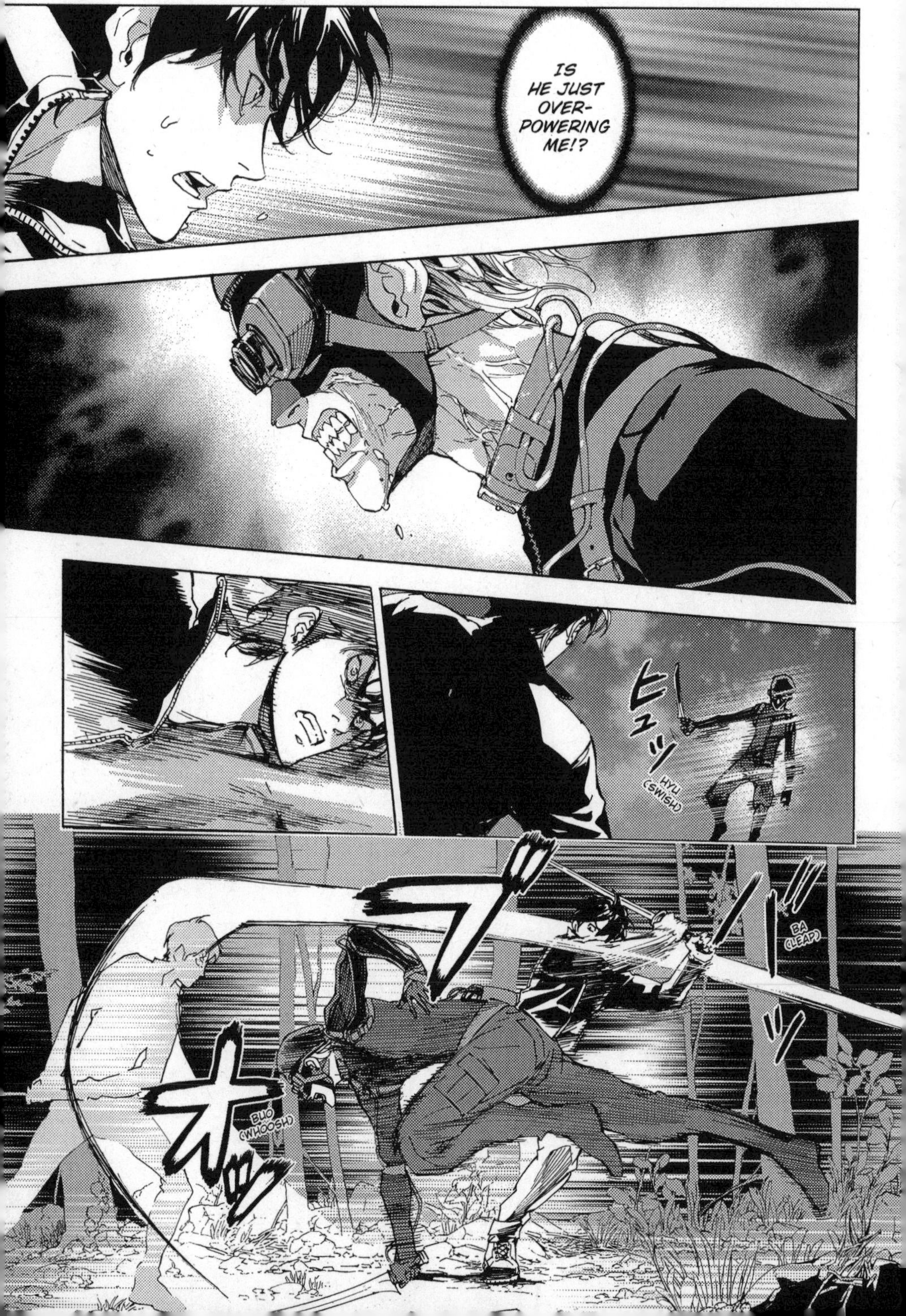
IS HE JUST OVER-POWERING ME!?
HYU (SWISH)
BA (LEAP)
BUO (WHOOSH)

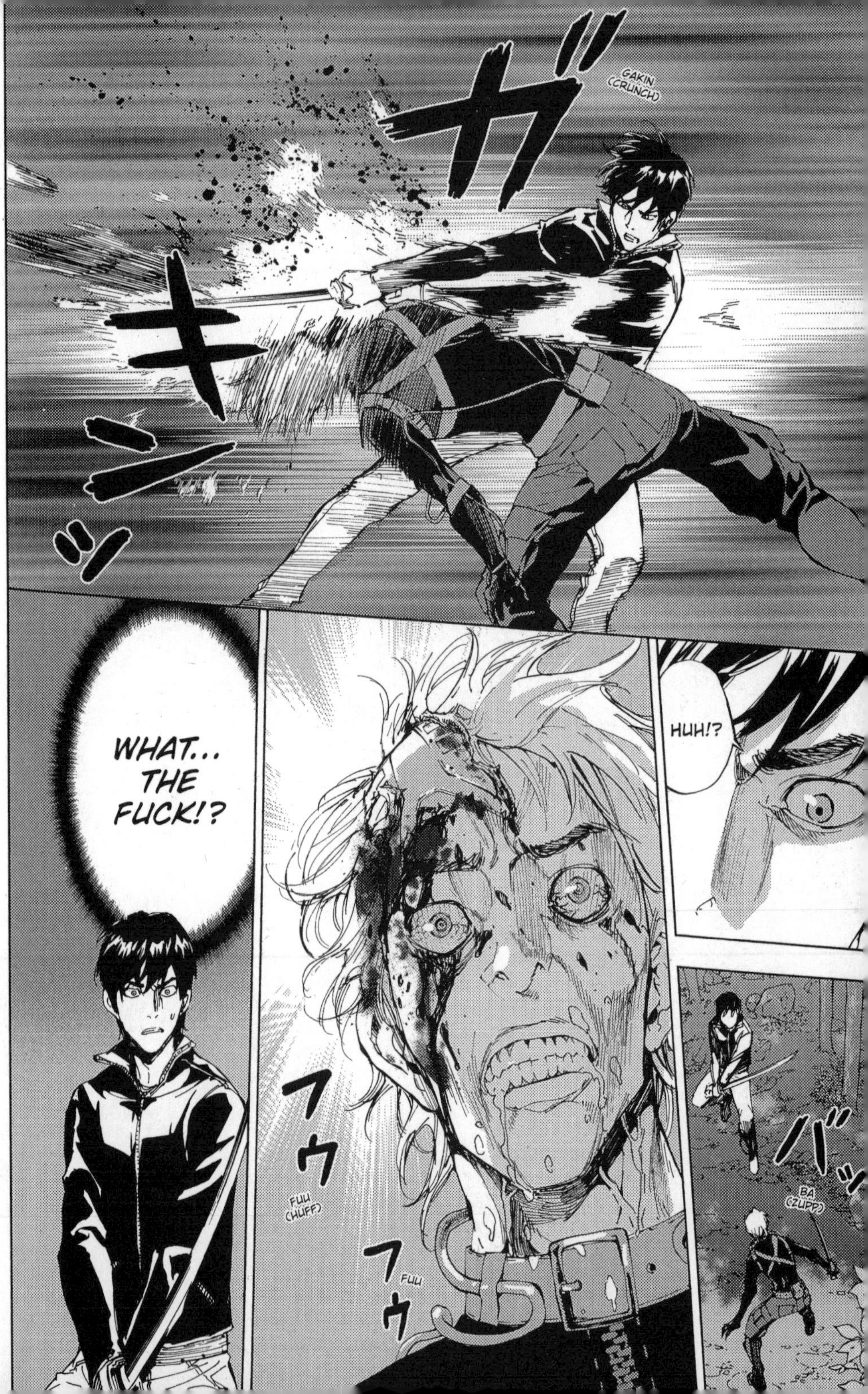
ガキンッ
GAKIN (CRUNCH)
HUH!?
バッ
BA (ZUPP)
フウ
FUU (HUFF)
フウ
FUU
WHAT... THE FUCK!?

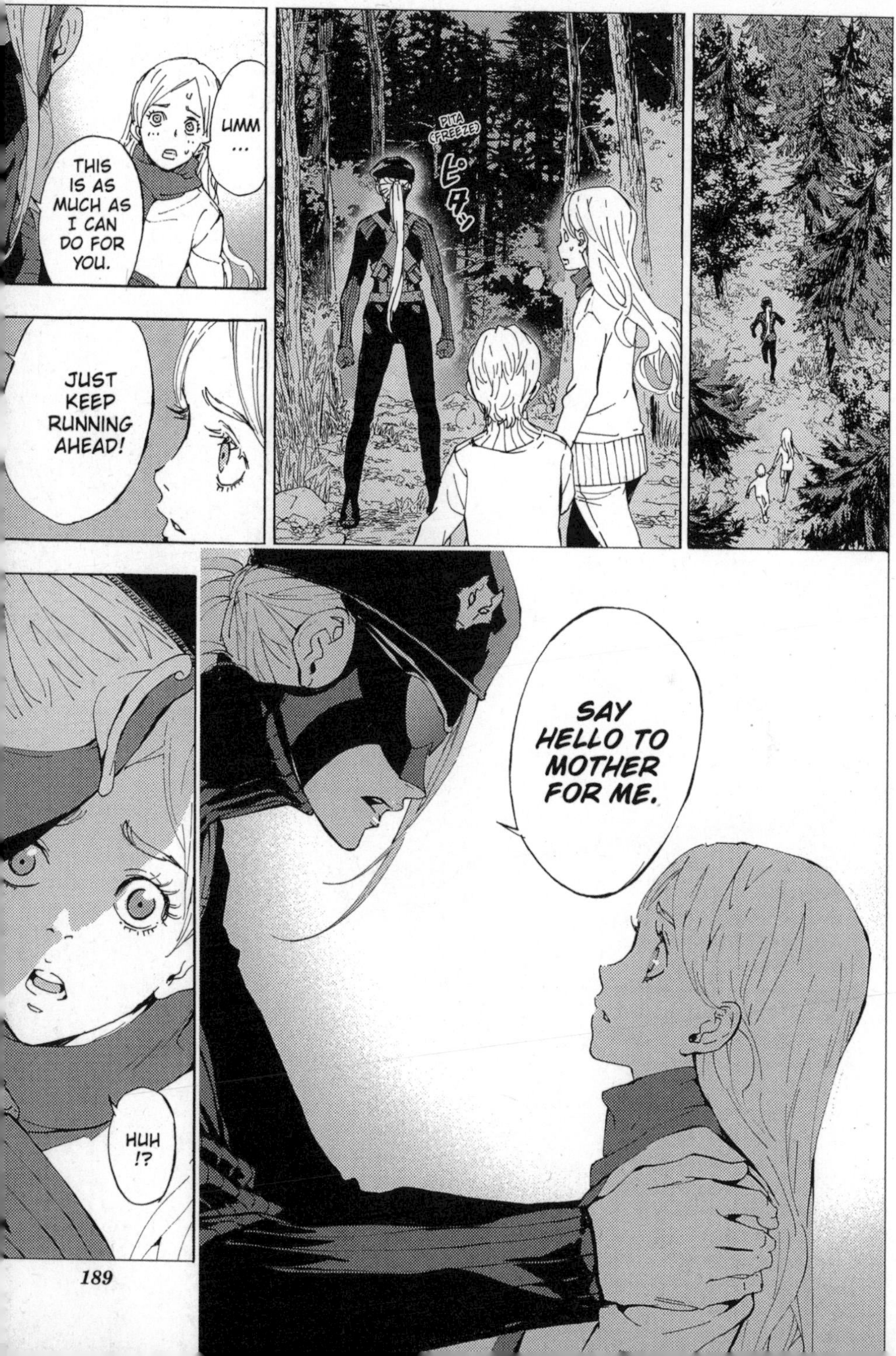
PITA (FREEZE)
ピタッ
UMM ...
THIS IS AS MUCH AS I CAN DO FOR YOU.
JUST KEEP RUNNING AHEAD!
SAY HELLO TO MOTHER FOR ME.
HUH !?

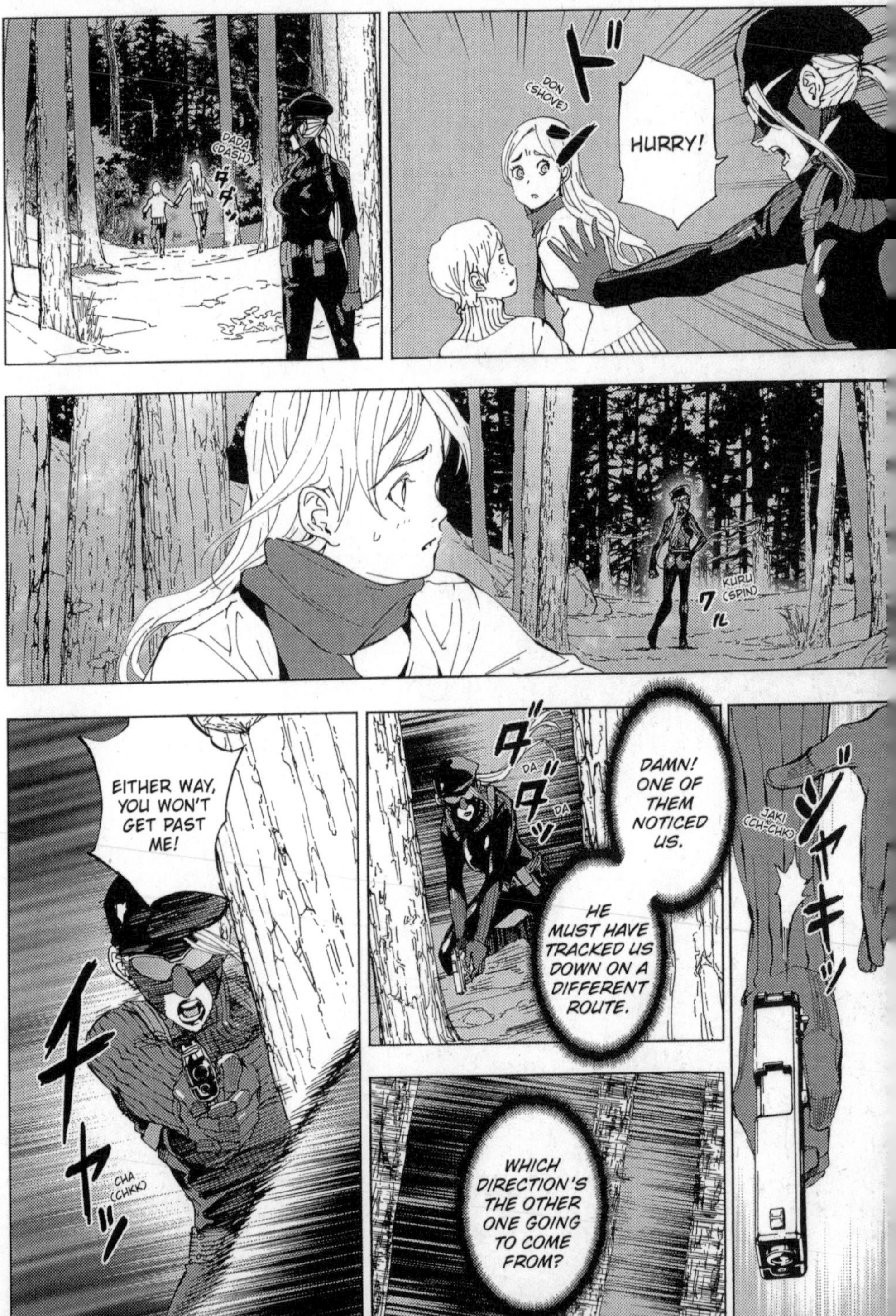
ド
DON (SHOVE)
HURRY!
DADA (DASH)
ダダッ
KURU (SPIN)
クル
ジャキッ
JAKI (CH-CHK)
DAMN! ONE OF THEM NOTICED US.
HE MUST HAVE TRACKED US DOWN ON A DIFFERENT ROUTE.
ダダッ
DA DA
WHICH DIRECTION'S THE OTHER ONE GOING TO COME FROM?
EITHER WAY, YOU WON'T GET PAST ME!
チャッ
CHA (CHKK)

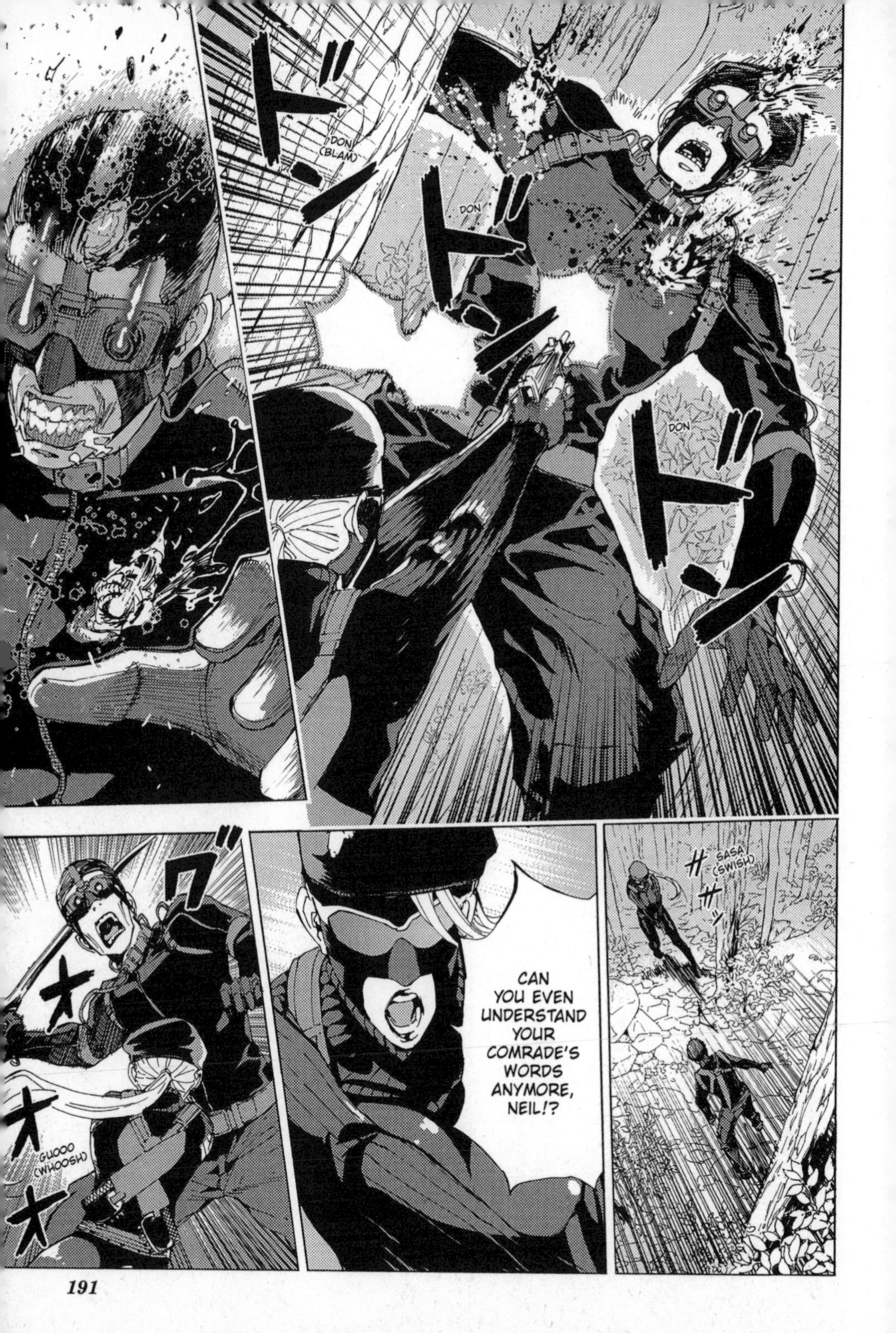

DON (BLAM)
DON
DON
SASA (SWISH)
CAN YOU EVEN UNDERSTAND YOUR COMRADE'S WORDS ANYMORE, NEIL!?
GUOOO (WHOOSH)

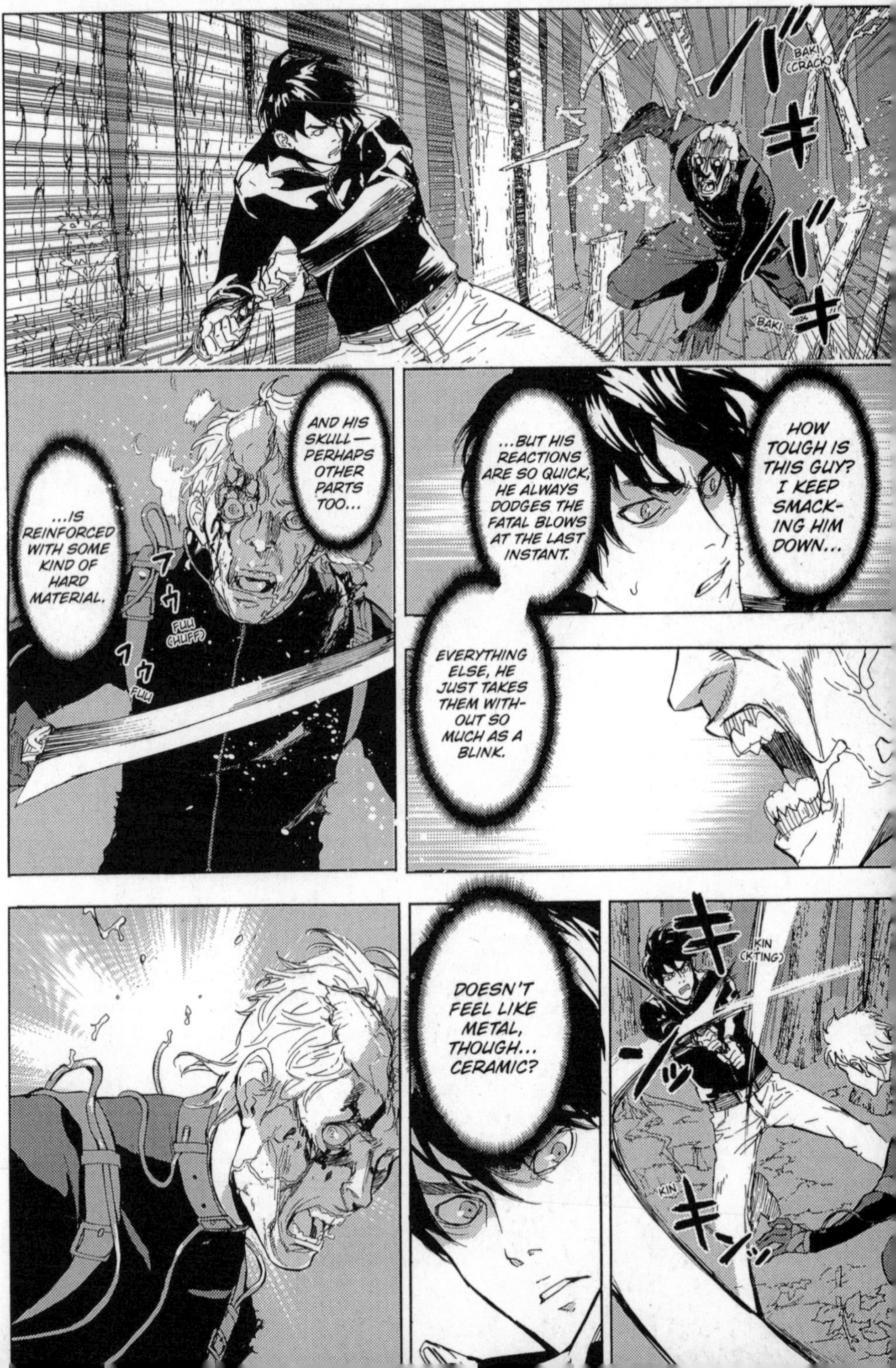

BAKI (CRACK)
BAKI
HOW TOUGH IS THIS GUY? I KEEP SMACKING HIM DOWN...
...BUT HIS REACTIONS ARE SO QUICK, HE ALWAYS DODGES THE FATAL BLOWS AT THE LAST INSTANT.
EVERYTHING ELSE, HE JUST TAKES THEM WITHOUT SO MUCH AS A BLINK.
AND HIS SKULL—PERHAPS OTHER PARTS TOO...
...IS REINFORCED WITH SOME KIND OF HARD MATERIAL.
FUU (HUFF)
FUU
KIN (K'TING)
KIN
DOESN'T FEEL LIKE METAL, THOUGH... CERAMIC?

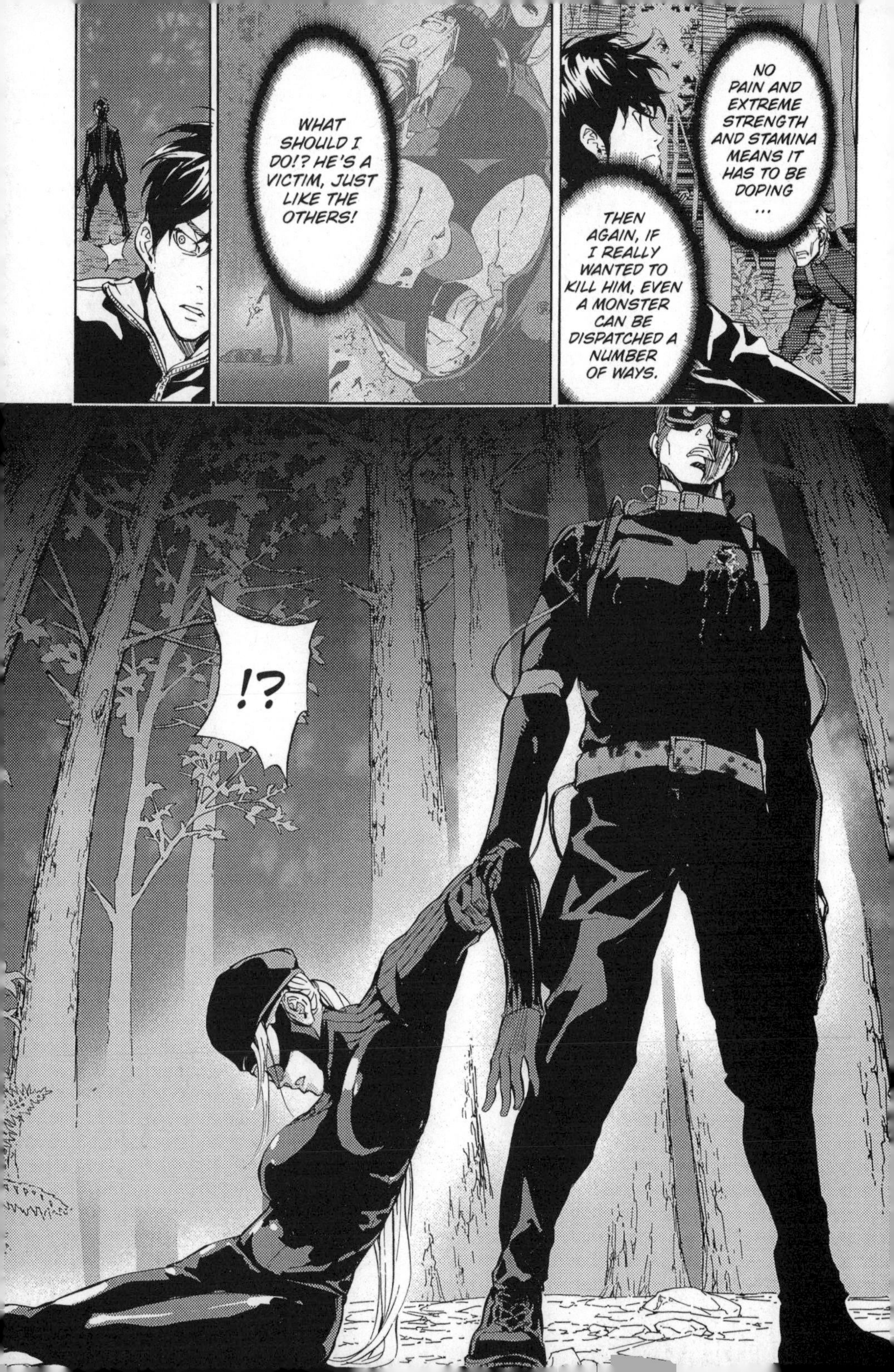
NO PAIN AND EXTREME STRENGTH AND STAMINA MEANS IT HAS TO BE DOPING ...
THEN AGAIN, IF I REALLY WANTED TO KILL HIM, EVEN A MONSTER CAN BE DISPATCHED A NUMBER OF WAYS.
WHAT SHOULD I DO!? HE'S A VICTIM, JUST LIKE THE OTHERS!
!?

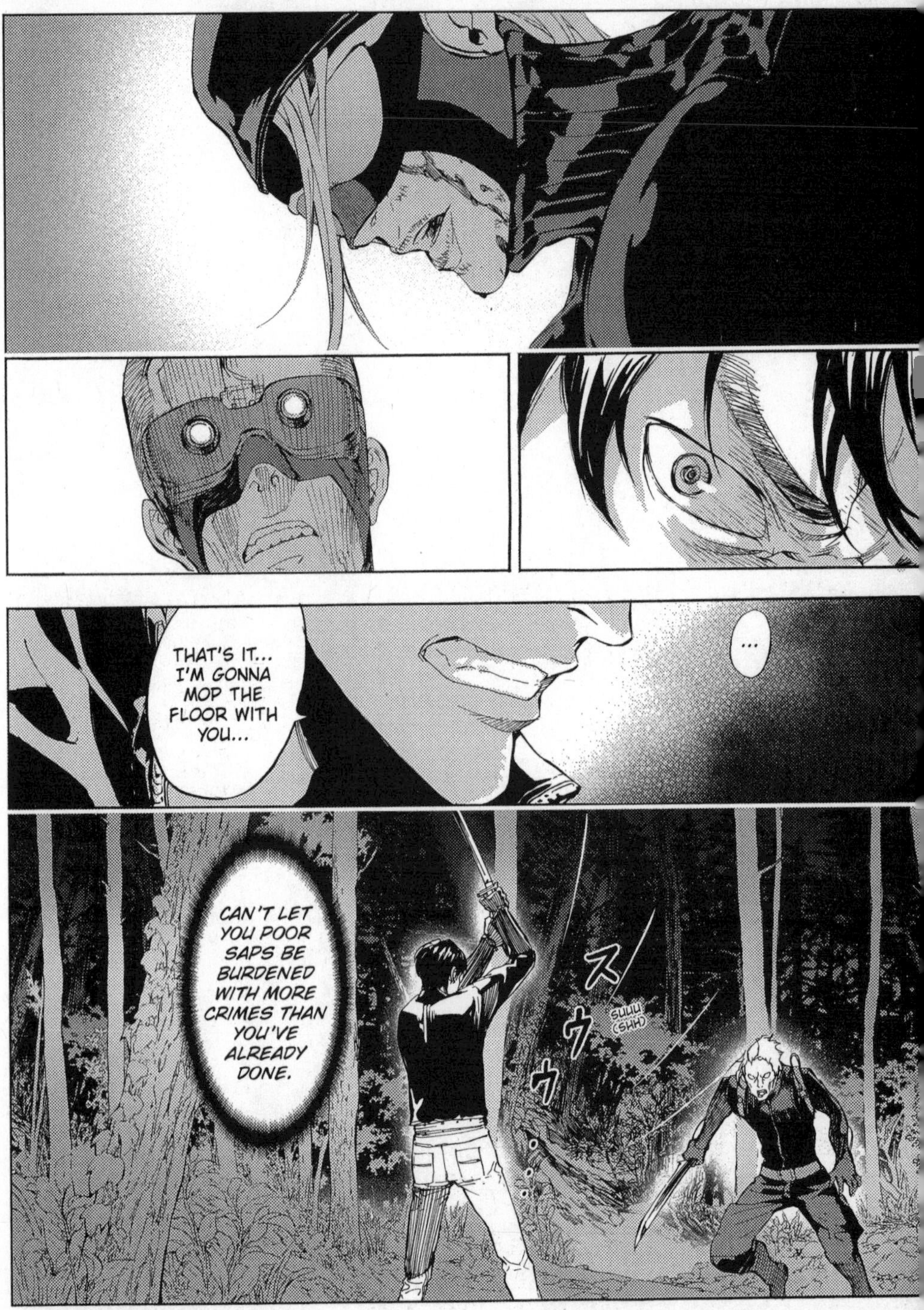
...
THAT'S IT... I'M GONNA MOP THE FLOOR WITH YOU...
SUUU (SHH)
CAN'T LET YOU POOR SAPS BE BURDENED WITH MORE CRIMES THAN YOU'VE ALREADY DONE.

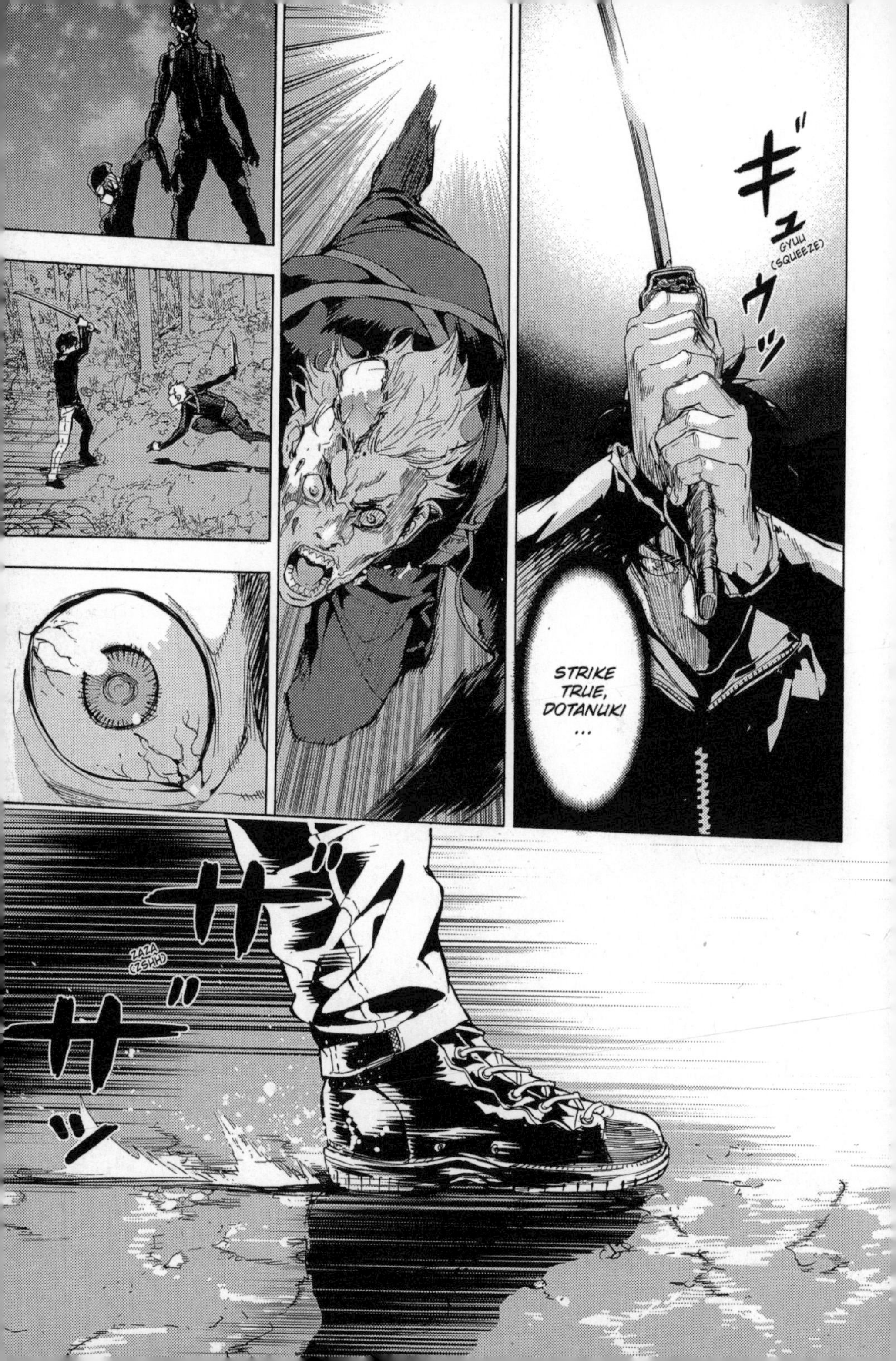
ギュウッ
GYUU (SQUEEZE)
STRIKE TRUE, DOTANUKI ...
ザザザッ
ZAZA (ZSHH)

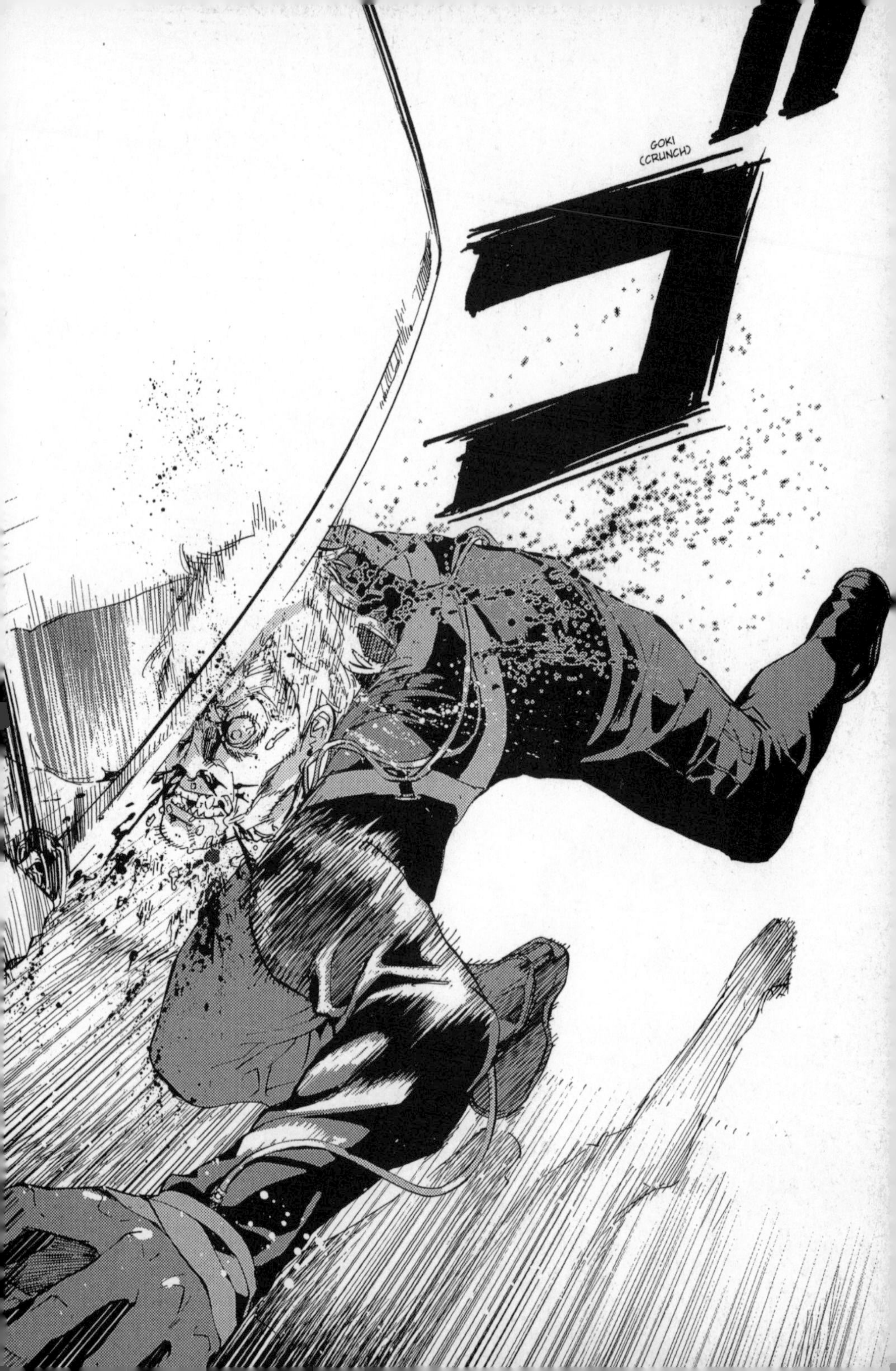
GOKI
(CRUNCH)

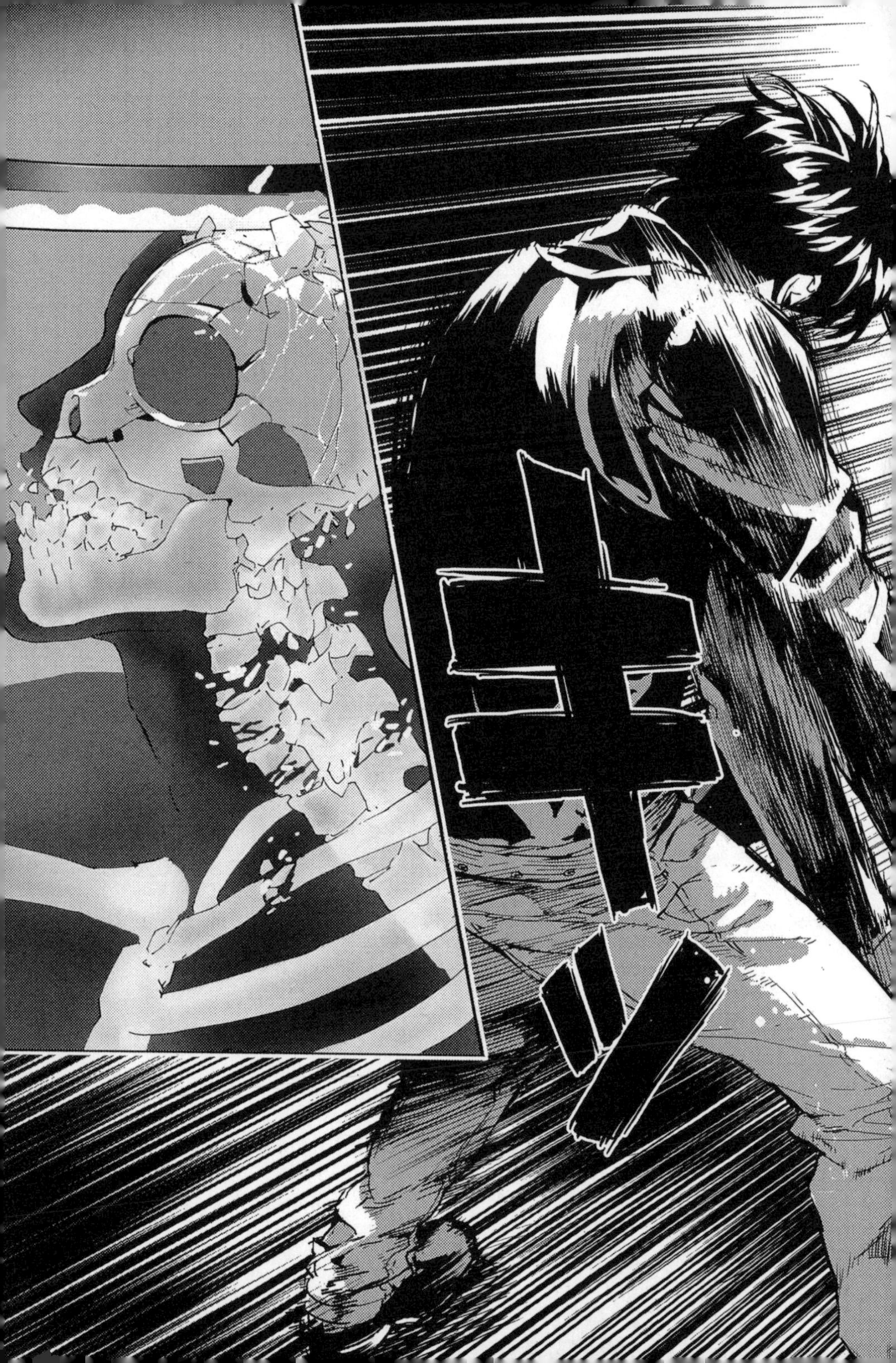
キッ

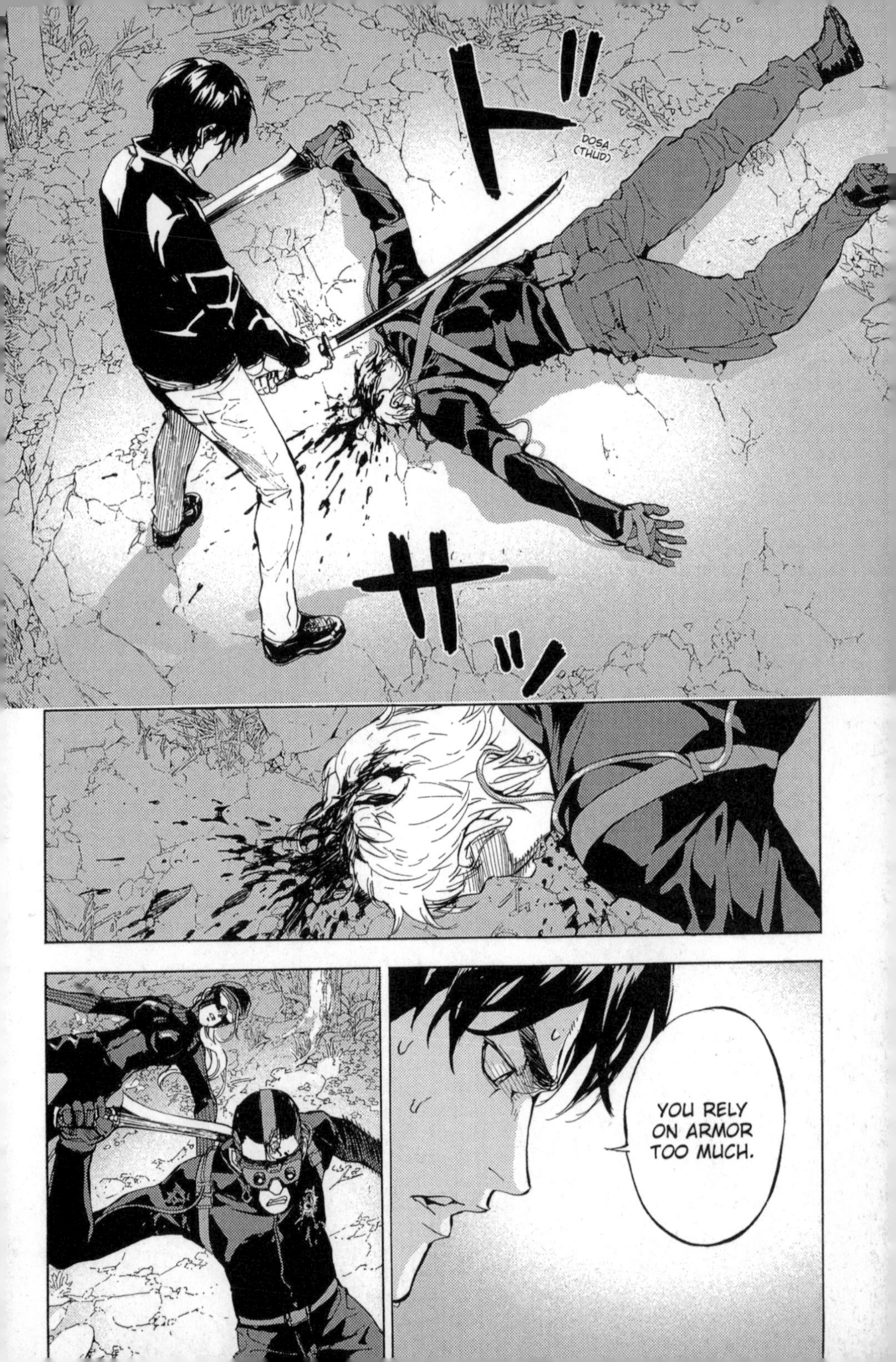
DOSA
(THUD)
YOU RELY ON ARMOR TOO MUCH.

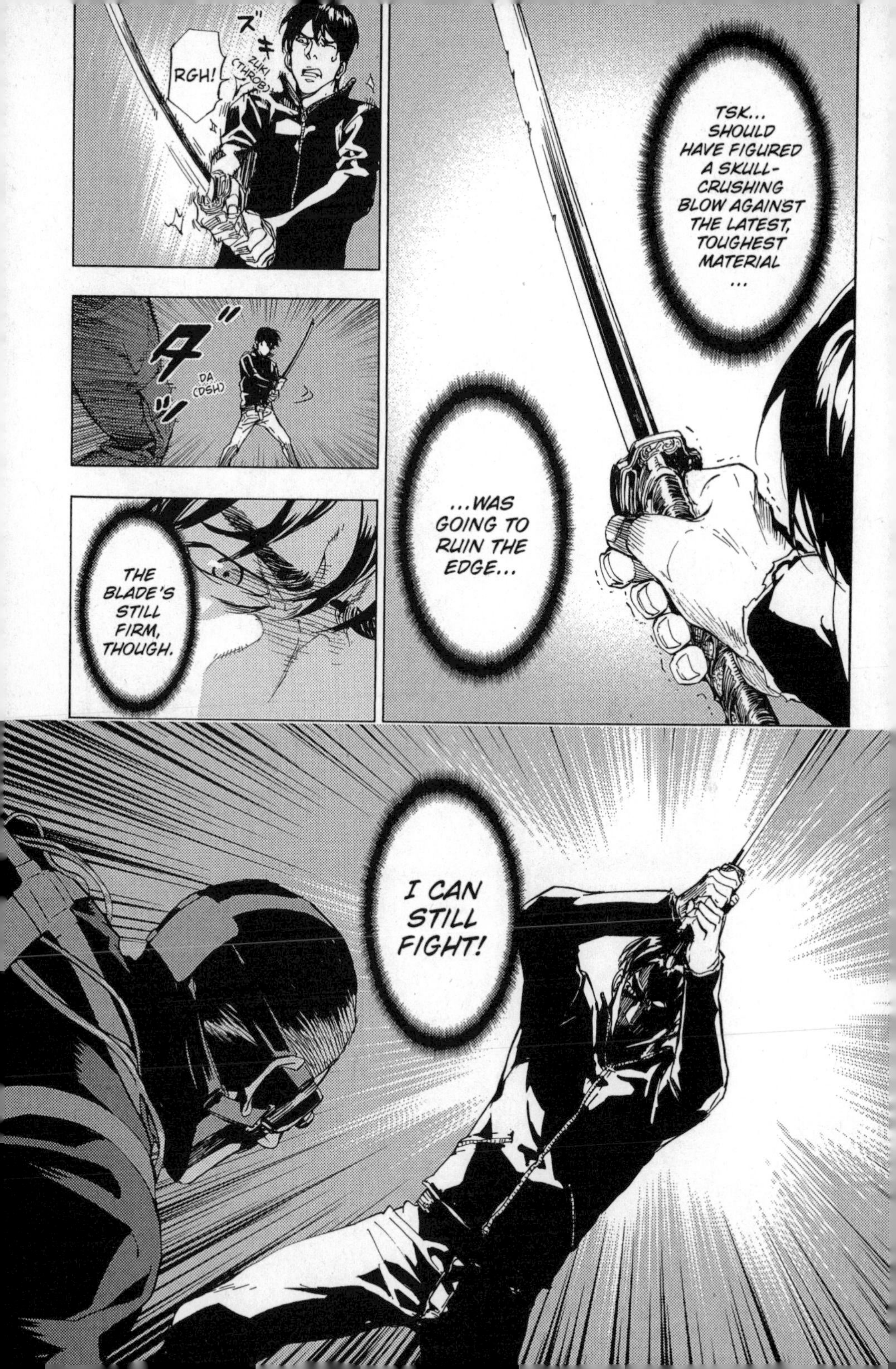
TSK... SHOULD HAVE FIGURED A SKULL-CRUSHING BLOW AGAINST THE LATEST, TOUGHEST MATERIAL ...
...WAS GOING TO RUIN THE EDGE...
ズキ
ZUKI (THROB)
RGH!
ダッ
DA (DSH)
THE BLADE'S STILL FIRM, THOUGH.
I CAN STILL FIGHT!

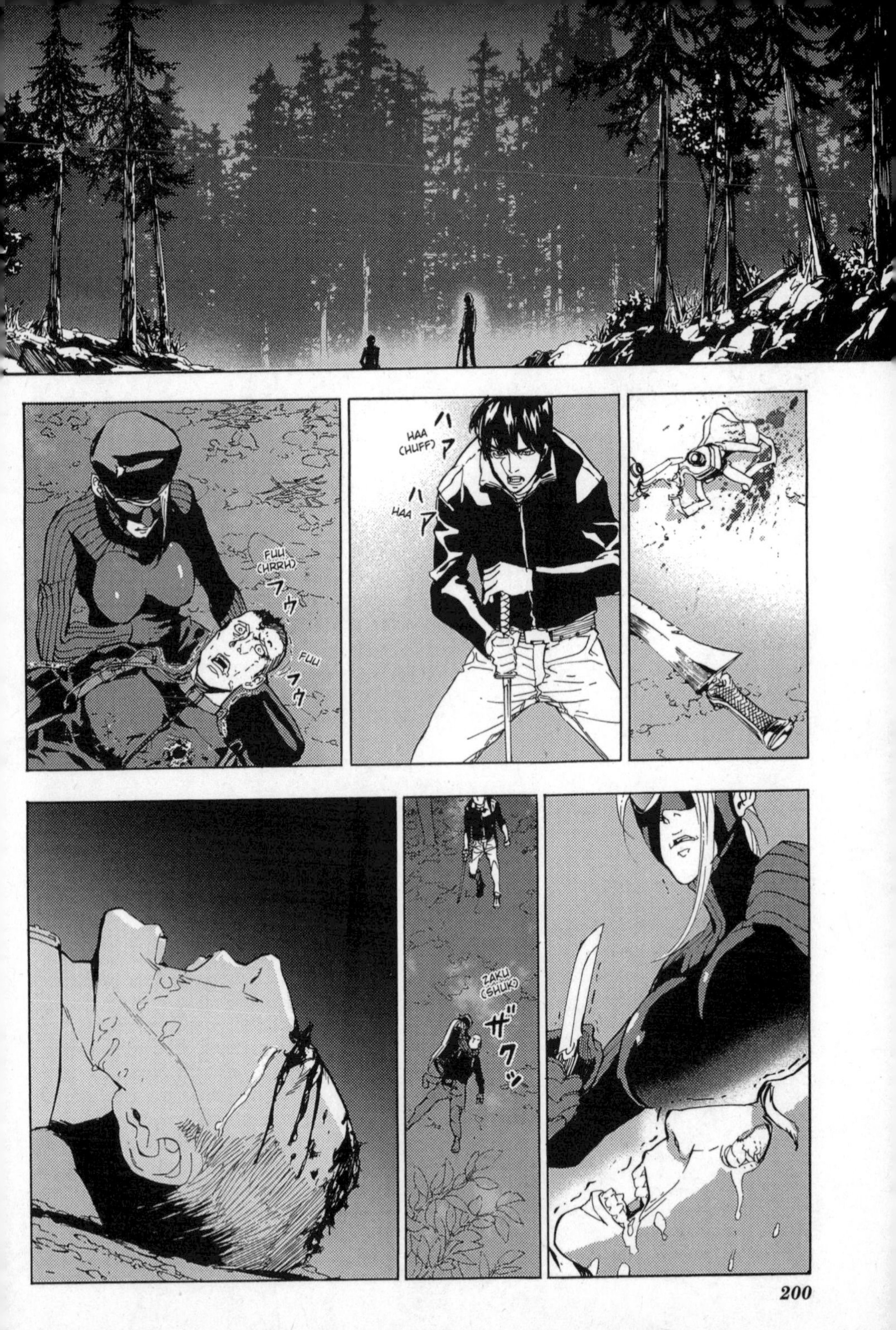
HAA (CHUFF)
ハア
HAA
ハア
FUU (HRRH)
フウ
FUU
フウ
ZAKU (SHUK)
ザクッ

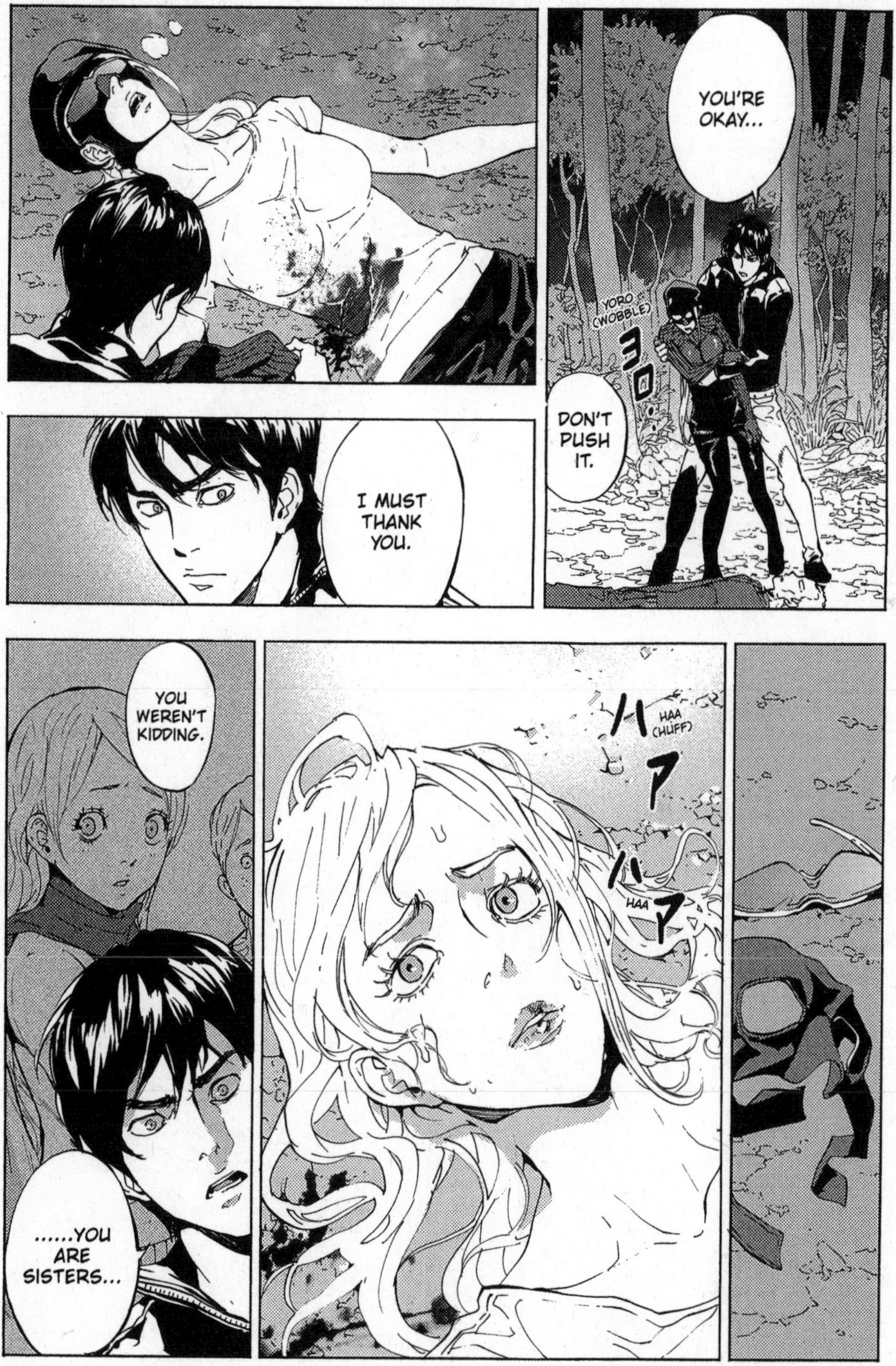
YOU'RE OKAY...
YORO (WOBBLE)
ヨロ
DON'T PUSH IT.
I MUST THANK YOU.
HAA (CHUFF)
ハア
HAA
ハア
YOU WEREN'T KIDDING.
......YOU ARE SISTERS...

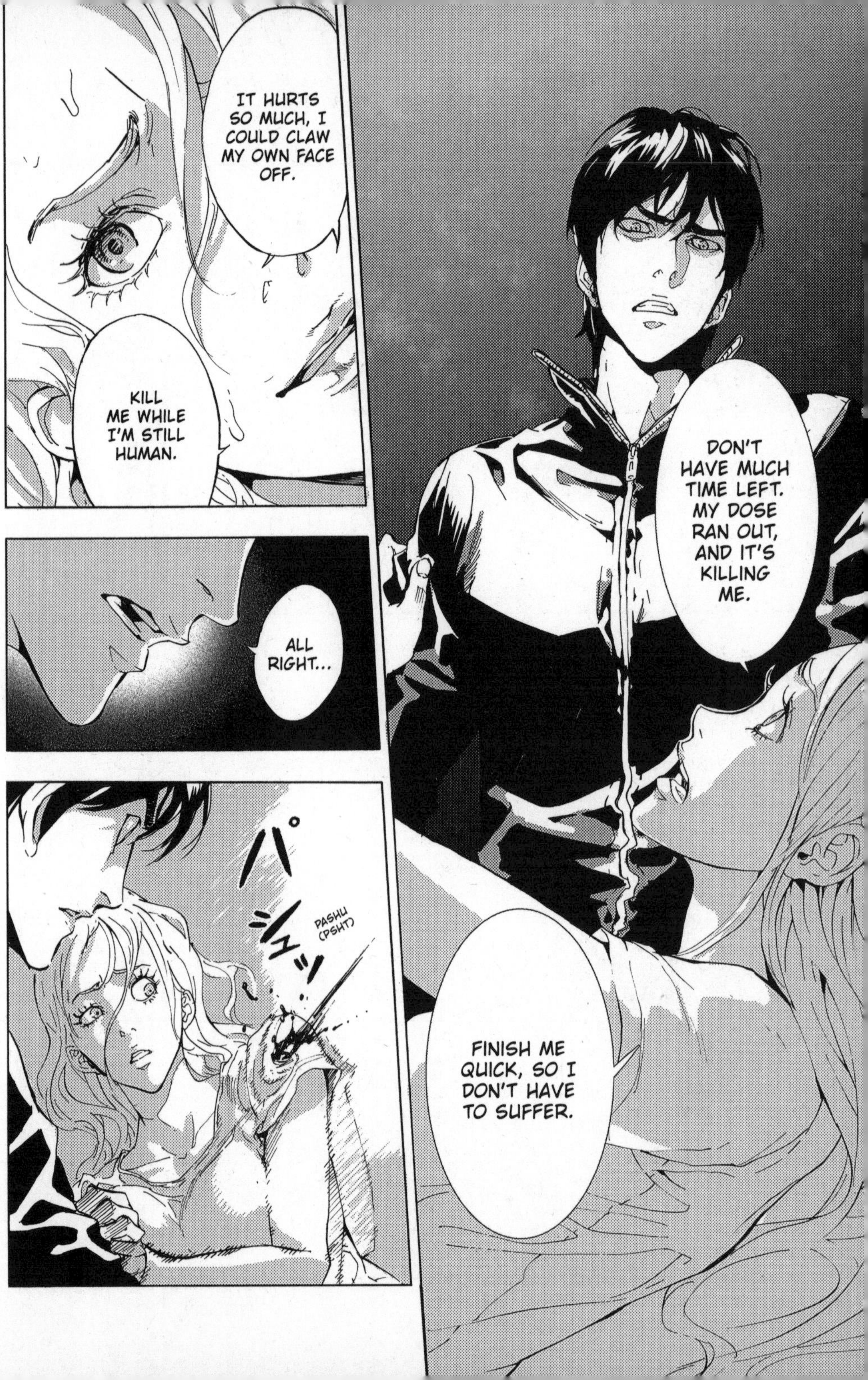
DON'T HAVE MUCH TIME LEFT. MY DOSE RAN OUT, AND IT'S KILLING ME.
FINISH ME QUICK, SO I DON'T HAVE TO SUFFER.
IT HURTS SO MUCH, I COULD CLAW MY OWN FACE OFF.
KILL ME WHILE I'M STILL HUMAN.
ALL RIGHT...
PASHU (PSHT)

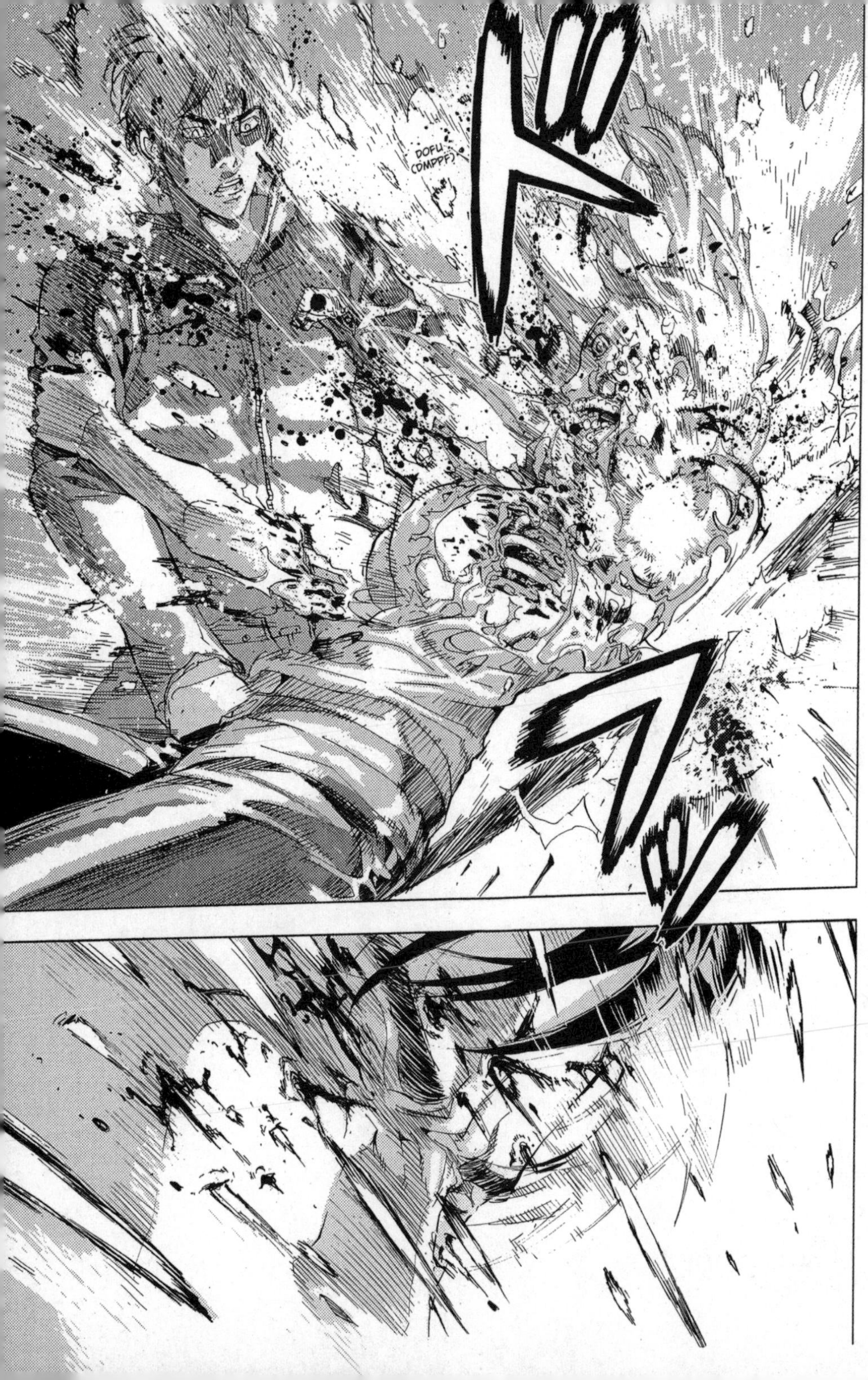
DOFU
(DMPPF)

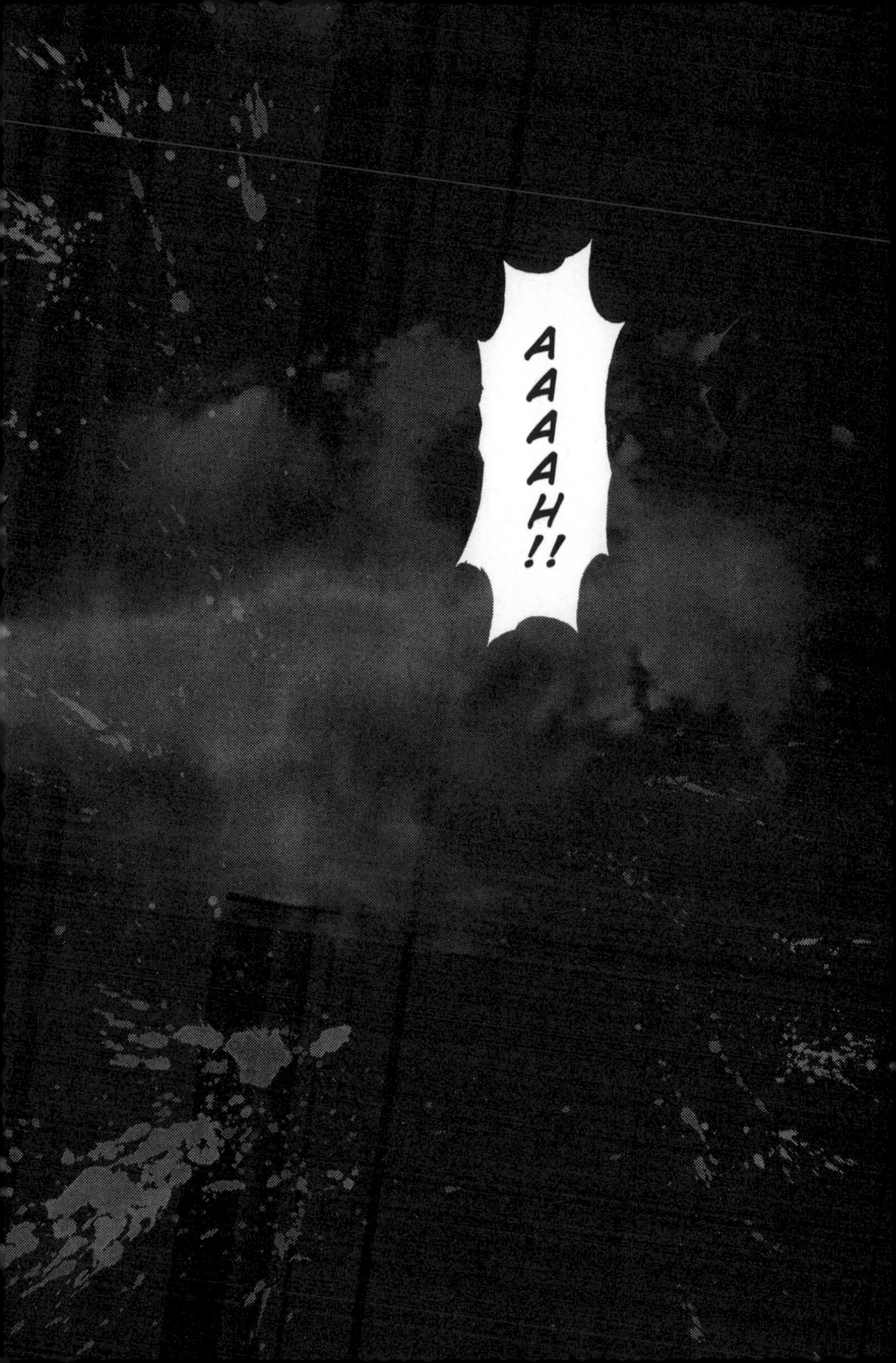
AAAAH!!

Until Death do us Part

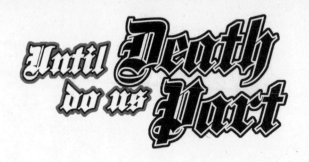

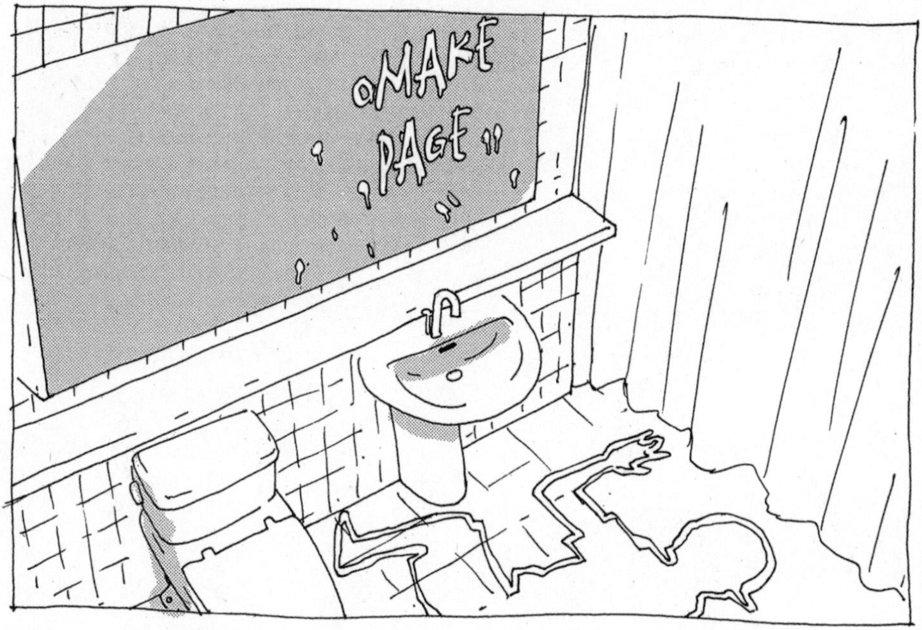
oMAKE
PAGE

I HAD AN ACCIDENT.

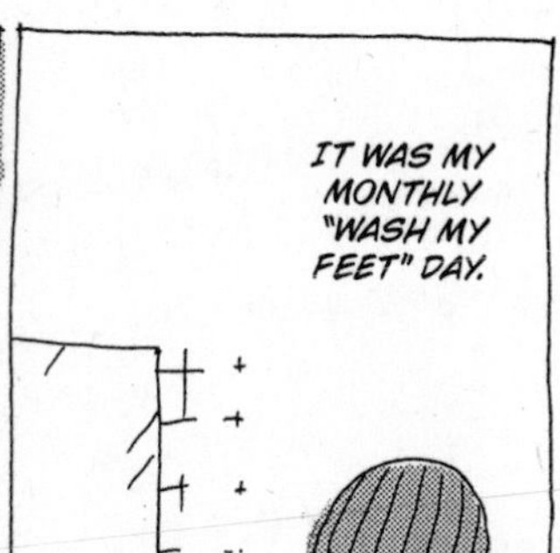
IT WAS MY MONTHLY "WASH MY FEET" DAY.

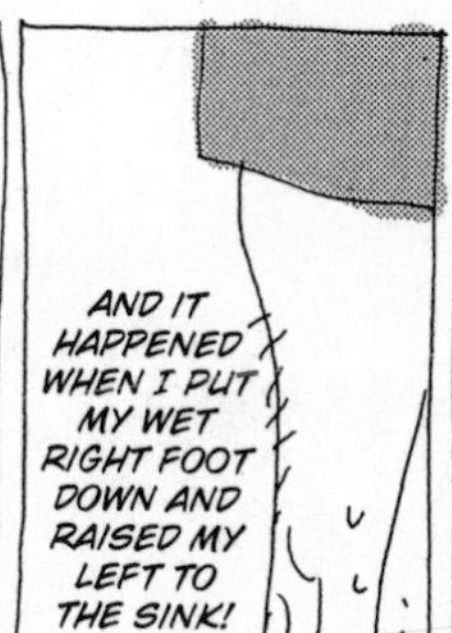
AND IT HAPPENED WHEN I PUT MY WET RIGHT FOOT DOWN AND RAISED MY LEFT TO THE SINK!

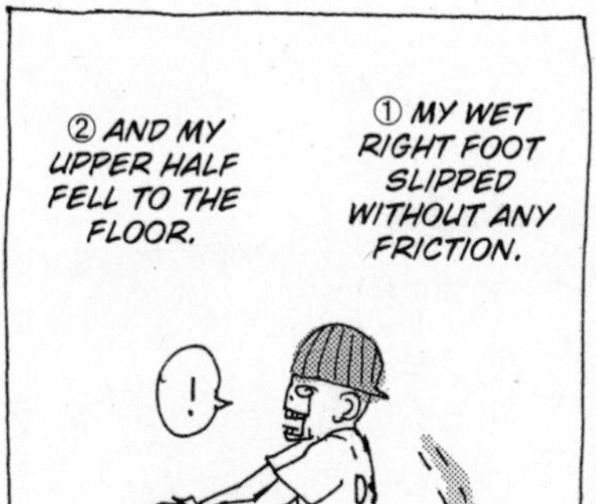
① MY WET RIGHT FOOT SLIPPED WITHOUT ANY FRICTION.
② AND MY UPPER HALF FELL TO THE FLOOR.
!
* BASED ON OBSERVATION OF THE ACCIDENT SCENE, DUE TO THE VICTIM'S UNCERTAIN MEMORY.

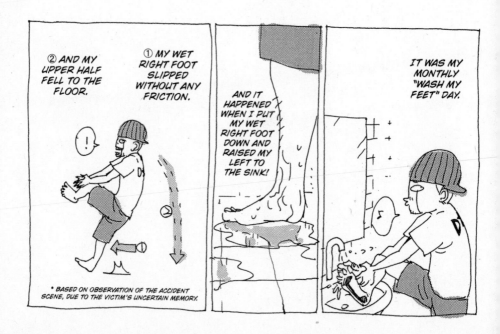

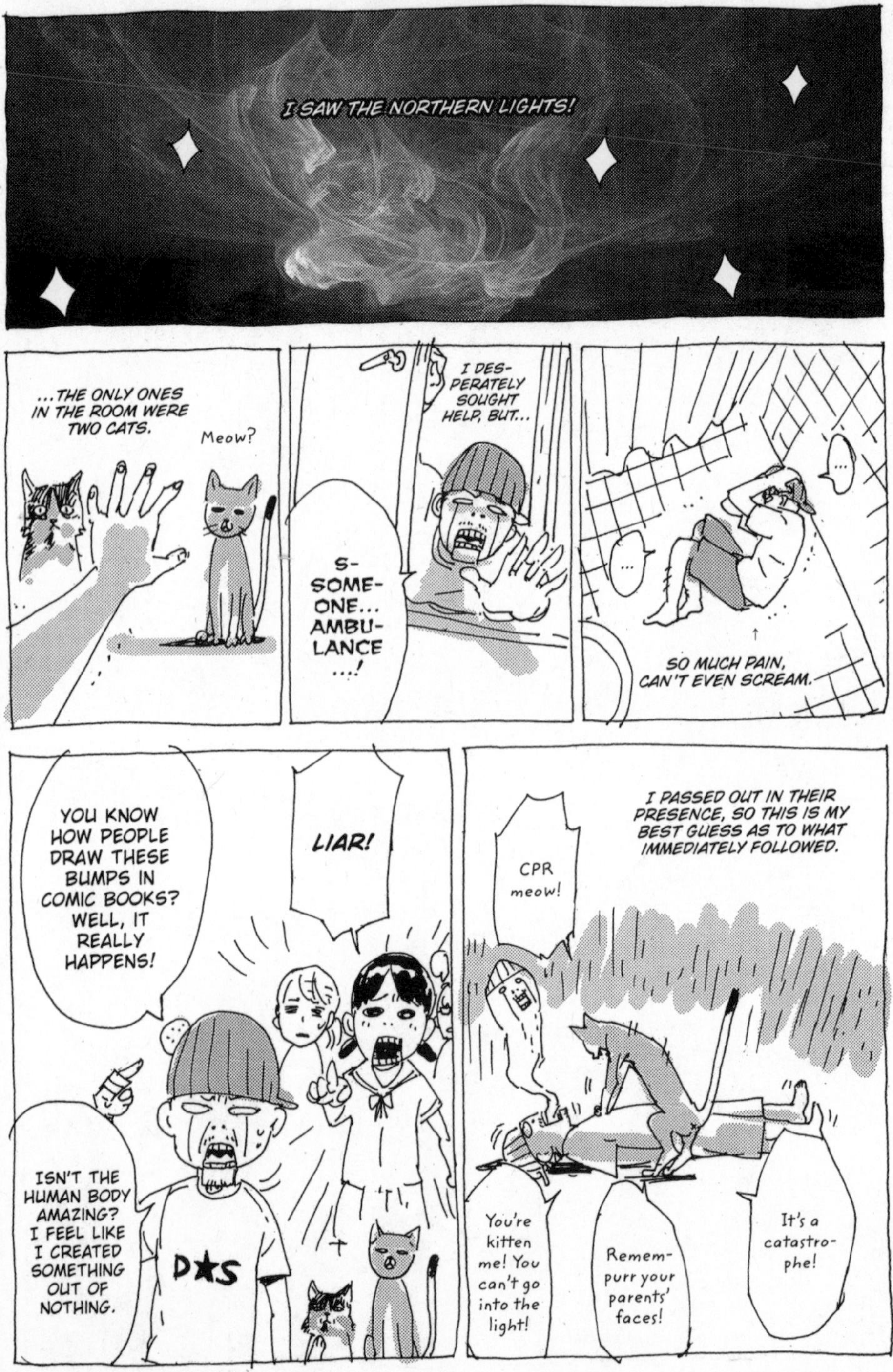
I SAW THE NORTHERN LIGHTS!
...
...
SO MUCH PAIN, CAN'T EVEN SCREAM.
I DES-PERATELY SOUGHT HELP, BUT...
S-SOME-ONE... AMBU-LANCE ...!
...THE ONLY ONES IN THE ROOM WERE TWO CATS.
Meow?
I PASSED OUT IN THEIR PRESENCE, SO THIS IS MY BEST GUESS AS TO WHAT IMMEDIATELY FOLLOWED.
CPR meow!
It's a catastro-phe!
Remem-purr your parents' faces!
You're kitten me! You can't go into the light!
LIAR!
YOU KNOW HOW PEOPLE DRAW THESE BUMPS IN COMIC BOOKS? WELL, IT REALLY HAPPENS!
ISN'T THE HUMAN BODY AMAZING? I FEEL LIKE I CREATED SOMETHING OUT OF NOTHING.
D★S

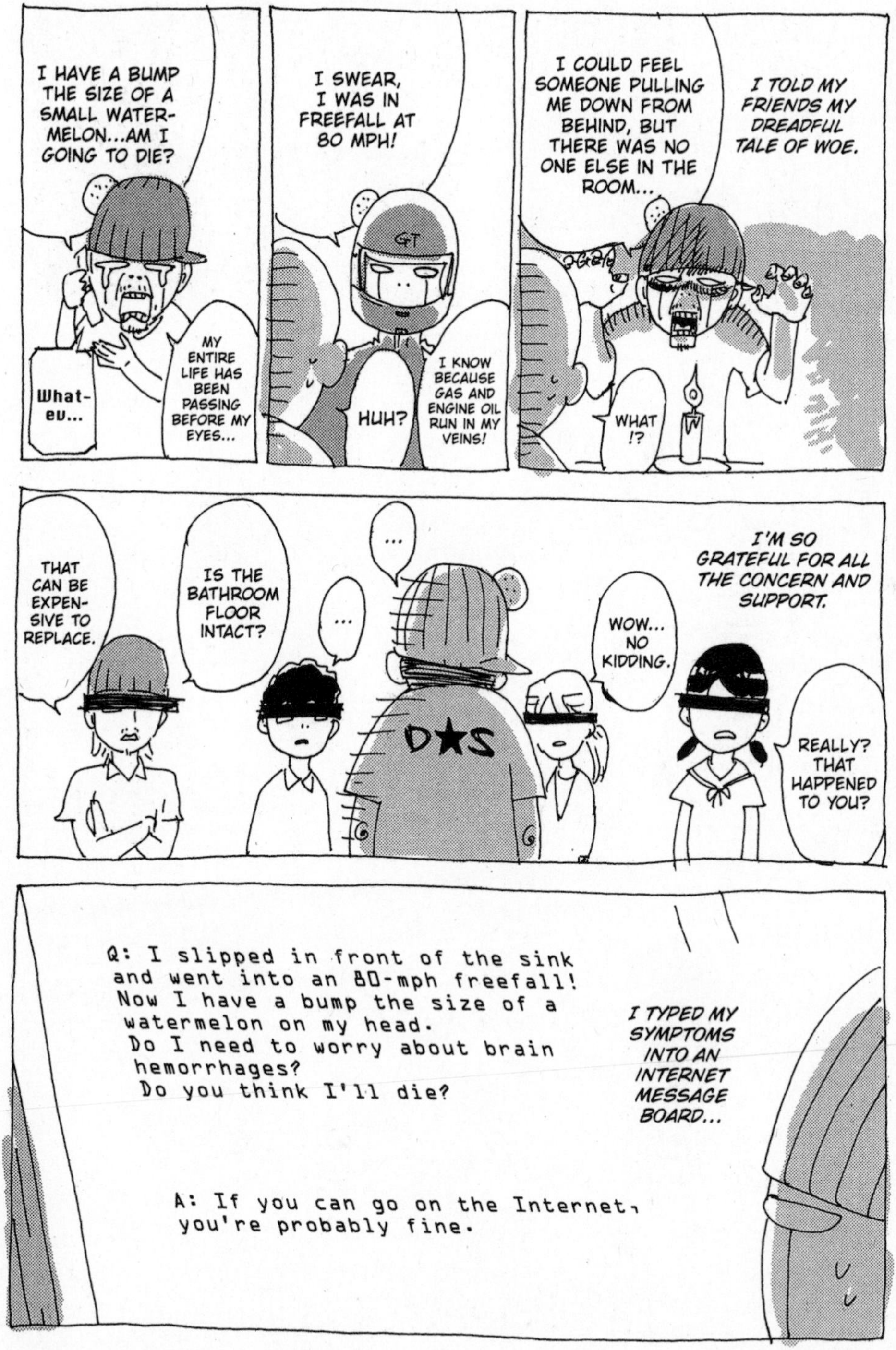
I TOLD MY FRIENDS MY DREADFUL TALE OF WOE.
I COULD FEEL SOMEONE PULLING ME DOWN FROM BEHIND, BUT THERE WAS NO ONE ELSE IN THE ROOM...
WHAT!?
I SWEAR, I WAS IN FREEFALL AT 80 MPH!
I KNOW BECAUSE GAS AND ENGINE OIL RUN IN MY VEINS!
HUH?
I HAVE A BUMP THE SIZE OF A SMALL WATER-MELON...AM I GOING TO DIE?
MY ENTIRE LIFE HAS BEEN PASSING BEFORE MY EYES...
Whatev...
I'M SO GRATEFUL FOR ALL THE CONCERN AND SUPPORT.
REALLY? THAT HAPPENED TO YOU?
WOW... NO KIDDING.
...
IS THE BATHROOM FLOOR INTACT?
...
THAT CAN BE EXPENSIVE TO REPLACE.
D★S
I TYPED MY SYMPTOMS INTO AN INTERNET MESSAGE BOARD...
Q: I slipped in front of the sink and went into an 80-mph freefall! Now I have a bump the size of a watermelon on my head. Do I need to worry about brain hemorrhages? Do you think I'll die?
A: If you can go on the Internet, you're probably fine.

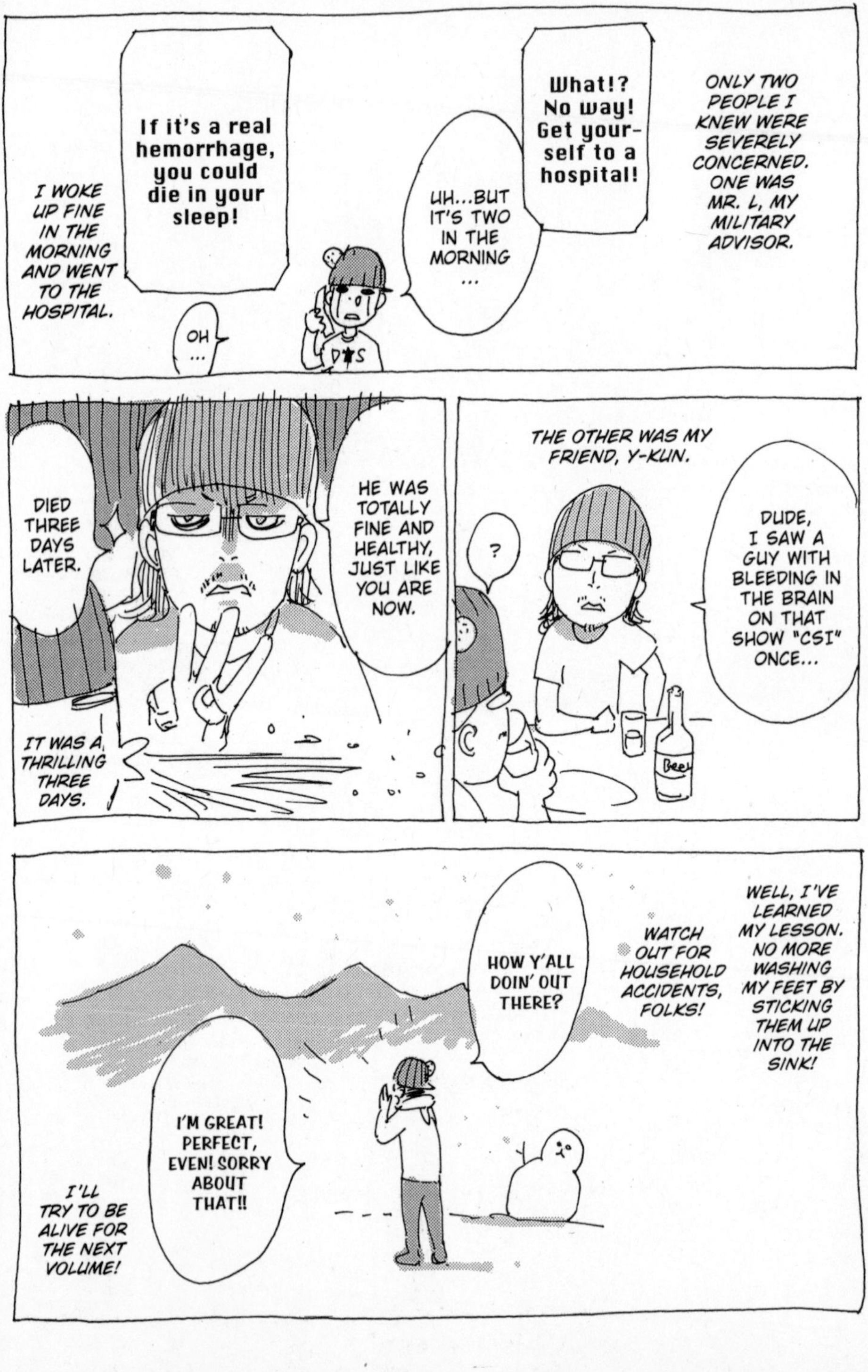
ONLY TWO PEOPLE I KNEW WERE SEVERELY CONCERNED. ONE WAS MR. L, MY MILITARY ADVISOR.
What!? No way! Get yourself to a hospital!
UH...BUT IT'S TWO IN THE MORNING...
If it's a real hemorrhage, you could die in your sleep!
OH...
I WOKE UP FINE IN THE MORNING AND WENT TO THE HOSPITAL.
THE OTHER WAS MY FRIEND, Y-KUN.
DUDE, I SAW A GUY WITH BLEEDING IN THE BRAIN ON THAT SHOW "CSI" ONCE...
?
HE WAS TOTALLY FINE AND HEALTHY, JUST LIKE YOU ARE NOW.
DIED THREE DAYS LATER.
IT WAS A THRILLING THREE DAYS.
WELL, I'VE LEARNED MY LESSON. NO MORE WASHING MY FEET BY STICKING THEM UP INTO THE SINK!
WATCH OUT FOR HOUSEHOLD ACCIDENTS, FOLKS!
HOW Y'ALL DOIN' OUT THERE?
I'M GREAT! PERFECT, EVEN! SORRY ABOUT THAT!!
I'LL TRY TO BE ALIVE FOR THE NEXT VOLUME!

Art Staff
Suri ♀: Chief Assistant
0-Second ♂: Background Art
Taurus ♀: Background Art

Military Advisor
Lee Hyun Seok (warmania)

SPECIAL THANKS
Shingo Takano

Crossover Planning
JESUS—Sajin Kouro, Yami no Aegis, Akatsuki no Aegis
Written by Kyouichi Nanatsuki,
Art by Yoshihide Fujiwara
(Shogakukan)

Design Assistance
Hitoshi Fukuchi.

Until Death do us Part

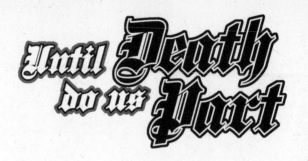

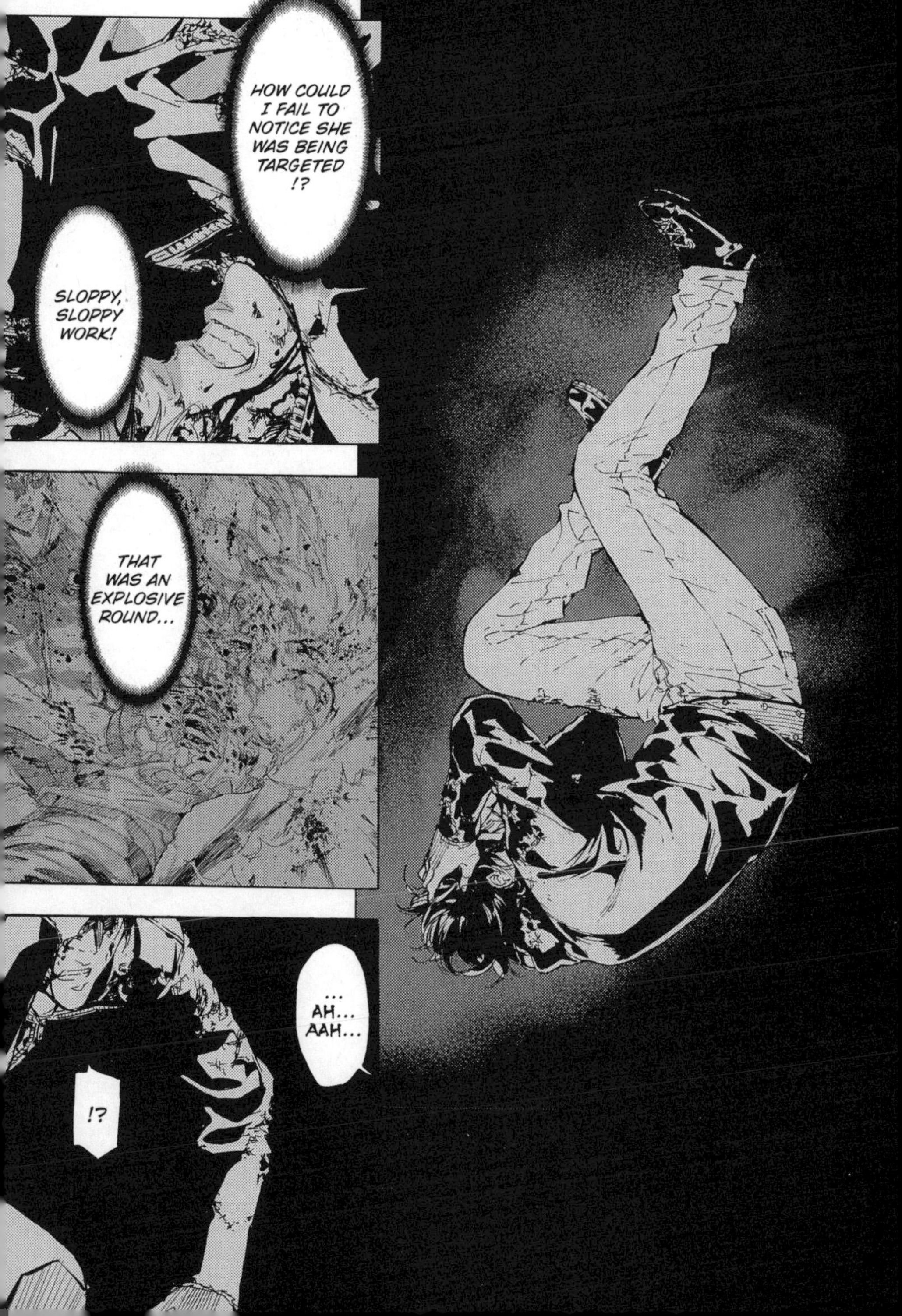
HOW COULD I FAIL TO NOTICE SHE WAS BEING TARGETED !?
SLOPPY, SLOPPY WORK!
THAT WAS AN EXPLOSIVE ROUND...
... AH... AAH...
!?

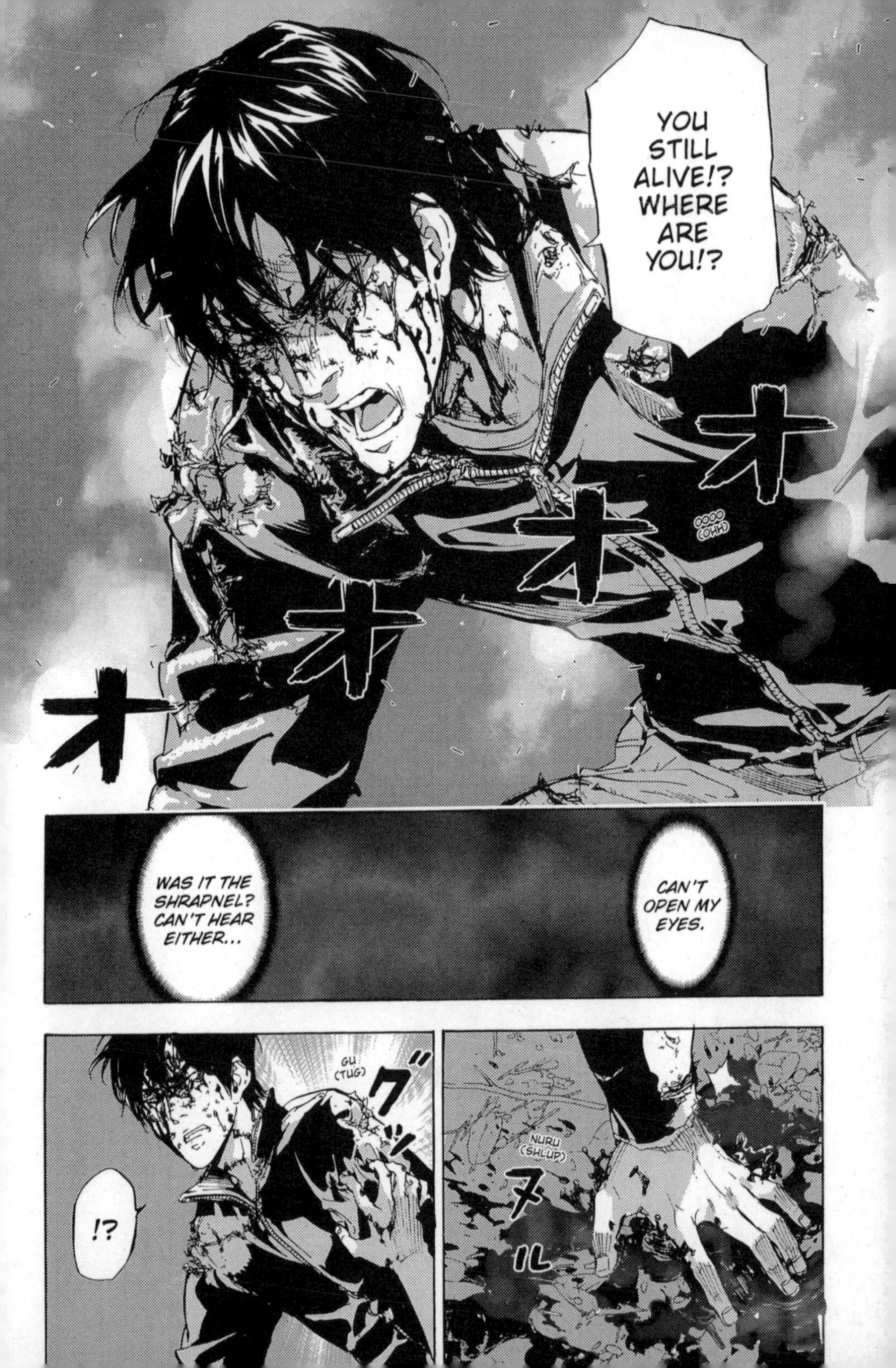
YOU STILL ALIVE!? WHERE ARE YOU!?
オオオオ
OOOO (OHH)
CAN'T OPEN MY EYES.
WAS IT THE SHRAPNEL? CAN'T HEAR EITHER...
NURU (SHLUP)
ヌル
GU (TUG)
グッ
!?

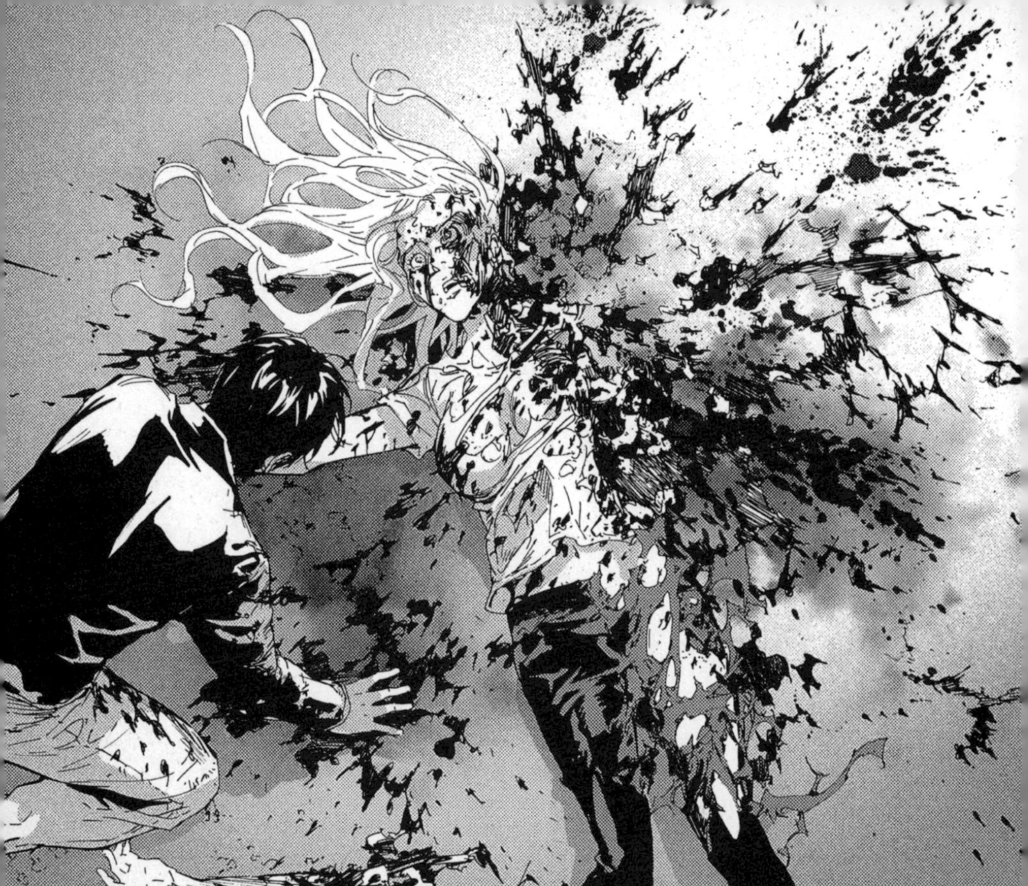
chapter 108

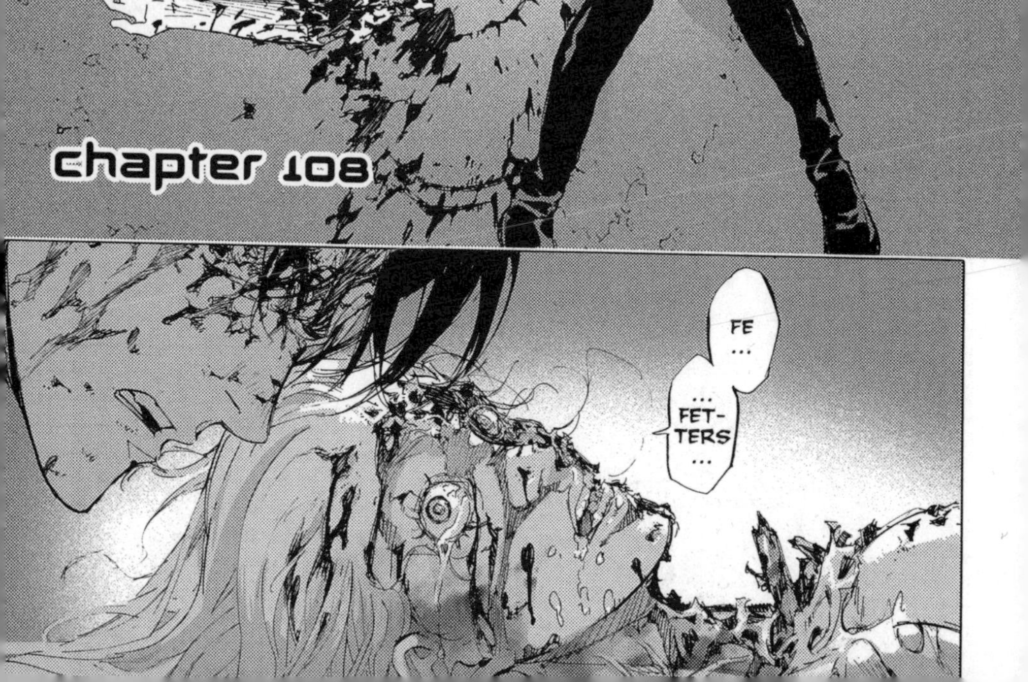
FE ...
... FET-TERS ...

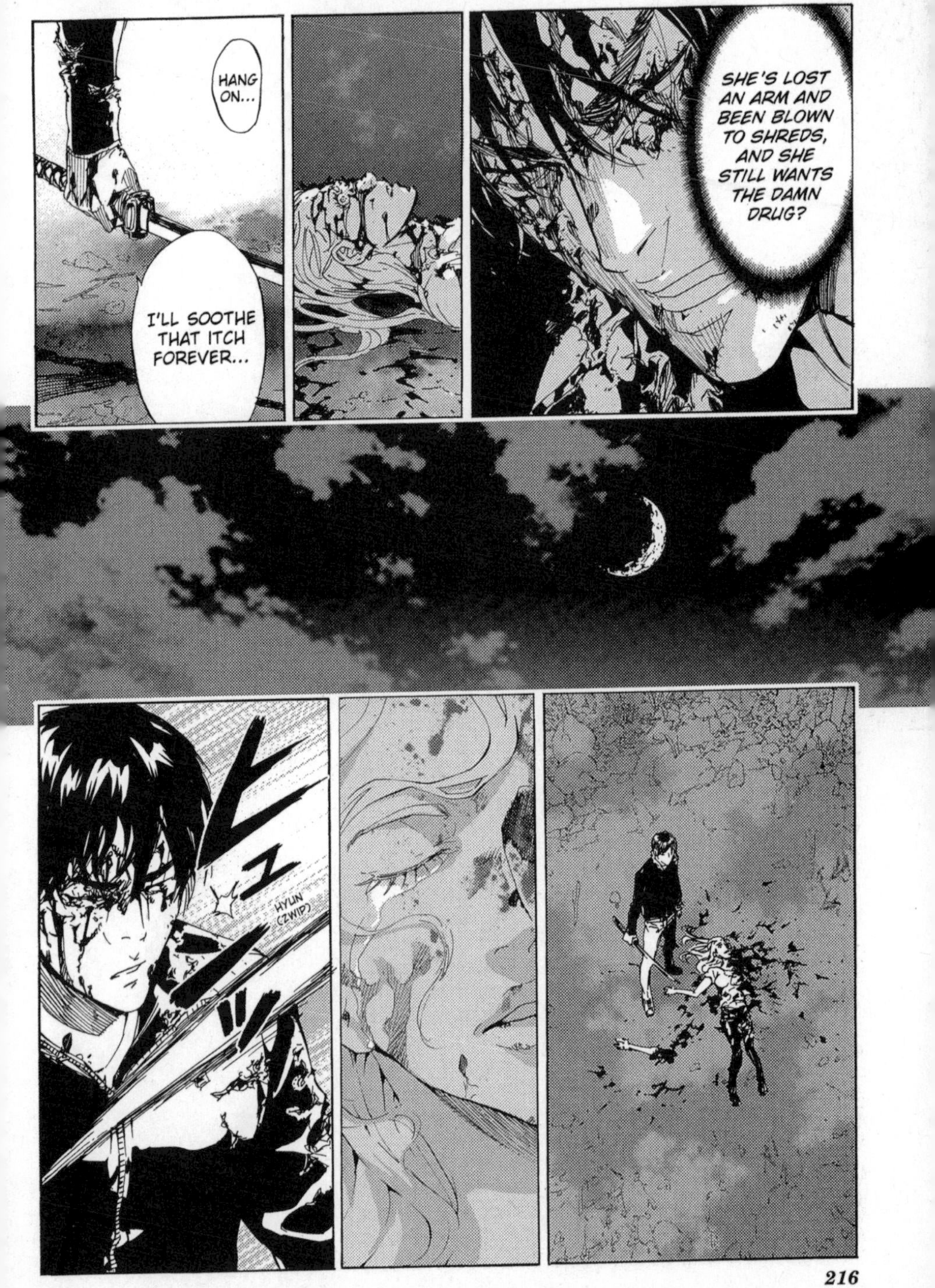
SHE'S LOST AN ARM AND BEEN BLOWN TO SHREDS, AND SHE STILL WANTS THE DAMN DRUG?
HANG ON...
I'LL SOOTHE THAT ITCH FOREVER...
HYUN (ZWIP)

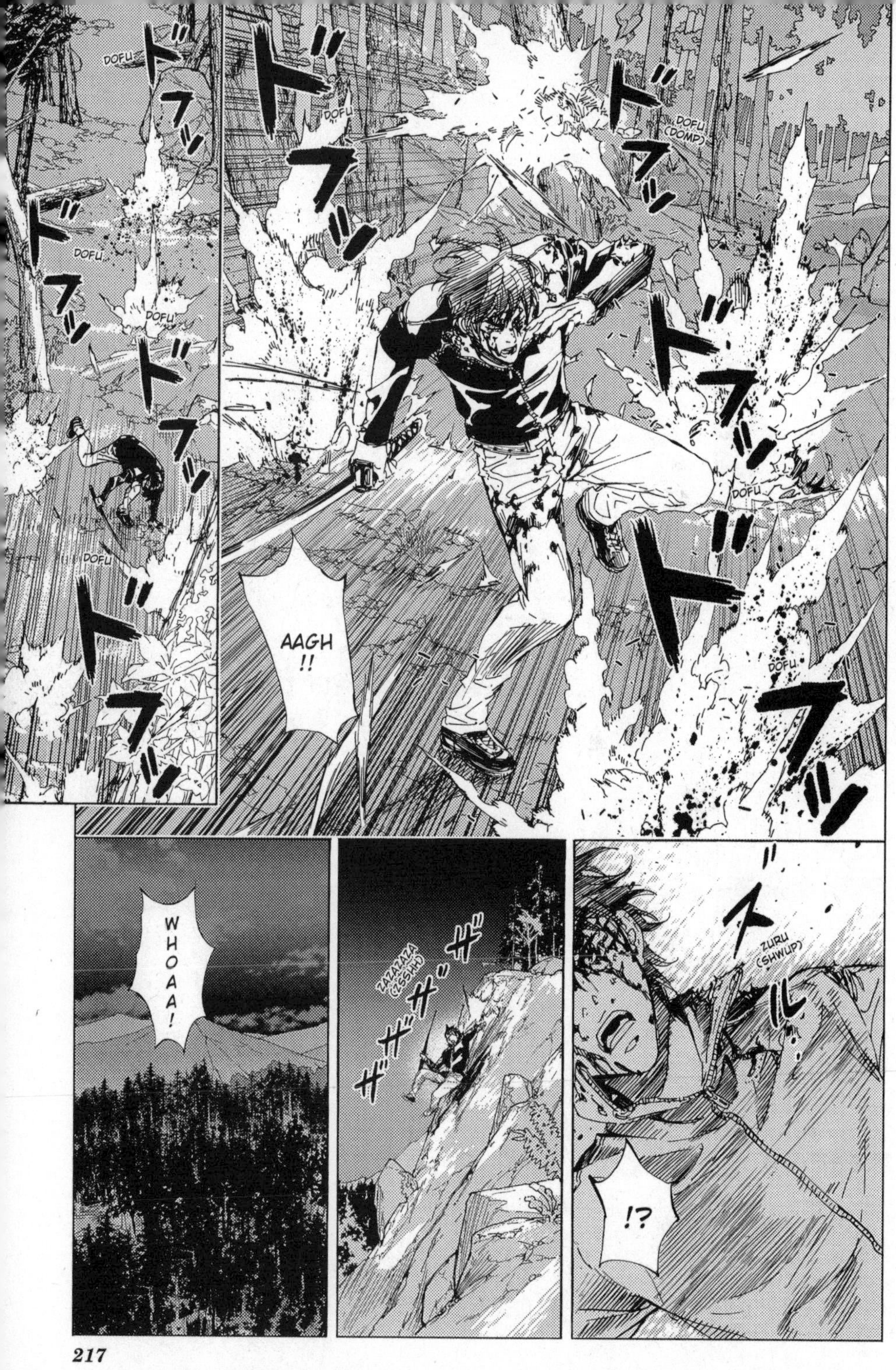

ドフッ
DOFU (DOMP)
ドフッ
DOFU
ドフッ
DOFU
ドフッ
DOFU
ドフッ
AAGH !!
ドフッ
DOFU
ドフッ
DOFU
ドフッ
DOFU
ドフッ
DOFU
ズル
ZURU (SHWUP)
!?
ザザザザ
ZAZAZAZA (ZSSHH)
WHOAAA!

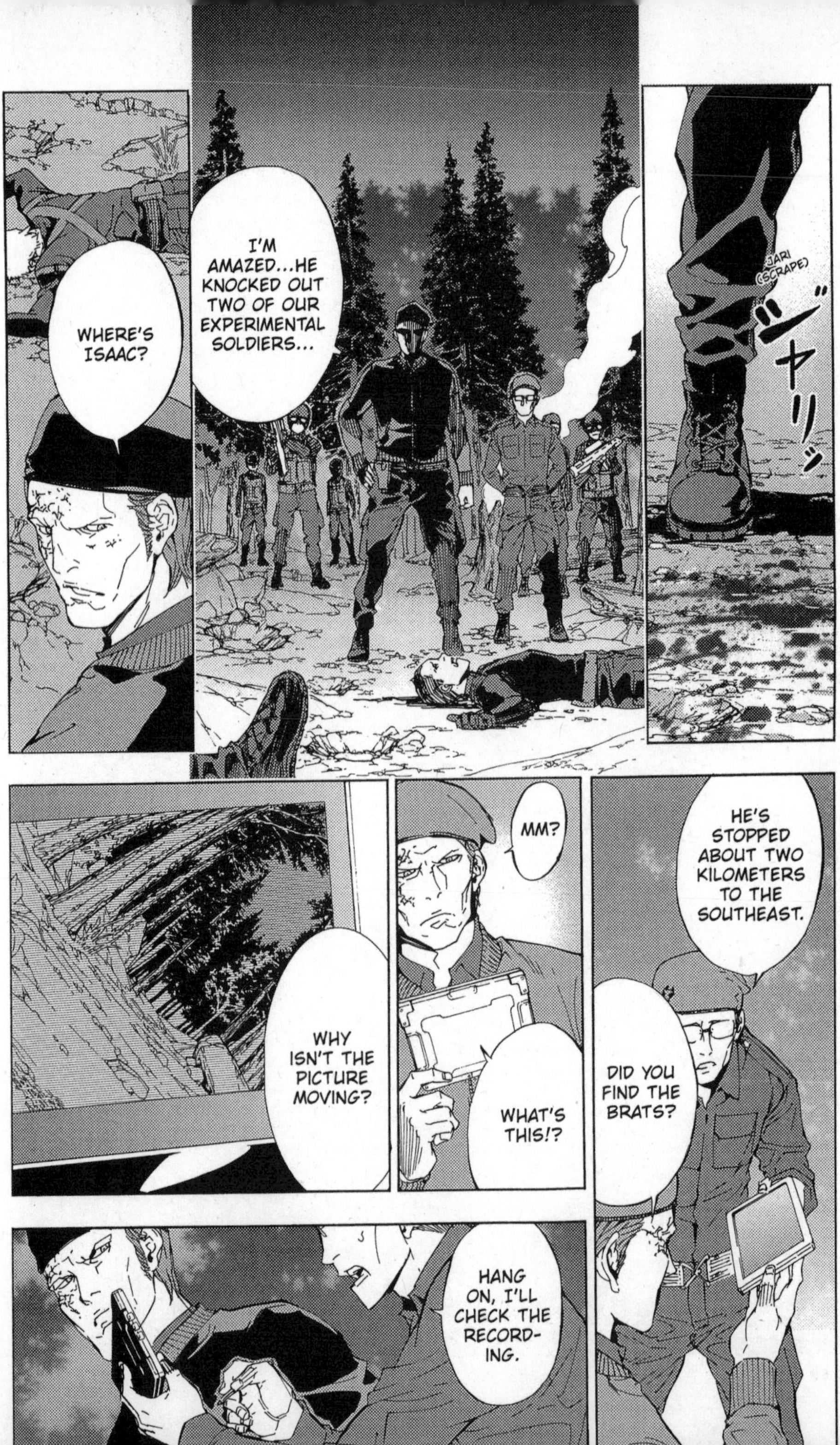

JARI (SCRAPE)
ジャリッ
I'M AMAZED...HE KNOCKED OUT TWO OF OUR EXPERIMENTAL SOLDIERS...
WHERE'S ISAAC?
HE'S STOPPED ABOUT TWO KILOMETERS TO THE SOUTHEAST.
DID YOU FIND THE BRATS?
MM?
WHAT'S THIS!?
WHY ISN'T THE PICTURE MOVING?
HANG ON, I'LL CHECK THE RECORDING.

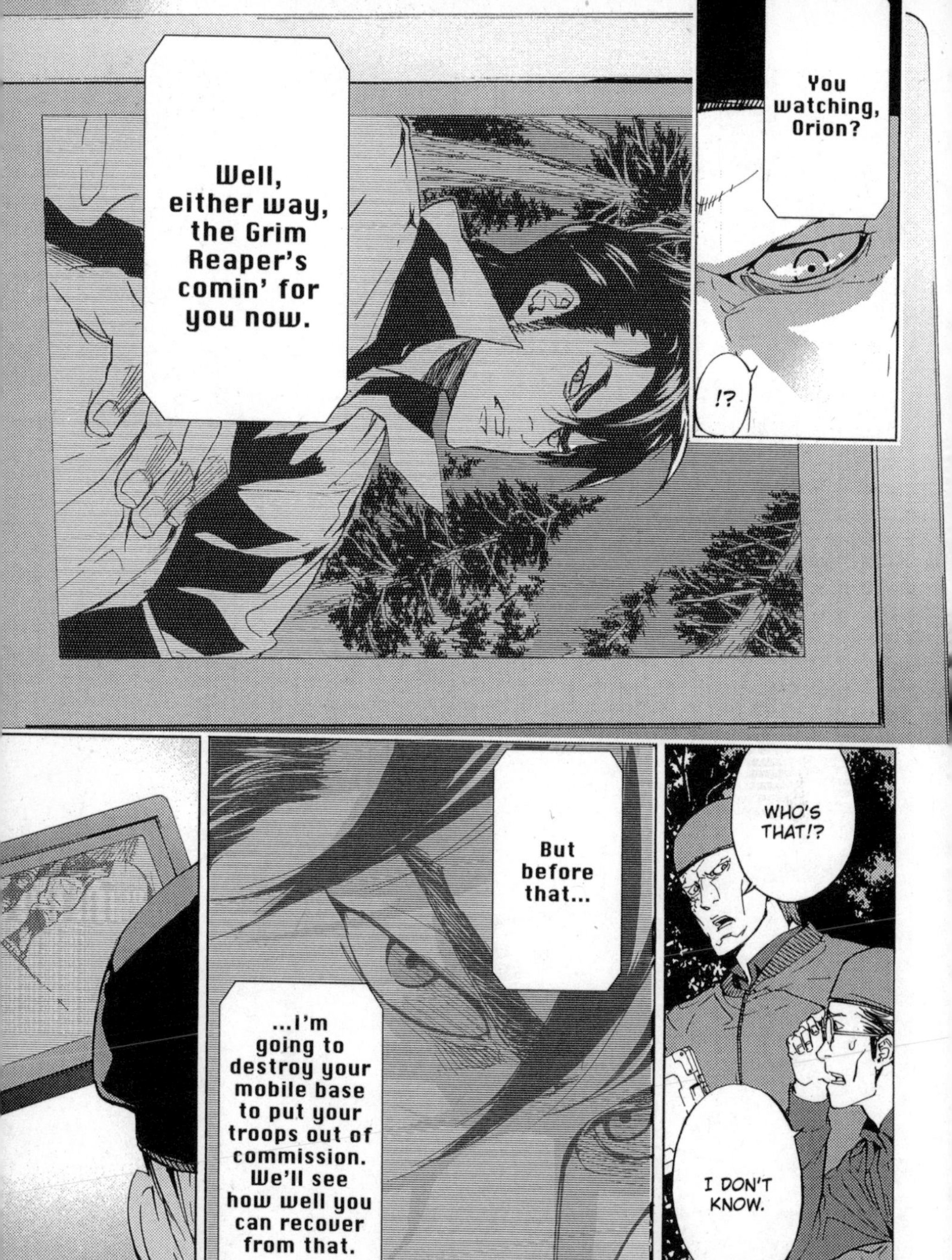
You watching, Orion?
!?
Well, either way, the Grim Reaper's comin' for you now.
WHO'S THAT!?
I DON'T KNOW.
But before that...
...I'm going to destroy your mobile base to put your troops out of commission. We'll see how well you can recover from that.

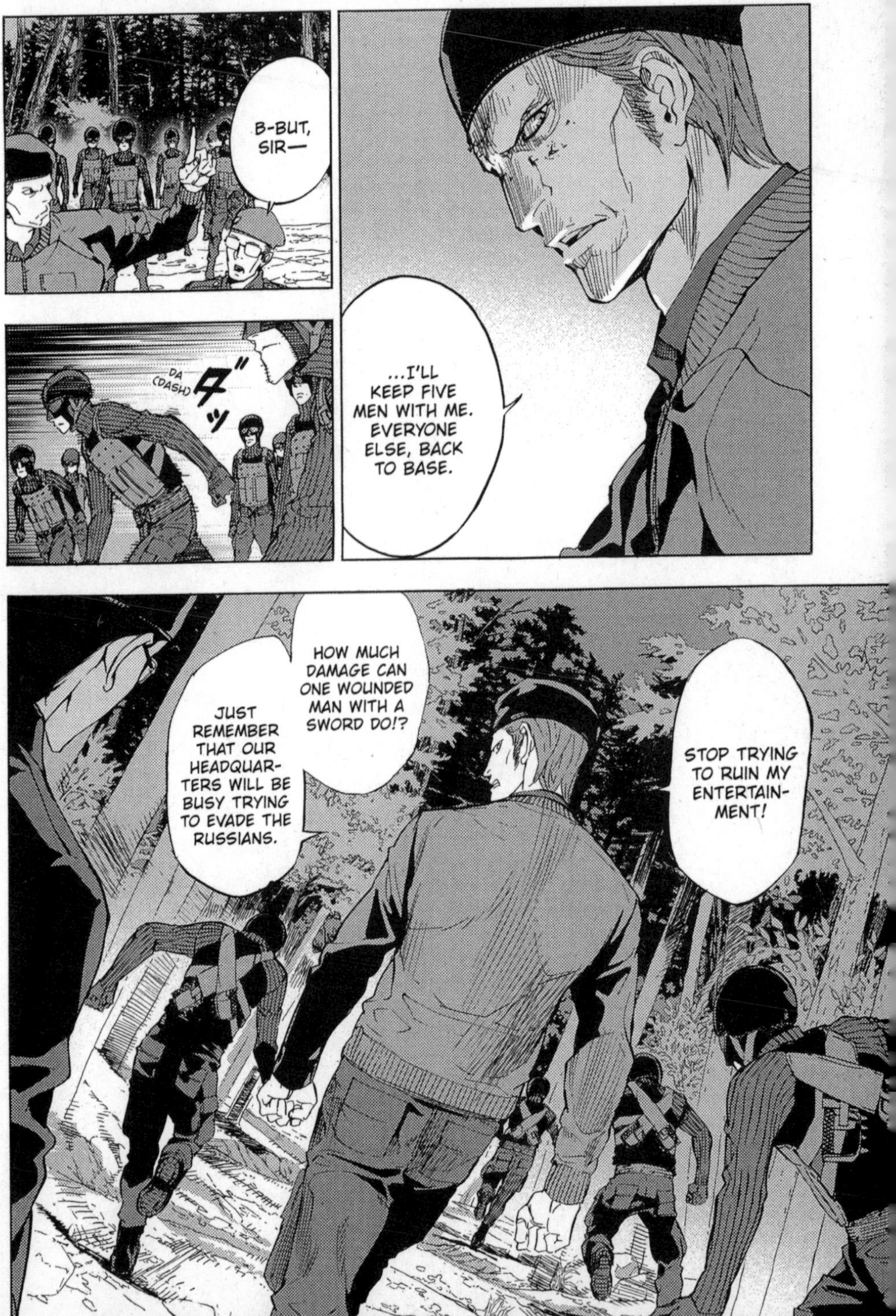
...I'LL KEEP FIVE MEN WITH ME. EVERYONE ELSE, BACK TO BASE.
B-BUT, SIR—
DA (DASH)
STOP TRYING TO RUIN MY ENTERTAIN-MENT!
HOW MUCH DAMAGE CAN ONE WOUNDED MAN WITH A SWORD DO!?
JUST REMEMBER THAT OUR HEADQUAR-TERS WILL BE BUSY TRYING TO EVADE THE RUSSIANS.

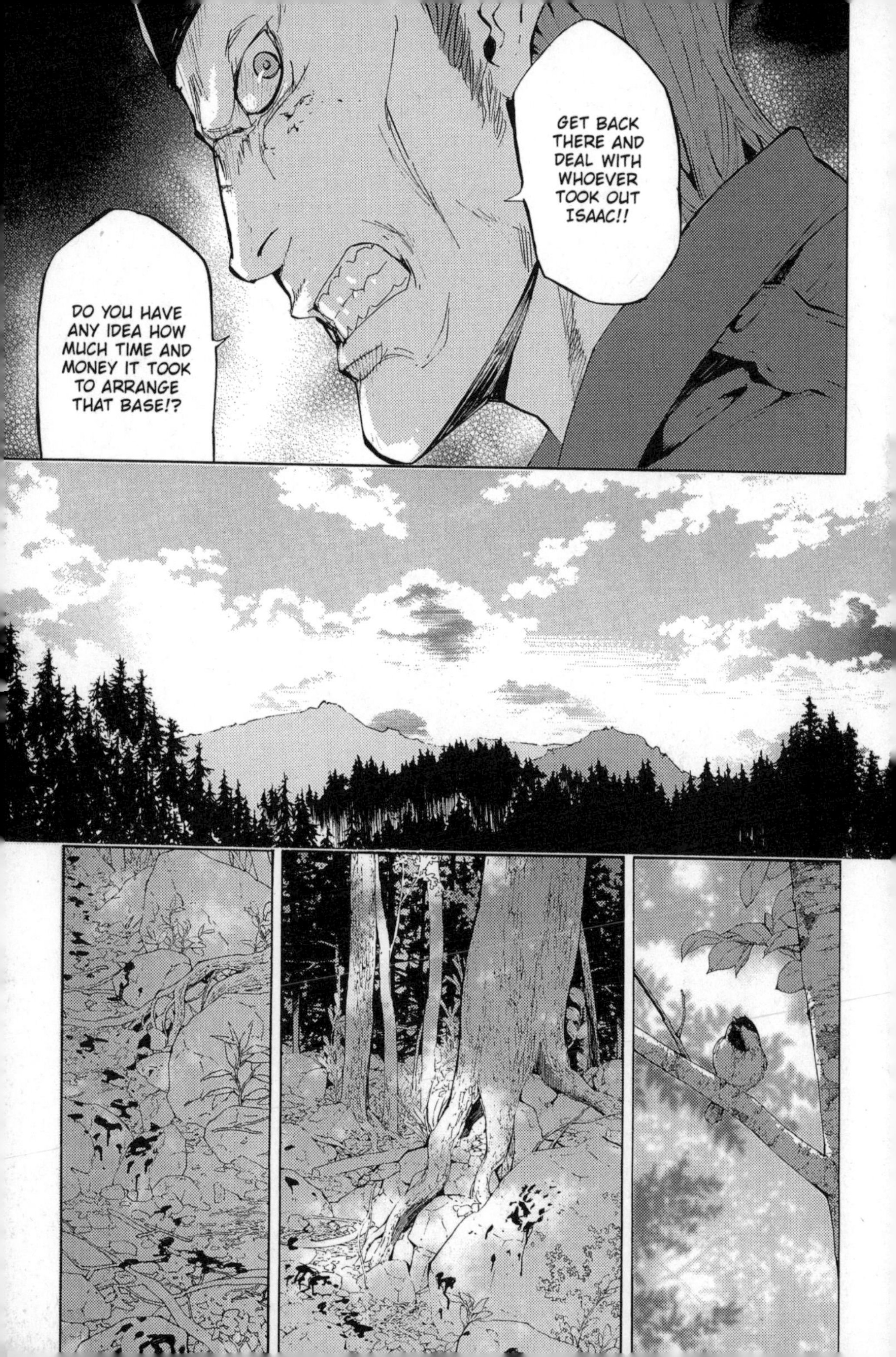
GET BACK THERE AND DEAL WITH WHOEVER TOOK OUT ISAAC!!
DO YOU HAVE ANY IDEA HOW MUCH TIME AND MONEY IT TOOK TO ARRANGE THAT BASE!?

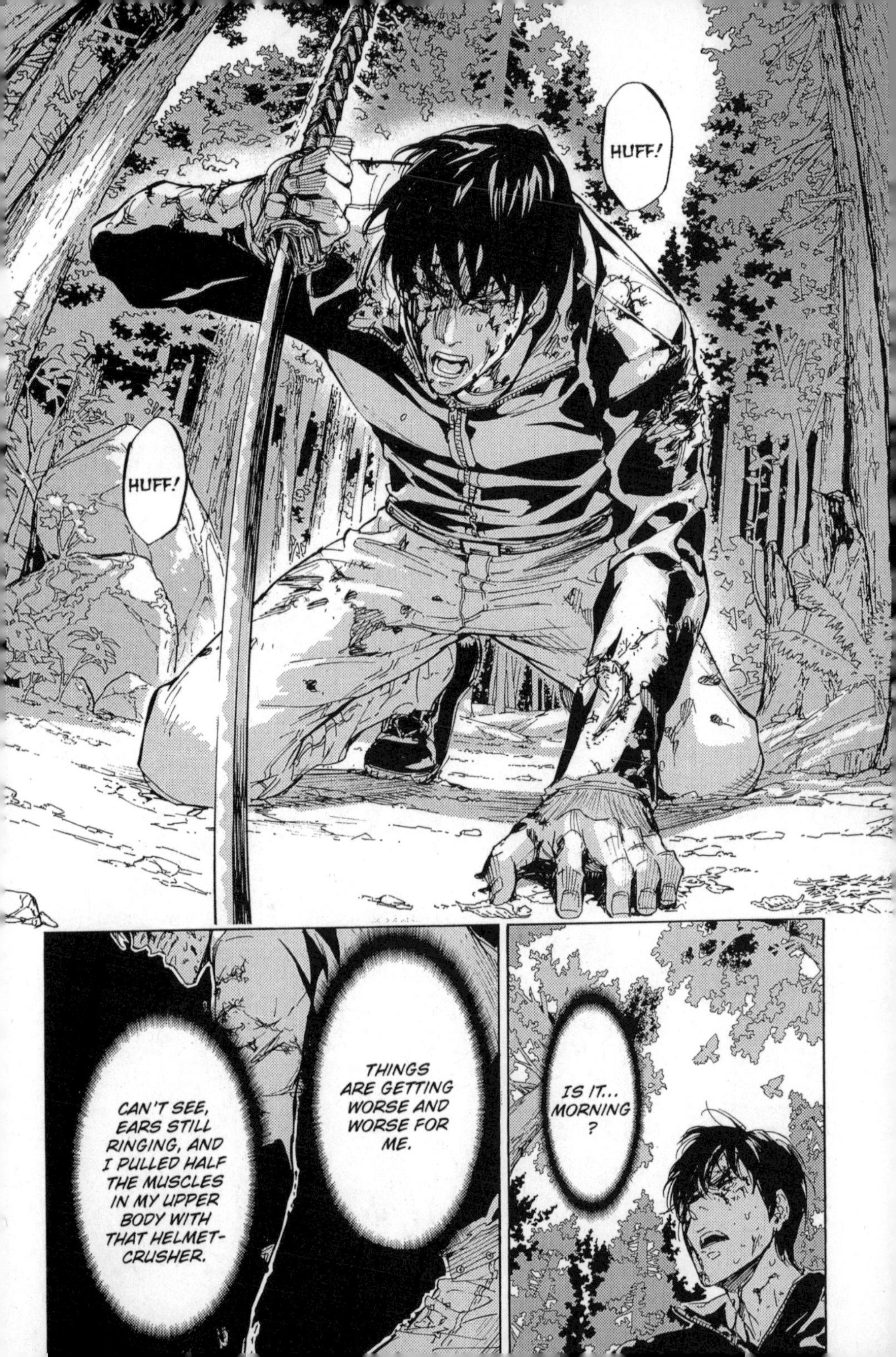
HUFF!
HUFF!
IS IT... MORNING?
THINGS ARE GETTING WORSE AND WORSE FOR ME.
CAN'T SEE, EARS STILL RINGING, AND I PULLED HALF THE MUSCLES IN MY UPPER BODY WITH THAT HELMET-CRUSHER.

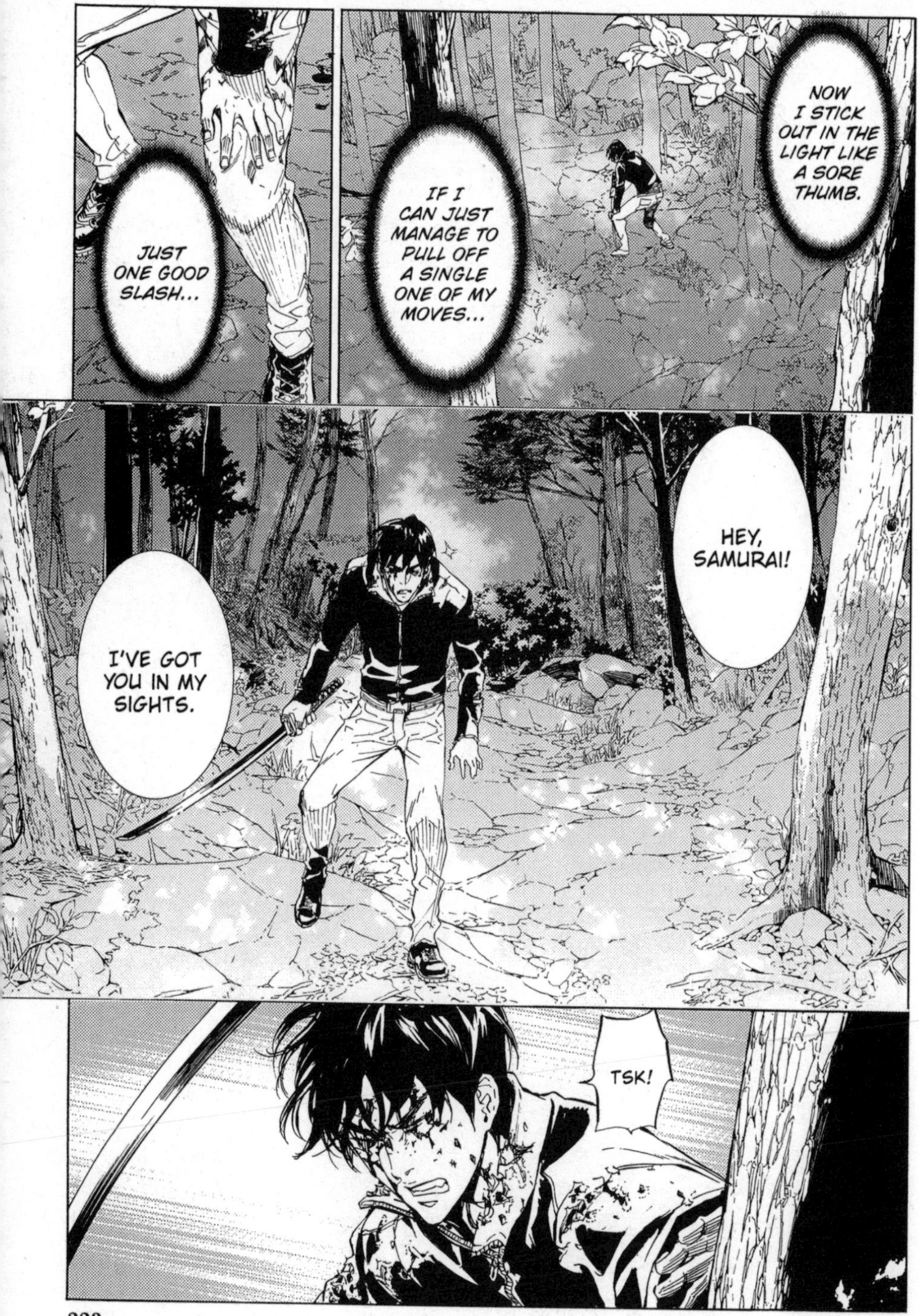
NOW I STICK OUT IN THE LIGHT LIKE A SORE THUMB.
IF I CAN JUST MANAGE TO PULL OFF A SINGLE ONE OF MY MOVES...
JUST ONE GOOD SLASH...
HEY, SAMURAI!
I'VE GOT YOU IN MY SIGHTS.
TSK!

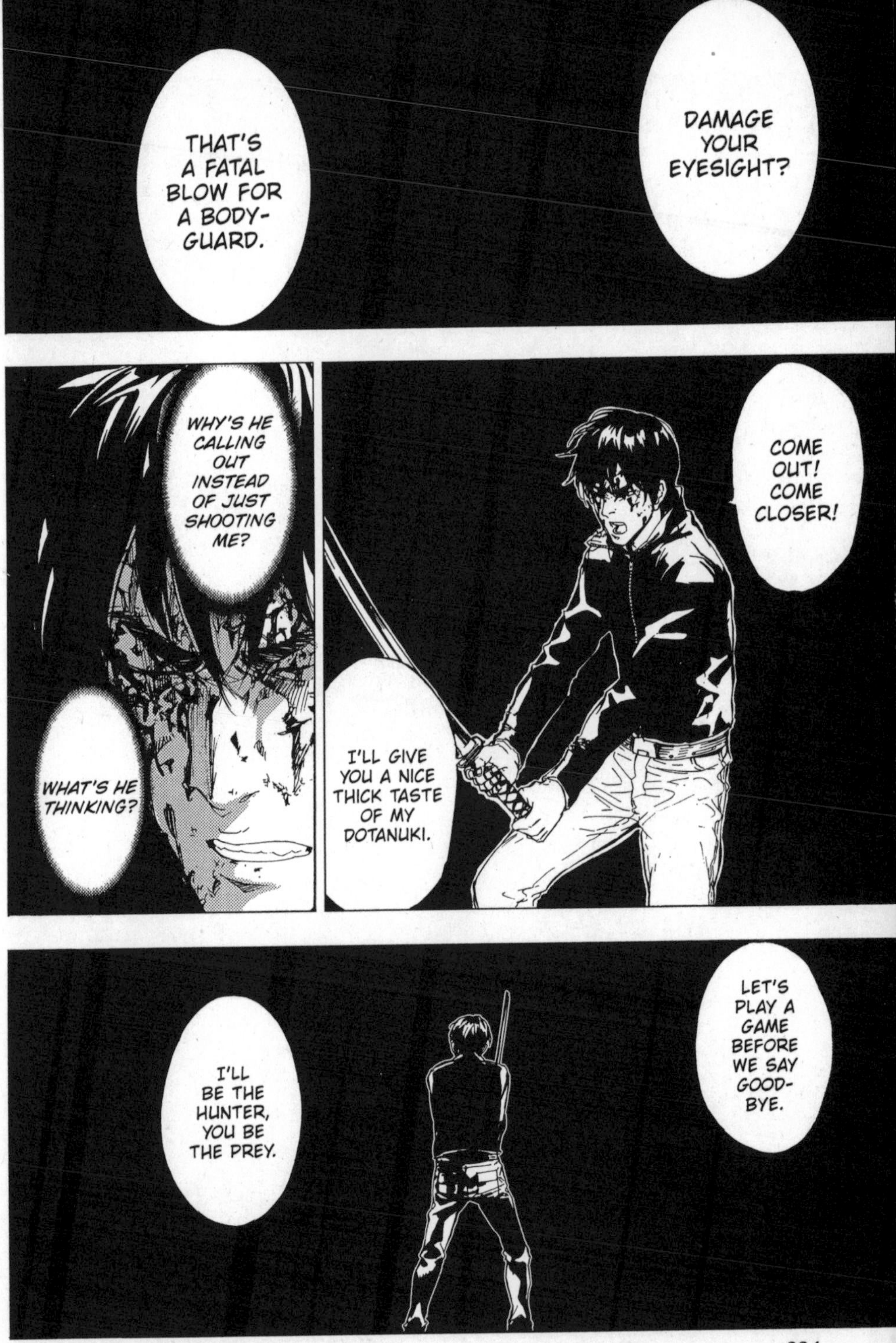
DAMAGE YOUR EYESIGHT?
THAT'S A FATAL BLOW FOR A BODY-GUARD.
COME OUT! COME CLOSER!
I'LL GIVE YOU A NICE THICK TASTE OF MY DOTANUKI.
WHY'S HE CALLING OUT INSTEAD OF JUST SHOOTING ME?
WHAT'S HE THINKING?
LET'S PLAY A GAME BEFORE WE SAY GOOD-BYE.
I'LL BE THE HUNTER, YOU BE THE PREY.

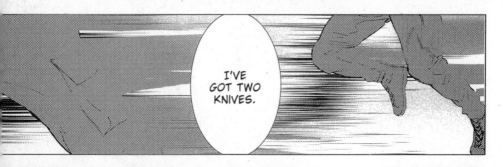

I'VE GOT TWO KNIVES.

IF YOU MANAGE TO EVADE ME, YOU MAY RETURN TO WHATEVER HOLE YOU CRAWLED OUT OF.

BUT NO CREATURE HAS YET EVADED MY GRASP!!

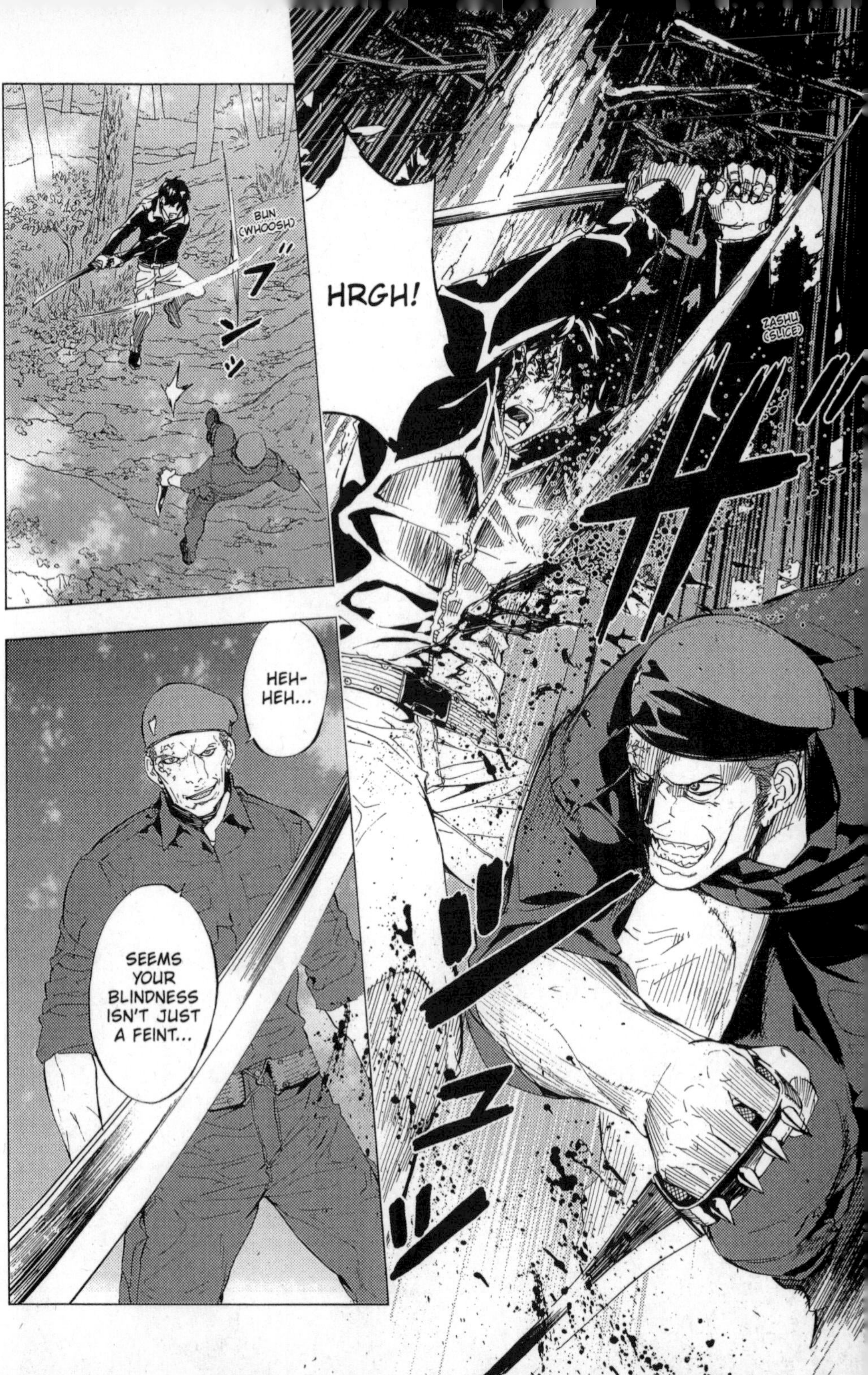
HRGH!
ZASHU (SLICE)
BUN (WHOOSH)
HEH-HEH...
SEEMS YOUR BLINDNESS ISN'T JUST A FEINT...

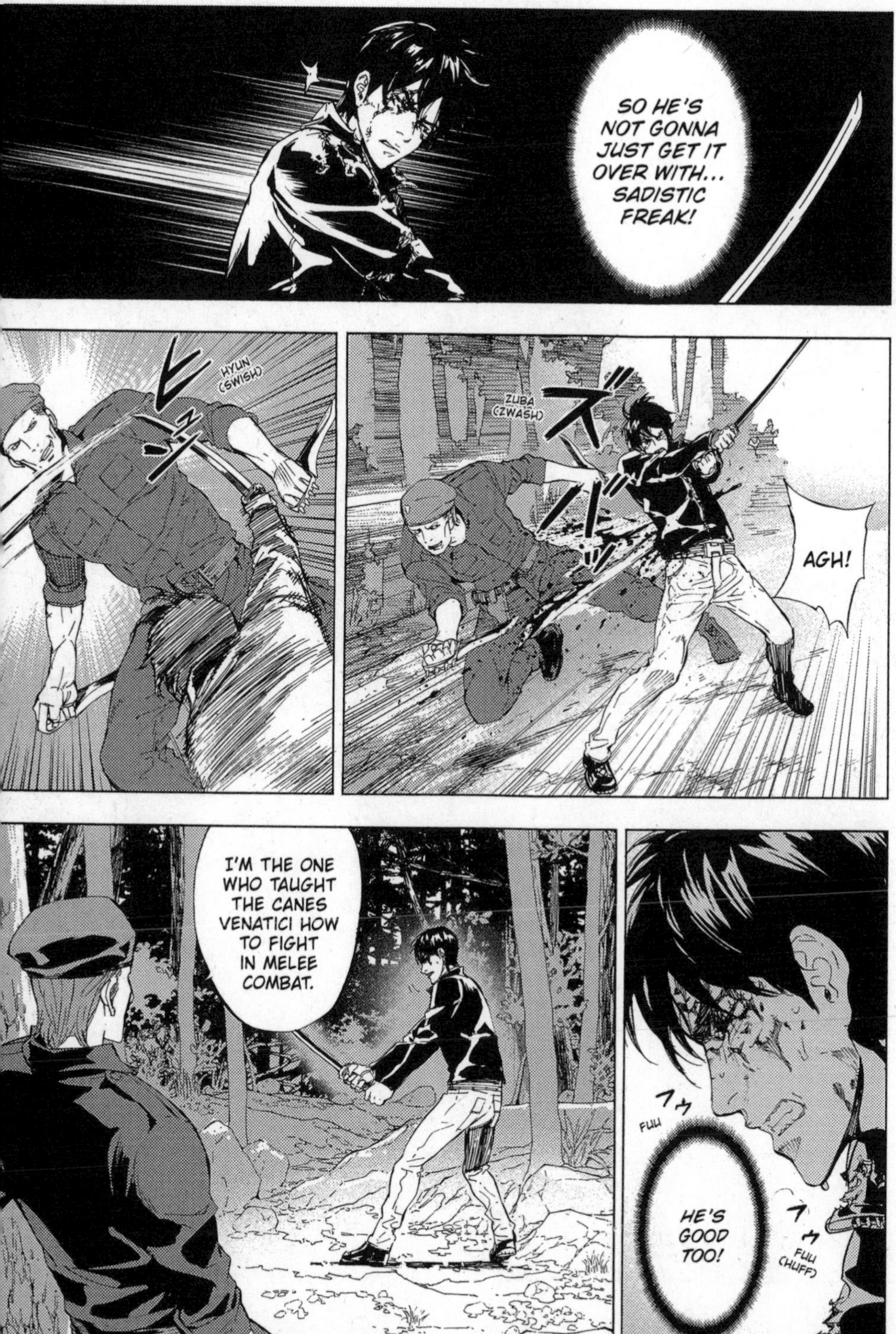
SO HE'S NOT GONNA JUST GET IT OVER WITH... SADISTIC FREAK!
ZUBA (ZWASH)
AGH!
HYUN (SWISH)
FUU
HE'S GOOD TOO!
FUU (HUFF)
I'M THE ONE WHO TAUGHT THE CANES VENATICI HOW TO FIGHT IN MELEE COMBAT.

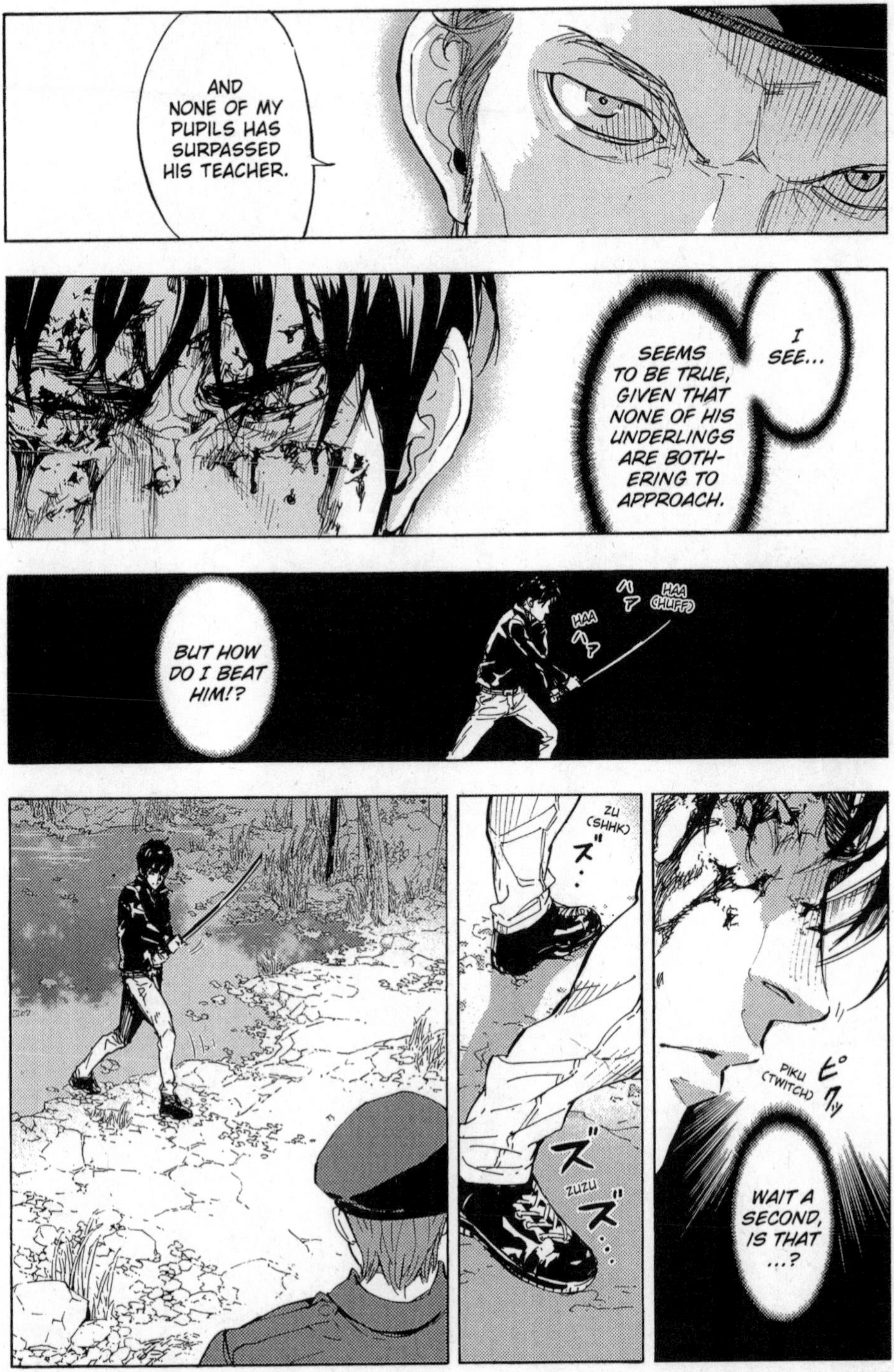
AND NONE OF MY PUPILS HAS SURPASSED HIS TEACHER.
I SEE...
SEEMS TO BE TRUE, GIVEN THAT NONE OF HIS UNDERLINGS ARE BOTH-ERING TO APPROACH.
HAA (HUFF)
HAA
BUT HOW DO I BEAT HIM!?
PIKU (TWITCH)
WAIT A SECOND, IS THAT ...?
ZU (SHHK)
ZUZU

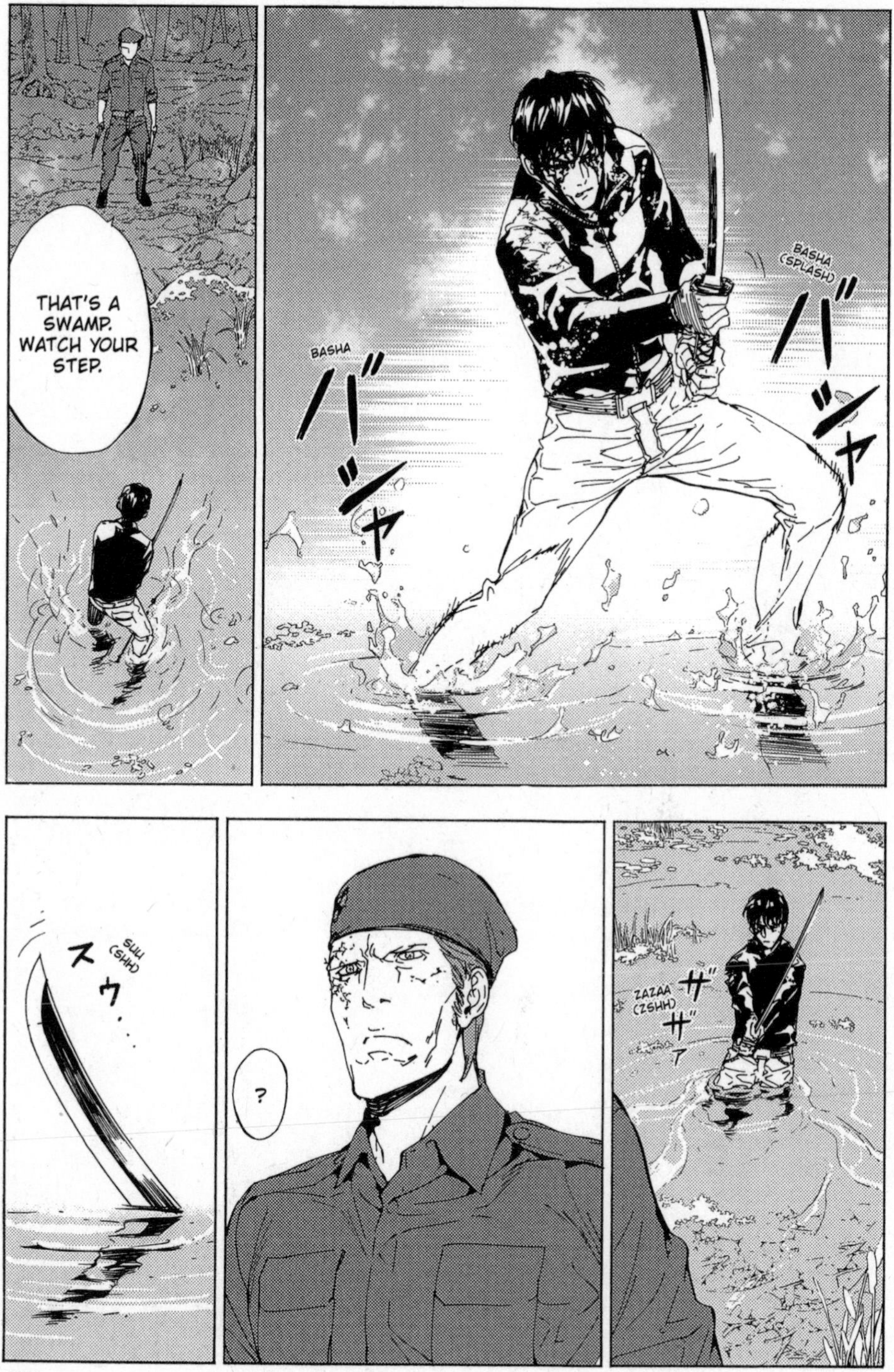
BASHA (SPLASH)
バシャ
BASHA
バシャ
THAT'S A SWAMP. WATCH YOUR STEP.
ZAZAA (ZSHH)
ザザァ
?
SUU (SHH)
スウ...

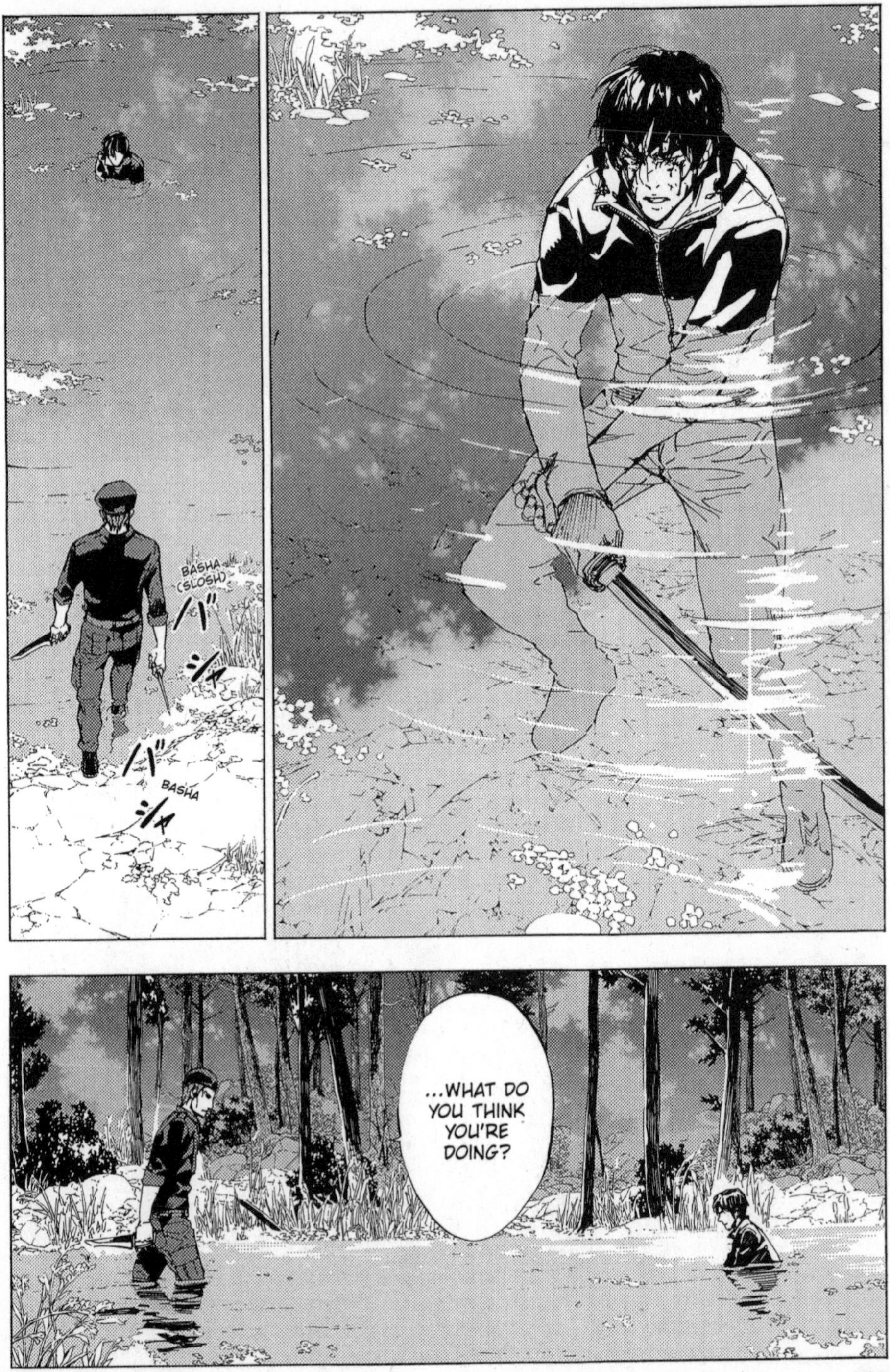
BASHA
(SLOSH)
バシャ
バシャ
BASHA
...WHAT DO YOU THINK YOU'RE DOING?

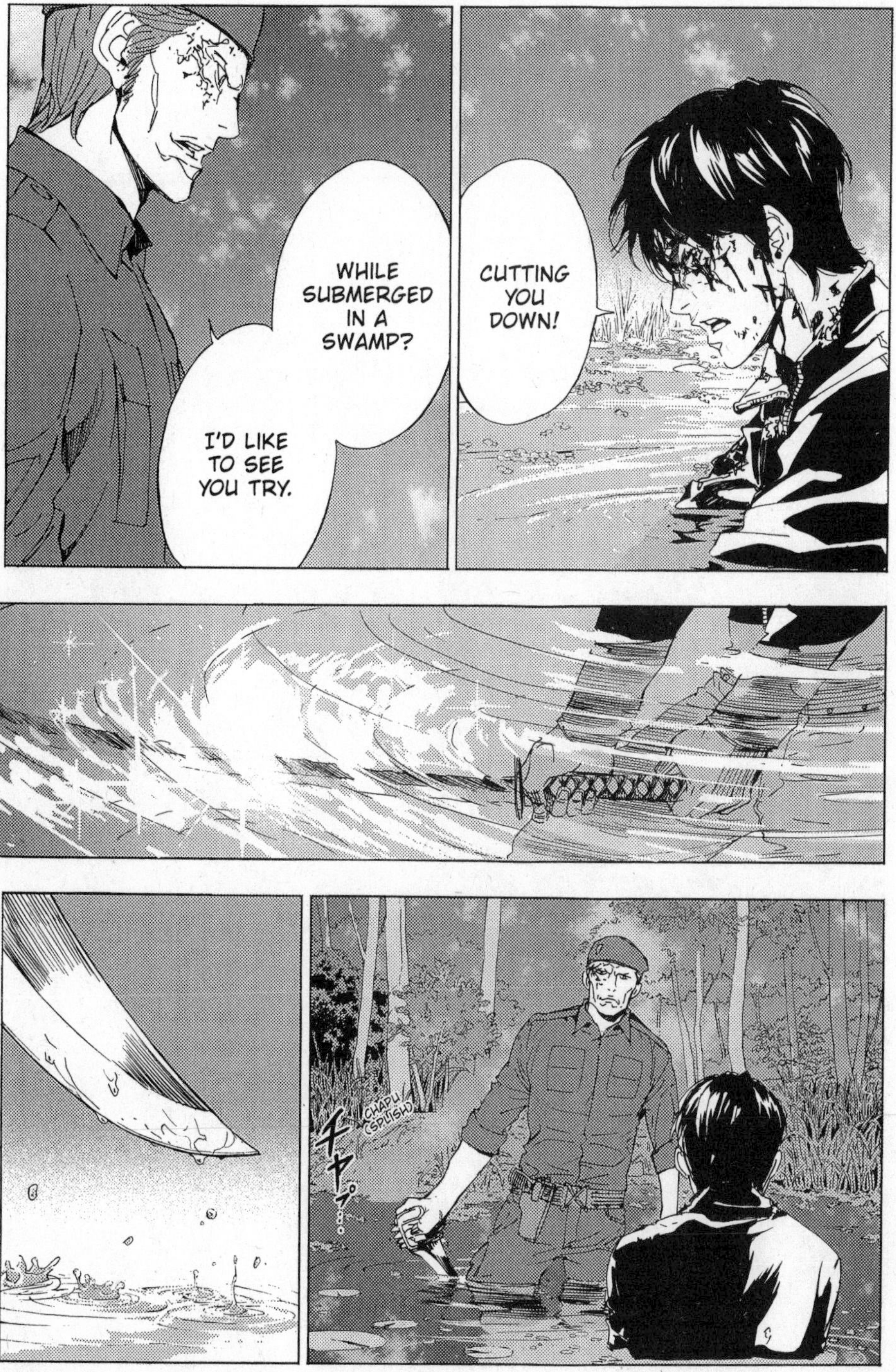
CUTTING YOU DOWN!
WHILE SUBMERGED IN A SWAMP?
I'D LIKE TO SEE YOU TRY.
チャプ…
CHAPU (SPLISH)

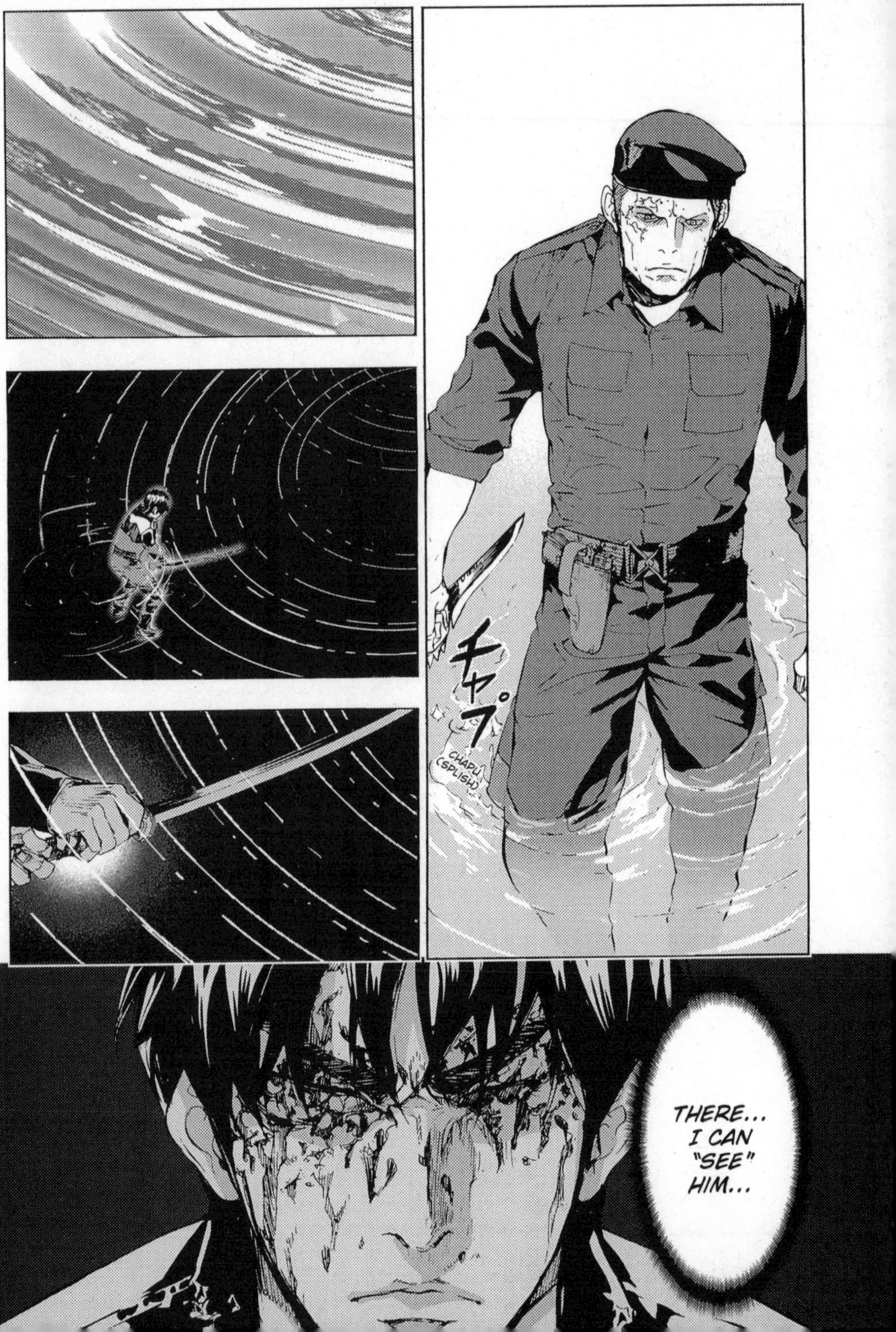
チャプ
CHAPU (SPLISH)
THERE... I CAN "SEE" HIM...

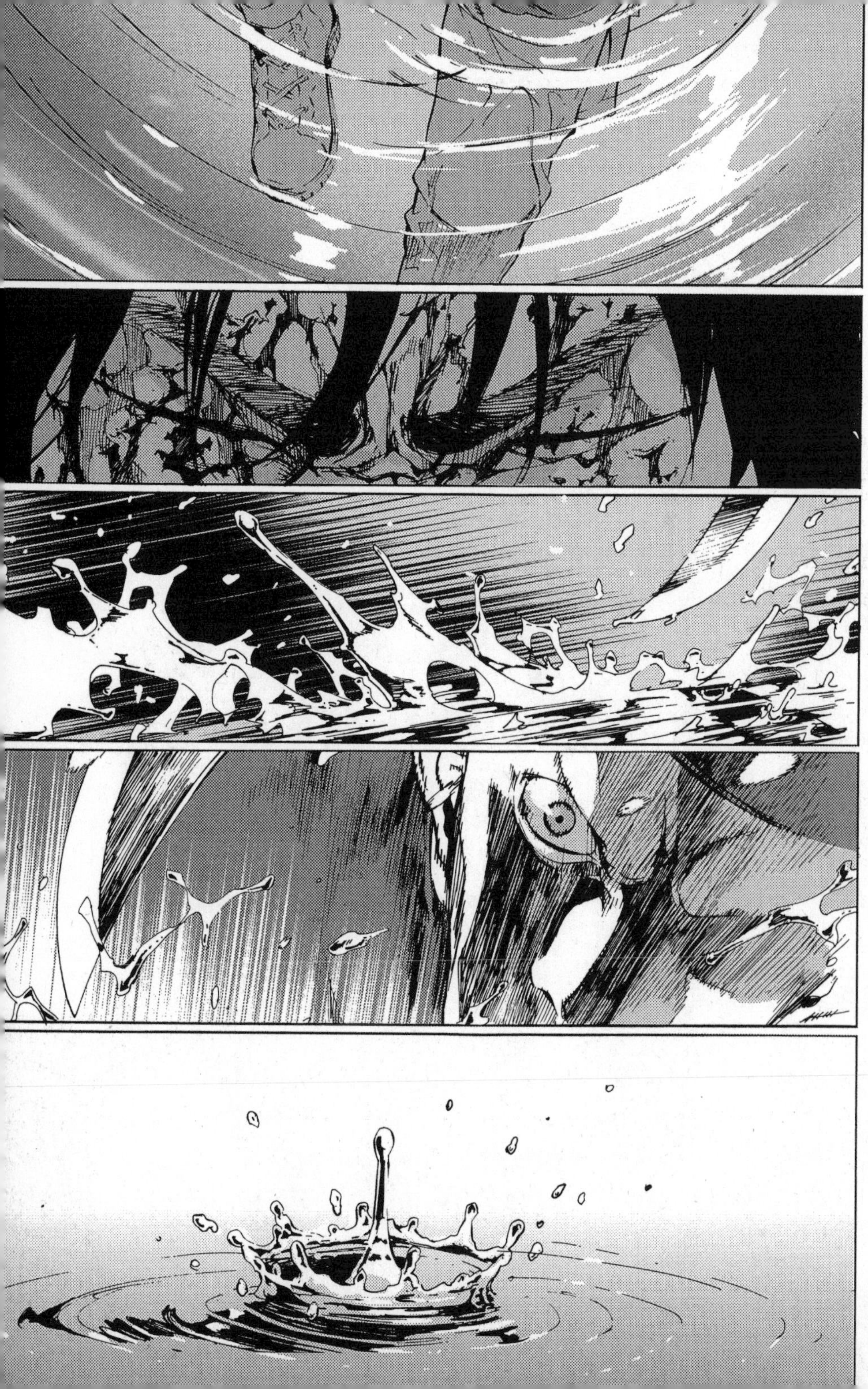

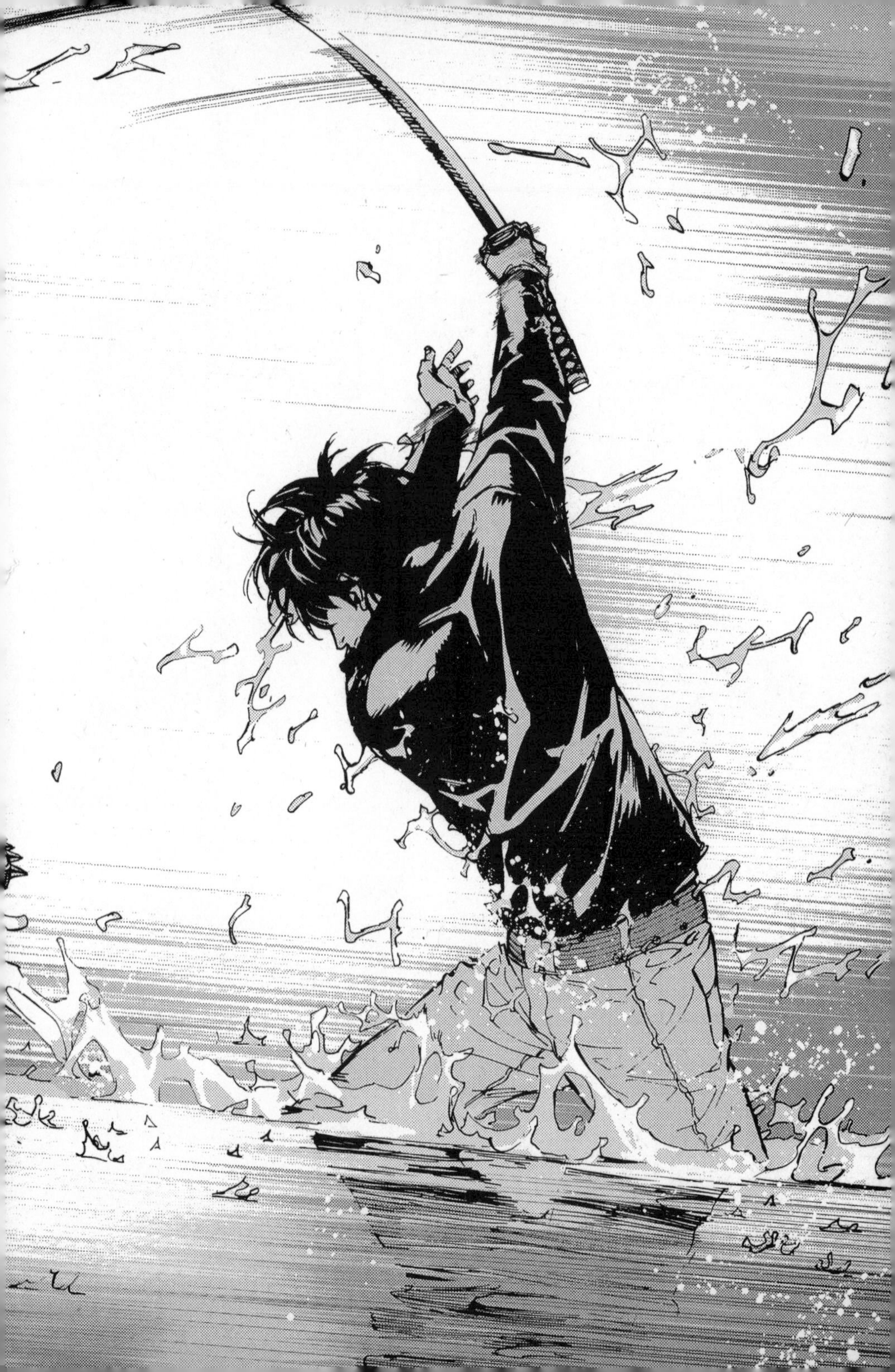

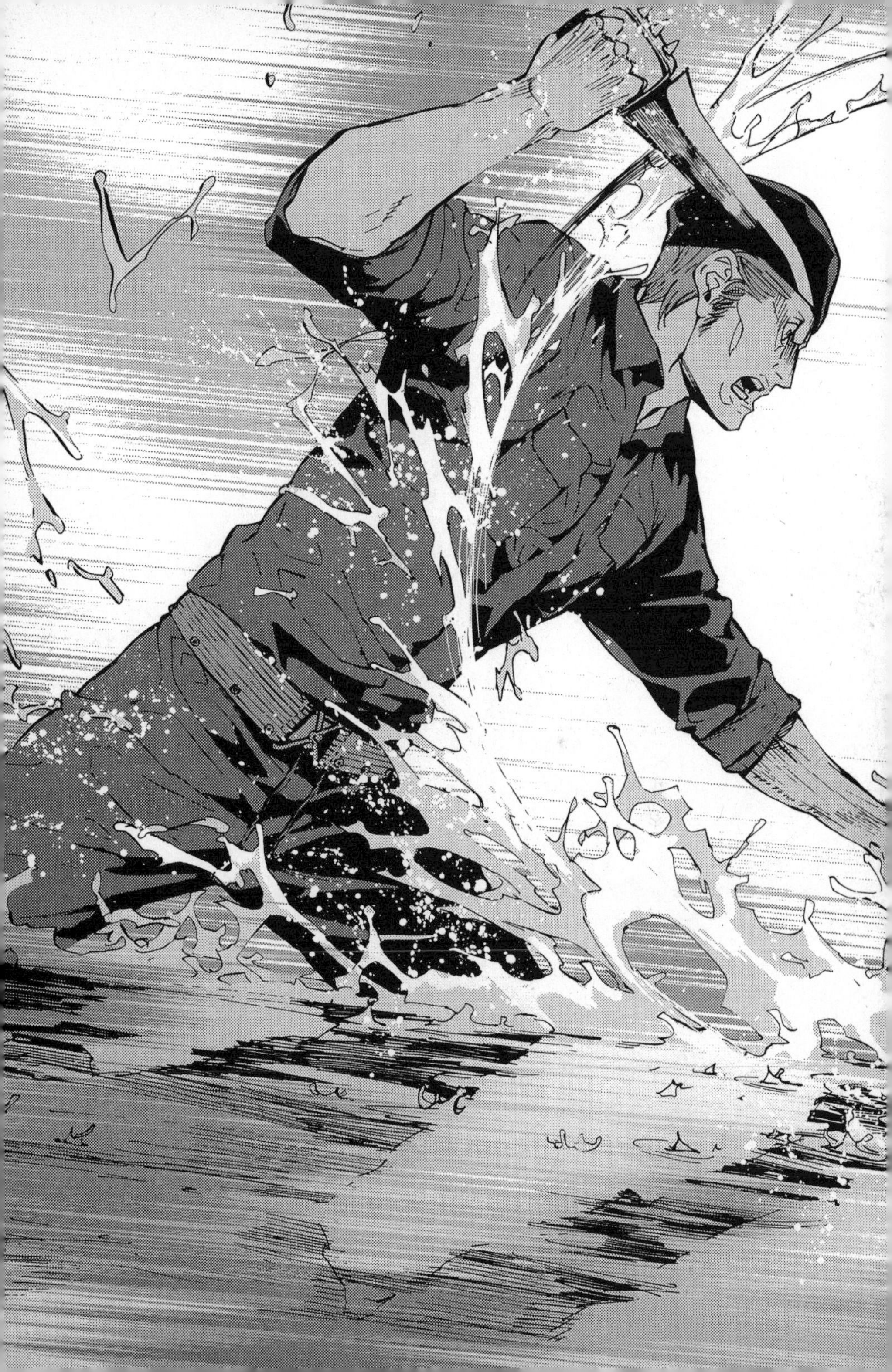

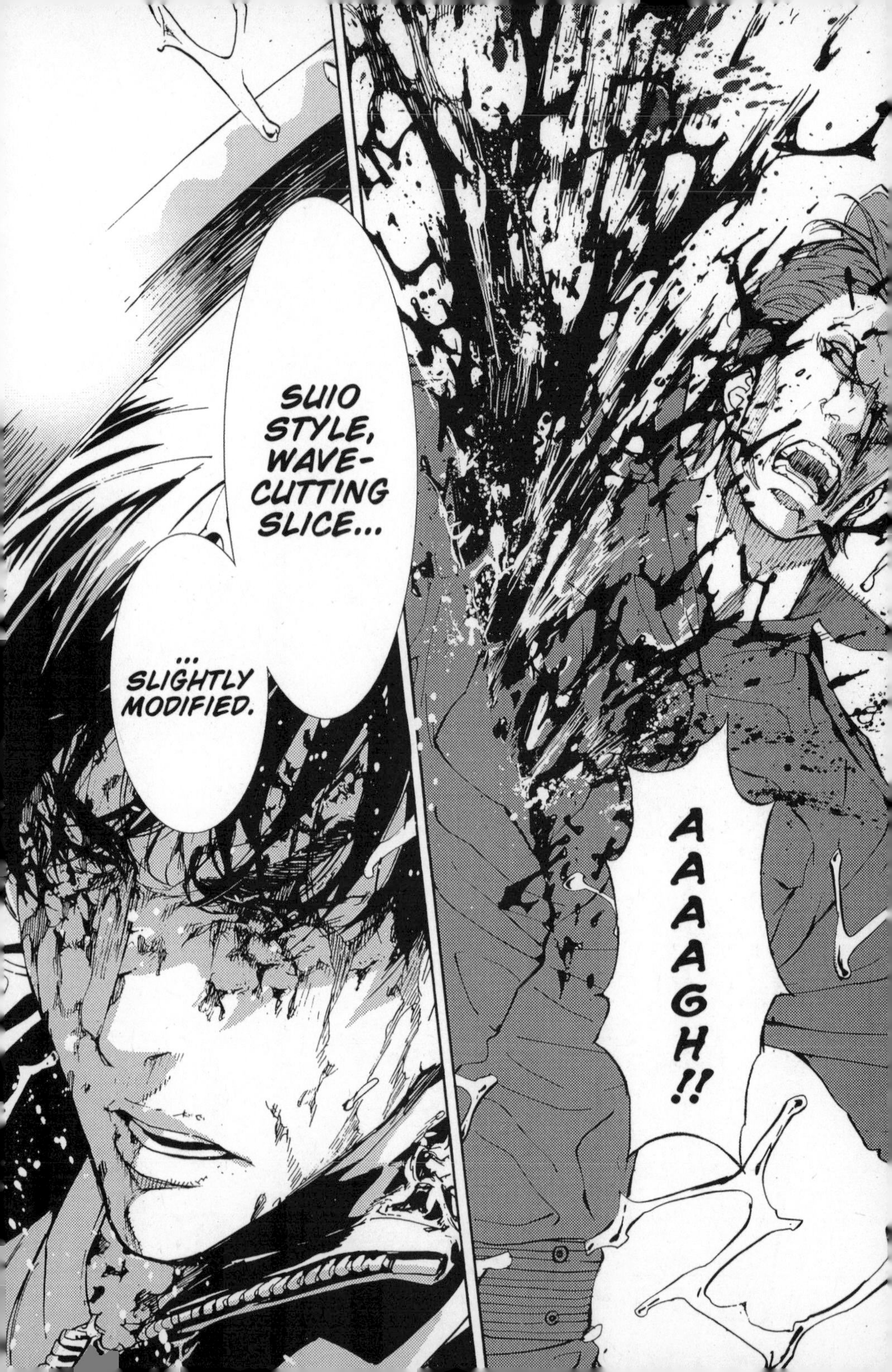
SUIO STYLE, WAVE-CUTTING SLICE...
...SLIGHTLY MODIFIED.
AAAAGH!!

Until Death do us Part

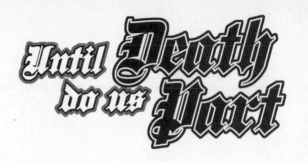

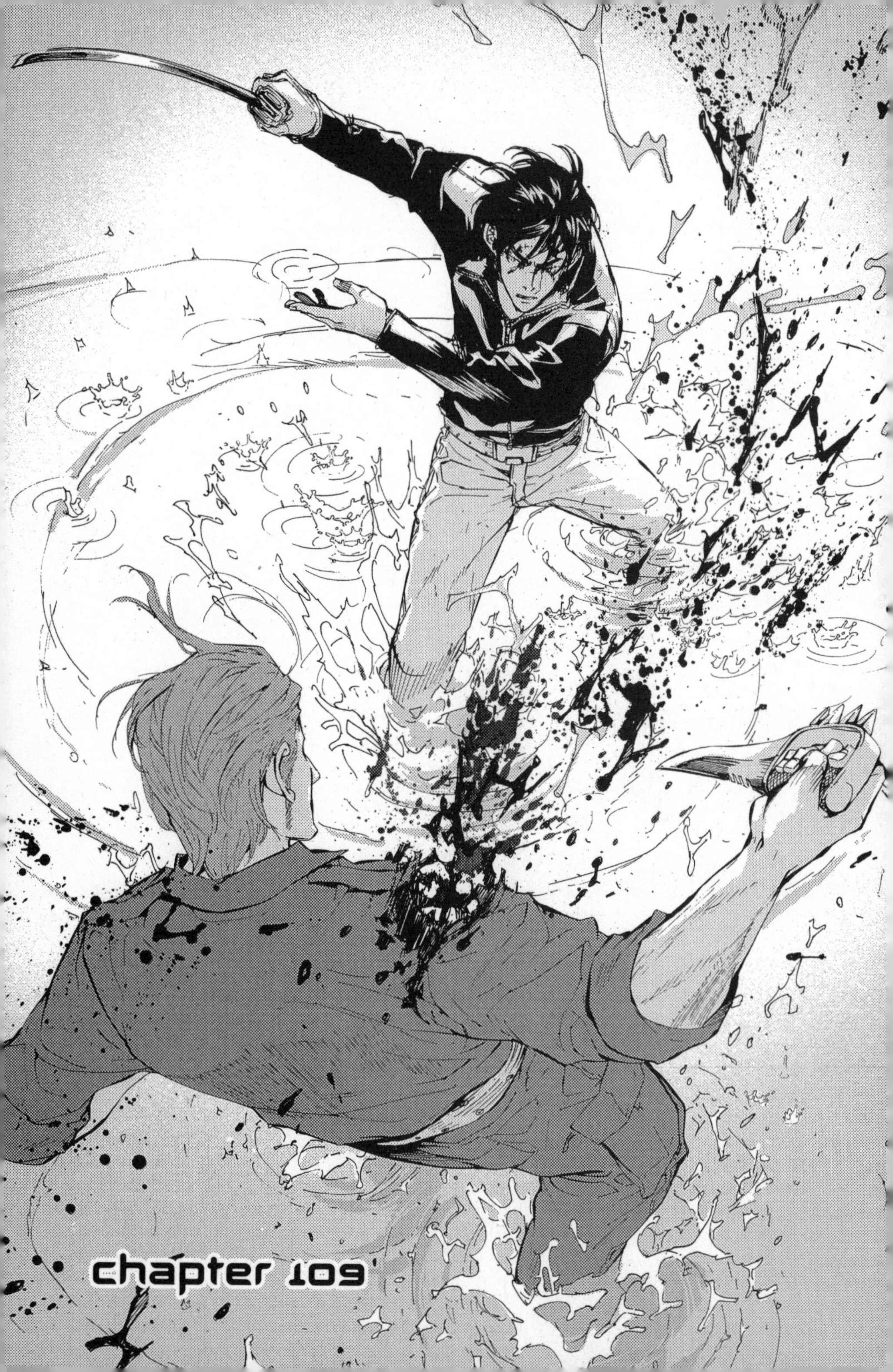
chapter 109

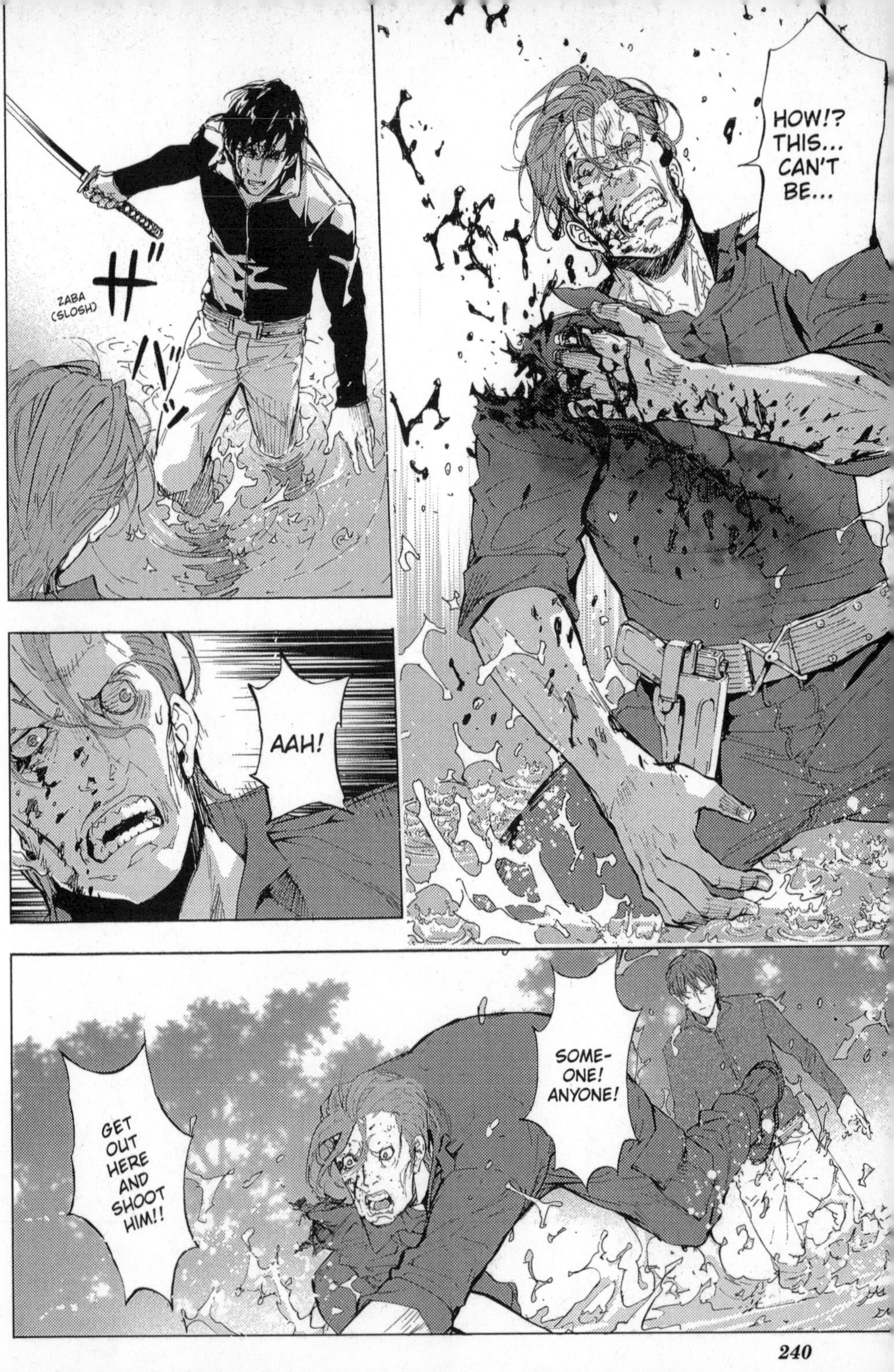
HOW!? THIS... CAN'T BE...
ZABA (SLOSH)
AAH!
SOME-ONE! ANYONE!
GET OUT HERE AND SHOOT HIM!!

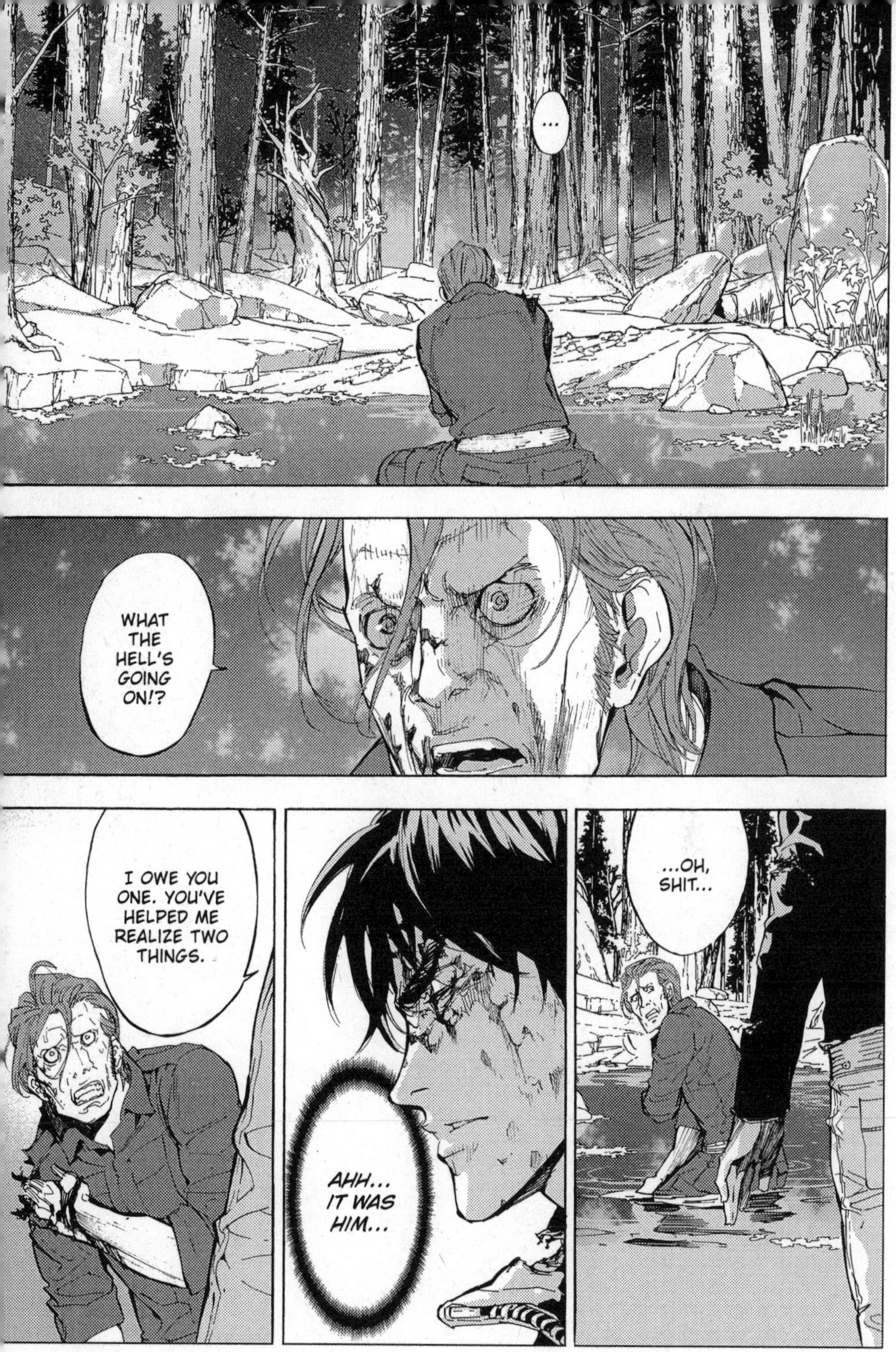
...
WHAT THE HELL'S GOING ON!?
...OH, SHIT...
AHH... IT WAS HIM...
I OWE YOU ONE. YOU'VE HELPED ME REALIZE TWO THINGS.

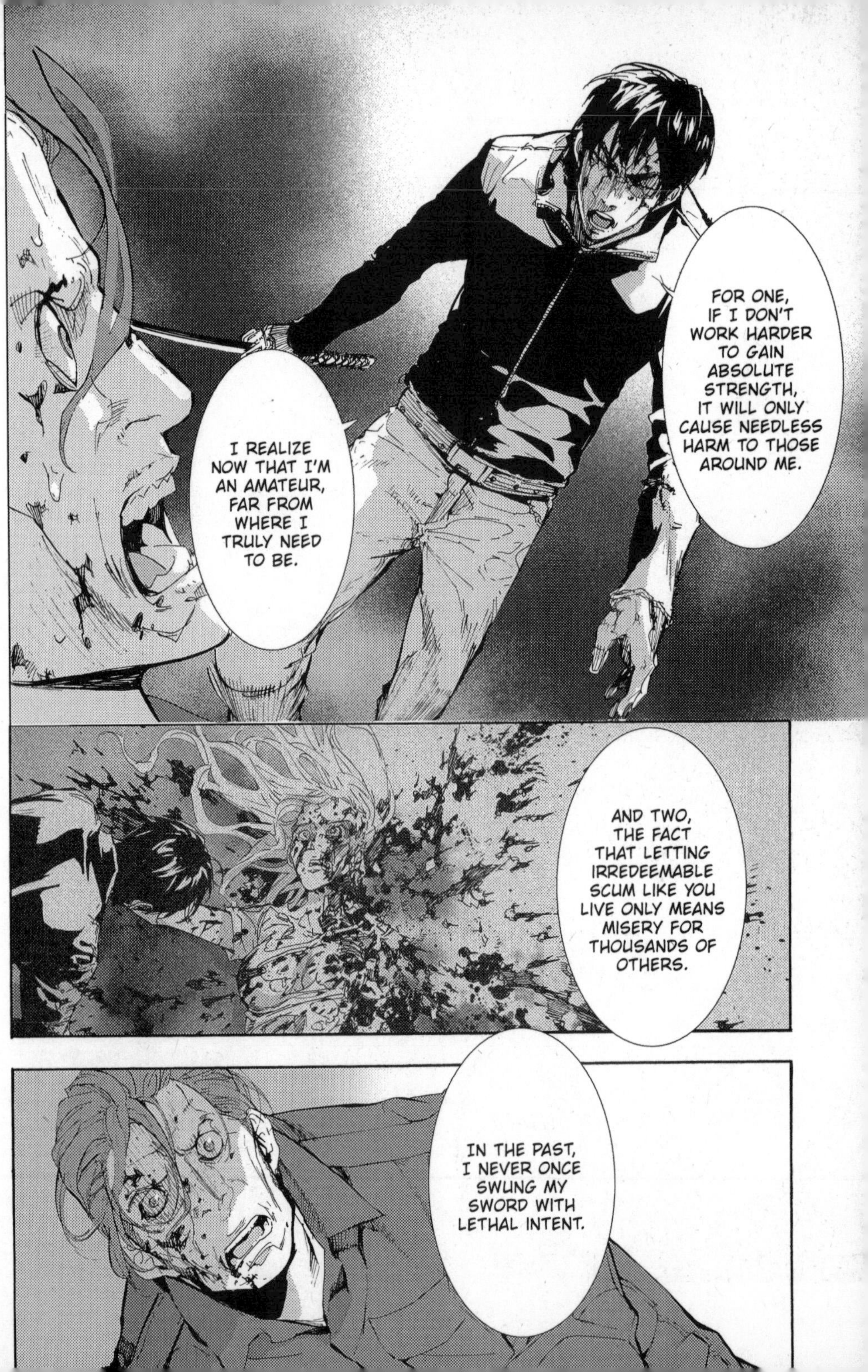
FOR ONE, IF I DON'T WORK HARDER TO GAIN ABSOLUTE STRENGTH, IT WILL ONLY CAUSE NEEDLESS HARM TO THOSE AROUND ME.
I REALIZE NOW THAT I'M AN AMATEUR, FAR FROM WHERE I TRULY NEED TO BE.
AND TWO, THE FACT THAT LETTING IRREDEEMABLE SCUM LIKE YOU LIVE ONLY MEANS MISERY FOR THOUSANDS OF OTHERS.
IN THE PAST, I NEVER ONCE SWUNG MY SWORD WITH LETHAL INTENT.

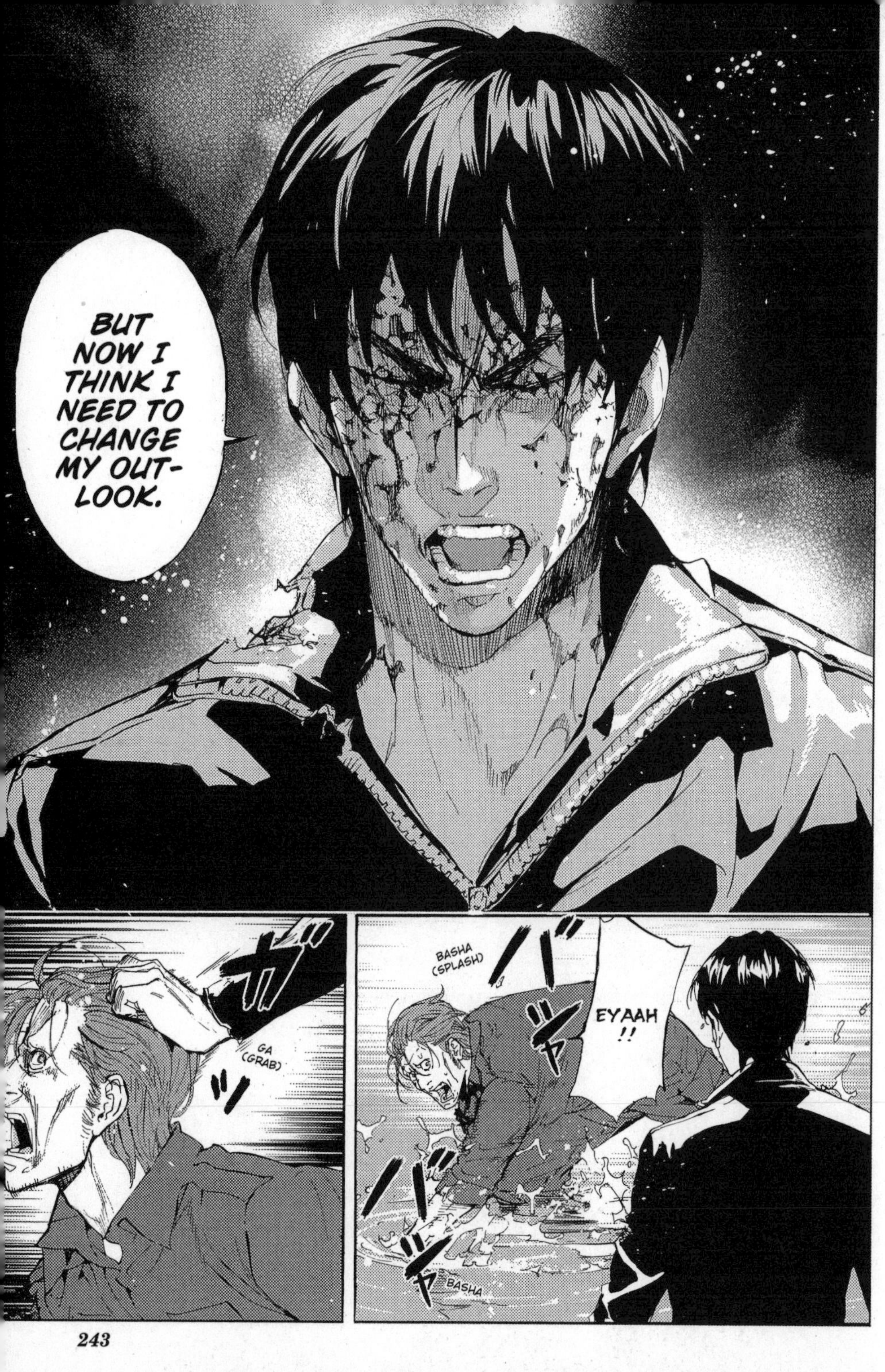
BUT NOW I THINK I NEED TO CHANGE MY OUT-LOOK.
BASHA (SPLASH)
EYAAH !!
BASHA
GA (GRAB)

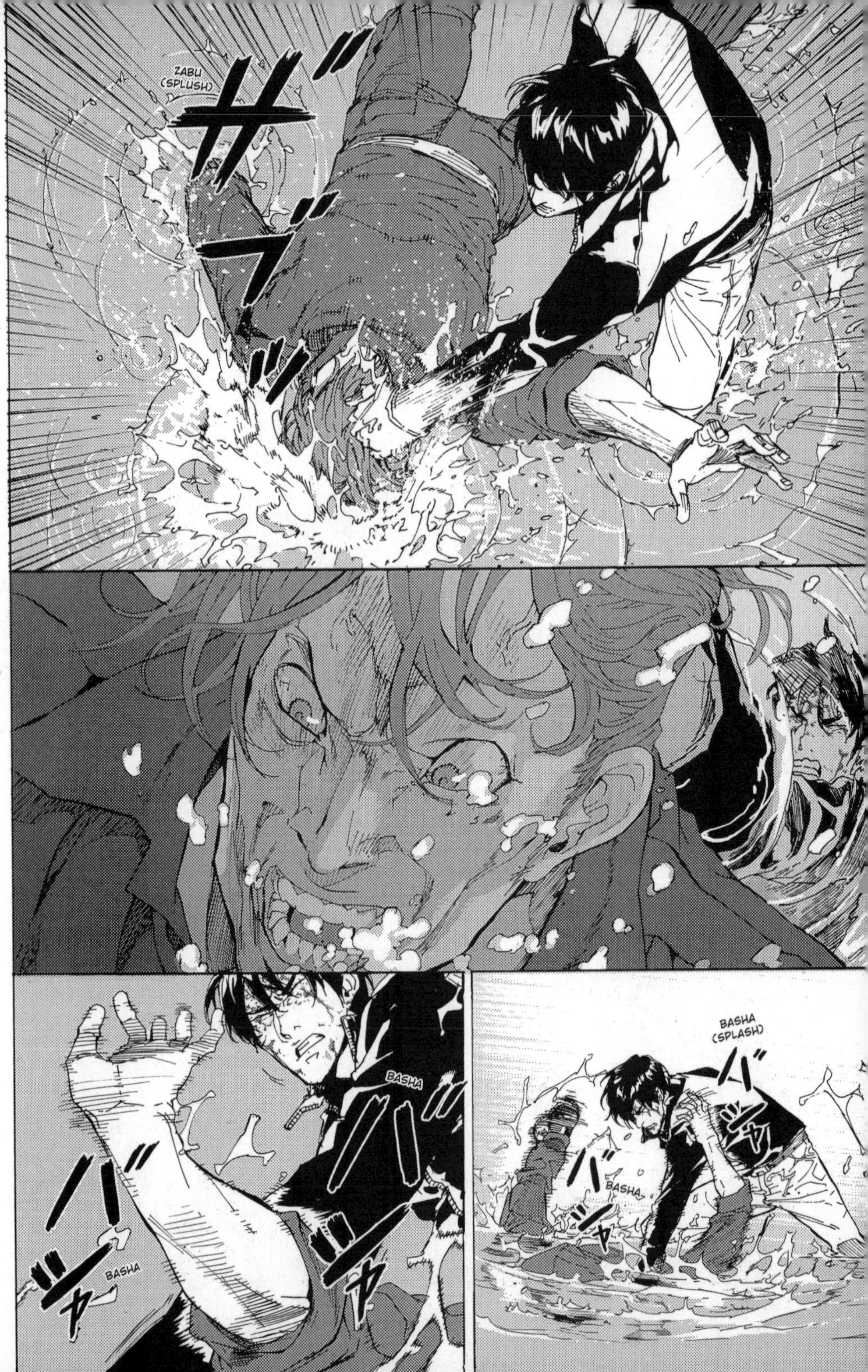
ZABU
(SPLUSH)
BASHA
(SPLASH)
BASHA
BASHA
BASHA

DIE.
ゴボッ
GOBO (BLUB)

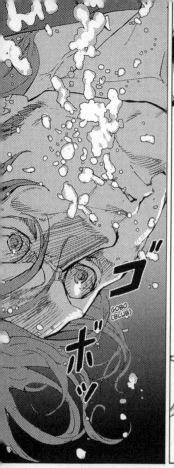

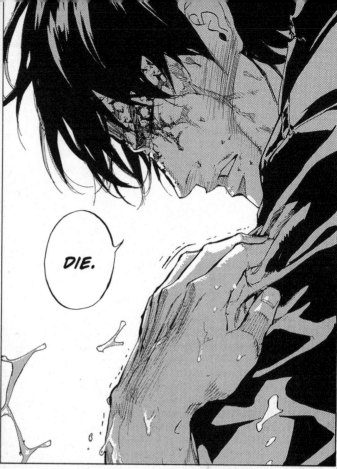

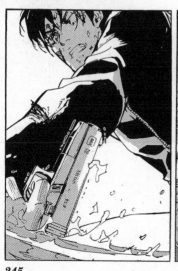

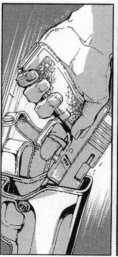

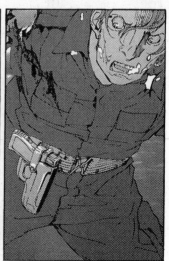

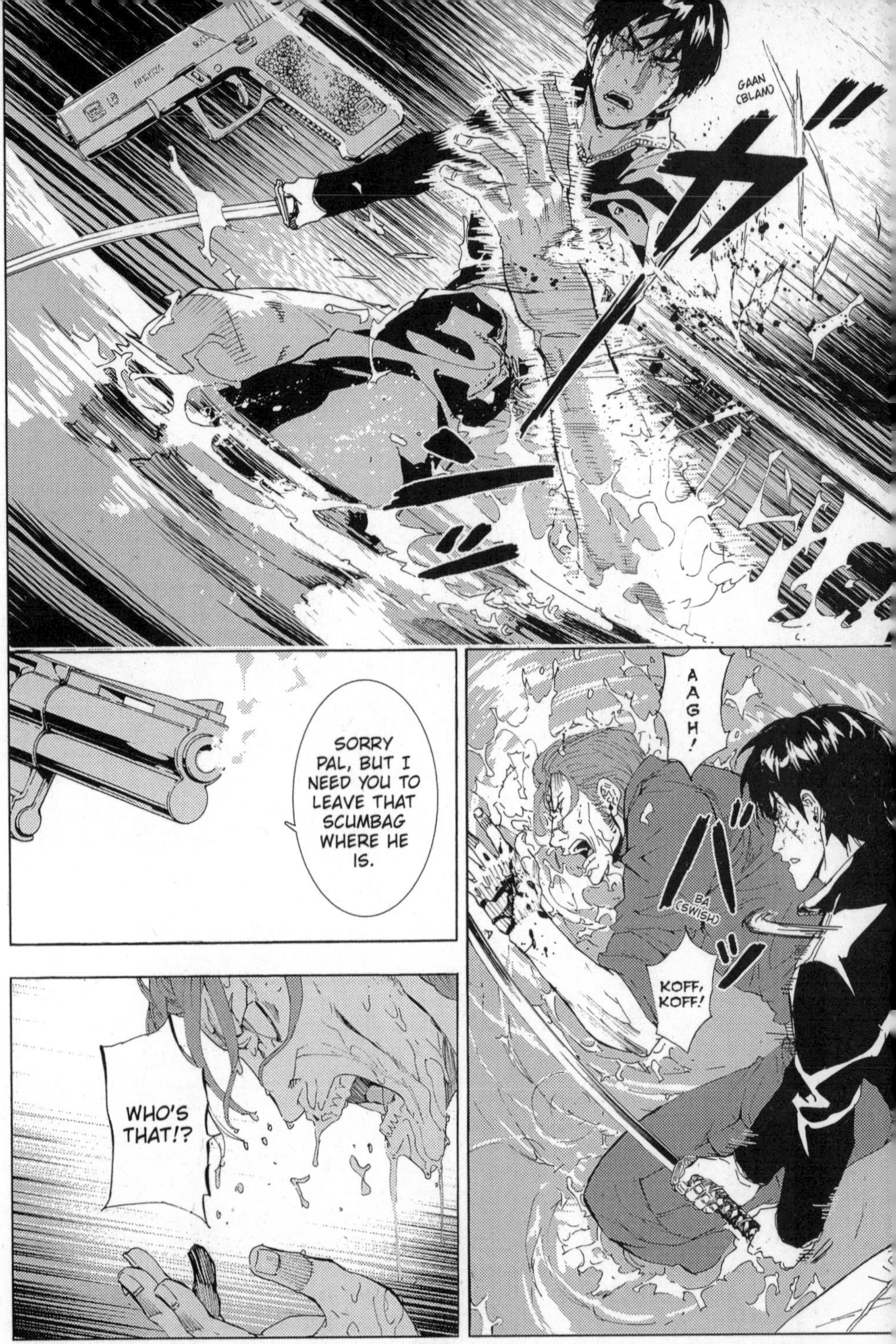
GAAN (BLAM)
AAGH!
BA (SWISH)
KOFF, KOFF!
SORRY PAL, BUT I NEED YOU TO LEAVE THAT SCUMBAG WHERE HE IS.
WHO'S THAT!?

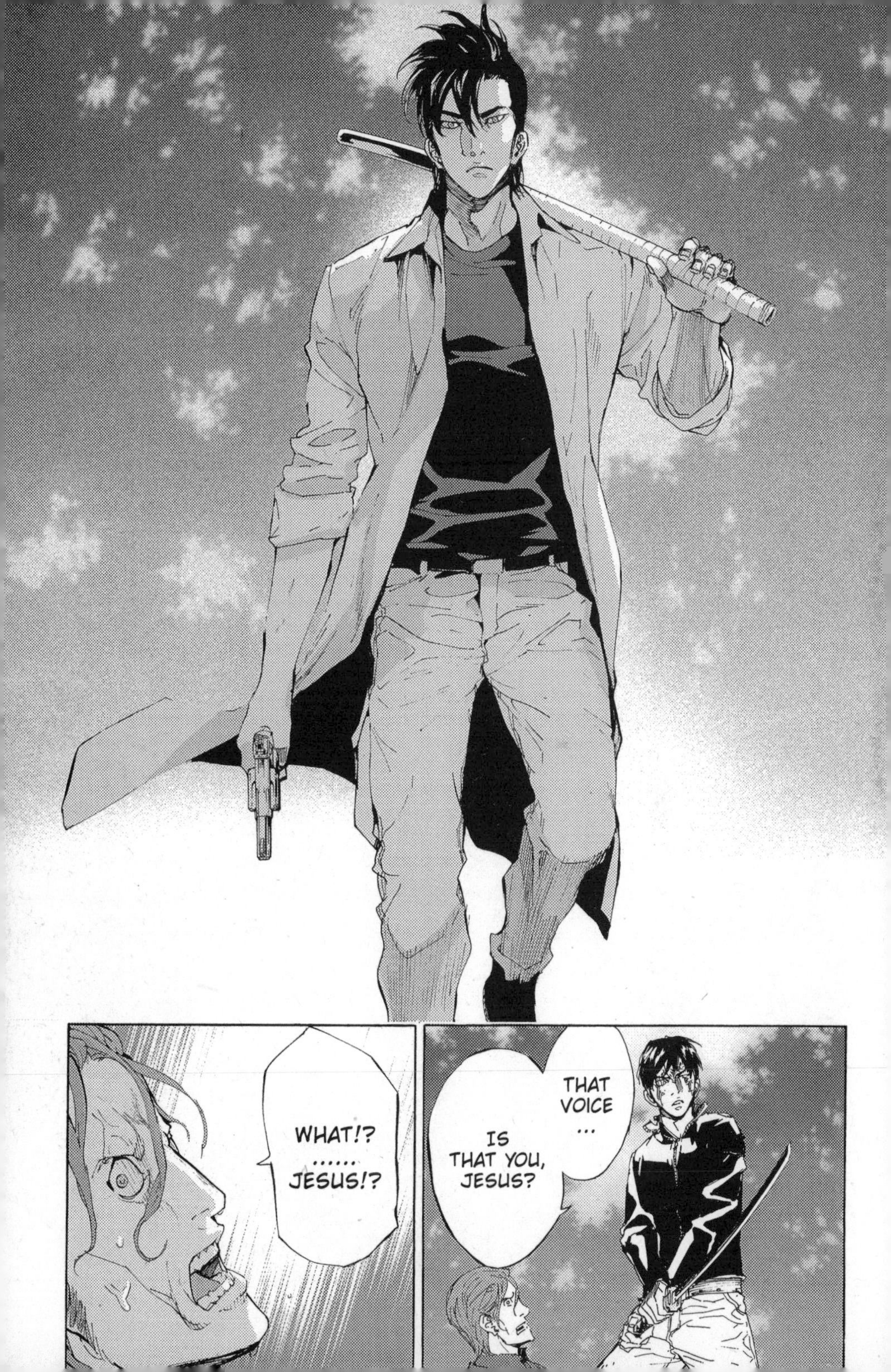
THAT VOICE ...
IS THAT YOU, JESUS?
WHAT!? .... JESUS!?

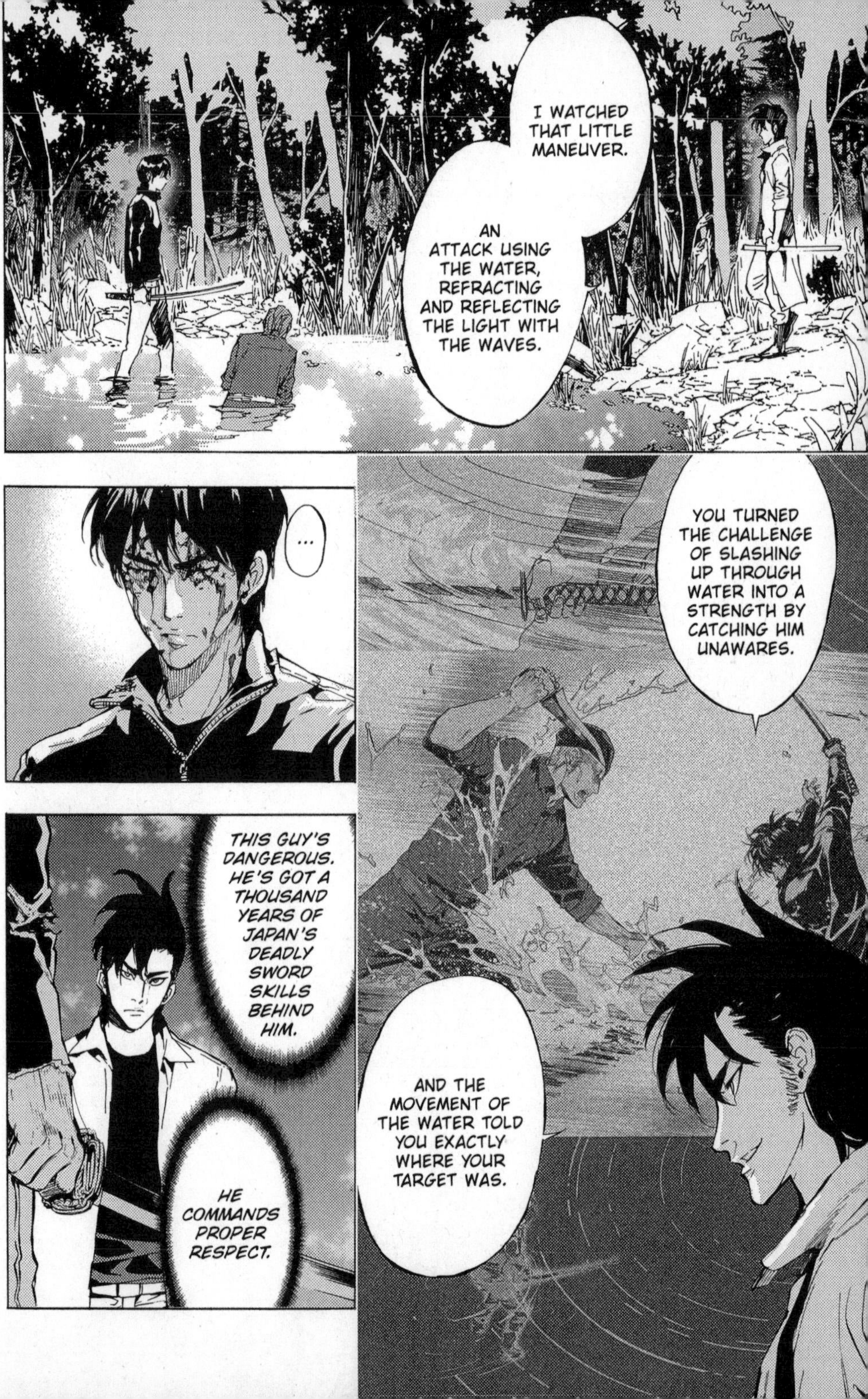
I WATCHED THAT LITTLE MANEUVER.
AN ATTACK USING THE WATER, REFRACTING AND REFLECTING THE LIGHT WITH THE WAVES.
YOU TURNED THE CHALLENGE OF SLASHING UP THROUGH WATER INTO A STRENGTH BY CATCHING HIM UNAWARES.
AND THE MOVEMENT OF THE WATER TOLD YOU EXACTLY WHERE YOUR TARGET WAS.
...
THIS GUY'S DANGEROUS. HE'S GOT A THOUSAND YEARS OF JAPAN'S DEADLY SWORD SKILLS BEHIND HIM.
HE COMMANDS PROPER RESPECT.

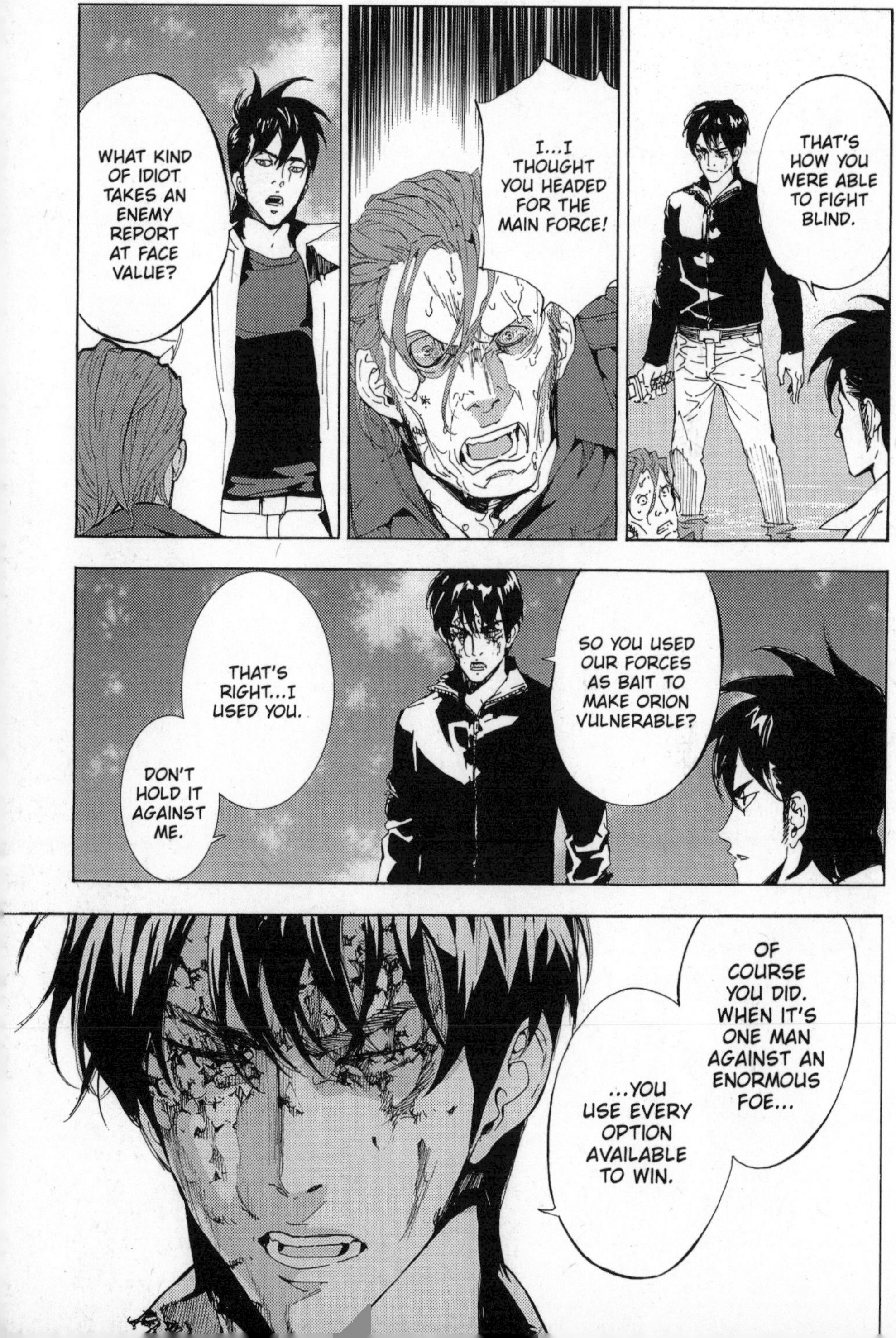
THAT'S HOW YOU WERE ABLE TO FIGHT BLIND.
I...I THOUGHT YOU HEADED FOR THE MAIN FORCE!
WHAT KIND OF IDIOT TAKES AN ENEMY REPORT AT FACE VALUE?
SO YOU USED OUR FORCES AS BAIT TO MAKE ORION VULNERABLE?
THAT'S RIGHT...I USED YOU.
DON'T HOLD IT AGAINST ME.
OF COURSE YOU DID. WHEN IT'S ONE MAN AGAINST AN ENORMOUS FOE...
...YOU USE EVERY OPTION AVAILABLE TO WIN.

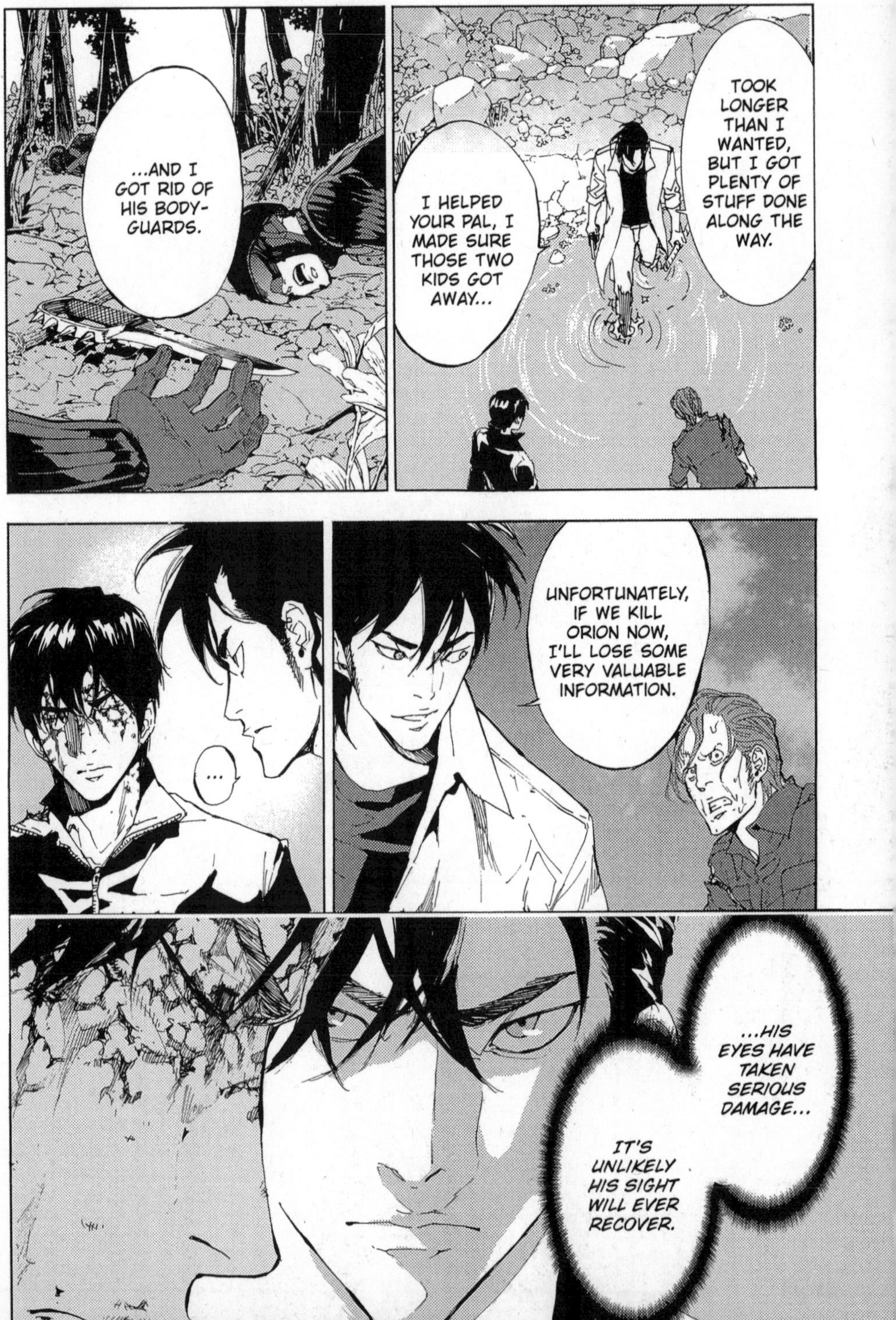
TOOK LONGER THAN I WANTED, BUT I GOT PLENTY OF STUFF DONE ALONG THE WAY.
I HELPED YOUR PAL, I MADE SURE THOSE TWO KIDS GOT AWAY...
...AND I GOT RID OF HIS BODY-GUARDS.
UNFORTUNATELY, IF WE KILL ORION NOW, I'LL LOSE SOME VERY VALUABLE INFORMATION.
...
...HIS EYES HAVE TAKEN SERIOUS DAMAGE...
IT'S UNLIKELY HIS SIGHT WILL EVER RECOVER.

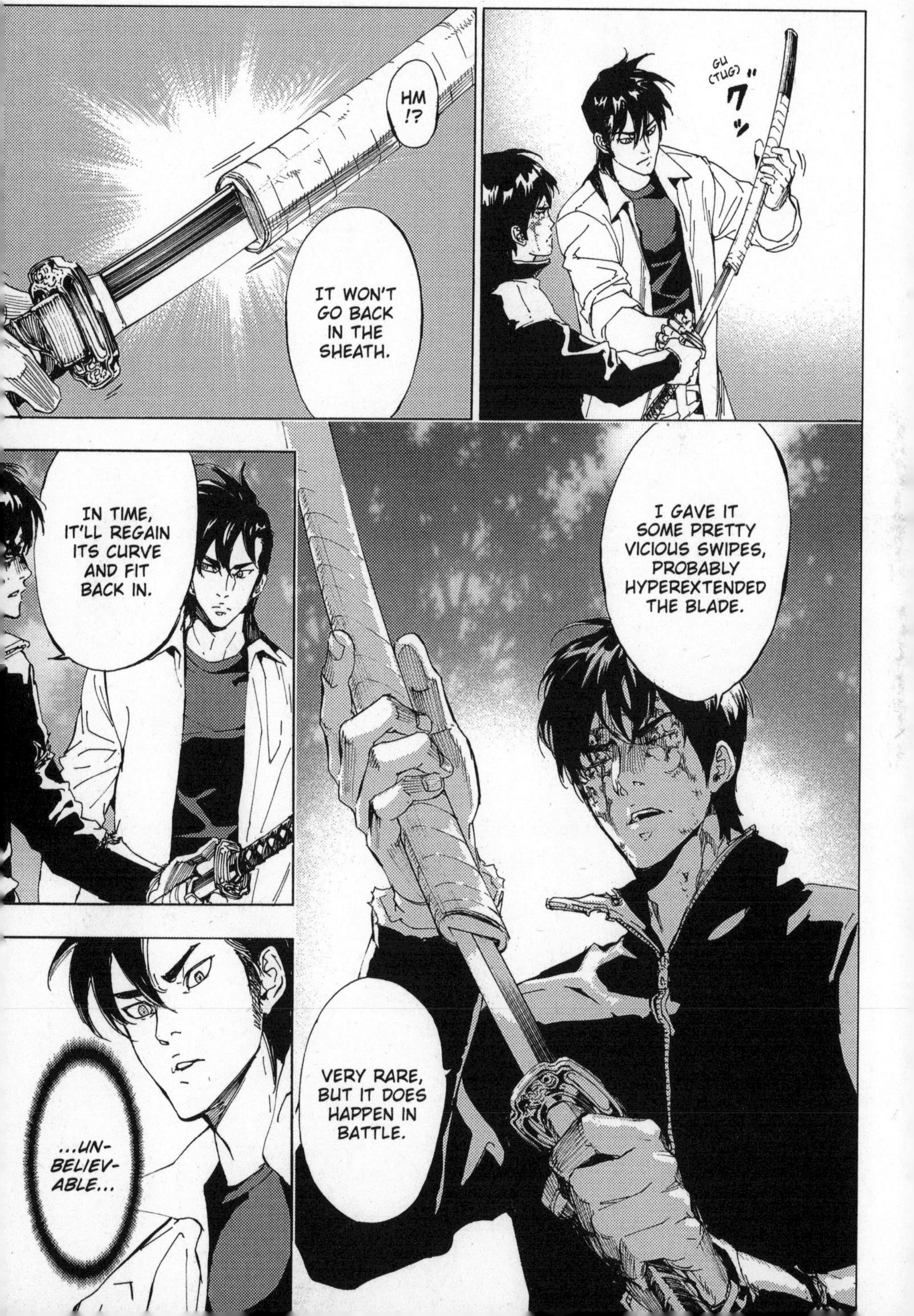
GU (TUG)
クッ
HM !?
IT WON'T GO BACK IN THE SHEATH.
I GAVE IT SOME PRETTY VICIOUS SWIPES, PROBABLY HYPEREXTENDED THE BLADE.
VERY RARE, BUT IT DOES HAPPEN IN BATTLE.
IN TIME, IT'LL REGAIN ITS CURVE AND FIT BACK IN.
...UN-BELIEV-ABLE...

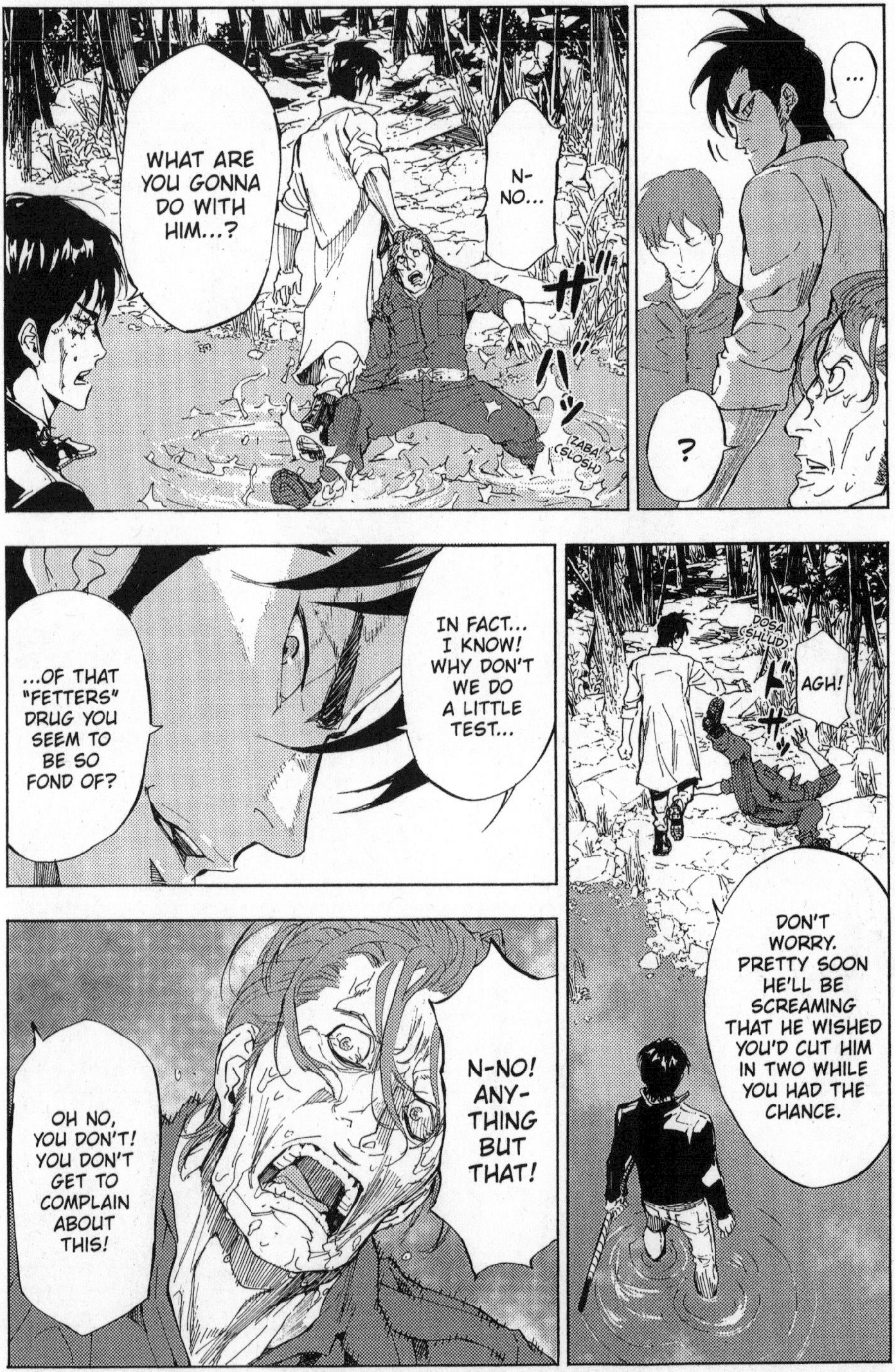
...
?
N-NO...
WHAT ARE YOU GONNA DO WITH HIM...?
ZABA! (SLOSH)
DOSA (SHLUD)
AGH!
DON'T WORRY. PRETTY SOON HE'LL BE SCREAMING THAT HE WISHED YOU'D CUT HIM IN TWO WHILE YOU HAD THE CHANCE.
IN FACT... I KNOW! WHY DON'T WE DO A LITTLE TEST...
...OF THAT "FETTERS" DRUG YOU SEEM TO BE SO FOND OF?
N-NO! ANYTHING BUT THAT!
OH NO, YOU DON'T! YOU DON'T GET TO COMPLAIN ABOUT THIS!

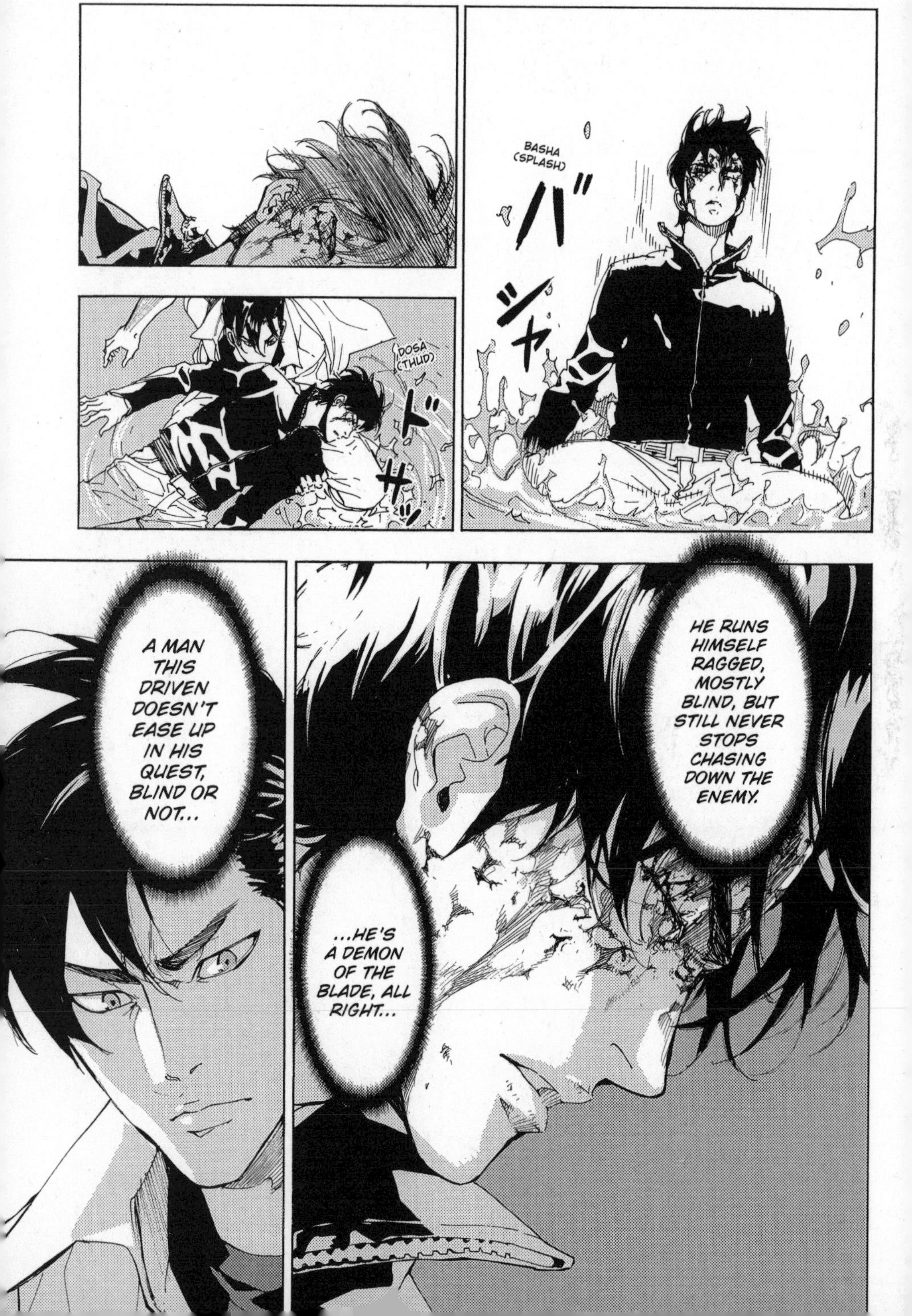
BASHA (SPLASH)
バシャ
DOSA (THUD)
ドサッ
HE RUNS HIMSELF RAGGED, MOSTLY BLIND, BUT STILL NEVER STOPS CHASING DOWN THE ENEMY.
...HE'S A DEMON OF THE BLADE, ALL RIGHT...
A MAN THIS DRIVEN DOESN'T EASE UP IN HIS QUEST, BLIND OR NOT...

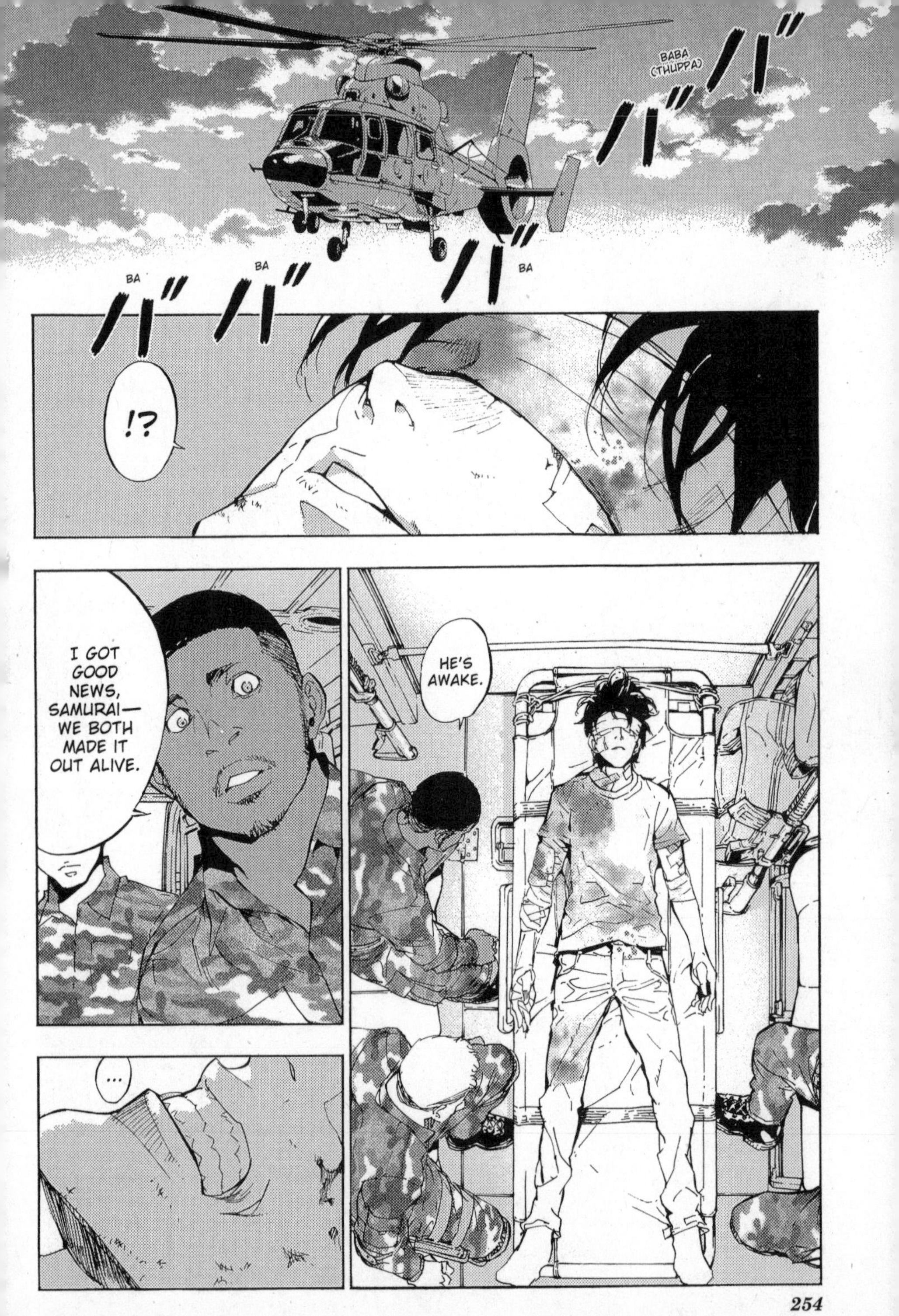
BABA (THUPPA)
BA
BA
BA
!?
HE'S AWAKE.
I GOT GOOD NEWS, SAMURAI—WE BOTH MADE IT OUT ALIVE.
...

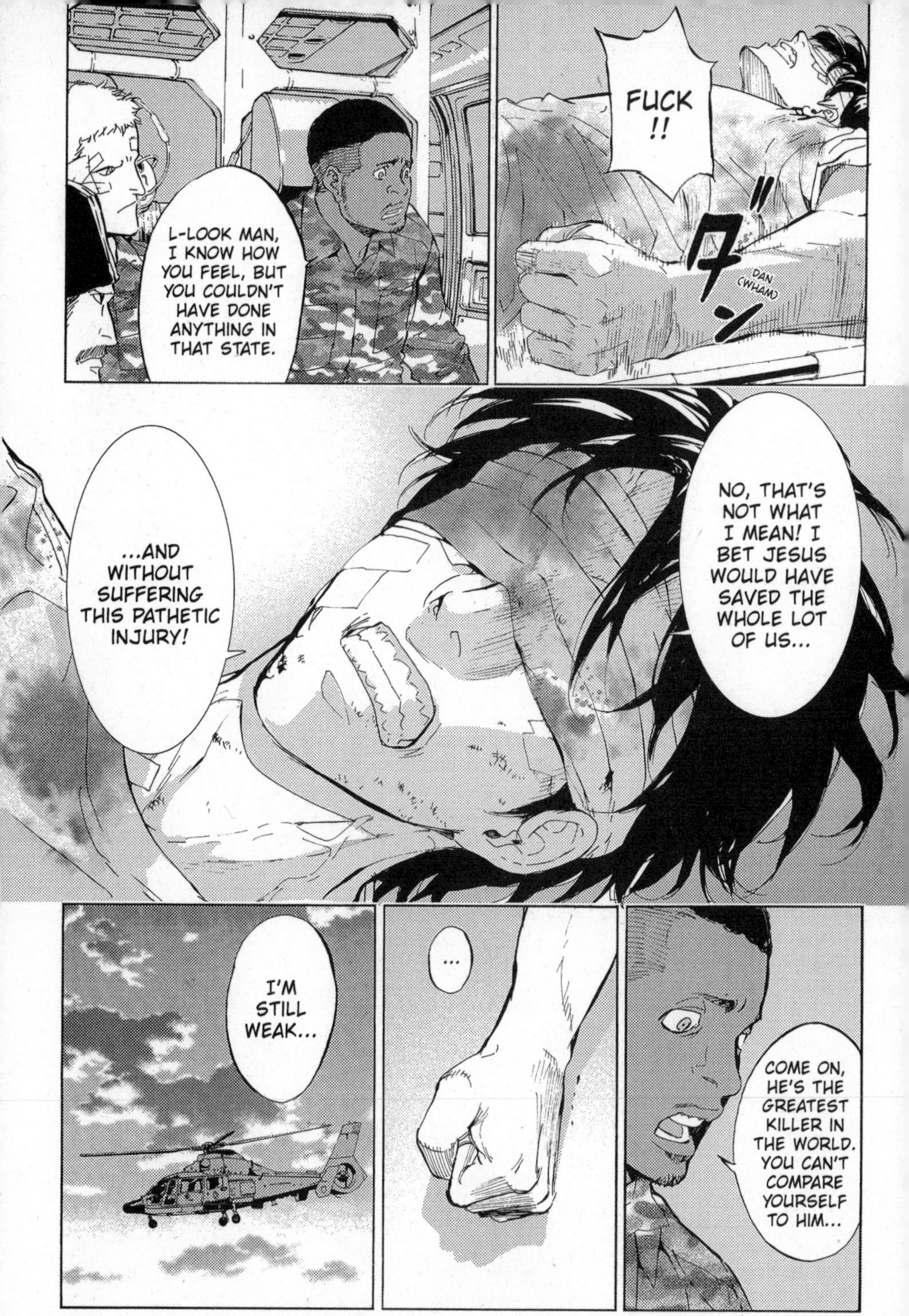
FUCK!!
ダン
DAN (WHAM)
L-LOOK MAN, I KNOW HOW YOU FEEL, BUT YOU COULDN'T HAVE DONE ANYTHING IN THAT STATE.
NO, THAT'S NOT WHAT I MEAN! I BET JESUS WOULD HAVE SAVED THE WHOLE LOT OF US...
...AND WITHOUT SUFFERING THIS PATHETIC INJURY!
COME ON, HE'S THE GREATEST KILLER IN THE WORLD. YOU CAN'T COMPARE YOURSELF TO HIM...
...
I'M STILL WEAK...

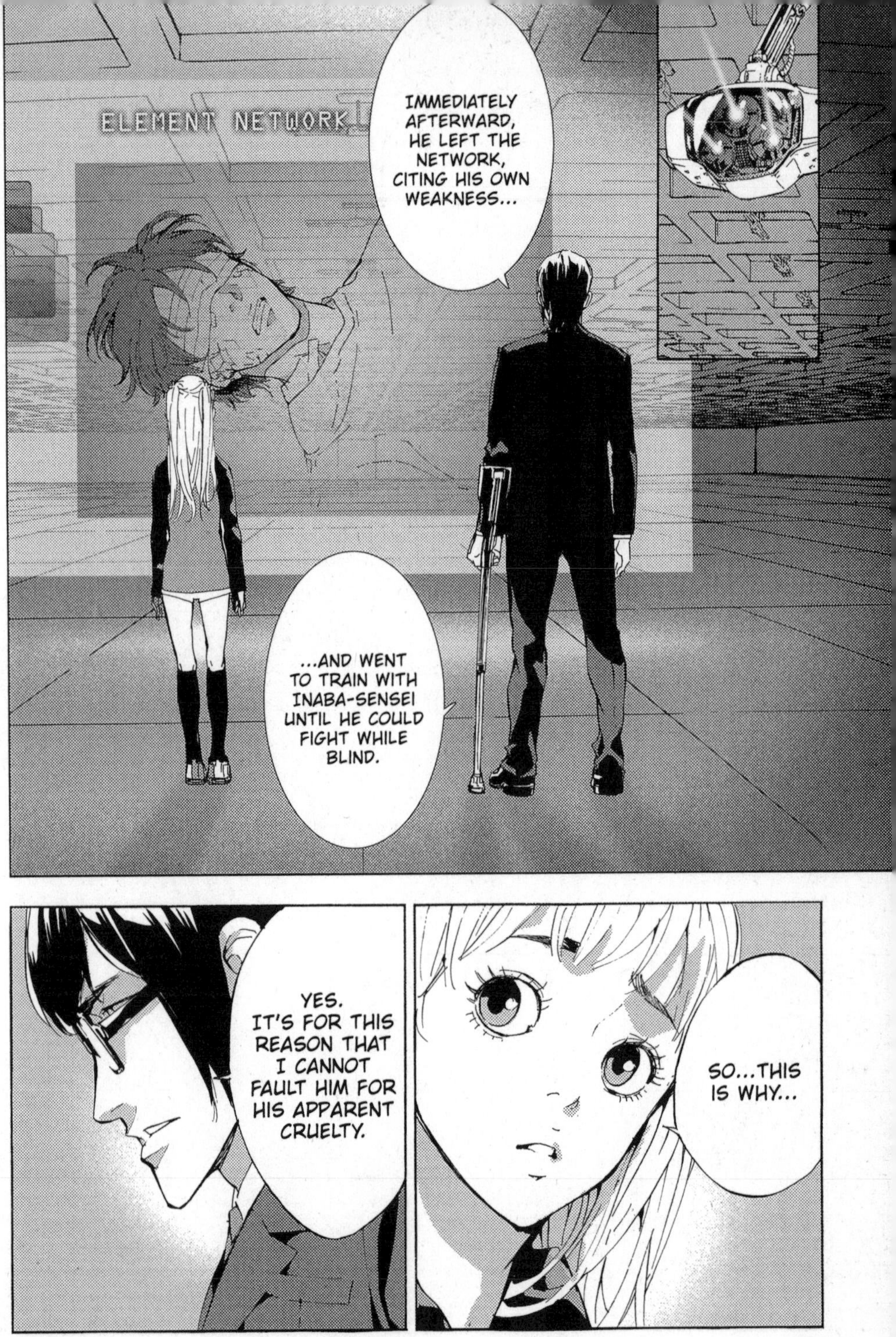
ELEMENT NETWORK
IMMEDIATELY AFTERWARD, HE LEFT THE NETWORK, CITING HIS OWN WEAKNESS...
...AND WENT TO TRAIN WITH INABA-SENSEI UNTIL HE COULD FIGHT WHILE BLIND.
SO...THIS IS WHY...
YES. IT'S FOR THIS REASON THAT I CANNOT FAULT HIM FOR HIS APPARENT CRUELTY.

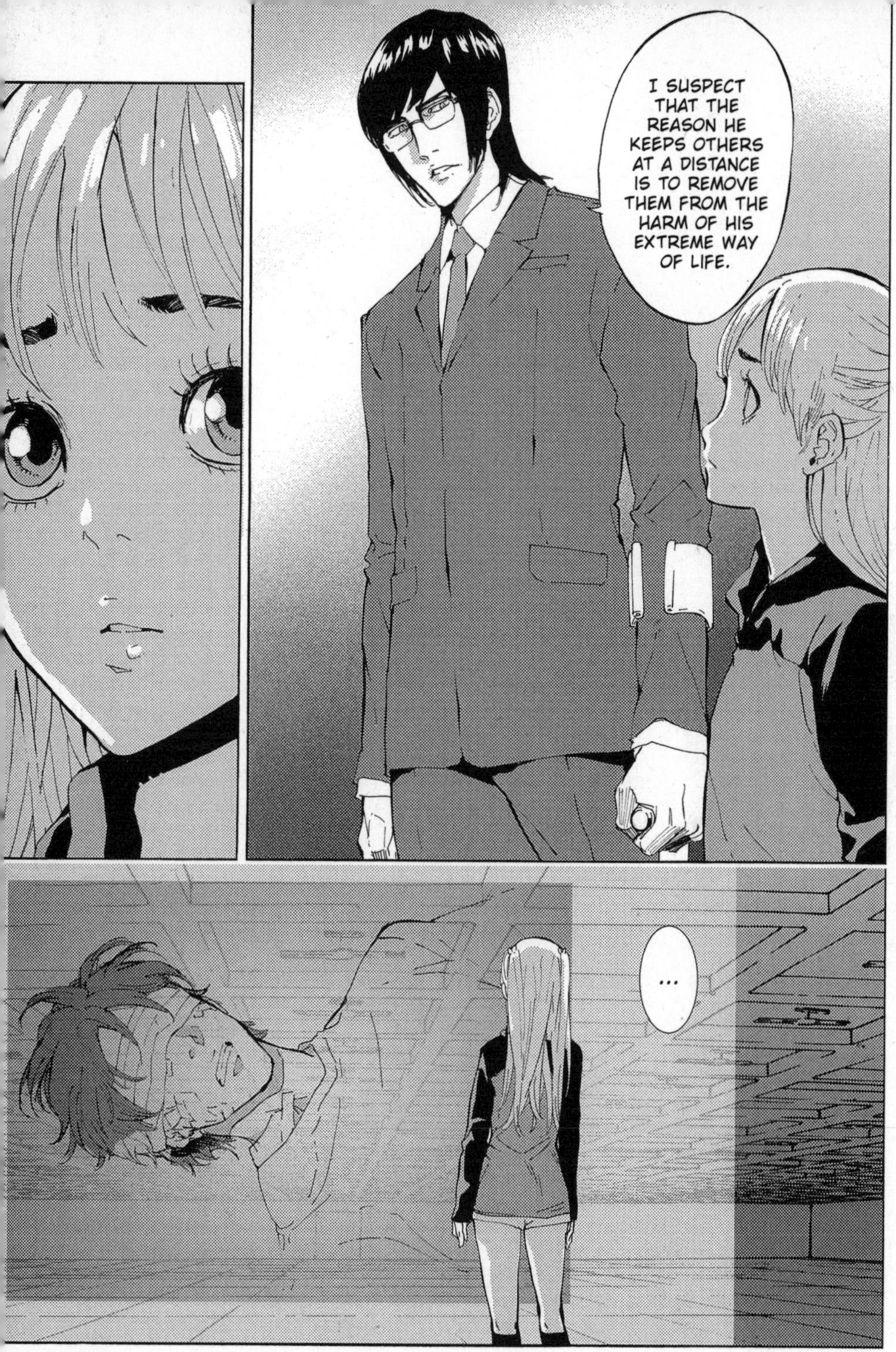
I SUSPECT THAT THE REASON HE KEEPS OTHERS AT A DISTANCE IS TO REMOVE THEM FROM THE HARM OF HIS EXTREME WAY OF LIFE.
...

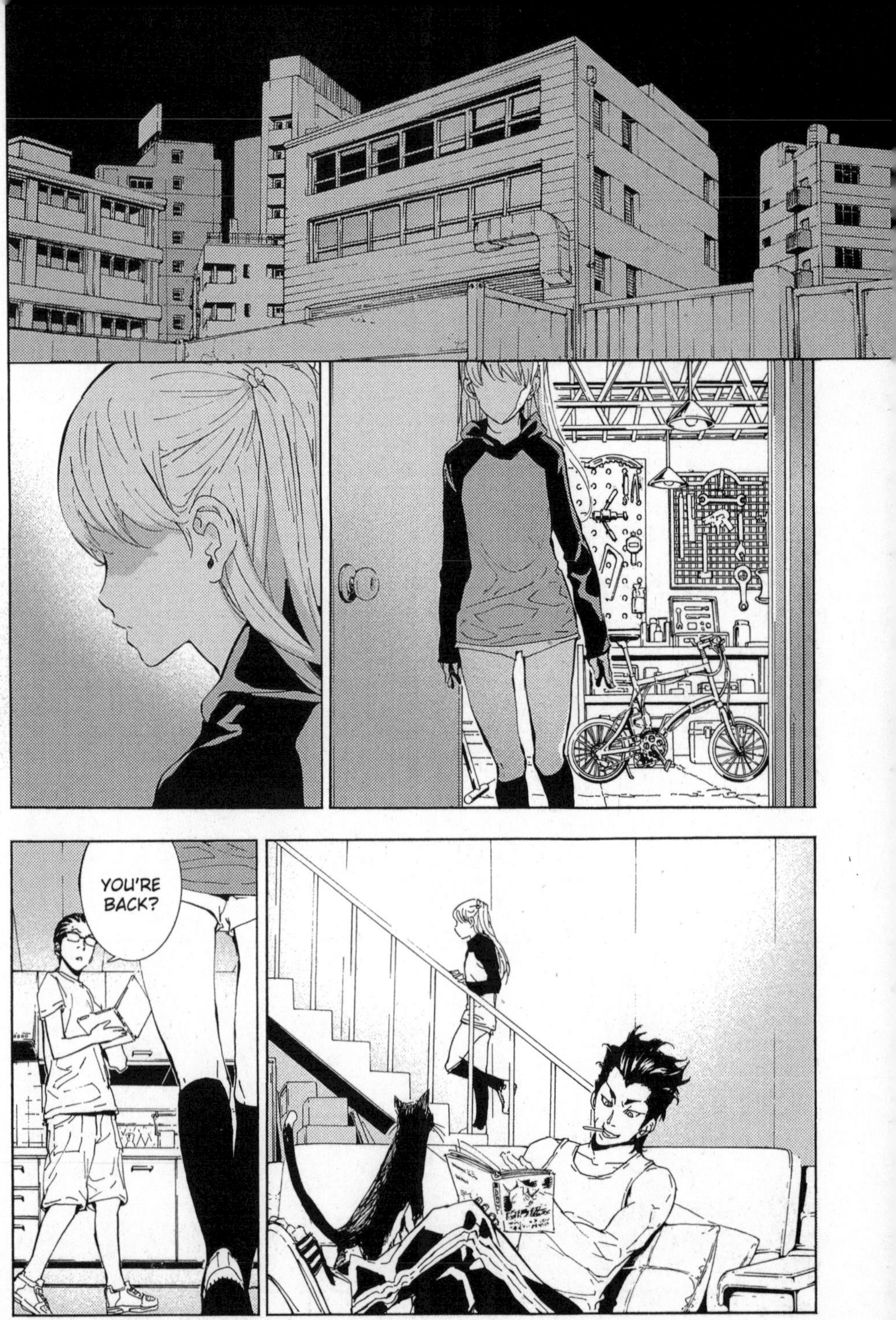
YOU'RE BACK?

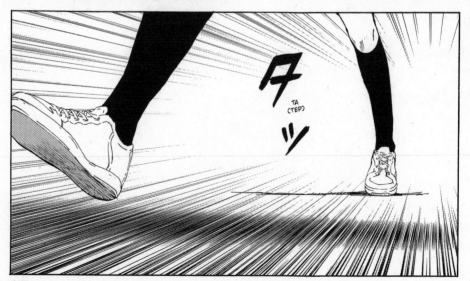

TA
(TEP)

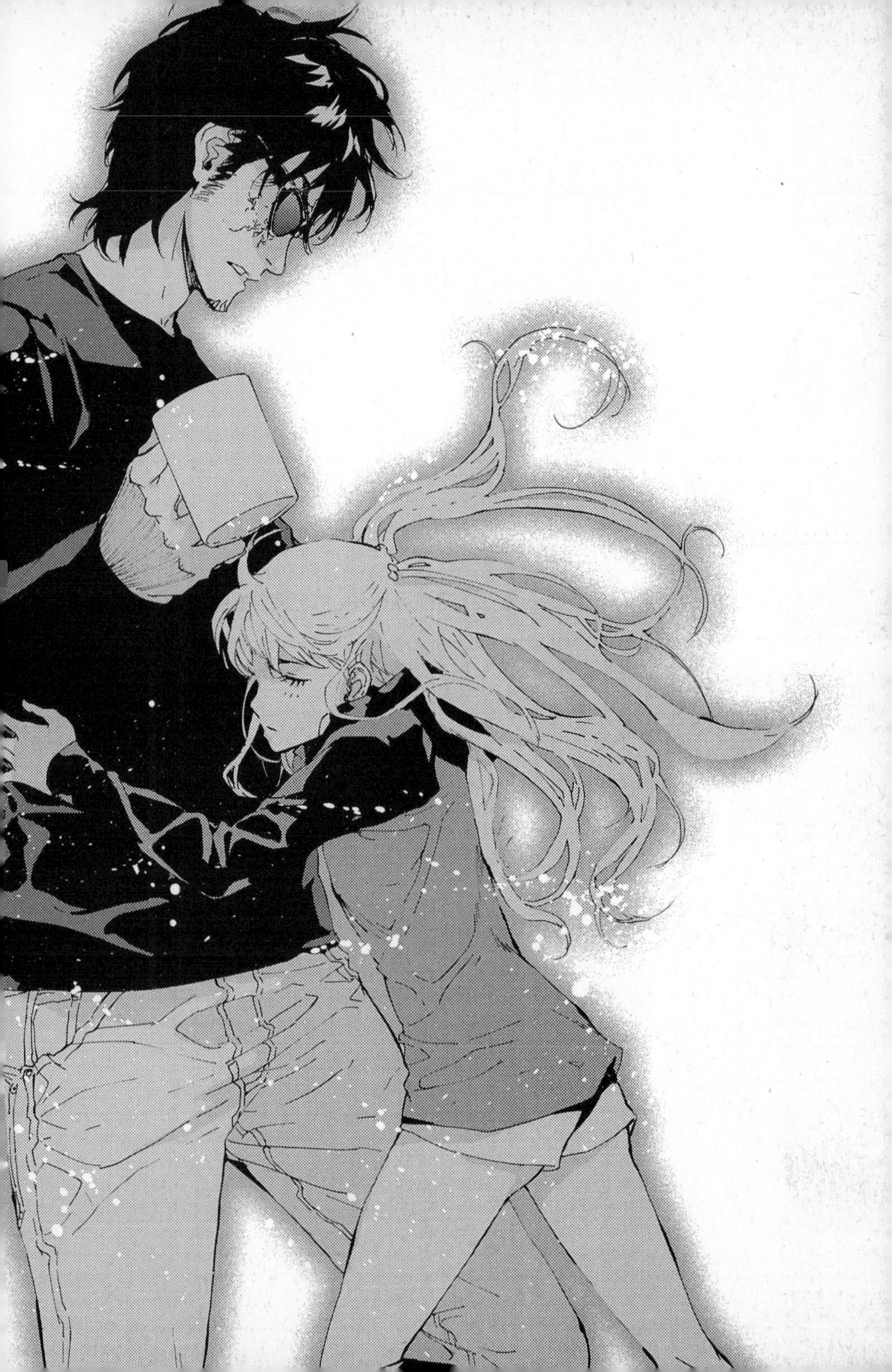

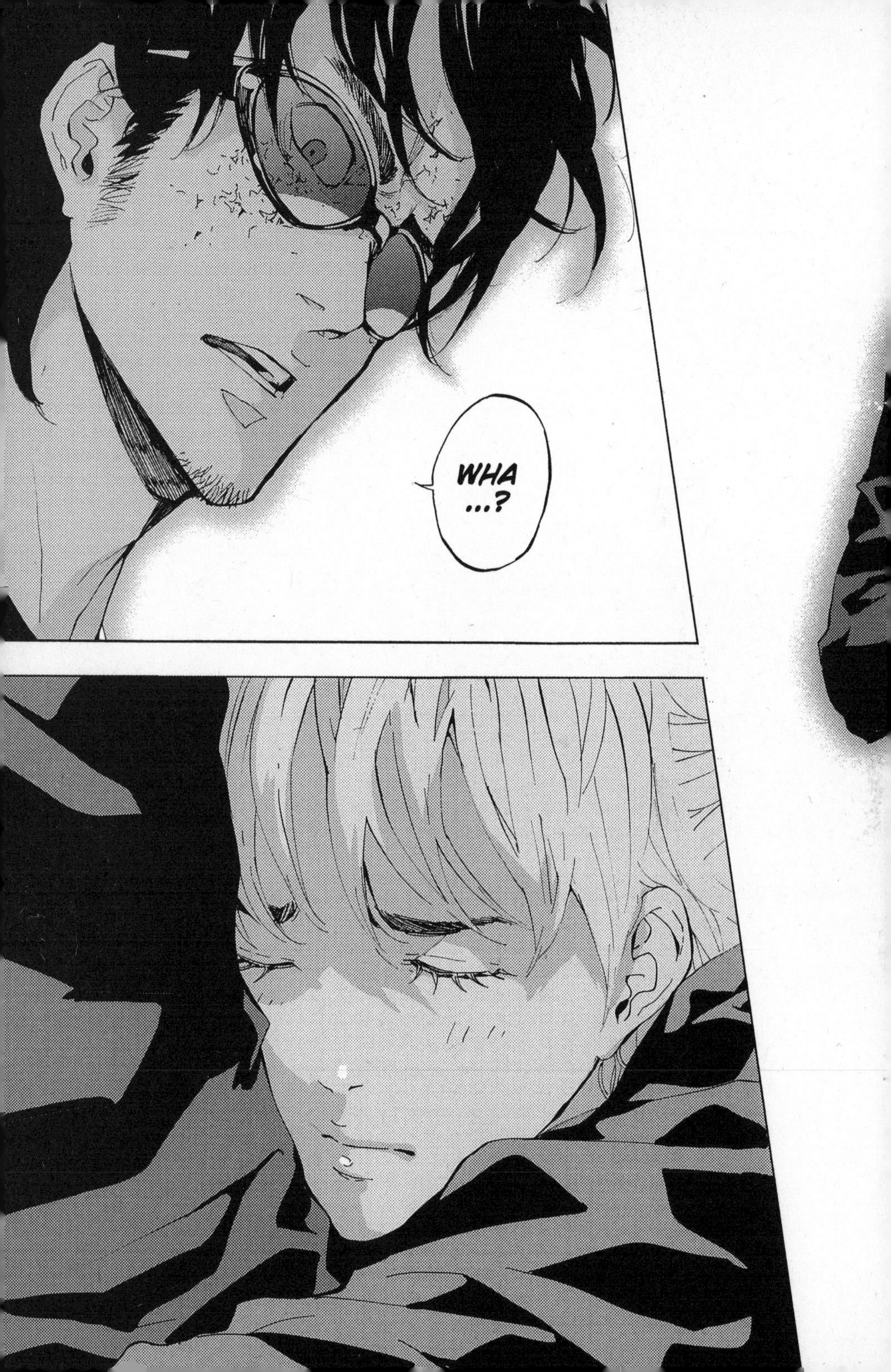
WHA ...?

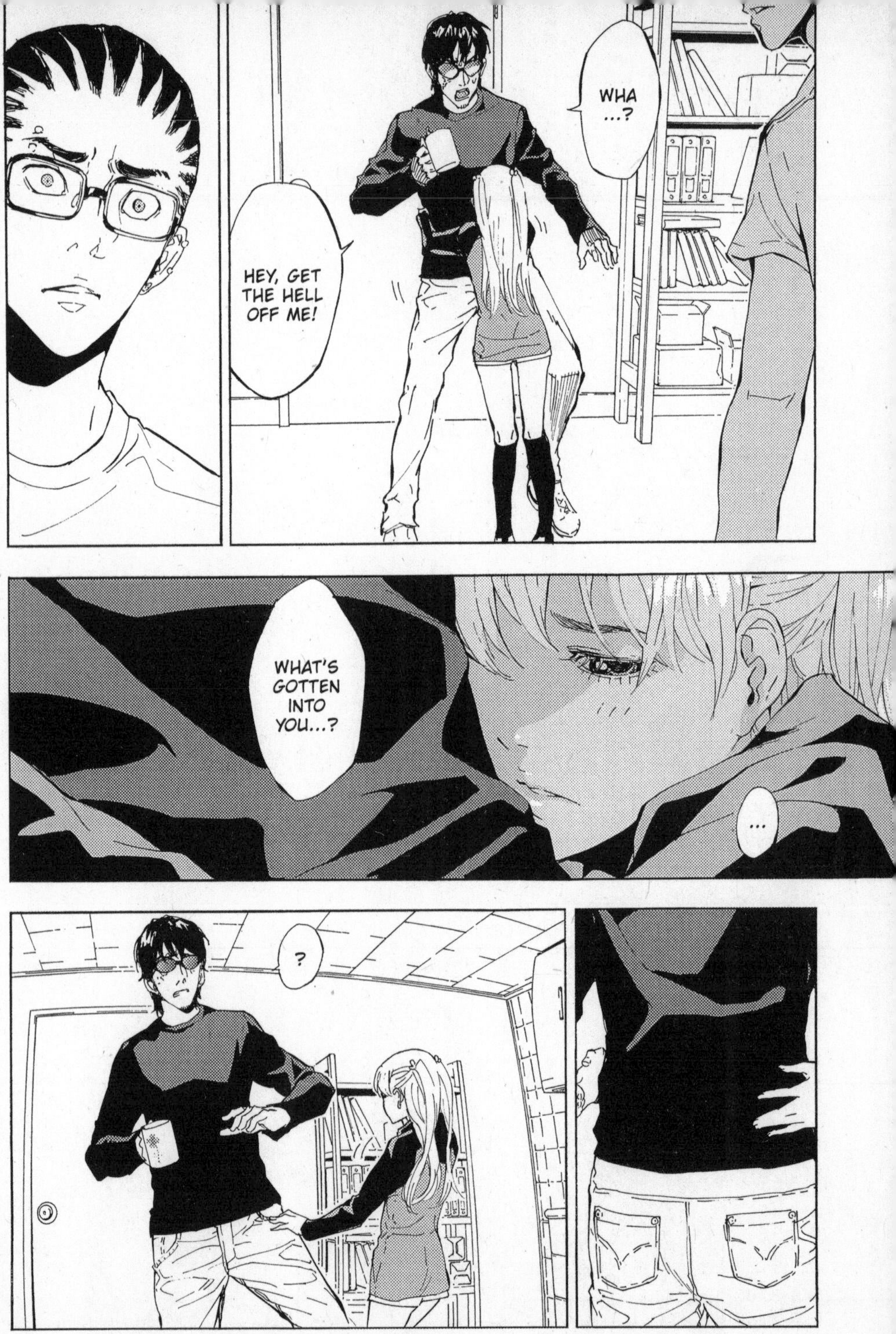
WHA ...?
HEY, GET THE HELL OFF ME!
WHAT'S GOTTEN INTO YOU...?
...
?

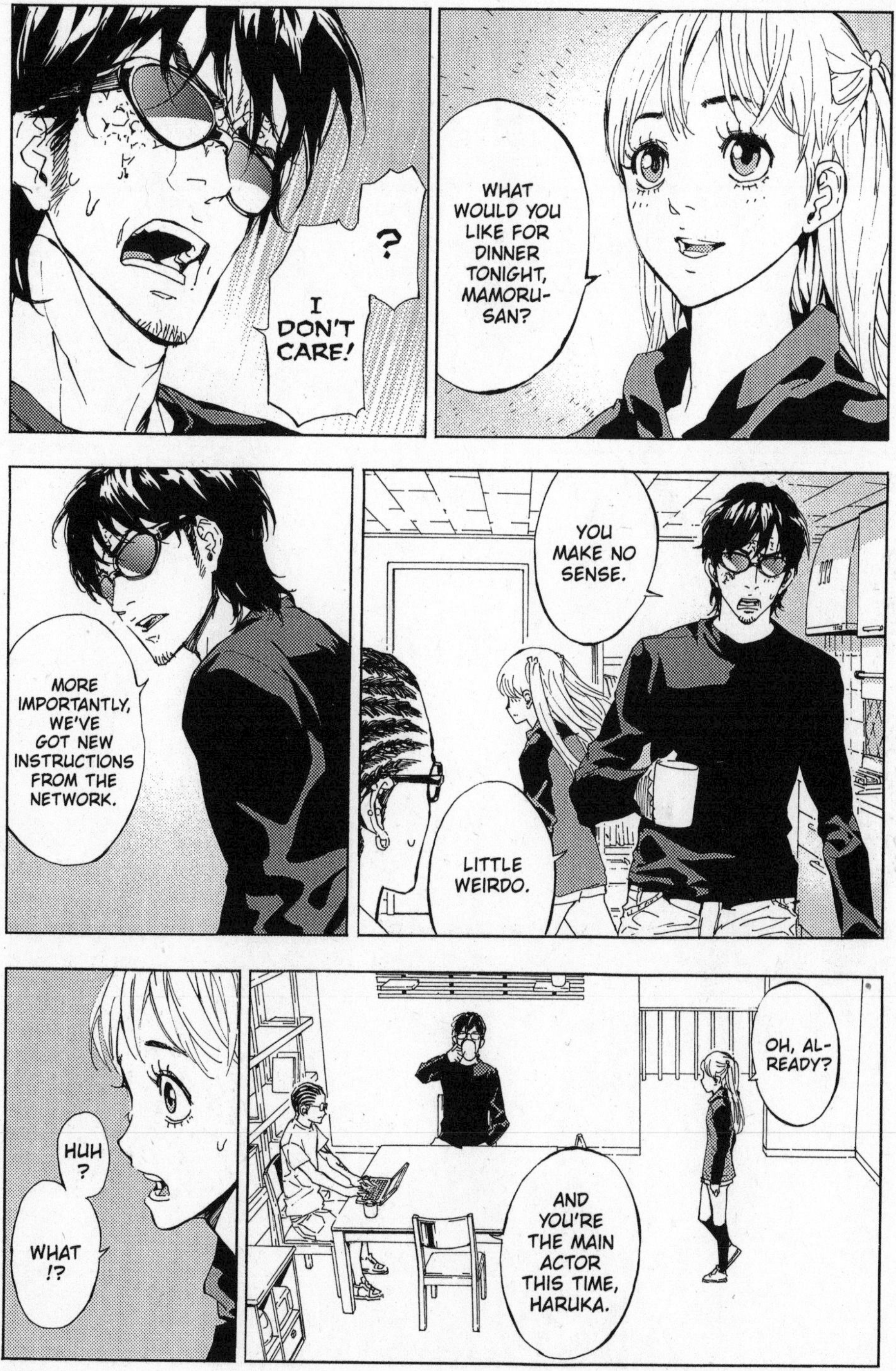
WHAT WOULD YOU LIKE FOR DINNER TONIGHT, MAMORU-SAN?
?
I DON'T CARE!
YOU MAKE NO SENSE.
LITTLE WEIRDO.
MORE IMPORTANTLY, WE'VE GOT NEW INSTRUCTIONS FROM THE NETWORK.
OH, AL-READY?
AND YOU'RE THE MAIN ACTOR THIS TIME, HARUKA.
HUH?
WHAT!?

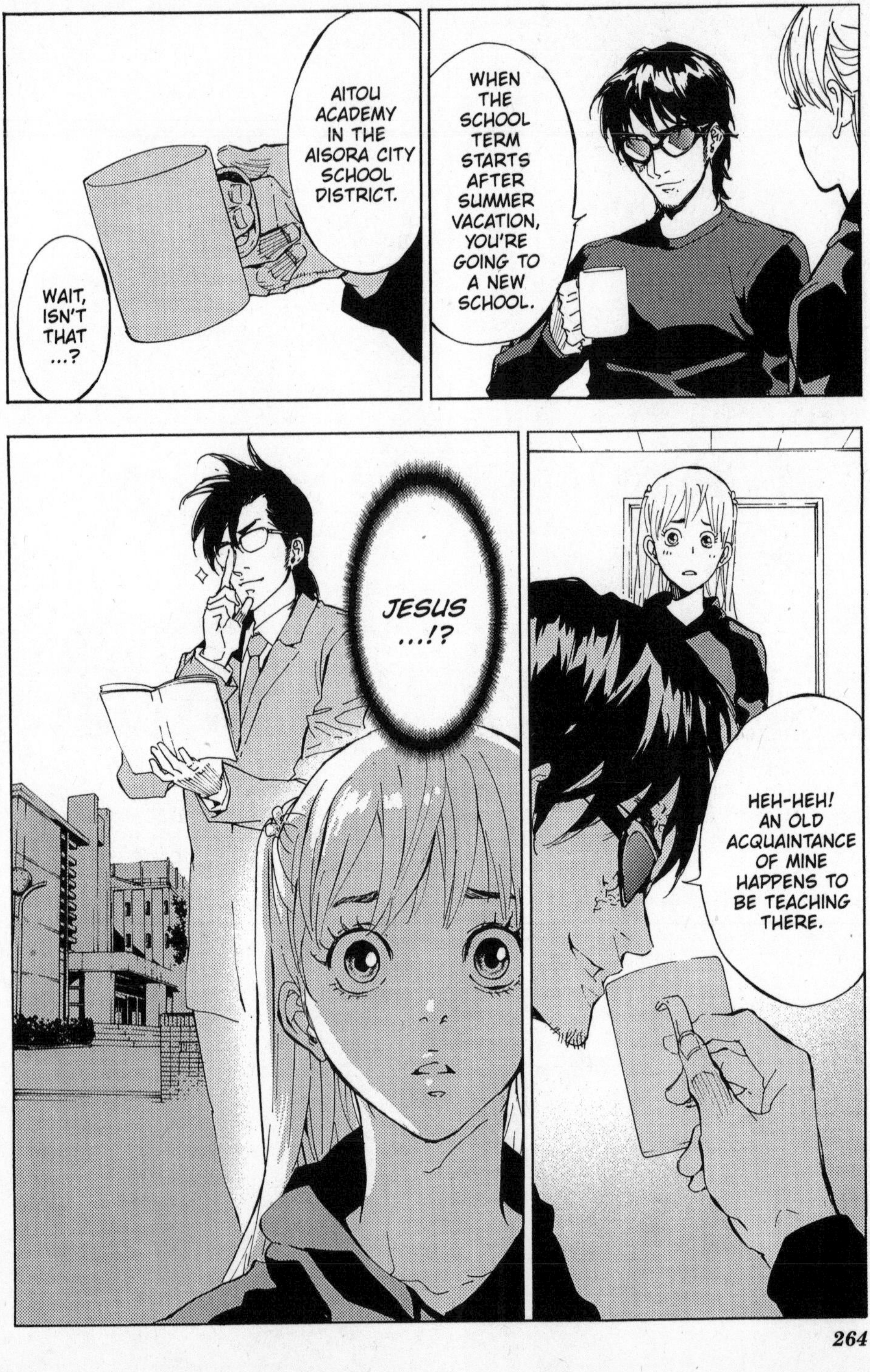
WHEN THE SCHOOL TERM STARTS AFTER SUMMER VACATION, YOU'RE GOING TO A NEW SCHOOL.
AITOU ACADEMY IN THE AISORA CITY SCHOOL DISTRICT.
WAIT, ISN'T THAT ...?
HEH-HEH! AN OLD ACQUAINTANCE OF MINE HAPPENS TO BE TEACHING THERE.
JESUS ...!?

Until Death do us Part

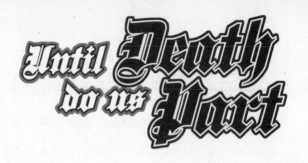

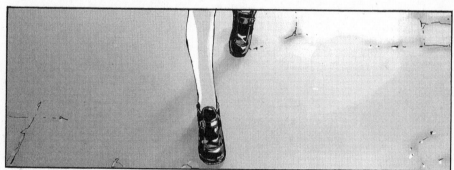

SCHOOL DOESN'T START FOR ANOTHER TEN DAYS, AND YOU'RE ALREADY RARING TO GO?

IGAWA-SAN.

OH?

chapter 110

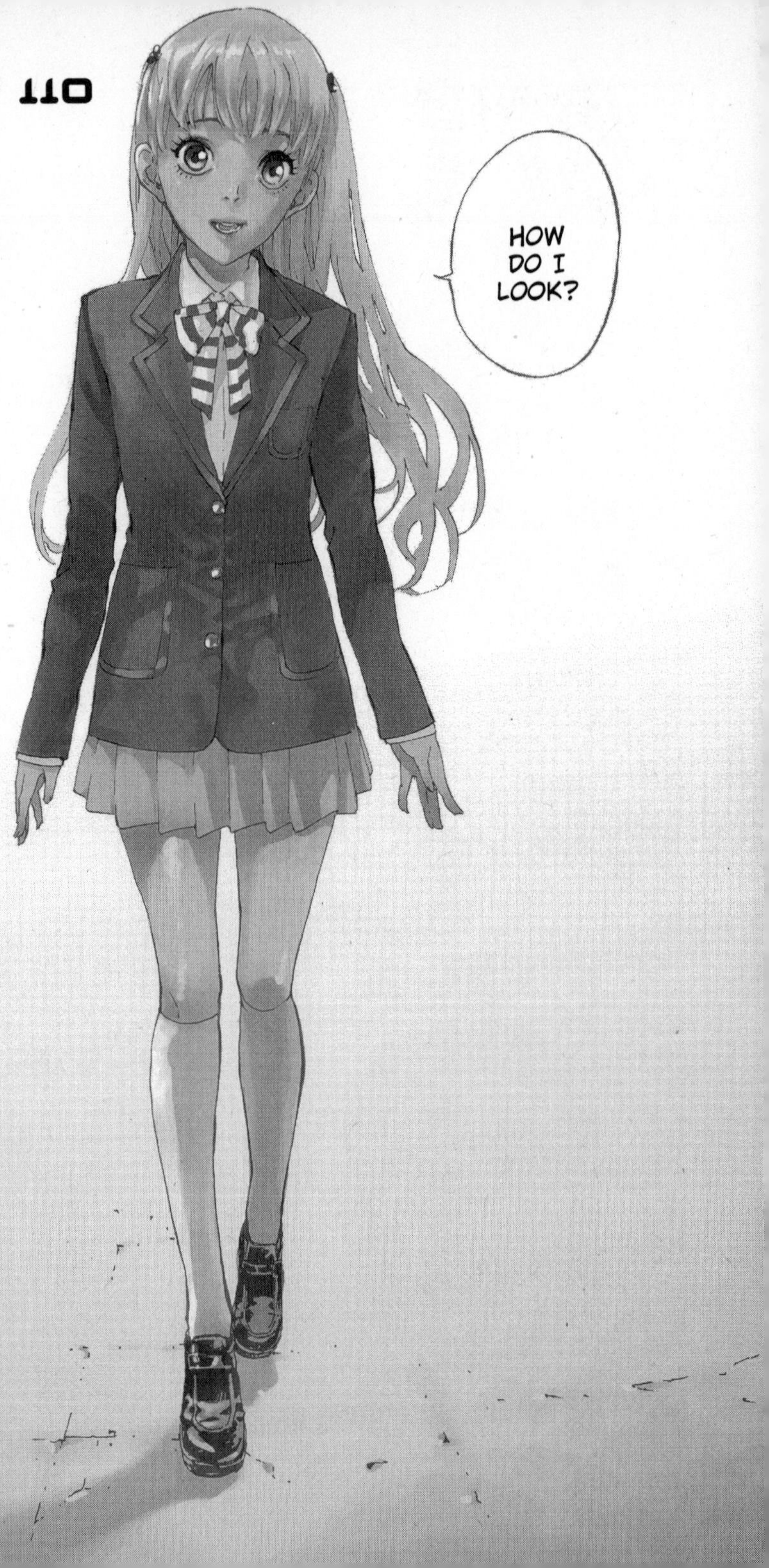
HOW DO I LOOK?

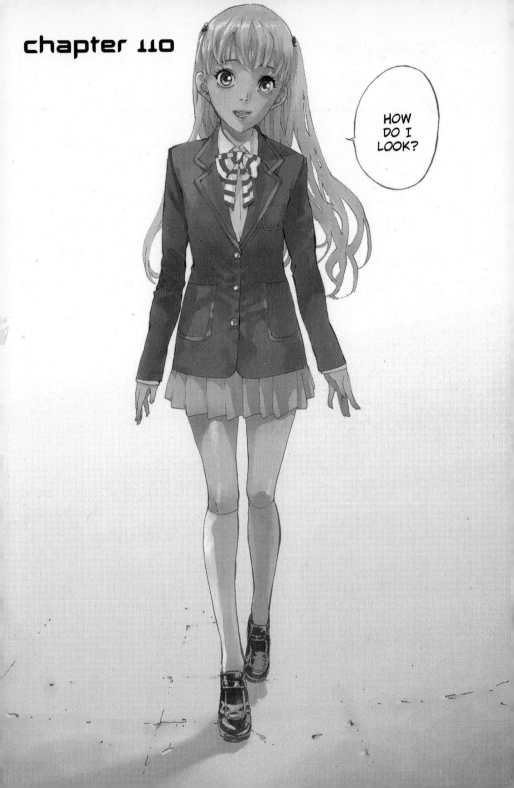

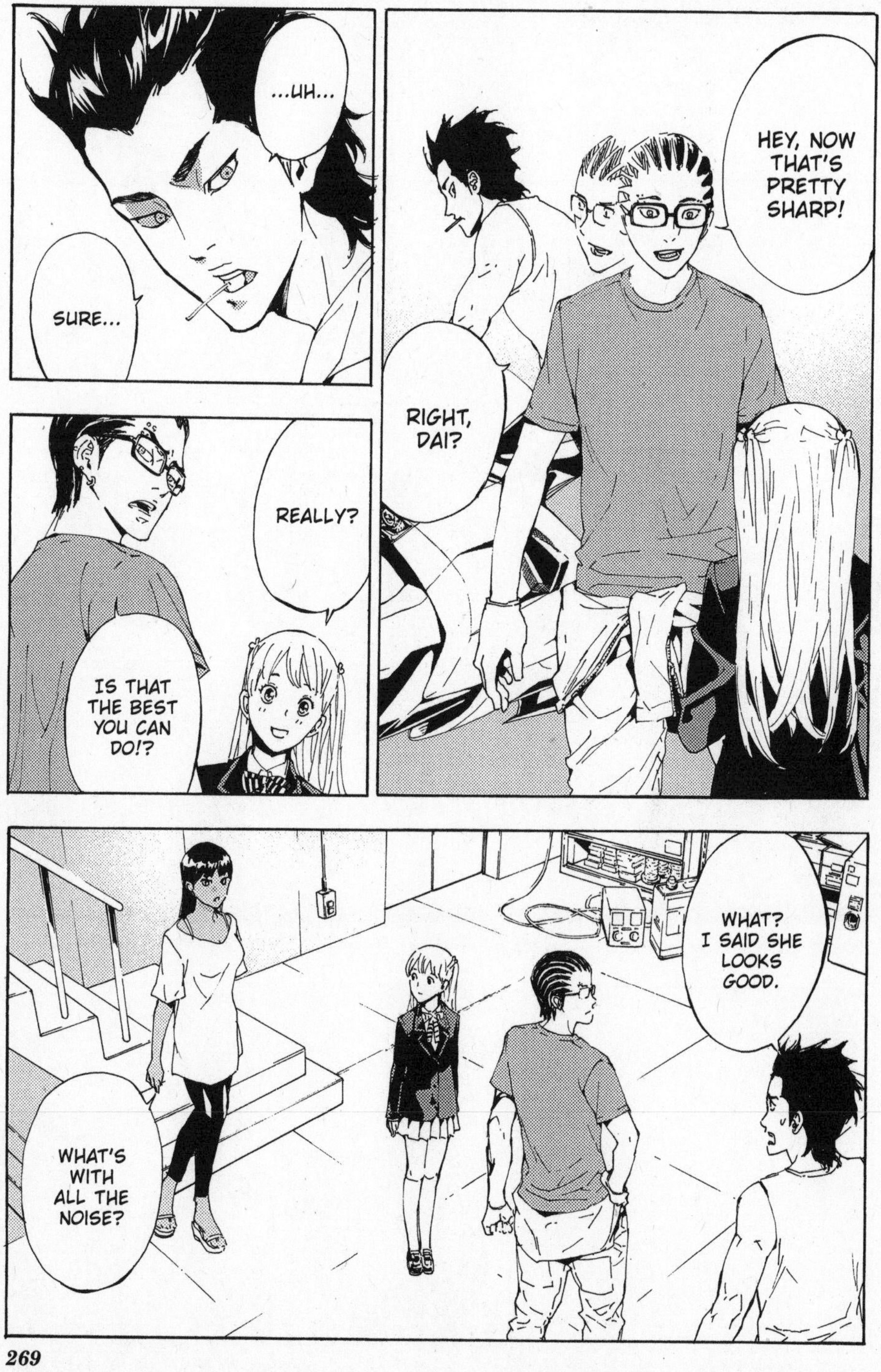
HEY, NOW THAT'S PRETTY SHARP!
RIGHT, DAI?
...UH...
SURE...
REALLY?
IS THAT THE BEST YOU CAN DO!?
WHAT? I SAID SHE LOOKS GOOD.
WHAT'S WITH ALL THE NOISE?

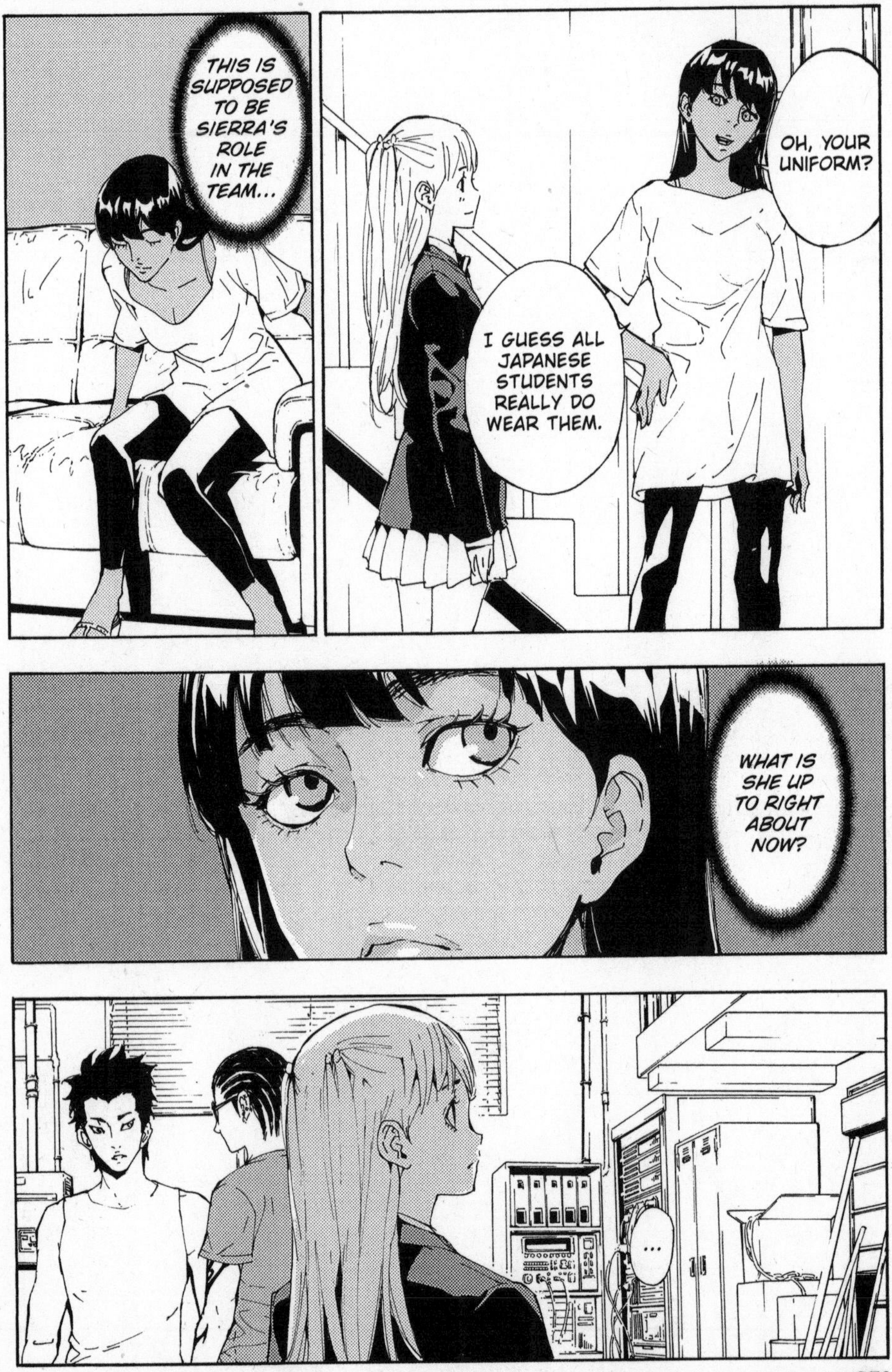
OH, YOUR UNIFORM?
I GUESS ALL JAPANESE STUDENTS REALLY DO WEAR THEM.
THIS IS SUPPOSED TO BE SIERRA'S ROLE IN THE TEAM...
WHAT IS SHE UP TO RIGHT ABOUT NOW?
...

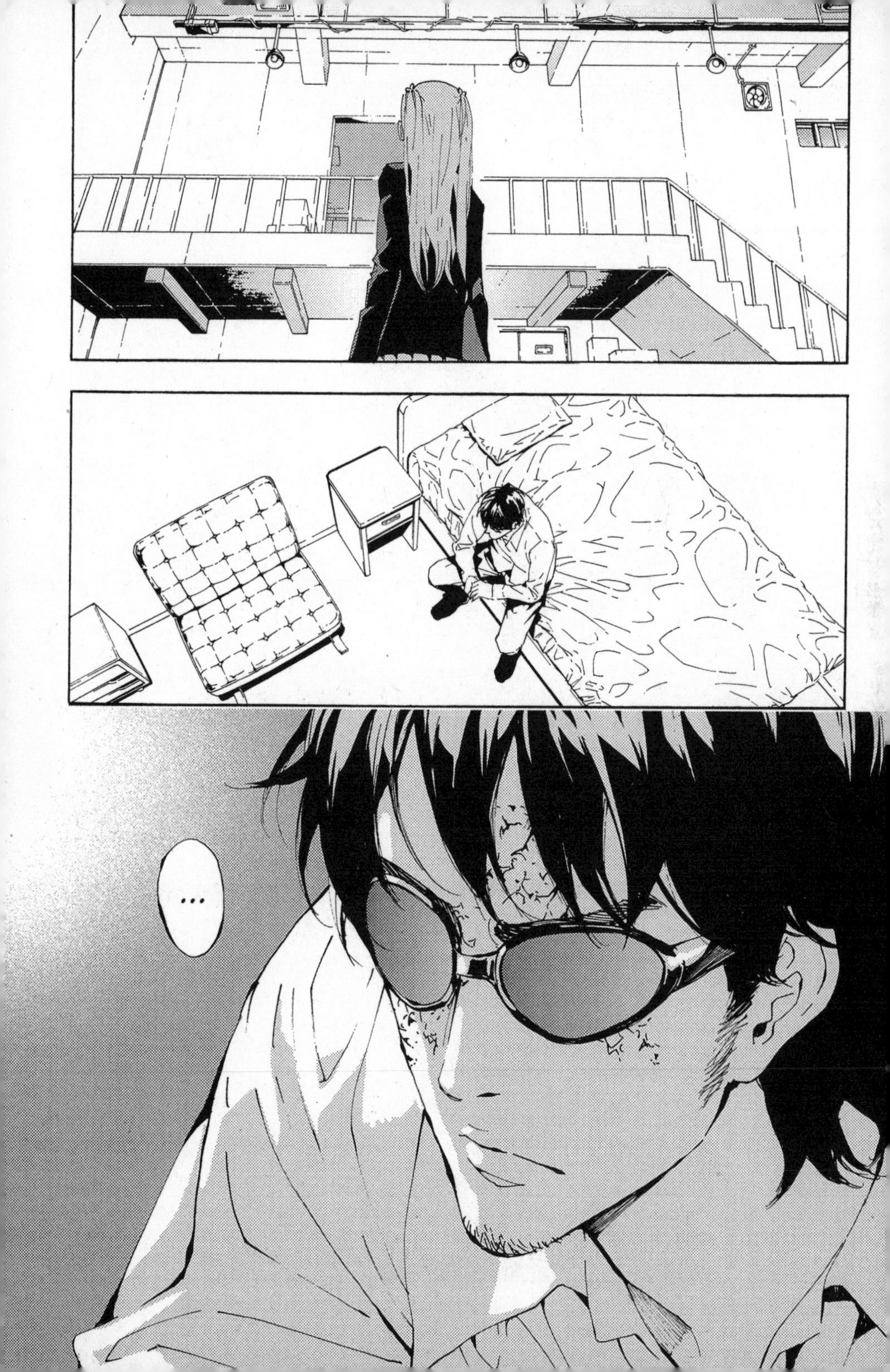
...

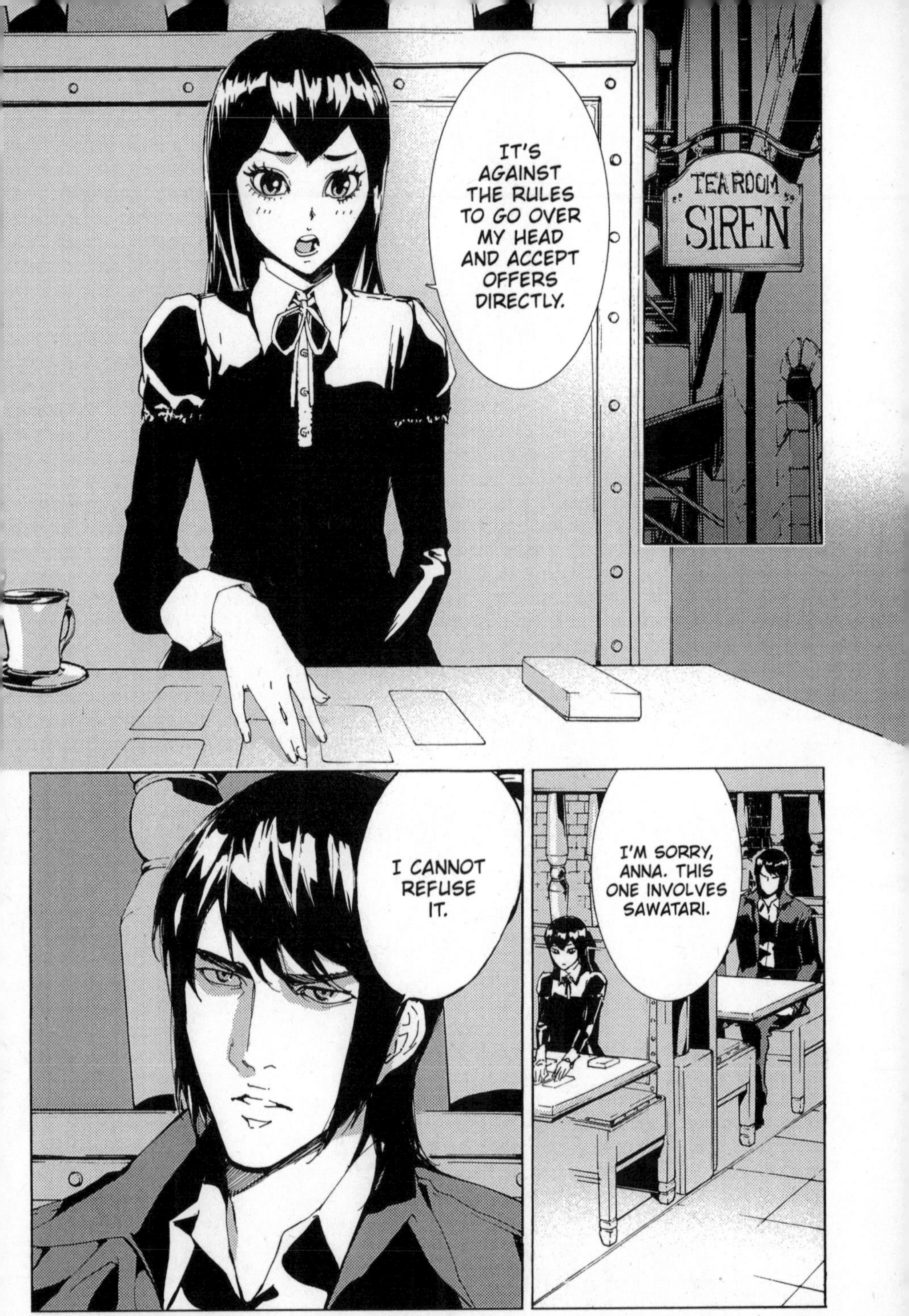
TEA ROOM
SIREN
IT'S AGAINST THE RULES TO GO OVER MY HEAD AND ACCEPT OFFERS DIRECTLY.
I'M SORRY, ANNA. THIS ONE INVOLVES SAWATARI.
I CANNOT REFUSE IT.

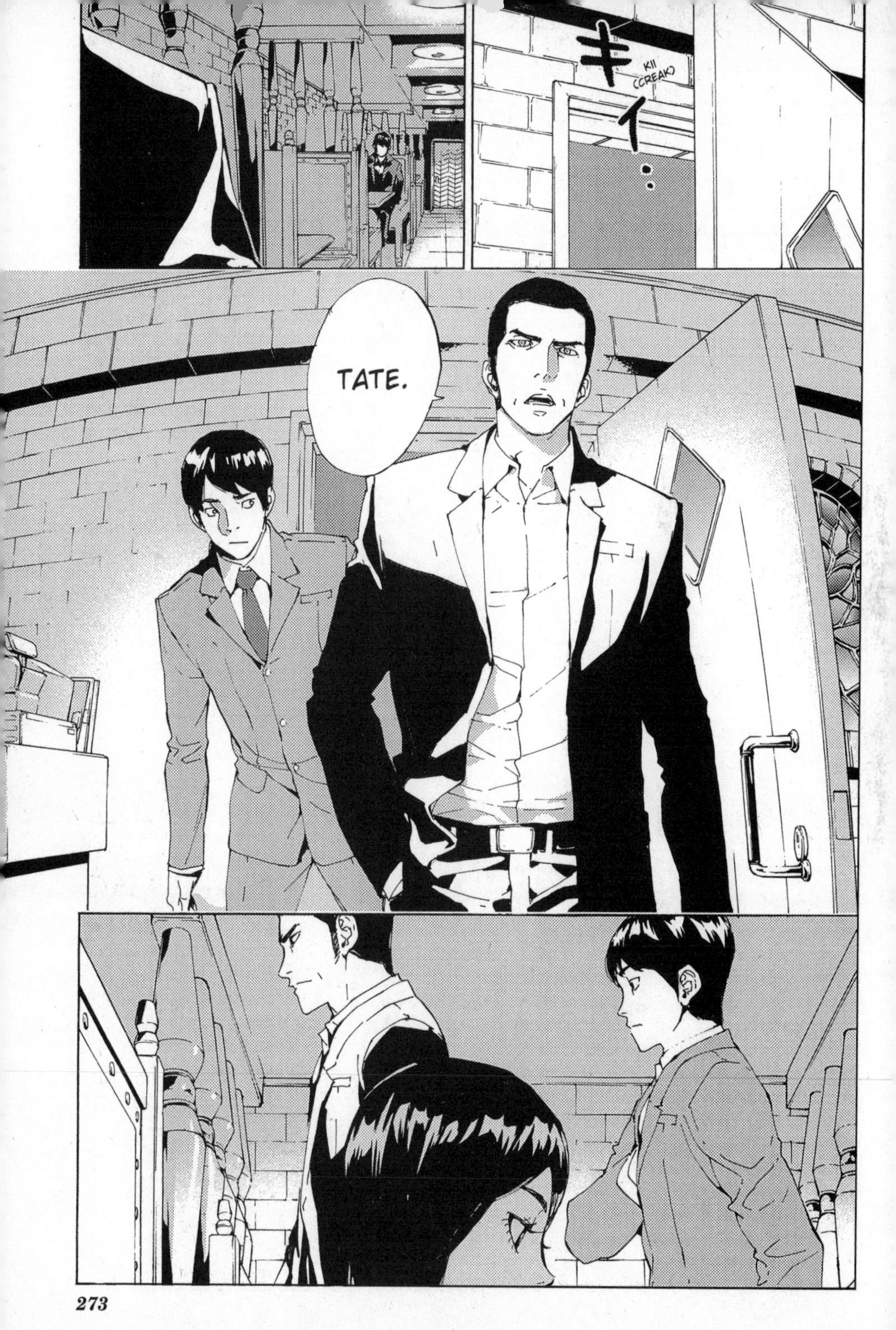
キイ…
KII (CREAK)
TATE.

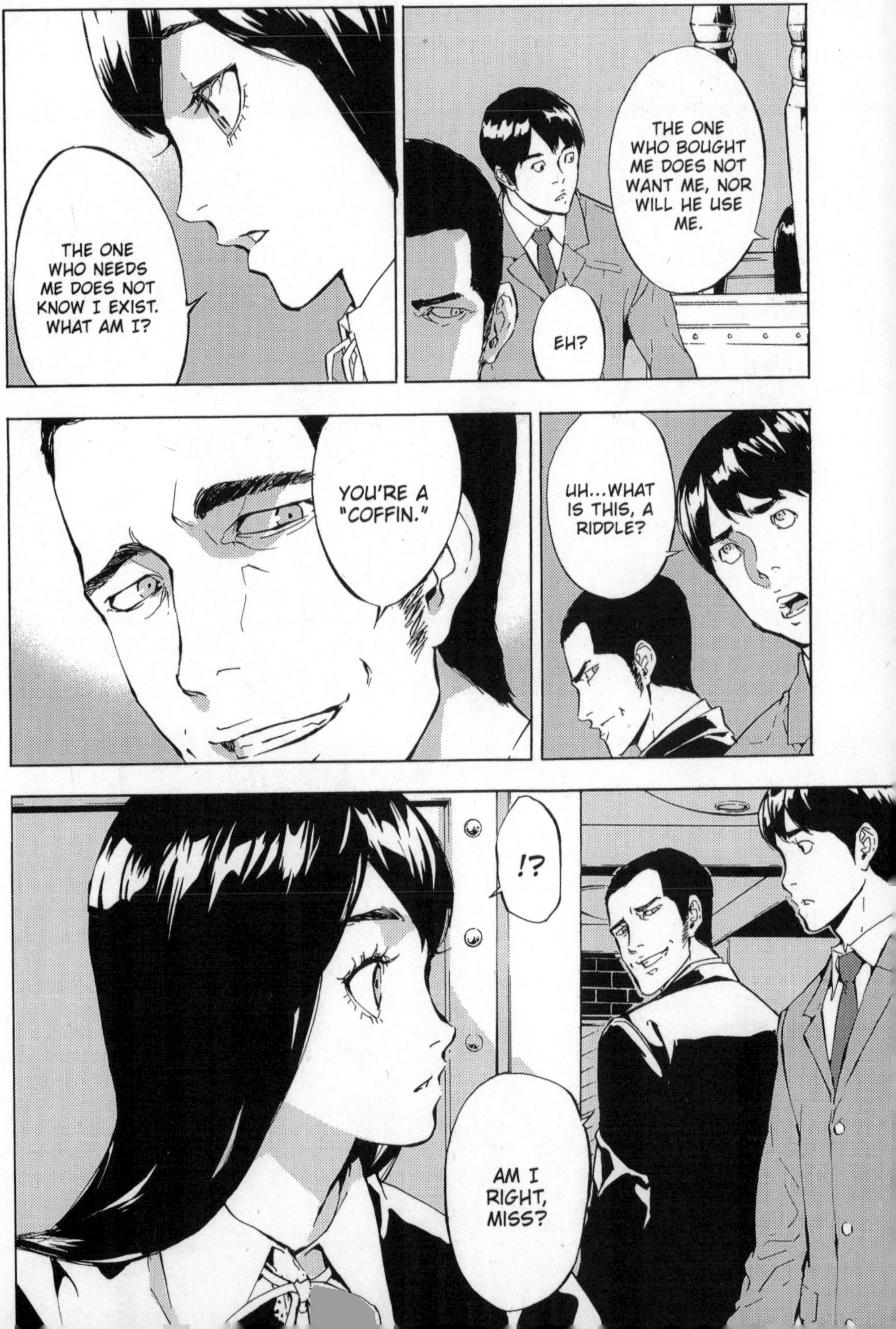
THE ONE WHO BOUGHT ME DOES NOT WANT ME, NOR WILL HE USE ME.
EH?
THE ONE WHO NEEDS ME DOES NOT KNOW I EXIST. WHAT AM I?
UH...WHAT IS THIS, A RIDDLE?
YOU'RE A "COFFIN."
!?
AM I RIGHT, MISS?

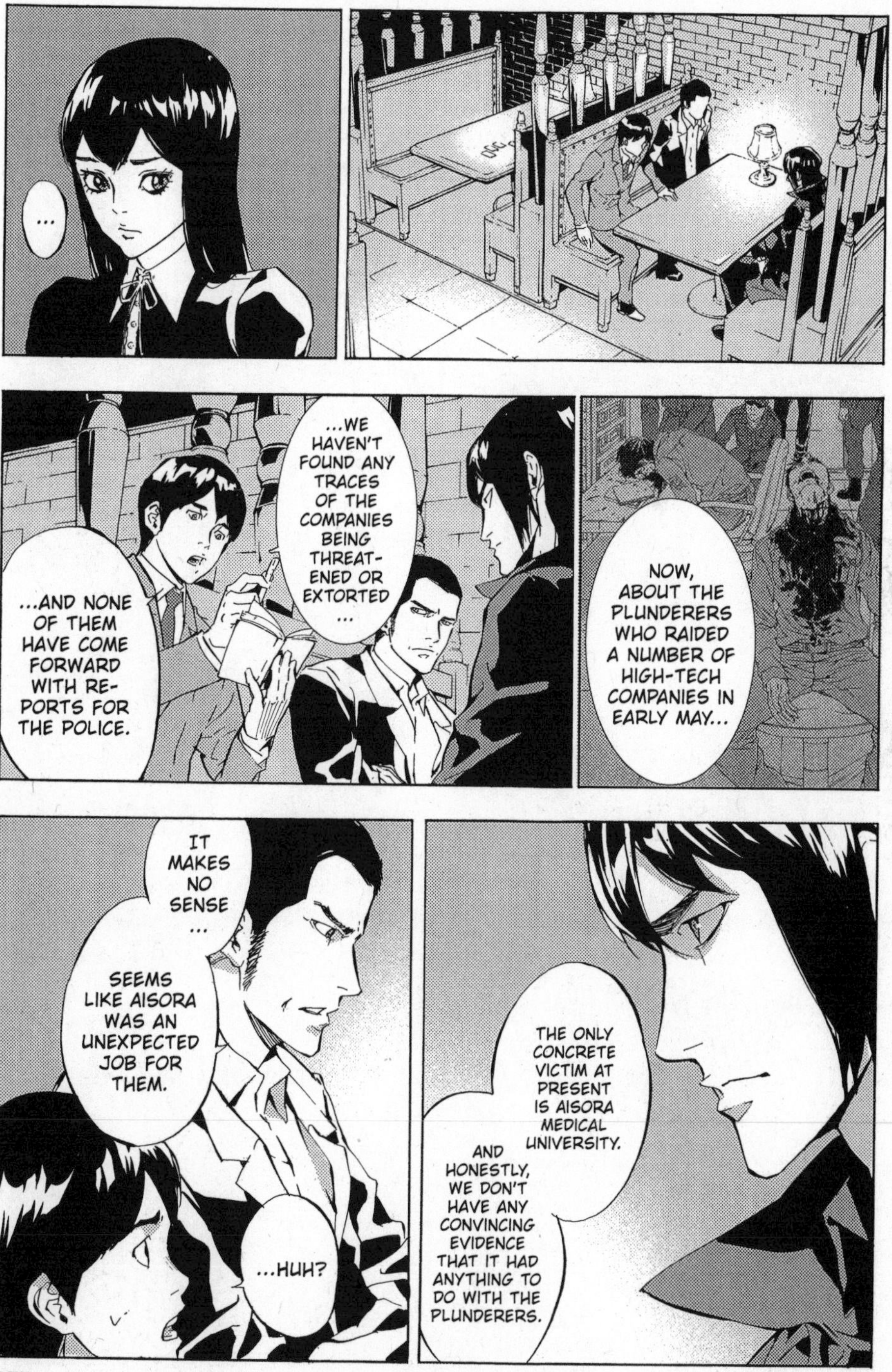
...
NOW, ABOUT THE PLUNDERERS WHO RAIDED A NUMBER OF HIGH-TECH COMPANIES IN EARLY MAY...
...WE HAVEN'T FOUND ANY TRACES OF THE COMPANIES BEING THREAT-ENED OR EXTORTED ...
...AND NONE OF THEM HAVE COME FORWARD WITH RE-PORTS FOR THE POLICE.
THE ONLY CONCRETE VICTIM AT PRESENT IS AISORA MEDICAL UNIVERSITY.
AND HONESTLY, WE DON'T HAVE ANY CONVINCING EVIDENCE THAT IT HAD ANYTHING TO DO WITH THE PLUNDERERS.
IT MAKES NO SENSE ...
SEEMS LIKE AISORA WAS AN UNEXPECTED JOB FOR THEM.
...HUH?

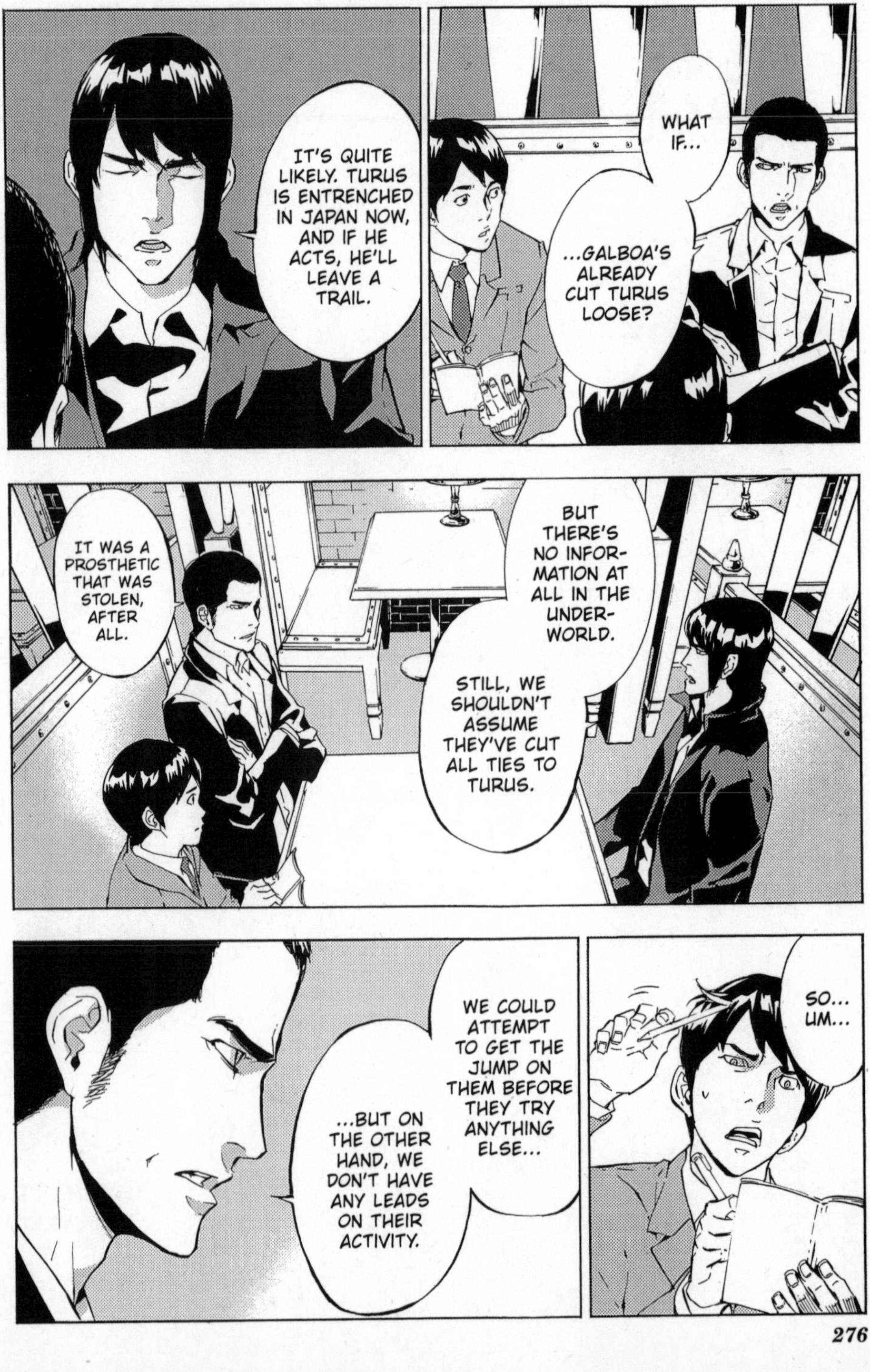
WHAT IF...
...GALBOA'S ALREADY CUT TURUS LOOSE?
IT'S QUITE LIKELY. TURUS IS ENTRENCHED IN JAPAN NOW, AND IF HE ACTS, HE'LL LEAVE A TRAIL.
BUT THERE'S NO INFORMATION AT ALL IN THE UNDERWORLD.
STILL, WE SHOULDN'T ASSUME THEY'VE CUT ALL TIES TO TURUS.
IT WAS A PROSTHETIC THAT WAS STOLEN, AFTER ALL.
SO... UM...
WE COULD ATTEMPT TO GET THE JUMP ON THEM BEFORE THEY TRY ANYTHING ELSE...
...BUT ON THE OTHER HAND, WE DON'T HAVE ANY LEADS ON THEIR ACTIVITY.

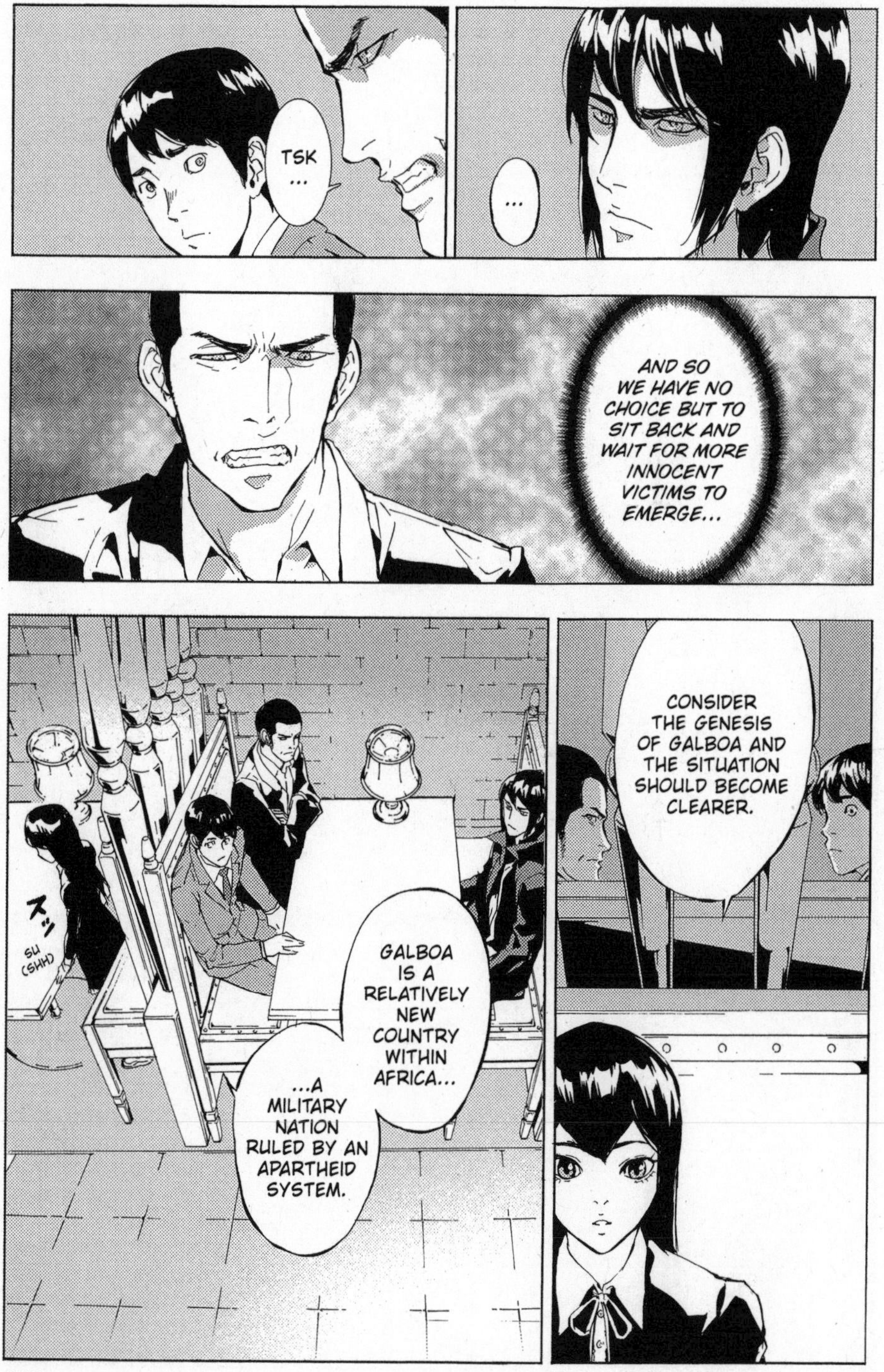
...
TSK ...
AND SO WE HAVE NO CHOICE BUT TO SIT BACK AND WAIT FOR MORE INNOCENT VICTIMS TO EMERGE...
CONSIDER THE GENESIS OF GALBOA AND THE SITUATION SHOULD BECOME CLEARER.
GALBOA IS A RELATIVELY NEW COUNTRY WITHIN AFRICA...
...A MILITARY NATION RULED BY AN APARTHEID SYSTEM.
スッ
SU (SHH)

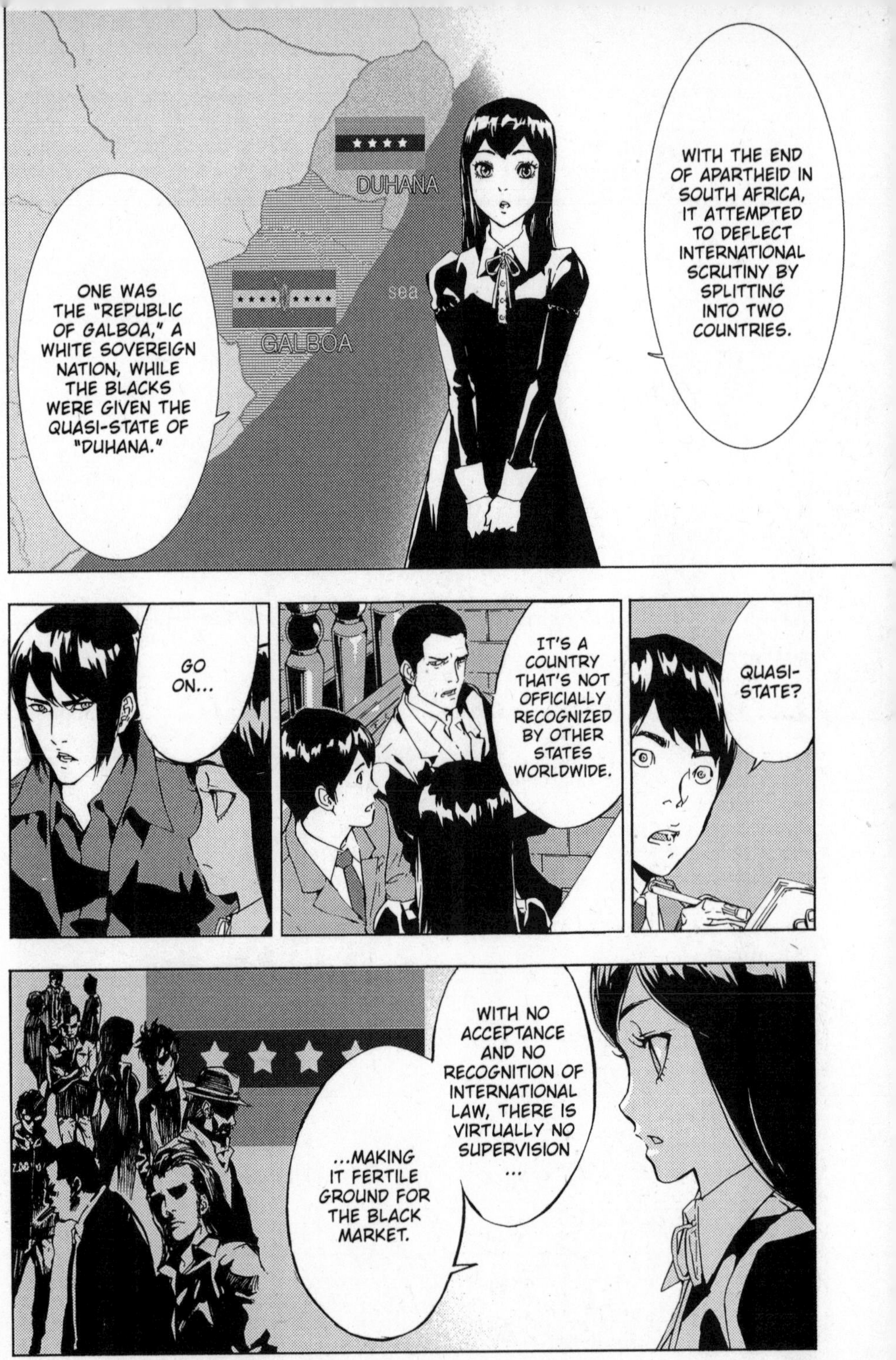
WITH THE END OF APARTHEID IN SOUTH AFRICA, IT ATTEMPTED TO DEFLECT INTERNATIONAL SCRUTINY BY SPLITTING INTO TWO COUNTRIES.
DUHANA
sea
GALBOA
ONE WAS THE "REPUBLIC OF GALBOA," A WHITE SOVEREIGN NATION, WHILE THE BLACKS WERE GIVEN THE QUASI-STATE OF "DUHANA."
QUASI-STATE?
IT'S A COUNTRY THAT'S NOT OFFICIALLY RECOGNIZED BY OTHER STATES WORLDWIDE.
GO ON...
WITH NO ACCEPTANCE AND NO RECOGNITION OF INTERNATIONAL LAW, THERE IS VIRTUALLY NO SUPERVISION ...
...MAKING IT FERTILE GROUND FOR THE BLACK MARKET.

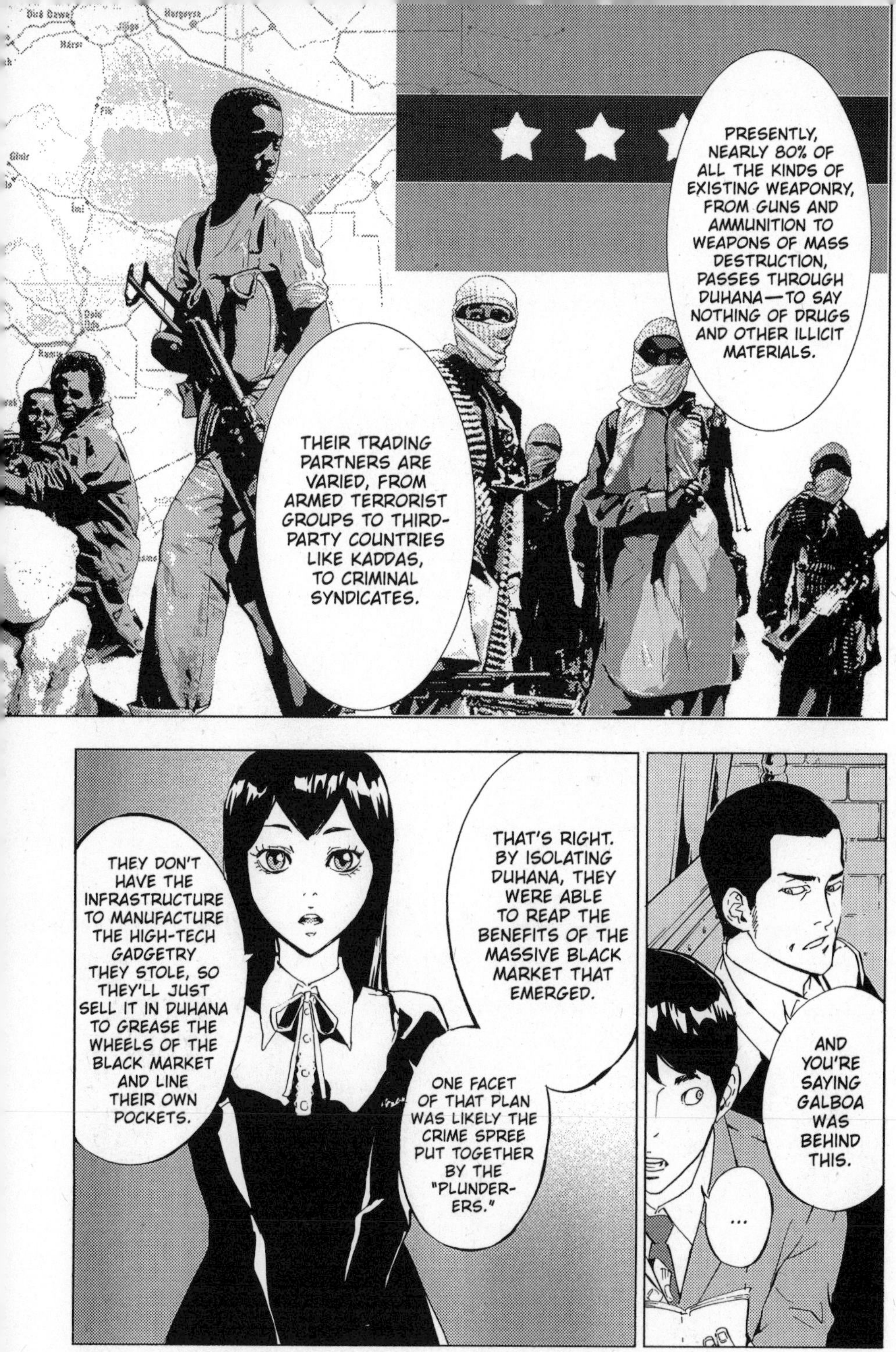
PRESENTLY, NEARLY 80% OF ALL THE KINDS OF EXISTING WEAPONRY, FROM GUNS AND AMMUNITION TO WEAPONS OF MASS DESTRUCTION, PASSES THROUGH DUHANA—TO SAY NOTHING OF DRUGS AND OTHER ILLICIT MATERIALS.
THEIR TRADING PARTNERS ARE VARIED, FROM ARMED TERRORIST GROUPS TO THIRD-PARTY COUNTRIES LIKE KADDAS, TO CRIMINAL SYNDICATES.
AND YOU'RE SAYING GALBOA WAS BEHIND THIS.
...
THAT'S RIGHT. BY ISOLATING DUHANA, THEY WERE ABLE TO REAP THE BENEFITS OF THE MASSIVE BLACK MARKET THAT EMERGED.
ONE FACET OF THAT PLAN WAS LIKELY THE CRIME SPREE PUT TOGETHER BY THE "PLUNDERERS."
THEY DON'T HAVE THE INFRASTRUCTURE TO MANUFACTURE THE HIGH-TECH GADGETRY THEY STOLE, SO THEY'LL JUST SELL IT IN DUHANA TO GREASE THE WHEELS OF THE BLACK MARKET AND LINE THEIR OWN POCKETS.

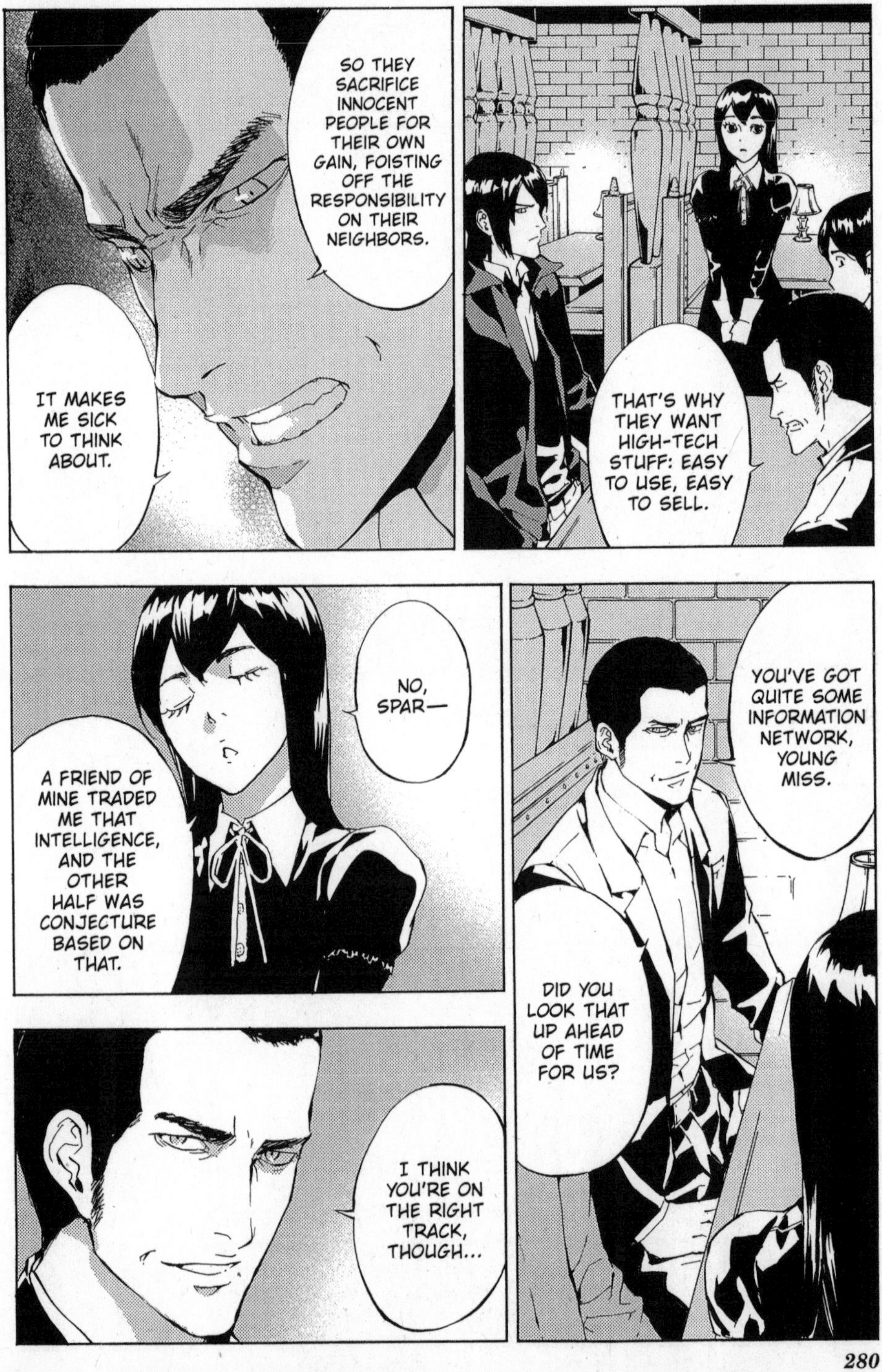

THAT'S WHY THEY WANT HIGH-TECH STUFF: EASY TO USE, EASY TO SELL.
SO THEY SACRIFICE INNOCENT PEOPLE FOR THEIR OWN GAIN, FOISTING OFF THE RESPONSIBILITY ON THEIR NEIGHBORS.
IT MAKES ME SICK TO THINK ABOUT.
YOU'VE GOT QUITE SOME INFORMATION NETWORK, YOUNG MISS.
DID YOU LOOK THAT UP AHEAD OF TIME FOR US?
NO, SPAR—
A FRIEND OF MINE TRADED ME THAT INTELLIGENCE, AND THE OTHER HALF WAS CONJECTURE BASED ON THAT.
I THINK YOU'RE ON THE RIGHT TRACK, THOUGH...

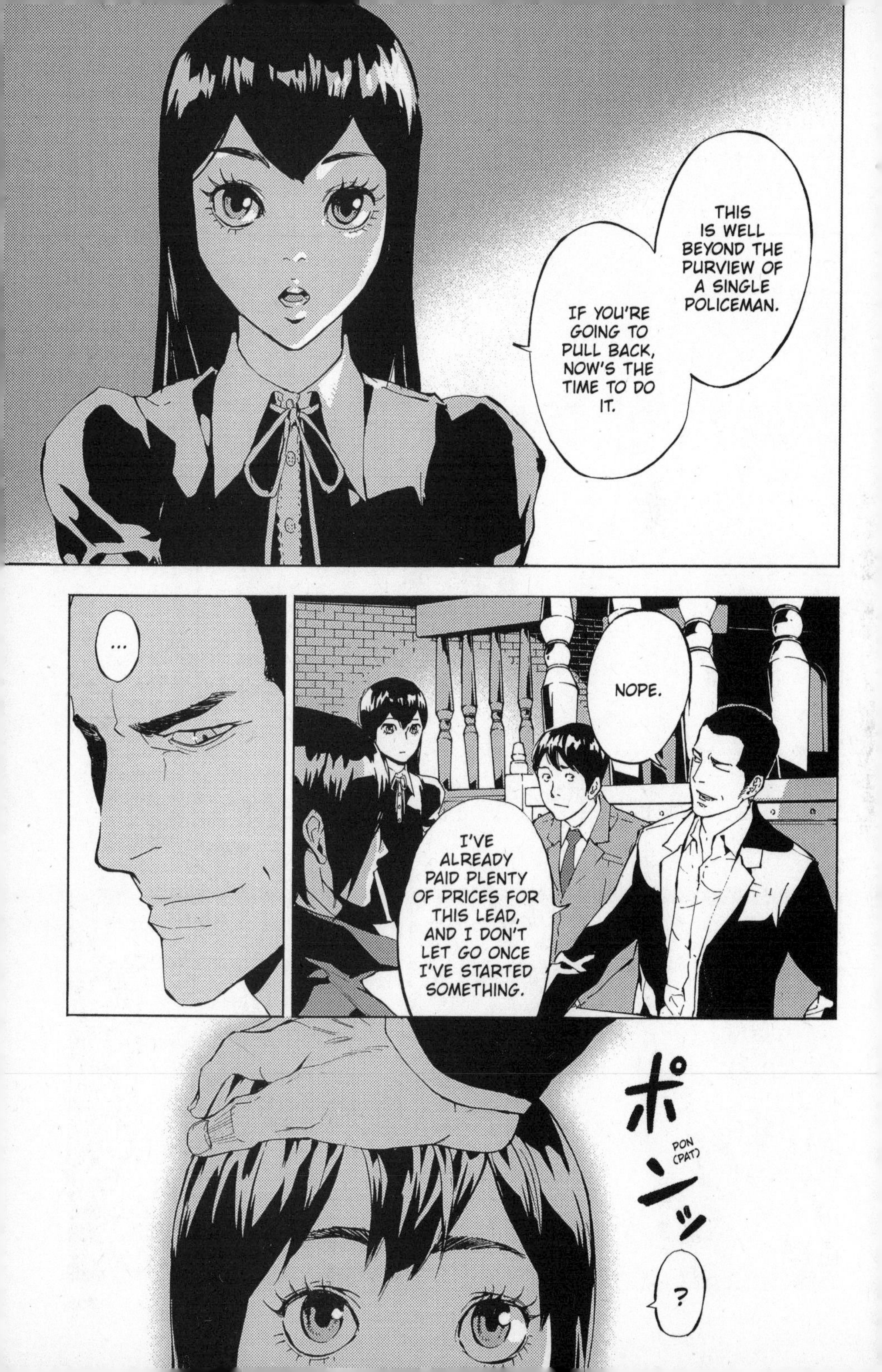
THIS IS WELL BEYOND THE PURVIEW OF A SINGLE POLICEMAN.
IF YOU'RE GOING TO PULL BACK, NOW'S THE TIME TO DO IT.
NOPE.
I'VE ALREADY PAID PLENTY OF PRICES FOR THIS LEAD, AND I DON'T LET GO ONCE I'VE STARTED SOMETHING.
...
ポンッ
PON (PAT)
?

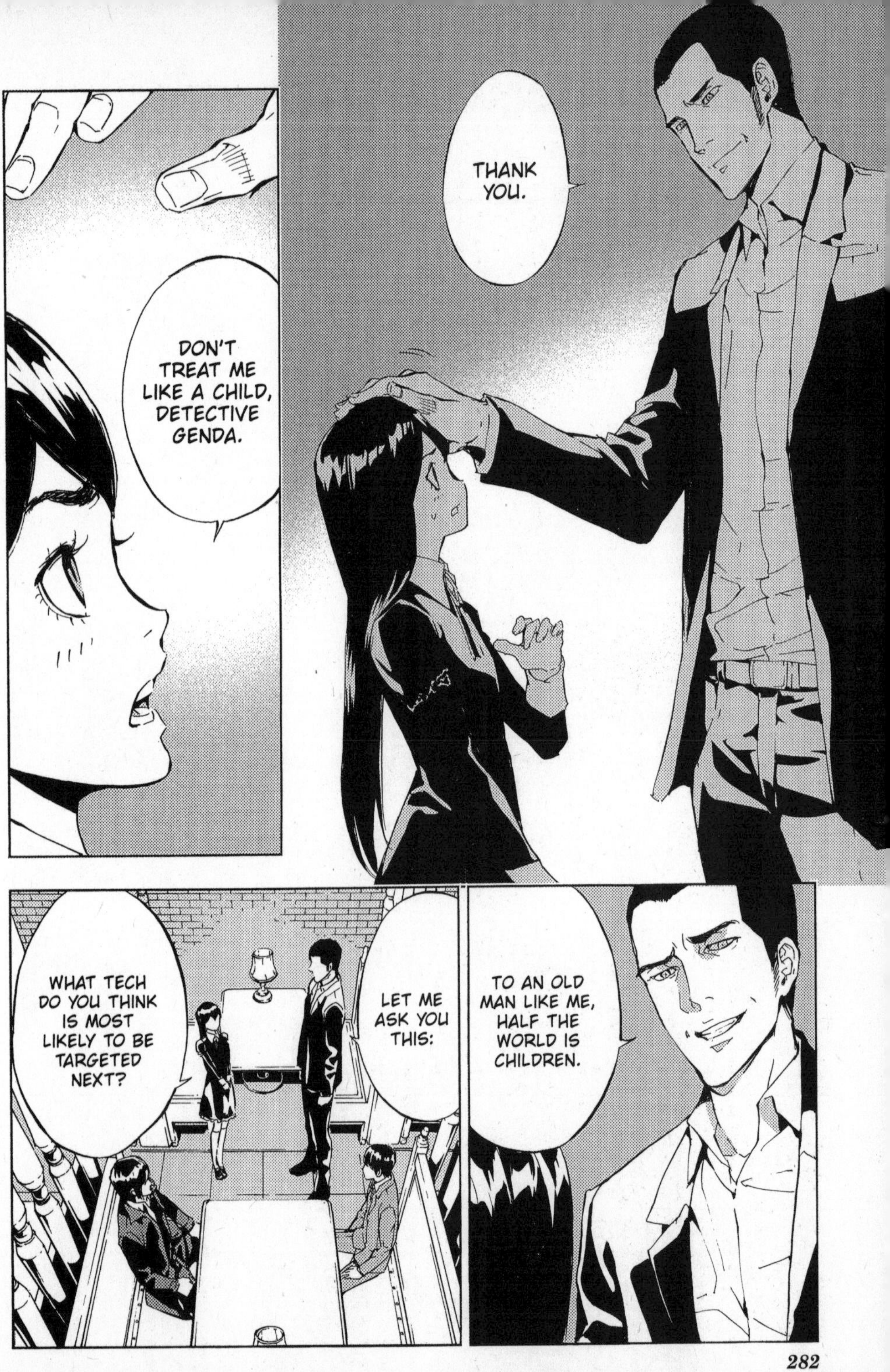
THANK YOU.
DON'T TREAT ME LIKE A CHILD, DETECTIVE GENDA.
TO AN OLD MAN LIKE ME, HALF THE WORLD IS CHILDREN.
LET ME ASK YOU THIS:
WHAT TECH DO YOU THINK IS MOST LIKELY TO BE TARGETED NEXT?

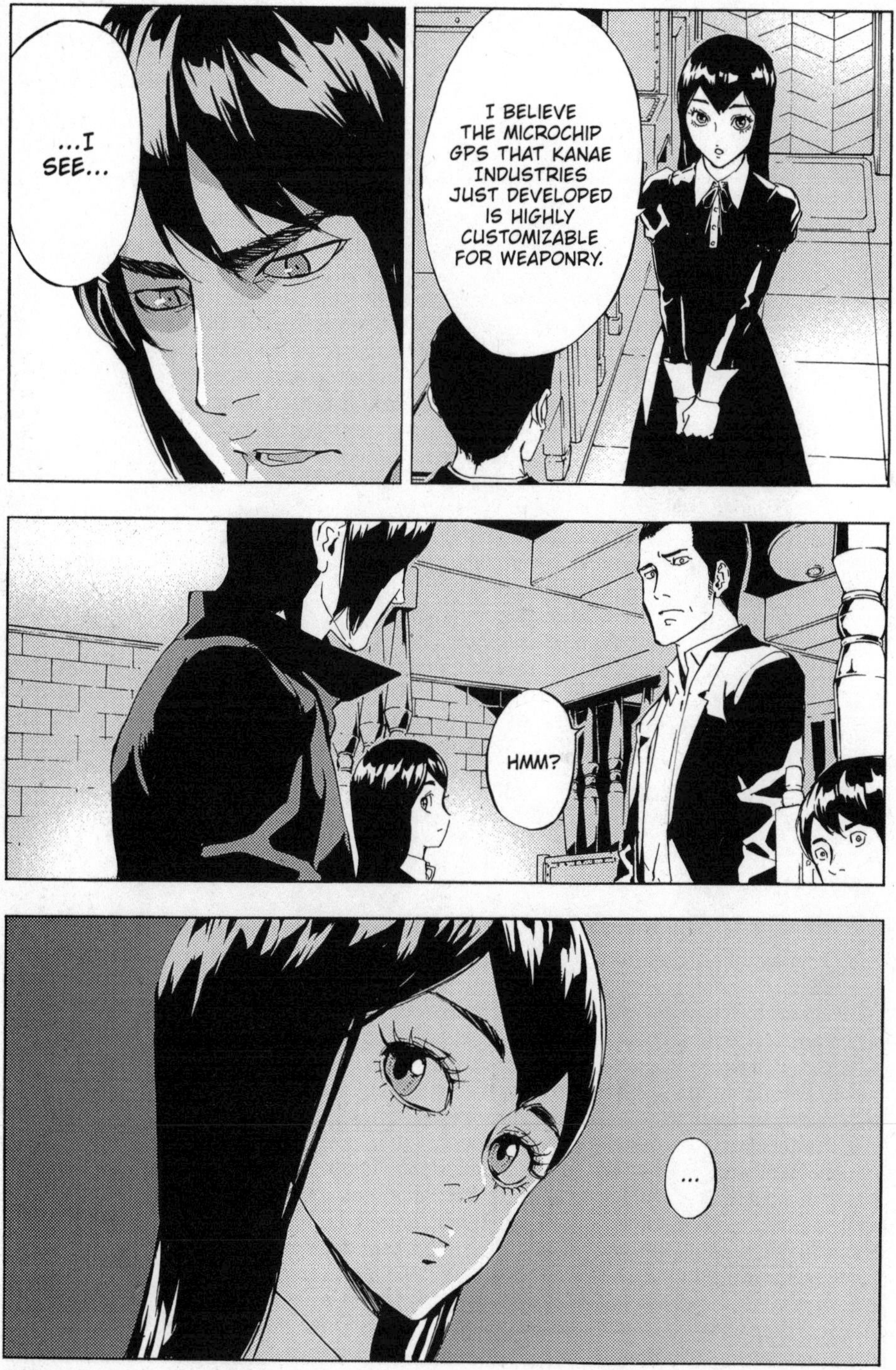
I BELIEVE THE MICROCHIP GPS THAT KANAE INDUSTRIES JUST DEVELOPED IS HIGHLY CUSTOMIZABLE FOR WEAPONRY.
...I SEE...
HMM?
...

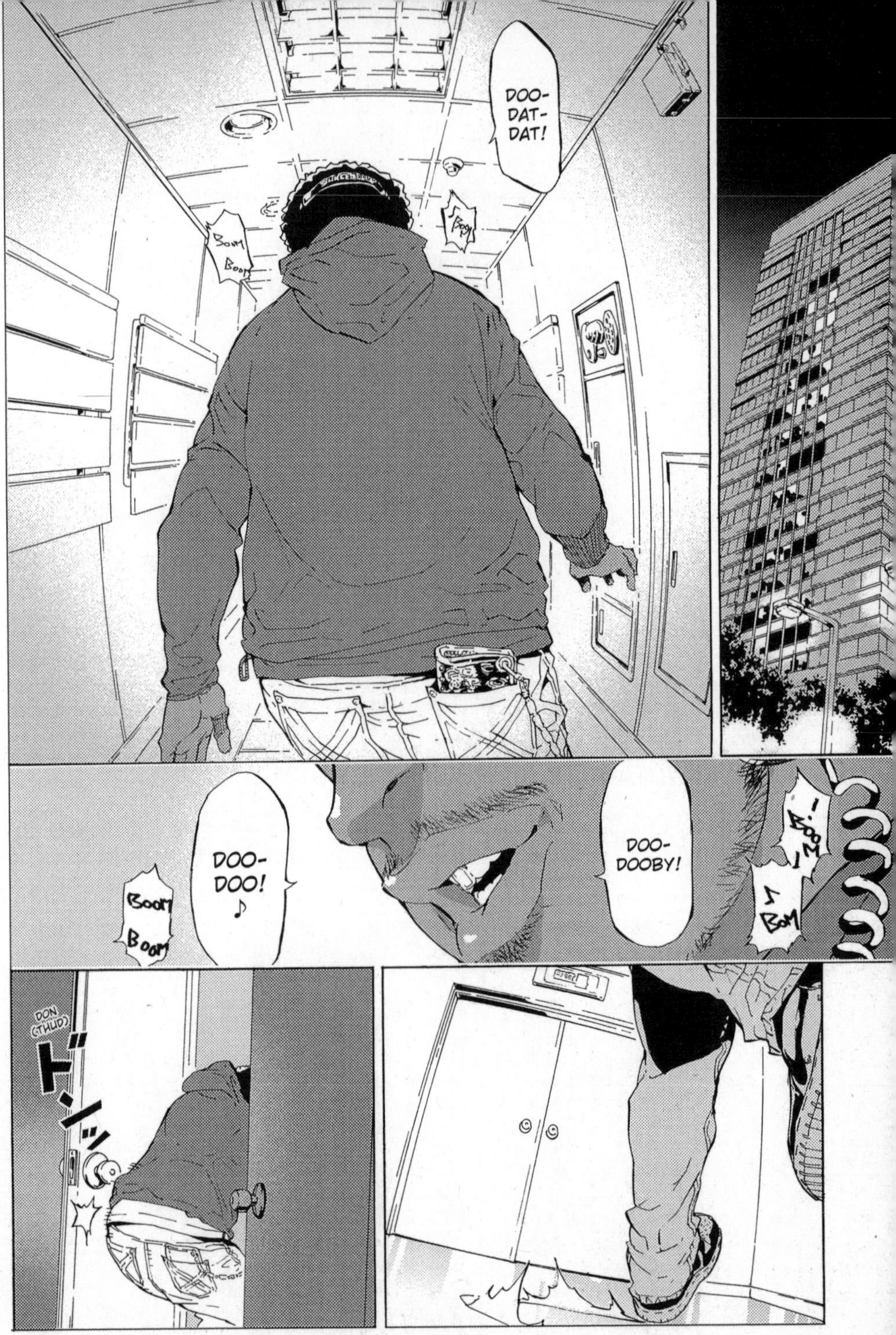

DOO-DAT-DAT!
♪Boom
Boom Boom
BOOM!
♪BOM
DOO-DOOBY!
DOO-DOO! ♪
Boom Boom
DON (THUD)
ドン

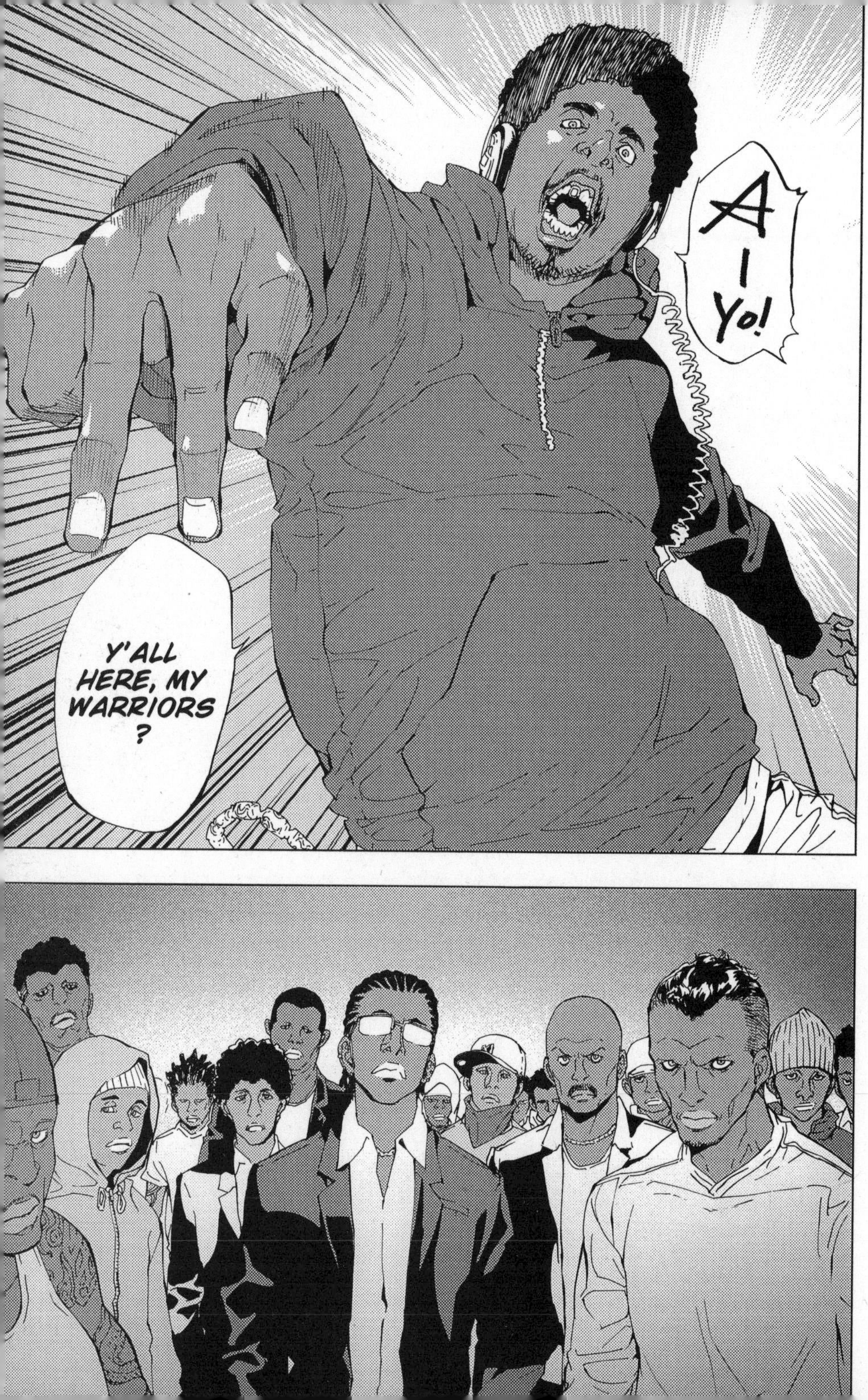
A I Yo!
Y'ALL HERE, MY WARRIORS?

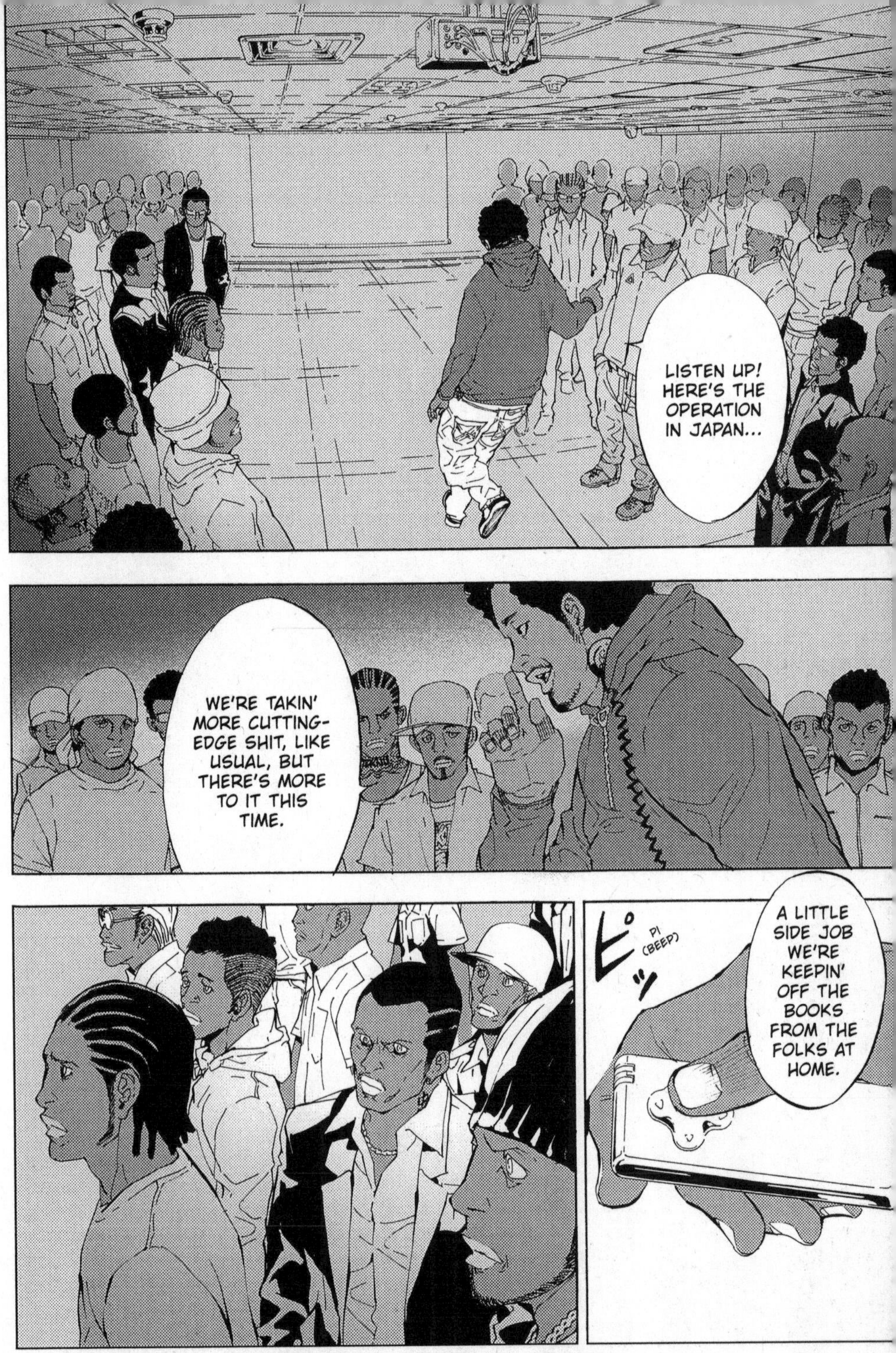
LISTEN UP! HERE'S THE OPERATION IN JAPAN...
WE'RE TAKIN' MORE CUTTING-EDGE SHIT, LIKE USUAL, BUT THERE'S MORE TO IT THIS TIME.
PI (BEEP)
A LITTLE SIDE JOB WE'RE KEEPIN' OFF THE BOOKS FROM THE FOLKS AT HOME.

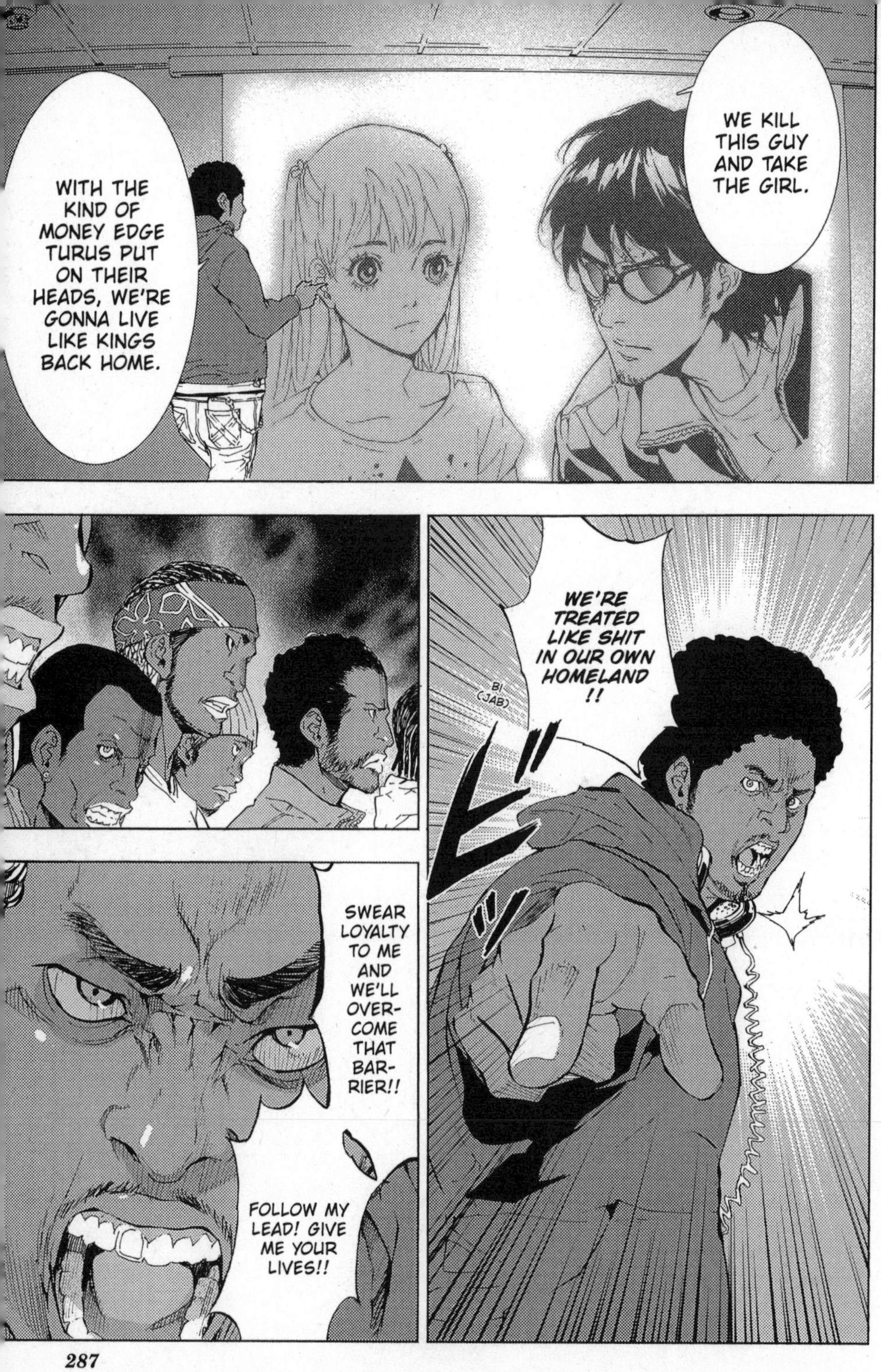
WE KILL THIS GUY AND TAKE THE GIRL.
WITH THE KIND OF MONEY EDGE TURUS PUT ON THEIR HEADS, WE'RE GONNA LIVE LIKE KINGS BACK HOME.
WE'RE TREATED LIKE SHIT IN OUR OWN HOMELAND!!
BI (JAB)
SWEAR LOYALTY TO ME AND WE'LL OVER-COME THAT BAR-RIER!!
FOLLOW MY LEAD! GIVE ME YOUR LIVES!!

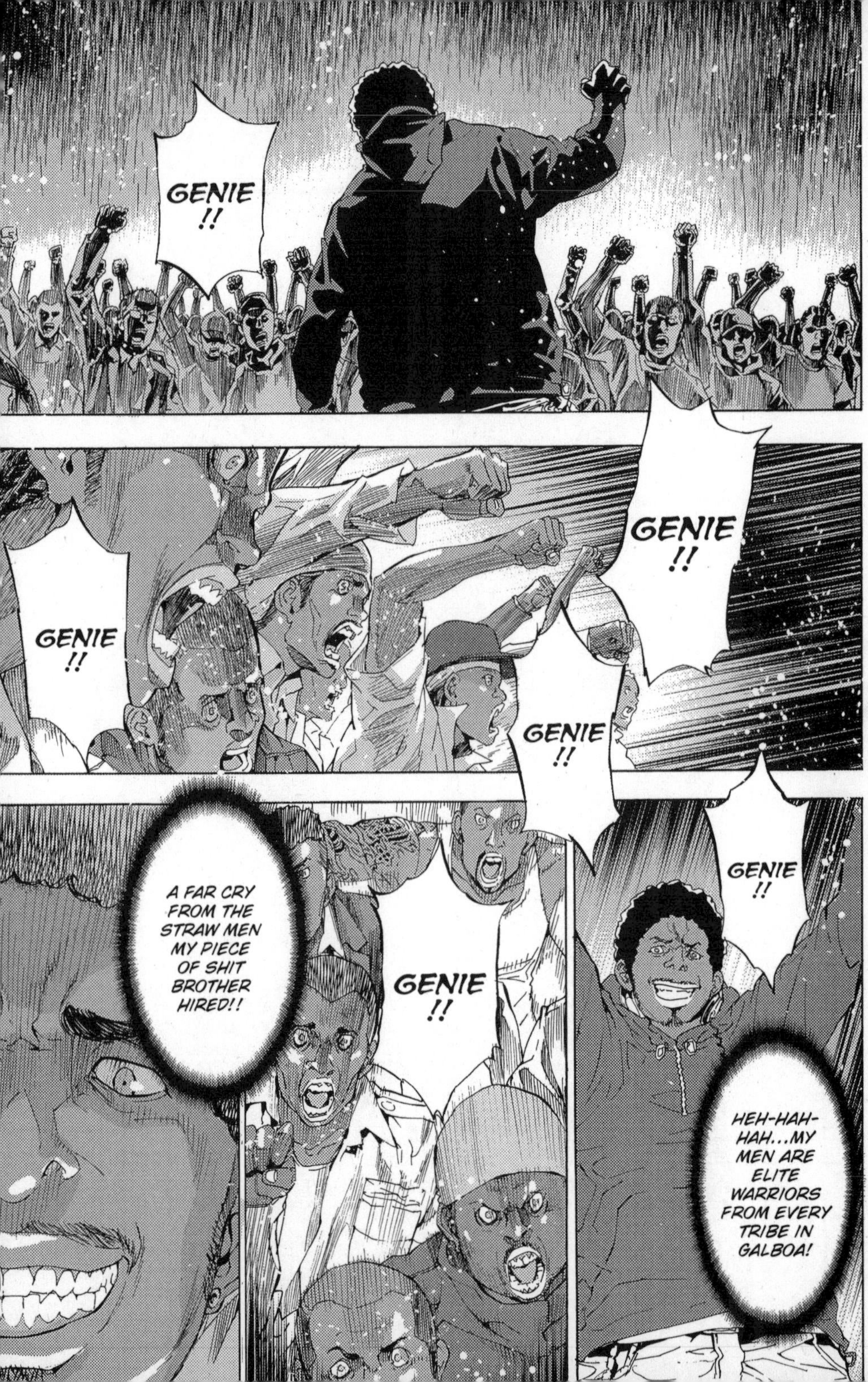
GENIE !!
GENIE !!
GENIE !!
GENIE !!
GENIE !!
HEH-HAH-HAH...MY MEN ARE ELITE WARRIORS FROM EVERY TRIBE IN GALBOA!
GENIE !!
A FAR CRY FROM THE STRAW MEN MY PIECE OF SHIT BROTHER HIRED!!

Until Death do us Part

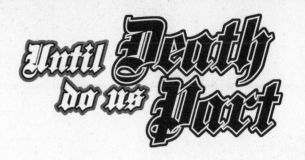

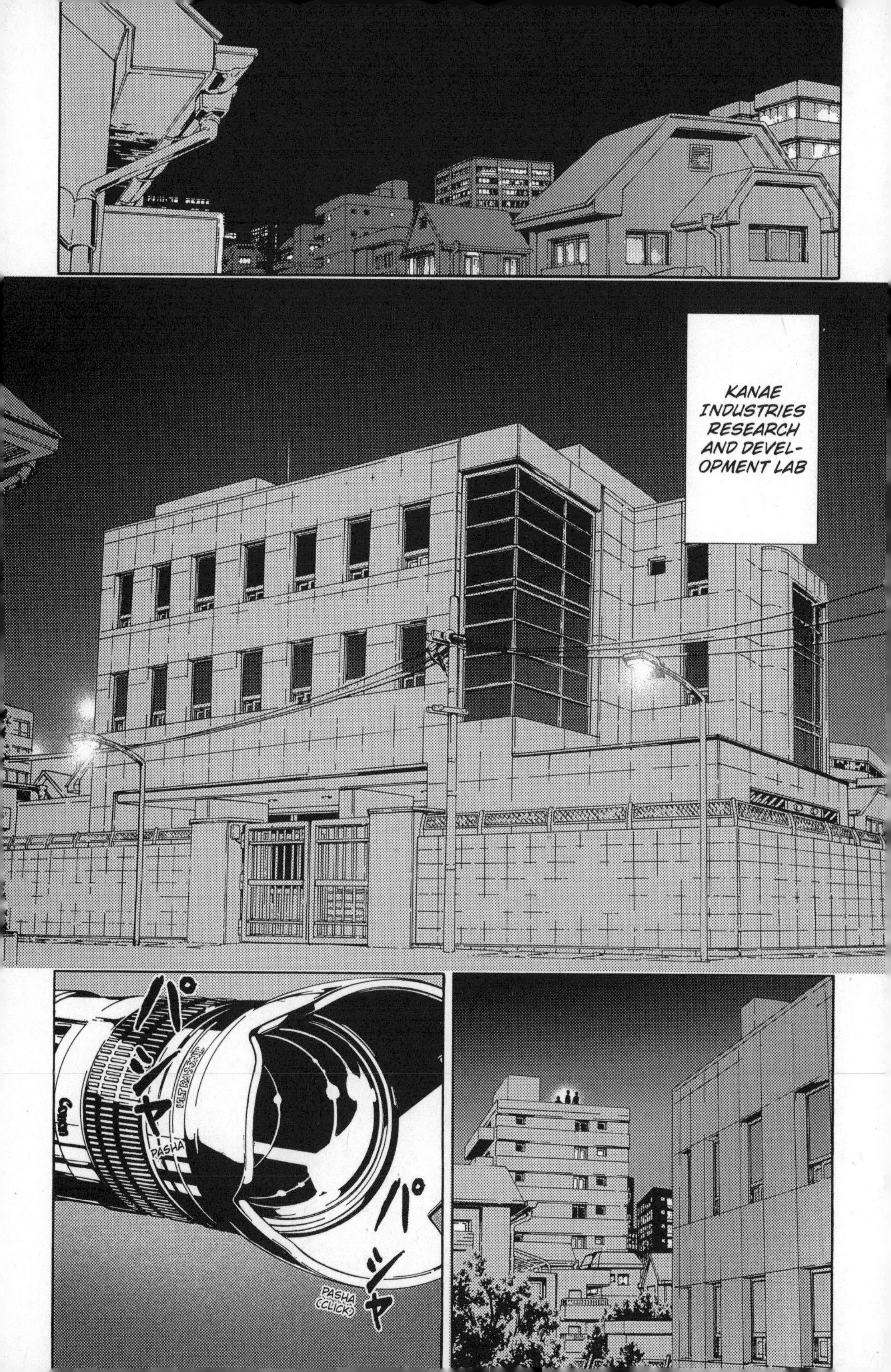
KANAE INDUSTRIES RESEARCH AND DEVEL-OPMENT LAB
パシャ
PASHA
パシャ
PASHA (CLICK)

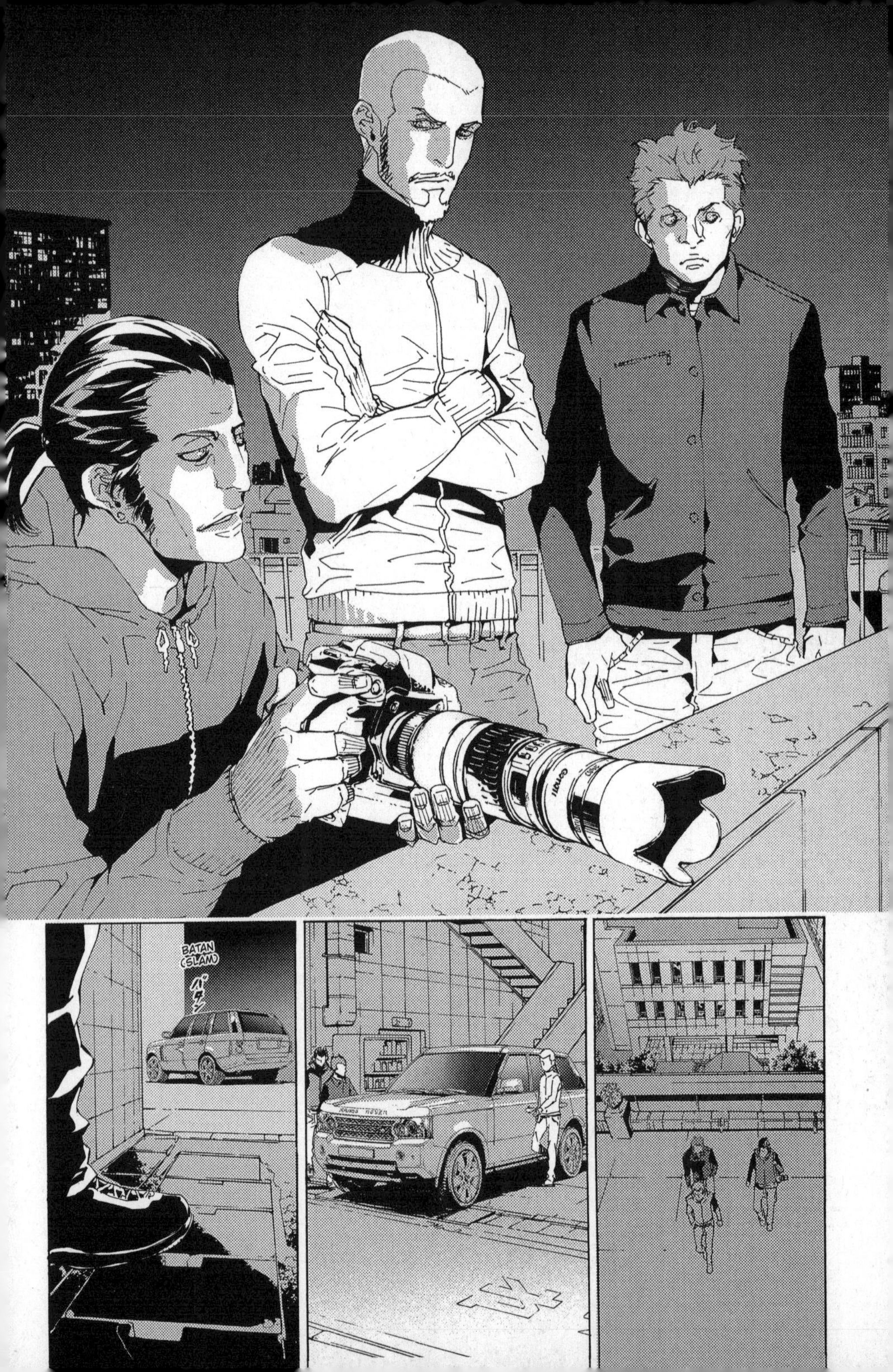
BATAN
(SLAM)

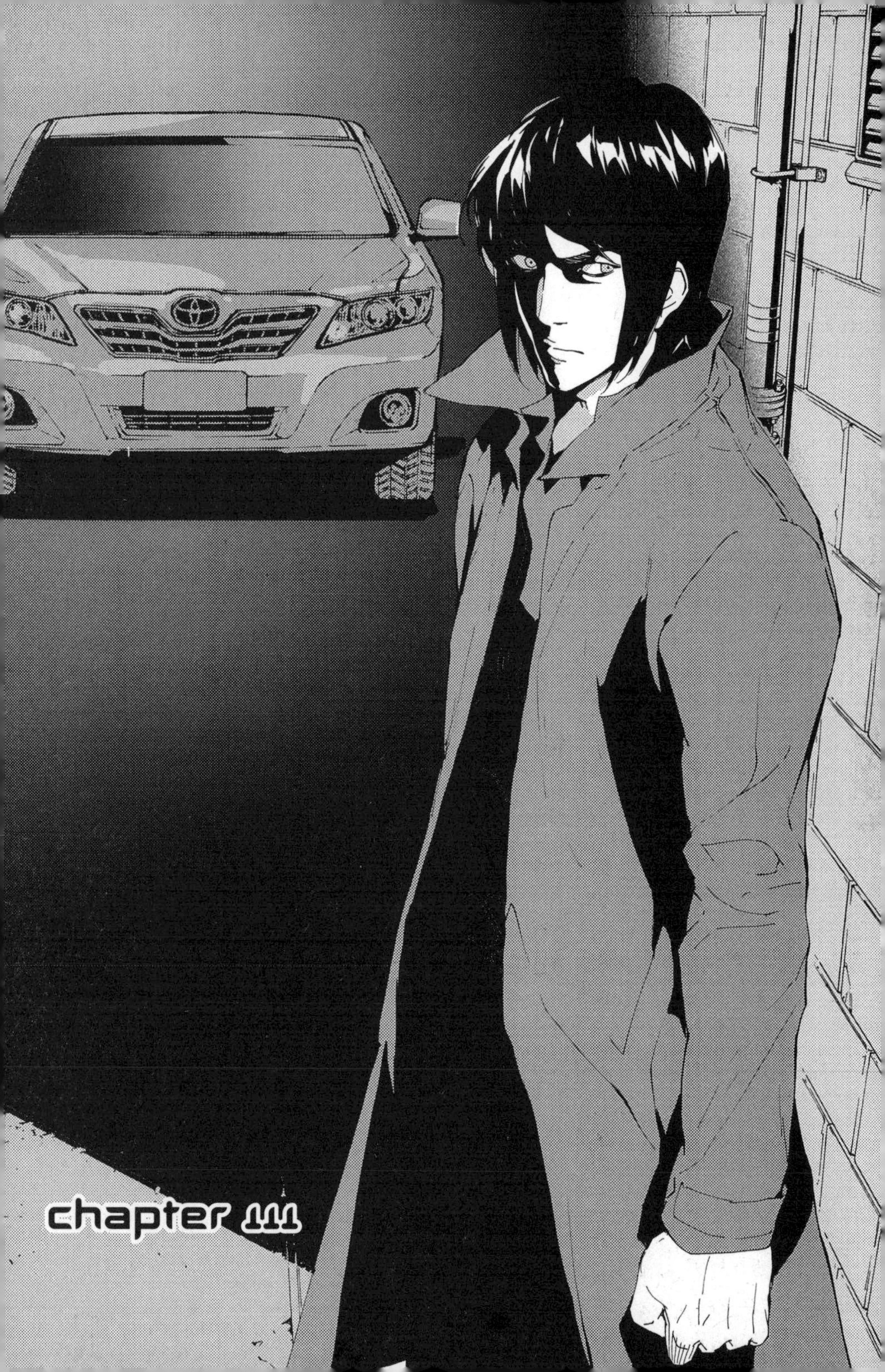
chapter 111

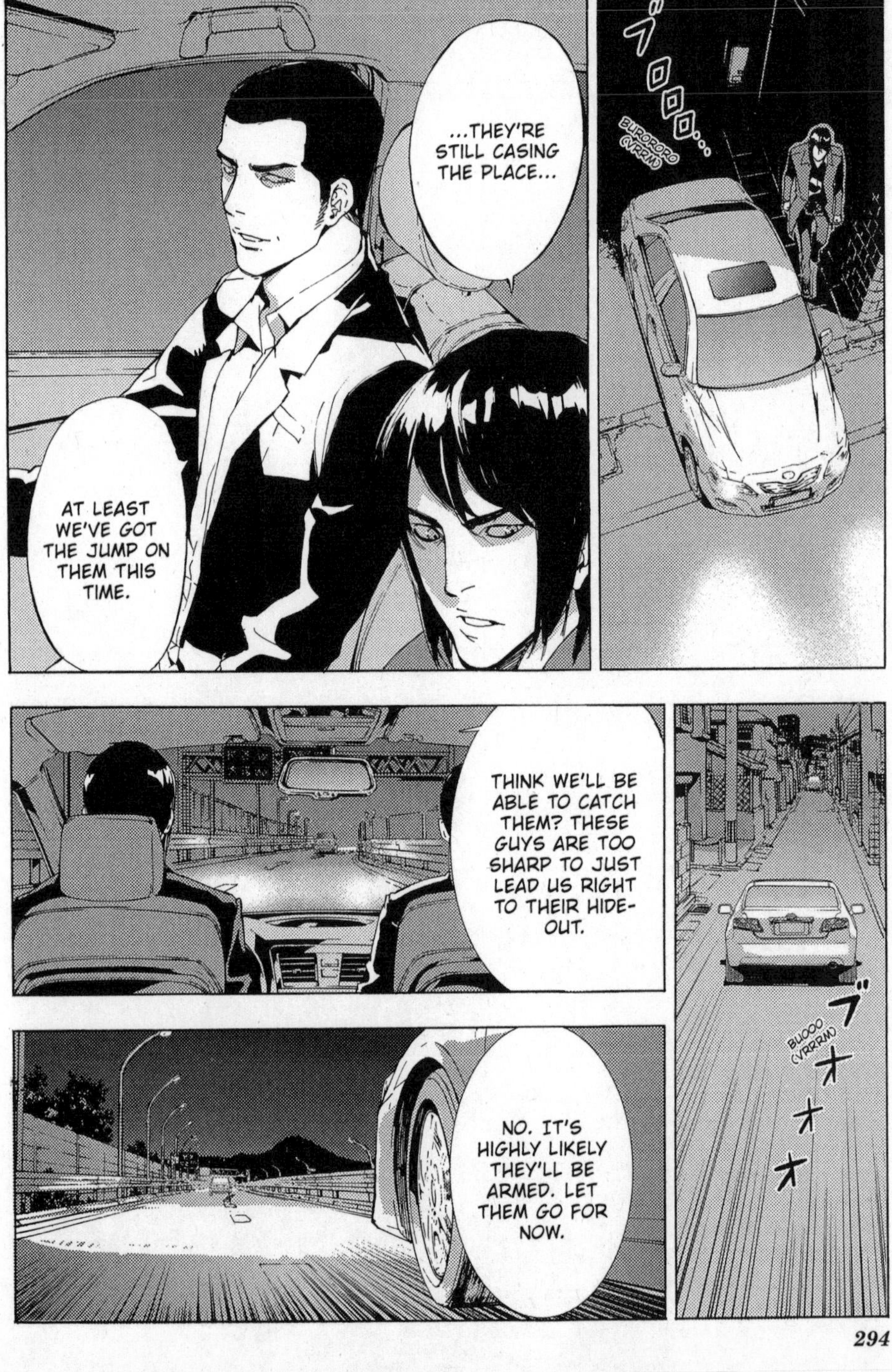
ブロロロ…
BURORORO (VRRM)
...THEY'RE STILL CASING THE PLACE...
AT LEAST WE'VE GOT THE JUMP ON THEM THIS TIME.
ブオオオ
BUOOO (VRRRM)
THINK WE'LL BE ABLE TO CATCH THEM? THESE GUYS ARE TOO SHARP TO JUST LEAD US RIGHT TO THEIR HIDE-OUT.
NO. IT'S HIGHLY LIKELY THEY'LL BE ARMED. LET THEM GO FOR NOW.

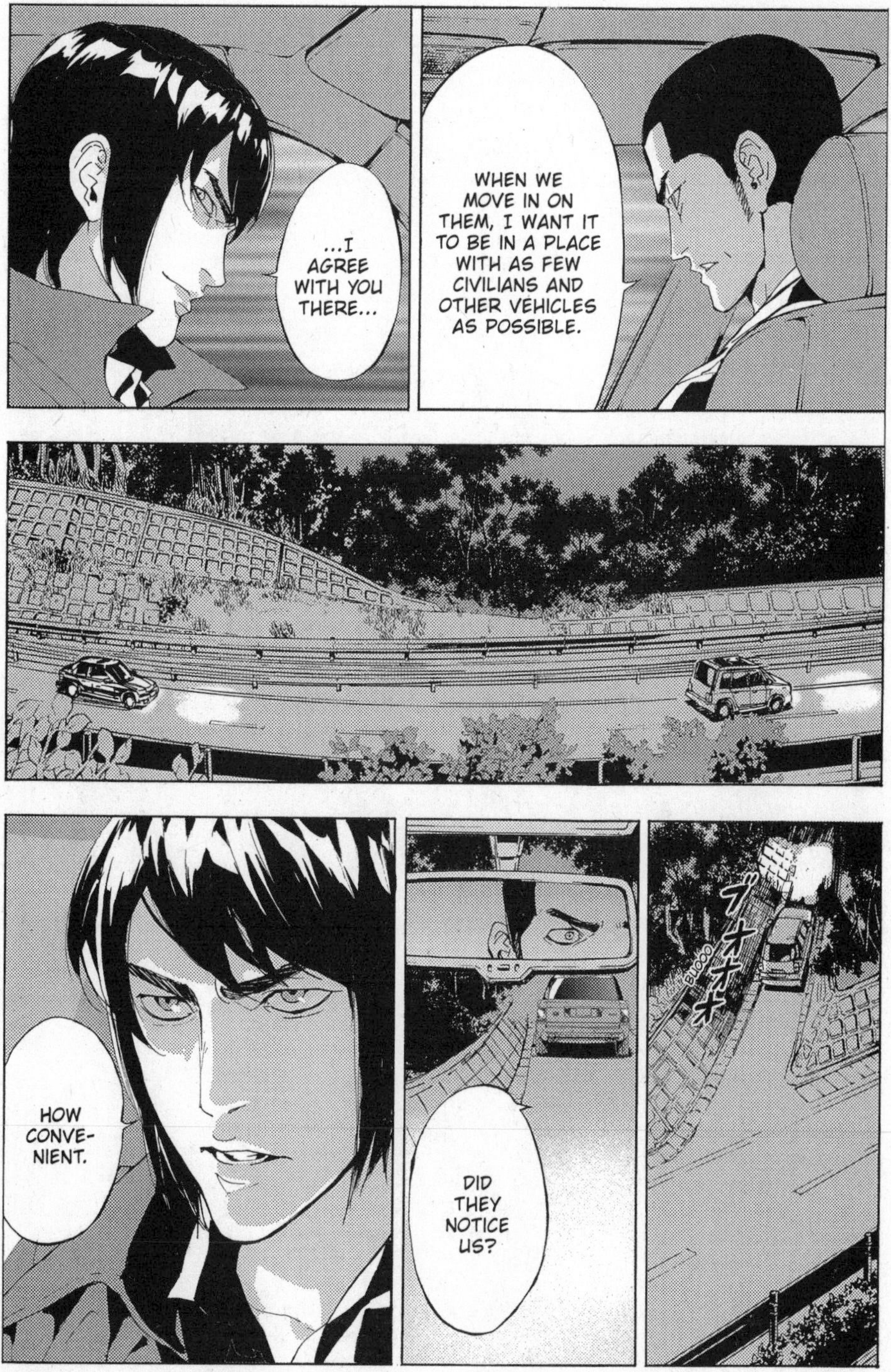
WHEN WE MOVE IN ON THEM, I WANT IT TO BE IN A PLACE WITH AS FEW CIVILIANS AND OTHER VEHICLES AS POSSIBLE.
...I AGREE WITH YOU THERE...
ブオオオ
BUOOO
DID THEY NOTICE US?
HOW CONVE-NIENT.

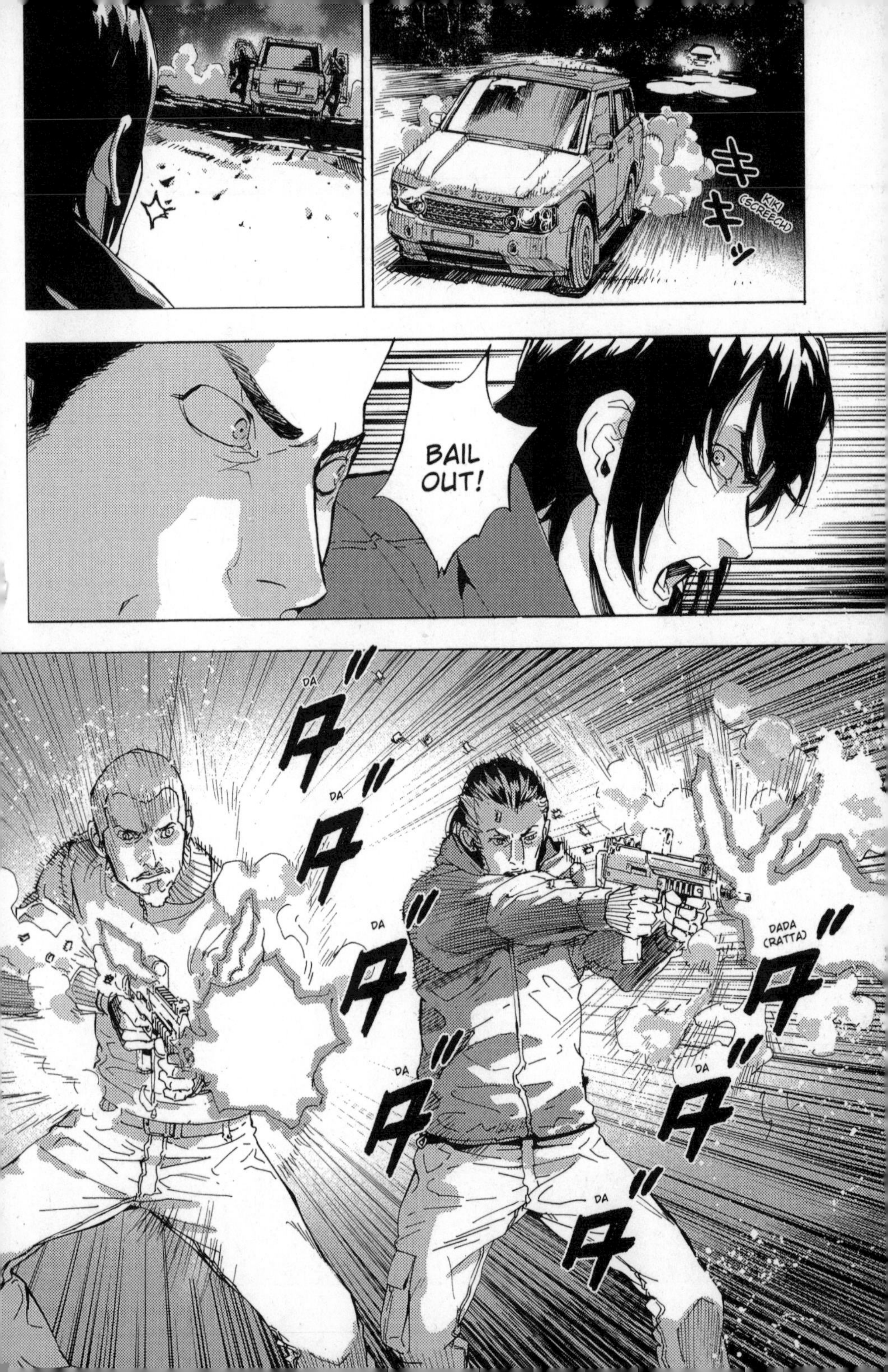
キキッ
KIKI (SCREECH)
BAIL OUT!
DA
ダ
DA
ダ
DA
ダ
DA
ダ
DA
ダ
DADA (RATTA)
ダダ
DA
ダ

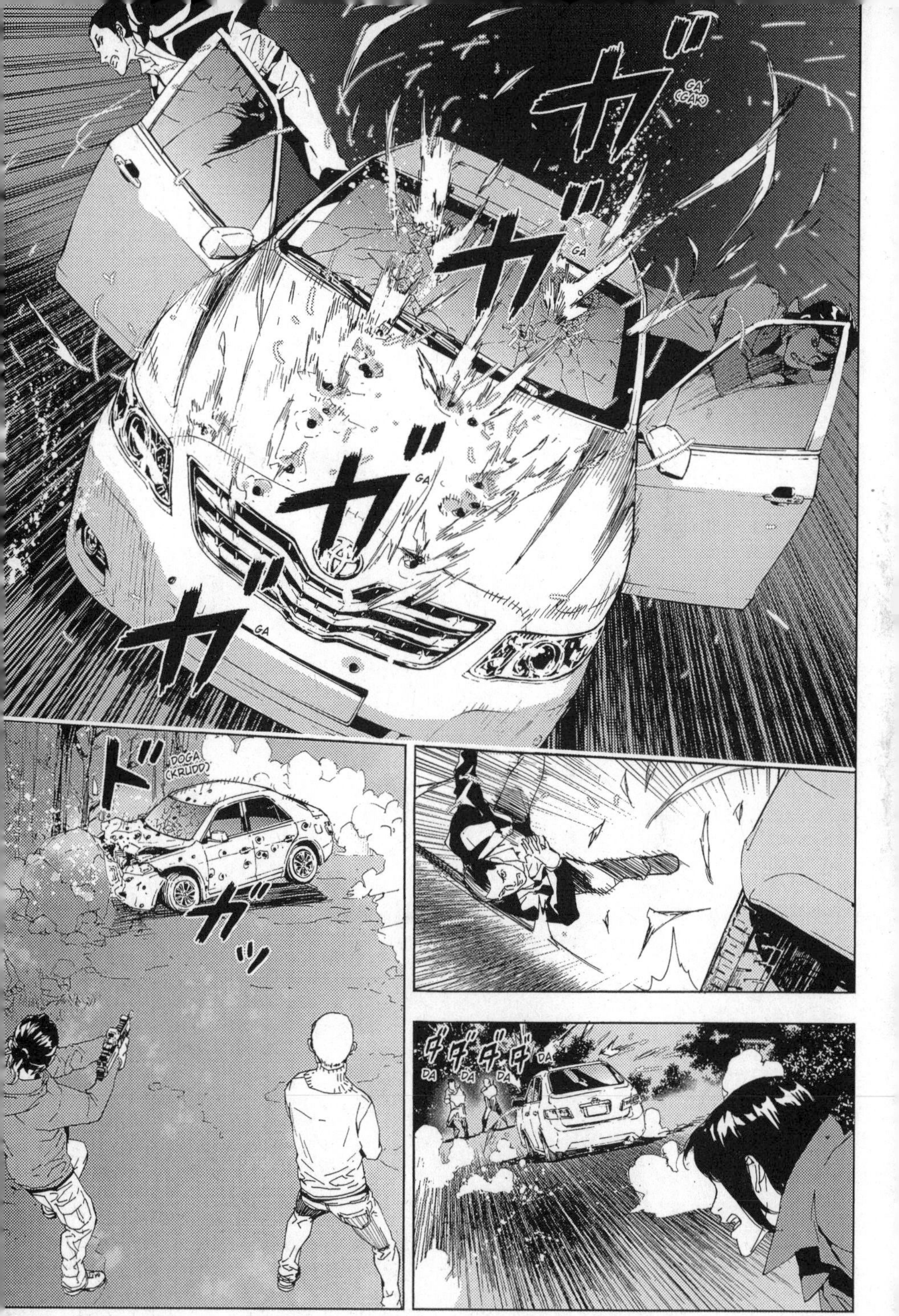
GA (GAK)
GA
GA
GA
DA
DA
DA
DA
DOGA (KRUDD)

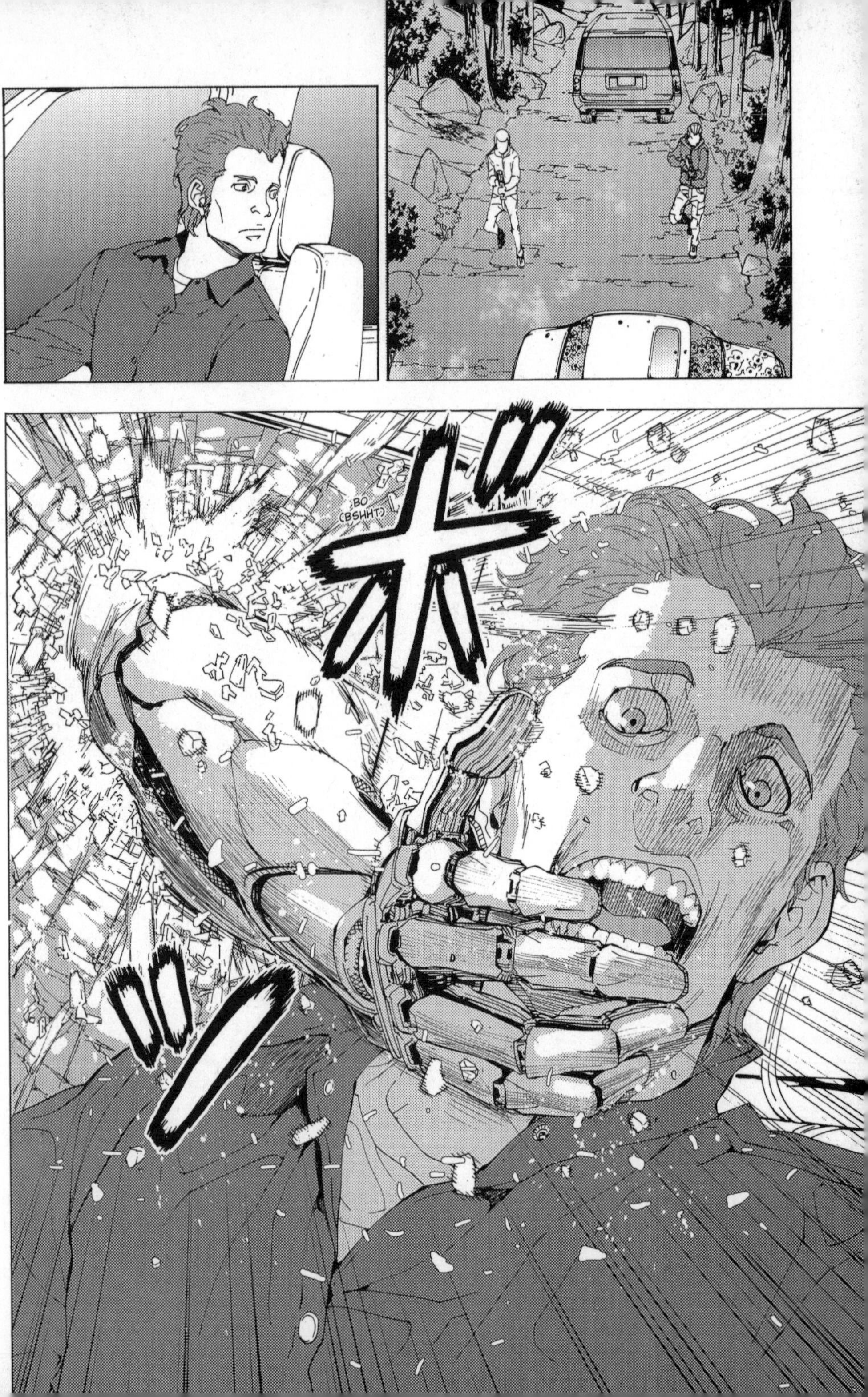
BO
(BSHHT)

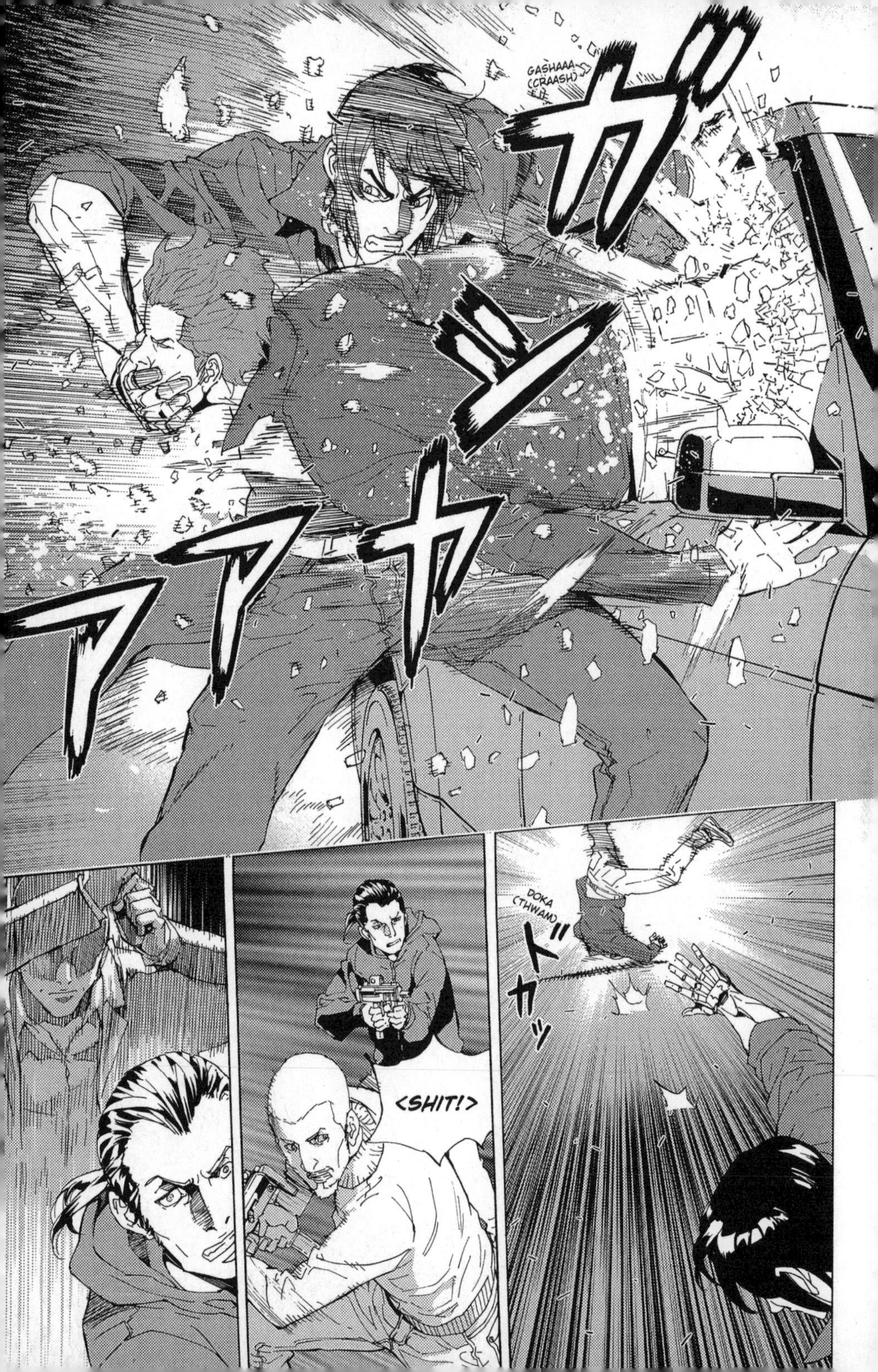
GASHAAA (CRAASH)
DOKA (THWAM)
ドカッ
<SHIT!>

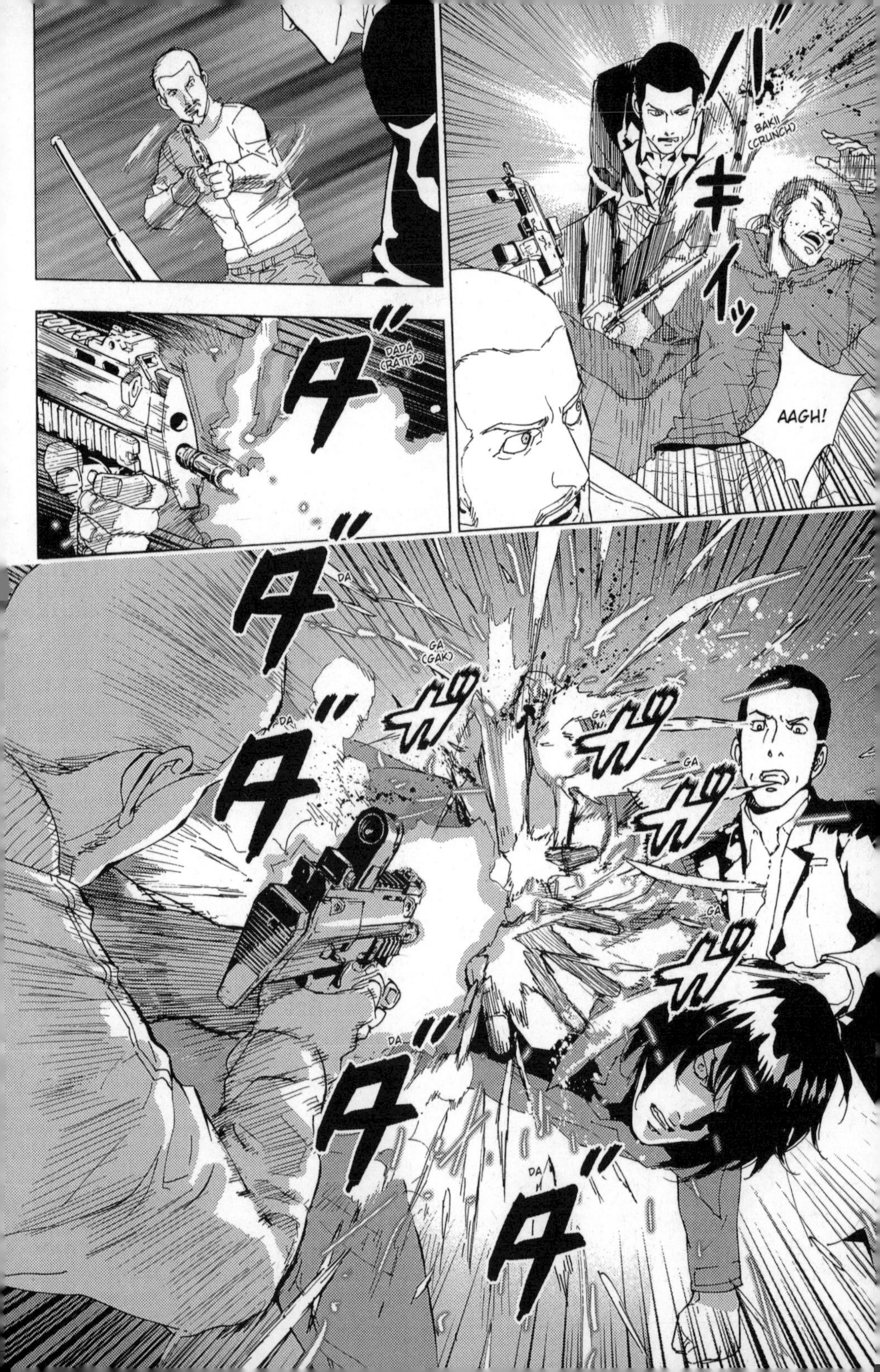
BAKII (CRUNCH)
AAGH!
DADA (RATTA)
GA
GA
GA
GA (GAK)
DA
DA
DA
DA

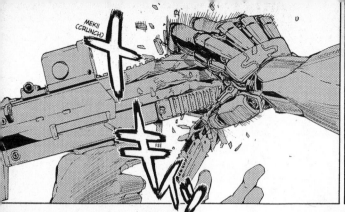

MEKII
(CRUNCH)

GA
(GRAB)

DOSU
(THWUD)

F-FUCKIN' MONSTER!

I'LL BE DAMNED...

DOSA
(DSHH)

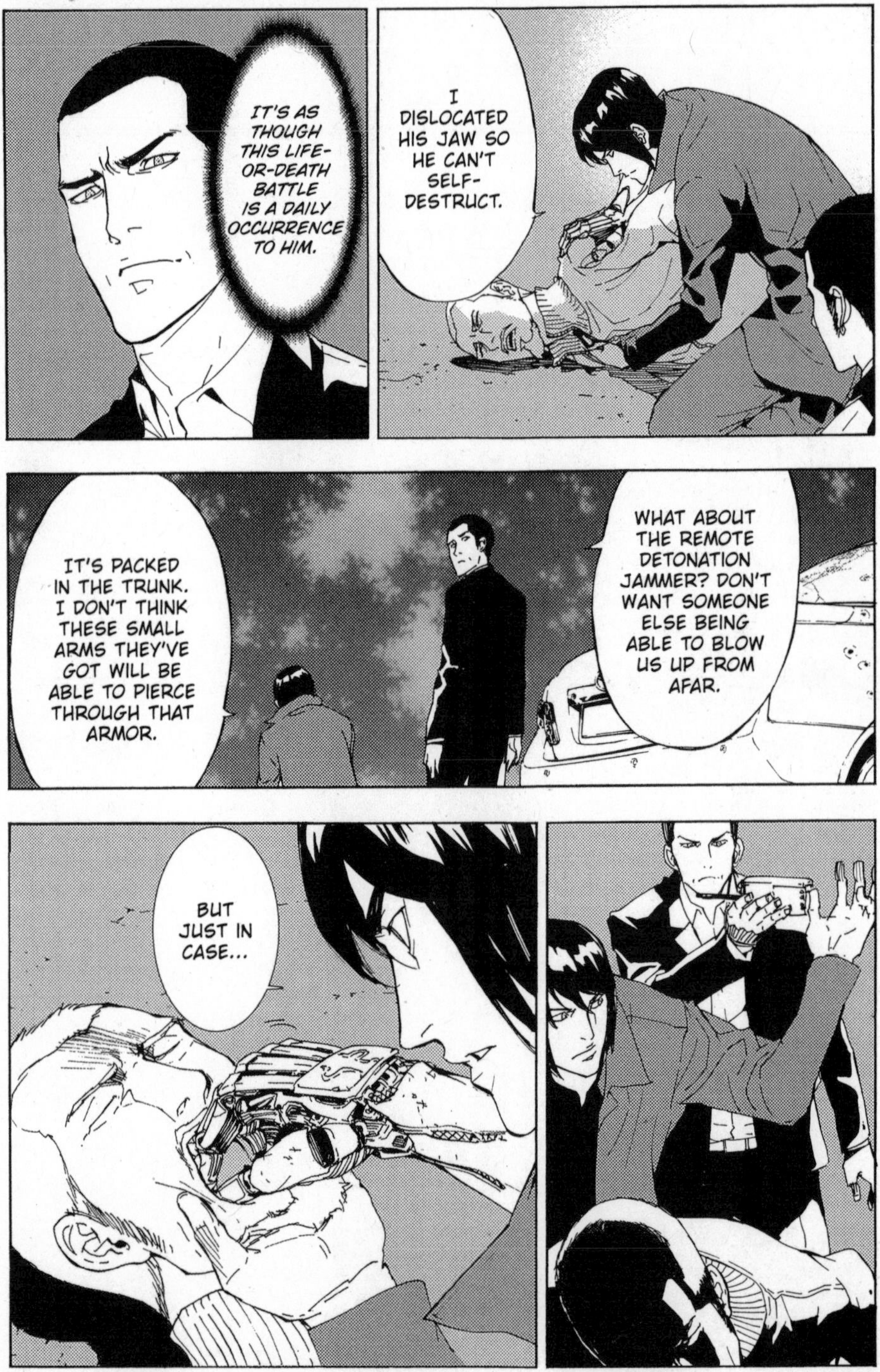
I DISLOCATED HIS JAW SO HE CAN'T SELF-DESTRUCT.
IT'S AS THOUGH THIS LIFE-OR-DEATH BATTLE IS A DAILY OCCURRENCE TO HIM.
WHAT ABOUT THE REMOTE DETONATION JAMMER? DON'T WANT SOMEONE ELSE BEING ABLE TO BLOW US UP FROM AFAR.
IT'S PACKED IN THE TRUNK. I DON'T THINK THESE SMALL ARMS THEY'VE GOT WILL BE ABLE TO PIERCE THROUGH THAT ARMOR.
BUT JUST IN CASE...

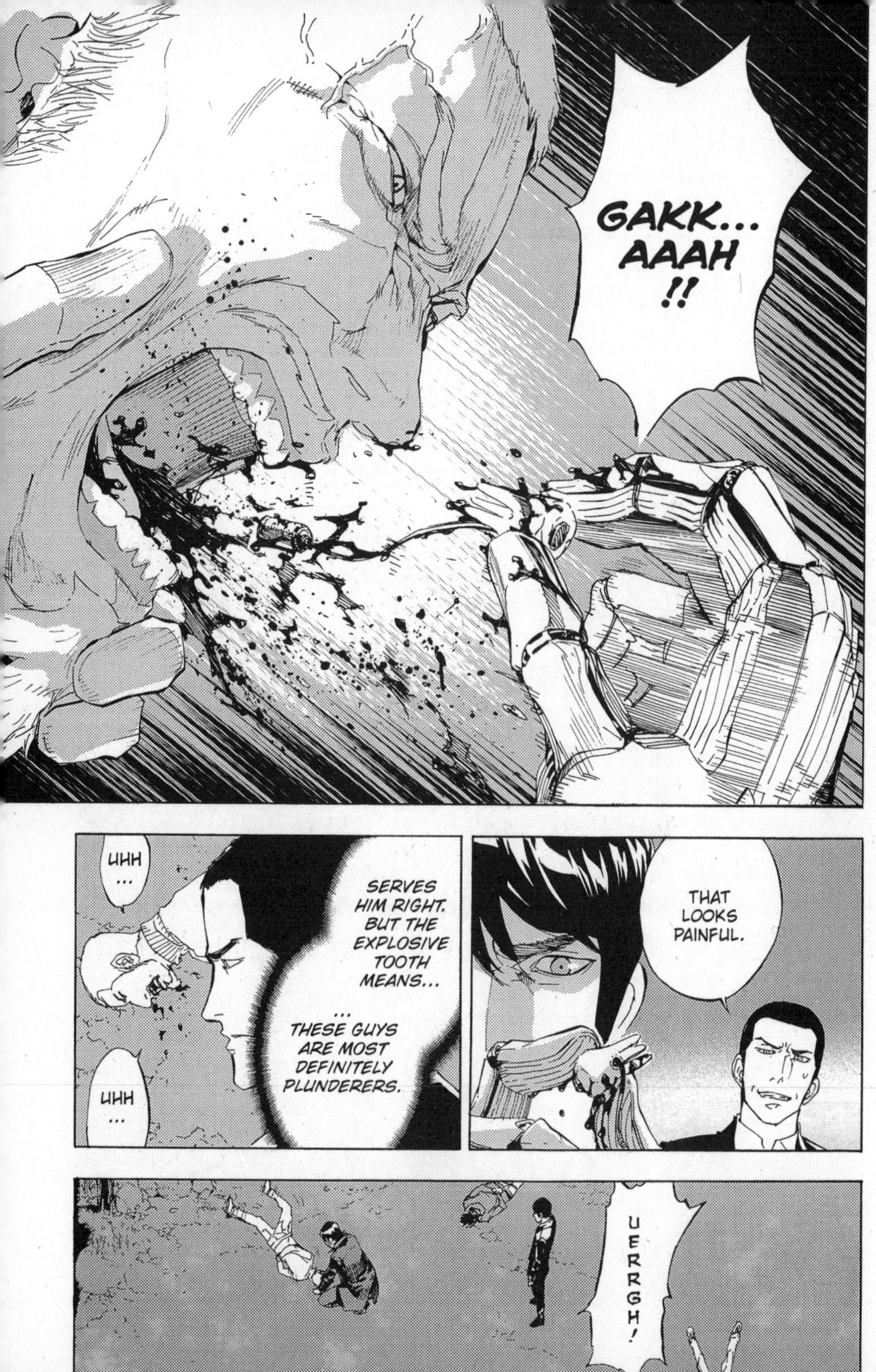
GAKK... AAAH !!
THAT LOOKS PAINFUL.
SERVES HIM RIGHT. BUT THE EXPLOSIVE TOOTH MEANS...
... THESE GUYS ARE MOST DEFINITELY PLUNDERERS.
UHH ...
UHH ...
UERRGH!

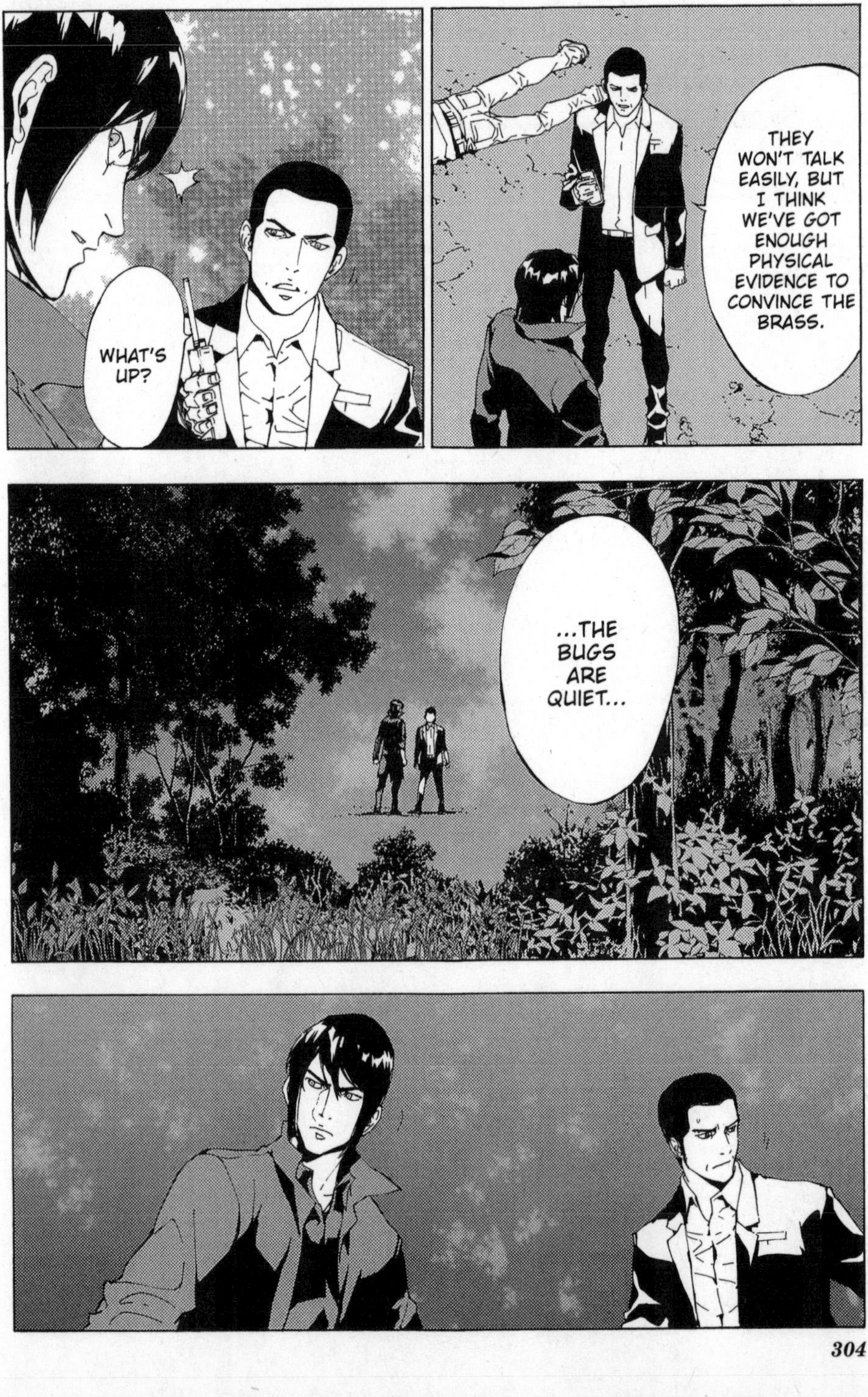
THEY WON'T TALK EASILY, BUT I THINK WE'VE GOT ENOUGH PHYSICAL EVIDENCE TO CONVINCE THE BRASS.
WHAT'S UP?
...THE BUGS ARE QUIET...

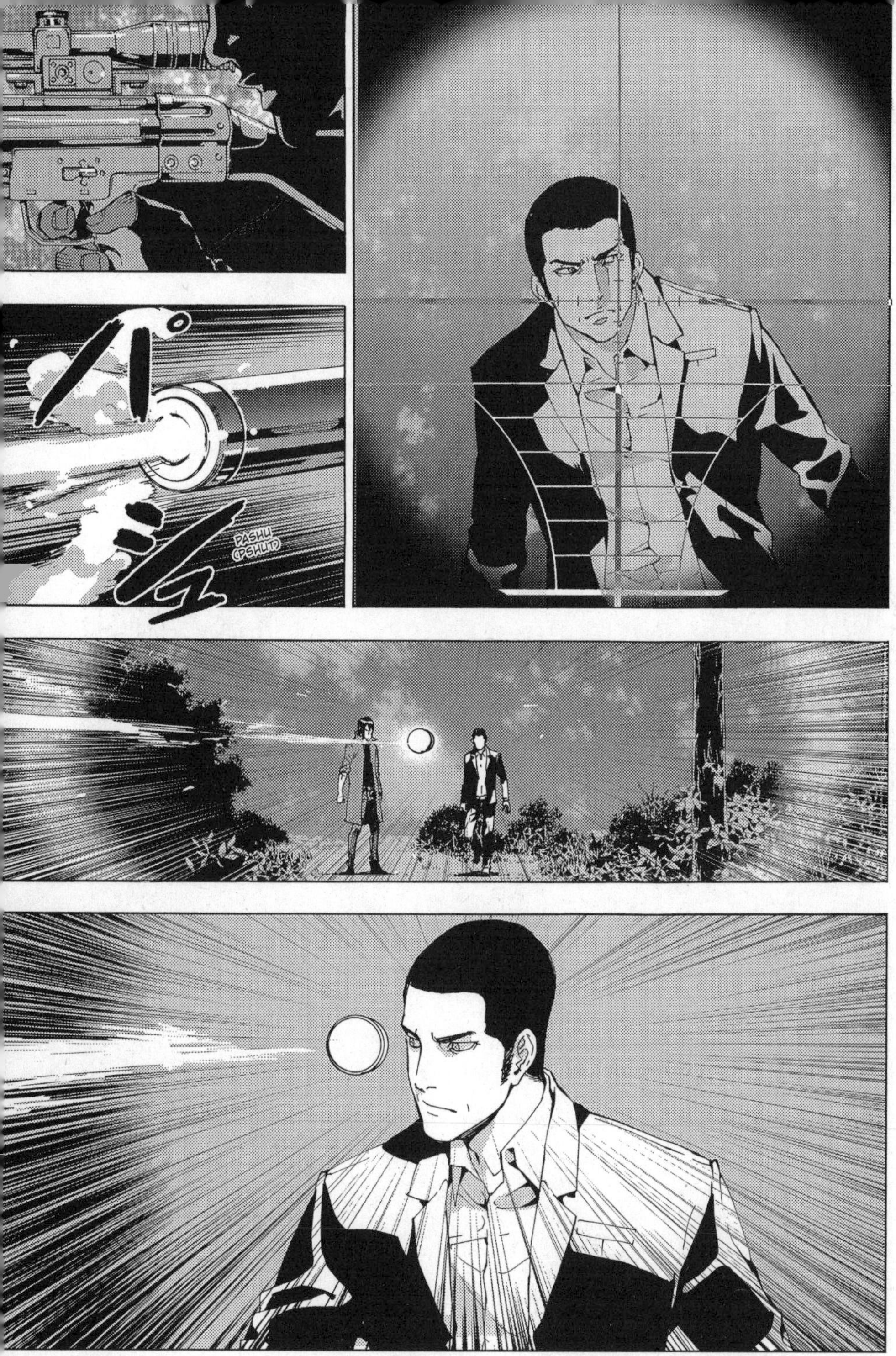
PASHU
(PSHU!)

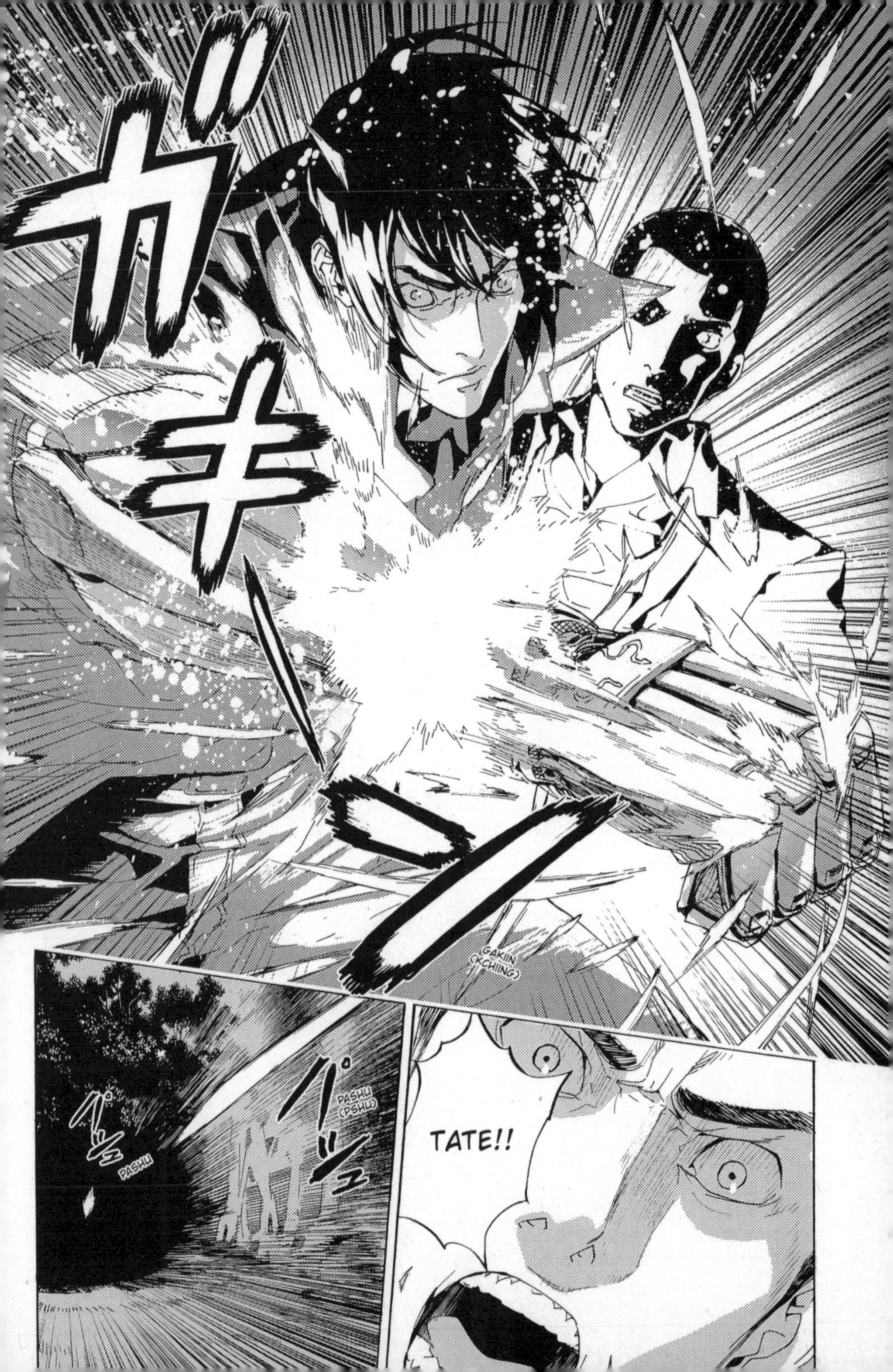
GAKIIN (KCHIING)
TATE!!
PASHU (PSHU)
PASHU

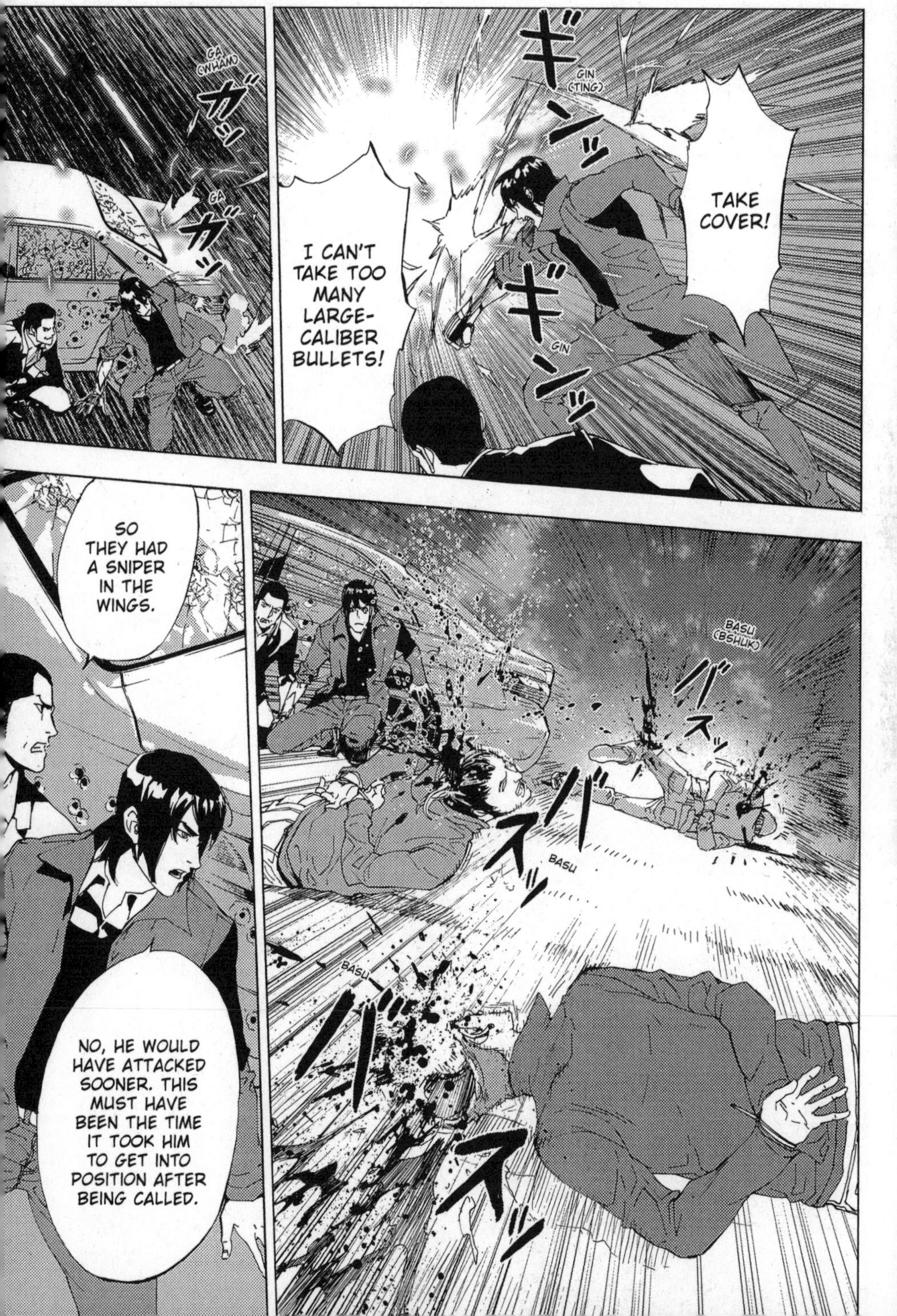
GIN (TING)
TAKE COVER!
I CAN'T TAKE TOO MANY LARGE-CALIBER BULLETS!
GIN
GA (WHAM)
GA
BASU (BSHUK)
BASU
BASU
SO THEY HAD A SNIPER IN THE WINGS.
NO, HE WOULD HAVE ATTACKED SOONER. THIS MUST HAVE BEEN THE TIME IT TOOK HIM TO GET INTO POSITION AFTER BEING CALLED.

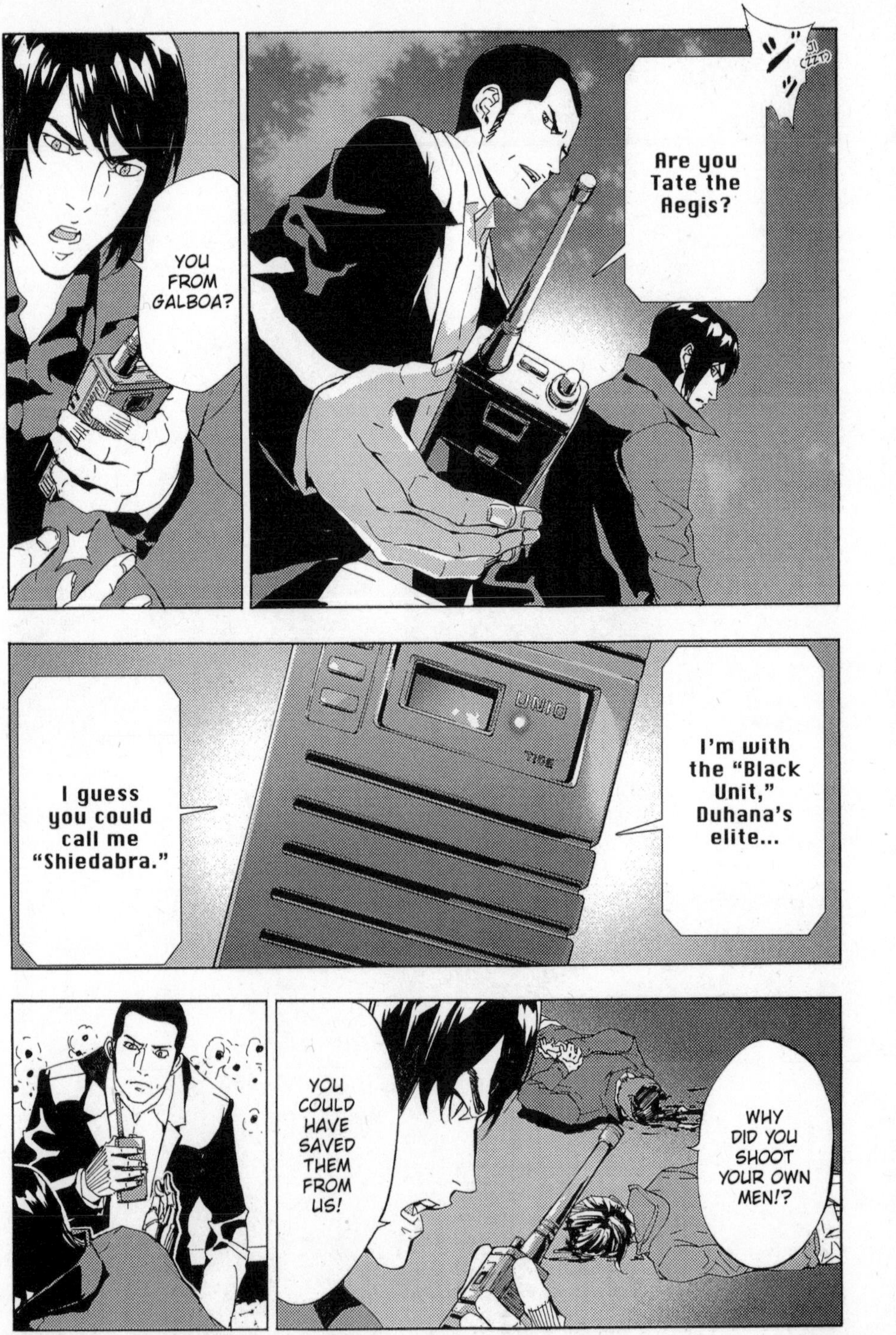
JI (ZZZT)
Are you Tate the Aegis?
YOU FROM GALBOA?
I'm with the "Black Unit," Duhana's elite...
I guess you could call me "Shiedabra."
WHY DID YOU SHOOT YOUR OWN MEN!?
YOU COULD HAVE SAVED THEM FROM US!

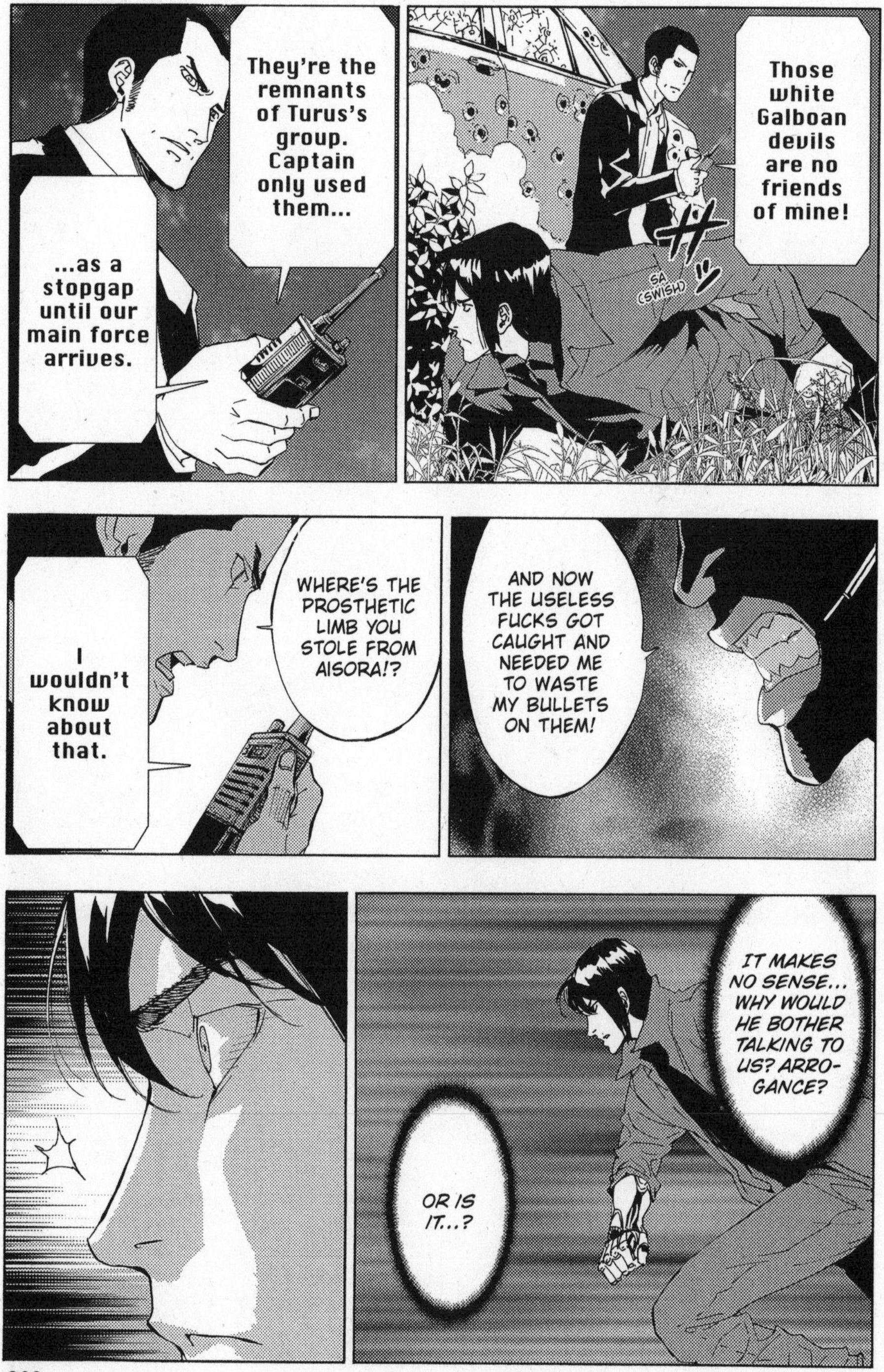
Those white Galboan devils are no friends of mine!
SA (SWISH)
They're the remnants of Turus's group. Captain only used them...
...as a stopgap until our main force arrives.
AND NOW THE USELESS FUCKS GOT CAUGHT AND NEEDED ME TO WASTE MY BULLETS ON THEM!
WHERE'S THE PROSTHETIC LIMB YOU STOLE FROM AISORA!?
I wouldn't know about that.
IT MAKES NO SENSE... WHY WOULD HE BOTHER TALKING TO US? ARROGANCE?
OR IS IT...?

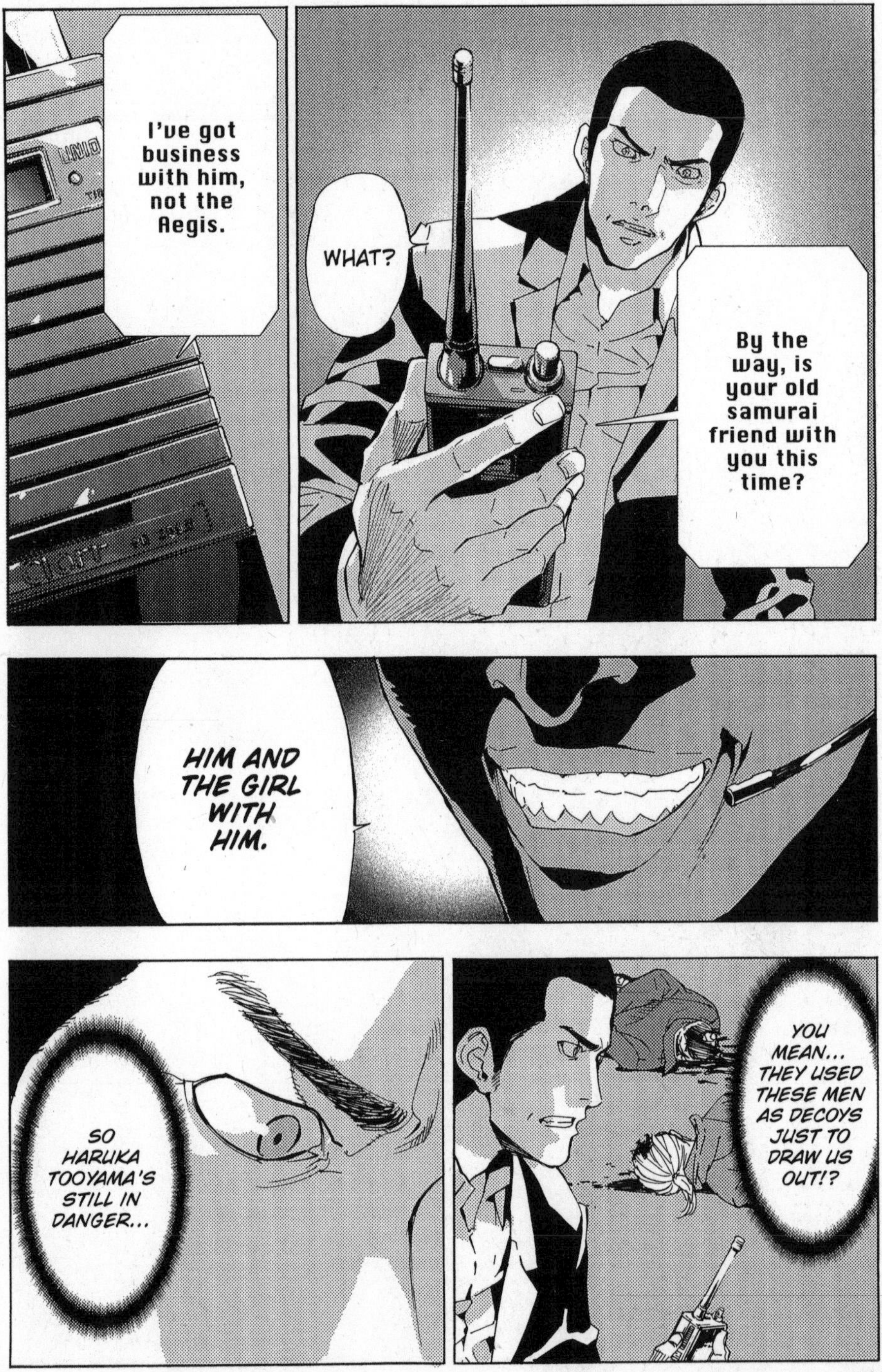
By the way, is your old samurai friend with you this time?
WHAT?
I've got business with him, not the Aegis.
HIM AND THE GIRL WITH HIM.
YOU MEAN... THEY USED THESE MEN AS DECOYS JUST TO DRAW US OUT!?
SO HARUKA TOOYAMA'S STILL IN DANGER...

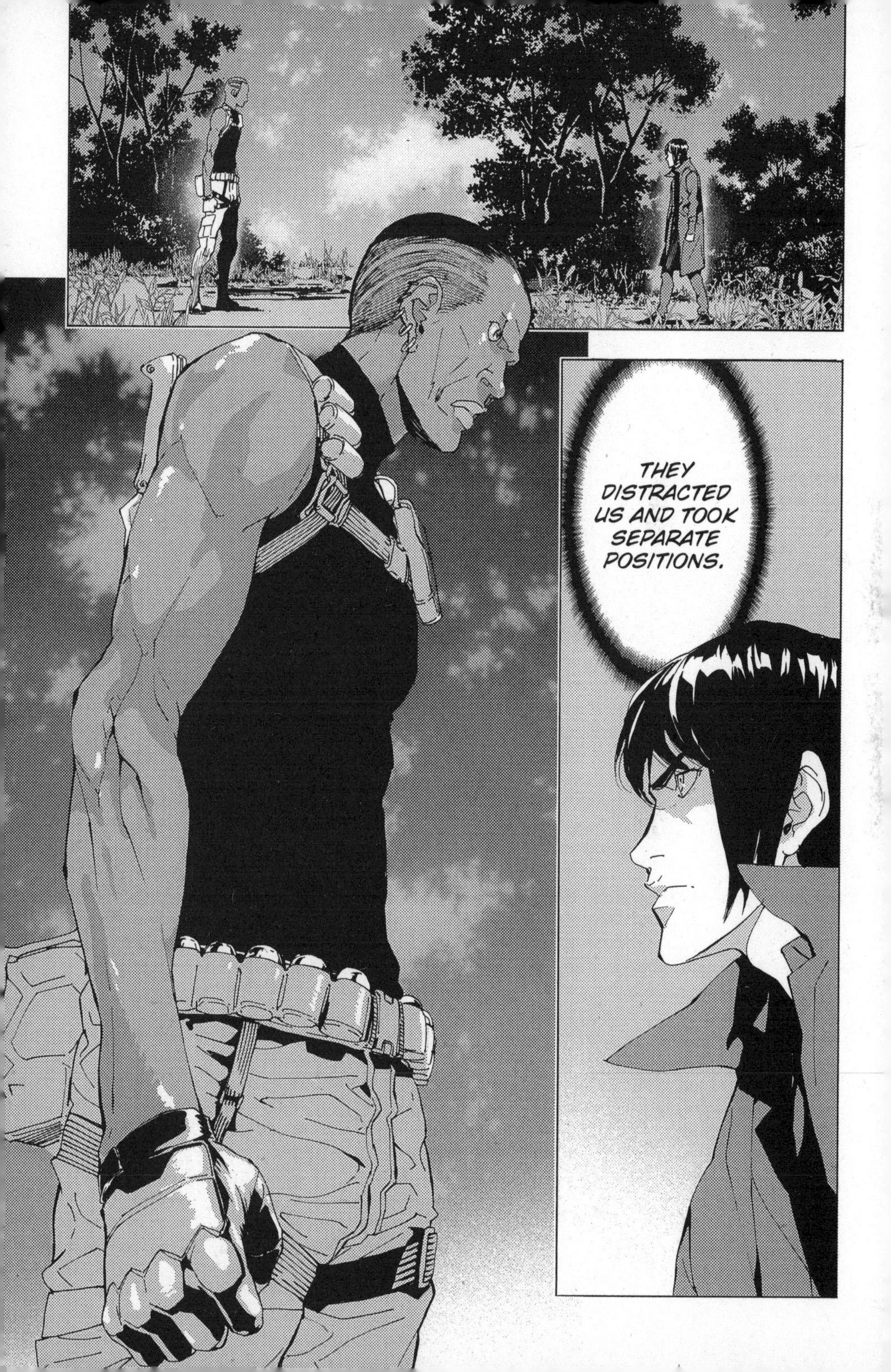
THEY DISTRACTED US AND TOOK SEPARATE POSITIONS.

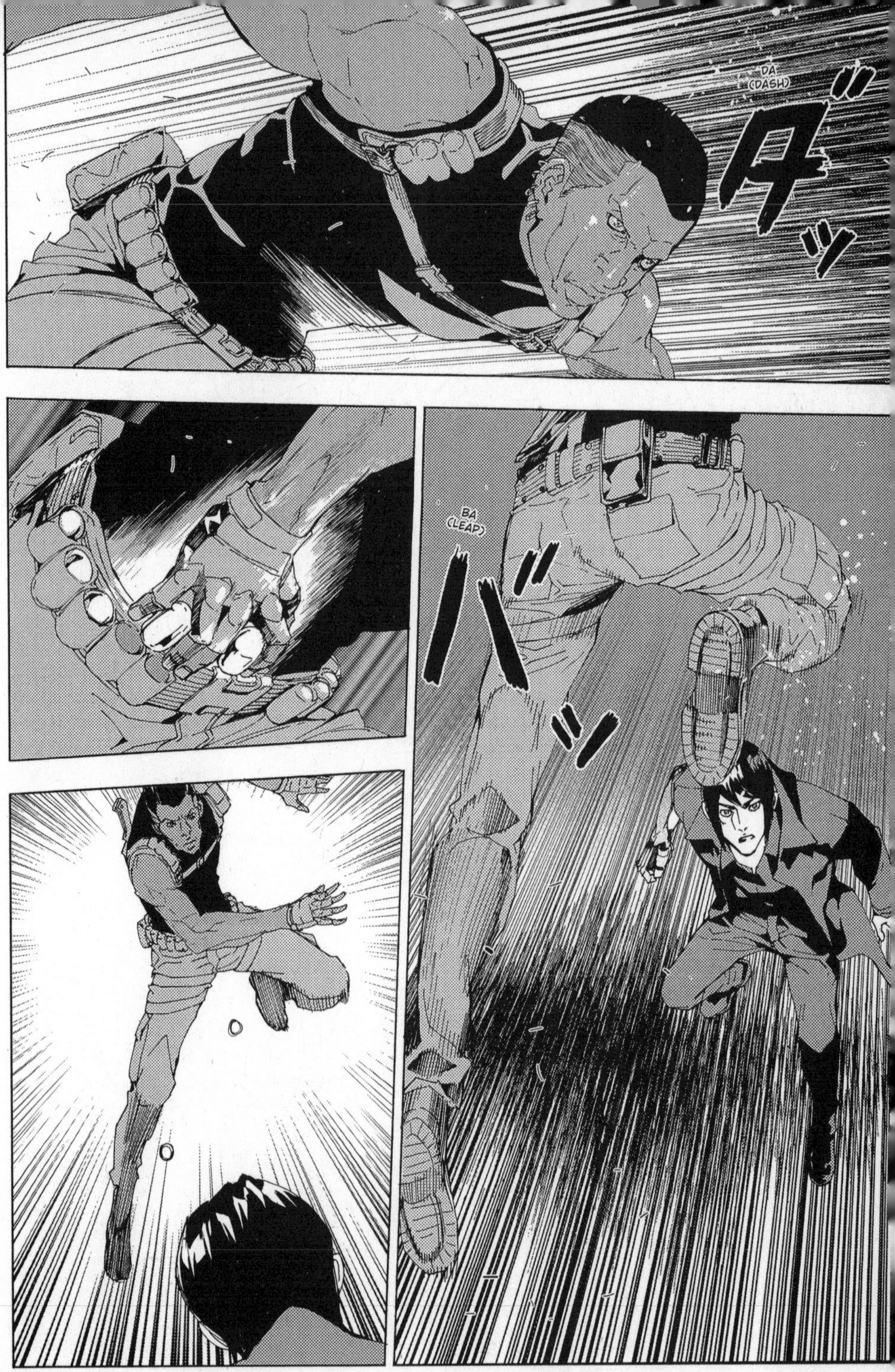
DA
(DASH)
ダッ
BA
(LEAP)
バッ

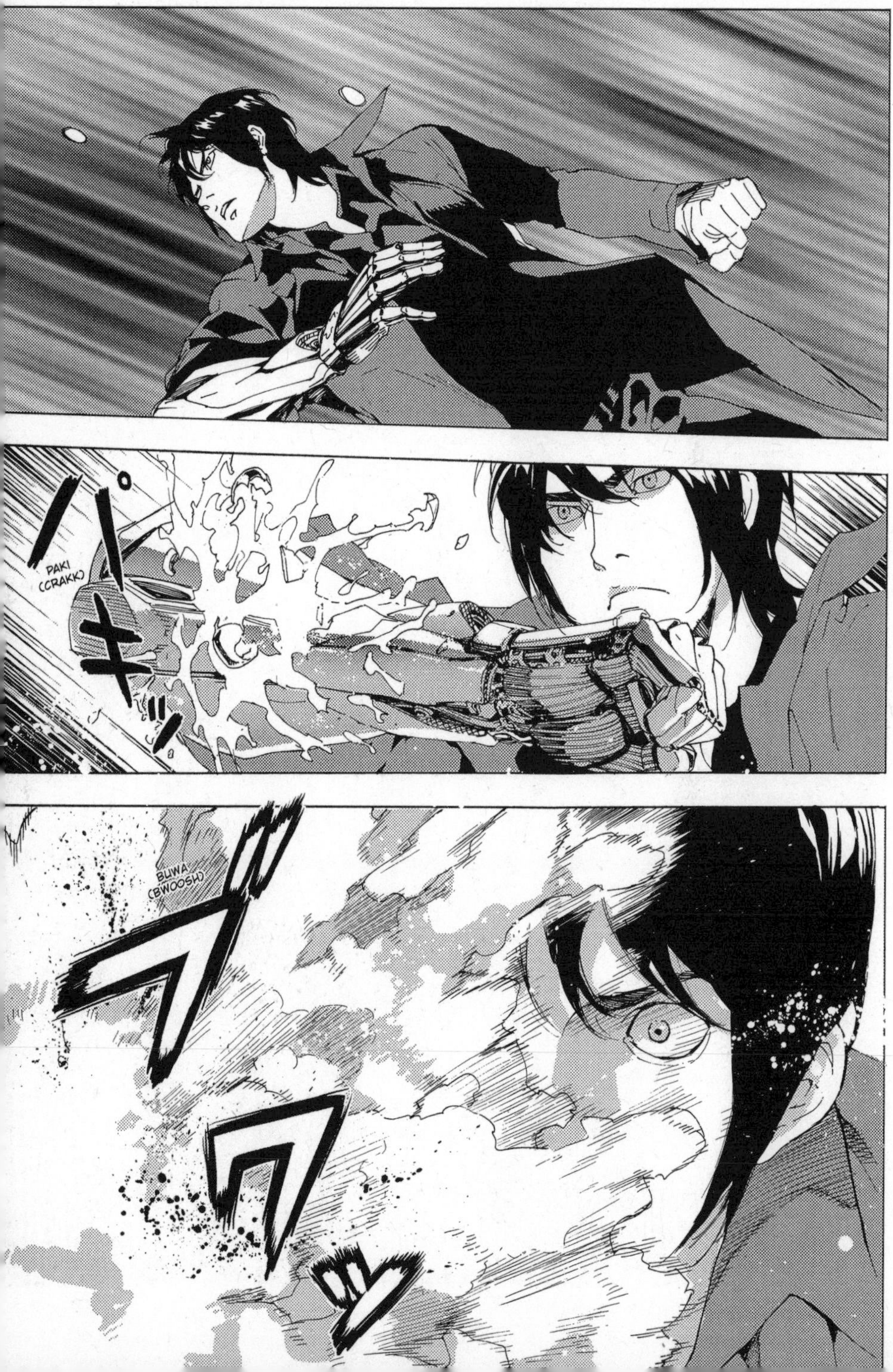
パキッ
PAKI (CRAKK)
ブワッ
BUWA (BWOOSH)

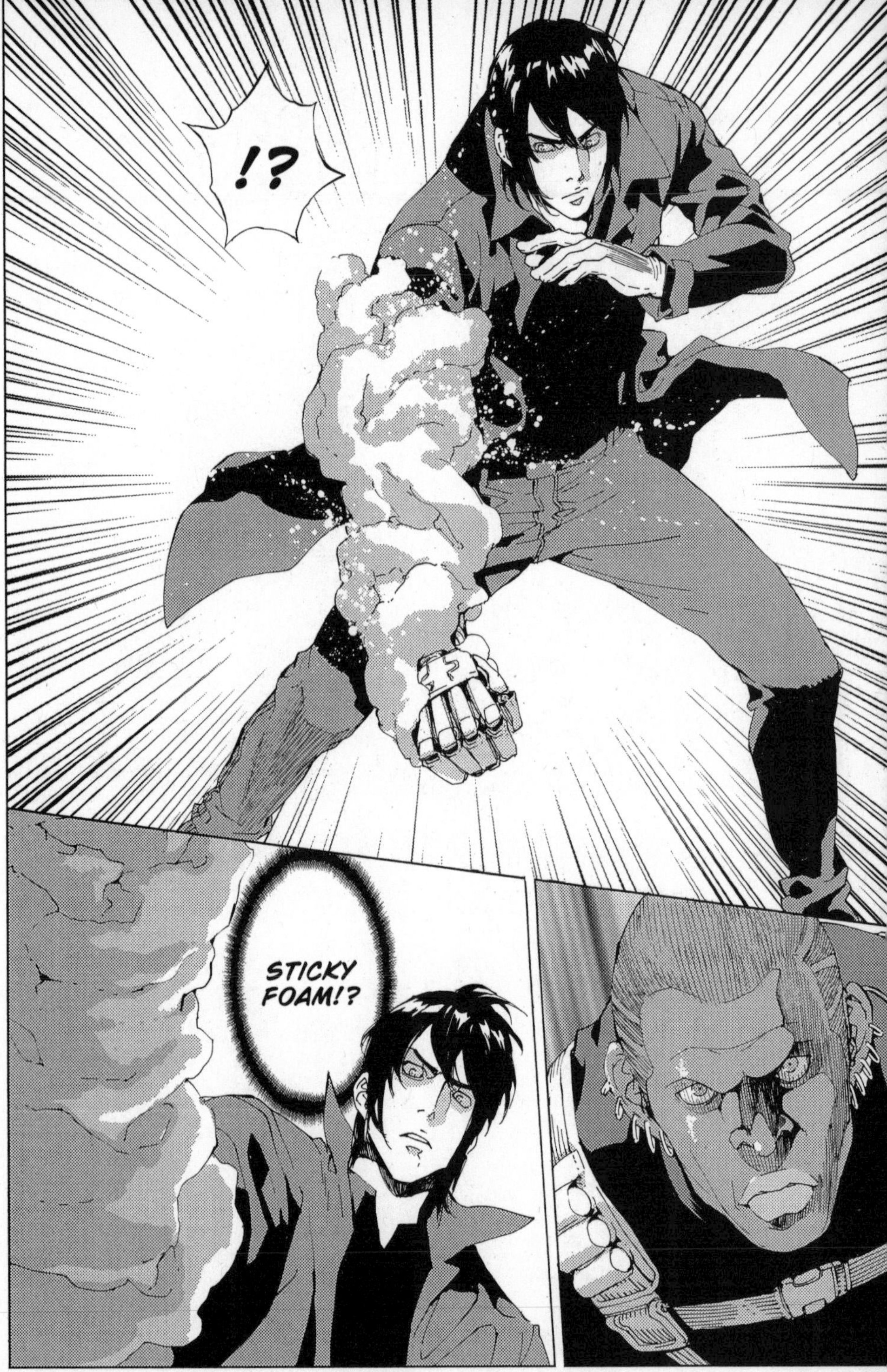
!?
STICKY FOAM!?

chapter 112

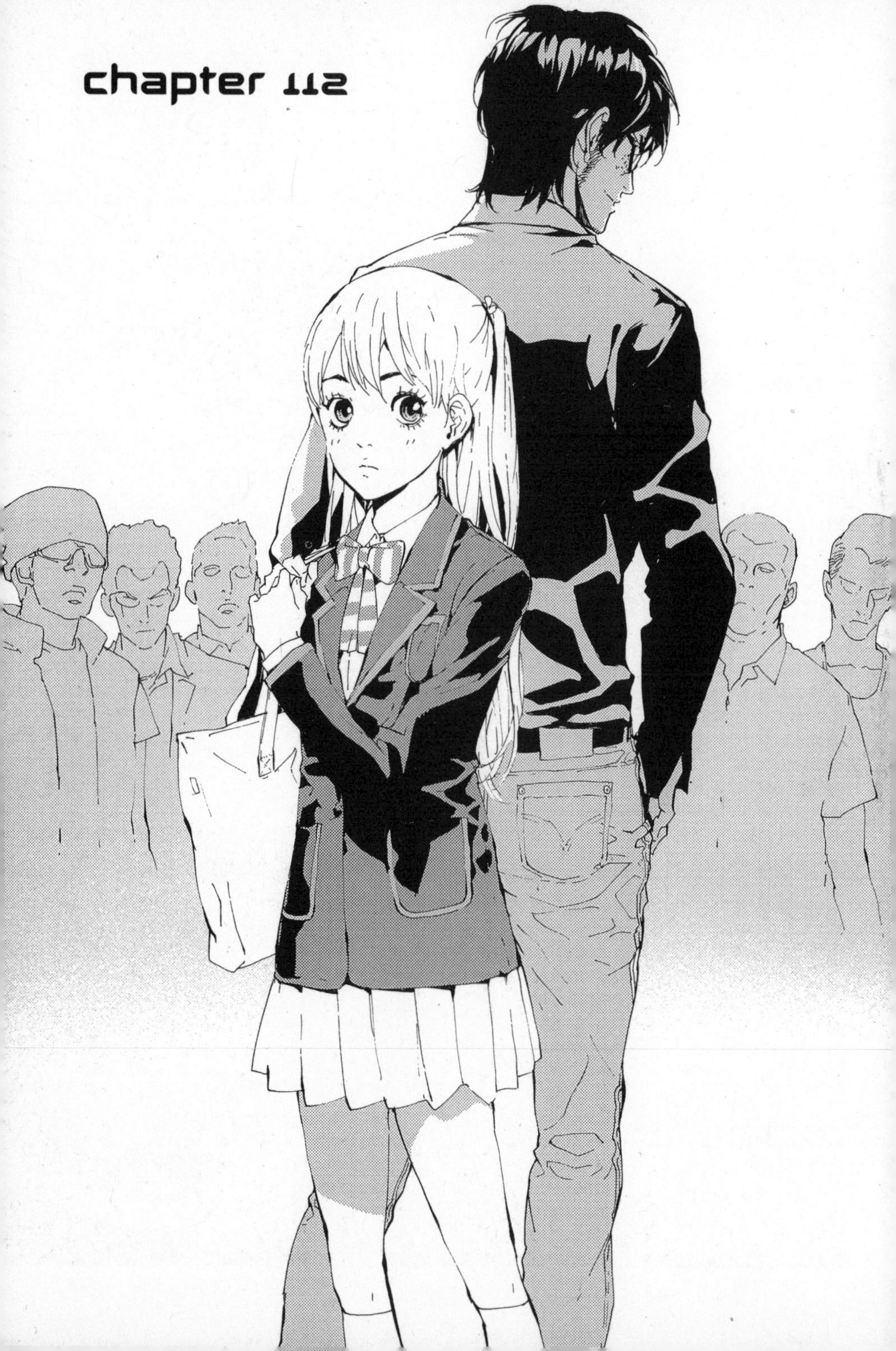

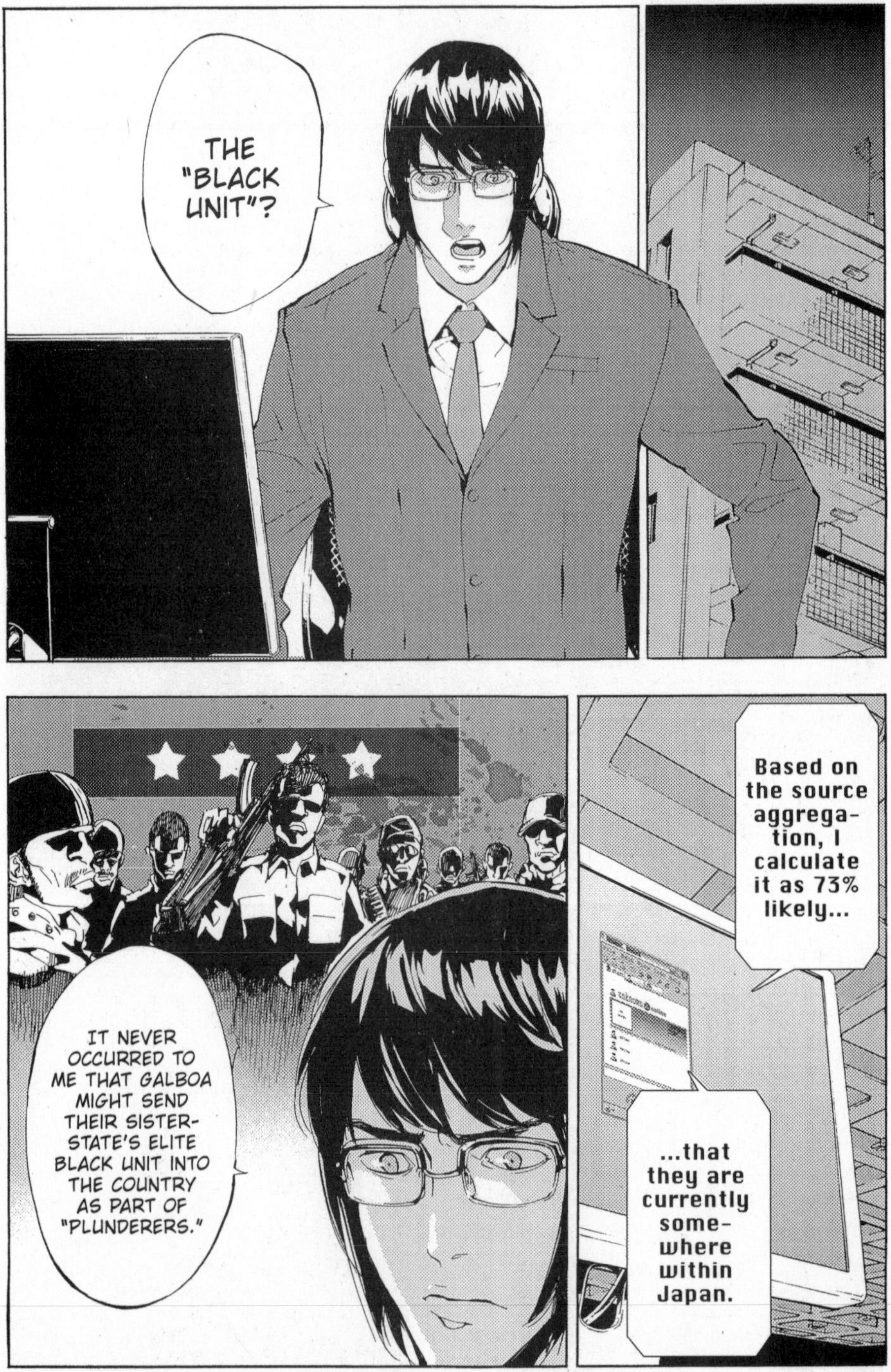
THE "BLACK UNIT"?
Based on the source aggregation, I calculate it as 73% likely...
...that they are currently somewhere within Japan.
IT NEVER OCCURRED TO ME THAT GALBOA MIGHT SEND THEIR SISTER-STATE'S ELITE BLACK UNIT INTO THE COUNTRY AS PART OF "PLUNDERERS."

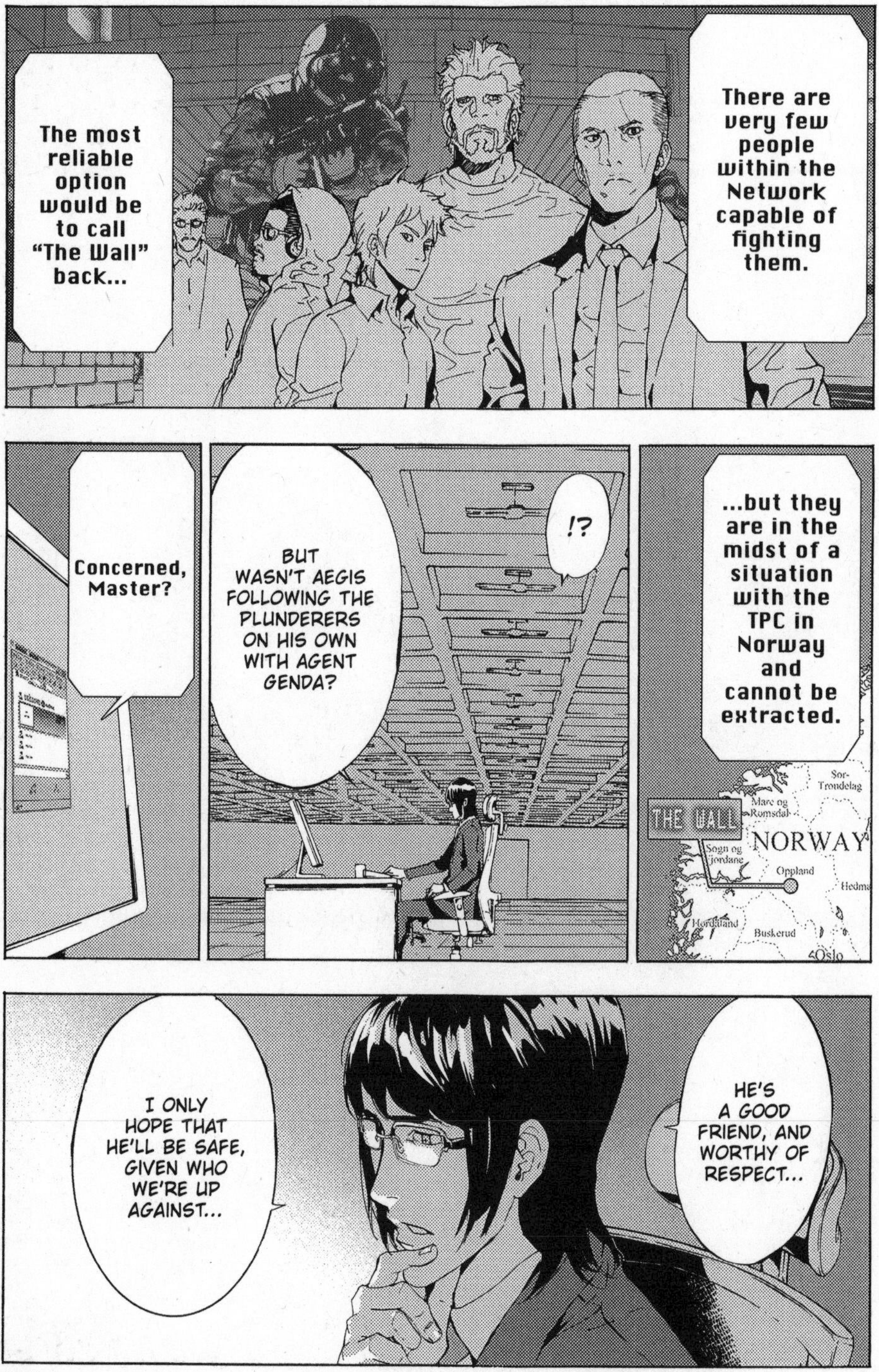
There are very few people within the Network capable of fighting them.
The most reliable option would be to call "The Wall" back...
...but they are in the midst of a situation with the TPC in Norway and cannot be extracted.
THE WALL
Sor-Trondelag
Mare og Romsdal
NORWAY
Sogn og Fjordane
Oppland
Hordaland
Buskerud
Oslo
!?
BUT WASN'T AEGIS FOLLOWING THE PLUNDERERS ON HIS OWN WITH AGENT GENDA?
Concerned, Master?
HE'S A GOOD FRIEND, AND WORTHY OF RESPECT...
I ONLY HOPE THAT HE'LL BE SAFE, GIVEN WHO WE'RE UP AGAINST...

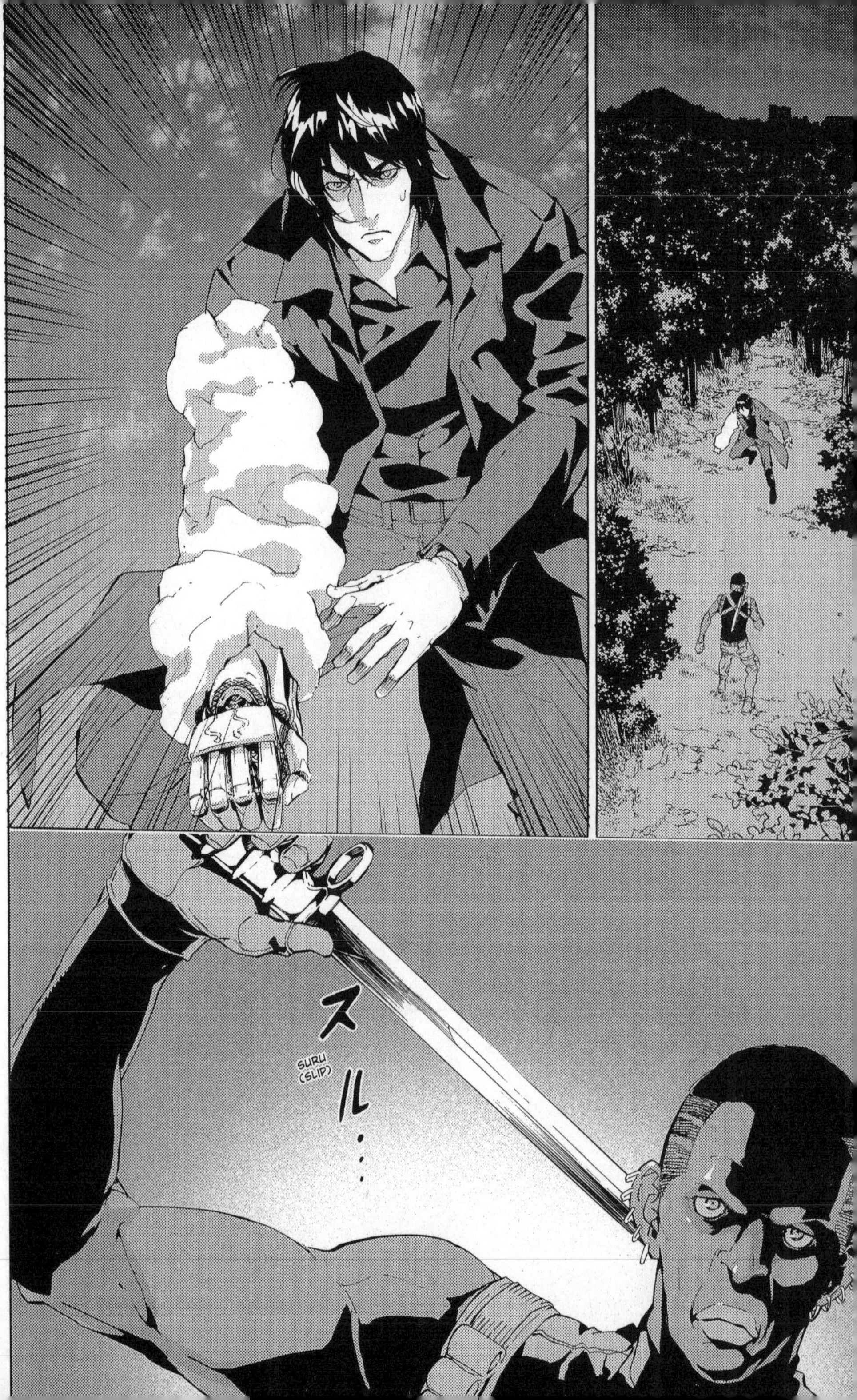
スル…
SURU (SLIP)

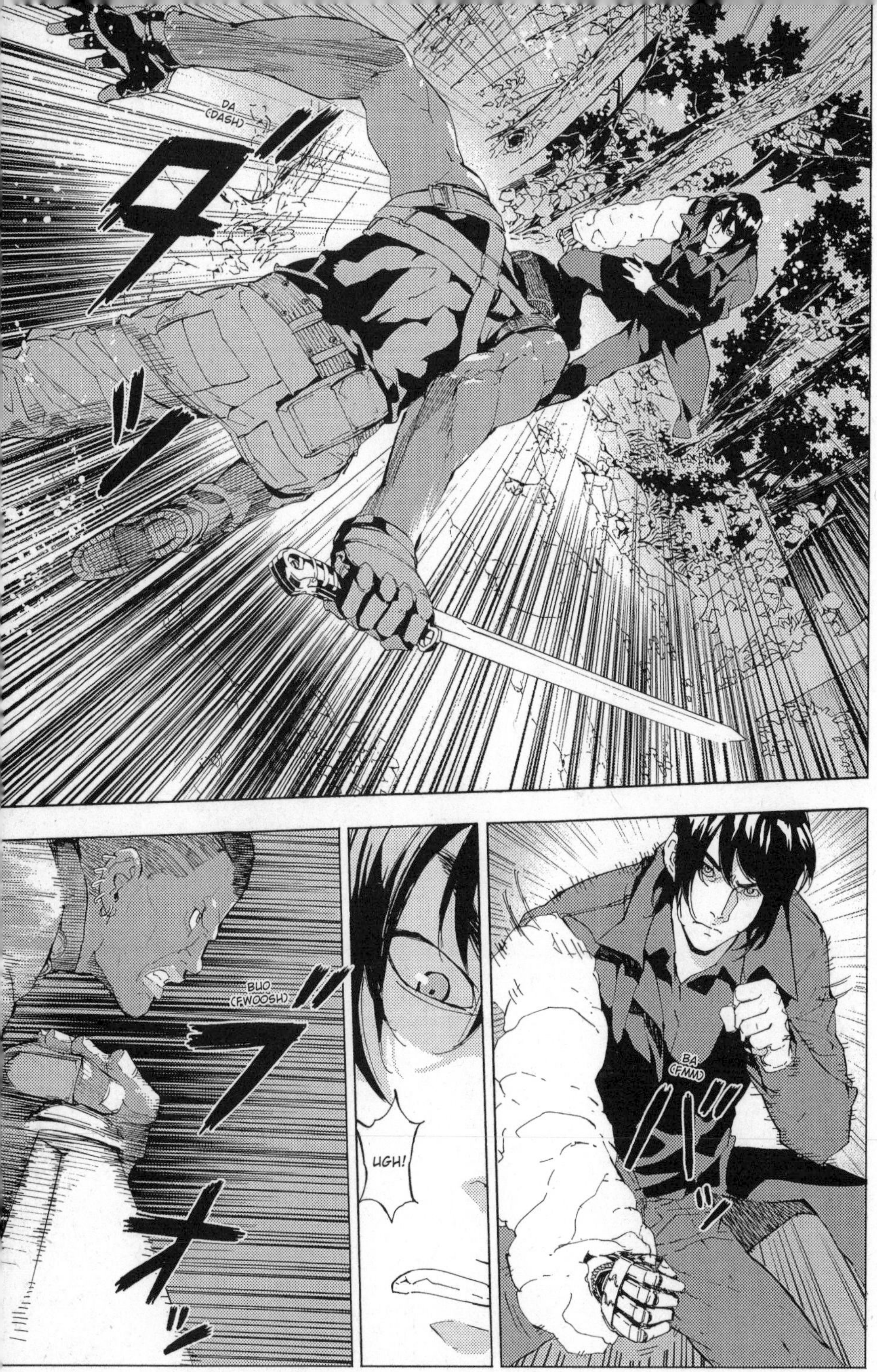
DA
(DASH)
BA
(FMM)
UGH!
BUO
(FWOOSH)

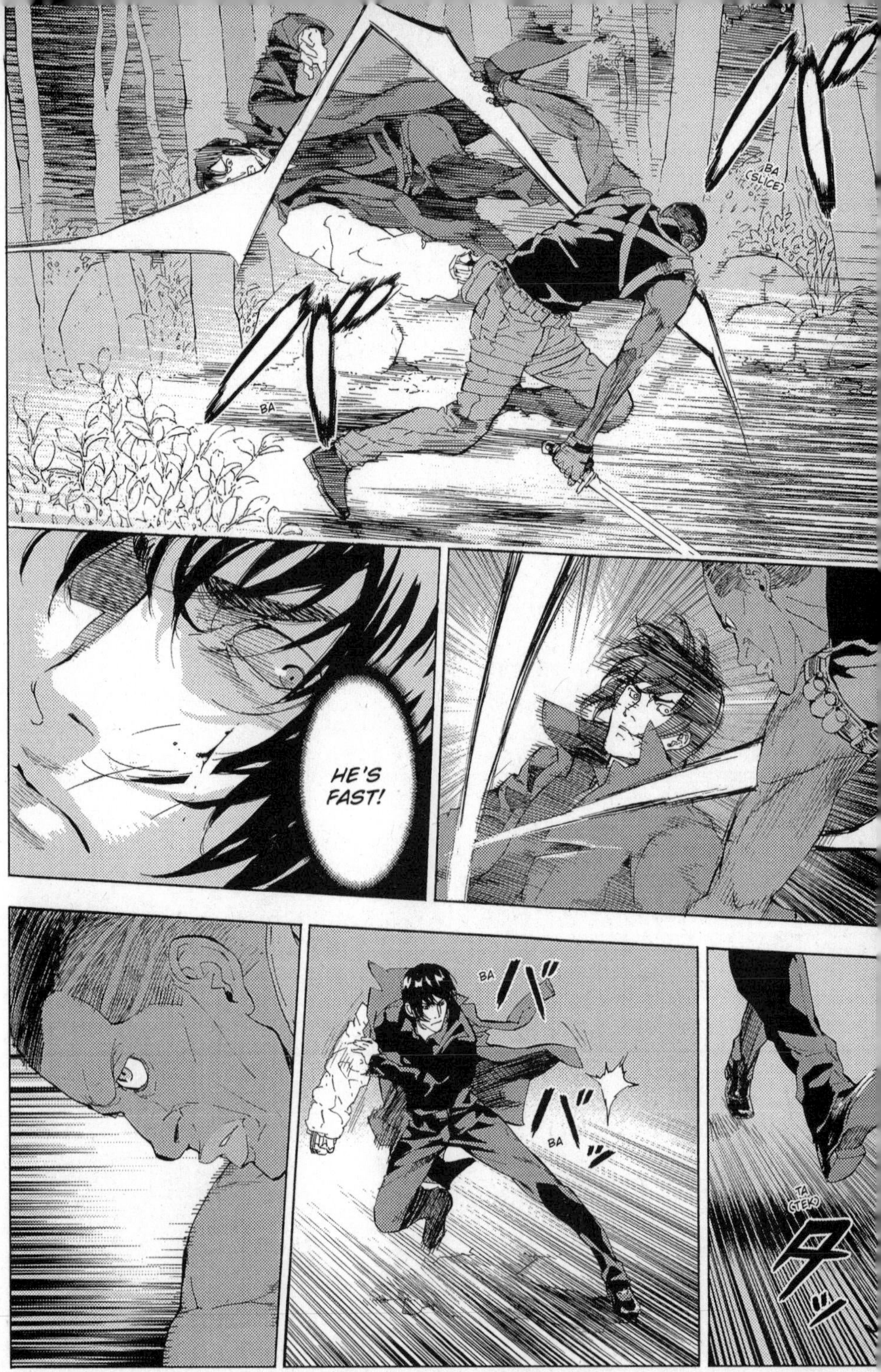
BA (SLICE)
BA
HE'S FAST!
TA (TEK)
タッ
BA
バ
BA
バッ

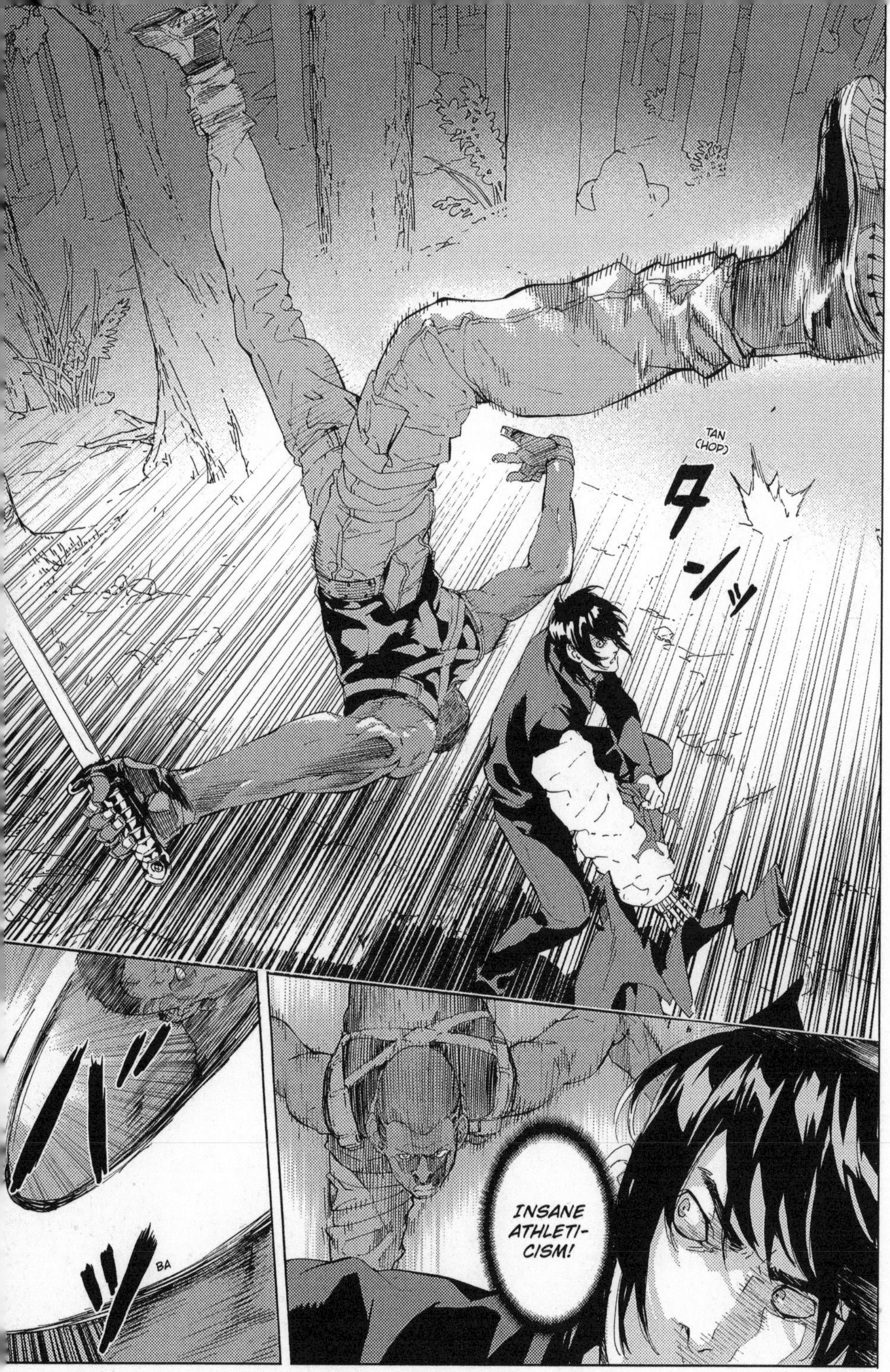
タンッ
TAN (HOP)
INSANE ATHLETI-CISM!
バッ
BA

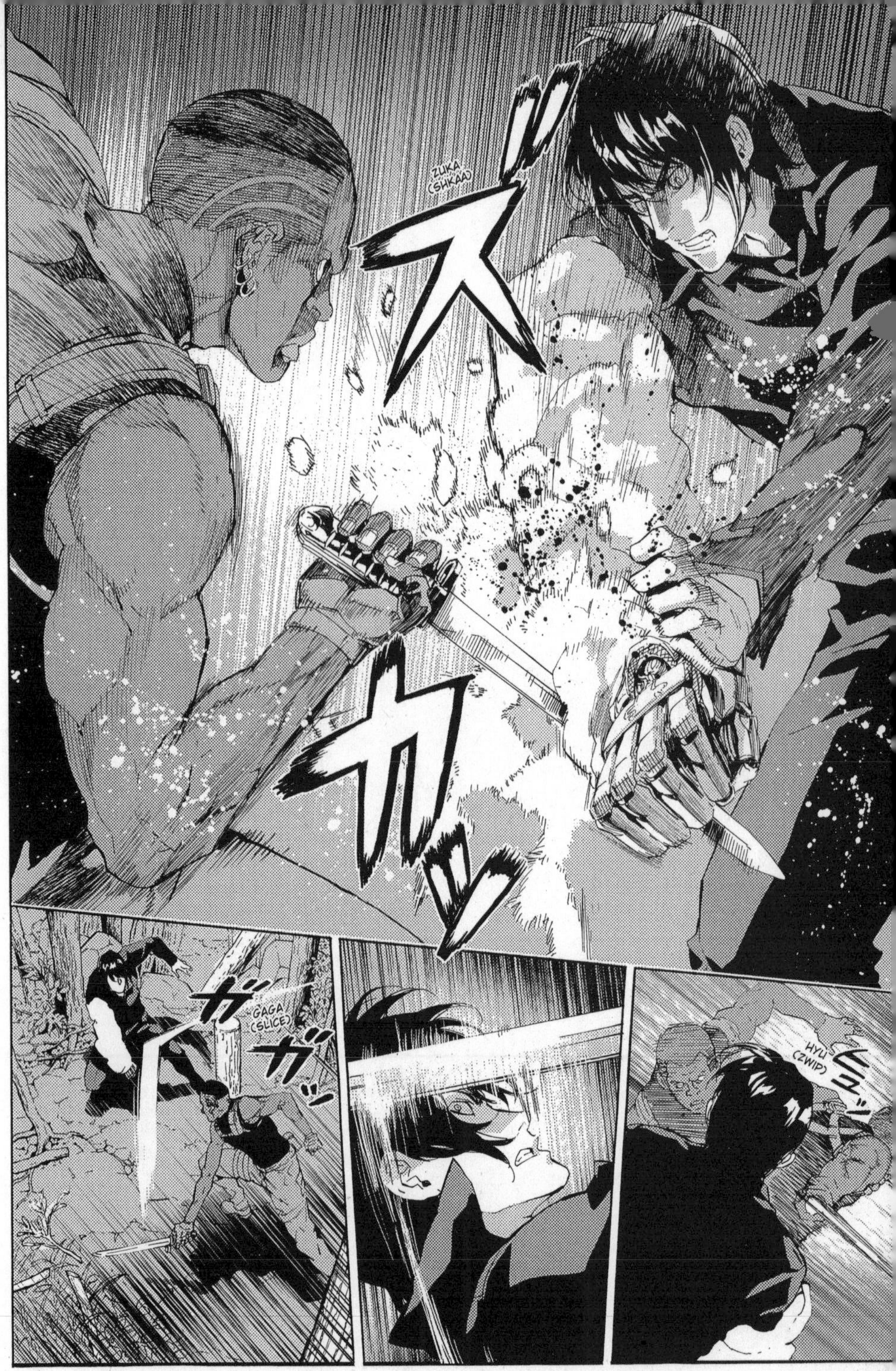
ズ
ZUKA (SHKAA)
カッ
ヒュッ
HYU (ZWIP)
ガガッ
GAGA (SLICE)

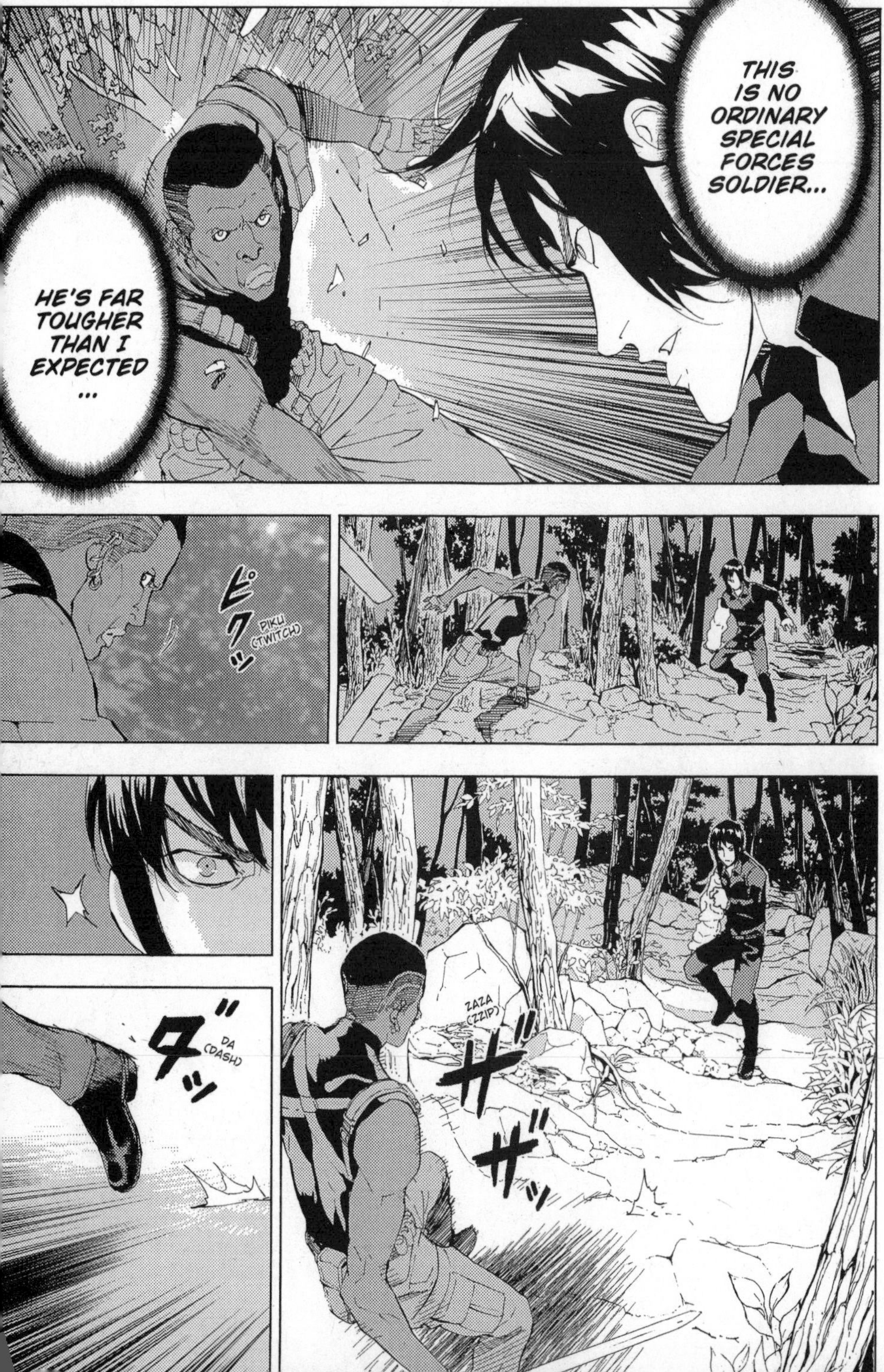
THIS IS NO ORDINARY SPECIAL FORCES SOLDIER...
HE'S FAR TOUGHER THAN I EXPECTED...
ピクッ
PIKU (TWITCH)
ザザッ
ZAZA (ZZIP)
ダッ
DA (DASH)

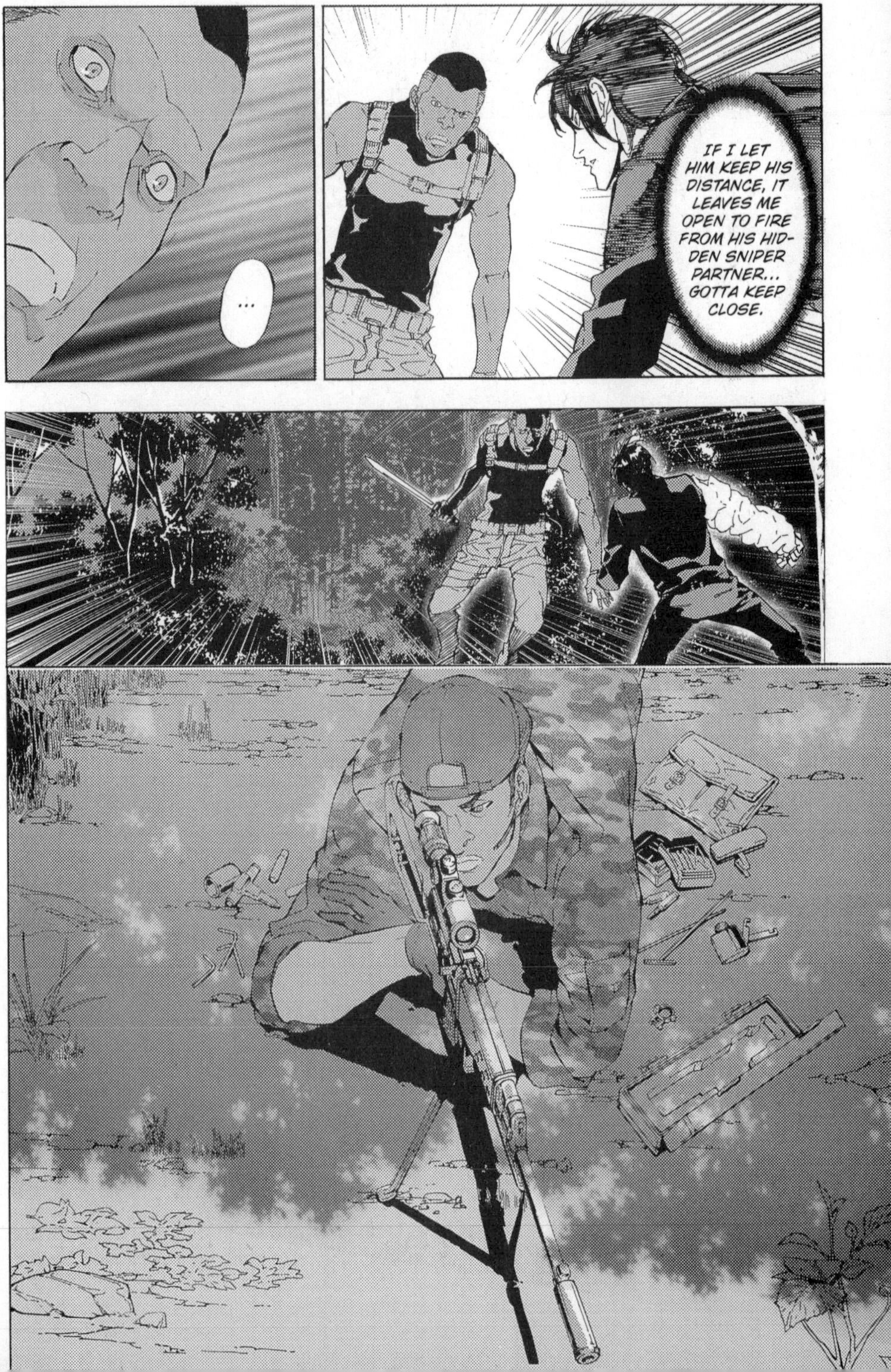
IF I LET HIM KEEP HIS DISTANCE, IT LEAVES ME OPEN TO FIRE FROM HIS HID-DEN SNIPER PARTNER... GOTTA KEEP CLOSE.
...

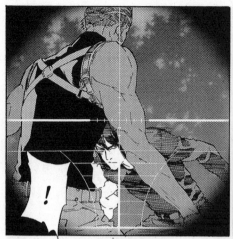

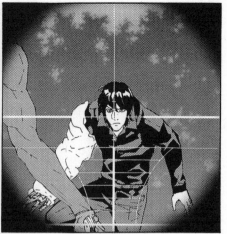

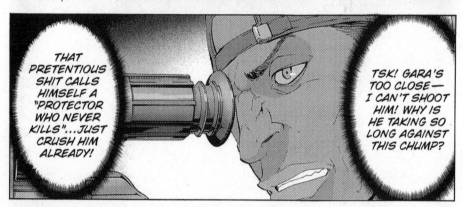

!
TSK! GARA'S TOO CLOSE— I CAN'T SHOOT HIM! WHY IS HE TAKING SO LONG AGAINST THIS CHUMP?
THAT PRETENTIOUS SHIT CALLS HIMSELF A "PROTECTOR WHO NEVER KILLS"...JUST CRUSH HIM ALREADY!
BUT STILL... HE KEEPS MOVING TO KEEP GARA'S BODY DIRECTLY IN MY LINE OF FIRE.
THE FACT THAT HE'S EVADING GARA'S ATTACKS TELLS ME HOW GOOD THIS GUY IS.
WON'T BE ENOUGH TO STOP ME FROM DOING MY JOB, THOUGH.
SHISHI (SHKK)

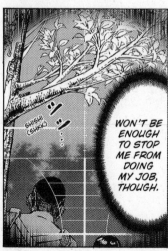

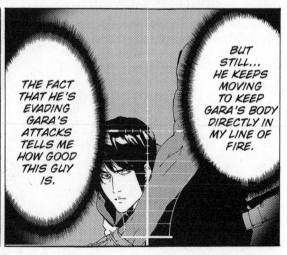

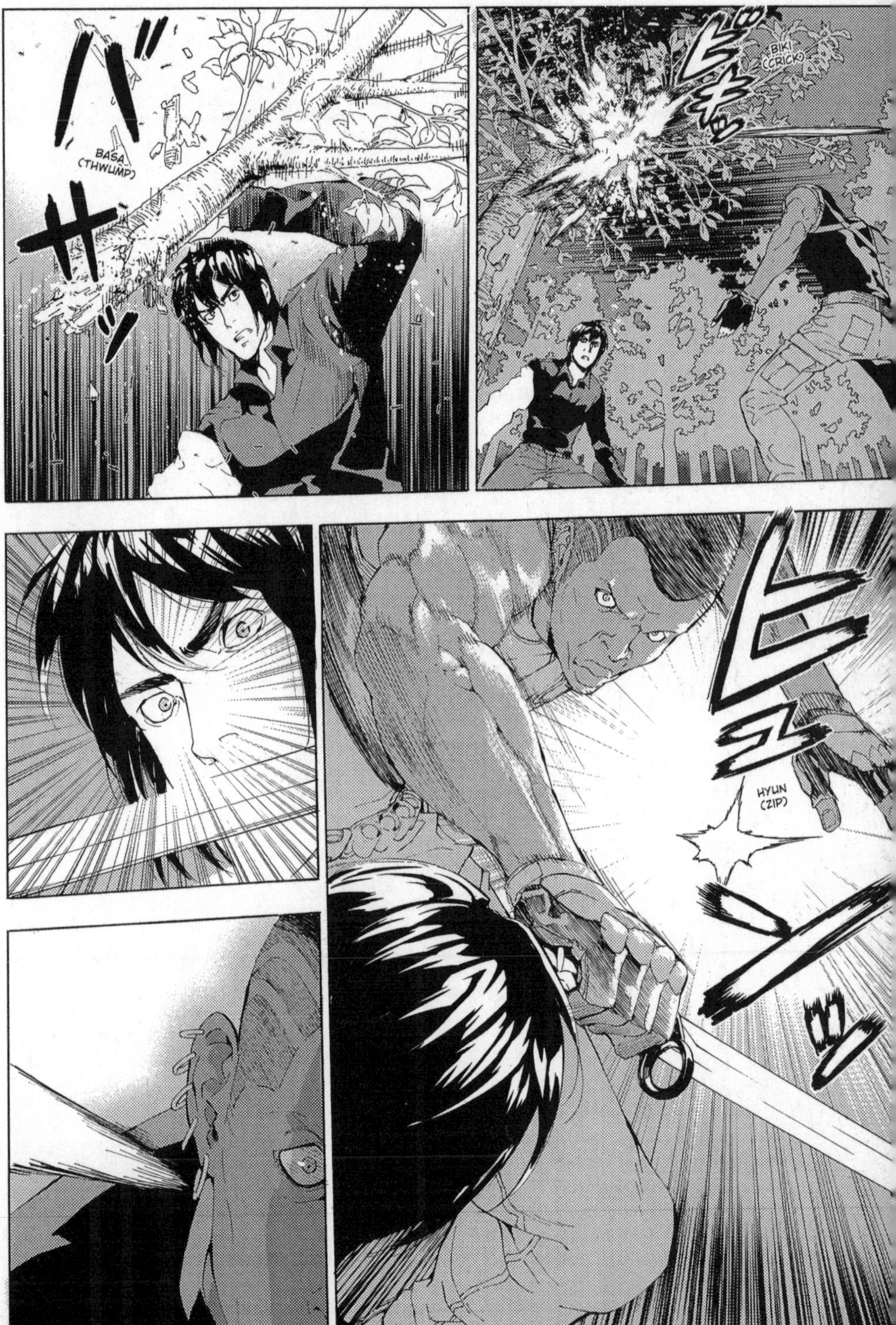
BIKI (CRICK)
BASA (THWUMP)
HYUN (ZIP)

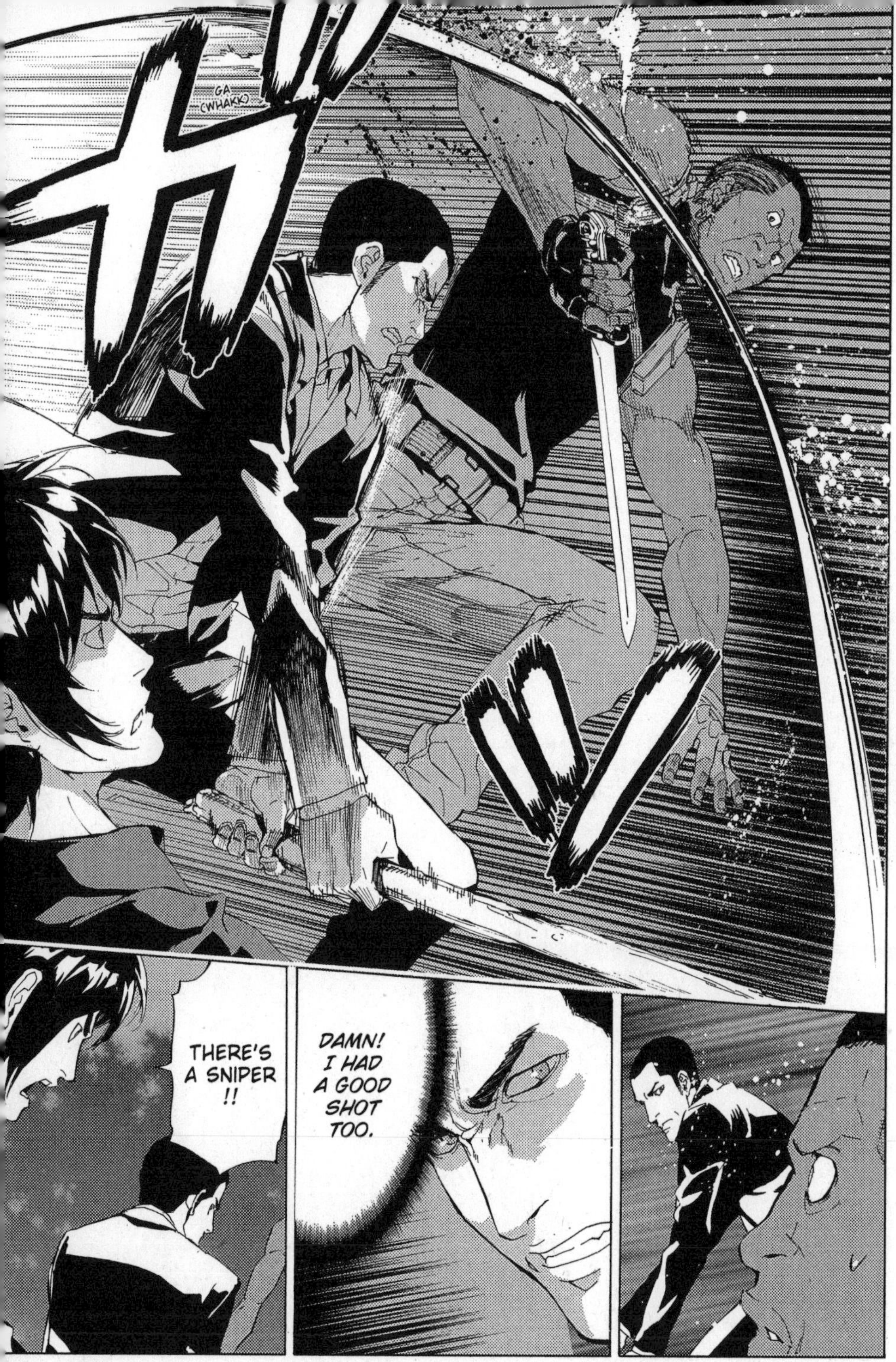
GA (WHAKK)
DAMN! I HAD A GOOD SHOT TOO.
THERE'S A SNIPER !!

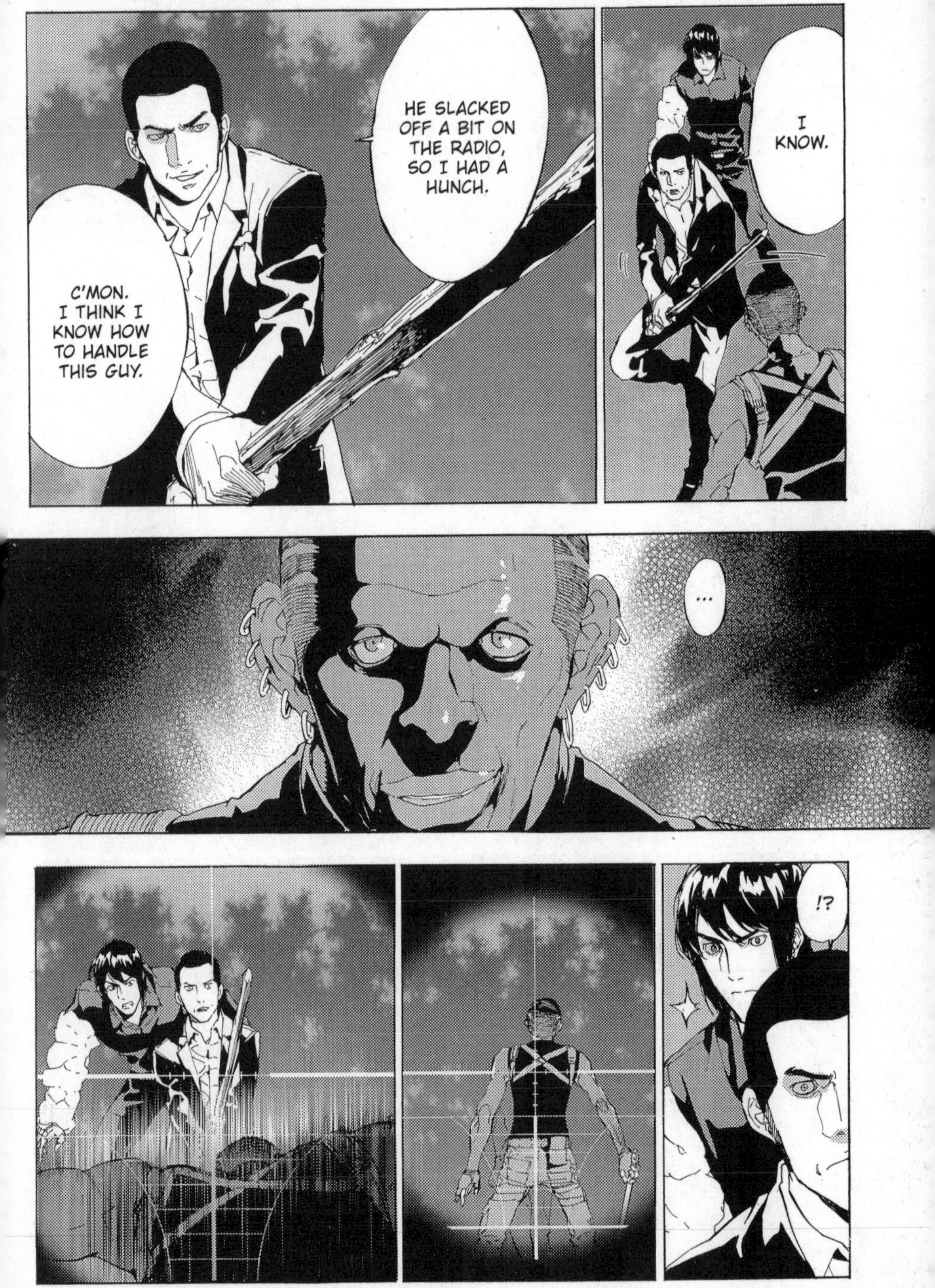
I KNOW.
HE SLACKED OFF A BIT ON THE RADIO, SO I HAD A HUNCH.
C'MON. I THINK I KNOW HOW TO HANDLE THIS GUY.
...
!?

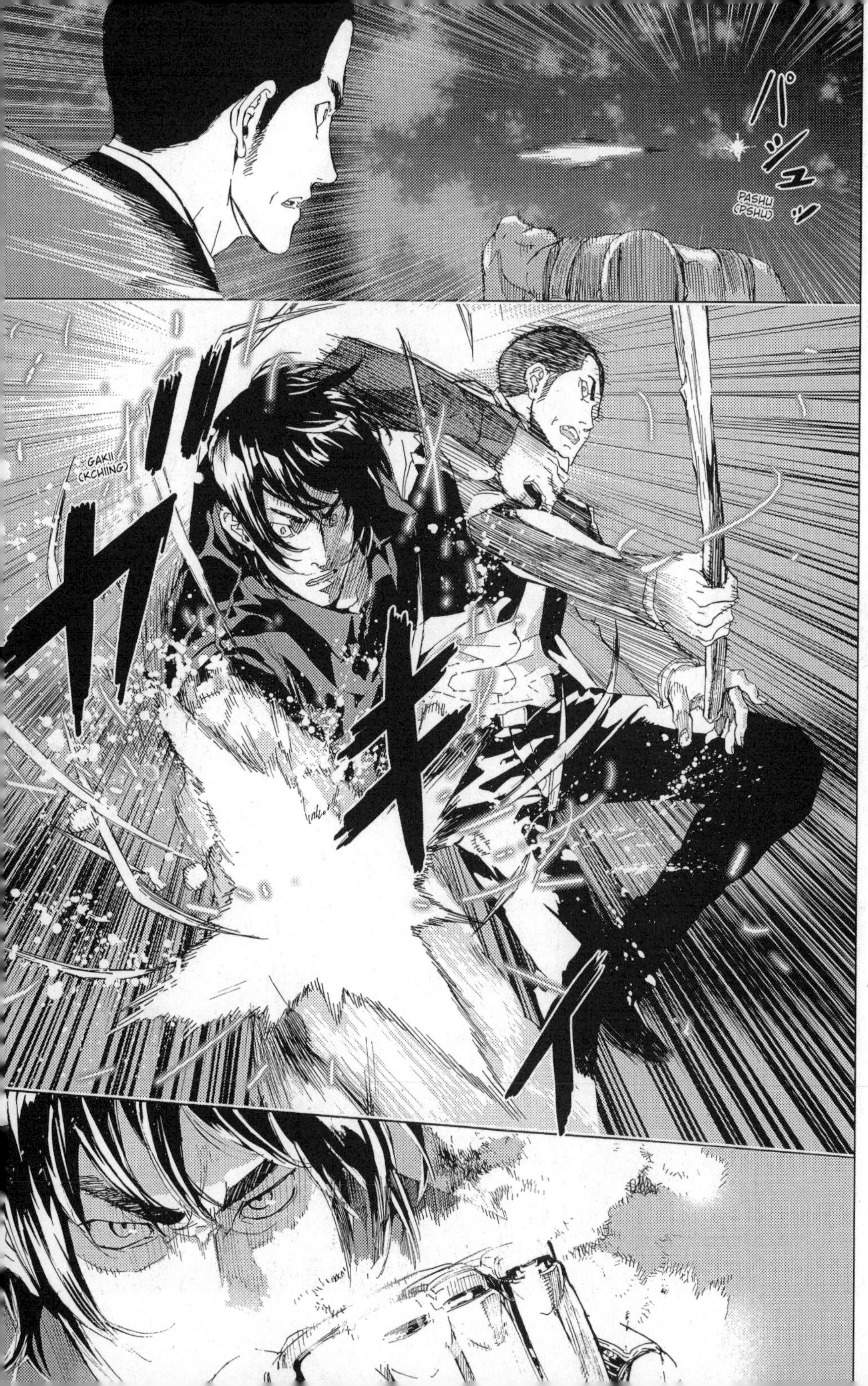

パシュッ
PASHU (PSHU)
ガキイ
GAKII (KCHIING)

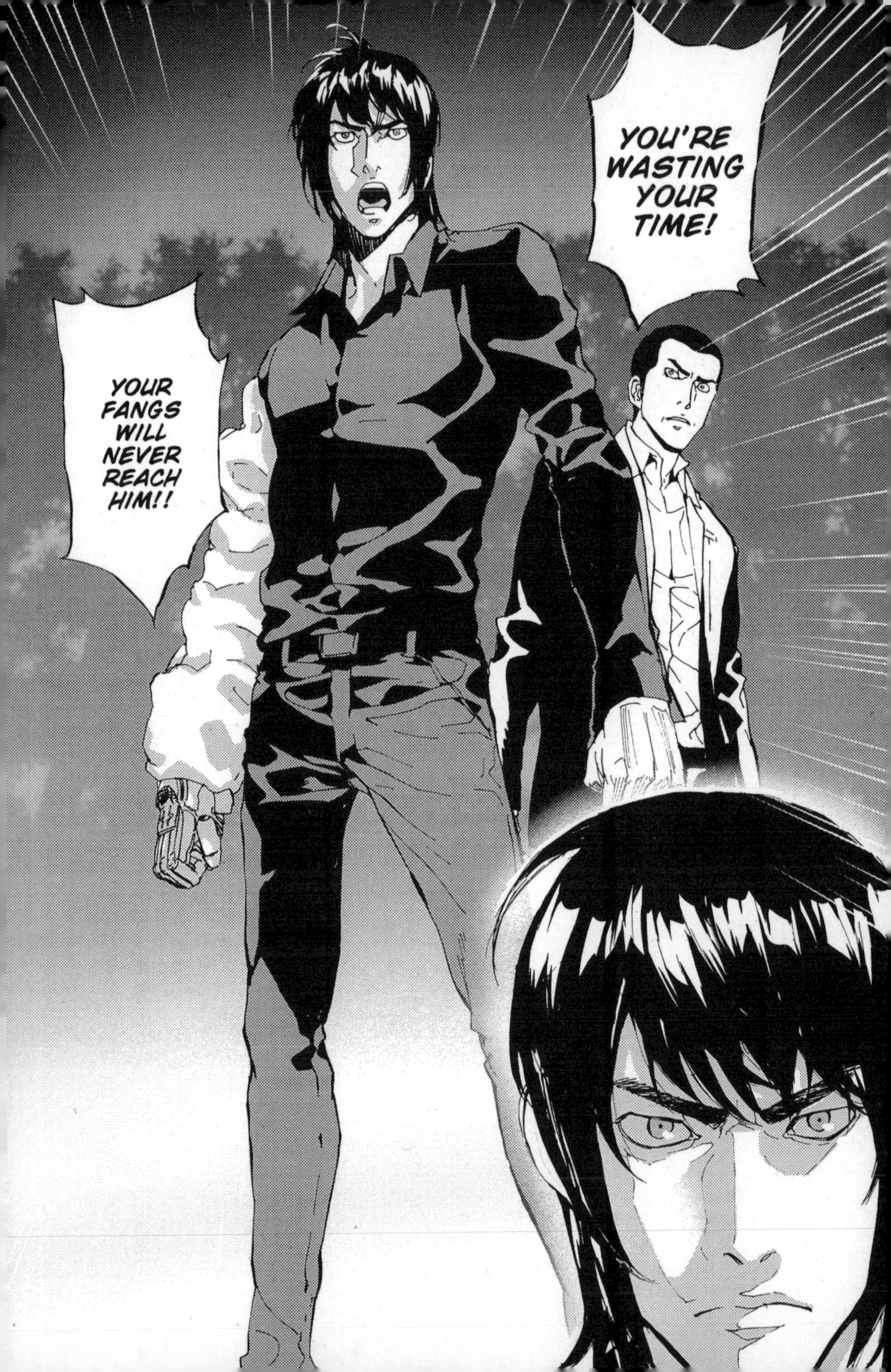
YOU'RE WASTING YOUR TIME!
YOUR FANGS WILL NEVER REACH HIM!!

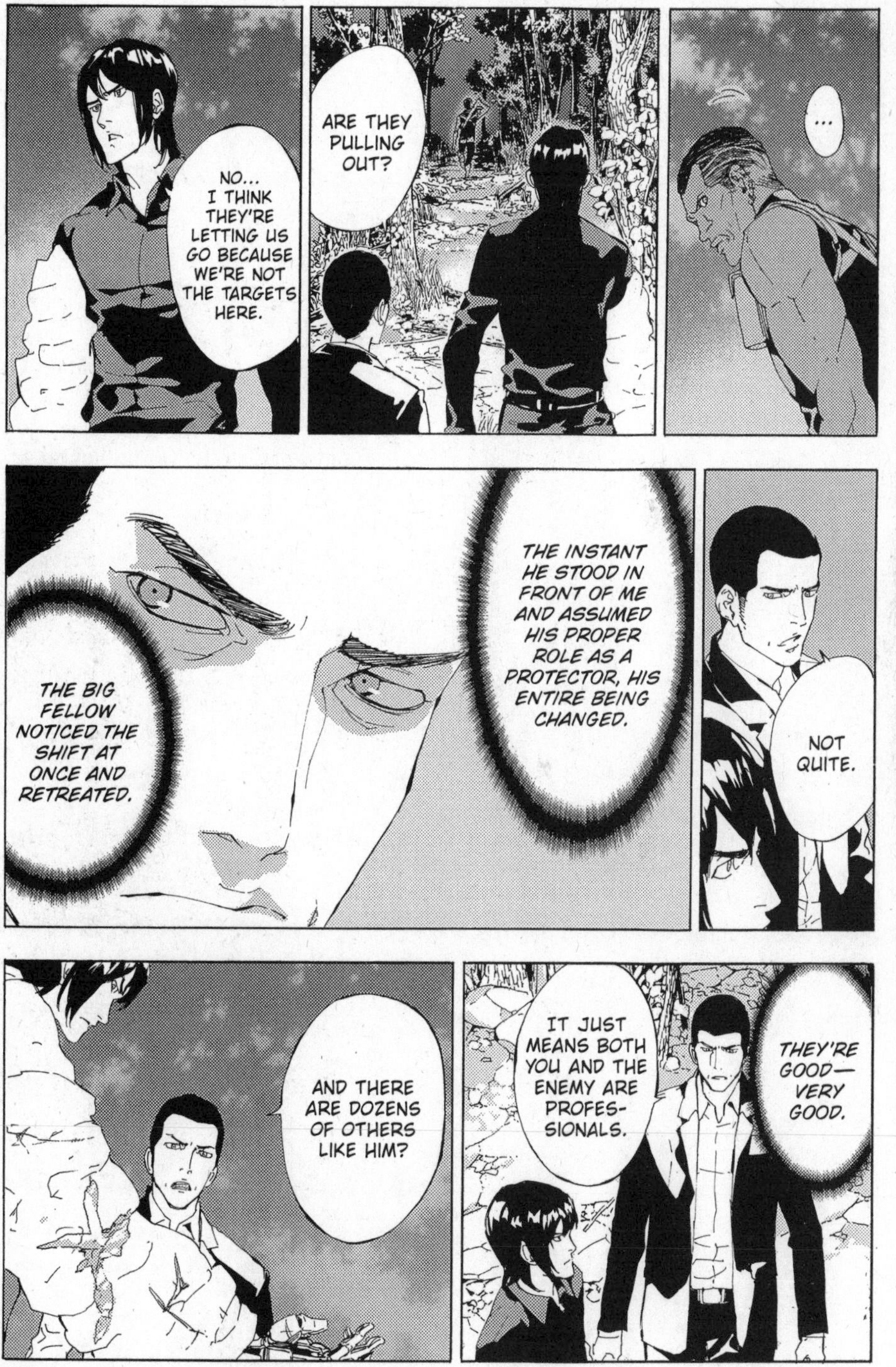
...
ARE THEY PULLING OUT?
NO... I THINK THEY'RE LETTING US GO BECAUSE WE'RE NOT THE TARGETS HERE.
NOT QUITE.
THE INSTANT HE STOOD IN FRONT OF ME AND ASSUMED HIS PROPER ROLE AS A PROTECTOR, HIS ENTIRE BEING CHANGED.
THE BIG FELLOW NOTICED THE SHIFT AT ONCE AND RETREATED.
THEY'RE GOOD—VERY GOOD.
IT JUST MEANS BOTH YOU AND THE ENEMY ARE PROFES-SIONALS.
AND THERE ARE DOZENS OF OTHERS LIKE HIM?

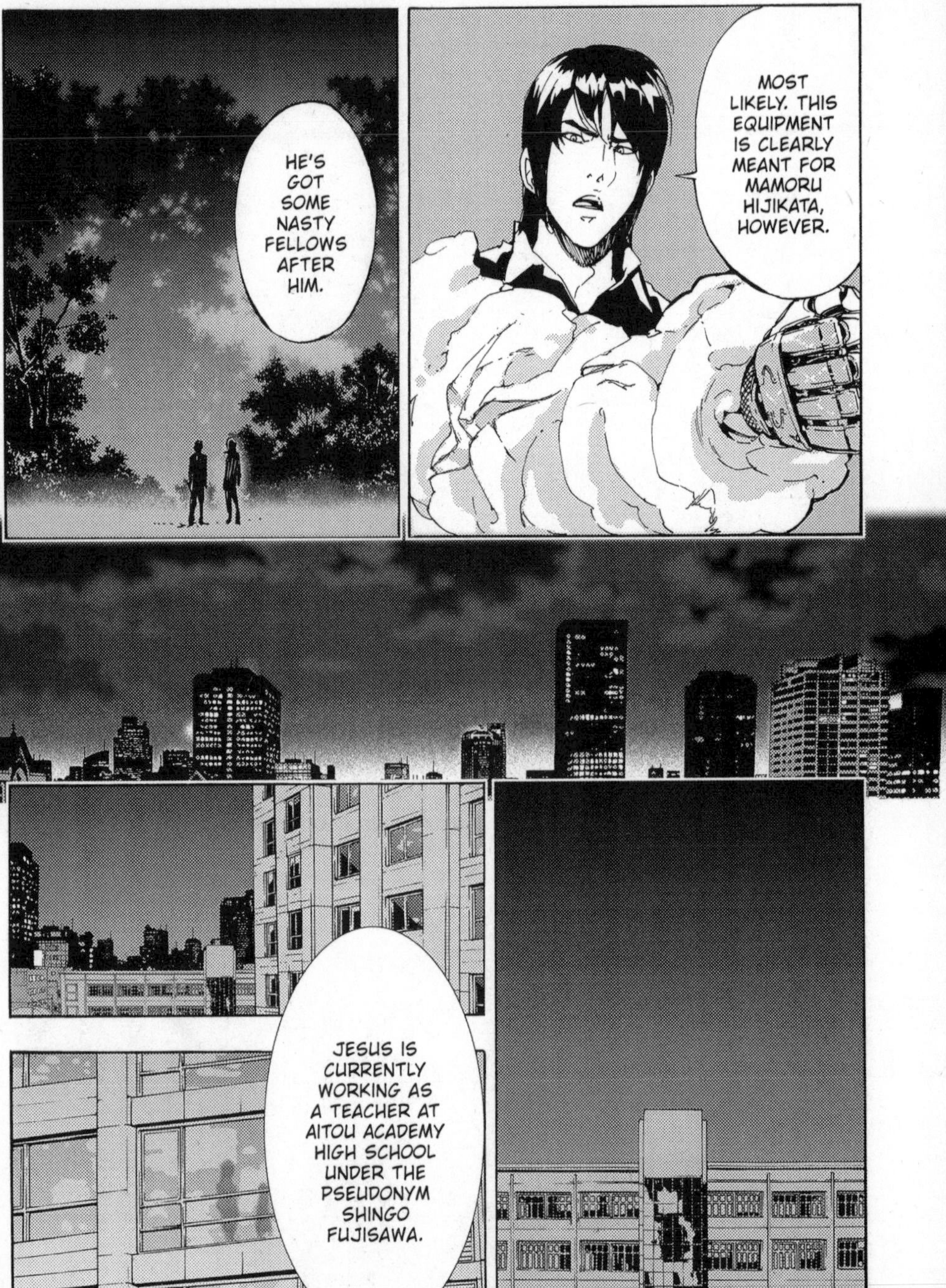
MOST LIKELY. THIS EQUIPMENT IS CLEARLY MEANT FOR MAMORU HIJIKATA, HOWEVER.
HE'S GOT SOME NASTY FELLOWS AFTER HIM.
JESUS IS CURRENTLY WORKING AS A TEACHER AT AITOU ACADEMY HIGH SCHOOL UNDER THE PSEUDONYM SHINGO FUJISAWA.

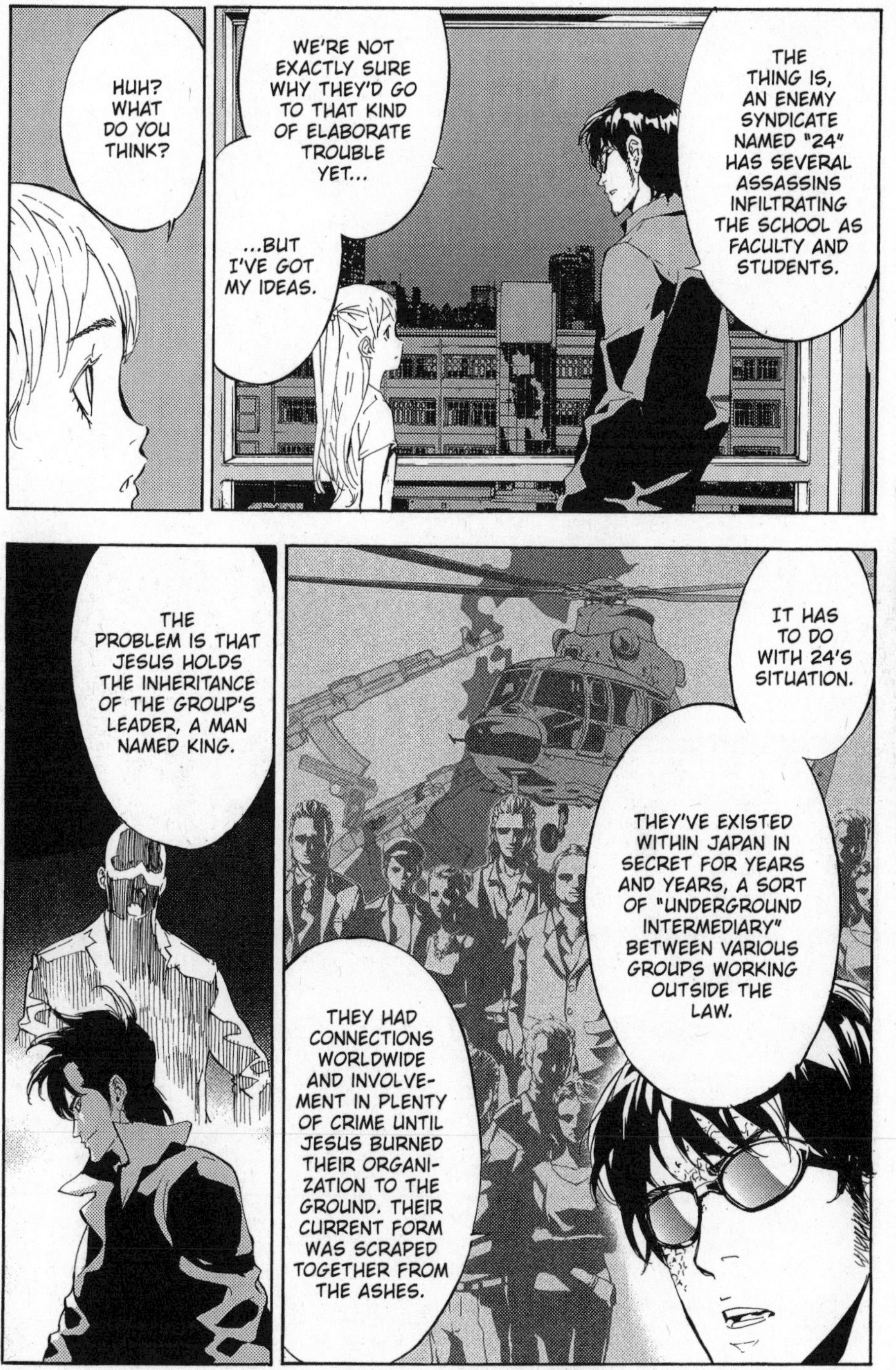
THE THING IS, AN ENEMY SYNDICATE NAMED "24" HAS SEVERAL ASSASSINS INFILTRATING THE SCHOOL AS FACULTY AND STUDENTS.
WE'RE NOT EXACTLY SURE WHY THEY'D GO TO THAT KIND OF ELABORATE TROUBLE YET...
...BUT I'VE GOT MY IDEAS.
HUH? WHAT DO YOU THINK?
IT HAS TO DO WITH 24'S SITUATION.
THEY'VE EXISTED WITHIN JAPAN IN SECRET FOR YEARS AND YEARS, A SORT OF "UNDERGROUND INTERMEDIARY" BETWEEN VARIOUS GROUPS WORKING OUTSIDE THE LAW.
THEY HAD CONNECTIONS WORLDWIDE AND INVOLVE-MENT IN PLENTY OF CRIME UNTIL JESUS BURNED THEIR ORGANI-ZATION TO THE GROUND. THEIR CURRENT FORM WAS SCRAPED TOGETHER FROM THE ASHES.
THE PROBLEM IS THAT JESUS HOLDS THE INHERITANCE OF THE GROUP'S LEADER, A MAN NAMED KING.

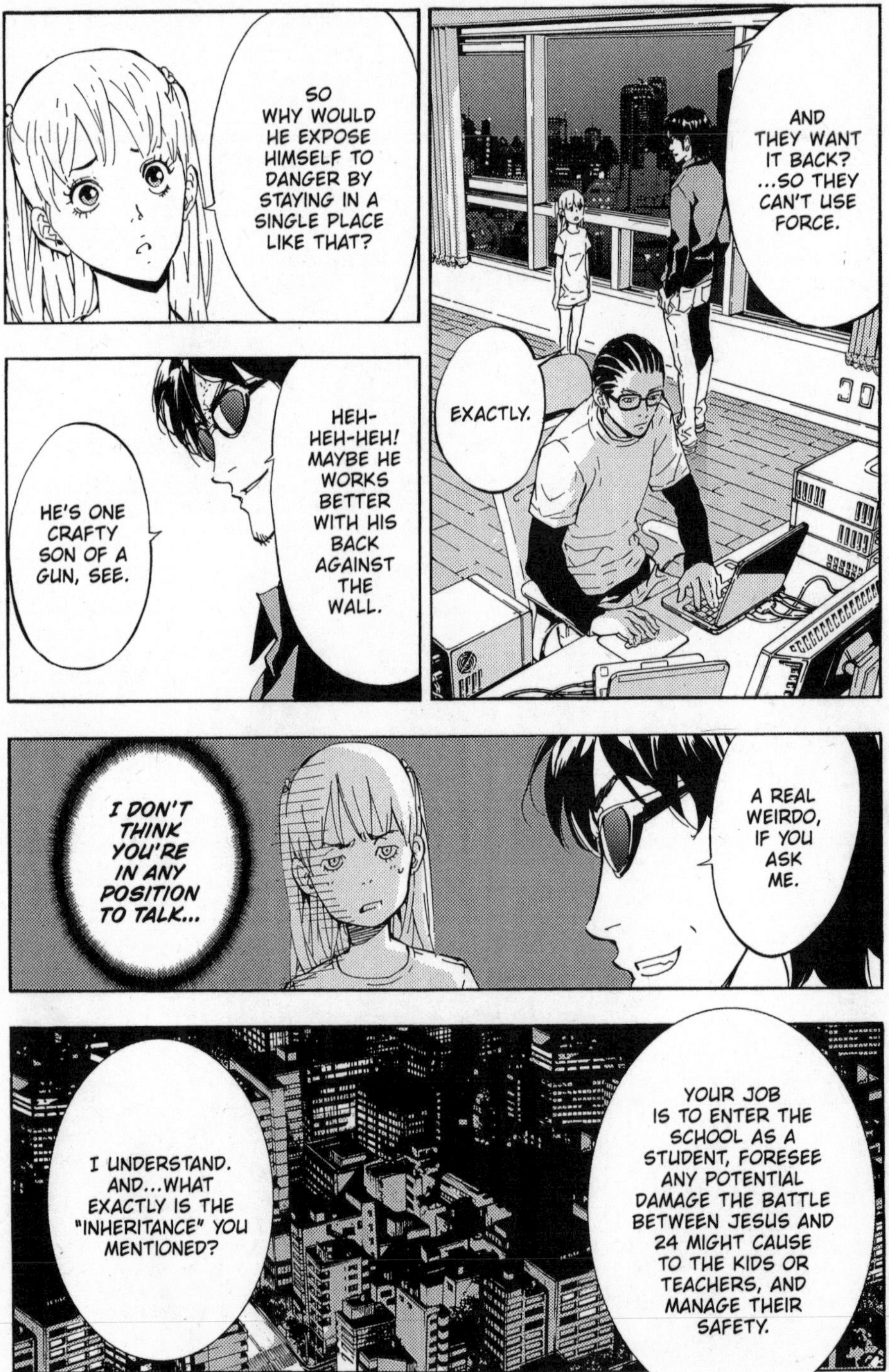
AND THEY WANT IT BACK? ...SO THEY CAN'T USE FORCE.
EXACTLY.
SO WHY WOULD HE EXPOSE HIMSELF TO DANGER BY STAYING IN A SINGLE PLACE LIKE THAT?
HEH-HEH-HEH! MAYBE HE WORKS BETTER WITH HIS BACK AGAINST THE WALL.
HE'S ONE CRAFTY SON OF A GUN, SEE.
A REAL WEIRDO, IF YOU ASK ME.
I DON'T THINK YOU'RE IN ANY POSITION TO TALK...
YOUR JOB IS TO ENTER THE SCHOOL AS A STUDENT, FORESEE ANY POTENTIAL DAMAGE THE BATTLE BETWEEN JESUS AND 24 MIGHT CAUSE TO THE KIDS OR TEACHERS, AND MANAGE THEIR SAFETY.
I UNDERSTAND. AND...WHAT EXACTLY IS THE "INHERITANCE" YOU MENTIONED?

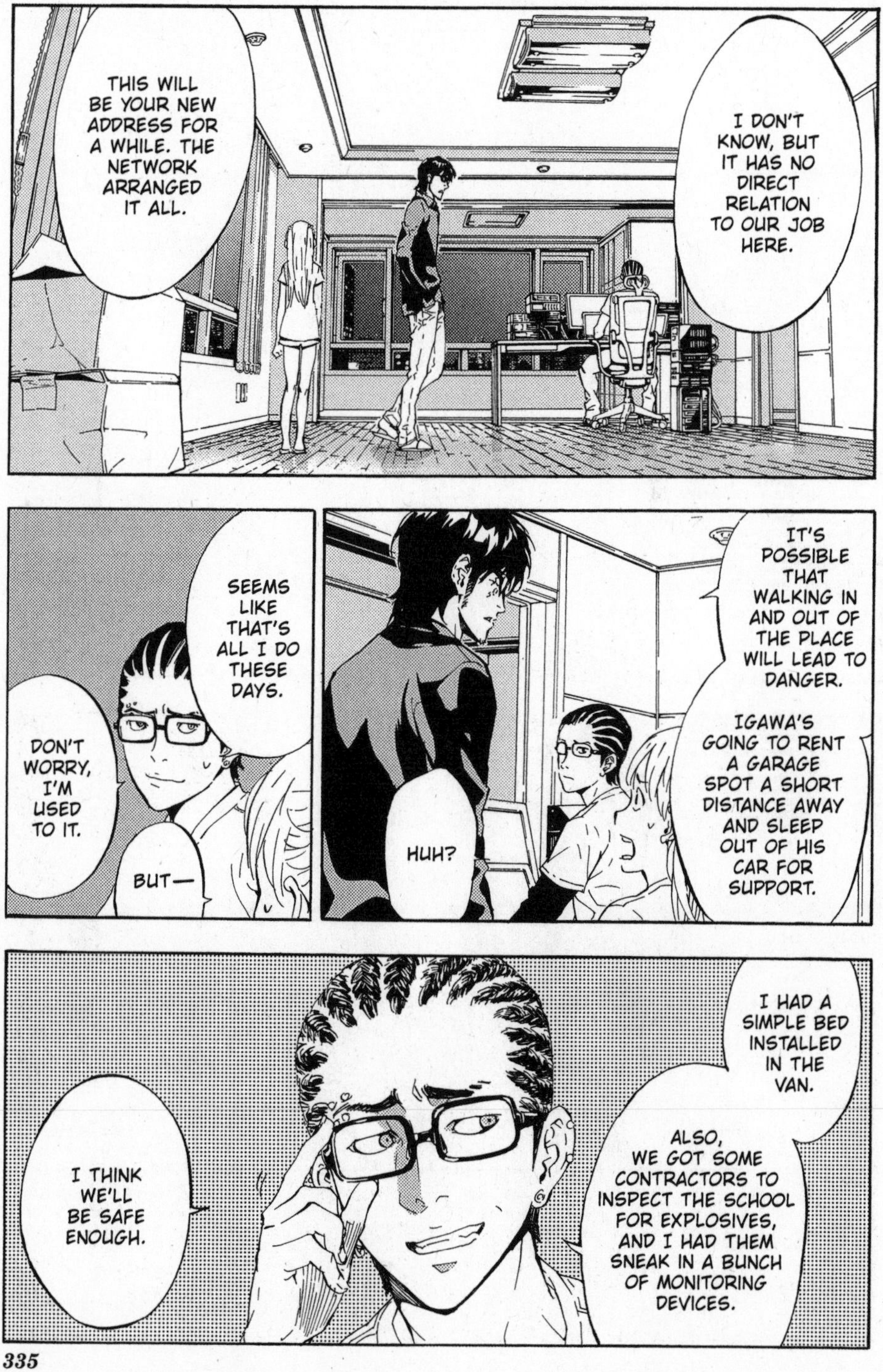
I DON'T KNOW, BUT IT HAS NO DIRECT RELATION TO OUR JOB HERE.
THIS WILL BE YOUR NEW ADDRESS FOR A WHILE. THE NETWORK ARRANGED IT ALL.
IT'S POSSIBLE THAT WALKING IN AND OUT OF THE PLACE WILL LEAD TO DANGER.
IGAWA'S GOING TO RENT A GARAGE SPOT A SHORT DISTANCE AWAY AND SLEEP OUT OF HIS CAR FOR SUPPORT.
HUH?
SEEMS LIKE THAT'S ALL I DO THESE DAYS.
DON'T WORRY, I'M USED TO IT.
BUT—
I HAD A SIMPLE BED INSTALLED IN THE VAN.
ALSO, WE GOT SOME CONTRACTORS TO INSPECT THE SCHOOL FOR EXPLOSIVES, AND I HAD THEM SNEAK IN A BUNCH OF MONITORING DEVICES.
I THINK WE'LL BE SAFE ENOUGH.

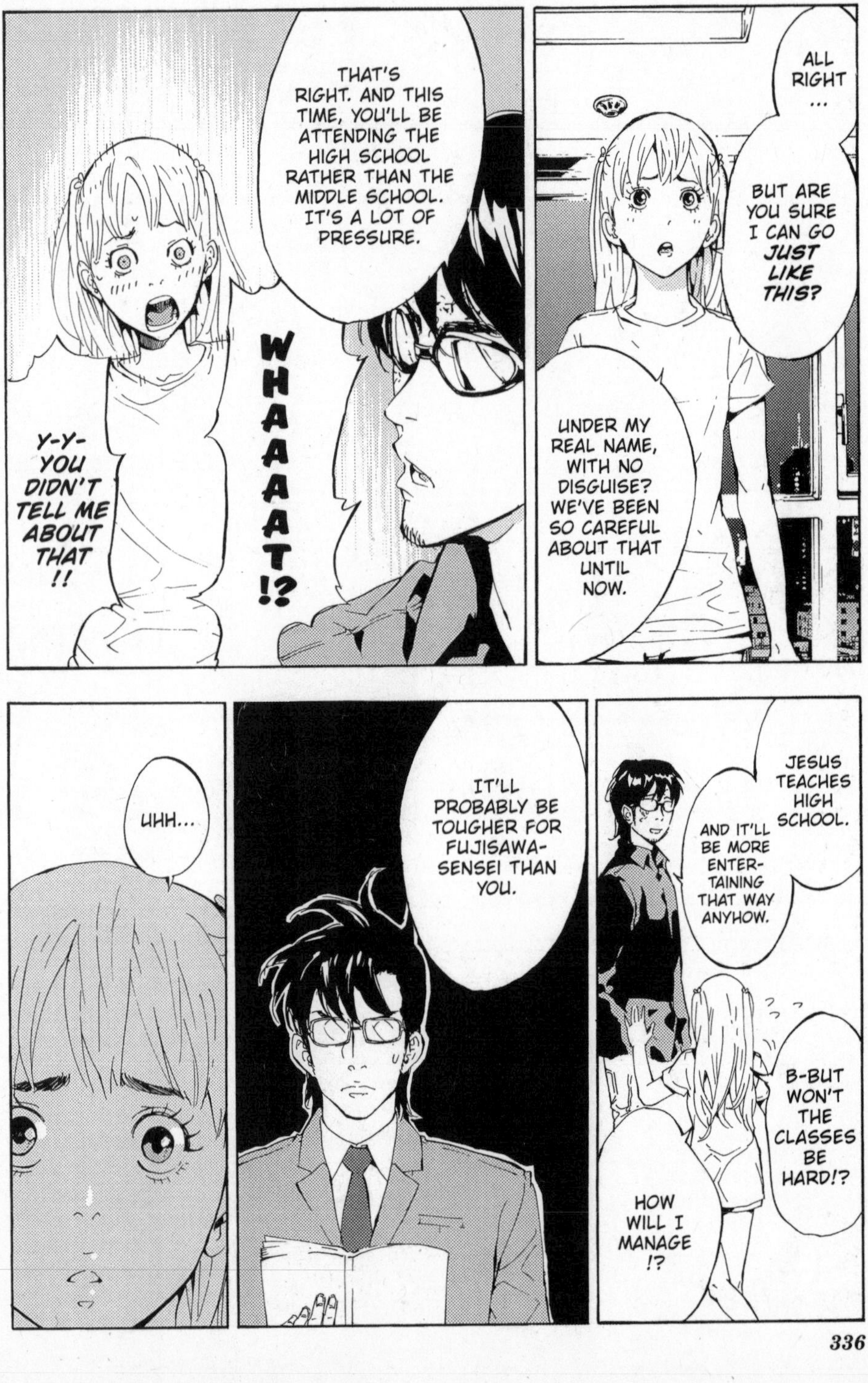
ALL RIGHT ...
BUT ARE YOU SURE I CAN GO JUST LIKE THIS?
UNDER MY REAL NAME, WITH NO DISGUISE? WE'VE BEEN SO CAREFUL ABOUT THAT UNTIL NOW.
THAT'S RIGHT. AND THIS TIME, YOU'LL BE ATTENDING THE HIGH SCHOOL RATHER THAN THE MIDDLE SCHOOL. IT'S A LOT OF PRESSURE.
WHAAAAAT!?
Y-Y-YOU DIDN'T TELL ME ABOUT THAT!!
JESUS TEACHES HIGH SCHOOL.
AND IT'LL BE MORE ENTER-TAINING THAT WAY ANYHOW.
B-BUT WON'T THE CLASSES BE HARD!?
HOW WILL I MANAGE!?
IT'LL PROBABLY BE TOUGHER FOR FUJISAWA-SENSEI THAN YOU.
UHH...

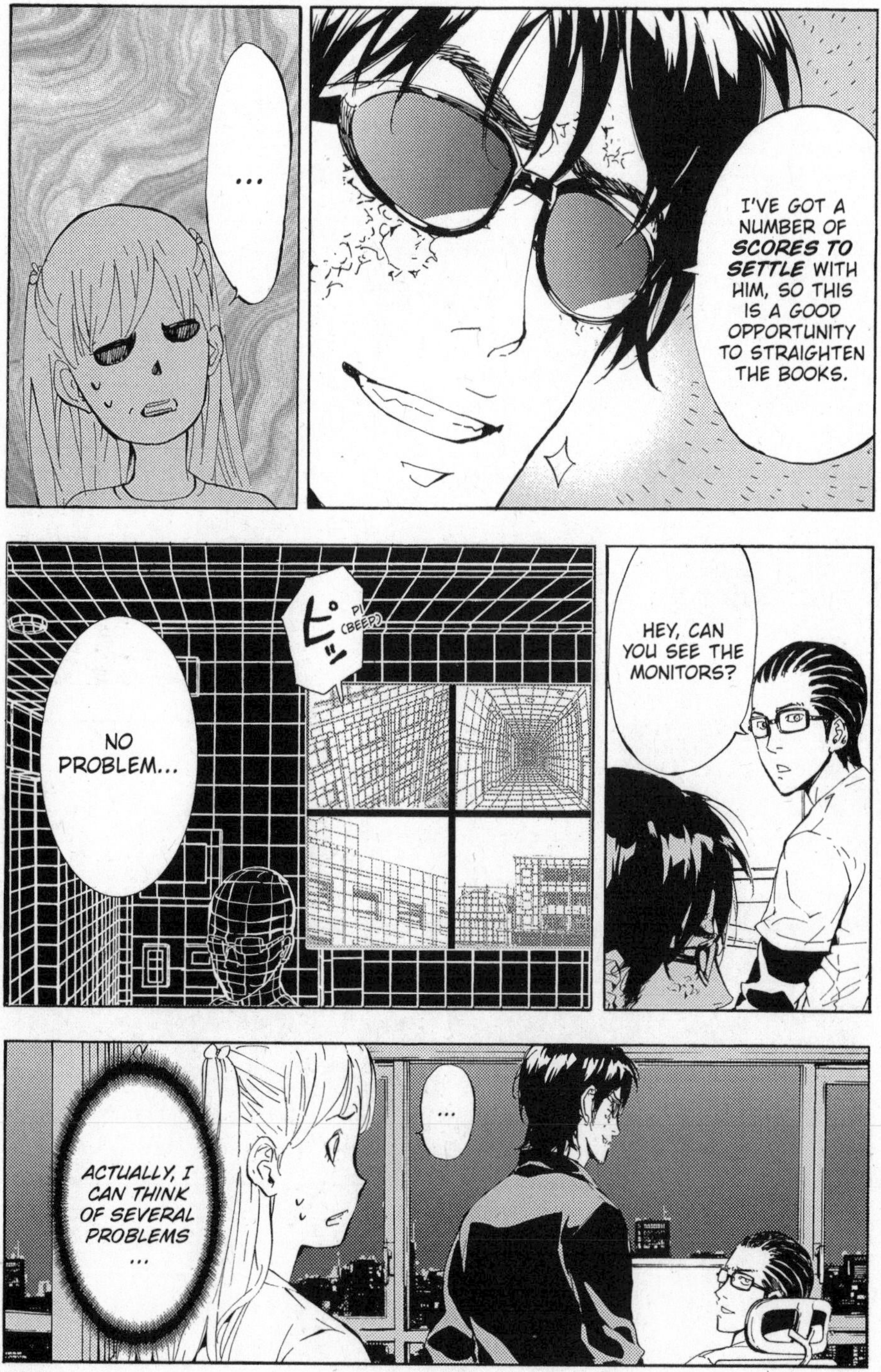
I'VE GOT A NUMBER OF ***SCORES TO SETTLE*** WITH HIM, SO THIS IS A GOOD OPPORTUNITY TO STRAIGHTEN THE BOOKS.
...
HEY, CAN YOU SEE THE MONITORS?
ピッ
PI (BEEP)
NO PROBLEM...
...
ACTUALLY, I CAN THINK OF SEVERAL PROBLEMS ...

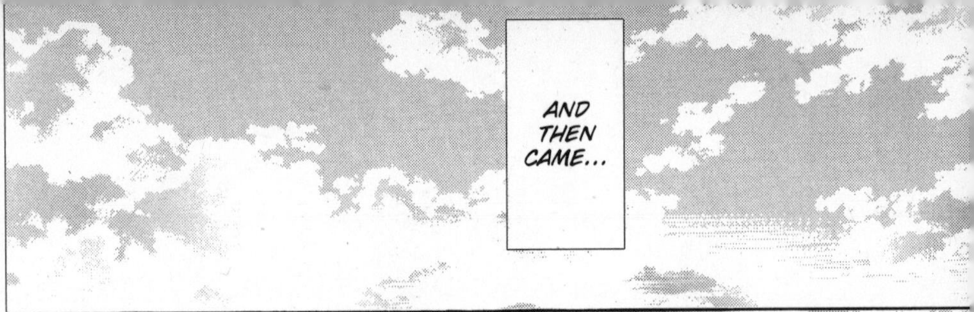
AND THEN CAME...

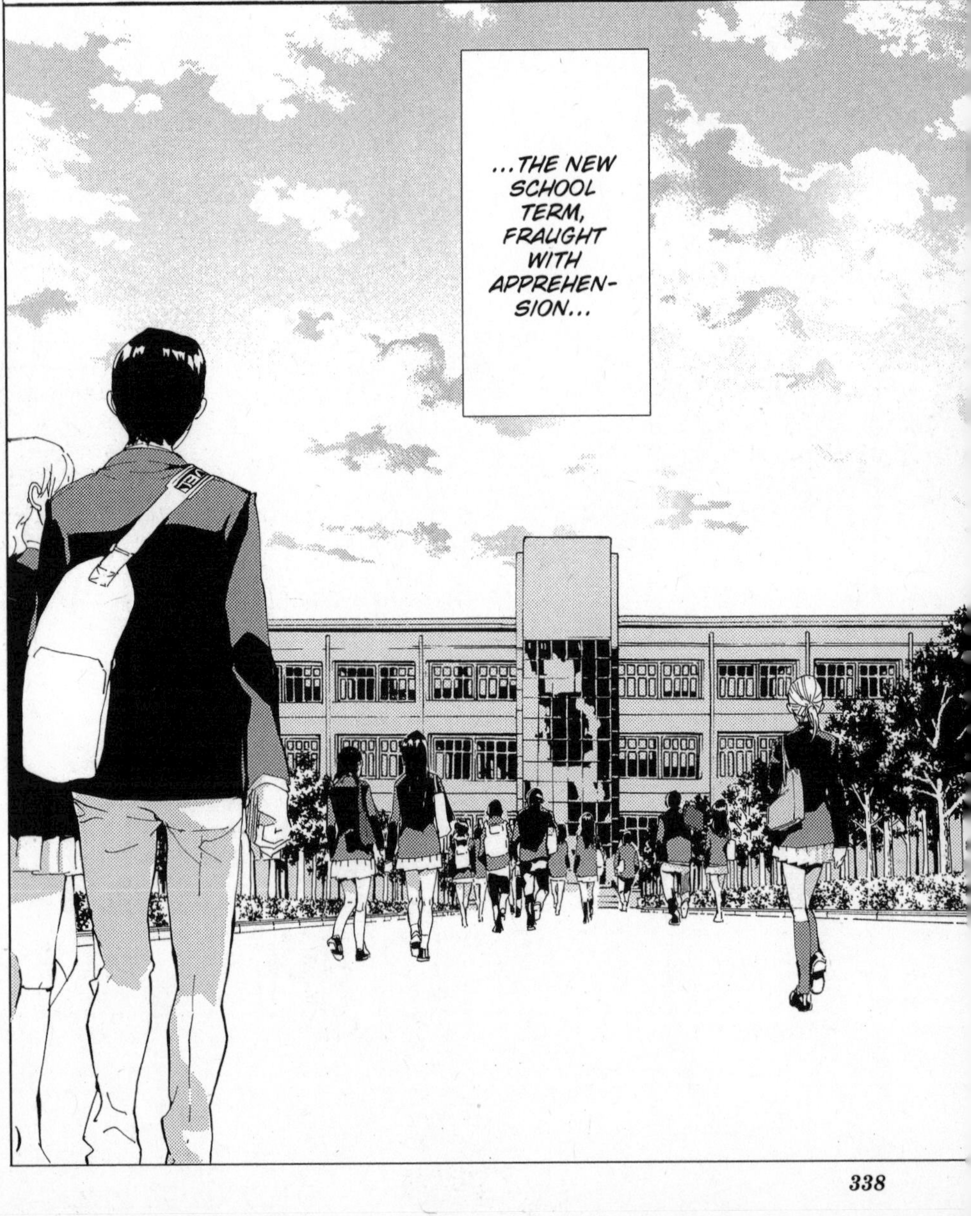
...THE NEW SCHOOL TERM, FRAUGHT WITH APPREHEN-SION...

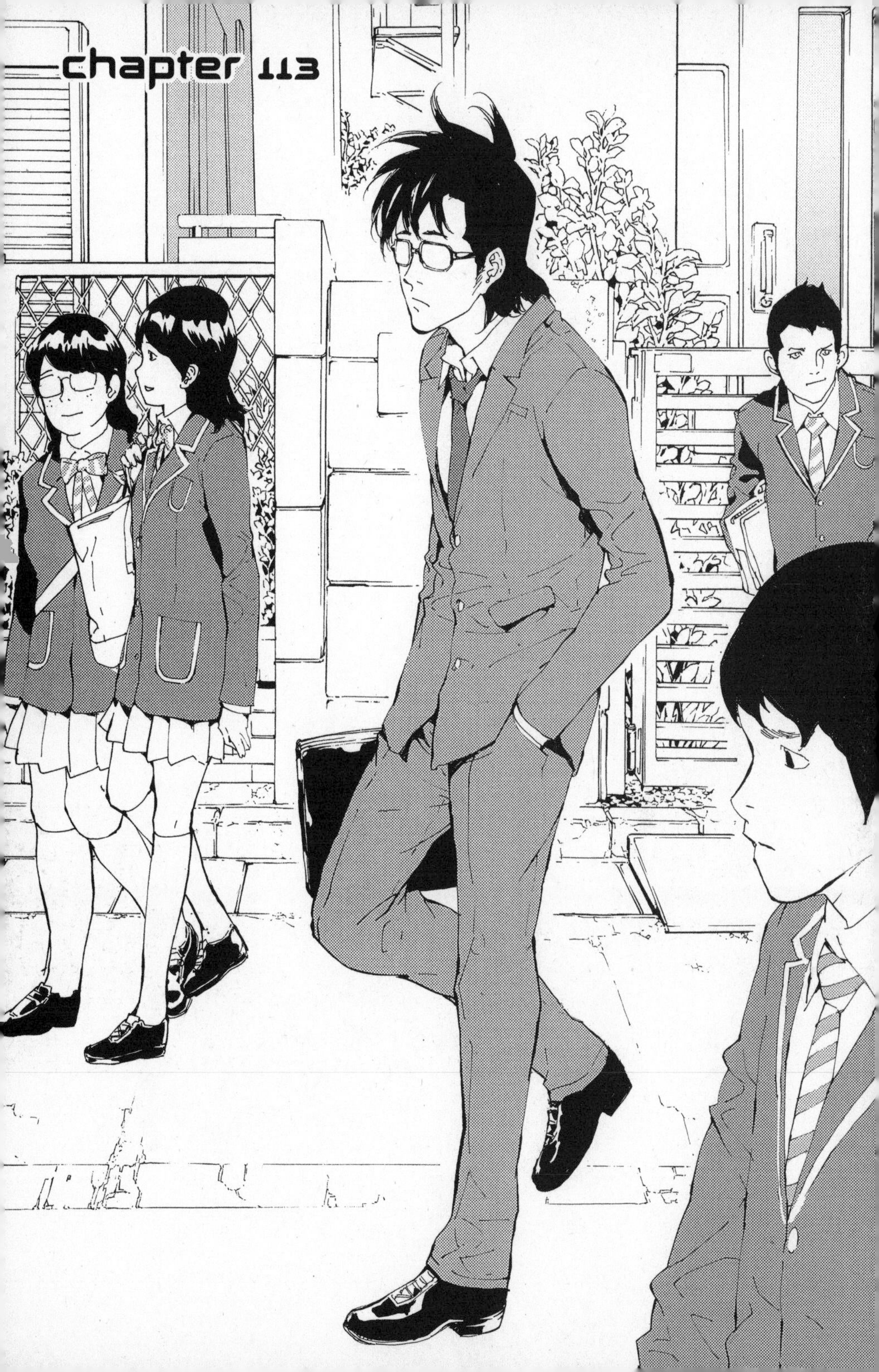
chapter 113

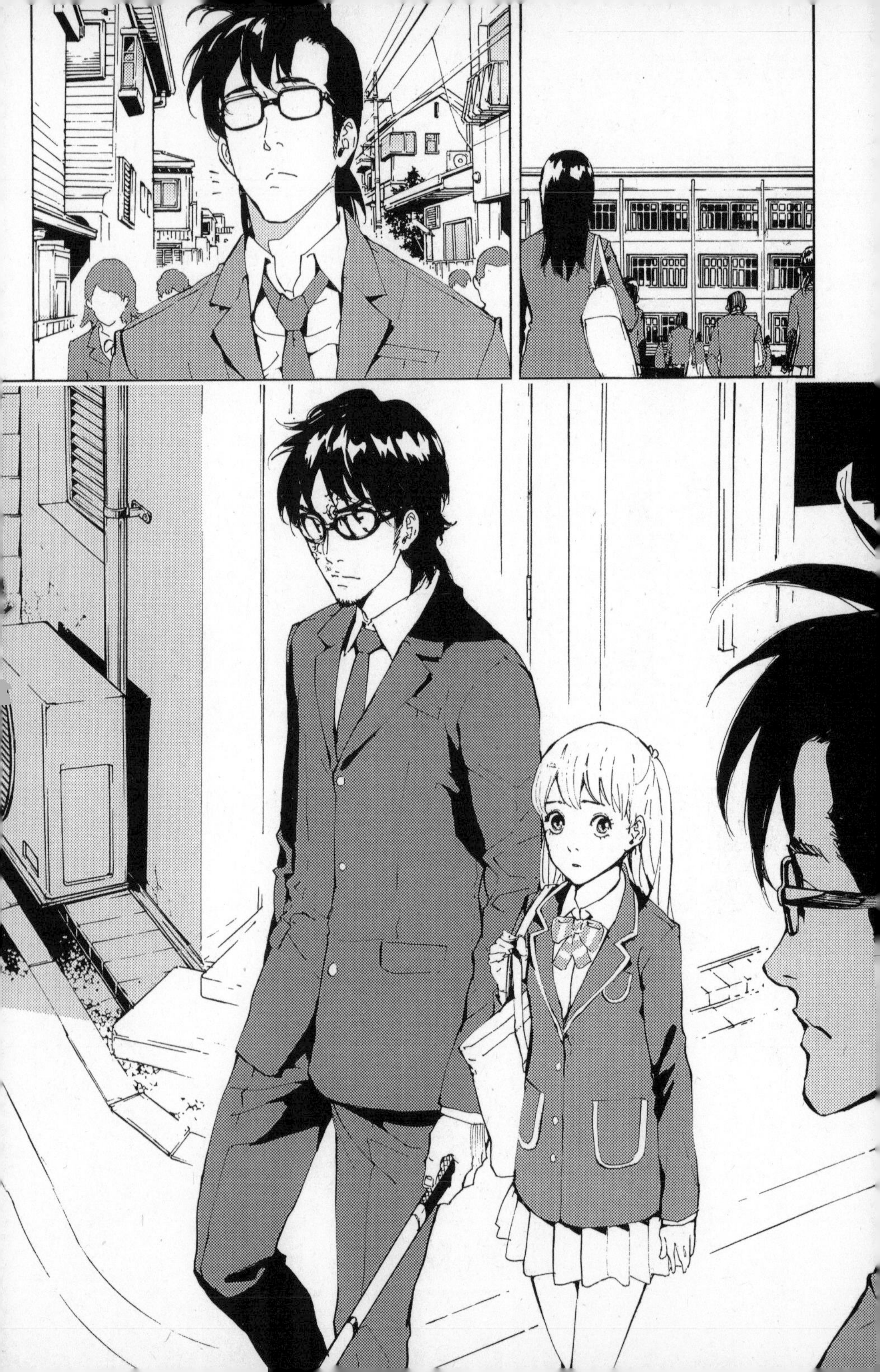

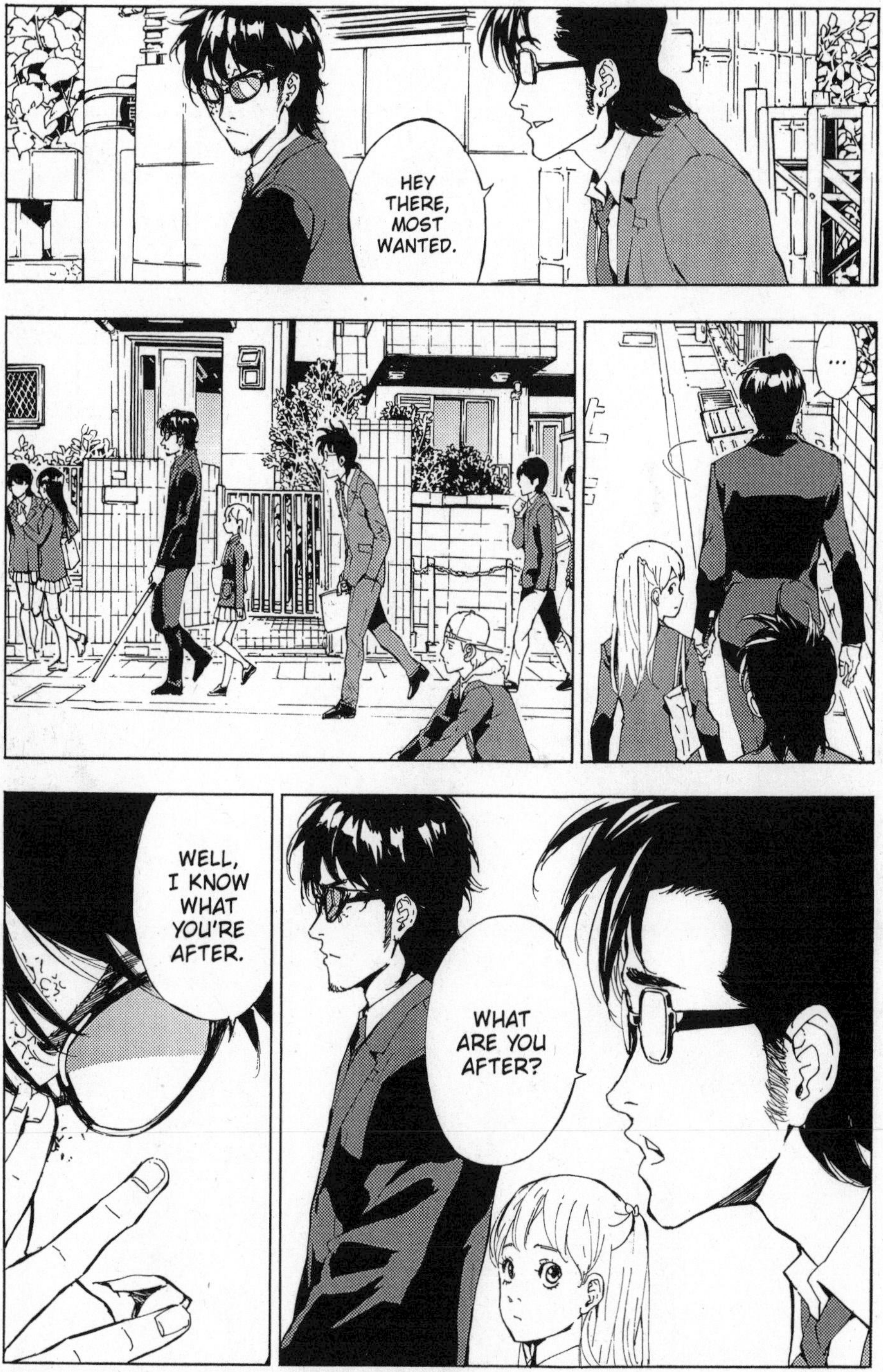
HEY THERE, MOST WANTED.
...
WHAT ARE YOU AFTER?
WELL, I KNOW WHAT YOU'RE AFTER.

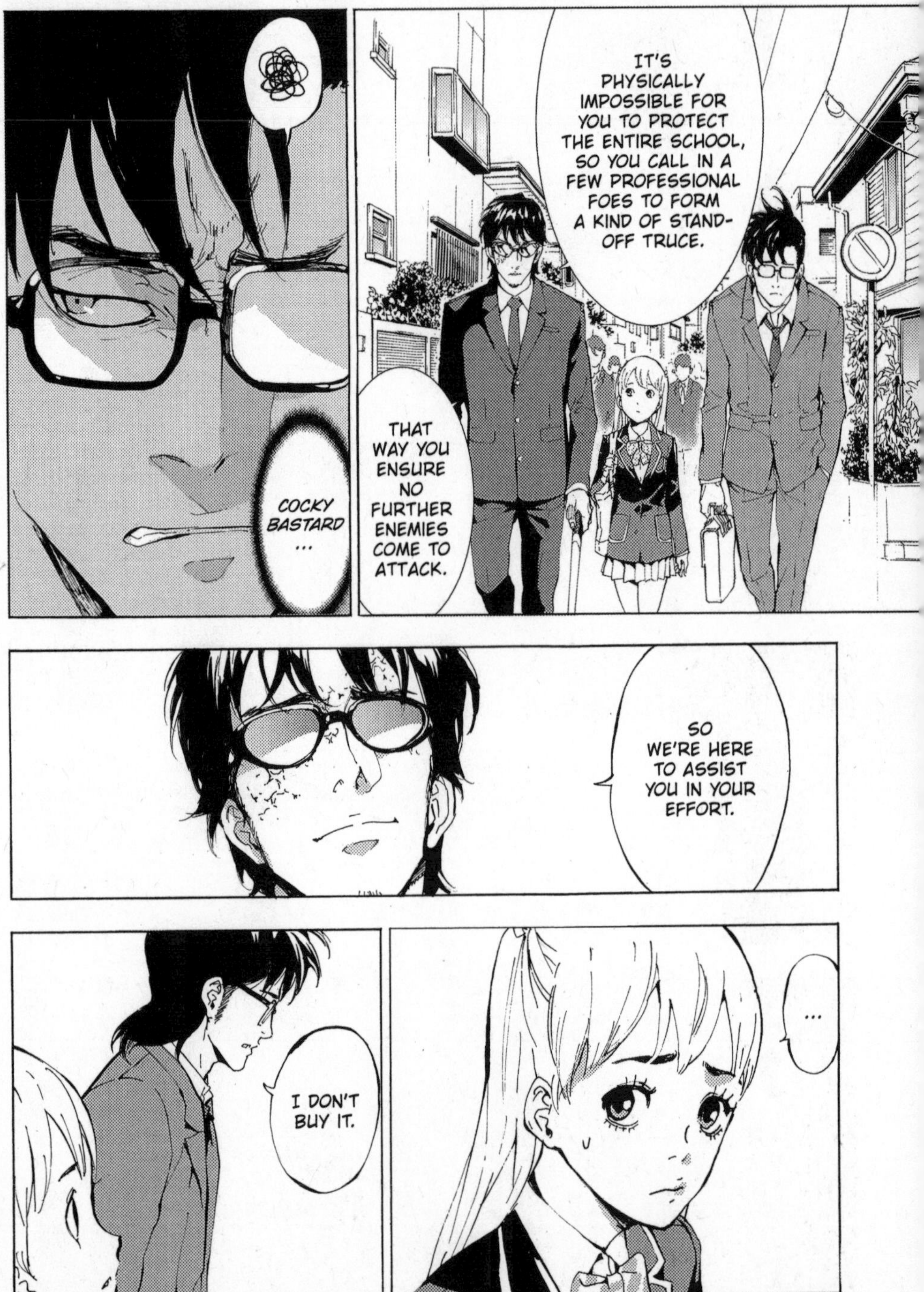
IT'S PHYSICALLY IMPOSSIBLE FOR YOU TO PROTECT THE ENTIRE SCHOOL, SO YOU CALL IN A FEW PROFESSIONAL FOES TO FORM A KIND OF STAND-OFF TRUCE.
THAT WAY YOU ENSURE NO FURTHER ENEMIES COME TO ATTACK.
COCKY BASTARD ...
SO WE'RE HERE TO ASSIST YOU IN YOUR EFFORT.
...
I DON'T BUY IT.

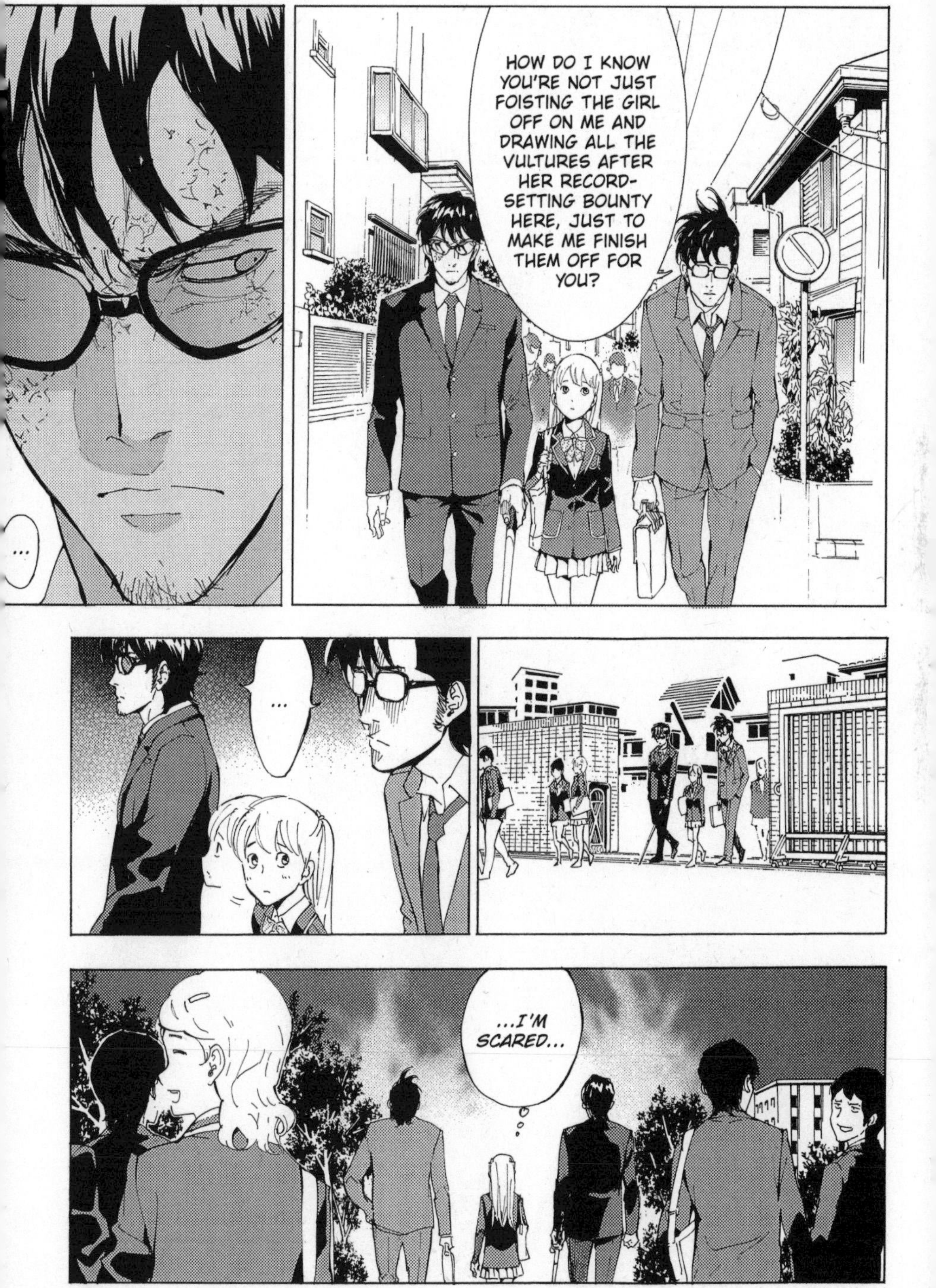
HOW DO I KNOW YOU'RE NOT JUST FOISTING THE GIRL OFF ON ME AND DRAWING ALL THE VULTURES AFTER HER RECORD-SETTING BOUNTY HERE, JUST TO MAKE ME FINISH THEM OFF FOR YOU?
...
...
...I'M SCARED...

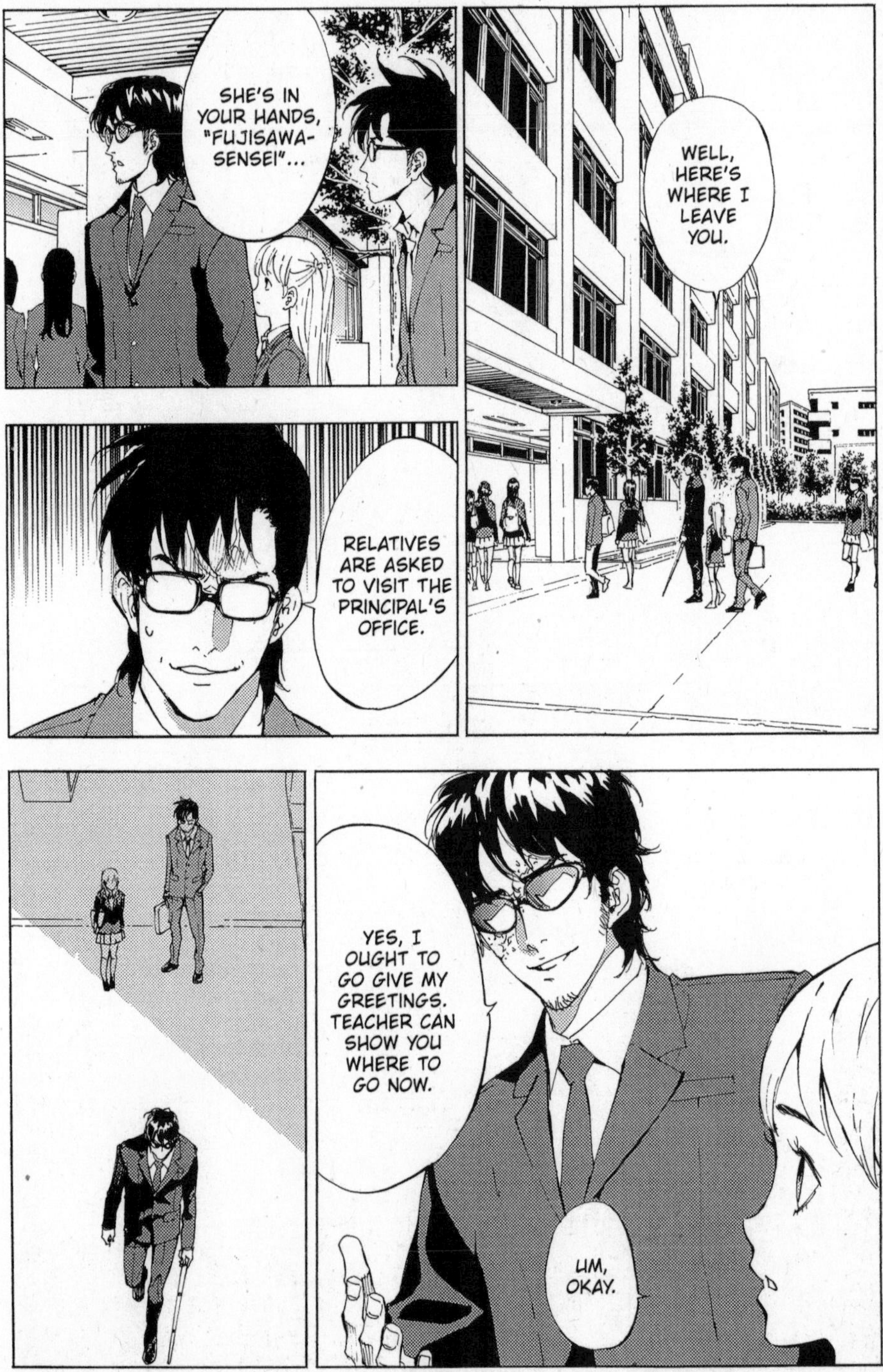
WELL, HERE'S WHERE I LEAVE YOU.
SHE'S IN YOUR HANDS, "FUJISAWA-SENSEI"...
RELATIVES ARE ASKED TO VISIT THE PRINCIPAL'S OFFICE.
YES, I OUGHT TO GO GIVE MY GREETINGS. TEACHER CAN SHOW YOU WHERE TO GO NOW.
UM, OKAY.

SO THIS IS HOW THE SON OF A BITCH GETS HIS PAYBACK...

...THERE'S ONE...

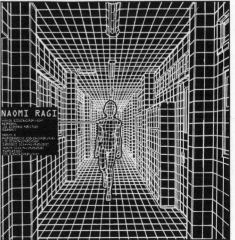

NAOMI RAGI

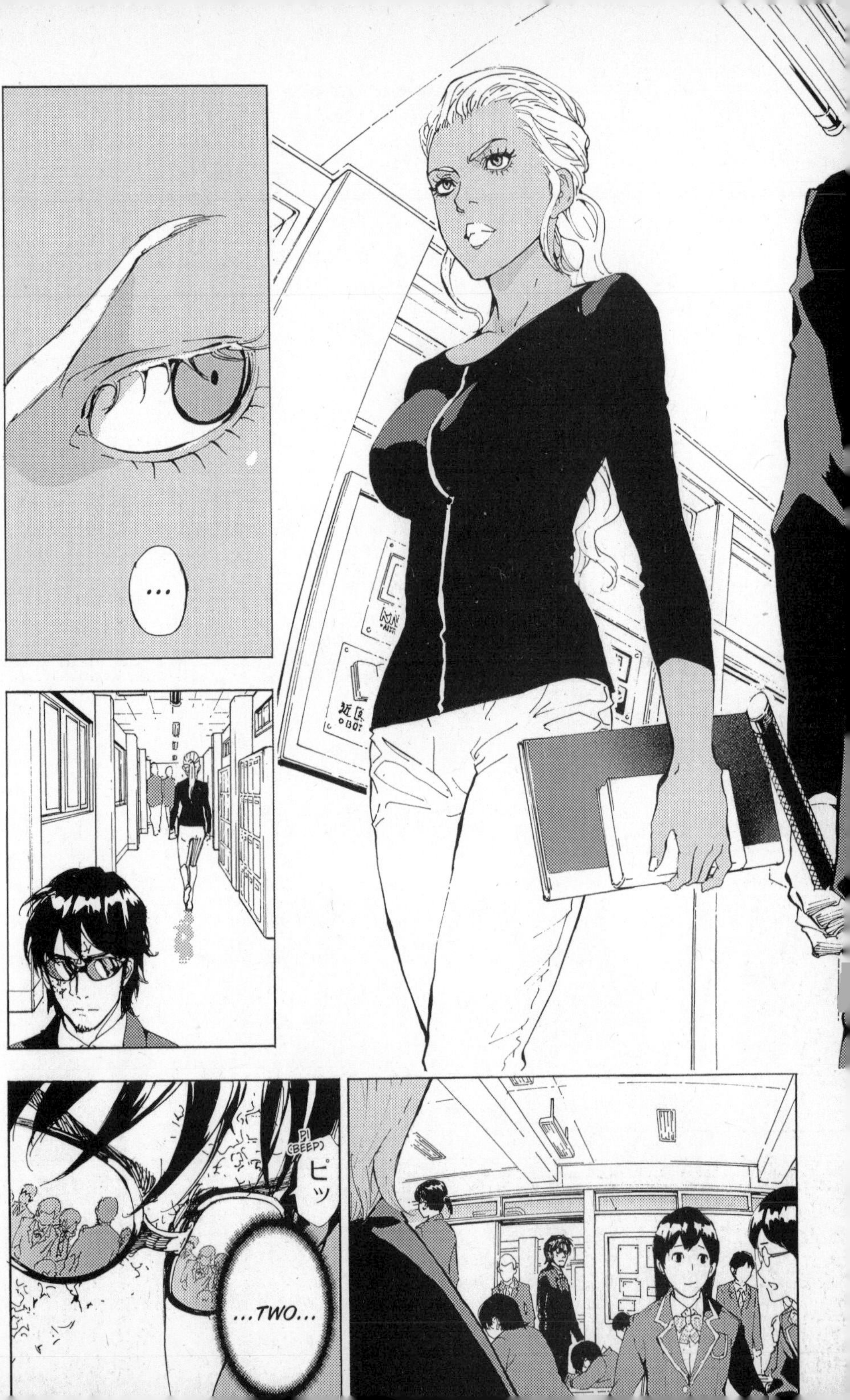
...
PI (BEEP)
ピッ
...TWO...

...

OJI KAIEDA

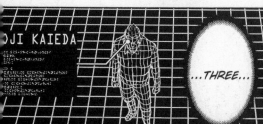

...THREE...

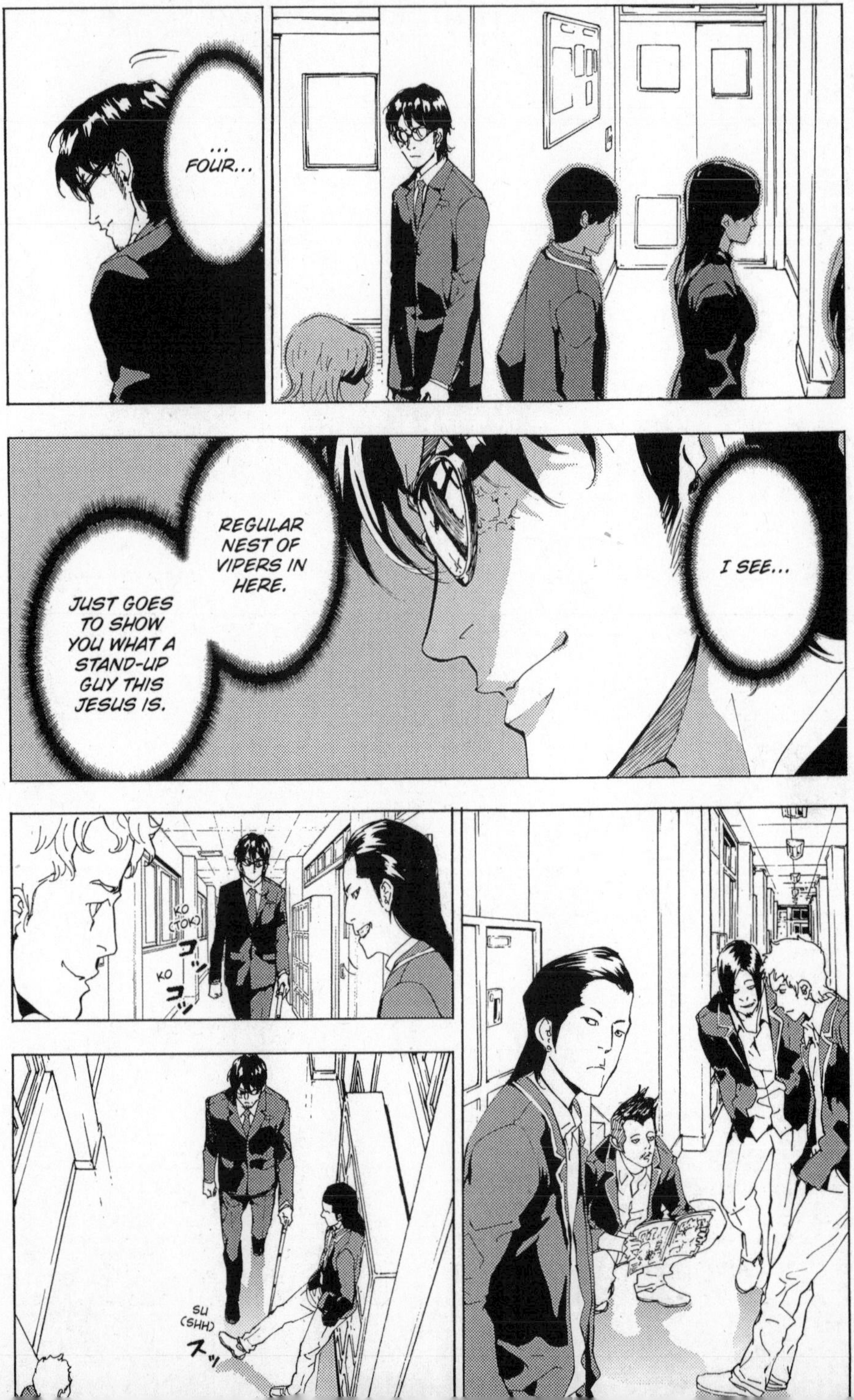
... FOUR...
I SEE...
REGULAR NEST OF VIPERS IN HERE.
JUST GOES TO SHOW YOU WHAT A STAND-UP GUY THIS JESUS IS.
KO (TOK)
コッ
KO
コッ
SU (SHH)
スッ

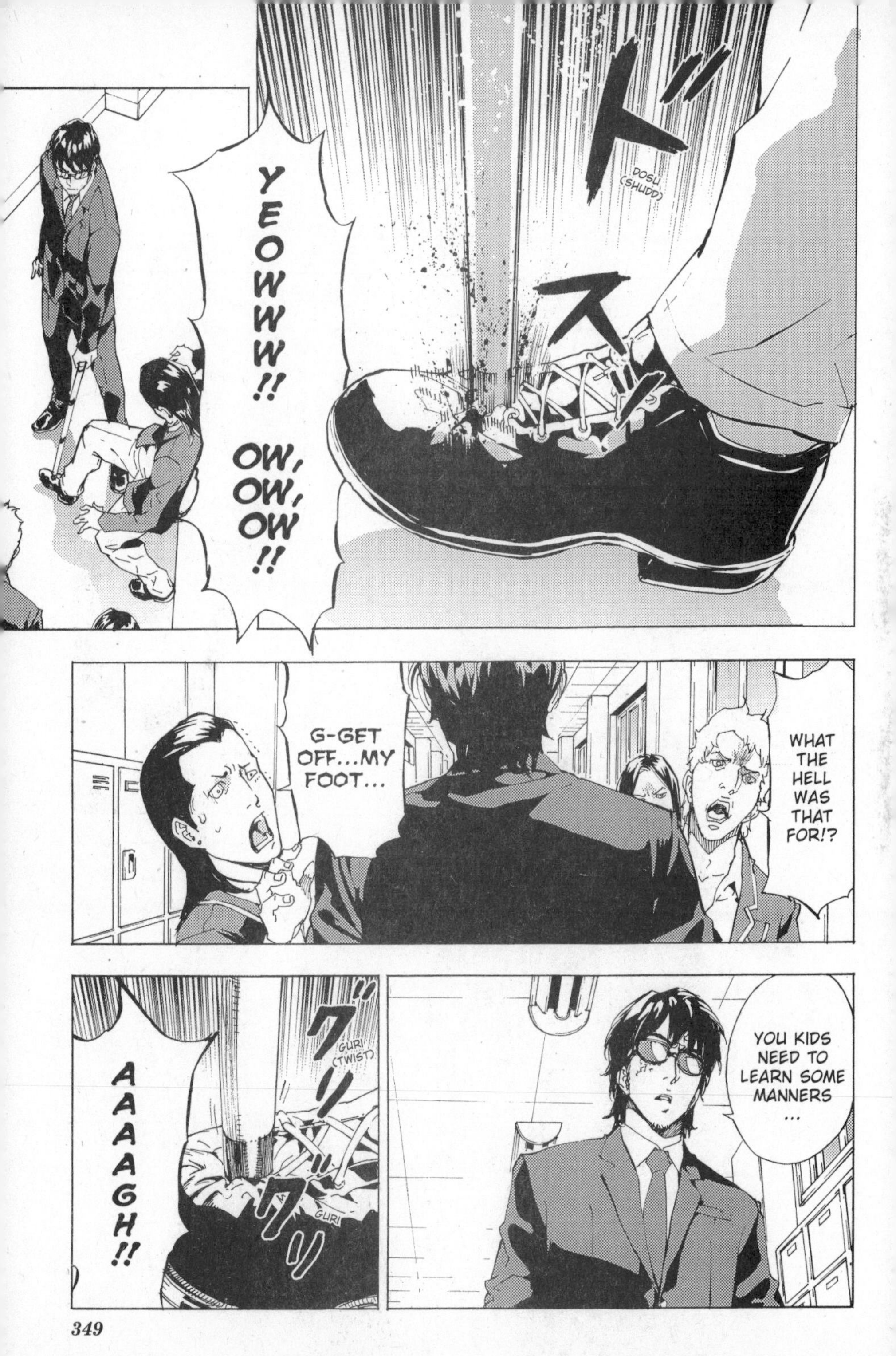

DOSU (SHUDD)
YEOWWWW!!
OW, OW, OW!!
WHAT THE HELL WAS THAT FOR!?
G-GET OFF...MY FOOT...
YOU KIDS NEED TO LEARN SOME MANNERS ...
GURI (TWIST)
AAAAAGH!!
GURI

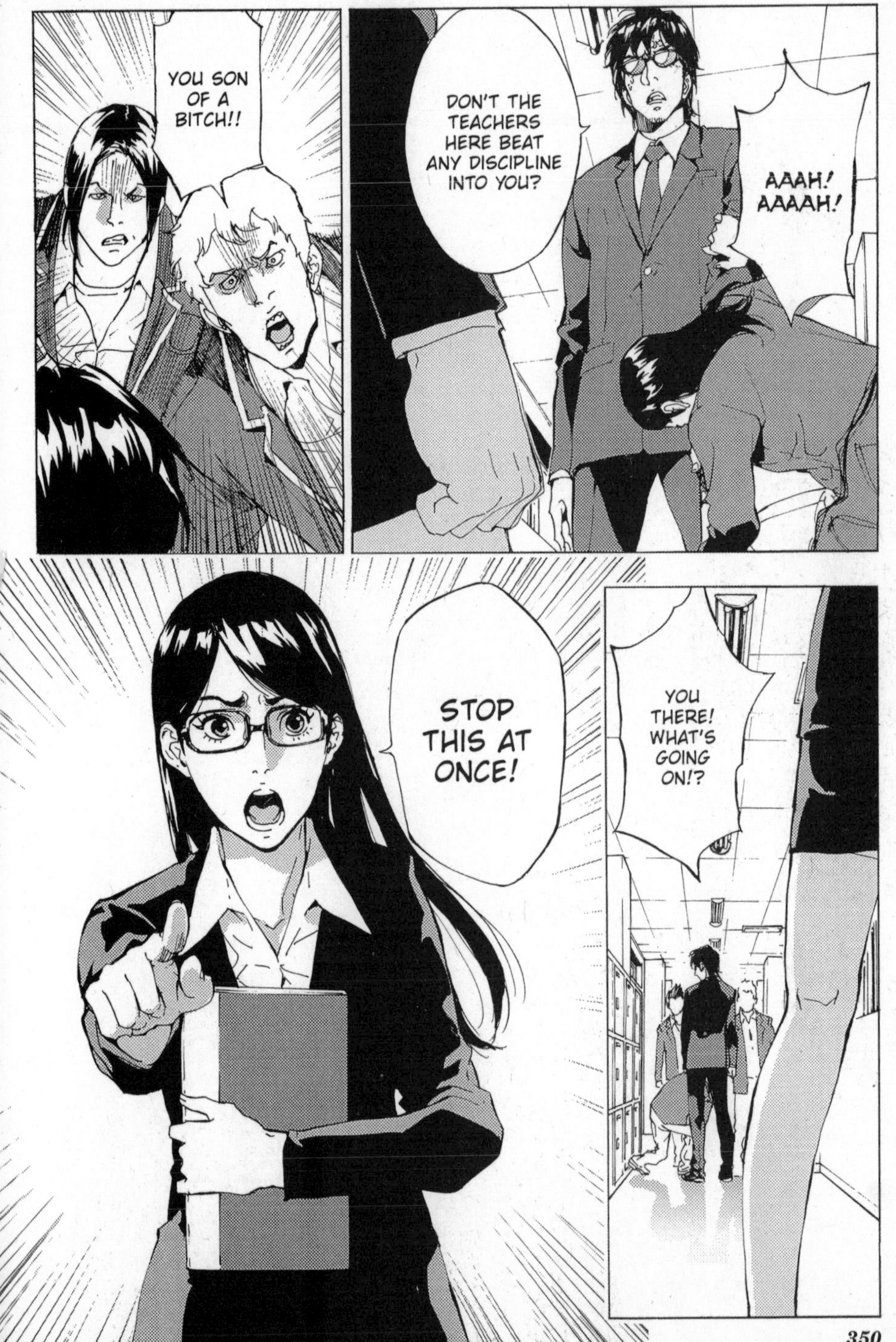
AAAH! AAAAH!
DON'T THE TEACHERS HERE BEAT ANY DISCIPLINE INTO YOU?
YOU SON OF A BITCH!!
YOU THERE! WHAT'S GOING ON!?
STOP THIS AT ONCE!

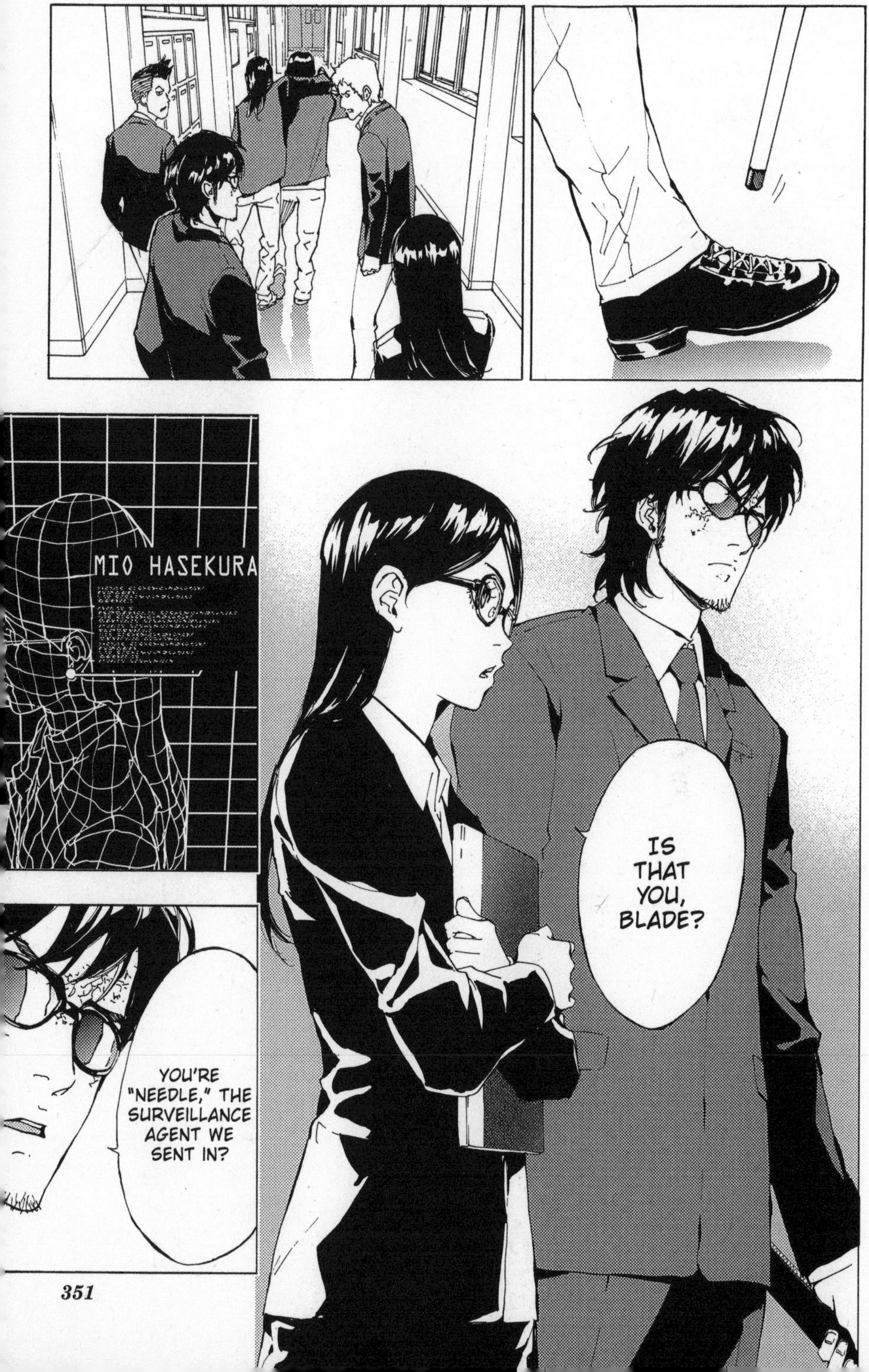
IS THAT YOU, BLADE?
MIO HASEKURA
YOU'RE "NEEDLE," THE SURVEILLANCE AGENT WE SENT IN?

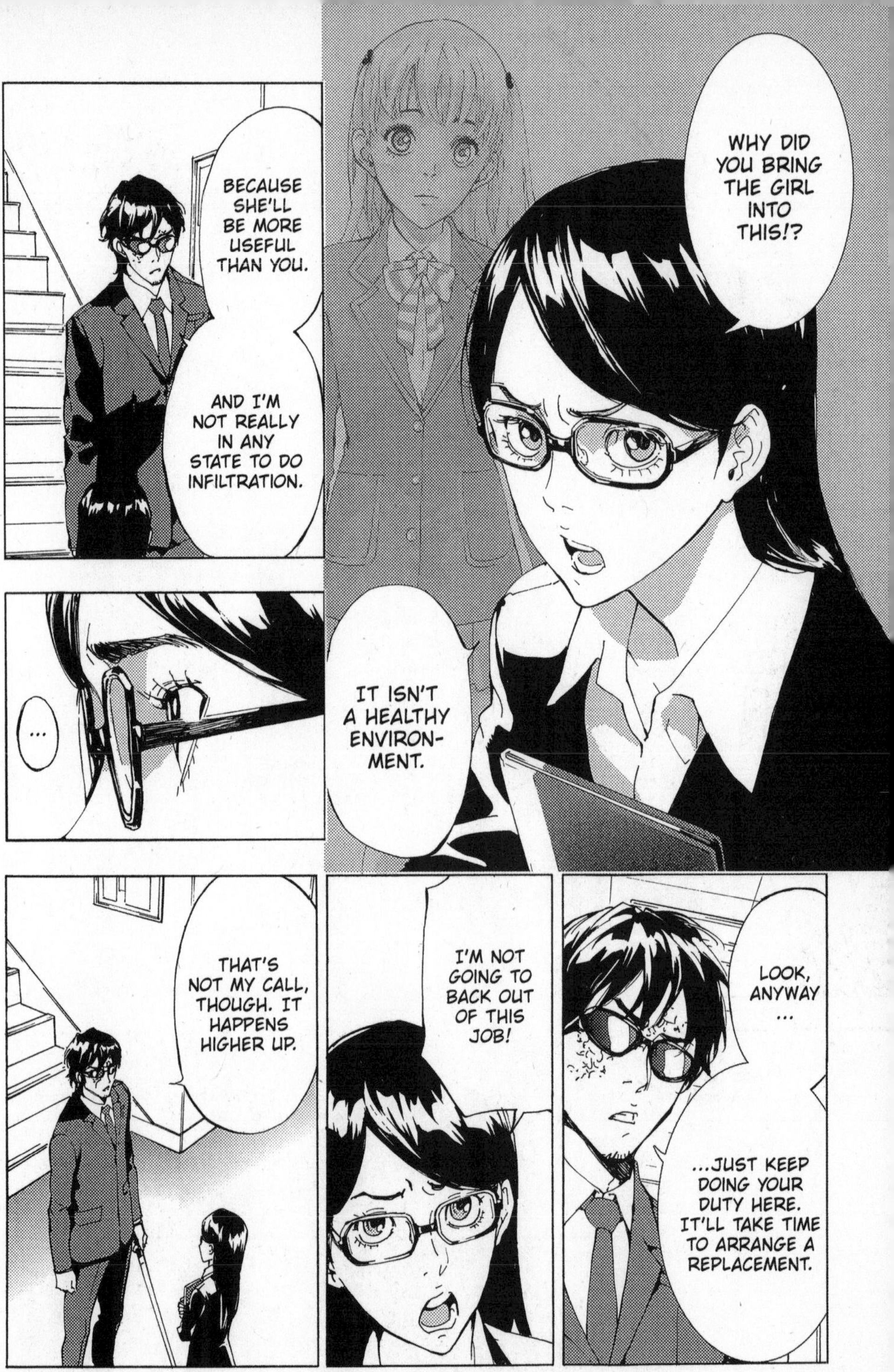
WHY DID YOU BRING THE GIRL INTO THIS!?
IT ISN'T A HEALTHY ENVIRONMENT.
BECAUSE SHE'LL BE MORE USEFUL THAN YOU.
AND I'M NOT REALLY IN ANY STATE TO DO INFILTRATION.
...
LOOK, ANYWAY ...
...JUST KEEP DOING YOUR DUTY HERE. IT'LL TAKE TIME TO ARRANGE A REPLACEMENT.
I'M NOT GOING TO BACK OUT OF THIS JOB!
THAT'S NOT MY CALL, THOUGH. IT HAPPENS HIGHER UP.

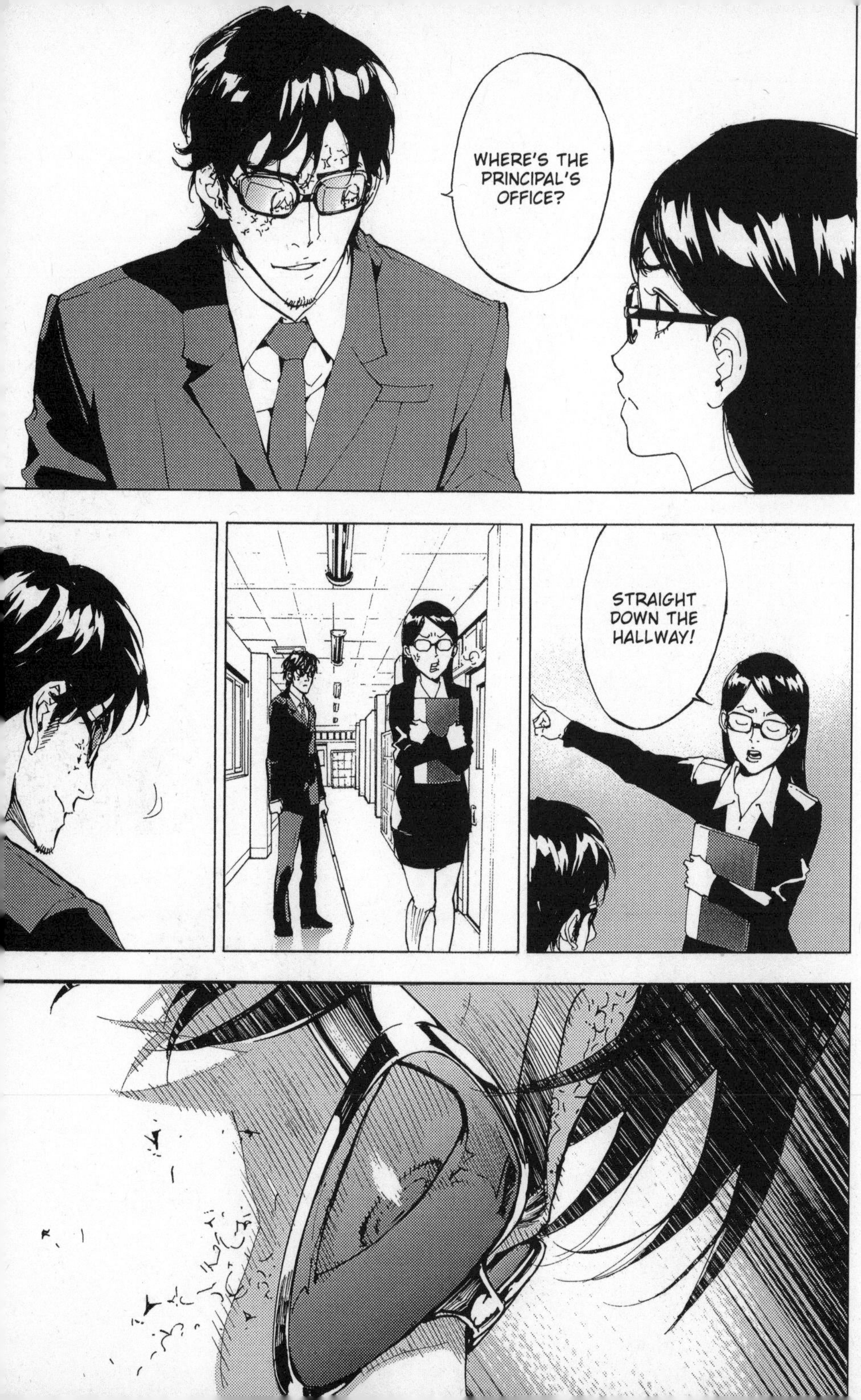
WHERE'S THE PRINCIPAL'S OFFICE?
STRAIGHT DOWN THE HALLWAY!

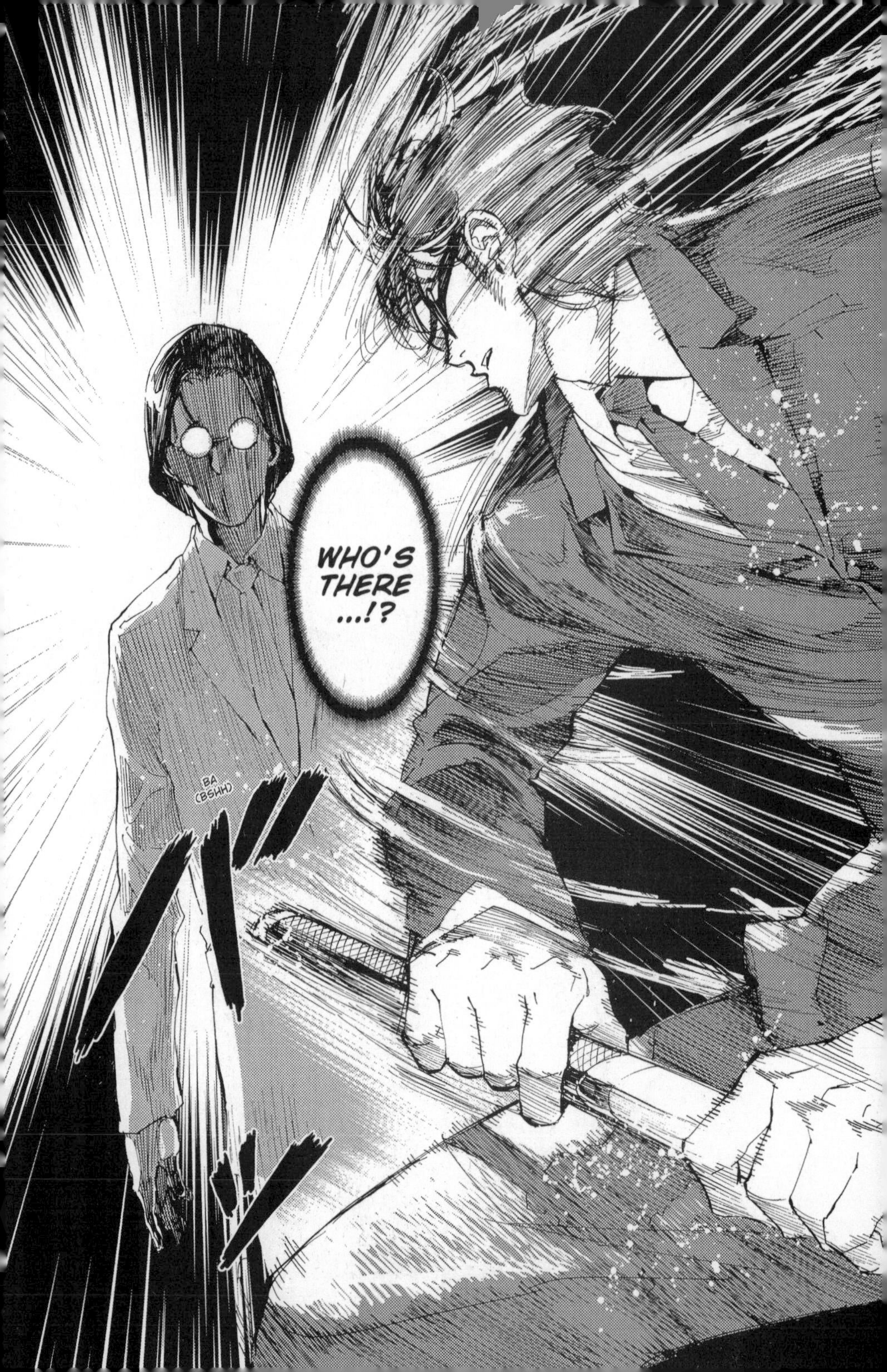
WHO'S THERE ...!?
BA (BSHH)

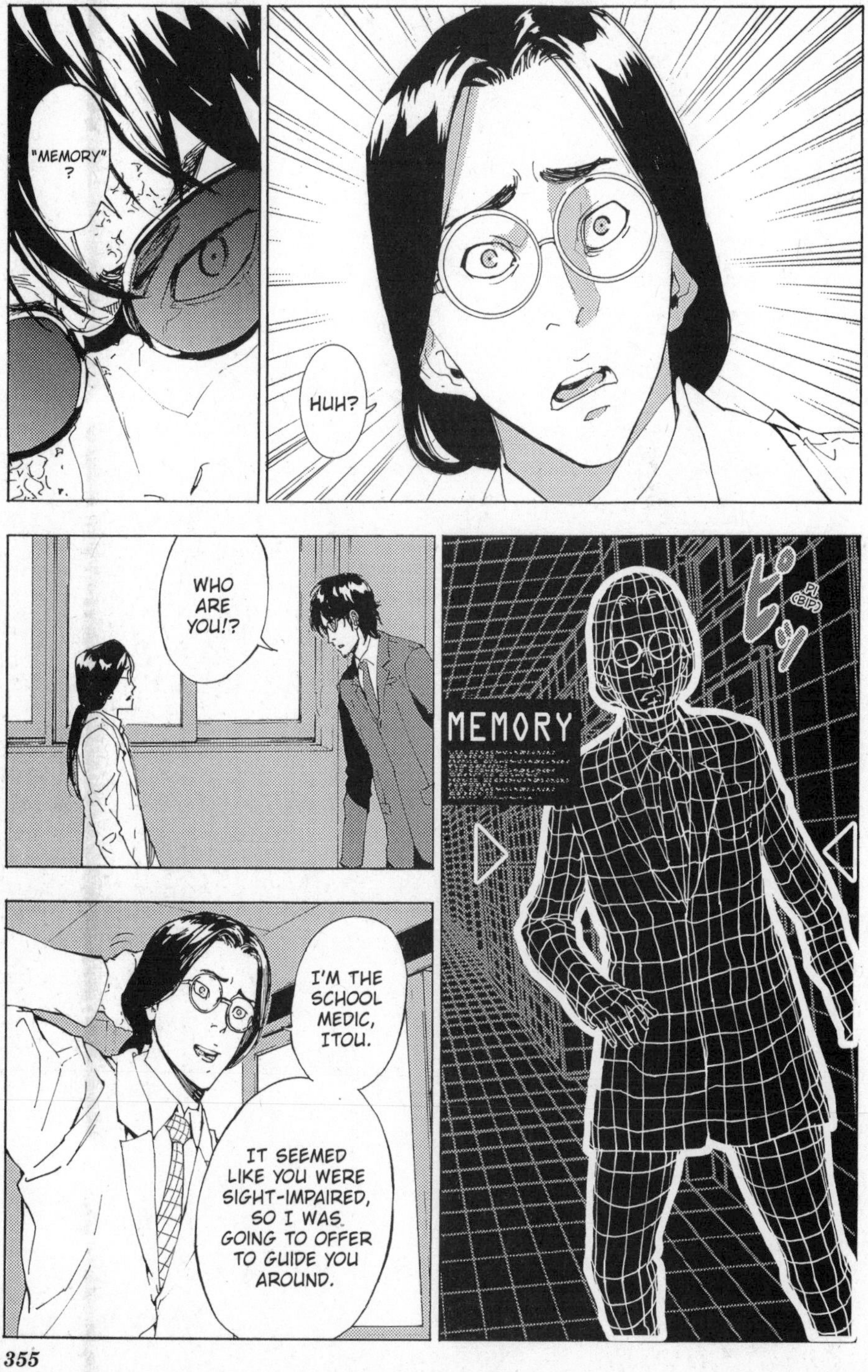
HUH?
"MEMORY"?
ピッ
PI. (BIP)
MEMORY
WHO ARE YOU!?
I'M THE SCHOOL MEDIC, ITOU.
IT SEEMED LIKE YOU WERE SIGHT-IMPAIRED, SO I WAS GOING TO OFFER TO GUIDE YOU AROUND.

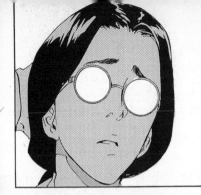

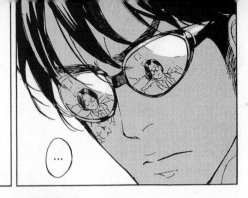

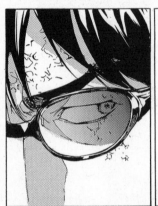

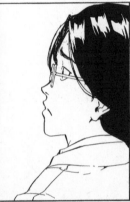

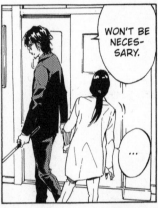

...
WON'T BE NECES-SARY.
...
...A FIFTH!? HE TOTALLY SLIPPED IN BEHIND ME UNDER MY RADAR.
THAT'S RIGHT, OUR AGENTS MENTIONED HIM IN THE REPORT. BUT I WASN'T EXPECTING A MAN OF THAT CALIBER ...

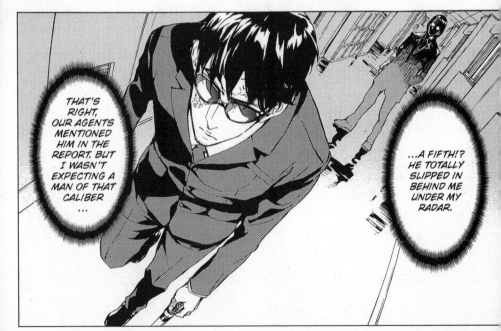

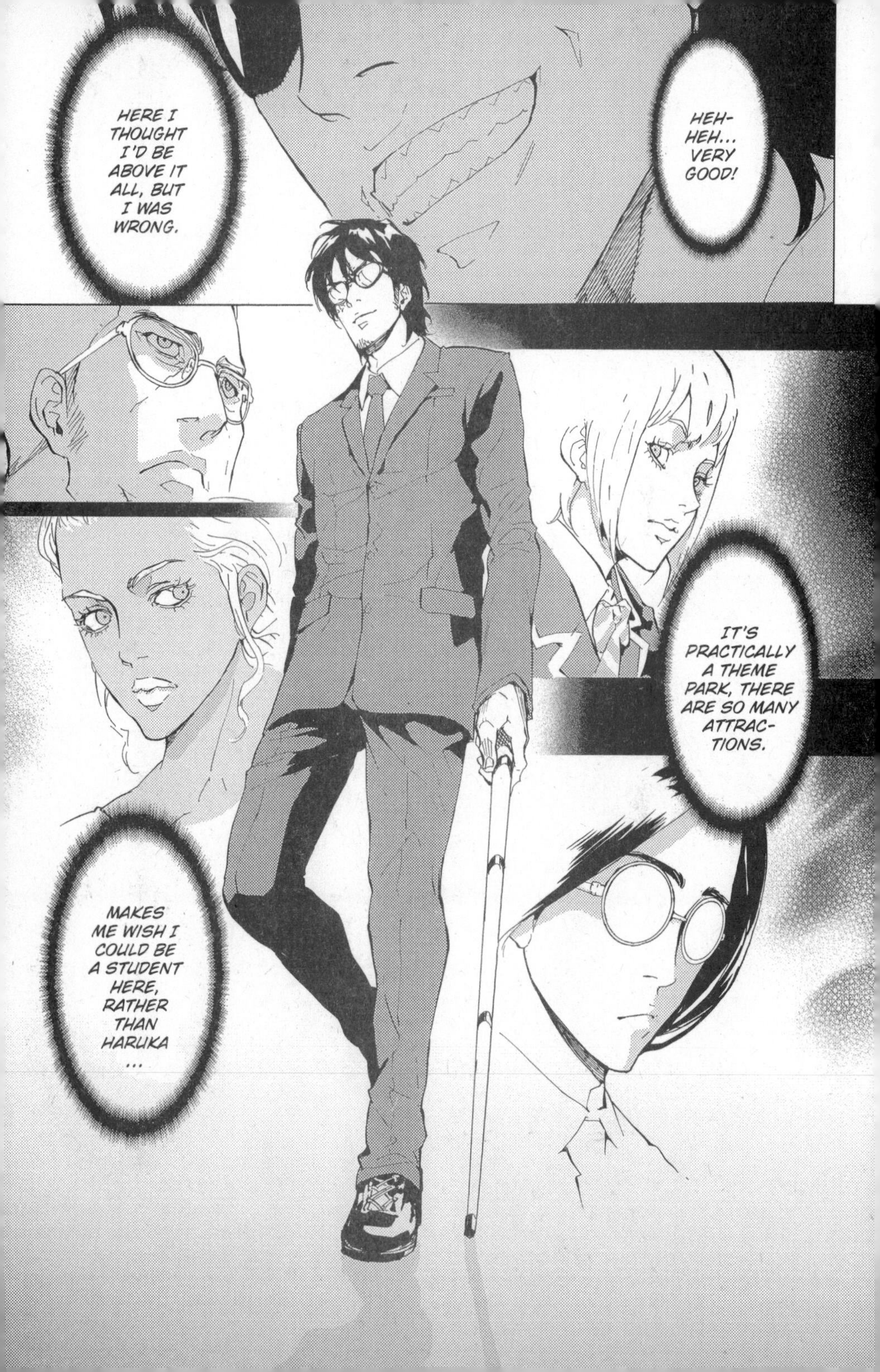
HEH-HEH... VERY GOOD!
HERE I THOUGHT I'D BE ABOVE IT ALL, BUT I WAS WRONG.
IT'S PRACTICALLY A THEME PARK, THERE ARE SO MANY ATTRACTIONS.
MAKES ME WISH I COULD BE A STUDENT HERE, RATHER THAN HARUKA...

...WHAT SHOULD I DO...?

...

MORNING.

GOOD MORNING!

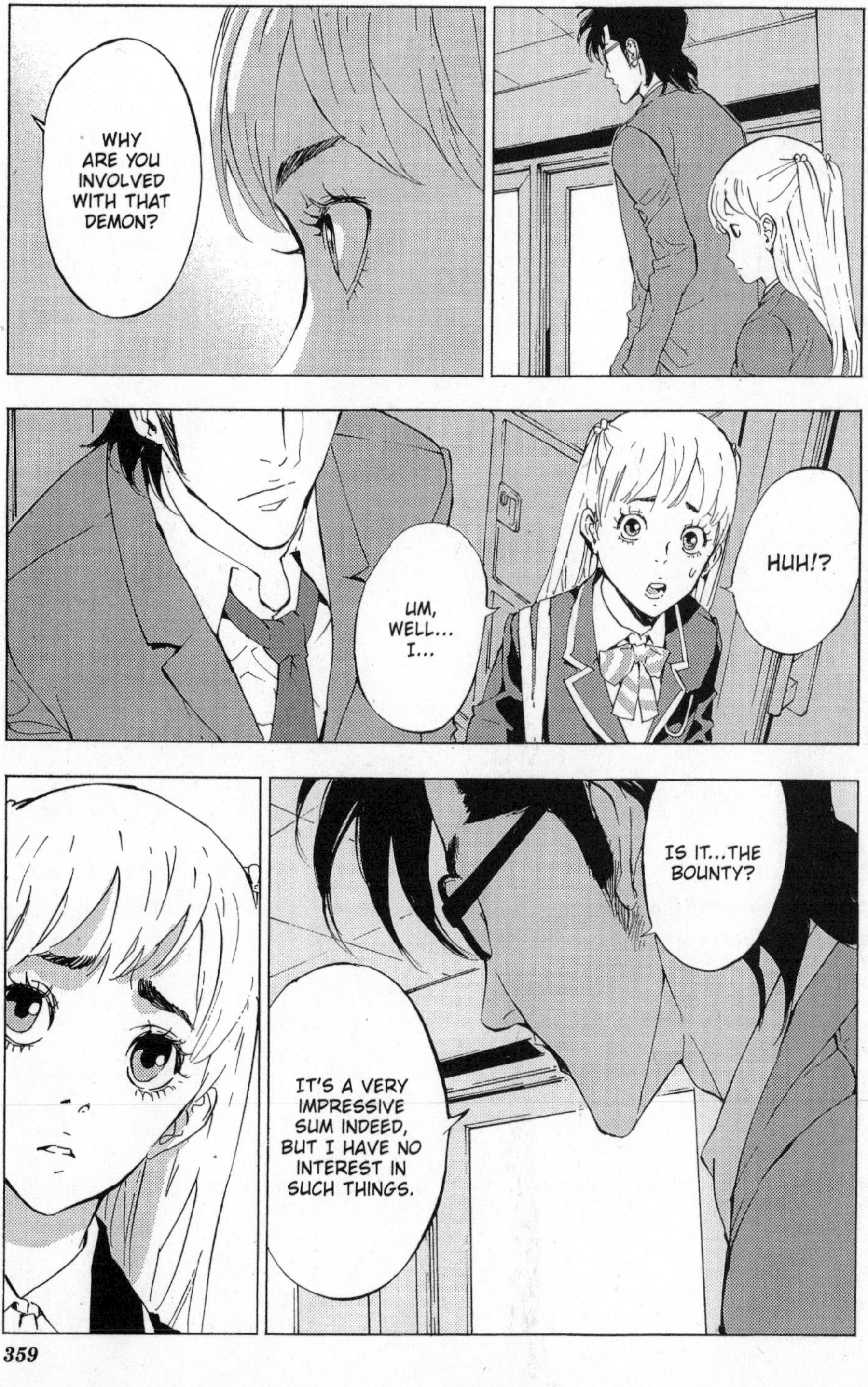
WHY ARE YOU INVOLVED WITH THAT DEMON?
HUH!?
UM, WELL... I...
IS IT...THE BOUNTY?
IT'S A VERY IMPRESSIVE SUM INDEED, BUT I HAVE NO INTEREST IN SUCH THINGS.

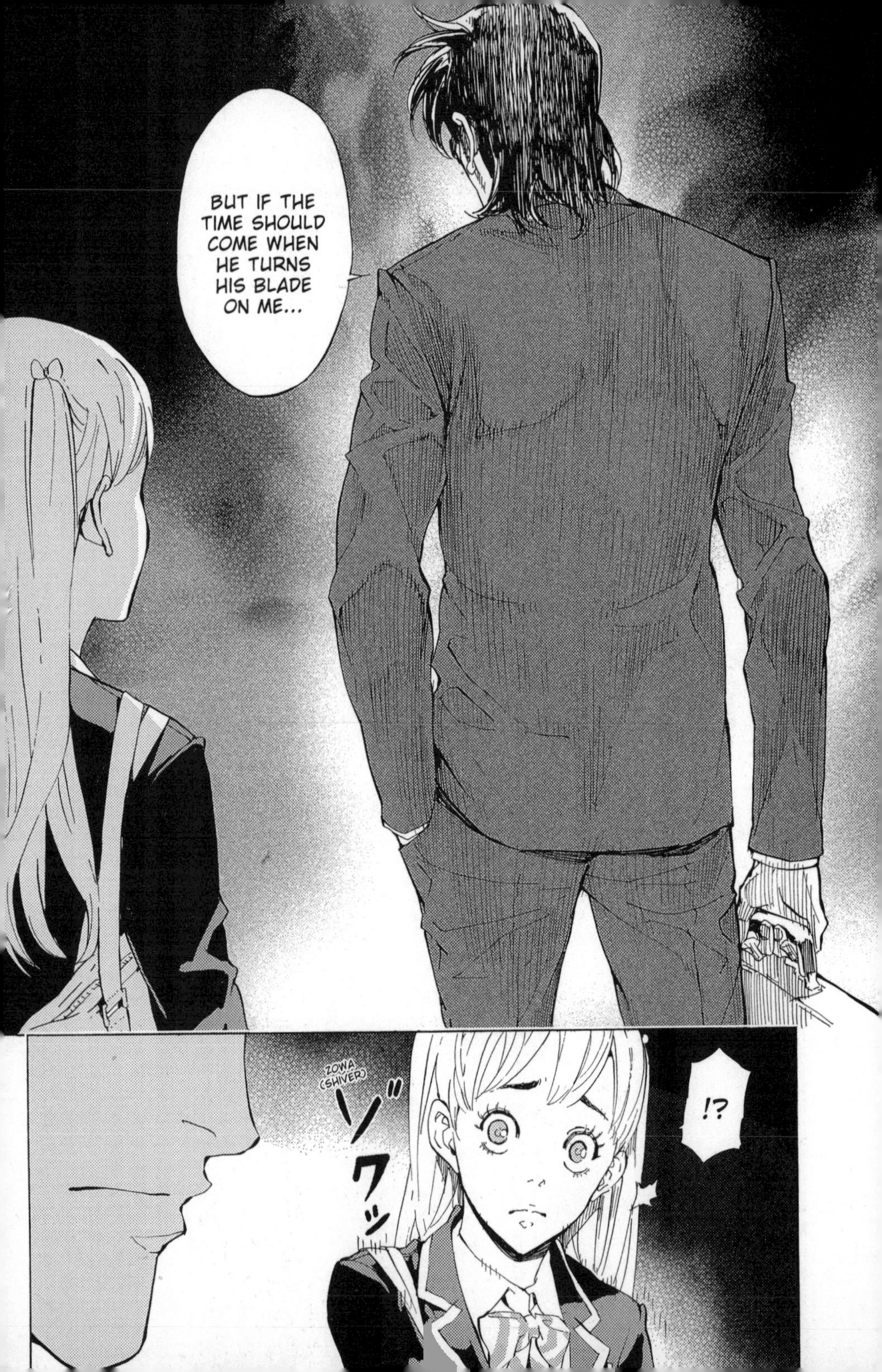
BUT IF THE TIME SHOULD COME WHEN HE TURNS HIS BLADE ON ME...
!?
ZOWA (SHIVER)
ゾワッ

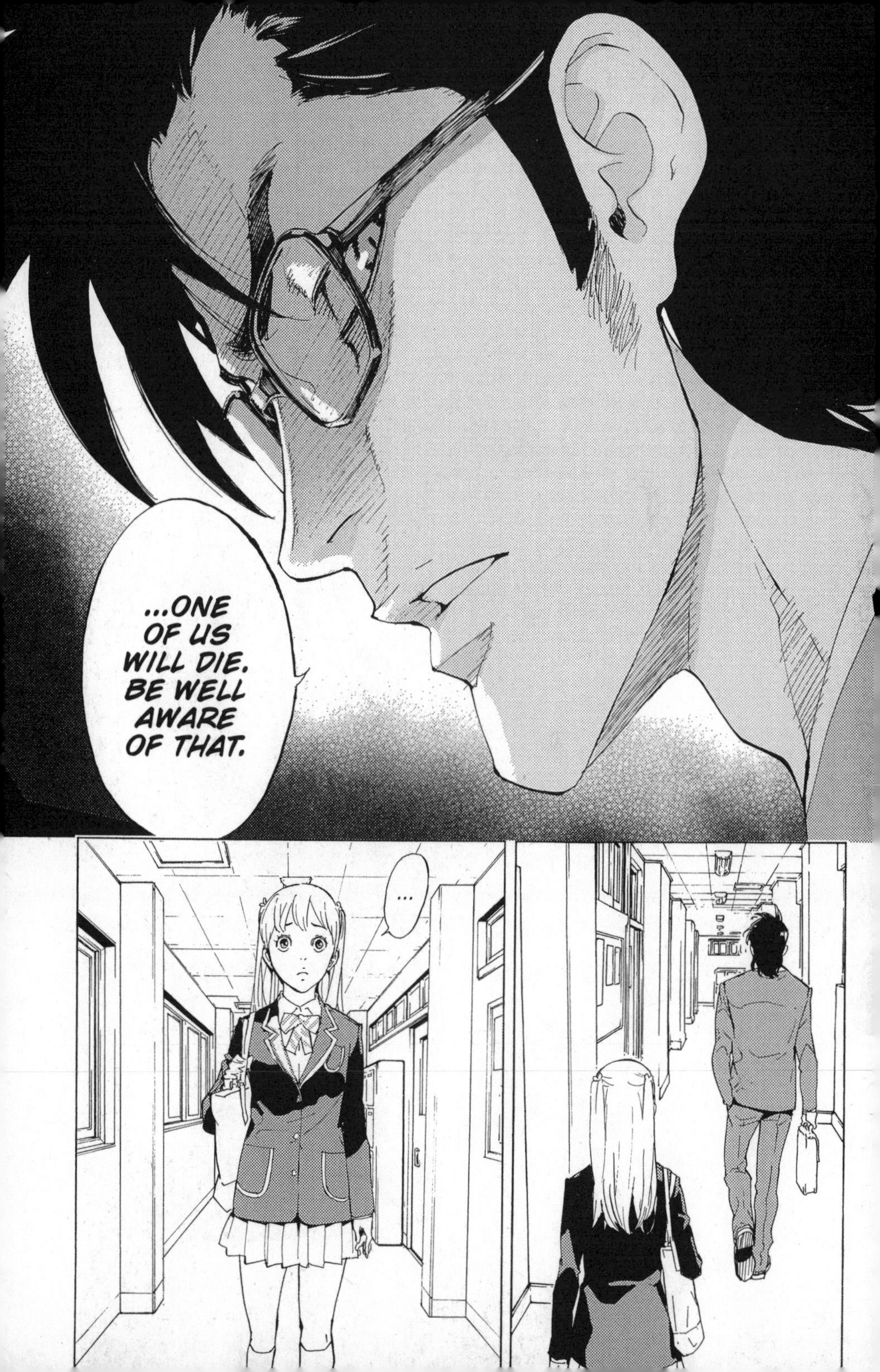
...ONE OF US WILL DIE. BE WELL AWARE OF THAT.
...

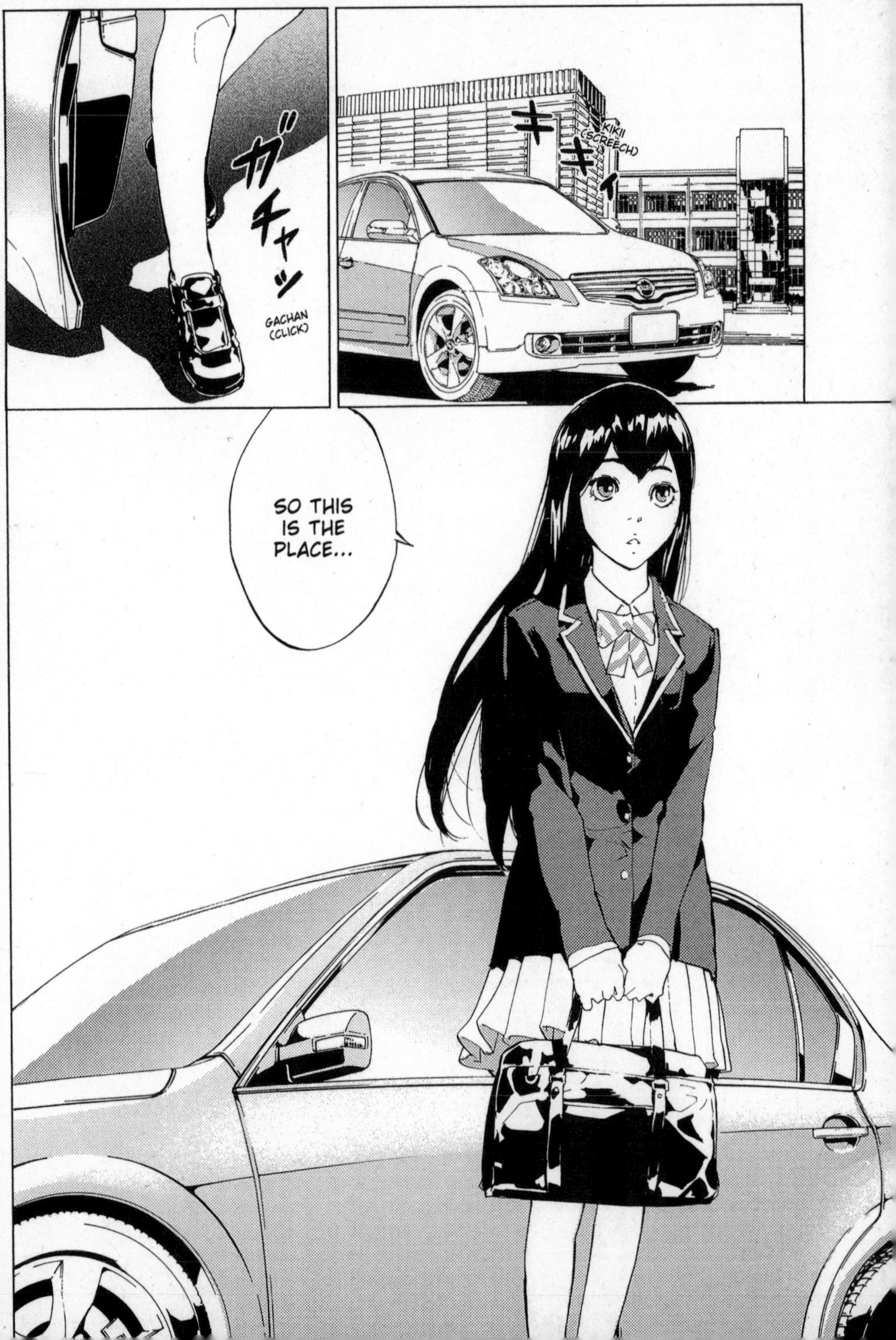
キキイ
KIKII (SCREECH)
ガチャッ
GACHAN (CLICK)
SO THIS IS THE PLACE...

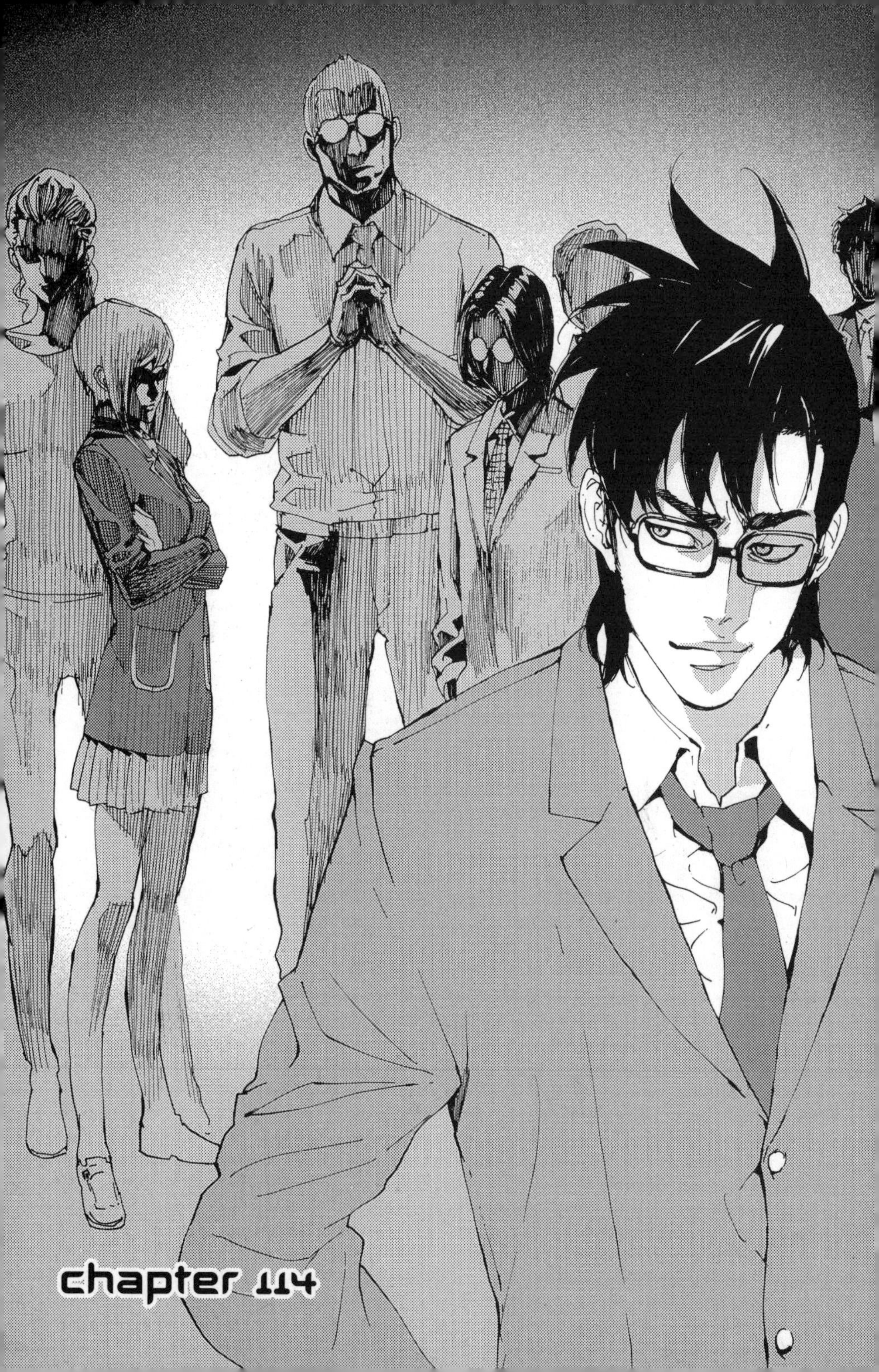
chapter 114

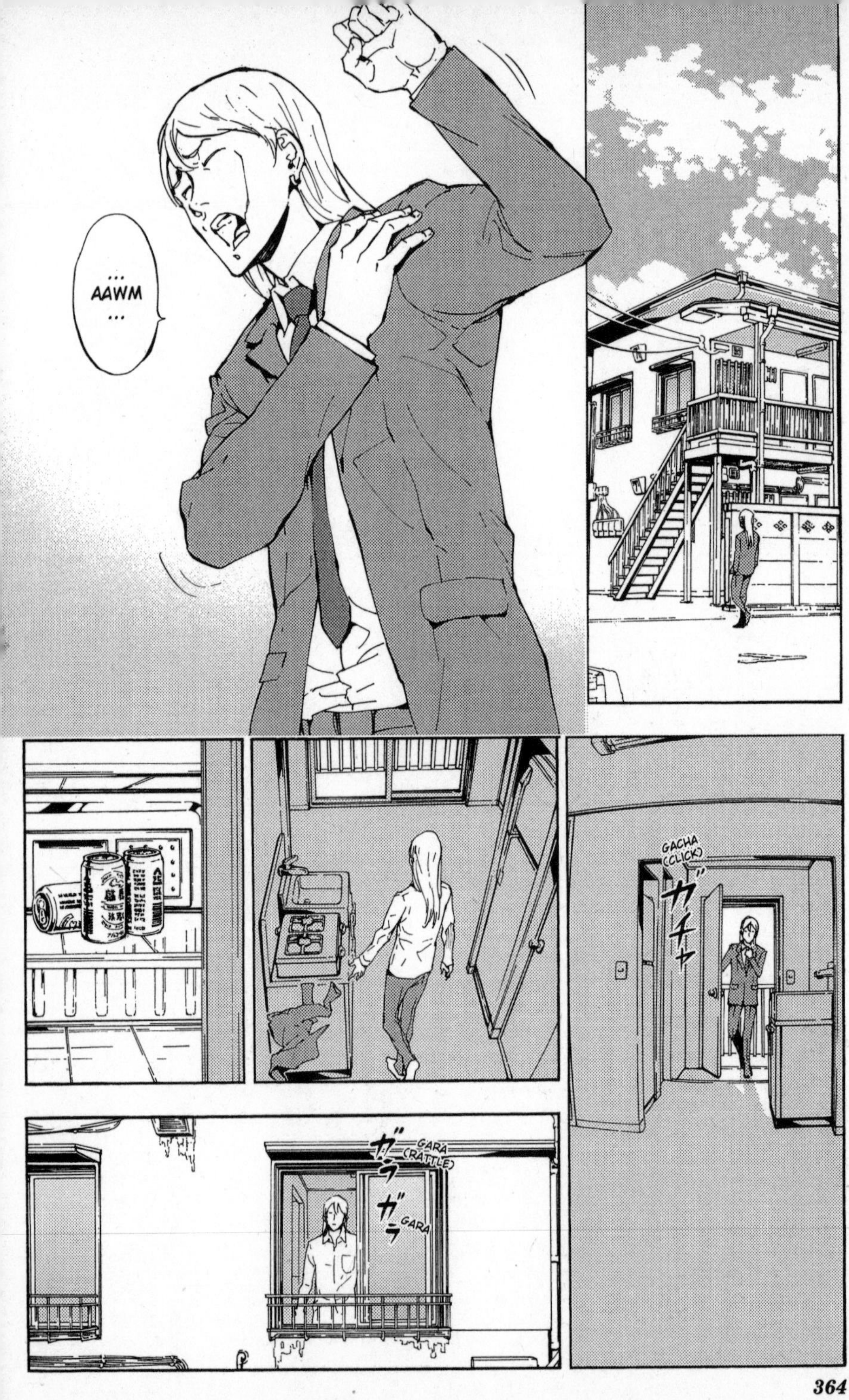

... AAWM ...
GACHA (CLICK)
ガチャ
GARA (RATTLE)
ガラ
GARA
ガラ

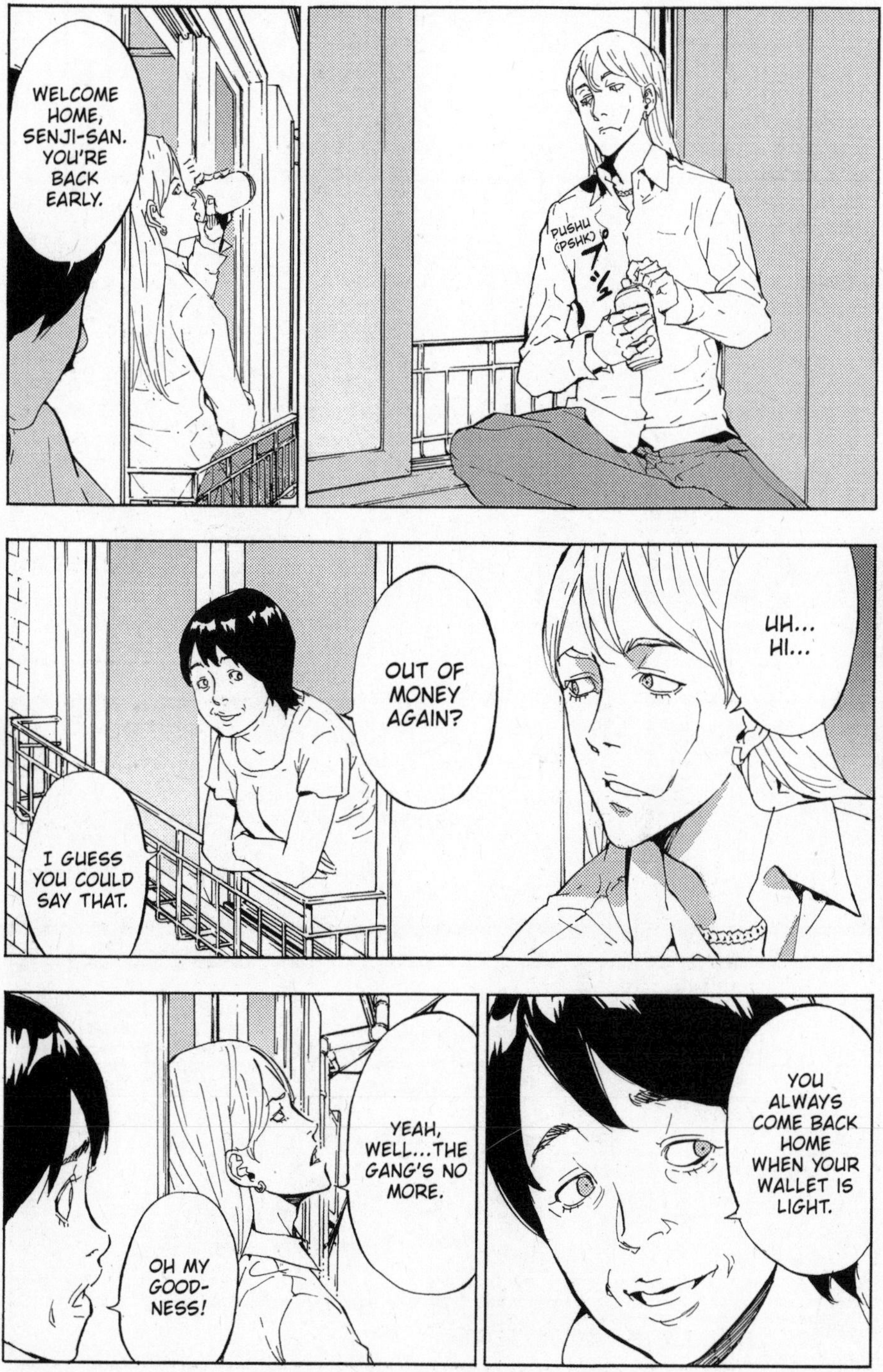
PUSHU (PSHK)
WELCOME HOME, SENJI-SAN. YOU'RE BACK EARLY.
UH... HI...
OUT OF MONEY AGAIN?
I GUESS YOU COULD SAY THAT.
YOU ALWAYS COME BACK HOME WHEN YOUR WALLET IS LIGHT.
YEAH, WELL...THE GANG'S NO MORE.
OH MY GOOD-NESS!

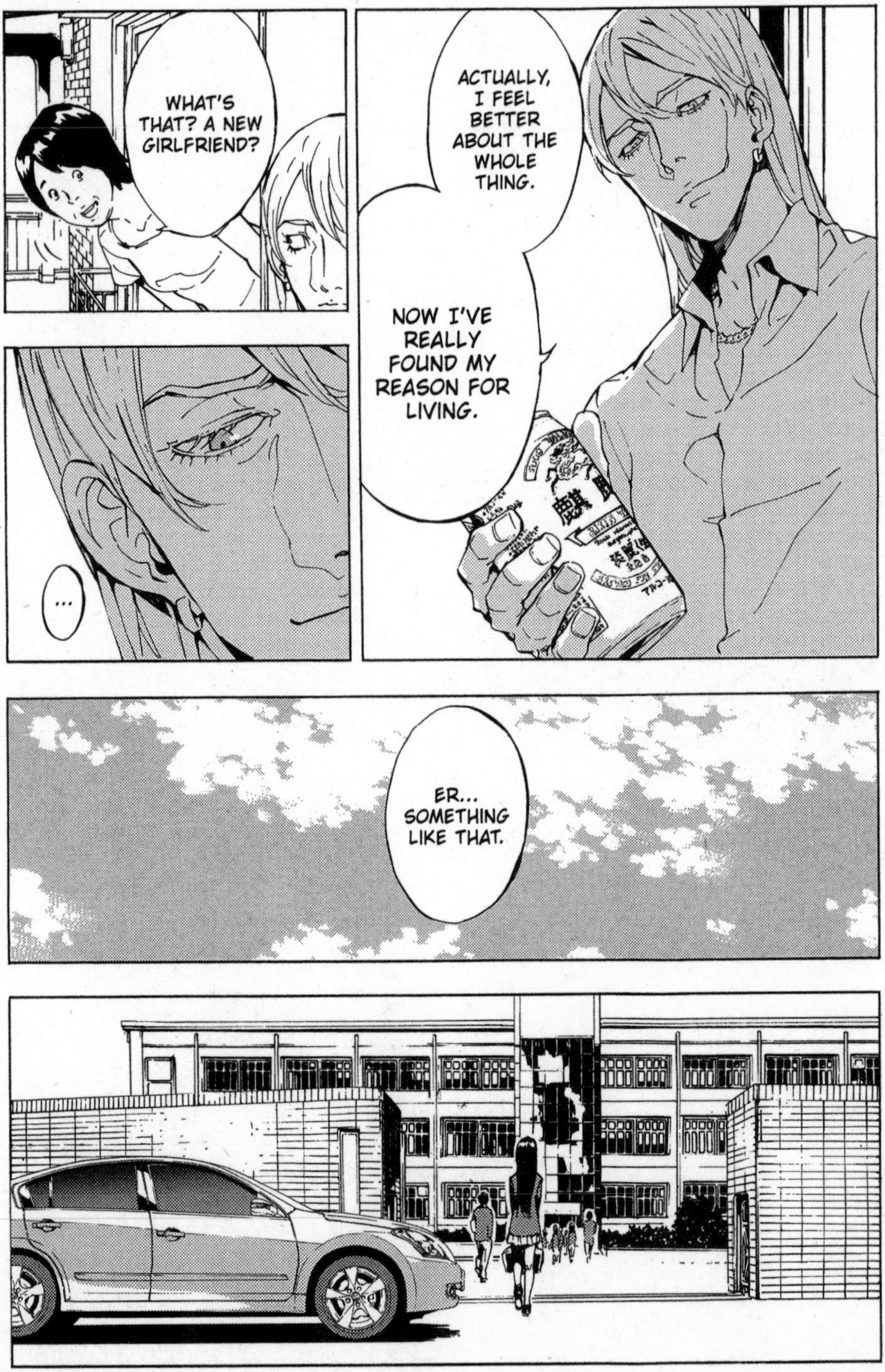
ACTUALLY, I FEEL BETTER ABOUT THE WHOLE THING.
NOW I'VE REALLY FOUND MY REASON FOR LIVING.
WHAT'S THAT? A NEW GIRLFRIEND?
...
ER... SOMETHING LIKE THAT.

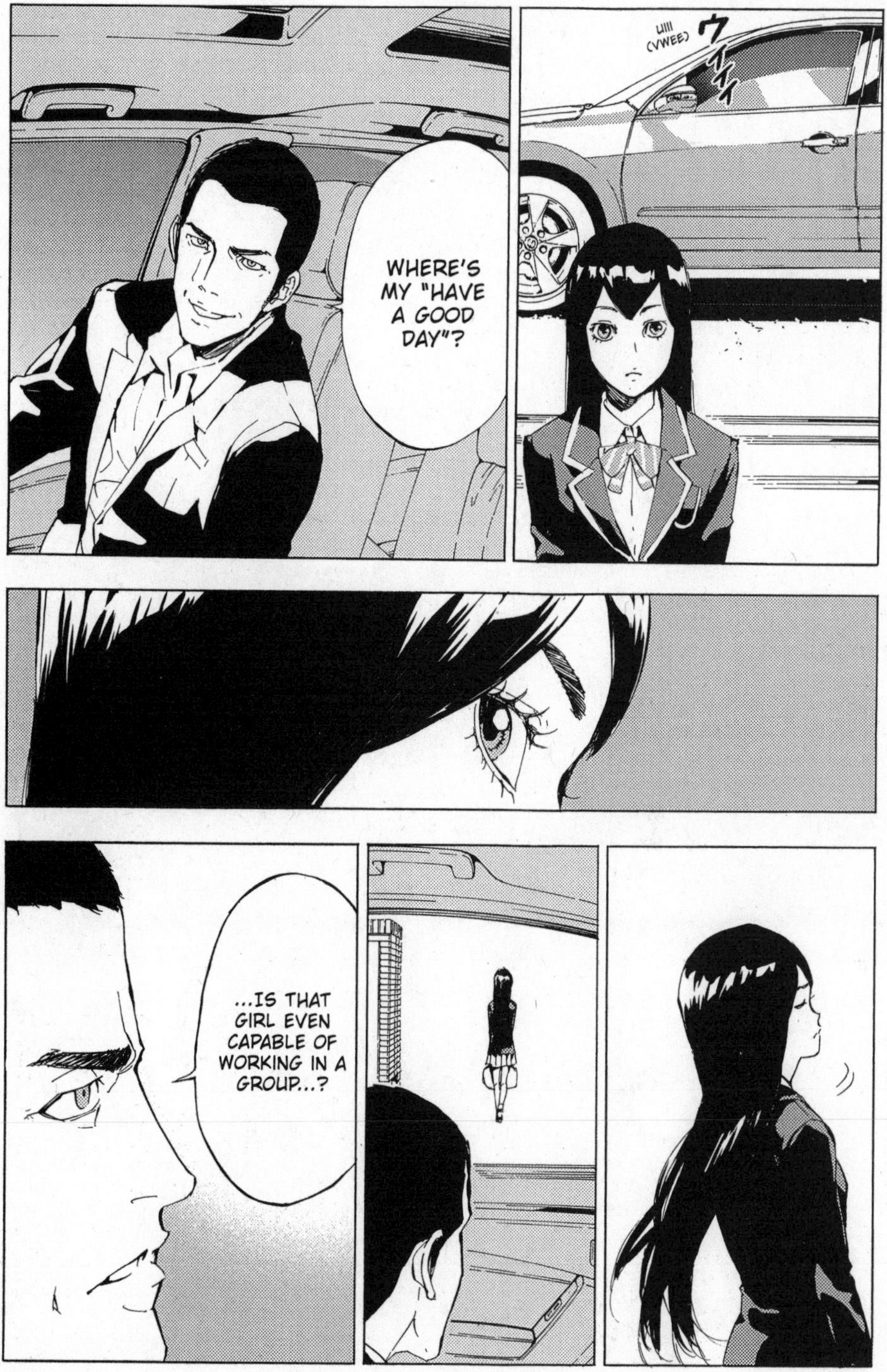
UIII (VWEE)
ウィィィ
WHERE'S MY "HAVE A GOOD DAY"?
...IS THAT GIRL EVEN CAPABLE OF WORKING IN A GROUP...?

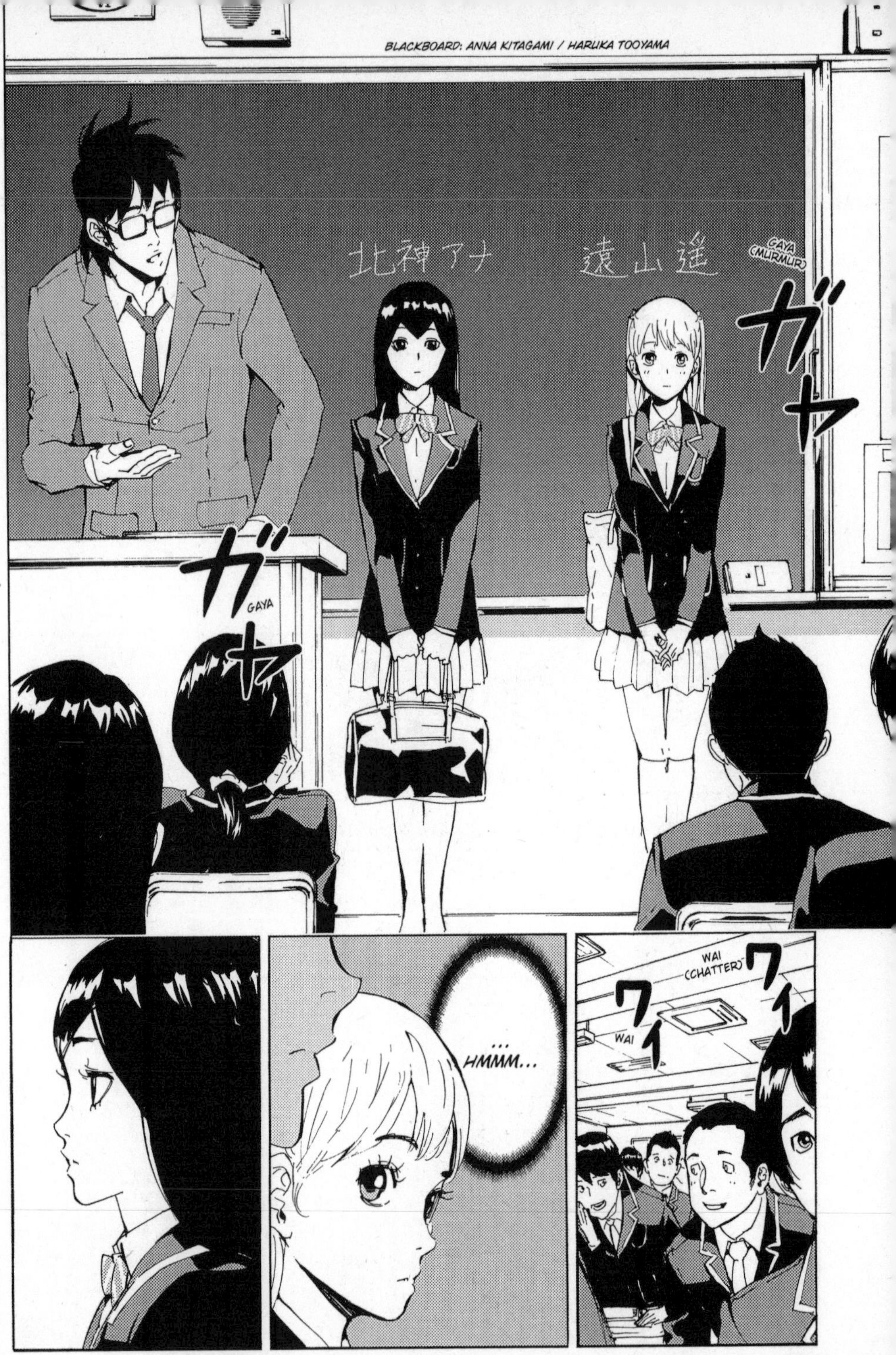
BLACKBOARD: ANNA KITAGAMI / HARUKA TOOYAMA
北神アナ
遠山遥
GAYA (MURMUR)
ガヤ
ガヤ
GAYA
WAI (CHATTER)
ワイ
WAI
ワイ
... HMMM...

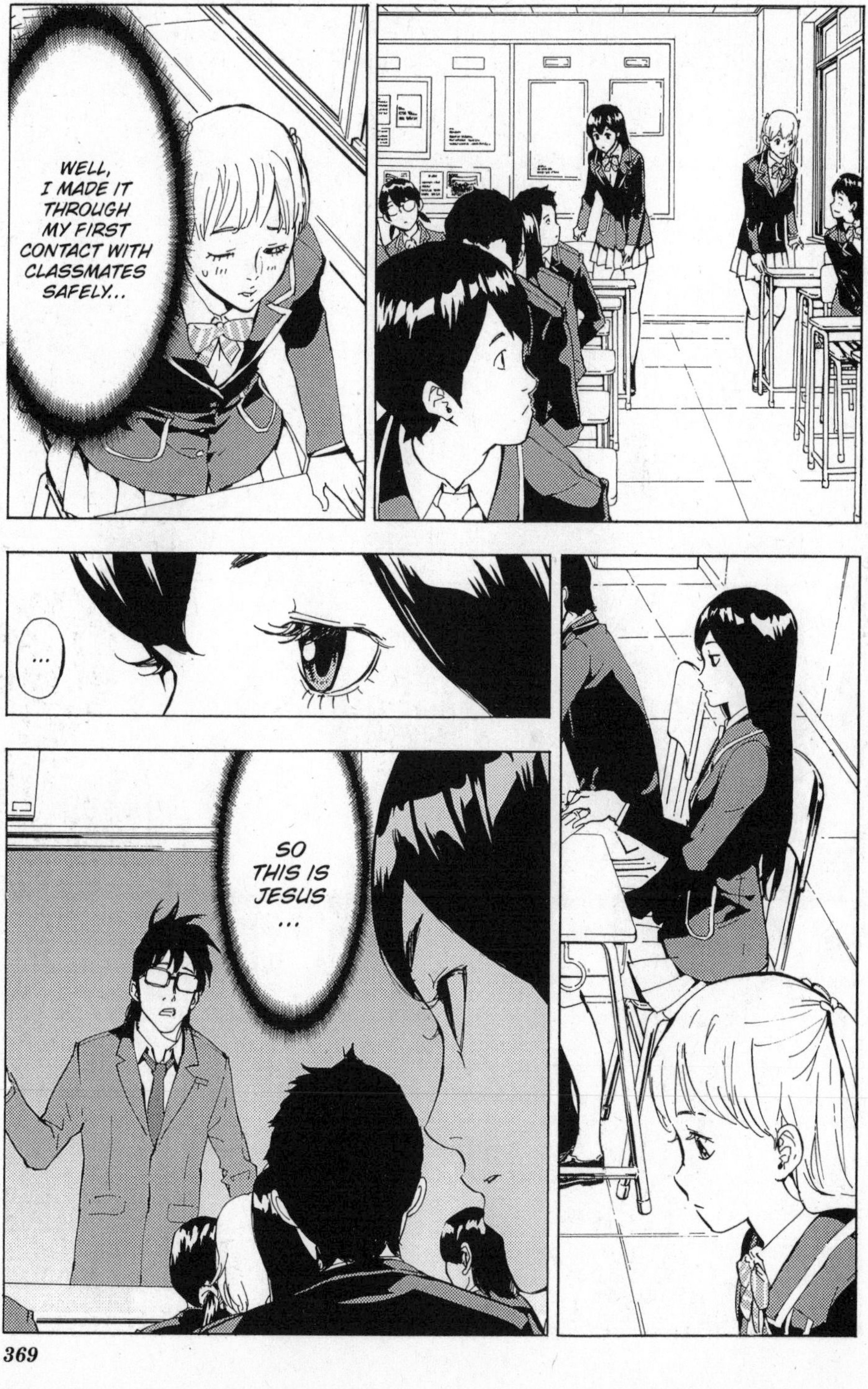
WELL, I MADE IT THROUGH MY FIRST CONTACT WITH CLASSMATES SAFELY...
...
SO THIS IS JESUS ...

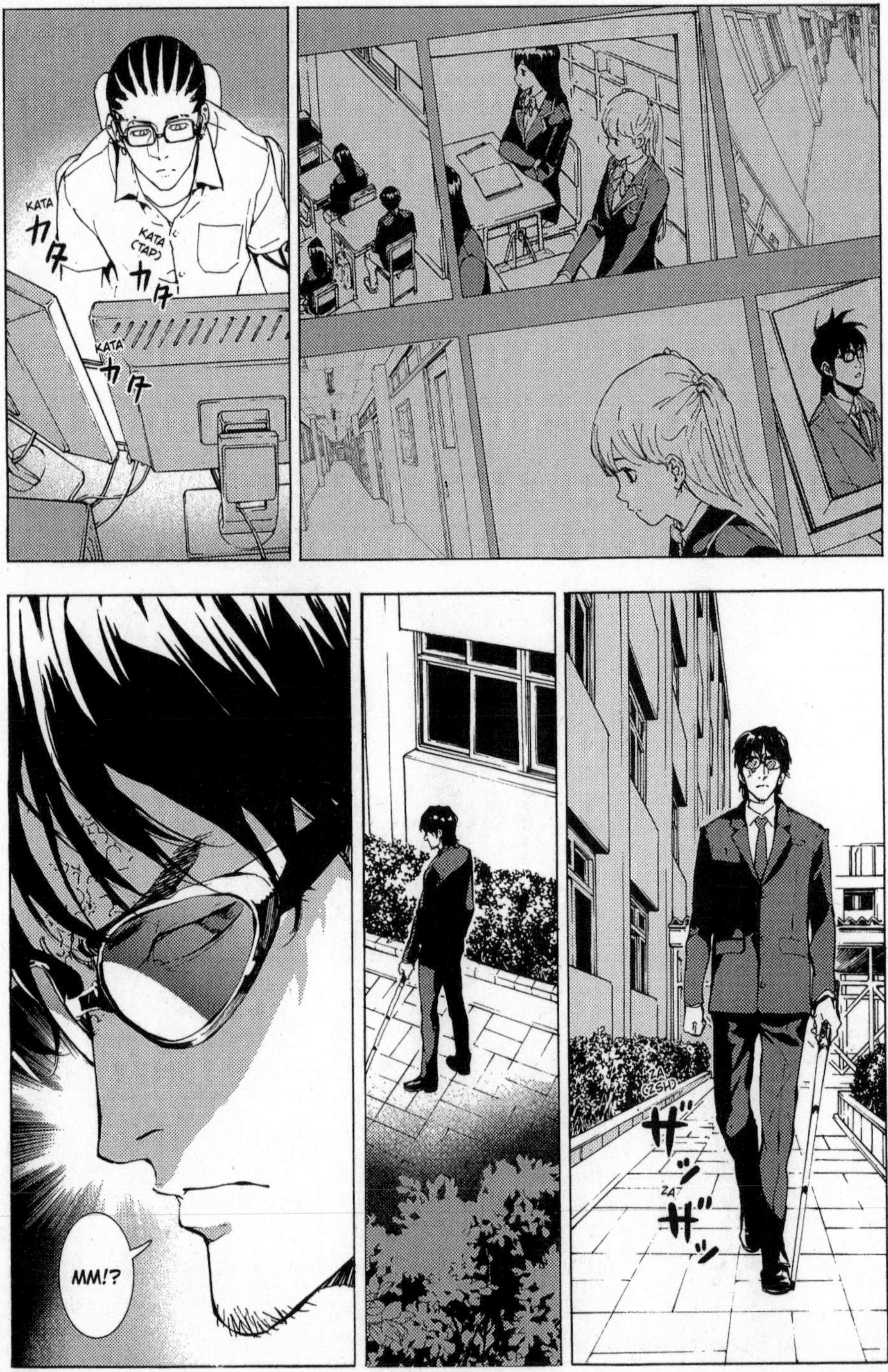
KATA
カタ
KATA (TAP)
カタ
KATA
カタ
ZA (ZSHD)
ザッ
ZA
ザッ
MM!?

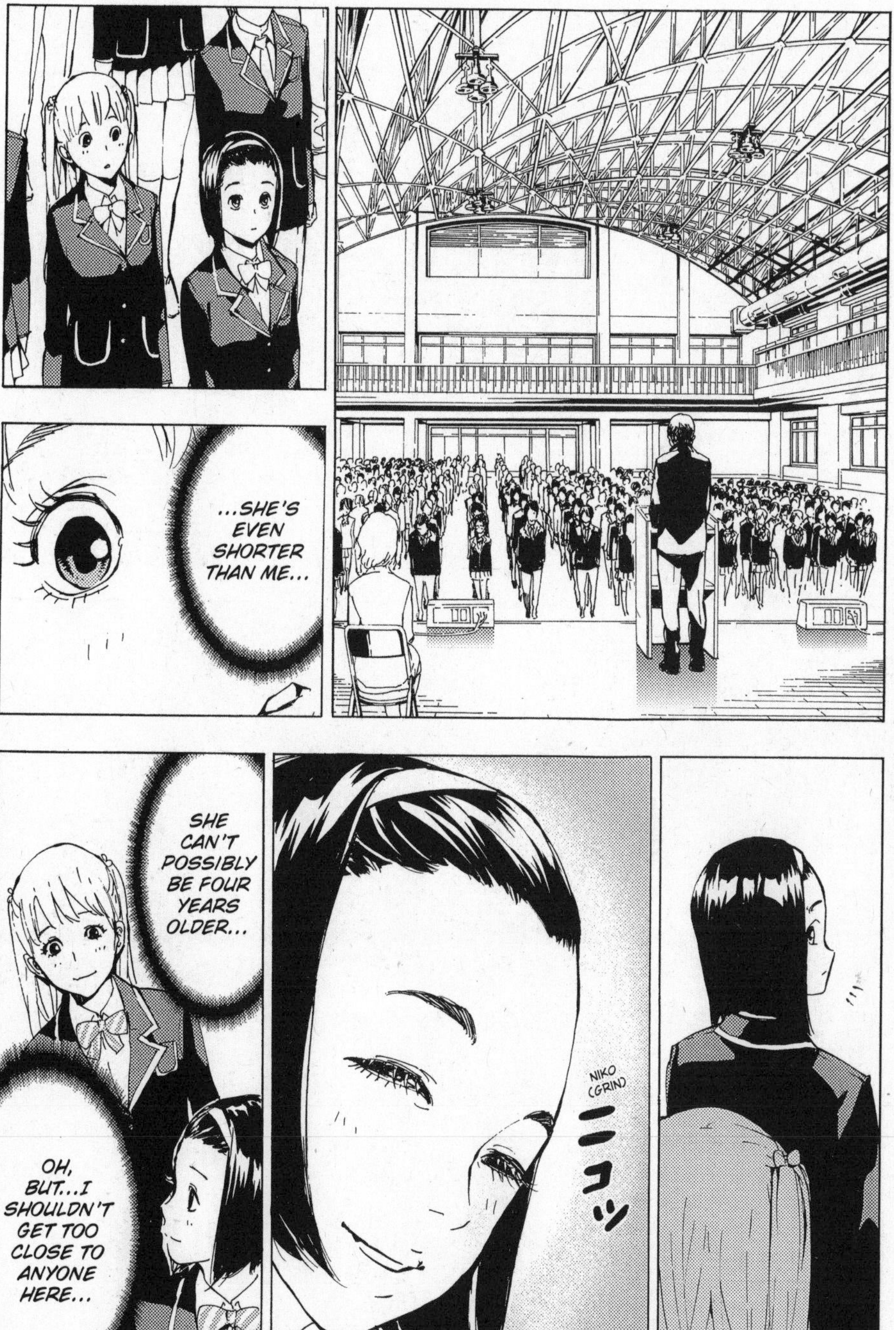
...SHE'S EVEN SHORTER THAN ME...
NIKO (GRIN)
ニコッ
SHE CAN'T POSSIBLY BE FOUR YEARS OLDER...
OH, BUT...I SHOULDN'T GET TOO CLOSE TO ANYONE HERE...

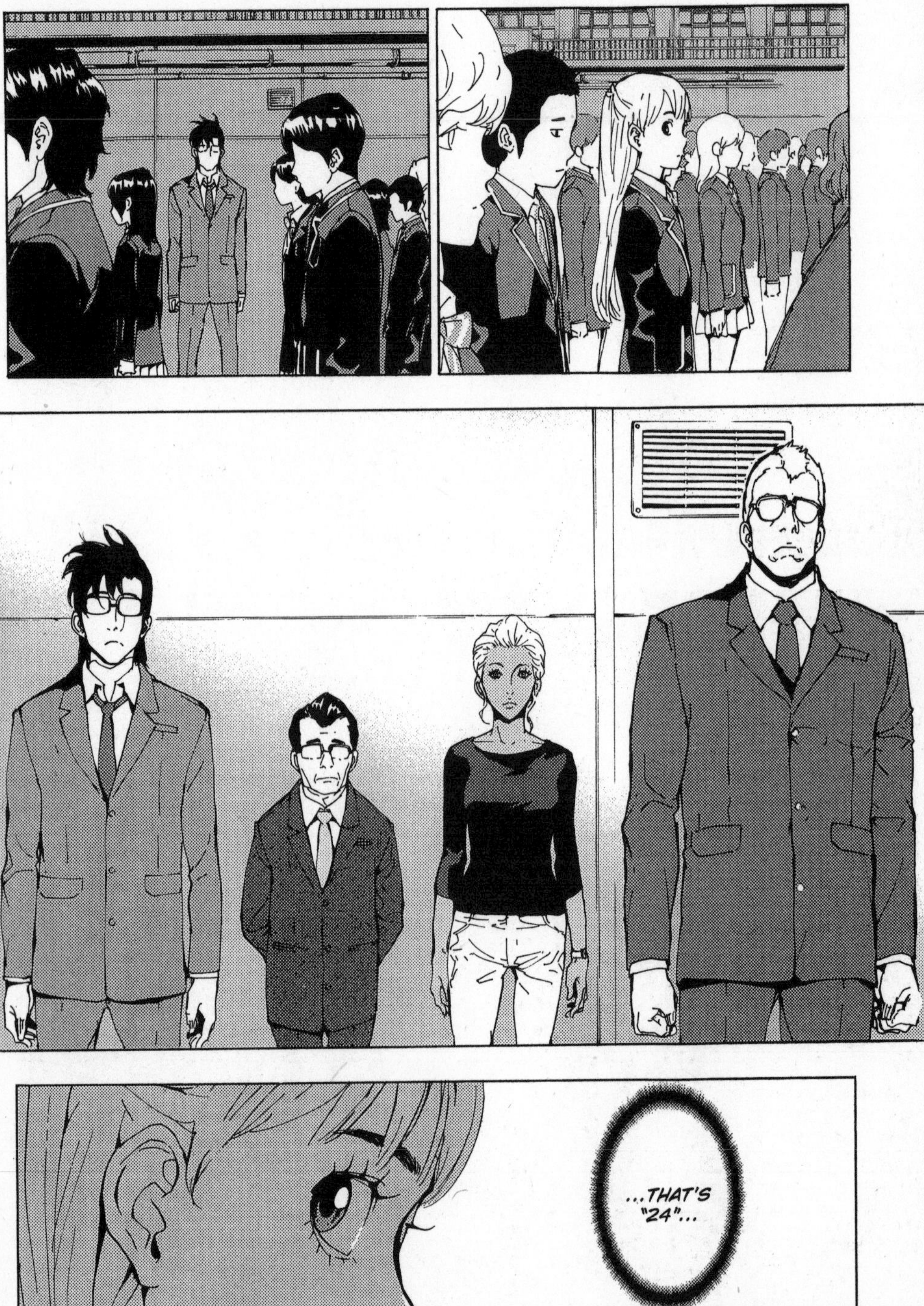
...THAT'S "24"...

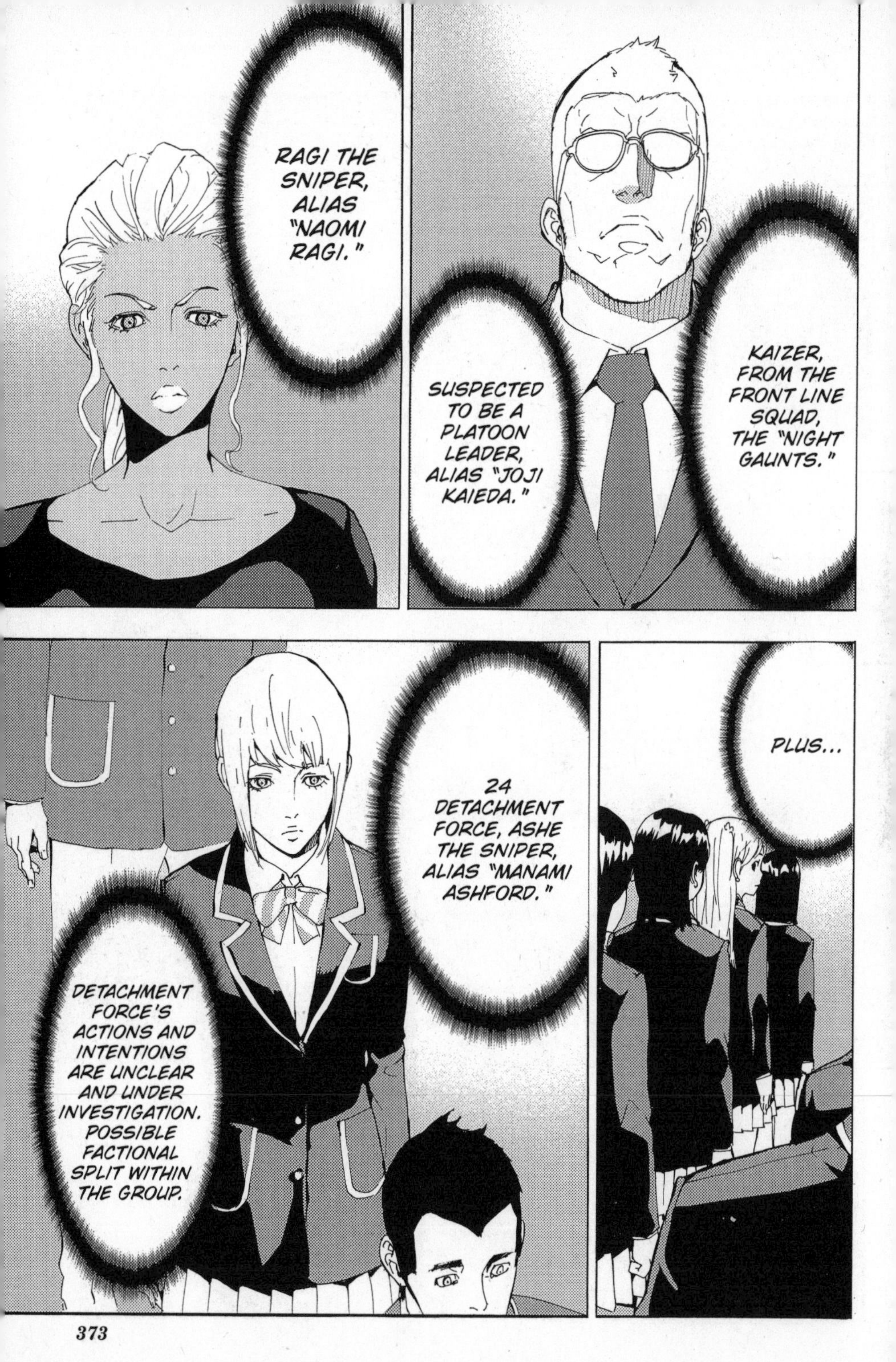
KAIZER, FROM THE FRONT LINE SQUAD, THE "NIGHT GAUNTS."
SUSPECTED TO BE A PLATOON LEADER, ALIAS "JOJI KAIEDA."
RAGI THE SNIPER, ALIAS "NAOMI RAGI."
PLUS...
24 DETACHMENT FORCE, ASHE THE SNIPER, ALIAS "MANAMI ASHFORD."
DETACHMENT FORCE'S ACTIONS AND INTENTIONS ARE UNCLEAR AND UNDER INVESTIGATION. POSSIBLE FACTIONAL SPLIT WITHIN THE GROUP.

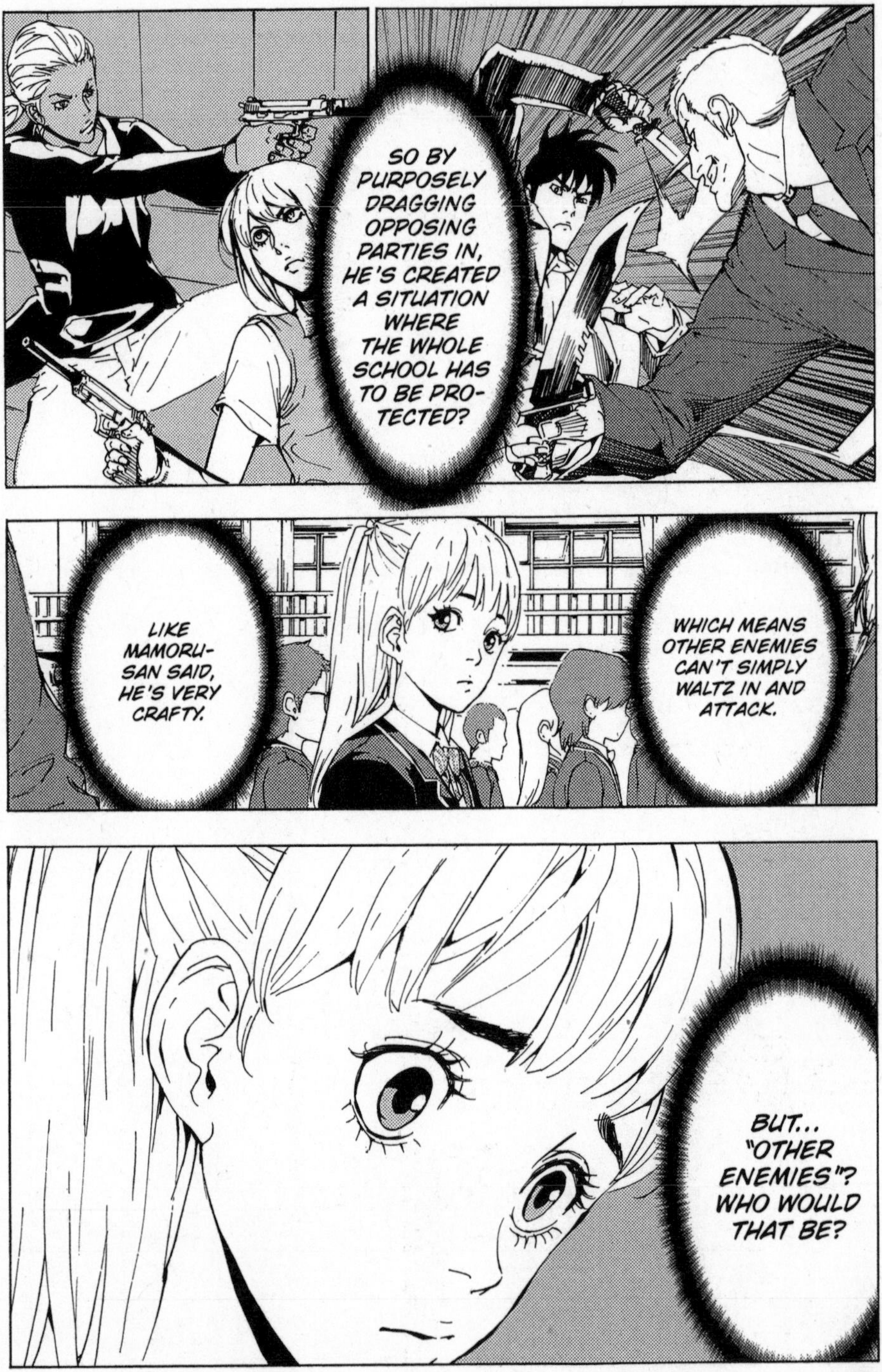
SO BY PURPOSELY DRAGGING OPPOSING PARTIES IN, HE'S CREATED A SITUATION WHERE THE WHOLE SCHOOL HAS TO BE PRO-TECTED?
WHICH MEANS OTHER ENEMIES CAN'T SIMPLY WALTZ IN AND ATTACK.
LIKE MAMORU-SAN SAID, HE'S VERY CRAFTY.
BUT... "OTHER ENEMIES"? WHO WOULD THAT BE?

NOW, YOU'LL NEED TO TURN IN YOUR SUMMER VACATION ASSIGNMENTS TO YOUR VARIOUS TEACHERS. ALSO...

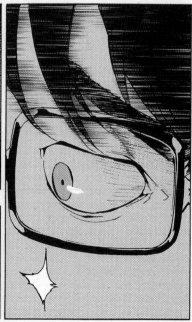

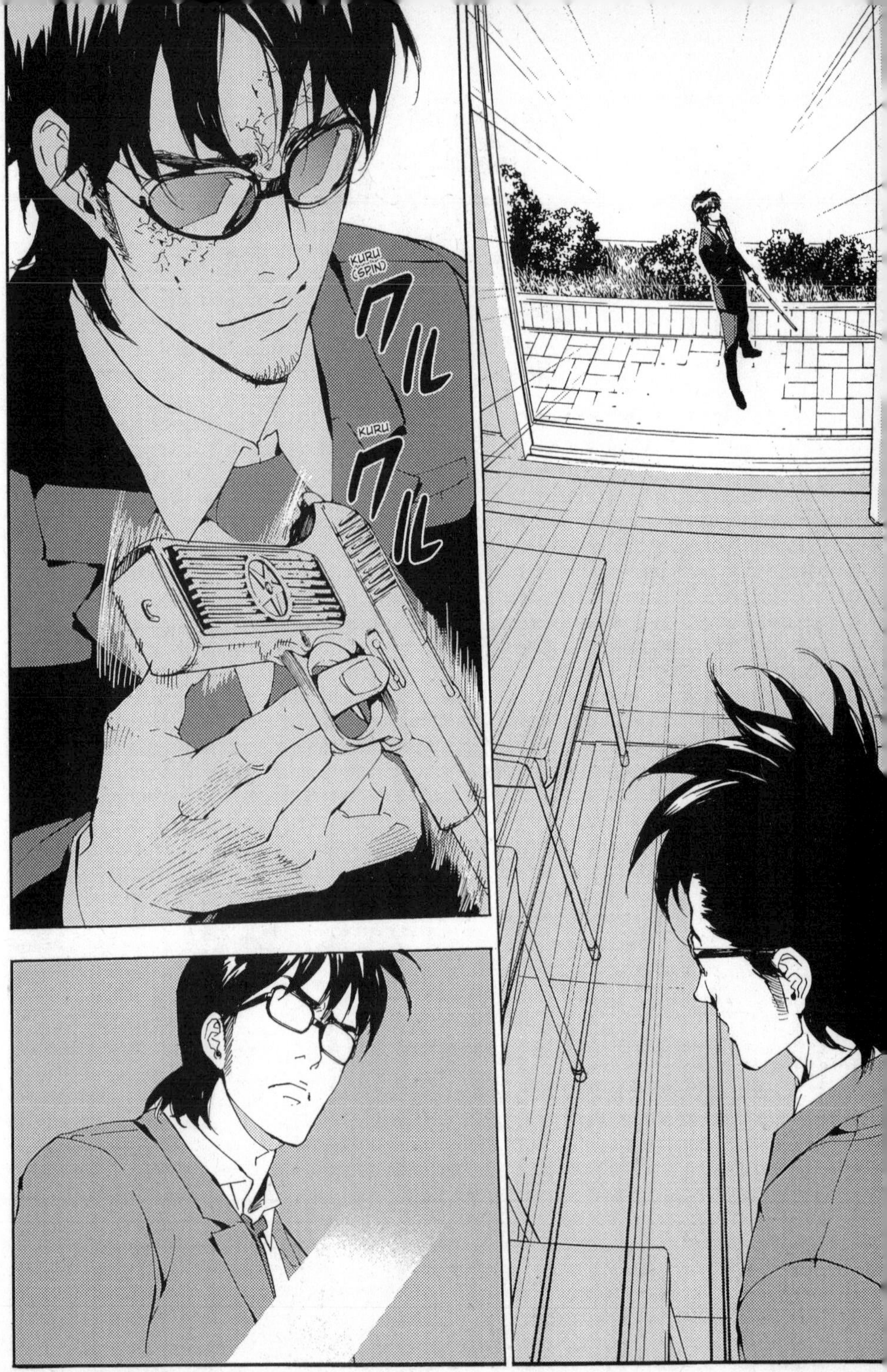
KURU (SPIN)
クル
KURU
クル

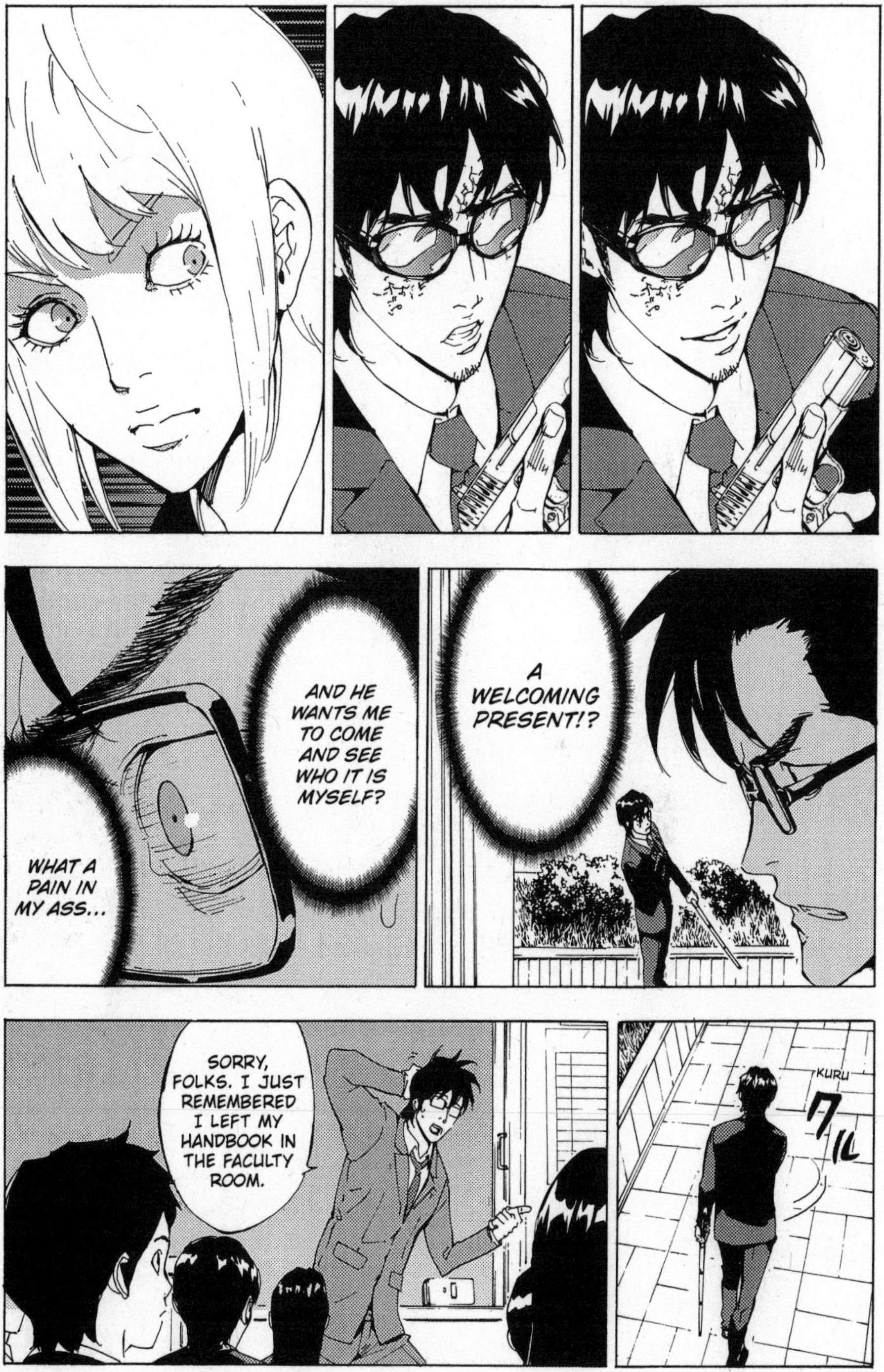
A WELCOMING PRESENT!?
AND HE WANTS ME TO COME AND SEE WHO IT IS MYSELF?
WHAT A PAIN IN MY ASS...
KURU
クル
SORRY, FOLKS. I JUST REMEMBERED I LEFT MY HANDBOOK IN THE FACULTY ROOM.

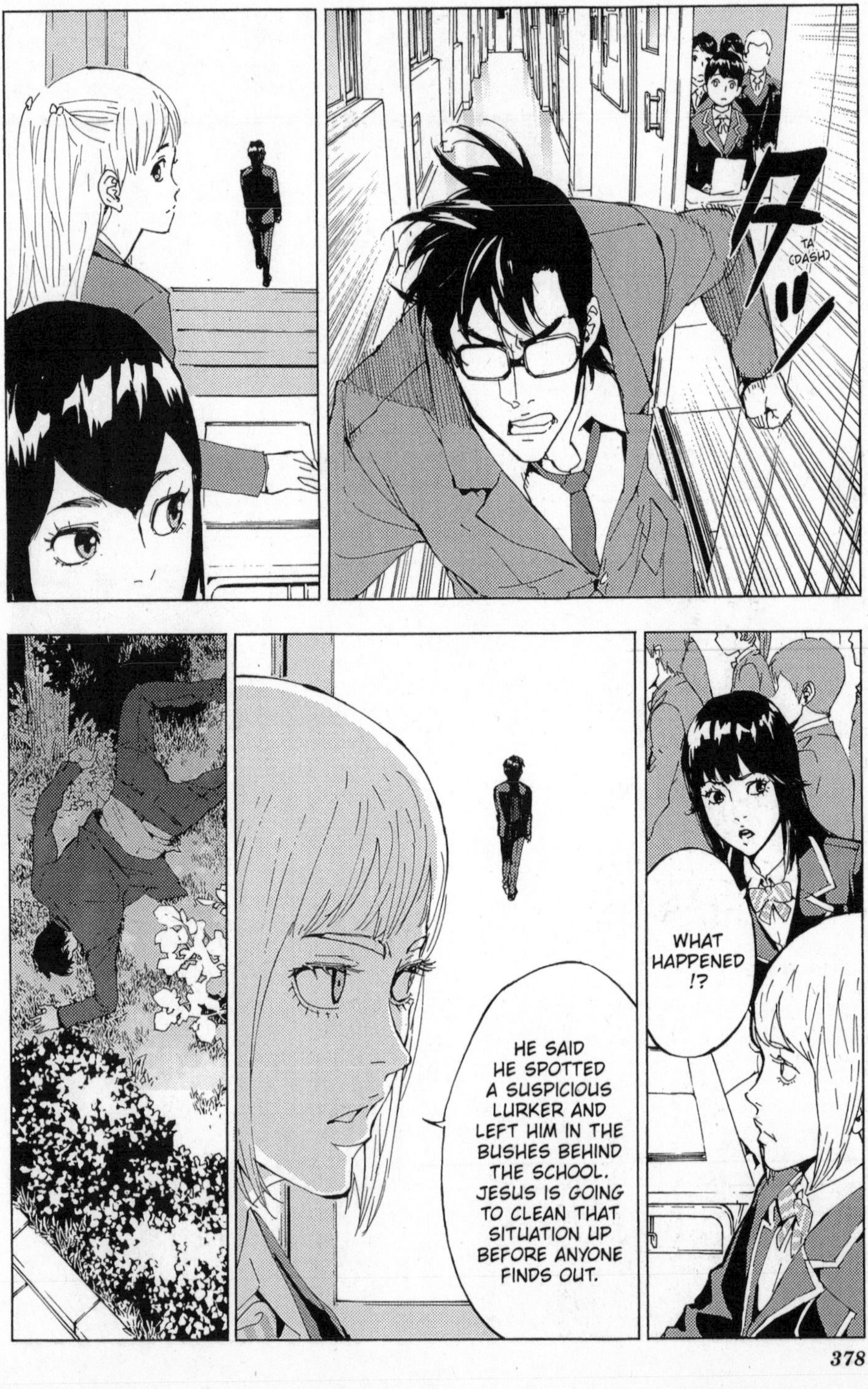
タッ
TA (DASH)
WHAT HAPPENED !?
HE SAID HE SPOTTED A SUSPICIOUS LURKER AND LEFT HIM IN THE BUSHES BEHIND THE SCHOOL. JESUS IS GOING TO CLEAN THAT SITUATION UP BEFORE ANYONE FINDS OUT.

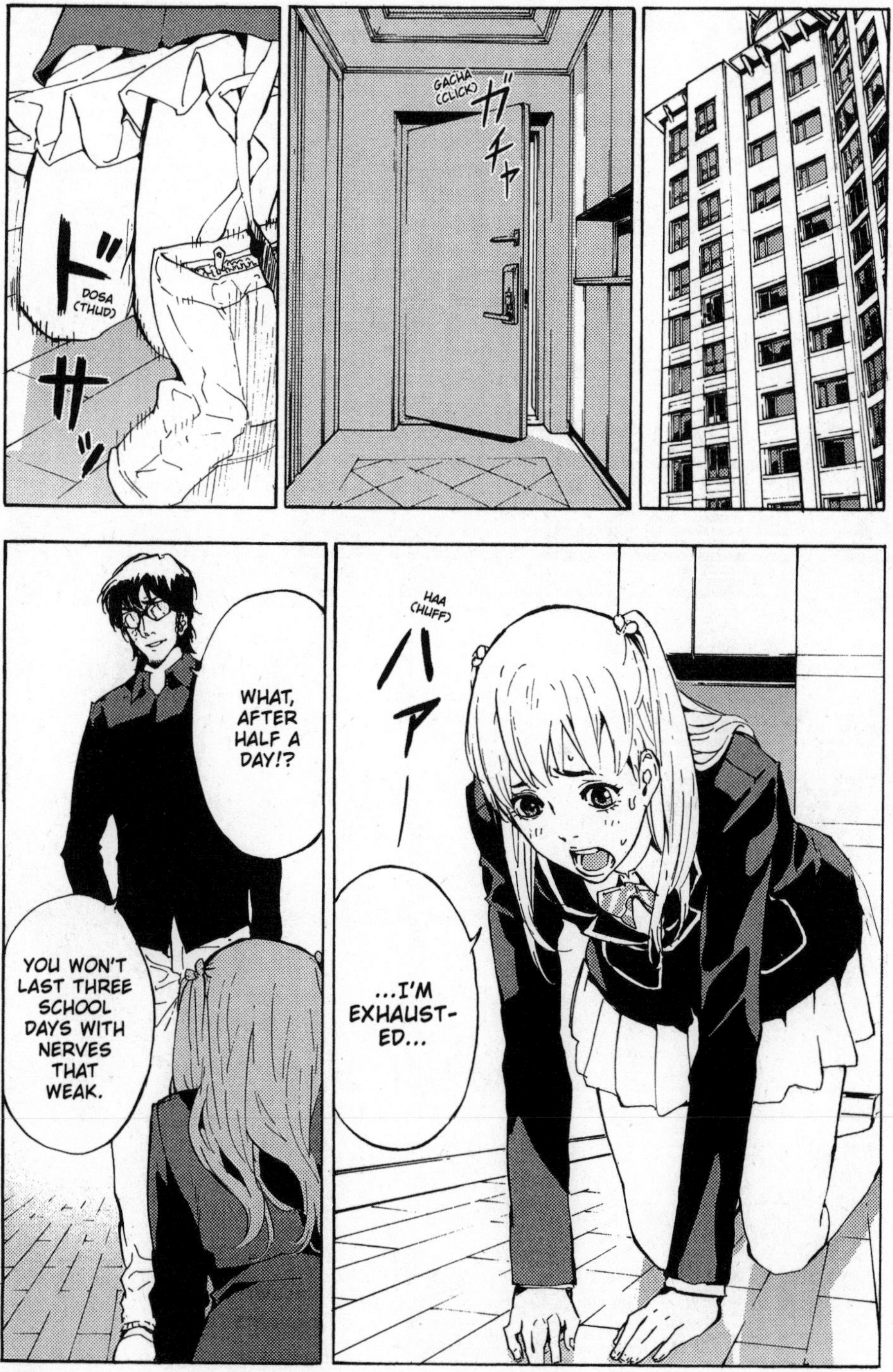
GACHA (CLICK)
ガチャ
DOSA (THUD)
ドサッ
HAA (HUFF)
ハアー
...I'M EXHAUST-ED...
WHAT, AFTER HALF A DAY!?
YOU WON'T LAST THREE SCHOOL DAYS WITH NERVES THAT WEAK.

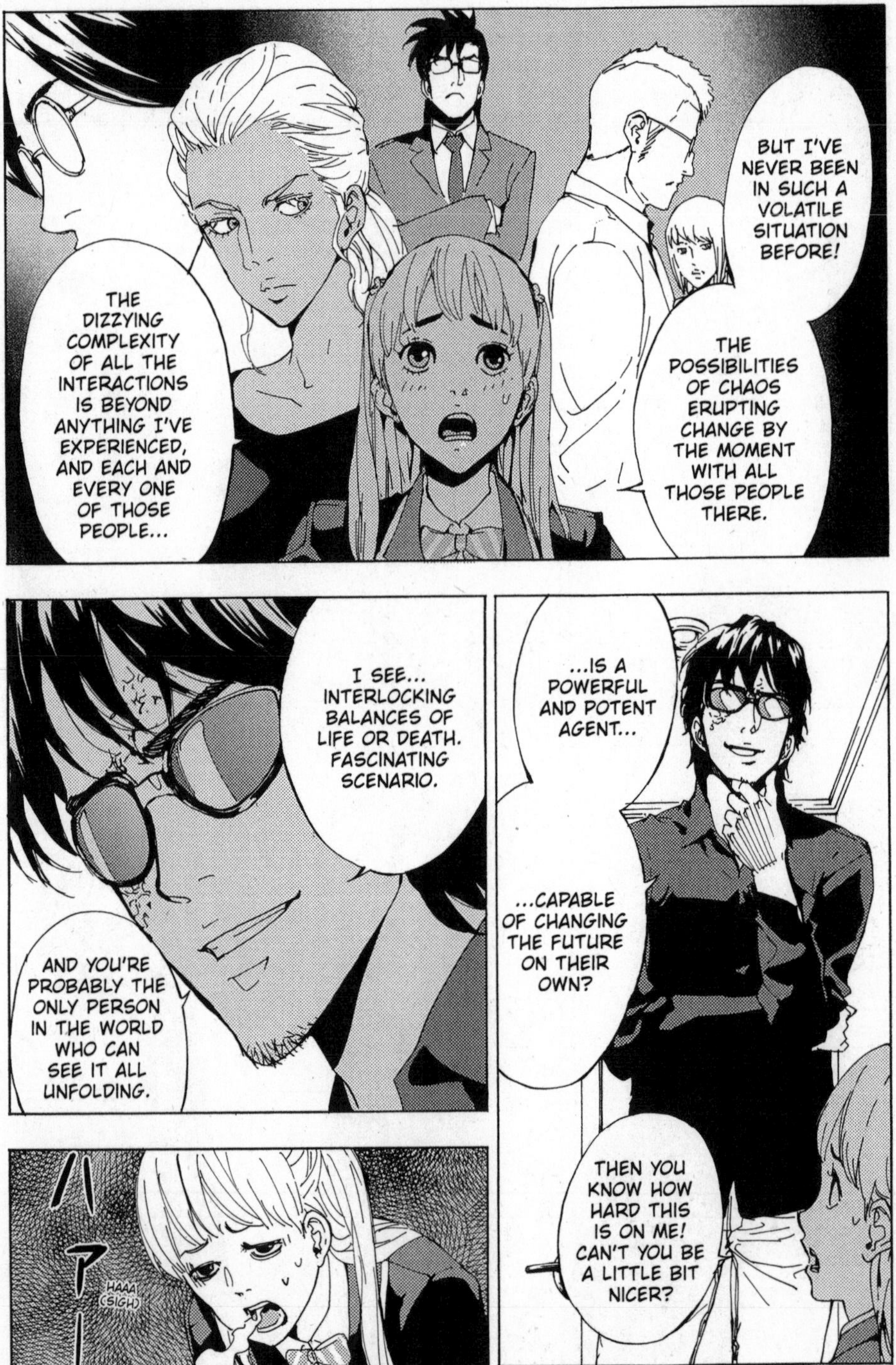
BUT I'VE NEVER BEEN IN SUCH A VOLATILE SITUATION BEFORE!
THE POSSIBILITIES OF CHAOS ERUPTING CHANGE BY THE MOMENT WITH ALL THOSE PEOPLE THERE.
THE DIZZYING COMPLEXITY OF ALL THE INTERACTIONS IS BEYOND ANYTHING I'VE EXPERIENCED, AND EACH AND EVERY ONE OF THOSE PEOPLE...
...IS A POWERFUL AND POTENT AGENT...
...CAPABLE OF CHANGING THE FUTURE ON THEIR OWN?
THEN YOU KNOW HOW HARD THIS IS ON ME! CAN'T YOU BE A LITTLE BIT NICER?
I SEE... INTERLOCKING BALANCES OF LIFE OR DEATH. FASCINATING SCENARIO.
AND YOU'RE PROBABLY THE ONLY PERSON IN THE WORLD WHO CAN SEE IT ALL UNFOLDING.
ハァー
HAAA (SIGH)

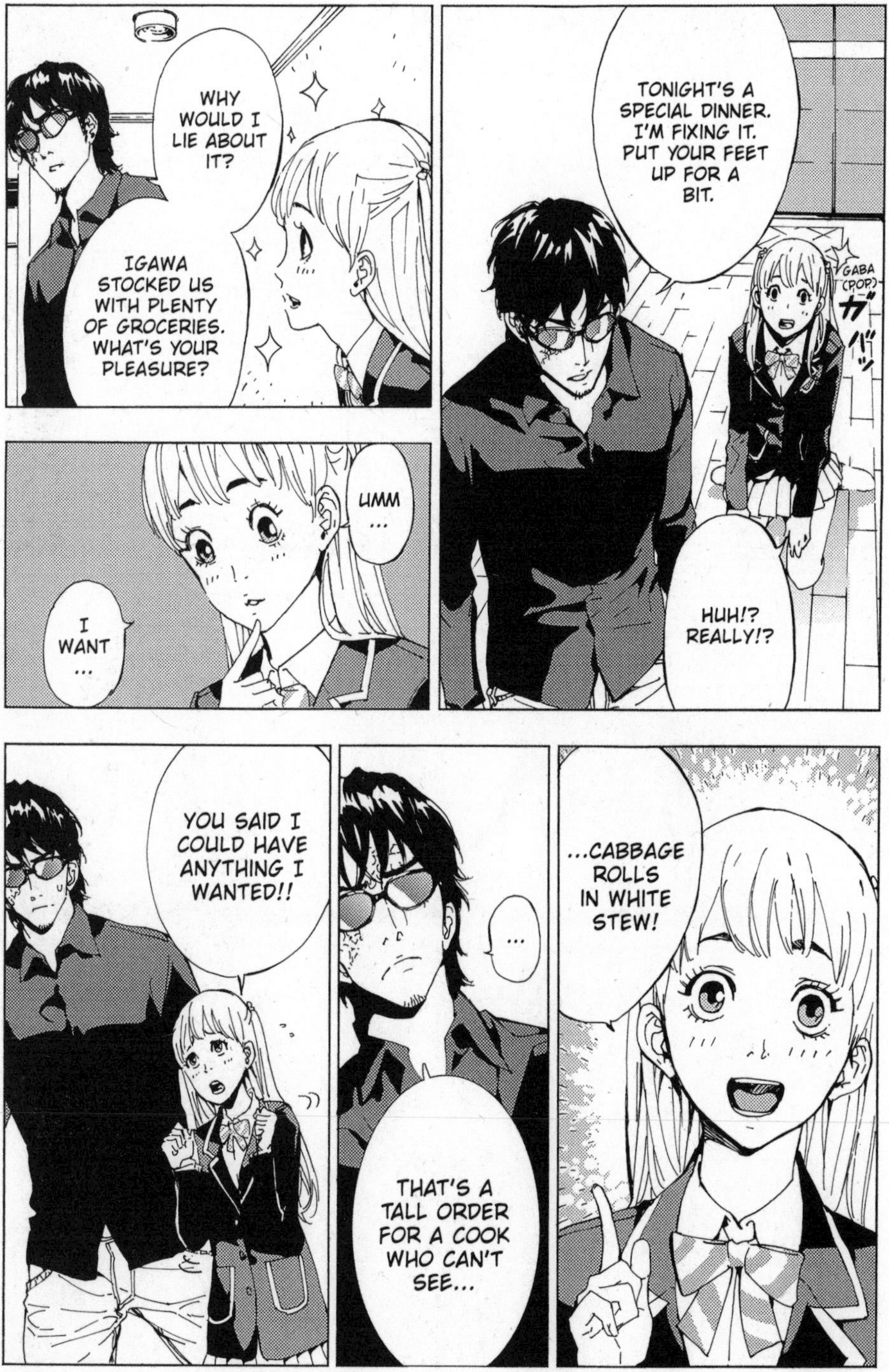
TONIGHT'S A SPECIAL DINNER. I'M FIXING IT. PUT YOUR FEET UP FOR A BIT.
GABA (POP)
ガバッ
HUH!? REALLY!?
WHY WOULD I LIE ABOUT IT?
IGAWA STOCKED US WITH PLENTY OF GROCERIES. WHAT'S YOUR PLEASURE?
UMM ...
I WANT ...
...CABBAGE ROLLS IN WHITE STEW!
...
THAT'S A TALL ORDER FOR A COOK WHO CAN'T SEE...
YOU SAID I COULD HAVE ANYTHING I WANTED!!

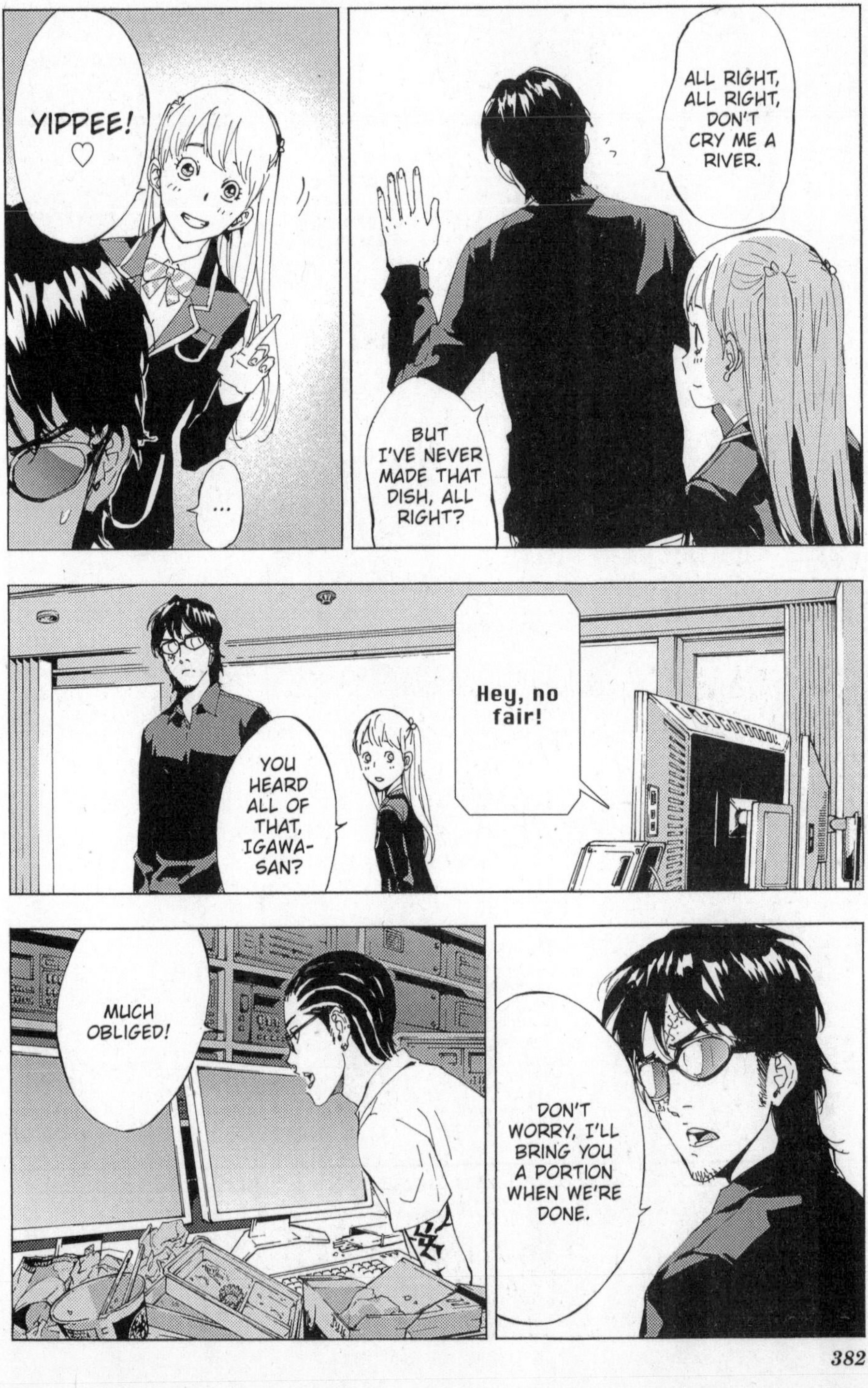
ALL RIGHT, ALL RIGHT, DON'T CRY ME A RIVER.
BUT I'VE NEVER MADE THAT DISH, ALL RIGHT?
YIPPEE! ♡
...
Hey, no fair!
YOU HEARD ALL OF THAT, IGAWA-SAN?
DON'T WORRY, I'LL BRING YOU A PORTION WHEN WE'RE DONE.
MUCH OBLIGED!

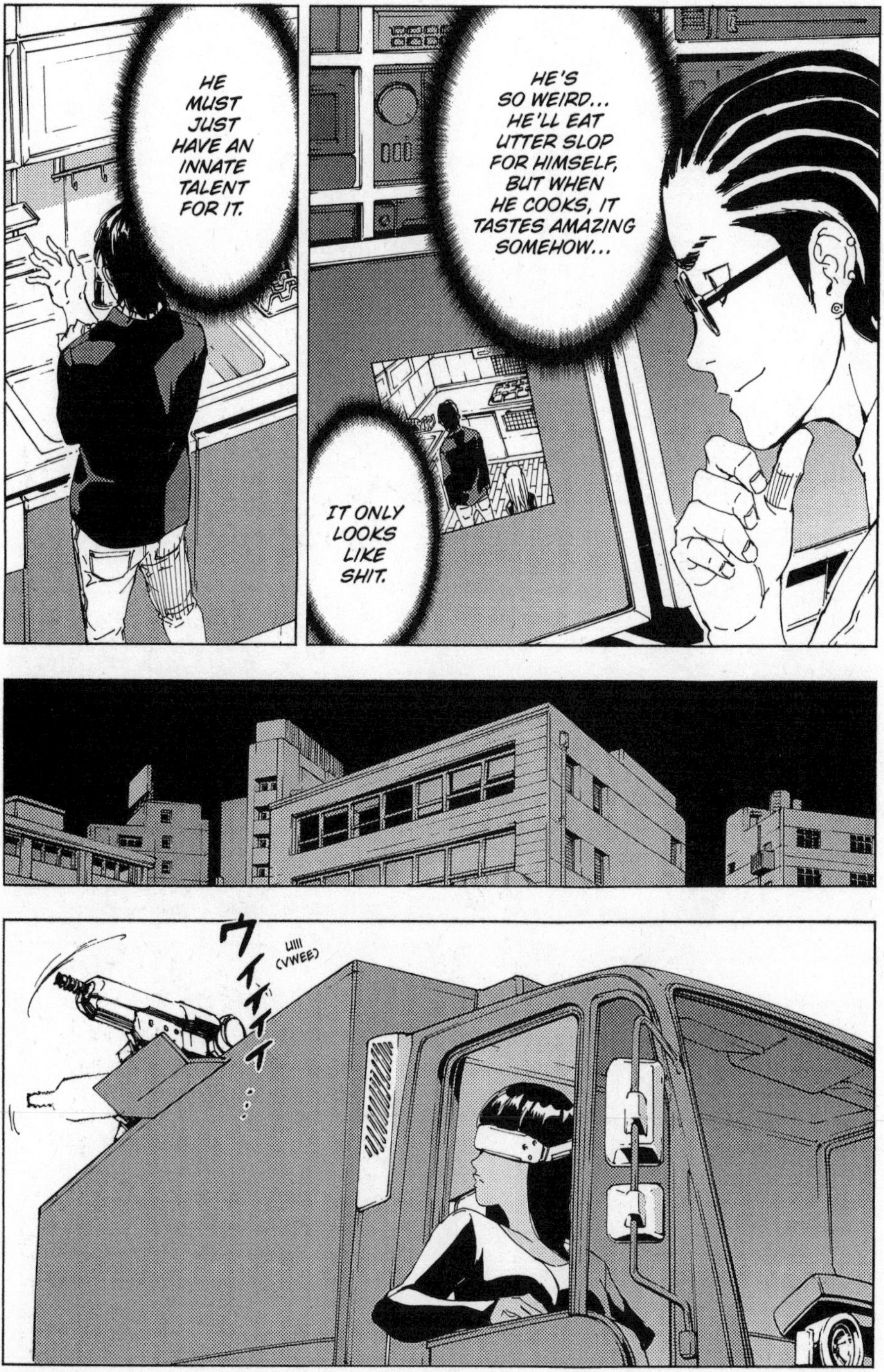
HE'S SO WEIRD... HE'LL EAT UTTER SLOP FOR HIMSELF, BUT WHEN HE COOKS, IT TASTES AMAZING SOMEHOW...
IT ONLY LOOKS LIKE SHIT.
HE MUST JUST HAVE AN INNATE TALENT FOR IT.
ウイイイイ...
UIII (VWEE)

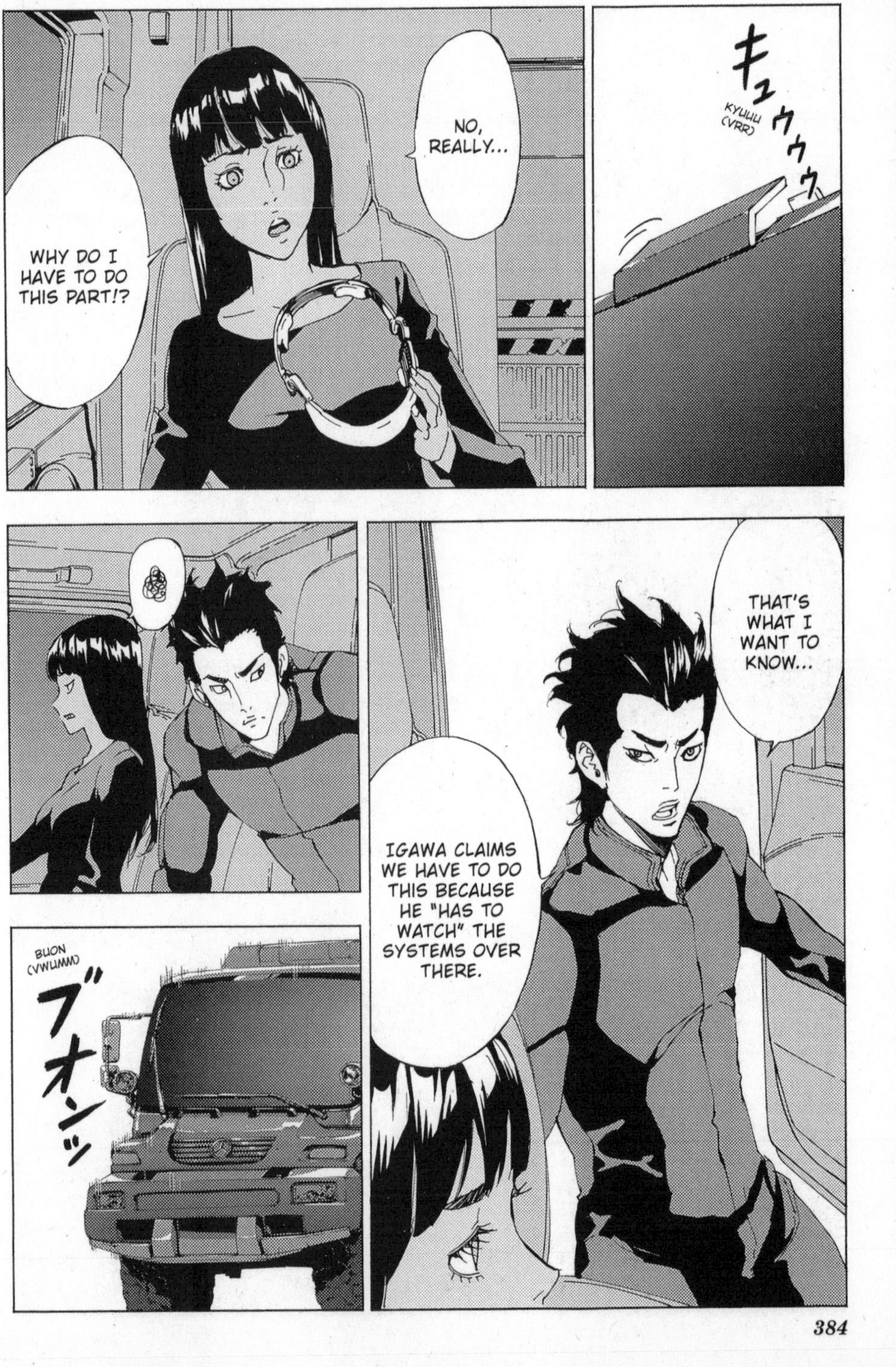
キュウウウ
KYUUU (VRR)
NO, REALLY...
WHY DO I HAVE TO DO THIS PART!?
THAT'S WHAT I WANT TO KNOW...
IGAWA CLAIMS WE HAVE TO DO THIS BECAUSE HE "HAS TO WATCH" THE SYSTEMS OVER THERE.
BUON (VWUMM)
ブオンッ

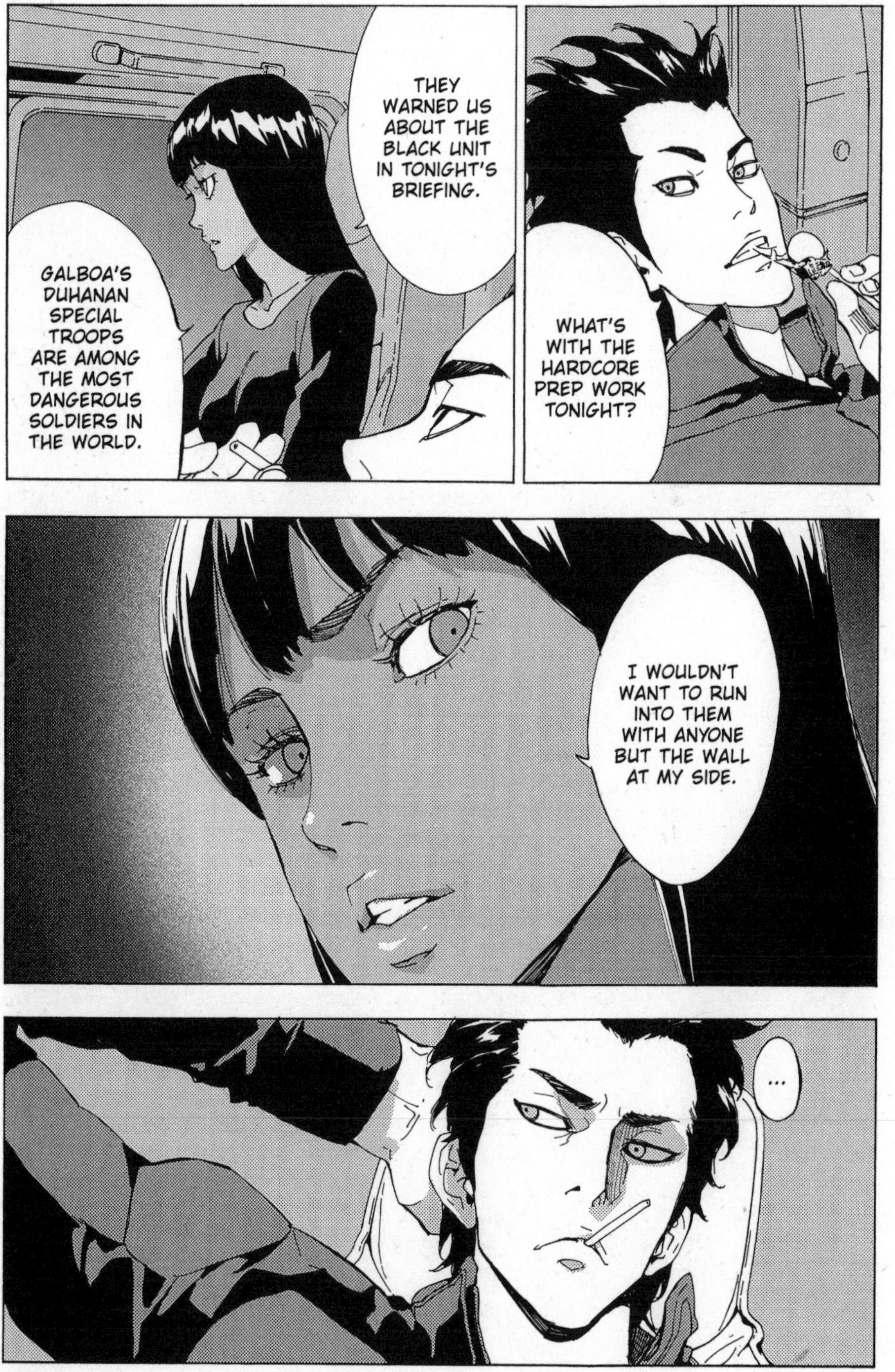
WHAT'S WITH THE HARDCORE PREP WORK TONIGHT?
THEY WARNED US ABOUT THE BLACK UNIT IN TONIGHT'S BRIEFING.
GALBOA'S DUHANAN SPECIAL TROOPS ARE AMONG THE MOST DANGEROUS SOLDIERS IN THE WORLD.
I WOULDN'T WANT TO RUN INTO THEM WITH ANYONE BUT THE WALL AT MY SIDE.
...

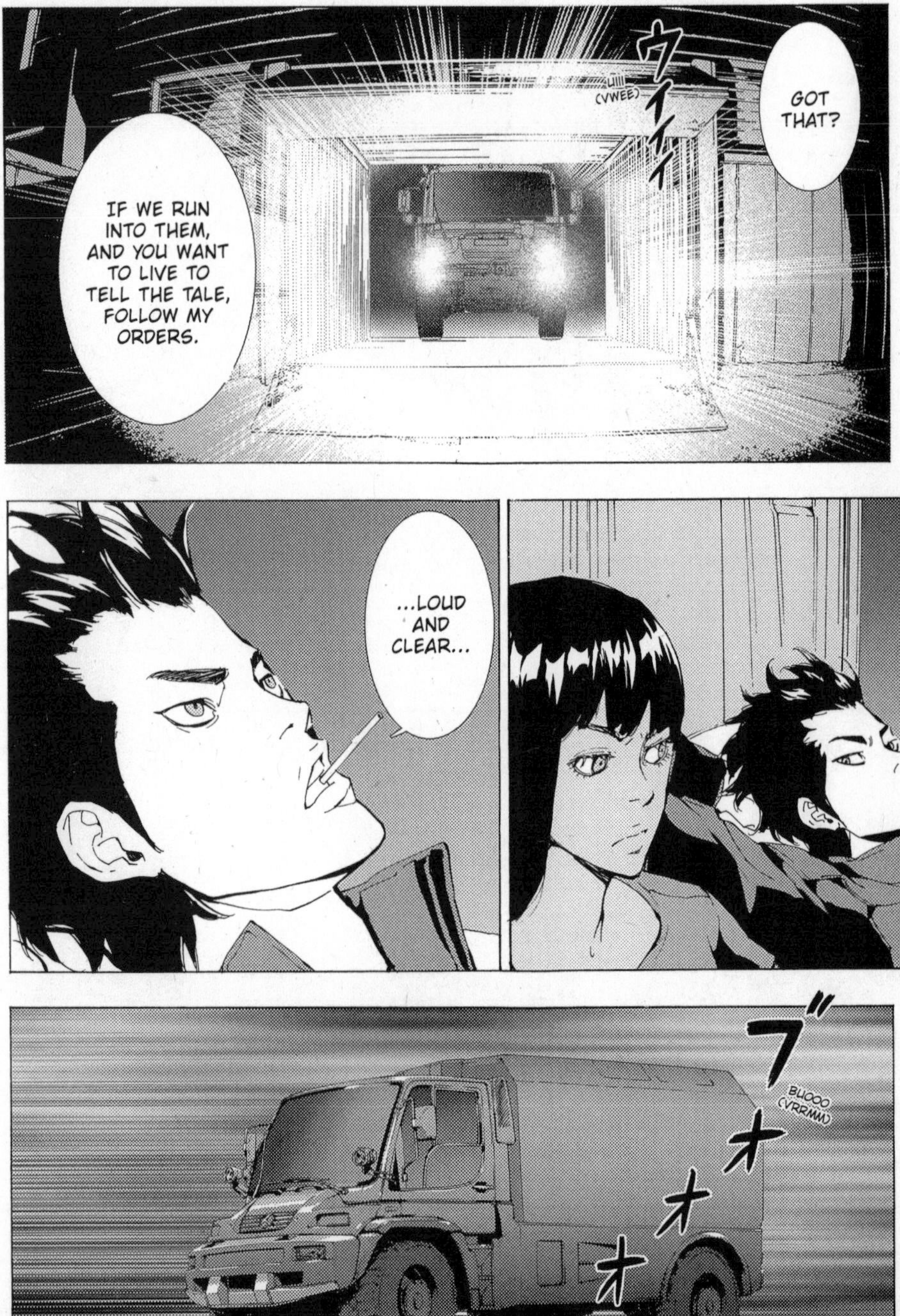
GOT THAT?
ウイイイ
UIII
(VWEE)
IF WE RUN INTO THEM, AND YOU WANT TO LIVE TO TELL THE TALE, FOLLOW MY ORDERS.
...LOUD AND CLEAR...
ブオオオ
BUOOO
(VRRMM)

Until Death do us Part

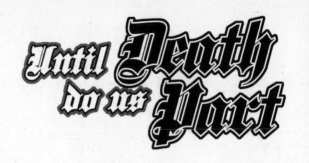

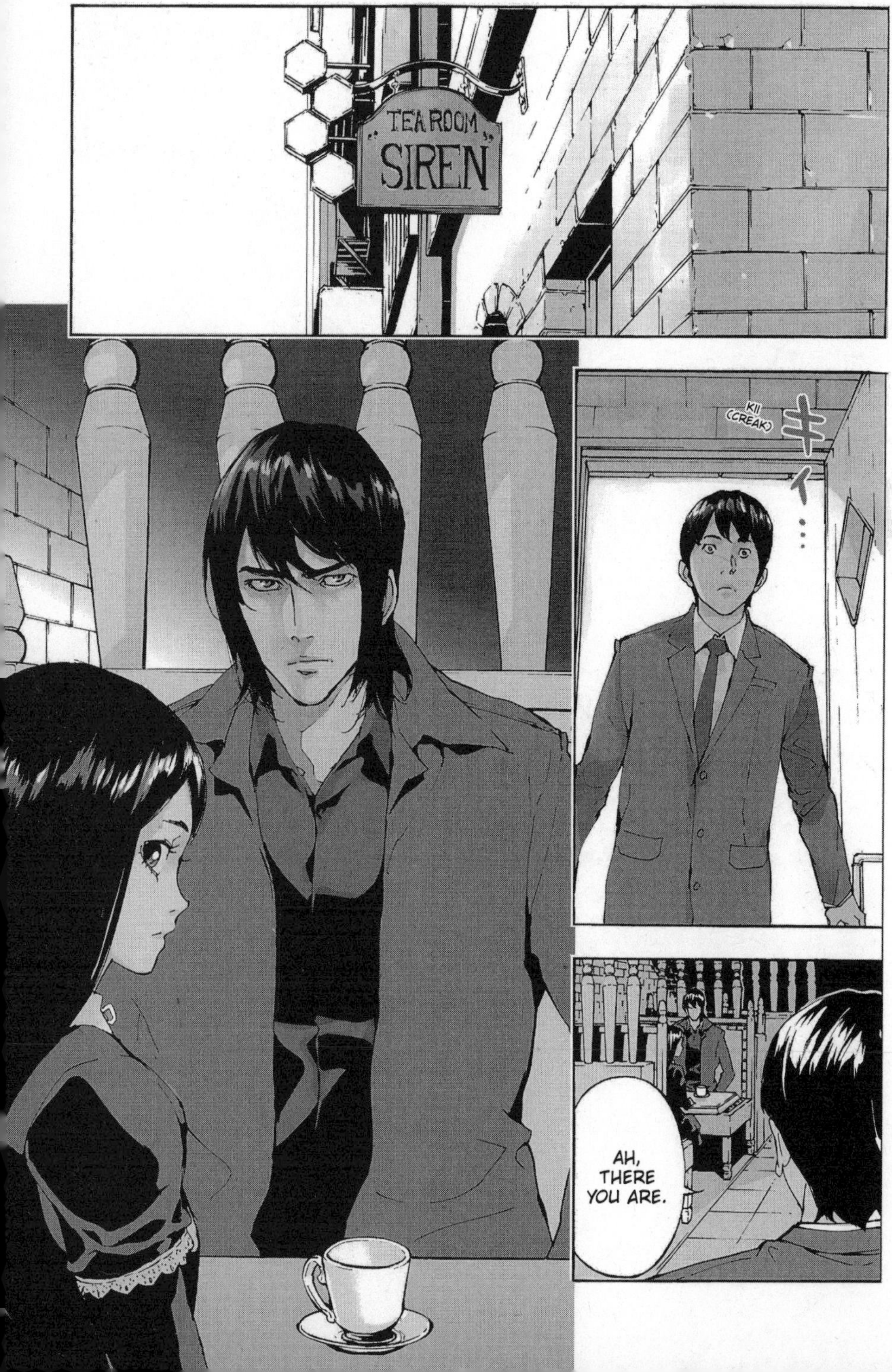
TEA ROOM
SIREN
KII (CREAK)
キイ…
AH, THERE YOU ARE.

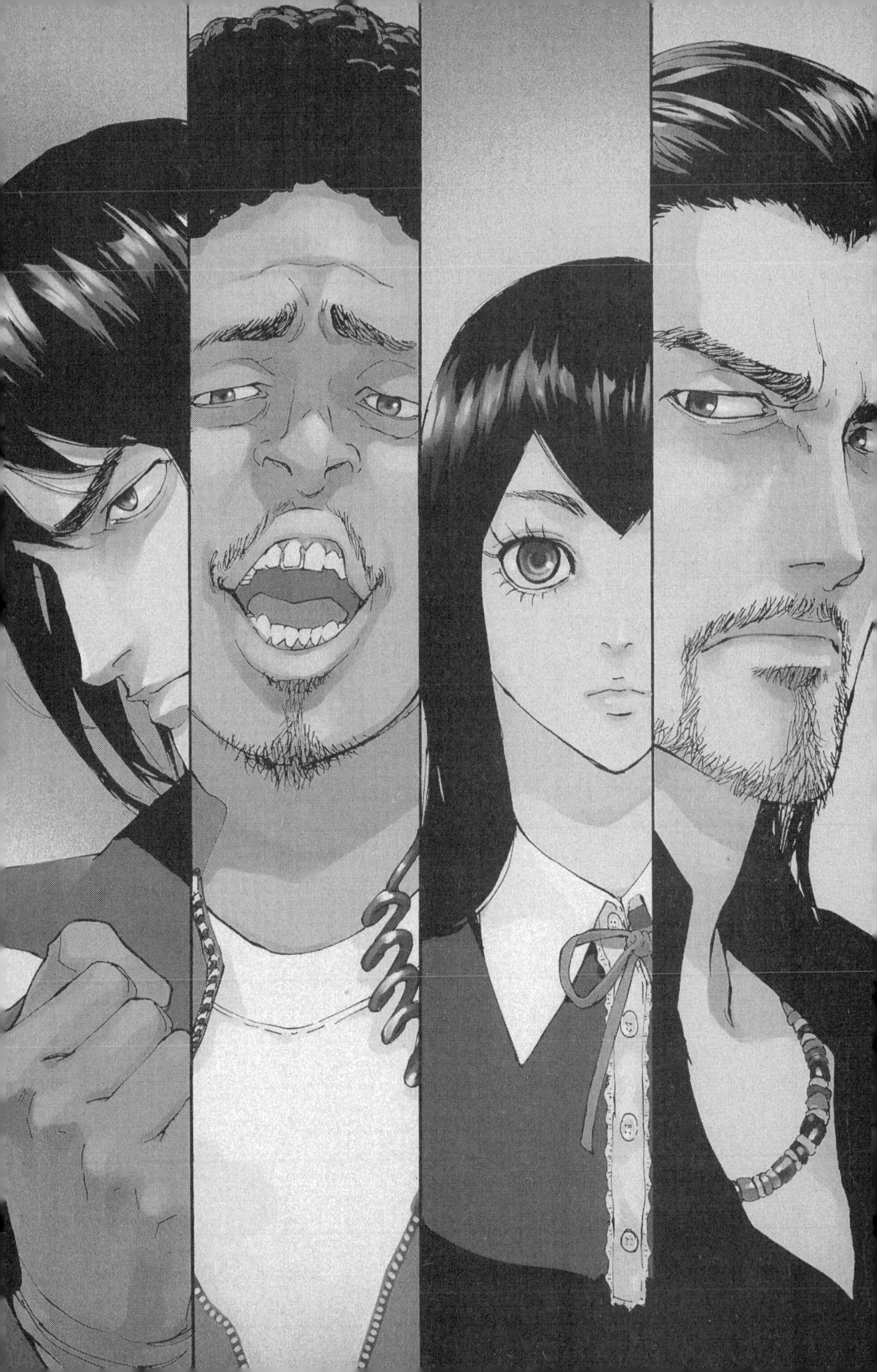

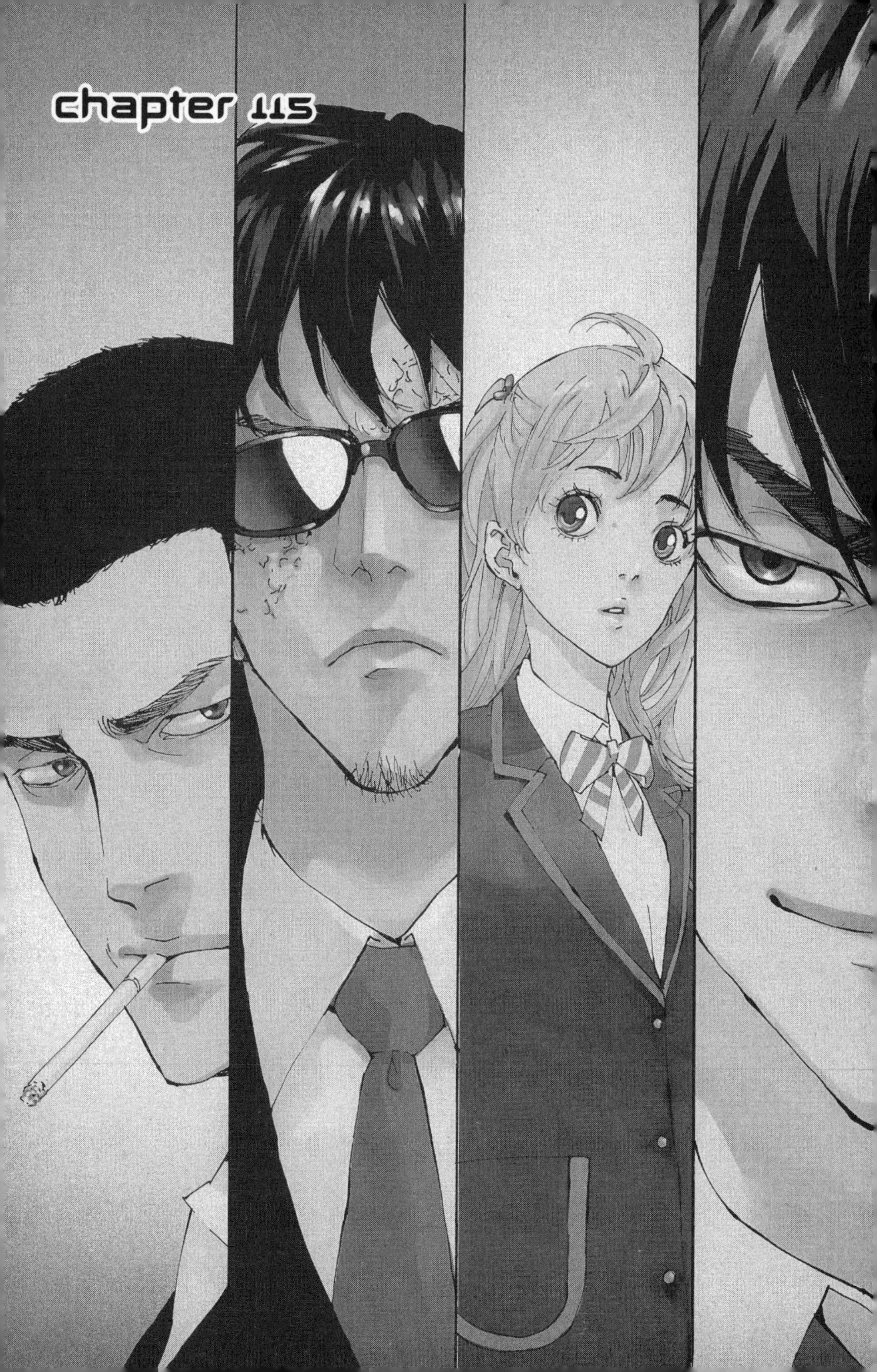
chapter 115

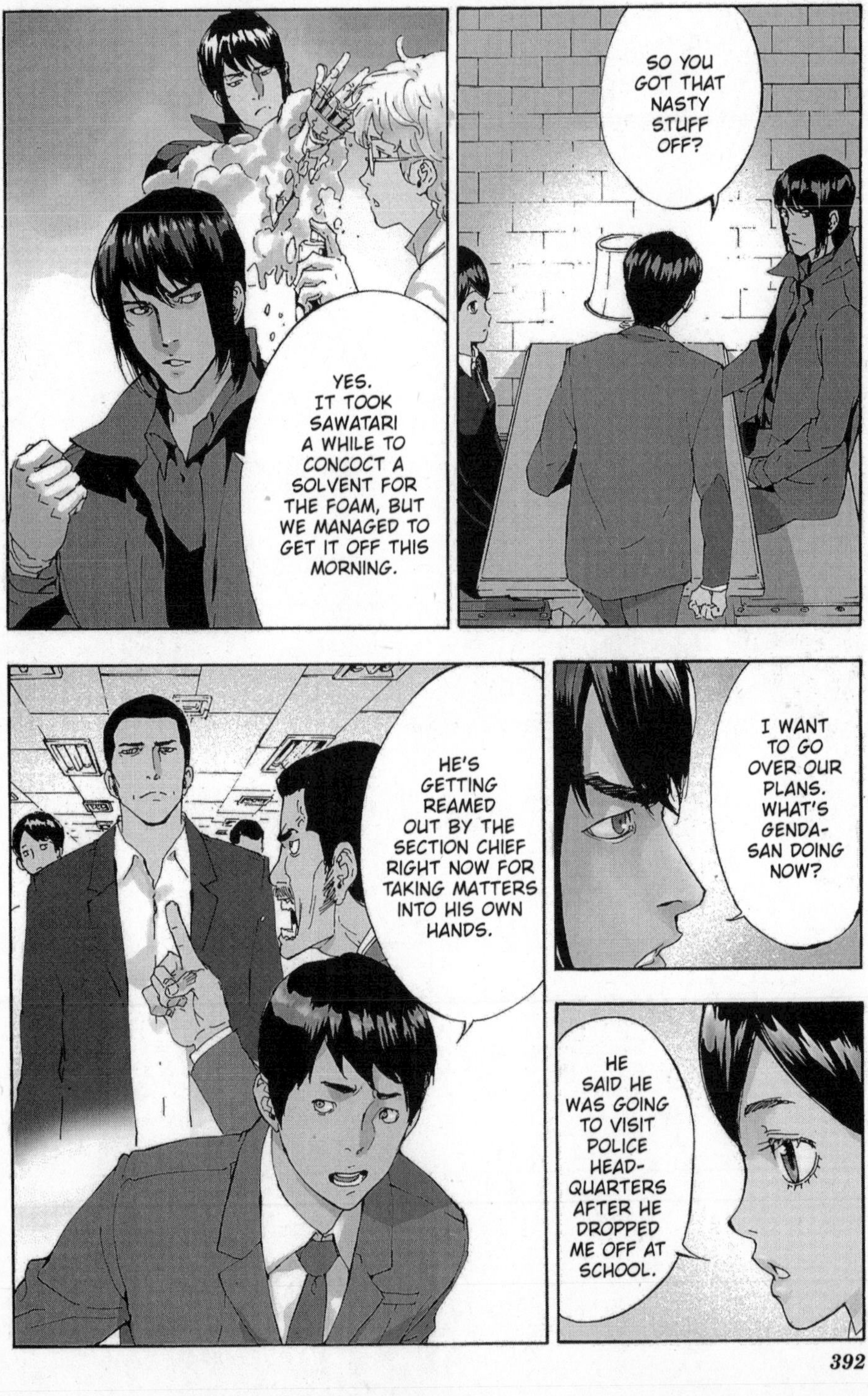
SO YOU GOT THAT NASTY STUFF OFF?
YES. IT TOOK SAWATARI A WHILE TO CONCOCT A SOLVENT FOR THE FOAM, BUT WE MANAGED TO GET IT OFF THIS MORNING.
I WANT TO GO OVER OUR PLANS. WHAT'S GENDA-SAN DOING NOW?
HE SAID HE WAS GOING TO VISIT POLICE HEAD-QUARTERS AFTER HE DROPPED ME OFF AT SCHOOL.
HE'S GETTING REAMED OUT BY THE SECTION CHIEF RIGHT NOW FOR TAKING MATTERS INTO HIS OWN HANDS.

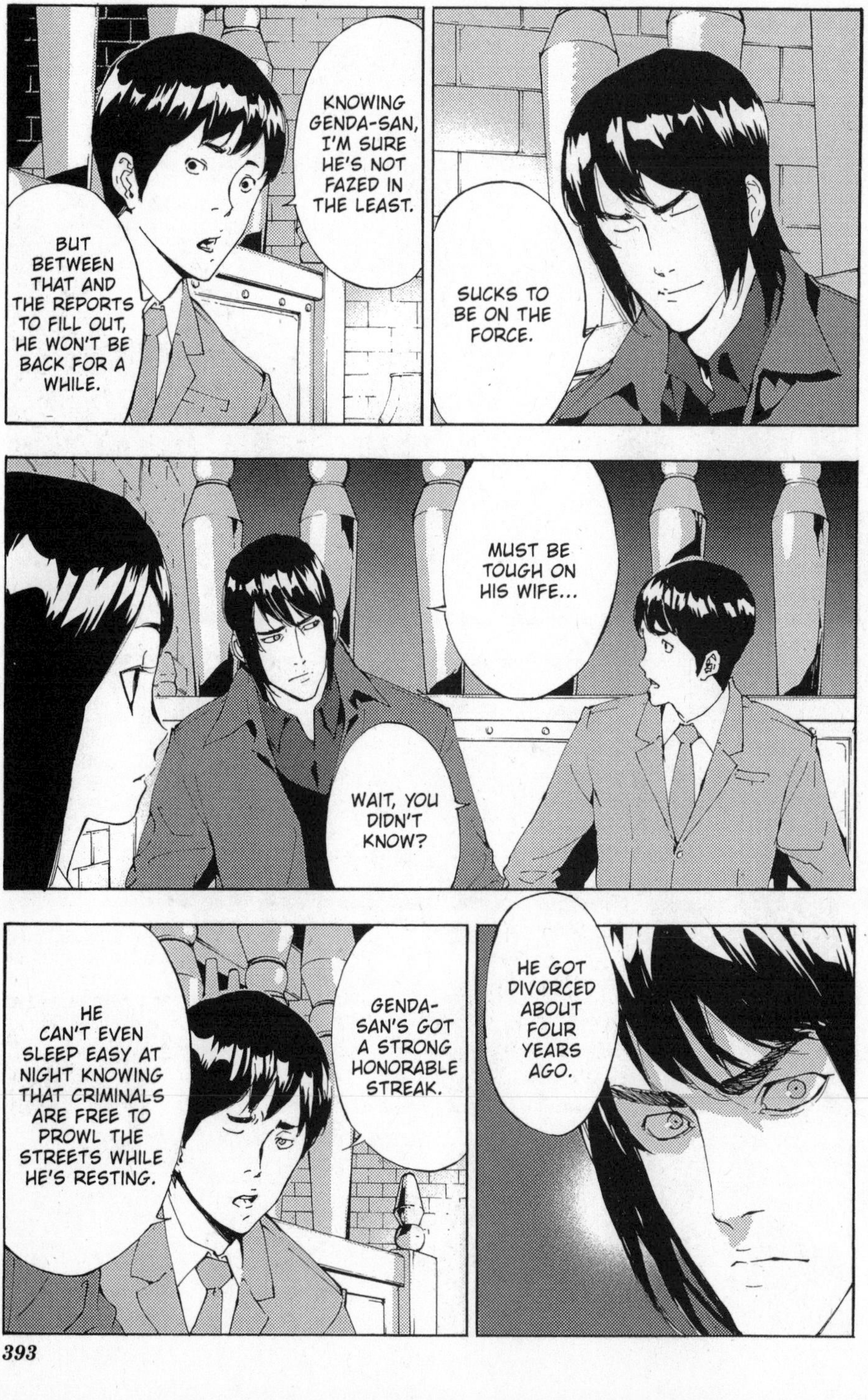
SUCKS TO BE ON THE FORCE.
KNOWING GENDA-SAN, I'M SURE HE'S NOT FAZED IN THE LEAST.
BUT BETWEEN THAT AND THE REPORTS TO FILL OUT, HE WON'T BE BACK FOR A WHILE.
MUST BE TOUGH ON HIS WIFE...
WAIT, YOU DIDN'T KNOW?
HE GOT DIVORCED ABOUT FOUR YEARS AGO.
GENDA-SAN'S GOT A STRONG HONORABLE STREAK.
HE CAN'T EVEN SLEEP EASY AT NIGHT KNOWING THAT CRIMINALS ARE FREE TO PROWL THE STREETS WHILE HE'S RESTING.

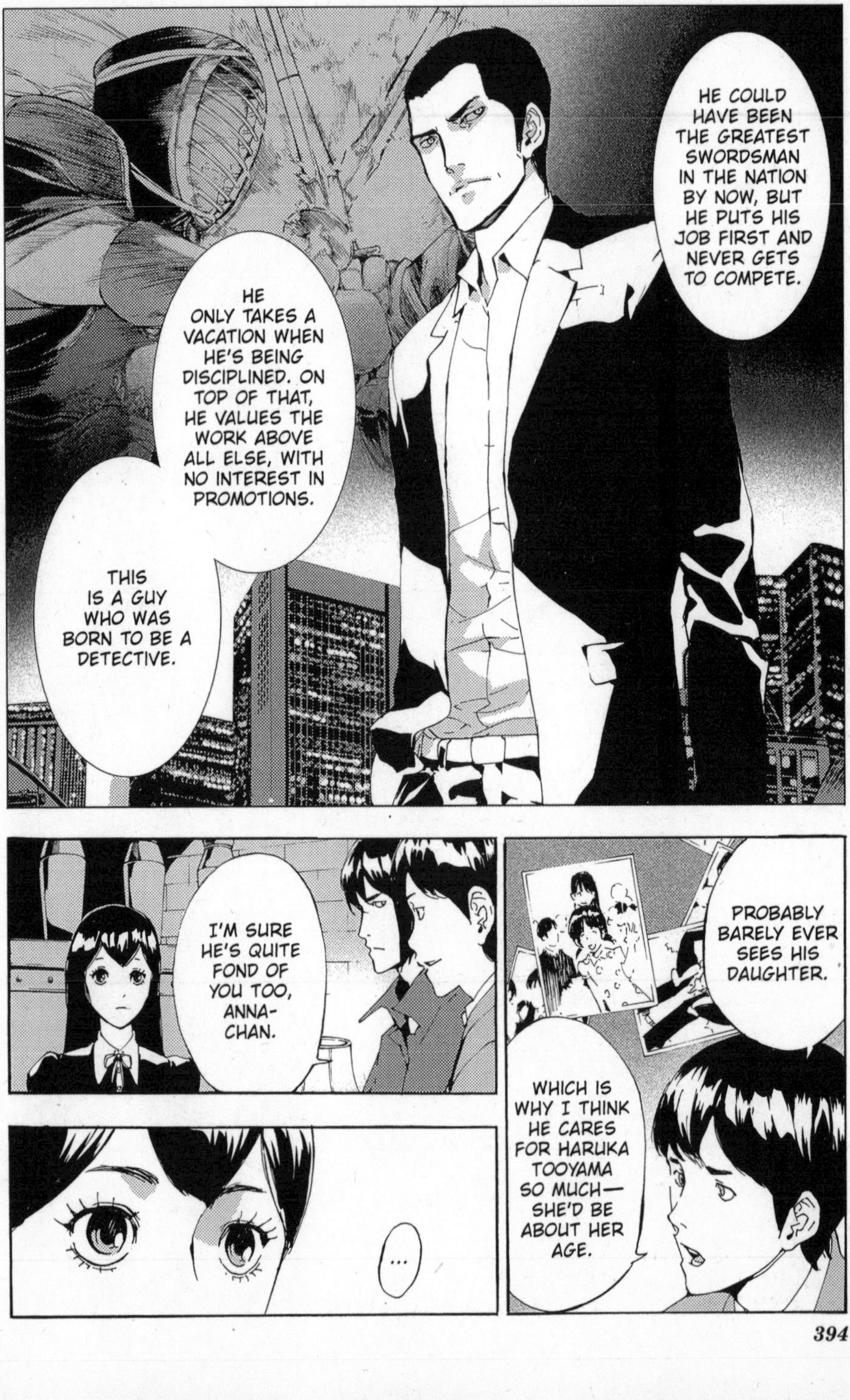
HE COULD HAVE BEEN THE GREATEST SWORDSMAN IN THE NATION BY NOW, BUT HE PUTS HIS JOB FIRST AND NEVER GETS TO COMPETE.
HE ONLY TAKES A VACATION WHEN HE'S BEING DISCIPLINED. ON TOP OF THAT, HE VALUES THE WORK ABOVE ALL ELSE, WITH NO INTEREST IN PROMOTIONS.
THIS IS A GUY WHO WAS BORN TO BE A DETECTIVE.
PROBABLY BARELY EVER SEES HIS DAUGHTER.
WHICH IS WHY I THINK HE CARES FOR HARUKA TOOYAMA SO MUCH— SHE'D BE ABOUT HER AGE.
I'M SURE HE'S QUITE FOND OF YOU TOO, ANNA-CHAN.
...

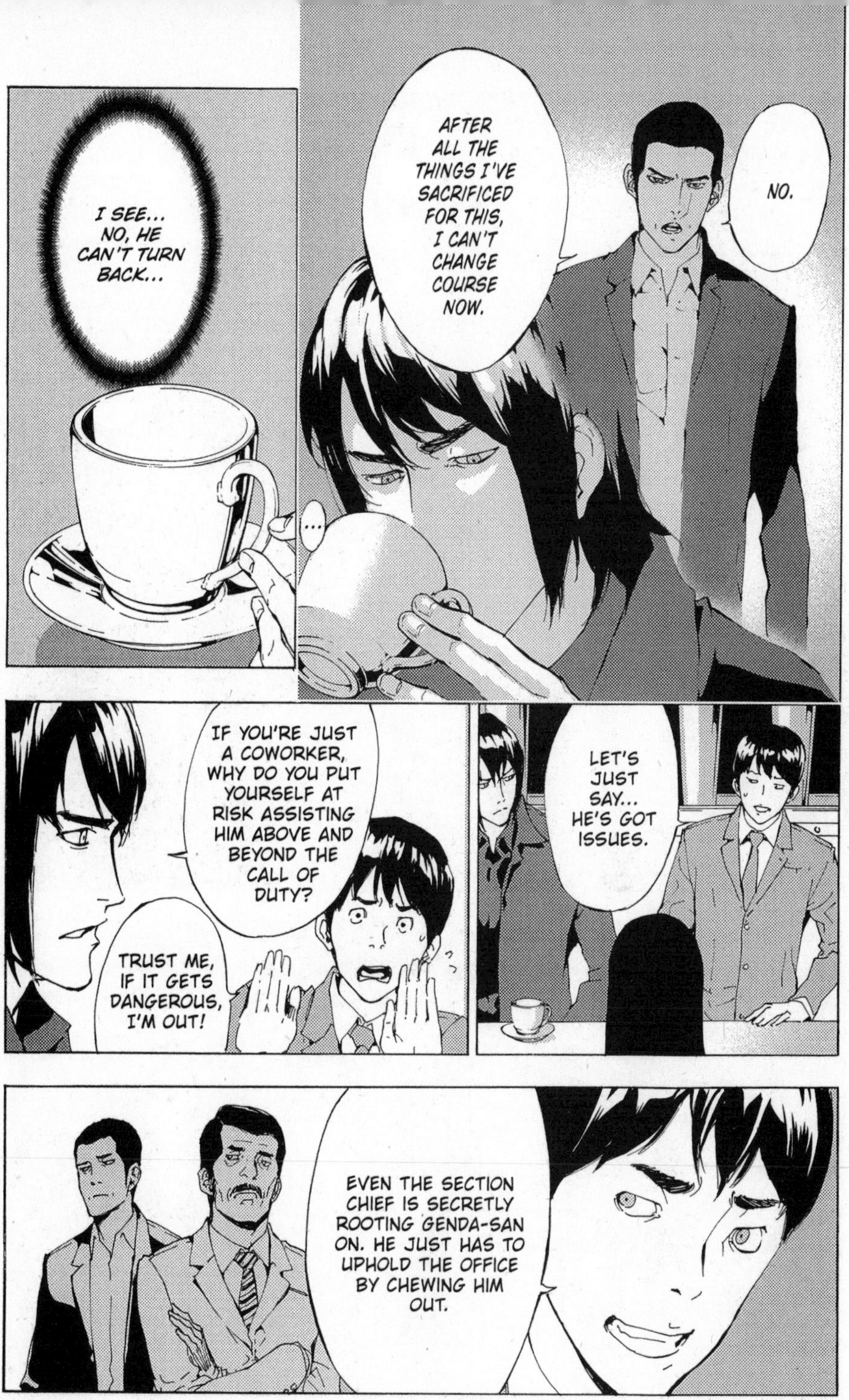
NO.
AFTER ALL THE THINGS I'VE SACRIFICED FOR THIS, I CAN'T CHANGE COURSE NOW.
...
I SEE... NO, HE CAN'T TURN BACK...
LET'S JUST SAY... HE'S GOT ISSUES.
IF YOU'RE JUST A COWORKER, WHY DO YOU PUT YOURSELF AT RISK ASSISTING HIM ABOVE AND BEYOND THE CALL OF DUTY?
TRUST ME, IF IT GETS DANGEROUS, I'M OUT!
EVEN THE SECTION CHIEF IS SECRETLY ROOTING GENDA-SAN ON. HE JUST HAS TO UPHOLD THE OFFICE BY CHEWING HIM OUT.

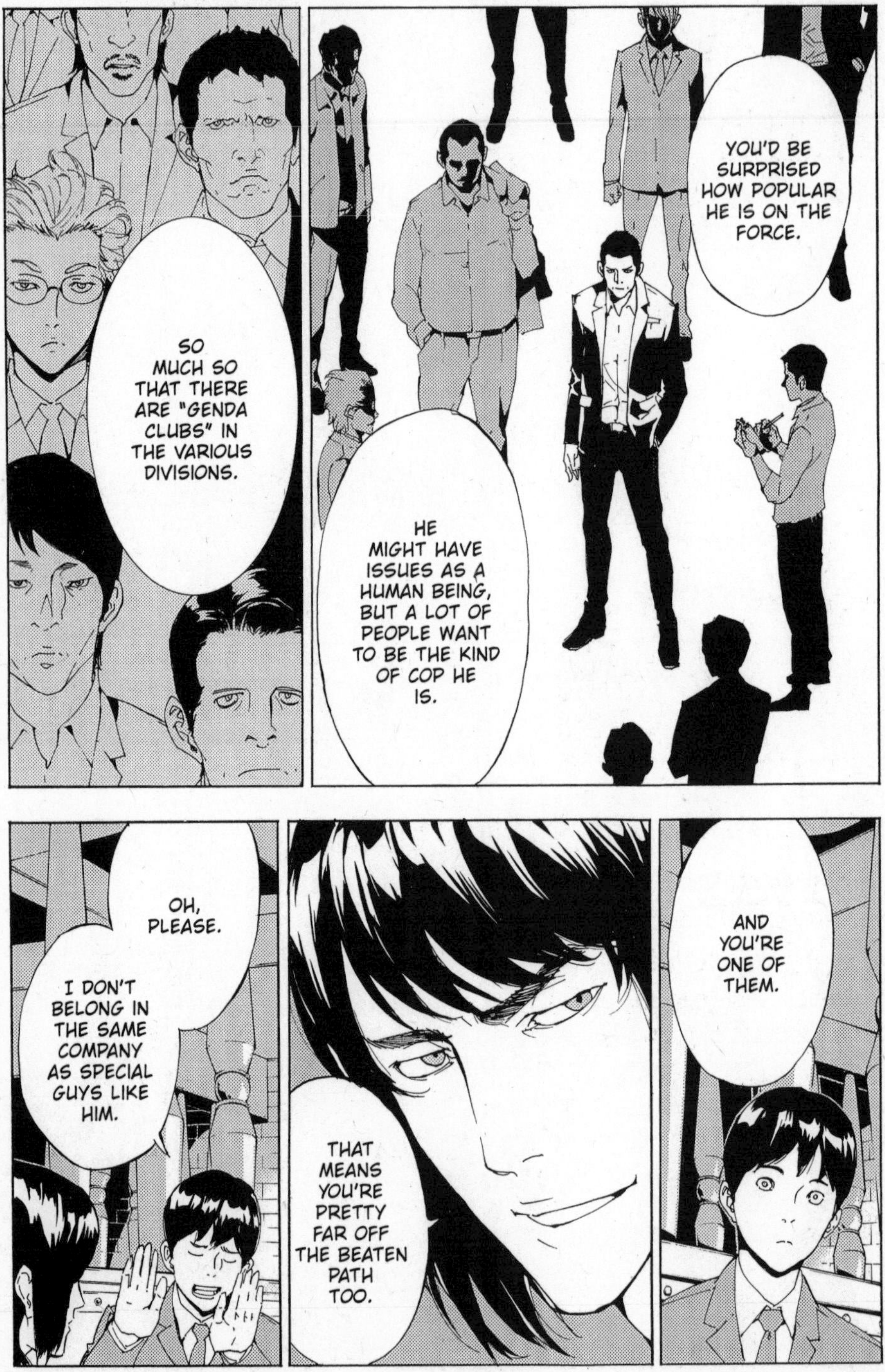
YOU'D BE SURPRISED HOW POPULAR HE IS ON THE FORCE.
HE MIGHT HAVE ISSUES AS A HUMAN BEING, BUT A LOT OF PEOPLE WANT TO BE THE KIND OF COP HE IS.
SO MUCH SO THAT THERE ARE "GENDA CLUBS" IN THE VARIOUS DIVISIONS.
AND YOU'RE ONE OF THEM.
THAT MEANS YOU'RE PRETTY FAR OFF THE BEATEN PATH TOO.
OH, PLEASE.
I DON'T BELONG IN THE SAME COMPANY AS SPECIAL GUYS LIKE HIM.

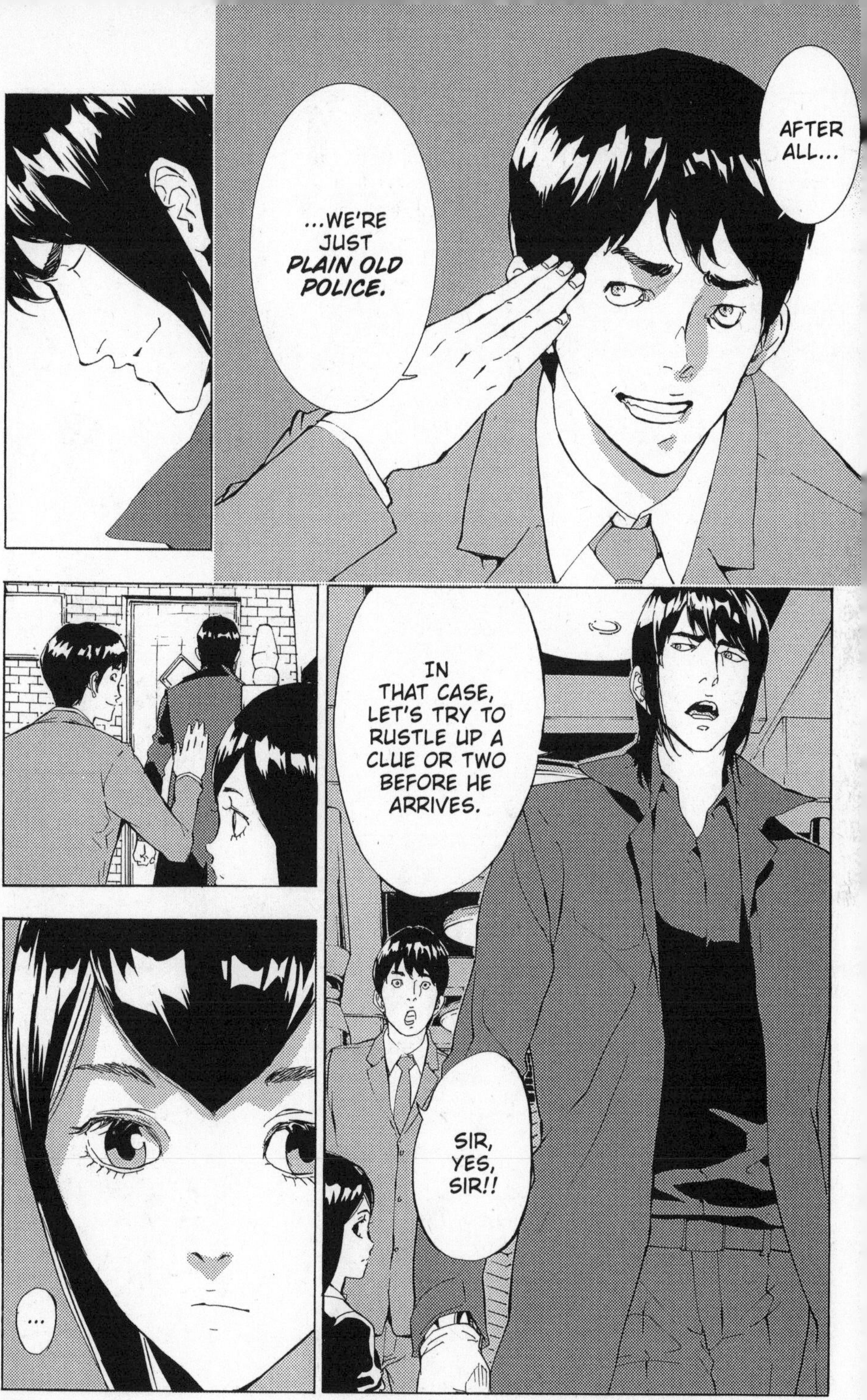
AFTER ALL...
...WE'RE JUST PLAIN OLD POLICE.
IN THAT CASE, LET'S TRY TO RUSTLE UP A CLUE OR TWO BEFORE HE ARRIVES.
SIR, YES, SIR!!
...

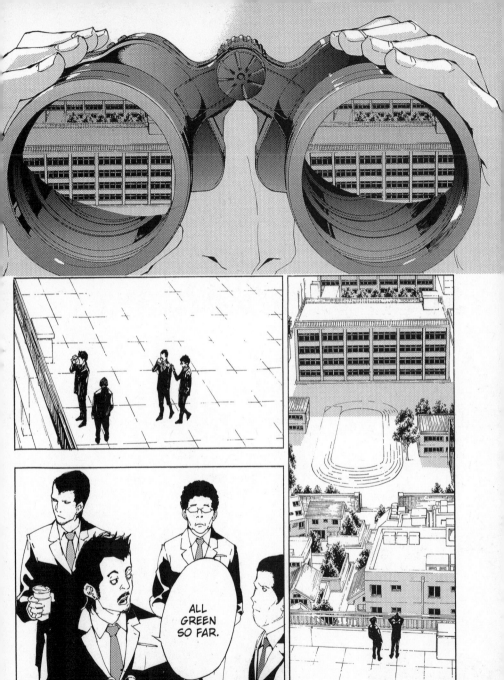

ALL GREEN SO FAR.

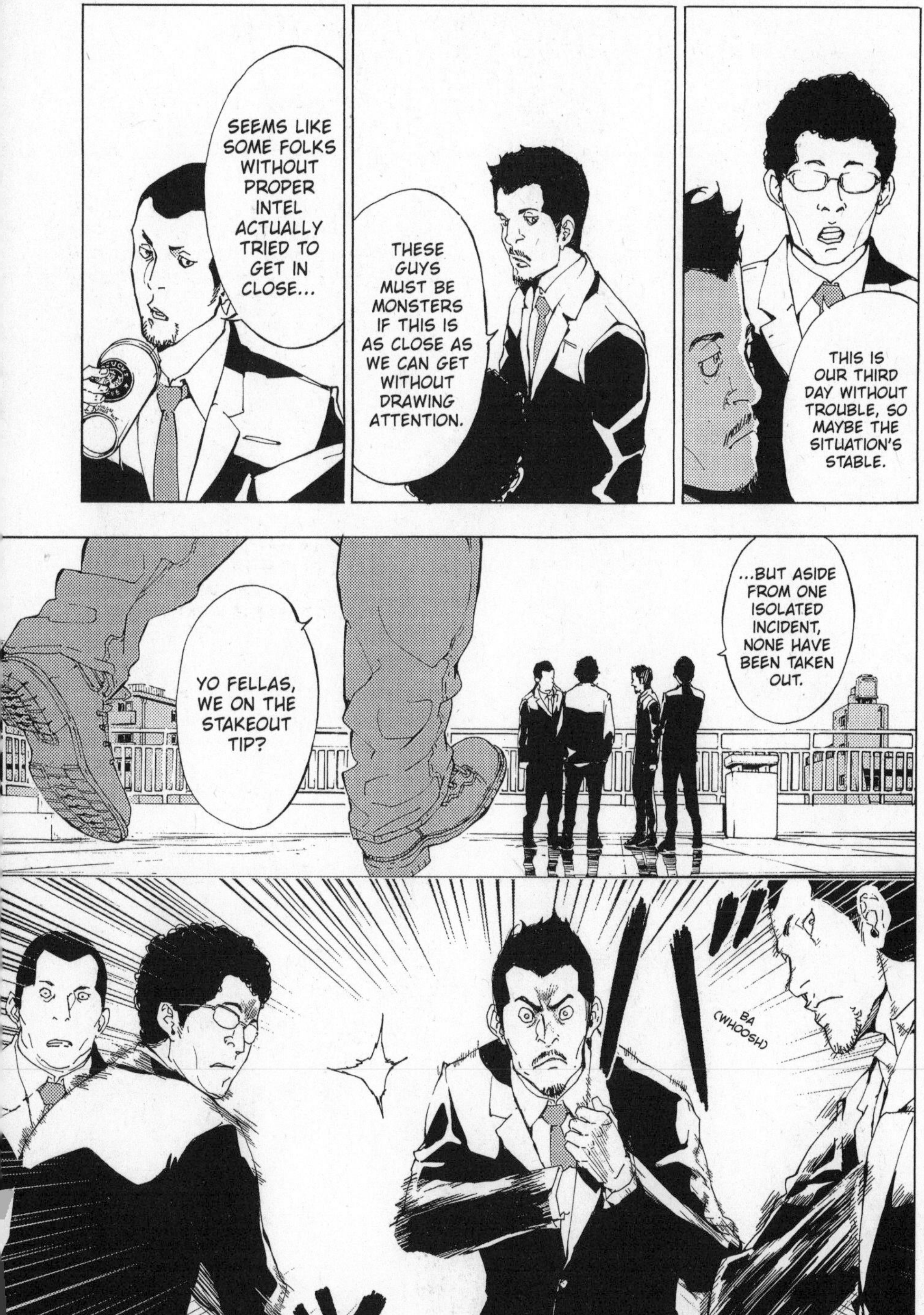
THIS IS OUR THIRD DAY WITHOUT TROUBLE, SO MAYBE THE SITUATION'S STABLE.
THESE GUYS MUST BE MONSTERS IF THIS IS AS CLOSE AS WE CAN GET WITHOUT DRAWING ATTENTION.
SEEMS LIKE SOME FOLKS WITHOUT PROPER INTEL ACTUALLY TRIED TO GET IN CLOSE...
...BUT ASIDE FROM ONE ISOLATED INCIDENT, NONE HAVE BEEN TAKEN OUT.
YO FELLAS, WE ON THE STAKEOUT TIP?
BA (WHOOSH)

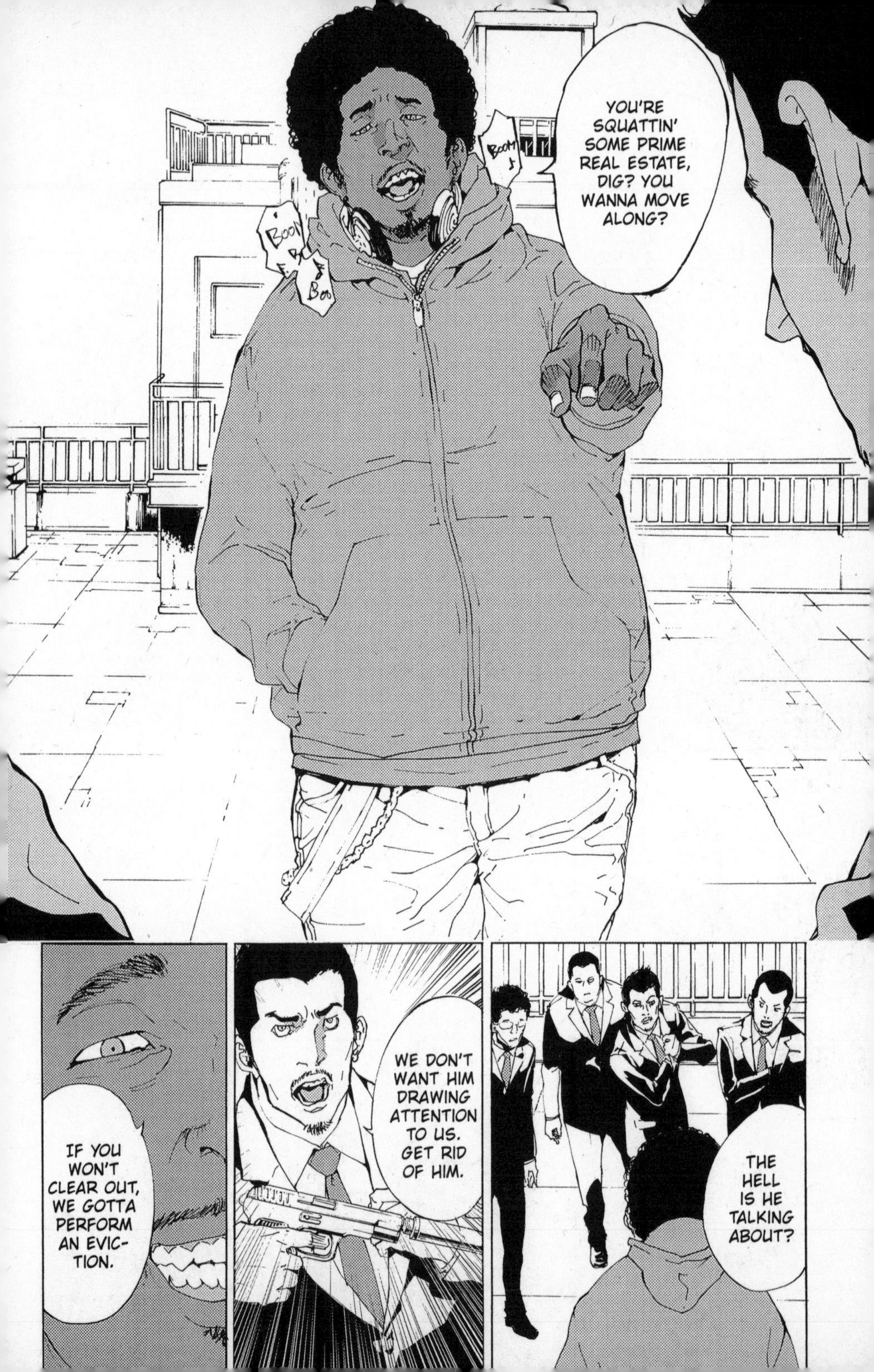
YOU'RE SQUATTIN' SOME PRIME REAL ESTATE, DIG? YOU WANNA MOVE ALONG?
THE HELL IS HE TALKING ABOUT?
WE DON'T WANT HIM DRAWING ATTENTION TO US. GET RID OF HIM.
IF YOU WON'T CLEAR OUT, WE GOTTA PERFORM AN EVICTION.

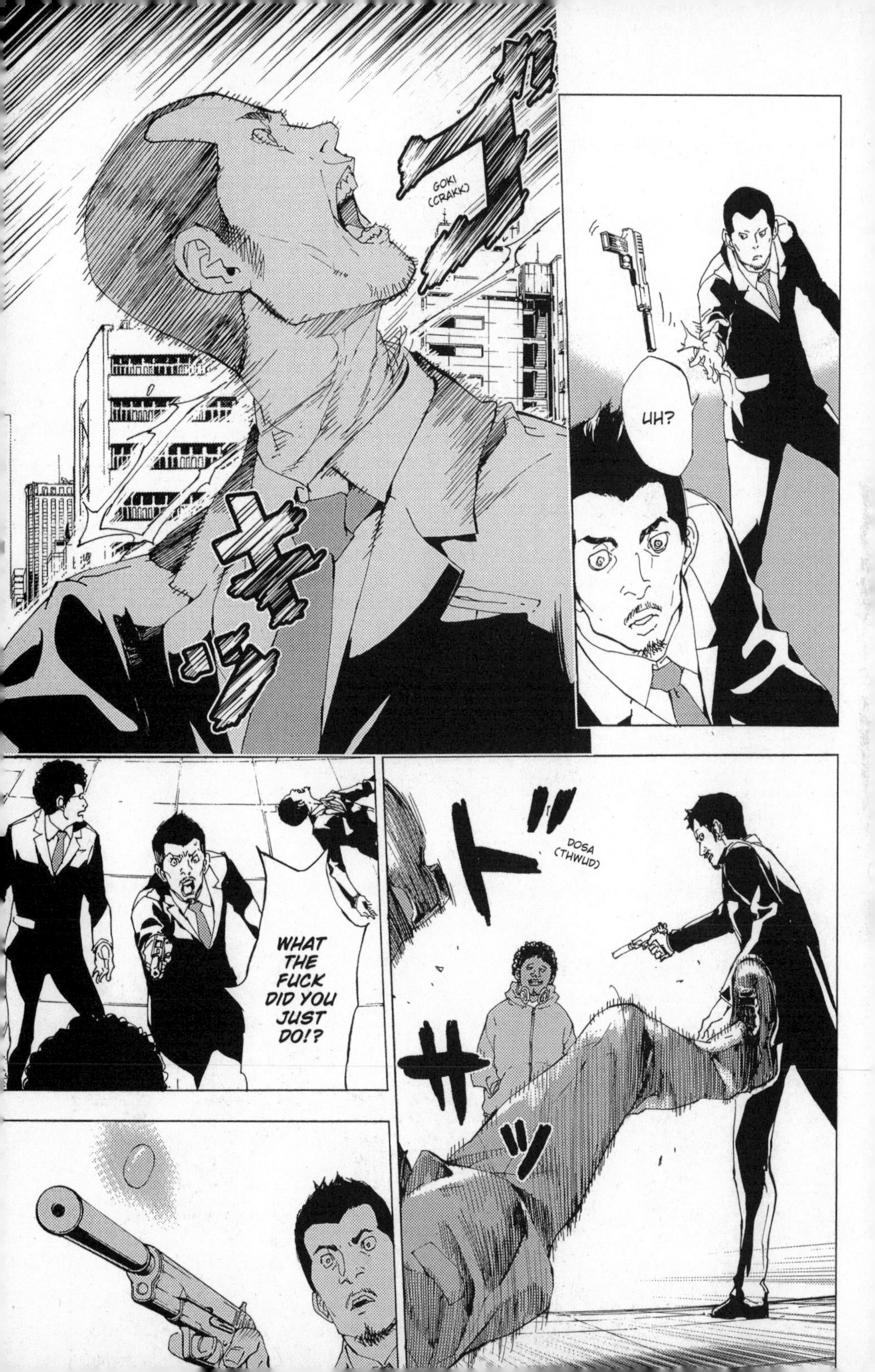
UH?
GOKI (CRAKK)
DOSA (THWUD)
WHAT THE FUCK DID YOU JUST DO!?

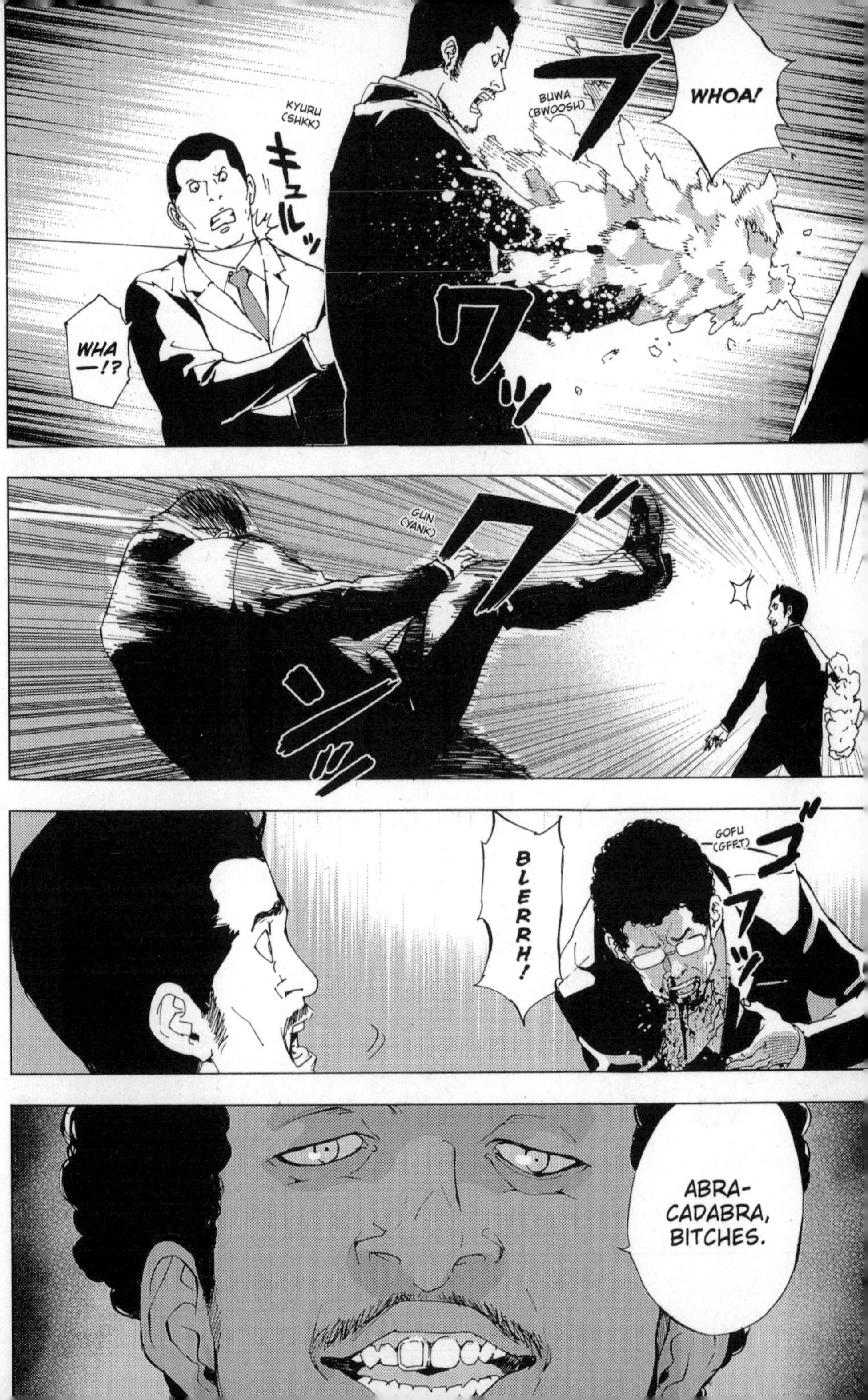
WHOA!
BUWA (BWOOSH)
KYURU (SHKK)
WHA—!?
GUN (YANK)
GOFU (GFFT)
BLERRH!
ABRA-CADABRA, BITCHES.

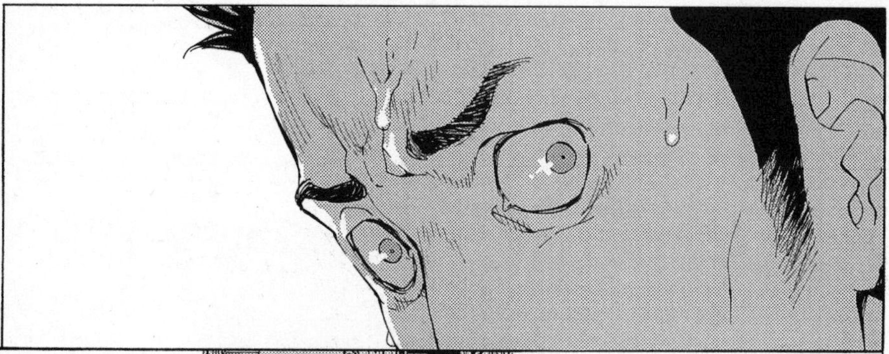
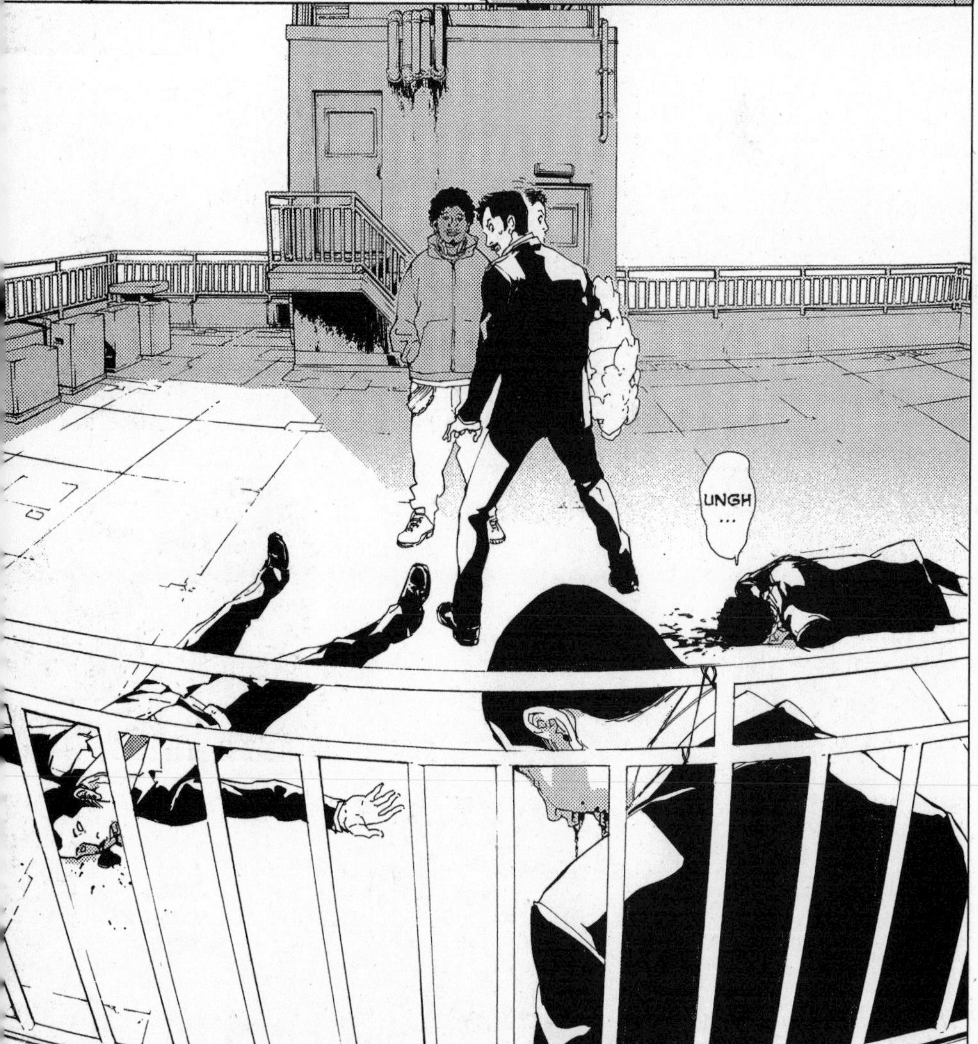
UNGH
...

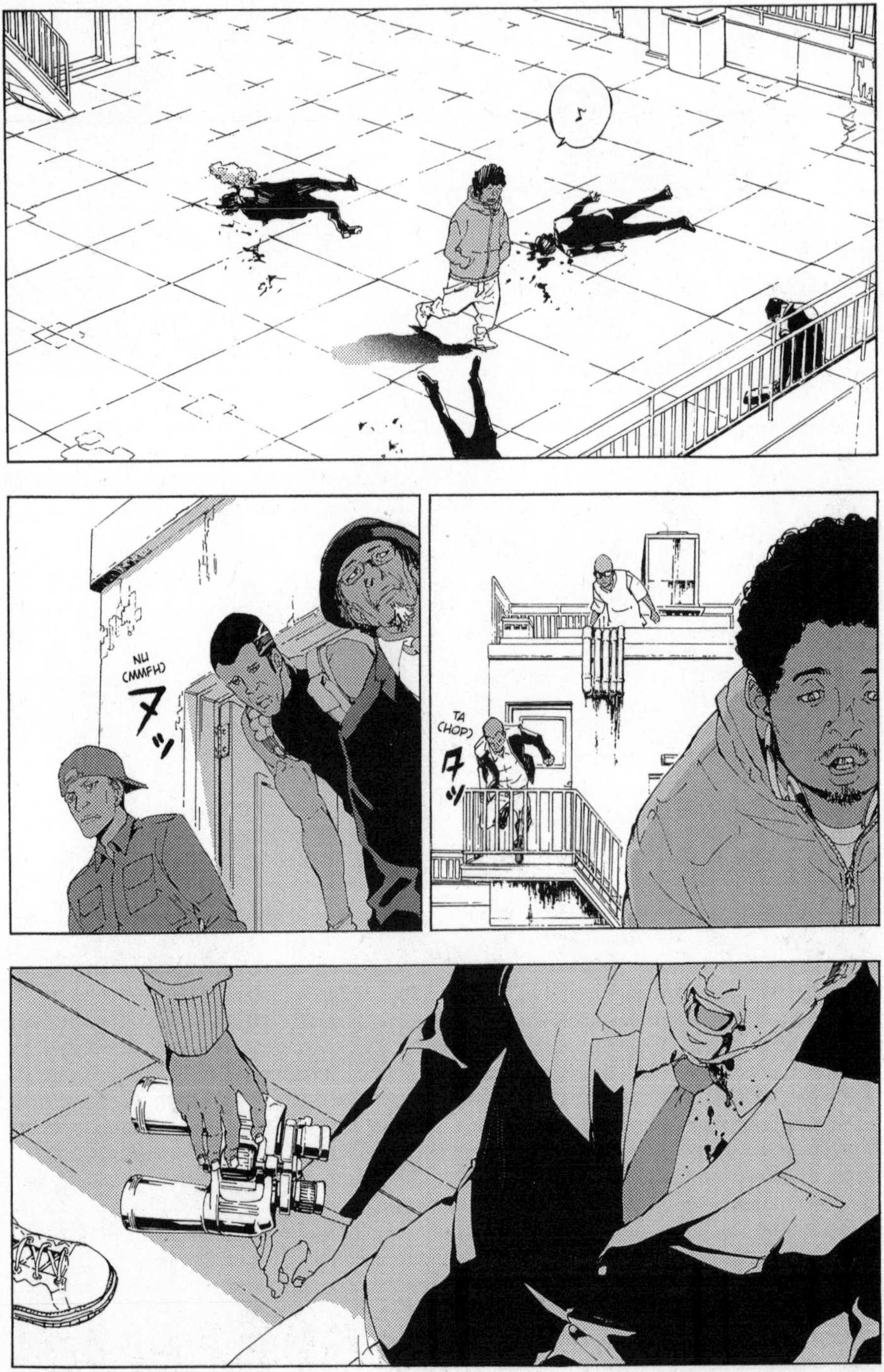
♪
TA (HOP)
タッ
NU (MMFH)
ヌッ

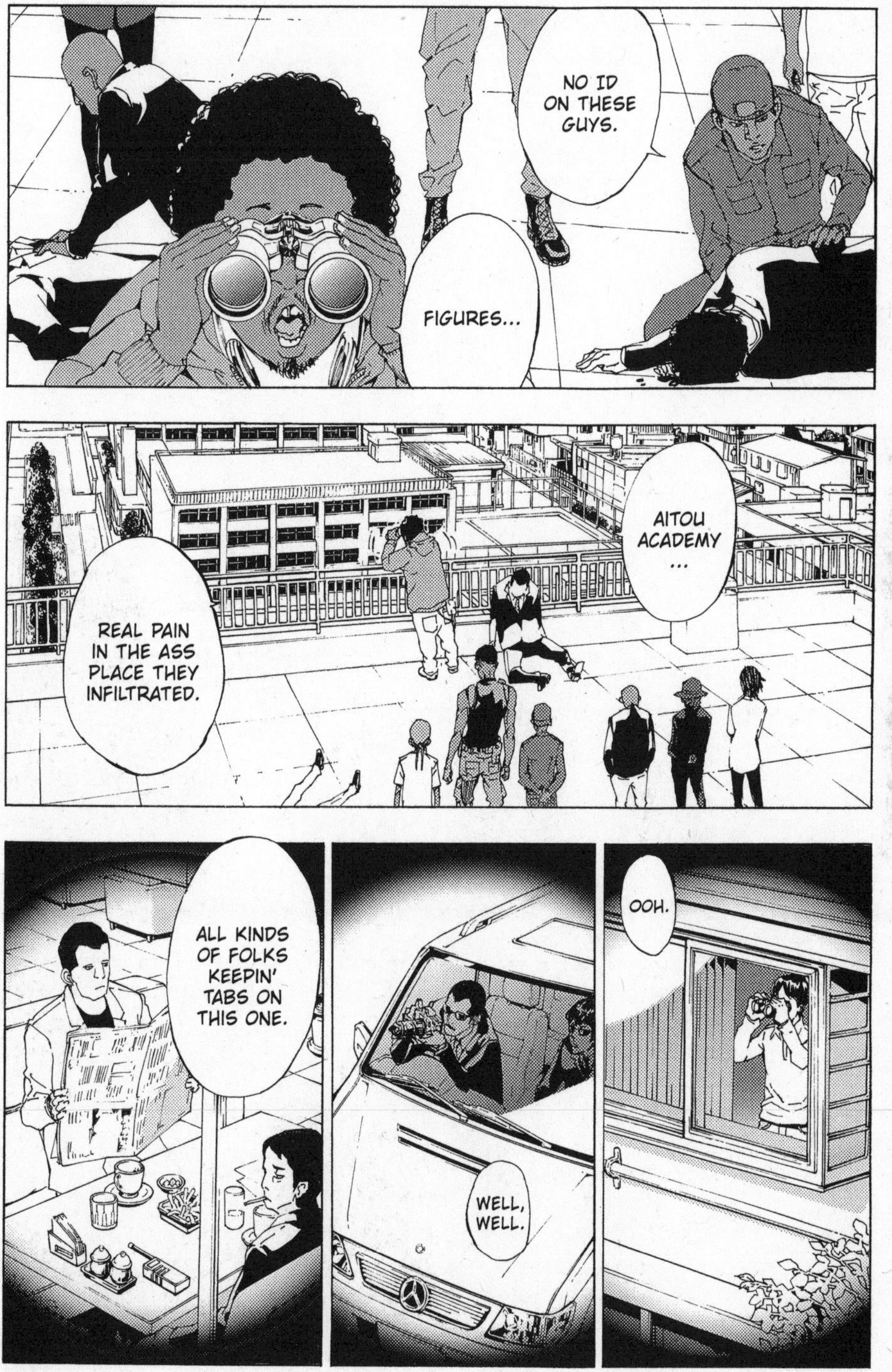
NO ID ON THESE GUYS.
FIGURES...
AITOU ACADEMY...
REAL PAIN IN THE ASS PLACE THEY INFILTRATED.
OOH.
WELL, WELL.
ALL KINDS OF FOLKS KEEPIN' TABS ON THIS ONE.

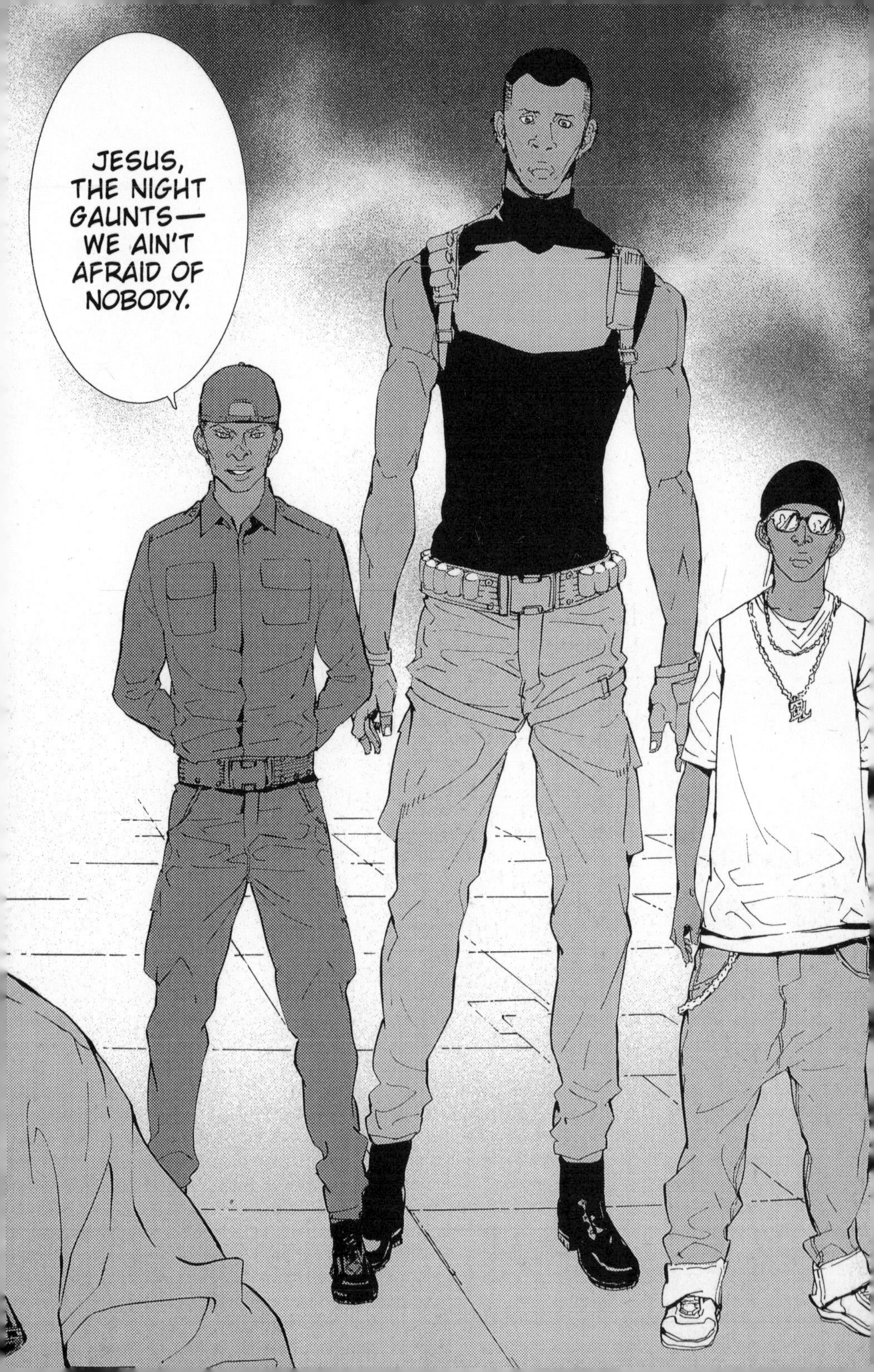
JESUS, THE NIGHT GAUNTS— WE AIN'T AFRAID OF NOBODY.

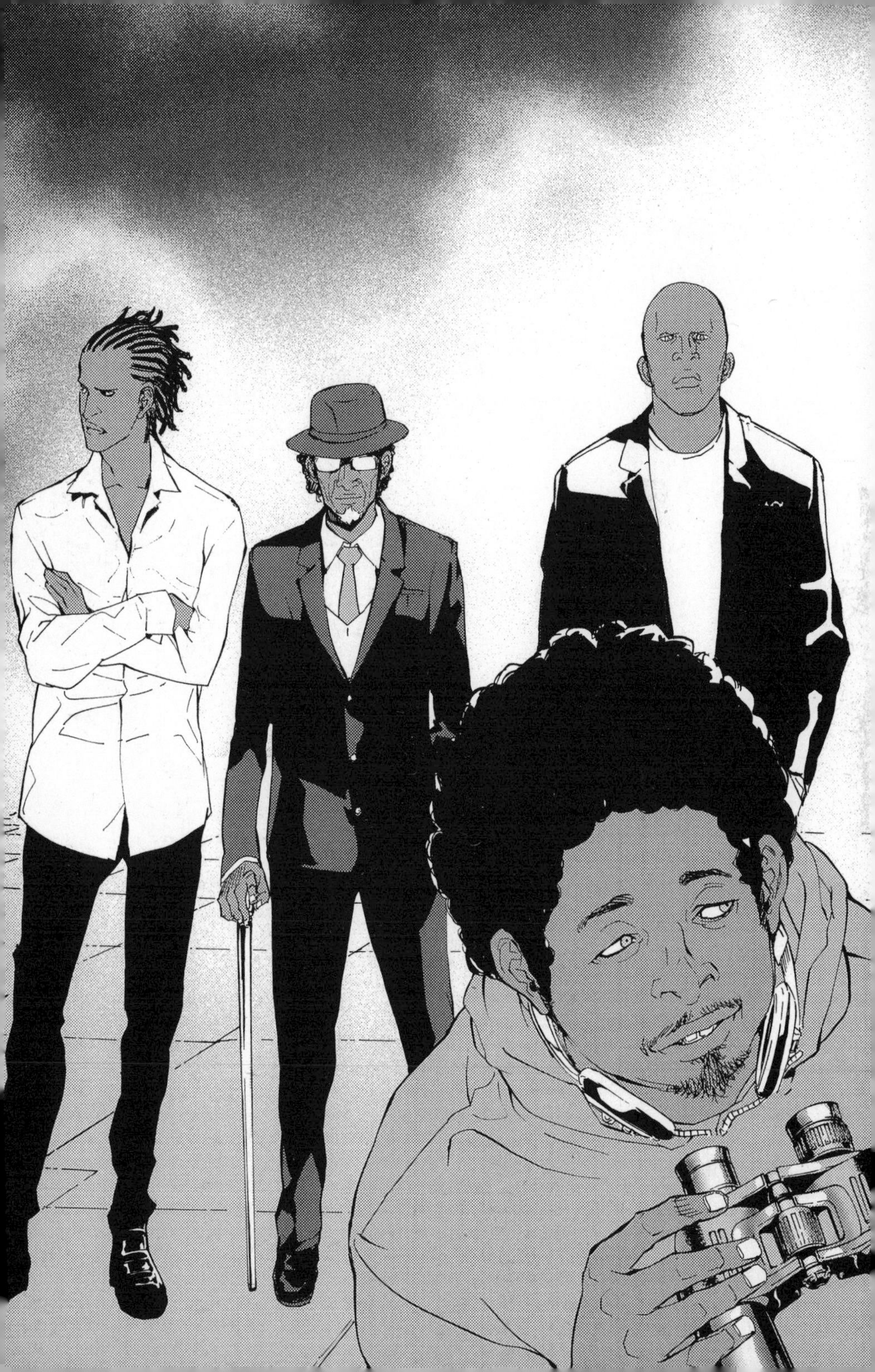

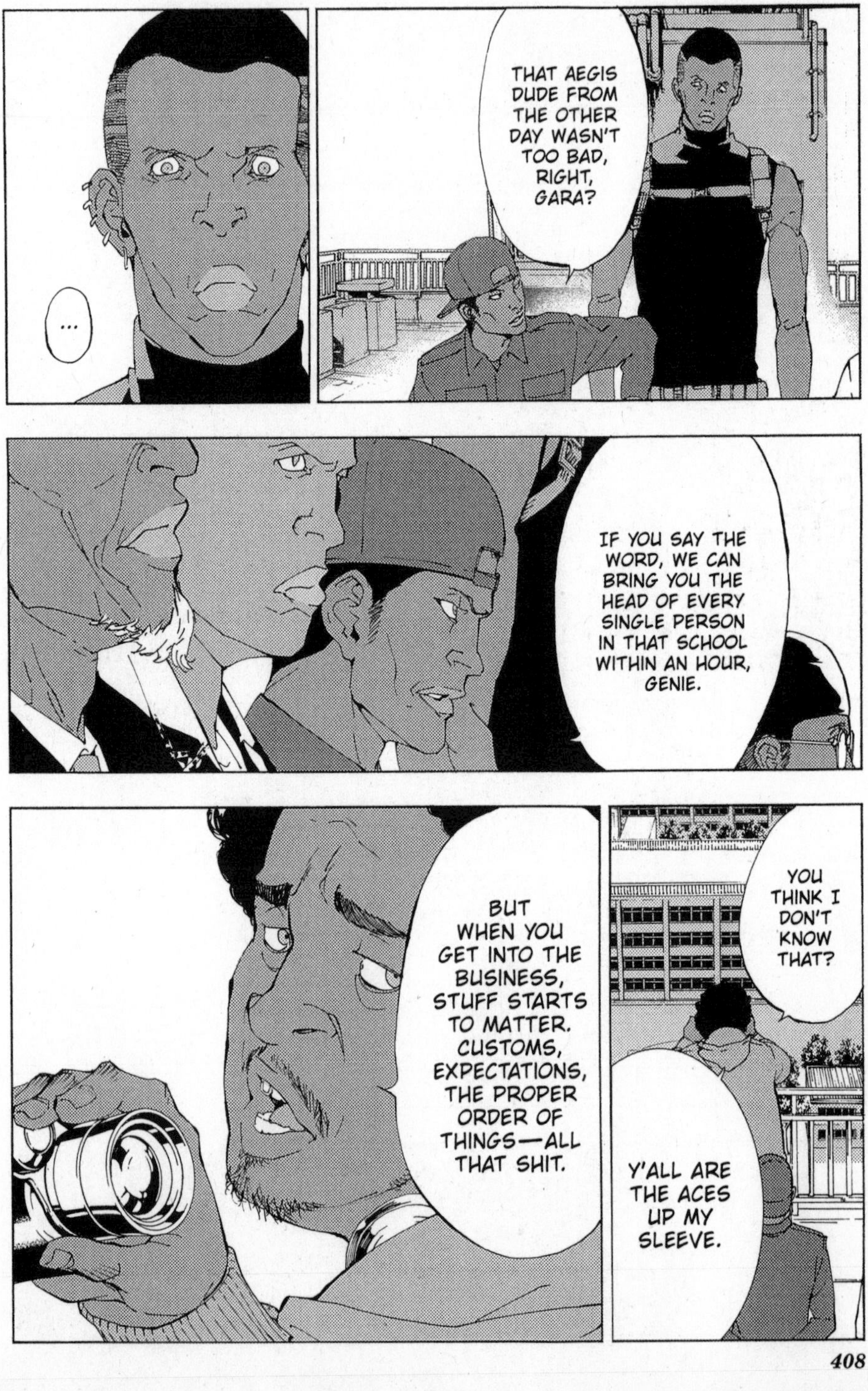
THAT AEGIS DUDE FROM THE OTHER DAY WASN'T TOO BAD, RIGHT, GARA?
...
IF YOU SAY THE WORD, WE CAN BRING YOU THE HEAD OF EVERY SINGLE PERSON IN THAT SCHOOL WITHIN AN HOUR, GENIE.
YOU THINK I DON'T KNOW THAT?
Y'ALL ARE THE ACES UP MY SLEEVE.
BUT WHEN YOU GET INTO THE BUSINESS, STUFF STARTS TO MATTER. CUSTOMS, EXPECTATIONS, THE PROPER ORDER OF THINGS—ALL THAT SHIT.

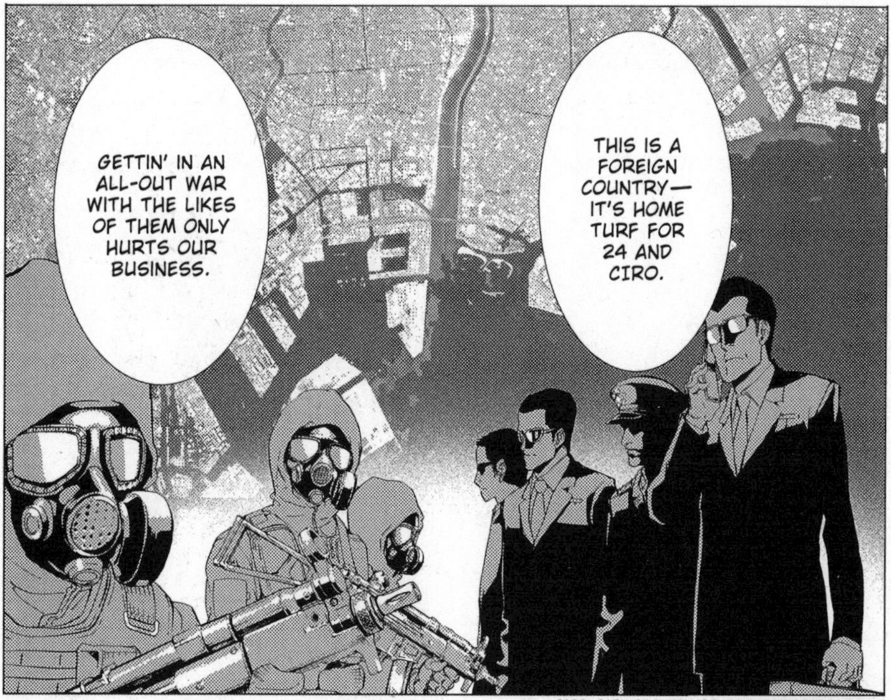
THIS IS A FOREIGN COUNTRY— IT'S HOME TURF FOR 24 AND CIRO.
GETTIN' IN AN ALL-OUT WAR WITH THE LIKES OF THEM ONLY HURTS OUR BUSINESS.

CIRO: CABINET INTELLIGENCE AND RESEARCH OFFICE

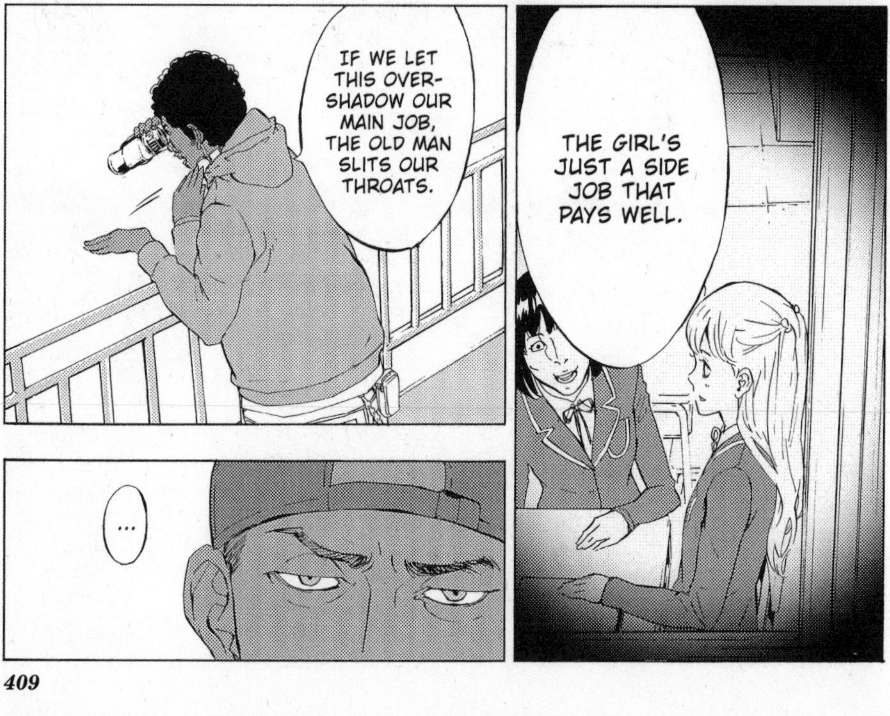
THE GIRL'S JUST A SIDE JOB THAT PAYS WELL.
IF WE LET THIS OVER-SHADOW OUR MAIN JOB, THE OLD MAN SLITS OUR THROATS.
...

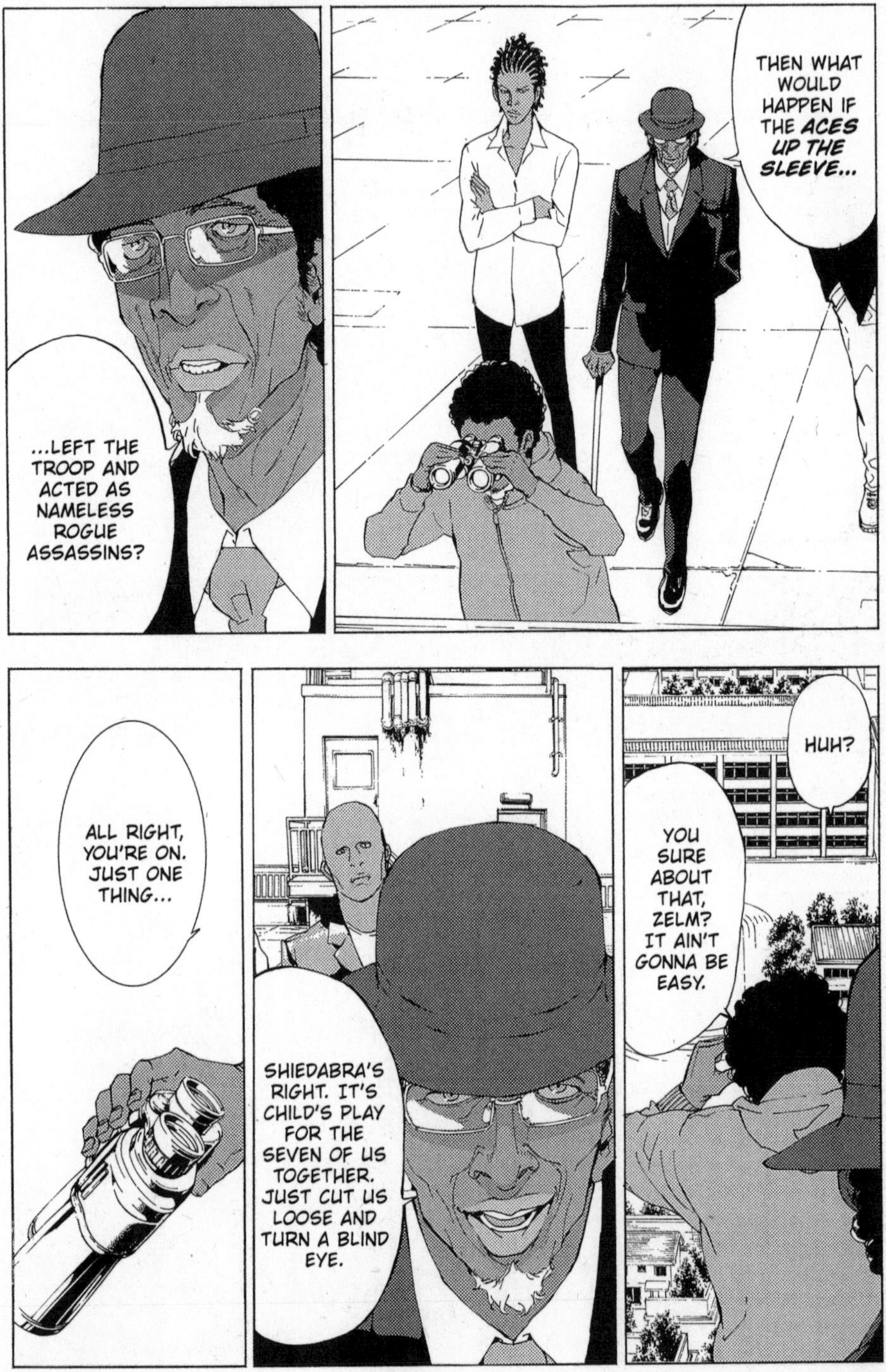
THEN WHAT WOULD HAPPEN IF THE *ACES UP THE SLEEVE...*
...LEFT THE TROOP AND ACTED AS NAMELESS ROGUE ASSASSINS?
HUH?
YOU SURE ABOUT THAT, ZELM? IT AIN'T GONNA BE EASY.
SHIEDABRA'S RIGHT. IT'S CHILD'S PLAY FOR THE SEVEN OF US TOGETHER. JUST CUT US LOOSE AND TURN A BLIND EYE.
ALL RIGHT, YOU'RE ON. JUST ONE THING...

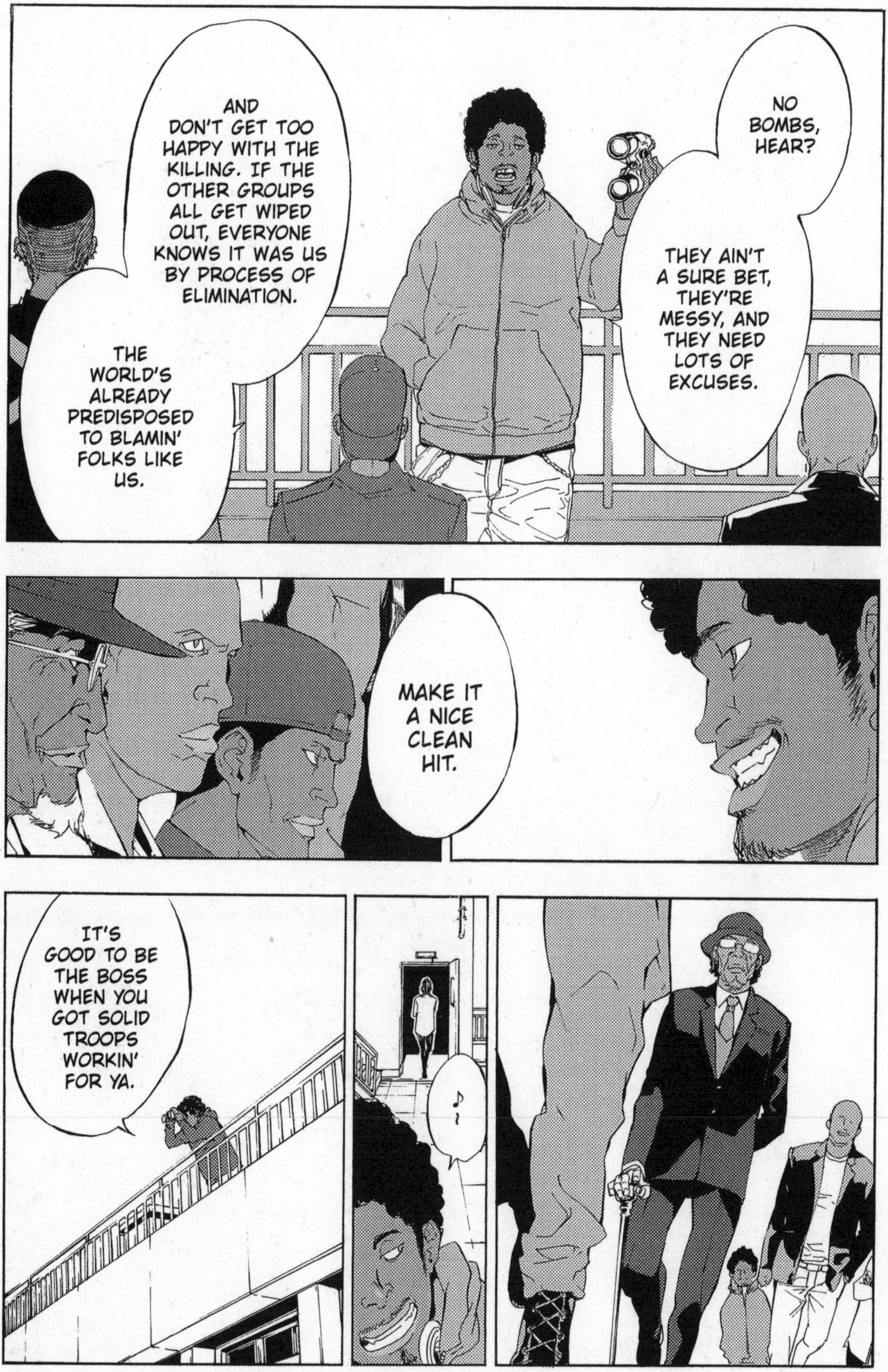
NO BOMBS, HEAR?
THEY AIN'T A SURE BET, THEY'RE MESSY, AND THEY NEED LOTS OF EXCUSES.
AND DON'T GET TOO HAPPY WITH THE KILLING. IF THE OTHER GROUPS ALL GET WIPED OUT, EVERYONE KNOWS IT WAS US BY PROCESS OF ELIMINATION.
THE WORLD'S ALREADY PREDISPOSED TO BLAMIN' FOLKS LIKE US.
MAKE IT A NICE CLEAN HIT.
♪~
IT'S GOOD TO BE THE BOSS WHEN YOU GOT SOLID TROOPS WORKIN' FOR YA.

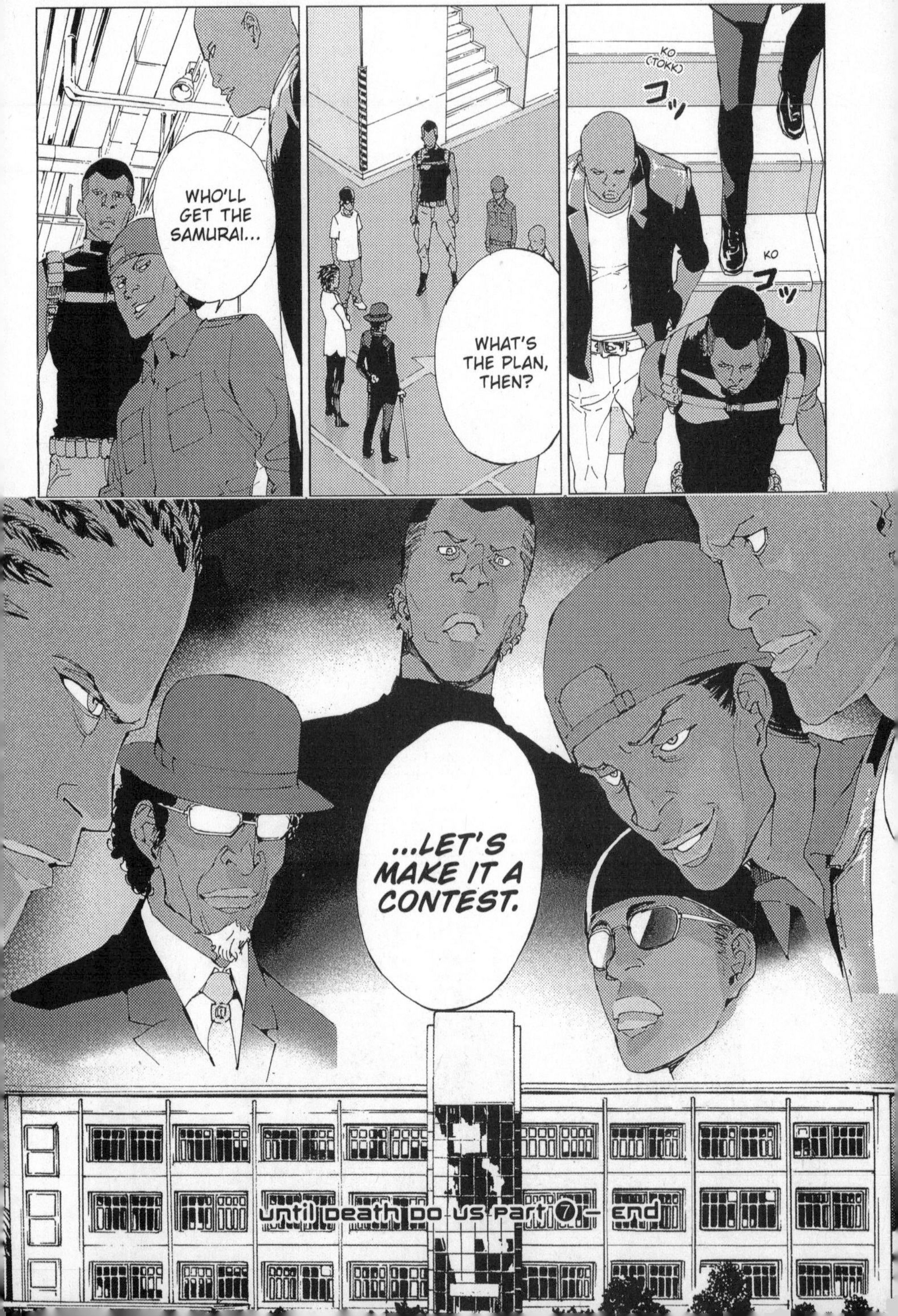
KO (TOKK)
コッ
KO
コッ
WHAT'S THE PLAN, THEN?
WHO'LL GET THE SAMURAI...
...LET'S MAKE IT A CONTEST.
until death do us part 7 - end

Until Death do us Part

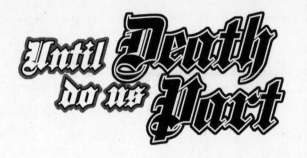

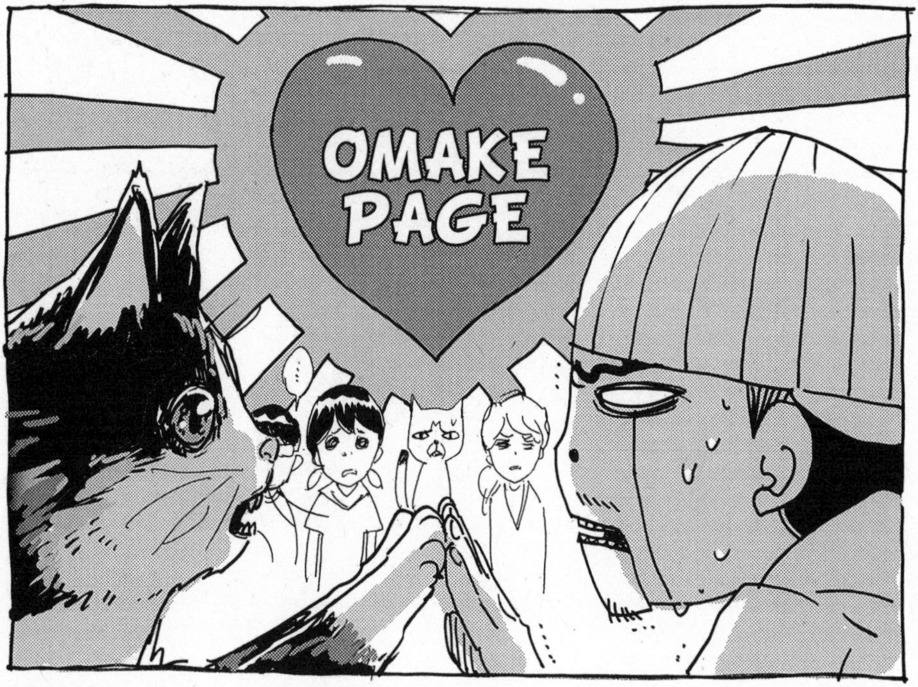
OMAKE PAGE

THIS IS THE STORY OF CARLOS AND CATHERINE, DOUBLE-S'S CATS, AND THEIR TRAGICOMIC LOVE LIVES...

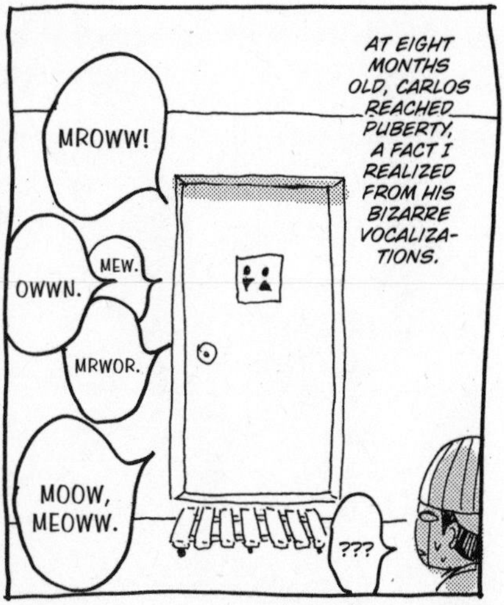
AT EIGHT MONTHS OLD, CARLOS REACHED PUBERTY, A FACT I REALIZED FROM HIS BIZARRE VOCALIZATIONS.
MROWW!
MEW.
OWWN.
MRWOR.
MOOW, MEOWW.
???

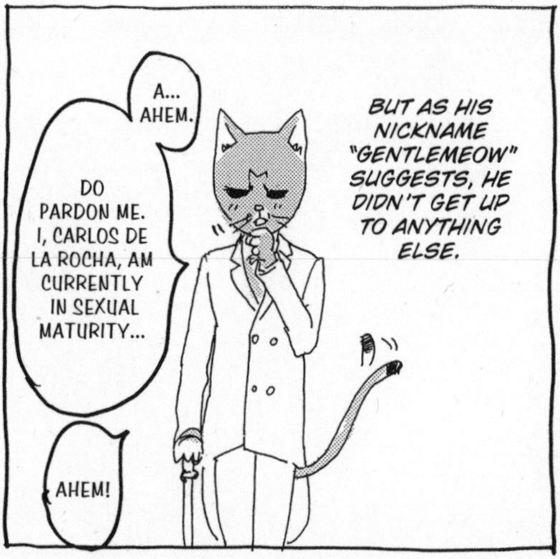
BUT AS HIS NICKNAME "GENTLEMEOW" SUGGESTS, HE DIDN'T GET UP TO ANYTHING ELSE.
A... AHEM.
DO PARDON ME. I, CARLOS DE LA ROCHA, AM CURRENTLY IN SEXUAL MATURITY...
AHEM!

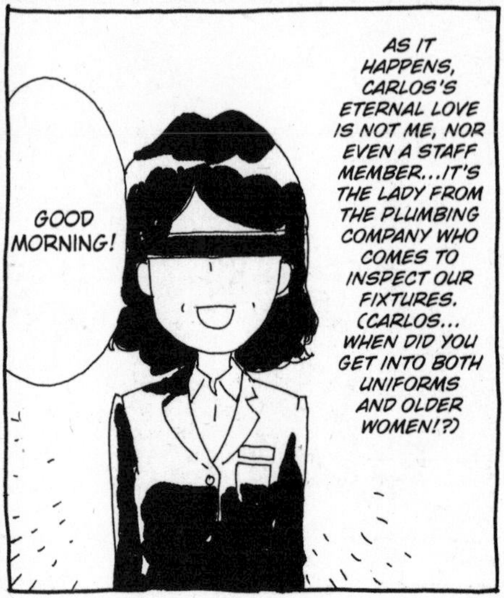
AS IT HAPPENS, CARLOS'S ETERNAL LOVE IS NOT ME, NOR EVEN A STAFF MEMBER...IT'S THE LADY FROM THE PLUMBING COMPANY WHO COMES TO INSPECT OUR FIXTURES. (CARLOS... WHEN DID YOU GET INTO BOTH UNIFORMS AND OLDER WOMEN!?)
GOOD MORNING!

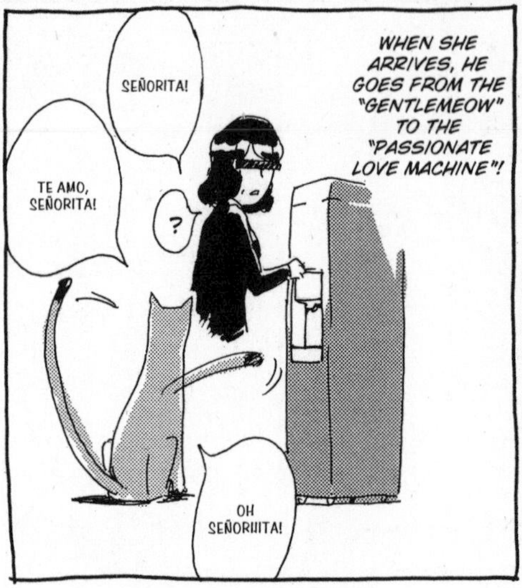
WHEN SHE ARRIVES, HE GOES FROM THE "GENTLEMEOW" TO THE "PASSIONATE LOVE MACHINE"!
SEÑORITA!
TE AMO, SEÑORITA!
?
OH SEÑORIIIITA!

BUT IT'S MY OTHER CAT, CATHERINE...WHOSE ISSUES WITH GOING INTO HEAT ARE A HUNDRED TIMES WORSE THAN ANYTHING I COULD IMAGINE...

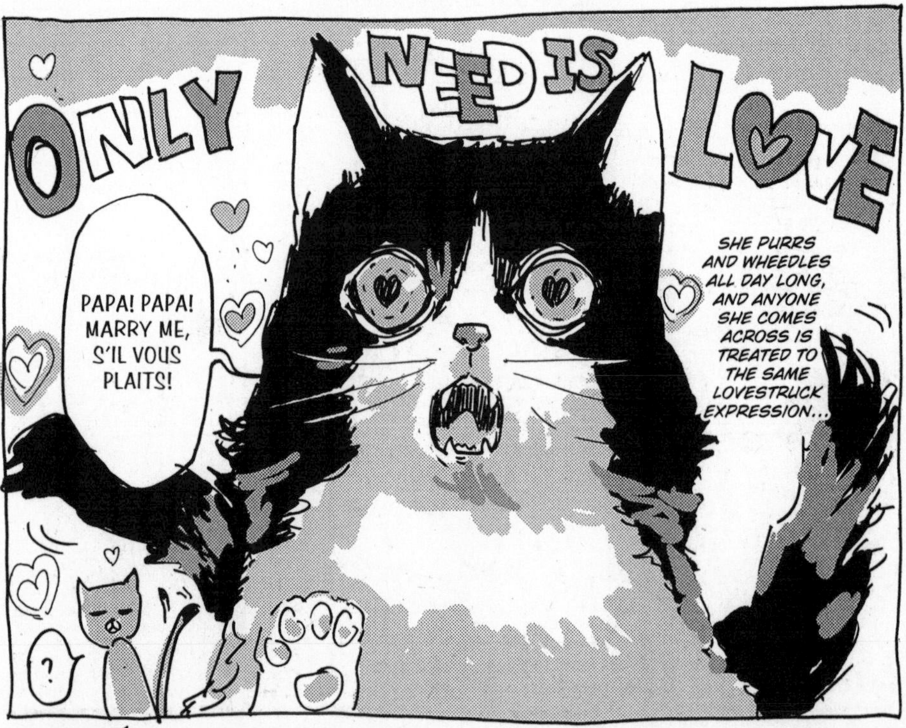
ONLY NEED IS LOVE
SHE PURRS AND WHEEDLES ALL DAY LONG, AND ANYONE SHE COMES ACROSS IS TREATED TO THE SAME LOVESTRUCK EXPRESSION...
PAPA! PAPA! MARRY ME, S'IL VOUS PLAITS!
?

MR. CARLOS IS ALREADY FIXED

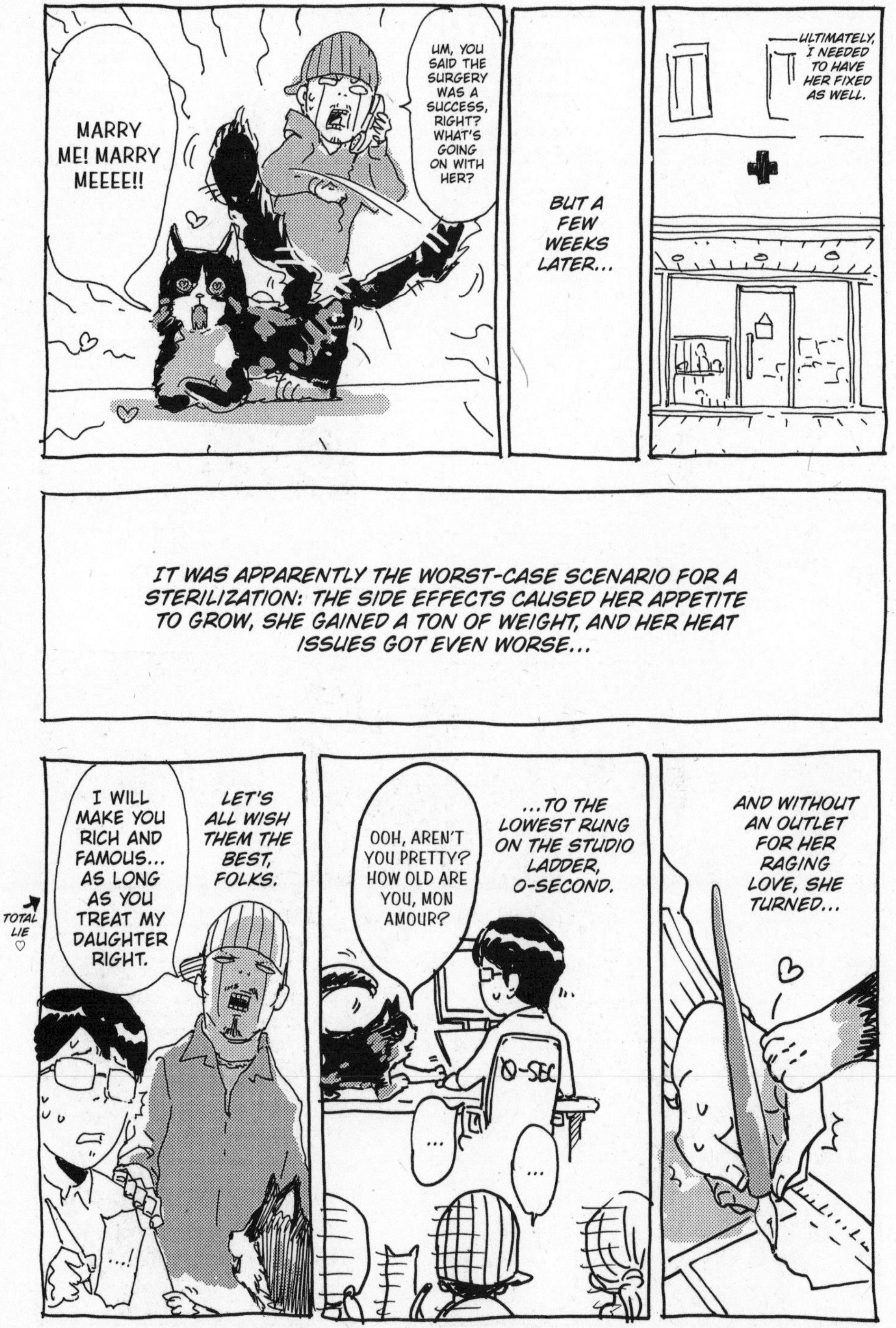
ULTIMATELY, I NEEDED TO HAVE HER FIXED AS WELL.
BUT A FEW WEEKS LATER...
UM, YOU SAID THE SURGERY WAS A SUCCESS, RIGHT? WHAT'S GOING ON WITH HER?
MARRY ME! MARRY MEEEE!!
IT WAS APPARENTLY THE WORST-CASE SCENARIO FOR A STERILIZATION: THE SIDE EFFECTS CAUSED HER APPETITE TO GROW, SHE GAINED A TON OF WEIGHT, AND HER HEAT ISSUES GOT EVEN WORSE...
AND WITHOUT AN OUTLET FOR HER RAGING LOVE, SHE TURNED...
...TO THE LOWEST RUNG ON THE STUDIO LADDER, O-SECOND.
OOH, AREN'T YOU PRETTY? HOW OLD ARE YOU, MON AMOUR?
O-SEC
...
...
LET'S ALL WISH THEM THE BEST, FOLKS.
I WILL MAKE YOU RICH AND FAMOUS... AS LONG AS YOU TREAT MY DAUGHTER RIGHT.
TOTAL LIE ♡
....!

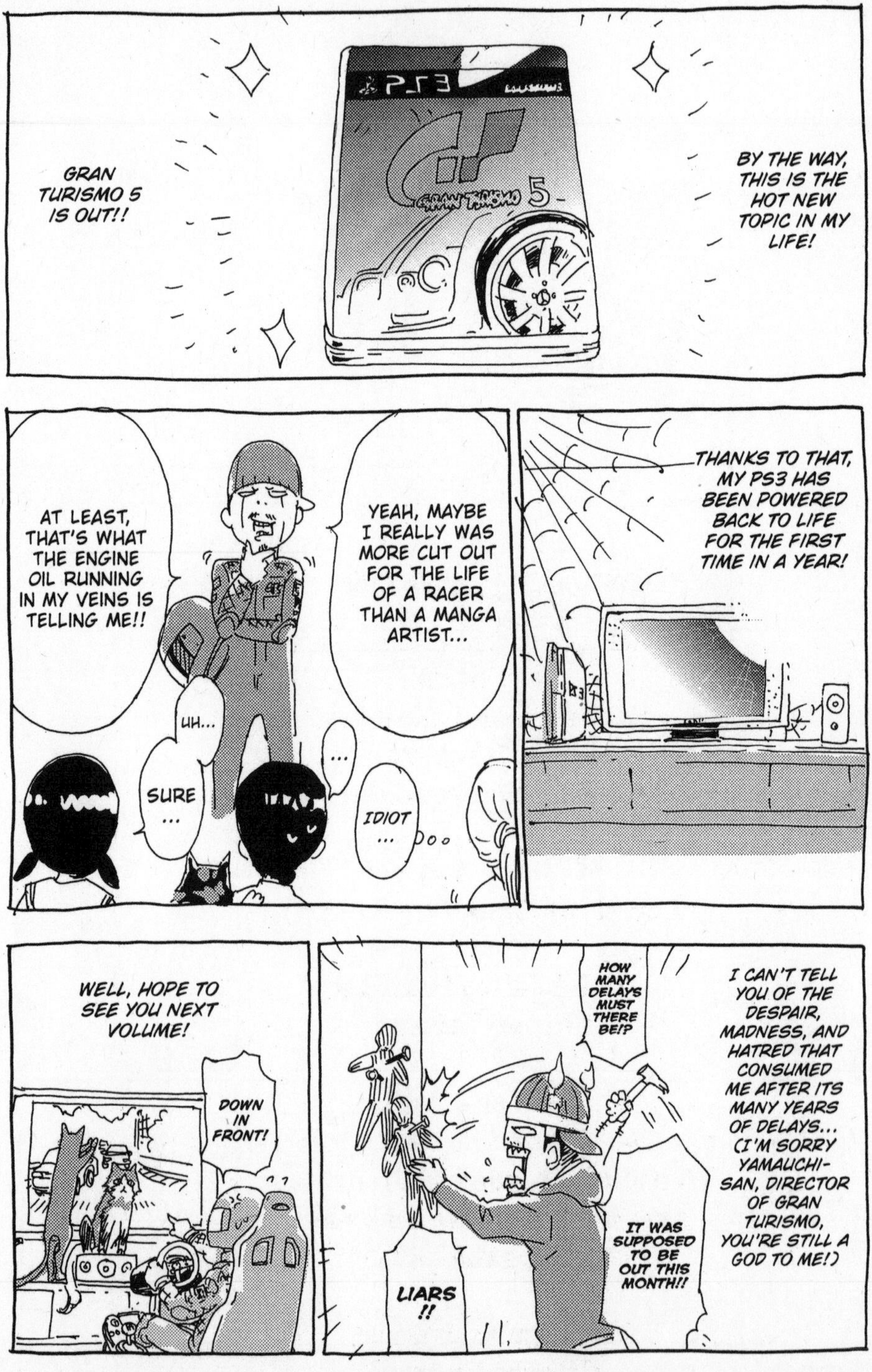
BY THE WAY, THIS IS THE HOT NEW TOPIC IN MY LIFE!
GRAN TURISMO 5 IS OUT!!
THANKS TO THAT, MY PS3 HAS BEEN POWERED BACK TO LIFE FOR THE FIRST TIME IN A YEAR!
YEAH, MAYBE I REALLY WAS MORE CUT OUT FOR THE LIFE OF A RACER THAN A MANGA ARTIST...
AT LEAST, THAT'S WHAT THE ENGINE OIL RUNNING IN MY VEINS IS TELLING ME!!
...
IDIOT...
UH...
SURE...
I CAN'T TELL YOU OF THE DESPAIR, MADNESS, AND HATRED THAT CONSUMED ME AFTER ITS MANY YEARS OF DELAYS... (I'M SORRY YAMAUCHI-SAN, DIRECTOR OF GRAN TURISMO, YOU'RE STILL A GOD TO ME!)
HOW MANY DELAYS MUST THERE BE!?
IT WAS SUPPOSED TO BE OUT THIS MONTH!!
LIARS!!
WELL, HOPE TO SEE YOU NEXT VOLUME!
DOWN IN FRONT!

Art Staff
Suri ♀: Chief Assistant
0-Second ♂: Background Art
Taurus ♀: Background Art

Military Advisor
Lee Hyun Seok (warmania)

SPECIAL THANKS
Shingo Takano

Crossover Planning
JESUS—Sajin Kouro, Yami no Aegis, Akatsuki no Aegis
Written by Kyouichi Nanatsuki,
Art by Yoshihide Fujiwara
(Shogakukan)

Design Assistance
Hitoshi Fukuchi

Until Death do us Part

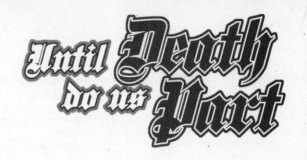

Translation Notes

Common Honorifics
no honorific: Indicates familiarity or closeness; if used without permission or reason, addressing someone in this manner would constitute an insult.
***-san*:** The Japanese equivalent of Mr./Mrs./Miss. If a situation calls for politeness, this is the fail-safe honorific.
***-sama*:** Conveys great respect; may also indicate that the social status of the speaker is lower than that of the addressee.
***-kun*:** Used most often when referring to boys, this indicates affection or familiarity. Occasionally used by older men among their peers, but it may also be used by anyone referring to a person of lower standing.
***-chan*:** An affectionate honorific indicating familiarity used mostly in reference to girls; also used in reference to cute persons or animals of either gender.
***-senpai*:** A suffix used to address upperclassmen or more experienced coworkers.
***-sensei*:** A respectful term for teachers, artists, or high-level professionals.

Yen conversion: While exchange rates fluctuate daily, a convenient conversion estimation is about ¥100 to 1 USD.

Page 58
Kaddas: A fictional Middle Eastern country from the setting of the manga *Jesus: Sajin Kouro* (by Kyouichi Nanatsuki and Yoshihide Fujiwara). Like Tate the Aegis from the previous volume, the character of Jesus and the evil Transplant Connection are crossover elements added to *Until Death Do Us Part*.

Page 81
Canes Venatici: The name of this mercenary outfit is also one of the eighty-eight major constellations. The Latin means "The Hunting Dogs."

Page 195
Dotanuki: A type of katana. Dotanuki is the name of a small village that was the home of a famous school/style of blacksmithing that produced many blades notable for their extreme hardiness. In recent years, the word *dotanuki* (spelled with different kanji from the historical blades) has come to signify a specific type of katana in a number of different manga/anime, most notably the blade of Ogami Itto, the main character of *Lone Wolf and Cub*.

Page 236
Suio style: An actual sword school dating back to the seventeenth century, specializing in *iaijutsu*, the art of quick-drawing the sword. The style's name means "water gull," because the founder dreamed of his skill being as effortless as a gull skimming over the water's surface. Similar to the use of *dotanuki*, this name was also used in *Lone Wolf and Cub*, although it was coincidental (author Kazuo Koike made it up before discovering that a real style with the same name existed). In that story, Ogami Itto utilizes the techniques in water similar to the way Mamoru does here.

UNTIL DEATH
DO US PART ⑦

HIROSHI TAKASHIGE
DOUBLE-S

Translation: Stephen Paul
Lettering: AndWorld Design

UNTIL DEATH DO US PART Vol. 13 and 14 © 2010, 2011 Hiroshi Takashige, DOUBLE-S / SQUARE ENIX CO., LTD. First published in Japan in 2010, 2011 by SQUARE ENIX CO., LTD. English translation rights arranged with SQUARE ENIX CO., LTD. and Hachette Book Group through Tuttle-Mori Agency, Inc.

Translation © 2014 by SQUARE ENIX CO., LTD.

Yen Press
Hachette Book Group
237 Park Avenue, New York, NY 10017

HachetteBookGroup.com
YenPress.com

Yen Press is an imprint of Hachette Book Group, Inc. The Yen Press name and logo are trademarks of Hachette Book Group, Inc.

First Yen Press Edition: September 2014

ISBN: 978-0-316-22431-4

10 9 8 7 6 5 4 3 2 1

BVG

Printed in the United States of America